SOUTH

FODOR'S MODERN GUIDES

are compiled, researched, and edited by an international team of travel writers, field correspondents, and editors. The series, which now almost covers the globe, was founded by Eugene Fodor.

OFFICES

New York & London

Editorial Staff for FODOR'S SOUTH 1982

Editor: CYNTHIA NELSON.

Area Editors: VICTOR BLOCK, CAROLYN CARTER, EDGAR CHEATHAM, PATRICIA CHEATHAM, RALPH DANFORD, BOB GRIFFIN, BERN KEATING, FLORENCE LEMKOWITZ, KAREN LINGO, JOHN D. PHILLIPS.

Contributing Editors: NICHOLAS ACOCELLA, MORRIS CUNNINGHAM, JIM DANCE, GEORGE DREHER, BETTY ELLISON, CALEB PIRTLE, KATHERINE SPIELMANN, HUGH WALKER.

Drawings: SANDRA LANG

Maps: DYNO LOWENSTEIN

FODOR'S

SOUTH
1982

**ALABAMA
FLORIDA
GEORGIA
KENTUCKY
LOUISIANA
MARYLAND
MISSISSIPPI
NORTH CAROLINA
SOUTH CAROLINA
TENNESSEE
VIRGINIA
WEST VIRGINIA**
plus
a side trip to
THE DELAWARE BEACHES

FODOR'S MODERN GUIDES, INC.
Distributed by
DAVID McKAY COMPANY, INC.
New York

All the following Guides are current (most of them also in
the Hodder and Stoughton British edition).

CURRENT FODOR'S COUNTRY AND AREA TITLES:

AUSTRALIA, NEW ZEALAND	INDIA & NEPAL
AND SOUTH PACIFIC	IRELAND
AUSTRIA	ISRAEL
BAJA CALIFORNIA	ITALY
BELGIUM AND	JAPAN AND KOREA
LUXEMBOURG	JORDAN AND HOLY LAND
BERMUDA	MEXICO
BRAZIL	NORTH AFRICA
CANADA	PEOPLE'S REPUBLIC
CARIBBEAN AND BAHAMAS	OF CHINA
CENTRAL AMERICA	PORTUGAL
EASTERN EUROPE	SCANDINAVIA
EGYPT	SOUTH AMERICA
EUROPE	SOUTHEAST ASIA
FRANCE	SOVIET UNION
GERMANY	SPAIN
GREAT BRITAIN	SWITZERLAND
GREECE	TURKEY
HOLLAND	YUGOSLAVIA

CITY GUIDES:

LONDON	ROME
NEW YORK CITY	WASHINGTON, D.C.
PARIS	

FODOR'S BUDGET SERIES:

BUDGET BRITAIN	BUDGET ITALY
BUDGET CARIBBEAN	BUDGET JAPAN
BUDGET EUROPE	BUDGET MEXICO
BUDGET FRANCE	BUDGET SPAIN
BUDGET GERMANY	BUDGET TRAVEL IN AMERICA

USA GUIDES:

USA (in one volume)	
ALASKA	NEW ENGLAND
CALIFORNIA	PENNSYLVANIA
COLORADO	SOUTH
FAR WEST	SOUTHWEST
FLORIDA	SUNBELT LEISURE
HAWAII	GUIDE

SPECIAL INTEREST SERIES:
CIVIL WAR SITES

CONTENTS

FACTS AT YOUR FINGERTIPS

When to Go 1; Planning Your Trip 1; Packing 2; Hints to the Motorist 3; What Will It Cost 4; Hotels & Motels 6; Hotel and Motel Categories 7; Dining Out 9; Restaurant Categories 10; Summer Sports 10; Winter Sports 11; Roughing It 11; Tipping 12; Hints to Handicapped Travelers 13

THE SOUTH, STATE BY STATE

v

CONTENTS

CONTENTS

FACTS AT YOUR FINGERTIPS

 WHEN TO GO. All in all, spring is probably the most attractive season in this part of the U.S. Cherry-blossoms are followed throughout the region by azaleas, dogwood, and camellias from April into May and apple blossoms in May.

Seasonal and special events occur throughout the year. Numerically speaking, however, summer has the most, followed by spring, fall and winter in that order. Festivals (folk, craft, art and music) tend to come in the summer, as do sports events. State and local fairs come mainly in August and September, though there are a few in early July and into October. Historical commemorations usually have no connection with the seasons and are likely to occur at any time of the year. The temperature averages in the winter generally run in the low 40's in inland areas, in the 60's at southern shores. Summer temperatures, modified by mountains in some areas, by sea breezes in others, range from the high 70's to the mid-80's, now and then, the low 90's. And so summer is becoming increasingly popular as more and more travelers note the tempering effect of Atlantic and Gulf breezes. Nine states border on salt water, making for over 10,000 miles of coastline.

Fairs and festivals, art shows, parades, and fiestas beckon from January through May, from mid-September through October. Perhaps the most popular is the clamorous, swashbuckling *Gasparilla Pirate Days*, held at Tampa the second week in February. Biggest off-season drawing cards are, of course, *Mardi Gras* (day before Lent) in New Orleans, and that city's *Spring Fiesta*, held each April. And of course, the *Kentucky Derby* acts as a magnet in early May. Other off-season events of great interest include: Christmas parades, bowl games, Indian expositions and powwows, and flower festivals.

 PLANNING YOUR TRIP. In the *Practical Information* sections for each of the separate states you will find detailed sources for information on general tourism, national and state parks, tours, gardens, festivals, sports, museums, historic sites and monuments, and much more. If you don't want to bother with reservations on your own, a travel agent won't cost you a cent, except for specific charges like telegrams. He gets his fee from the hotel or carrier he books for you. A travel agent can also help those who would prefer to take their vacations on a "package tour"—thus keeping planning to a minimum; and in explaining the details of the "travel now, pay later" vacation possibilities offered by the nation's carriers. Various tour operators offer package tours to the South, most of them to five main destinations: Washington, DC, New Orleans, Miami Beach, Walt Disney World and the Kentucky Derby. Here are a few suggestions: *Greyhound World Tours*, Greyhound Tower, Phoenix, Ariz. 85077; *Jefferson Tours*, 106 Glenwood Ave., Minneapolis, Minn. 55403; *Trailways Tours*, 1512 Commerce St., Dallas, Tex. 75201; *Travel Services*, 110 Kentucky Towers, 416 West Walnut St., Louisville, Ky. 40202; and *Tour Service*, 820 American Bank Tower, Austin, Tex.

If you don't belong to an auto club, now is the time to join one. They can be very helpful about routings and offering emergency service on the road. Two such are: the *American Automobile Association*, 1712 G St. NW, Washington, DC 20006; and the *Amoco Motor Club*, PO Box 7769, Chicago, Illinois 60680. In addition to its information services, the AAA has a nation-wide network of some 26,000 service stations which provide emergency repair service. The *Exxon Travel Club*, 450 Decoma, Houston, Texas 77002, provides information, low-cost insurance, and some legal services. The *National Travel Club,* Travel Building, Floral Park, NY 11001 offers information services, insurance, and tours. Some of the major oil companies will send maps and mark preferred routes on them if you tell them what you have in mind. Try: *Exxon Touring Service,* 811 Gatehouse Rd., Falls Church, Va. 20042; or 450 Decoma, Houston, Texas 77001; *ARCO Travel Service,* P.O. Box 93, Versailles, Ky. 40383; *Mobil Travel Service,* Box 25, Versailles, Ky. 40383; *Texaco Travel Service,* Box 1459, Houston, Texas 77001. The practice of giving away free road maps at gasoline stations has almost entirely disappeared, and the most convenient place to get them now is bookstores. The three major road atlases for the U.S. are those published by Rand McNally, Hammond, and Grosset. Most states have their own maps, which pinpoint attractions, list historical sites, parks, etc. Write to the tourist services, in the state or states you plan to visit for copies of current maps. The precise addresses of the various state tourist services are given in the *Practical Information* sections for each state. City chambers of commerce are also good sources of information.

Plan to board the pets, discontinue paper and milk deliveries, and tell your local police and fire departments when you'll be leaving, when you expect to return. Ask a kindly neighbor to keep an eye on your house or apartment; fully protect your swimming pool against intruders. Have a neighbor keep your mail, or have it held at the post office. Consider having your telephone disconnected, if you plan to be away more than a few weeks. Look into the purchase of trip insurance (including baggage), and make certain your auto, fire, and other policies are up-to-date. The *American Automobile Association* (AAA) offers both group personal accident insurance and bail bond protection as part of its annual membership. Today, most people who travel use credit cards for major expenses such as gas, repairs, lodgings, and some meals. Put most of your trip money into travelers' checks. Arrange to have your lawn mowed at the usual times, and leave that kindly neighbor your itinerary (insofar as possible), car license number, and a key to your home (and tell police and firemen he has it). If you qualify for Senior Citizen discounts be sure to have the proper membership cards and identification along. (See below at the end of the Hotels and Motels section.)

 PACKING. *What to take, what to wear.* Make a packing list for each member of the family. Then check off items as you pack them. It will save time, reduce confusion. Time-savers to carry along include extra photo film (plenty), suntan lotion, insect repellent, sufficient toothpaste, soap, etc. Always carry an extra pair of glasses, including sunglasses, particularly if they're prescription ones. A travel iron is always handy, as are plastic bags (small and large) for wet suits, socks, etc. They are also excellent, of course, for packing shoes, spillable cosmetics, and other easily-damaged items. Fun extras to carry include binoculars, a compass, and a magnifying glass—useful in reading those fine print maps.

All members of the family should have sturdy pairs of shoes with non-slip soles. Keep them handy in the back of the car. You never know when you may want to stop and clamber along a rocky trail. Carry rain gear in a separate bag in the back of the car (so no one will have to get out and hunt for it in a downpour en route).

Women will probably want to stick to one or two basic colors for their wardrobes, so that they can manage with one set of accessories. If possible, include one knit or jersey dress or a pants suit. A full-skirted traveling dress will show less wear and wrinkling. For dress-up evenings, take along a couple of "basic" dresses you can vary with a simple change of accessories. That way you can dress up or down to suit the occasion.

If you go in spring or summer plan to dress as lightly as possible, but have along a light sweater for overcast days, cool evenings, and air-conditioned interiors. Women should have sleeveless dresses of cotton, linen, or synthetic fabrics that breathe. For men, tropical-weight suits of synthetic blends that breathe easily and are wrinkle-resistant are best. Cotton shirts are more absorbent than synthetics. In the humid coastal areas and in heat-generating cities temperatures over 29°C (85°F) often build into thundershowers, so a lightweight raincoat that can double as an overcoat in cooler weather, or as a windbreaker over warmer clothes in winter, will be handy. November through March be prepared for cooler weather, especially as you go inland and into higher ground. Men will probably want a jacket along for dining out and a dress shirt and tie for the most formal occasions. Turtlenecks are widely accepted and are a comfortable accessory. Don't forget extra slacks.

Planning a lot of sun time? Don't forget something sufficiently cover-up to wear over swim suits en route to the pool, beach, or lakefront, and for those first few days when you're getting reacquainted with sun on tender skin.

 INSURANCE. In planning your trip, think about three kinds of insurance: property, medical, and automobile. The best person to consult about insuring your household furnishings and personal property is your insurance agent. For Americans, he is also the person to ask about whatever special adjustments might be advisable in medical coverage while traveling. Foreigners visiting the United States should bear in mind that medical expenses in this country can be astronomical compared to those elsewhere, and that the kind of protection that some countries (Britain, for example) extend not only to their own nationals but to visiting foreigners as well simply does not exist here.

Every state has some sort of Financial Responsibility law establishing minimum and maximum amounts for which you can be held liable in auto accidents. Most states require insurance to be offered, and 17 states require you to have it in order to register a car or get a license within their jurisdictions. In any case, it is almost essential to have third party coverage, or "liability insurance," as claims can run very high for both car repairs and, particularly, medical treatment. Insurance premiums vary according to place and person; they are generally highest for males under 25 and for drivers who live in large urban areas.

One possibility is the *American Automobile Association* (AAA), which offers both group personal accident insurance (from $2,500 to $3,750) and bail bond protection up to $5,000 as part of its annual membership (fee $25). The AAA can also arrange the validation of foreign driving permits for use in the United States. Foreigners should consider getting their insurance before leaving their own countries since short-term tourists will find it difficult and expensive to buy here. For the AAA, write to *AAA,* 1712 G Street N.W., Washington, D.C. 20006.

If you are over 50, write to the American Association of Retired Persons/AIM, P.O. Box 2400, Long Beach, Calif. 90801 for information about its auto insurance recommendations and other travel services.

 HINTS TO THE MOTORIST. Probably the first precaution you will take is to have your car thoroughly checked by your regular dealer or service station to make sure that everything is in good shape. Second, you may find it wise to join an auto club that can provide you with trip planning information, insurance coverage, and emergency and repair service along the way. Thirdly, the *National Institute for Automotive Service Excellence,* which tests and certifies the competence of auto mechanics, publishes a directory of about 10,000 repair shops all over the U.S. which employ certified mechanics. It is available from *NIASE,* Suite 515, 1825 K Street N.W., Washington, D.C. 20005. The main highways of the South are great for high-speed driving. Speed limit is 55 miles per hour, to conform to gas conservation laws. However, highway hypnosis can be a decided danger on roads that stretch for miles without a break. It results from steady driving over long distances at set speeds. Principal symptoms are drowsiness and the inability to concentrate on what you're doing. The cure: Vary your speed occasionally, stop to stretch your legs, have a cup of coffee or tea, take a little exercise, take a brief nap.

If you get stuck on any kind of road, pull off the highway onto the shoulder, raise the hood, attach something white (a handkerchief, scarf, or a piece of tissue) to the door handle on the driver's side, and sit inside and wait. This is especially effective on limited-access highways, usually patrolled vigilantly by state highway officers. A special warning to women stalled at night: Remain inside the car with doors locked, and make sure the Good Samaritan is indeed what he seems. It is easier to find telephones along the major highways these days, since their locations are more frequently marked than they used to be. If you are a member of an automobile club, call the nearest garage listed in your Emergency Road Service Directory. Or ask the operator for help.

The mountains you will encounter in the South will present no particular driving problem. The roads are engineered for the ordinary driver, being well graded, normally wide, and safe. Observe the posted speed signs, particularly for curves. Keep to the right, again especially on curves. Use your engine in second or low gear on long descents, in order to save your brakes. If your car stalls, and your temperature gauge is high, it could mean a vapor lock. Cool the fuel pump with a damp cloth for a few minutes.

Budget your vacation driving time as carefully as you do your money. It's no fun to go sightseeing after a neck-and-shoulder-wearying day behind the wheel. In the wide open spaces, 250 miles a day is enough. In congested areas, make it 200. In most of the South, you'll be able to do the 250 miles comfortably. Stop occasionally to stretch your legs, walk the dog, buy a postcard, or give the kids a nature lesson in the woods or a roadside wiener roast. Save the big push for a business trip.

Traveling by car with your pet dog or cat? More and more motels accept them, but be sure to check *before* you register. Some turn them down, some want to look first, some offer special facilities. If it's a firt-time trip for your pet, accustom it to car travel by short trips in the neighborhood. And when you're packing, include its favorite foods, bowls, and toys. Your dog may like to ride with its head out the window. Discourage this. Wind and dust particles can permanently damage its eyes. Dogs are especially susceptible to heat stroke. Don't leave your dog in a parked car on a hot day while you dawdle over lunch. Keep your dog's bowl handy for water during stops for gas; service station attendants are usually cooperative about this.

One tip for frequent motel stops along the road is to pack two suitcases—one for the final destination, and the other with items for overnight stops: pajamas, shaving gear, cosmetics, toothbrushes, fresh shirt or dress. Put overnight luggage into the trunk last, so it can be pulled out first on overnight stops. A safety hint: Don't string your suits and dresses on hangers along a chain or rod stretched across the back seat. This obstructs vision, and may cause an accident.

WHAT WILL IT COST? Two people can travel in the USA for an average of about $80 a day (not counting gasoline or other transportation costs), as you can see in the table below. Regionally, however, there are wide variations. The Northeast is the most expensive part of the country, followed by the Mid-Atlantic states, the Midwest, the South Central states, the Plains and Far West, and the Southeast, in that order. And within the South of course prices vary too. Mississippi is cheaper than Florida, West Virginia than Maryland.

In some areas you can cut expenses by traveling off-season, when hotel rates are usually lower. The budget-minded traveler can also find bargain accommodations at tourist homes or family-style YMCA's and YWCA's. Some state and federal parks also provide inexpensive lodging. And some 250 colleges in 41 states offer dormitory accommodations to tourists during vacations at single-room rates of $2-$10 per night, with meals from $0.60-$3.50. A directory of some 200 such bargains all over the U.S. is *Mort's Guide to Low-Cost Vacations and Lodgings on College Campuses, USA-Canada*, from CMG Publishing Co., P.O. Box 630, Princeton, N.J. 08540.

Another way to cut down on the cost of your trip is to look for out-of-the-way resorts. Travelers are frequently rewarded by discovering very attractive areas which haven't as yet begun to draw quantities of people.

Typical Expenses for Two People	
Room at *moderate* hotel or motel	$35.00 plus tax
Breakfast, including tip	5.00
Lunch at *inexpensive* restaurant, including tip	8.00
Dinner at *moderate* restaurant, including tip	20.00
Sightseeing bus tour	6.00
An evening drink	4.00
Admission to museum or historic site	2.00
	$80.00

If you are budgeting your trip, don't forget to set aside a realistic amount for the possible rental of sports equipment (perhaps including a boat or canoe), entrance fees to amusement and historical sites, etc. Allow for tolls for bridges and super-highways (this can be a major item), extra film for cameras, and souvenirs.

After lodging, your biggest expense will be food, and here you can make great economies if you are willing to eat simply in your room and to picnic. It will save you time and money, and it will help you enjoy your trip more. That beautiful scenery does not have to whiz by at 55 miles per hour. Many states have picnic and rest areas, often well-equipped and in scenic spots, even on highways and thruways, so finding a pleasant place to stop is usually not difficult. Before you leave home put together a picnic kit.

Sturdy plastic plates and cups are cheaper in the long run than throw-away paper ones; and the same goes for permanent metal flatware rather than the throw-away plastic kind. Pack a small electric pot and two thermoses, one for water and one for milk, tea, or coffee. In other words, one hot, and one cold. If you go by car, take along a small cooler. Bread, milk, cold cereal, jam, tea or instant coffee, bouillon cubes and instant soup packets, fruit, fresh vegetables that need no cooking (such as lettuce, cucumbers, carrots, tomatoes, and mushrooms), cold cuts, cheese, nuts, raisins, eggs (hard boil them in the electric pot in your room the night before)—with only things like these you can eat conveniently, cheaply, and well.

Even in restaurants there are ways to cut costs. 1) Always stop at the cash register and look over the menu *before* you sit down. 2) Have a few standard items like coffee, soup, side dishes, etc. to test the price range. 3) Look around to see what other people are actually getting for their money. How big are the portions? Is there more than one slice of tomato in the salad? 4) Order a complete dinner; a la carte *always* adds up to more, unless you see someone with an enormous Chef's Salad and decide that's all you need. 5) If there is a salad bar or any kind of smorgasbord, fill up there and save on desserts and extras. 6) Ask about smaller portions, at lower prices, for children. Most places are providing them now. 7) Go to a Chinese restaurant and order one less main dish than the number of people in your group. You'll still come away pleasantly full. 8) Ask for the Day's Special, House Special, or whatever it's called. Chances are that it will be better, and more abundant, than other dishes on the menu. 9) Remember that in many restaurants lunch may be a better bargain than dinner. 10) Insist on *no ice* in your beverages; you'll get 30%-50% more to drink. 11) Drink half your coffee then ask for a refill; usually it won't be charged. 12) Below, in the section on restaurants we suggest some chains that offer good value for your money.

If you like a drink before dinner or bed, bring your own bottle. Most hotels and motels supply ice free or for very little, but the markup on alcoholic beverages in restaurants, bars, lounges and dining rooms is enormous, and in some states peculiar laws apply regarding alcohol consumption. And in any case, a good domestic dry white wine makes a fine aperitif and is much cheaper than a cocktail.

 HOTELS AND MOTELS. *General Hints.* Don't be one of those who take pot luck for lodgings. You'll waste a lot of time hunting for a place, and often won't be happy with the accommodations you finally find. If you are without reservations, begin looking early in the afternoon. If you have reservations, but expect to arrive later than five or six P.M., advise the hotel or motel in advance. Some places will not, unless advised, hold reservations after six P.M. And if you hope to get a room at the hotel's *minimum* rate, be sure to reserve ahead or arrive very early.

If you are planning to stay in a popular resort region, at the height of the season, reserve well in advance. Include a deposit for all places except motels (and for motels if they request one). Many chain or associated motels and hotels will make advance reservations for you at affiliated hostelries along your route.

A number of hotels and motels have one-day laundry and dry-cleaning services, and many motels have coin laundries. Most motels, but not all, have telephones in the rooms. If you want to be sure of room service, however, better stay at a hotel. Many motels have swimming pools, and even beachfront hotels frequently have a pool. Even some motels in the hearts of large cities have pools. An advantage at motels is the free parking. There's seldom a charge for parking at country and resort hotels.

Hotel and motel chains. In addition to the hundreds of excellent independent motels and hotels throughout the country, there are also many that belong to national or regional chains. A major advantage of the chains, to many travelers, is the ease of making reservations en route, or at one fell swoop in advance. If you are a guest at a member hotel or motel, the management will be delighted to secure you a sure booking at one of its affiliated hotels for the coming evening—at no costs to you. Chains also usually have toll-free WATS (800) lines to assist you in making reservations on your own. This, of course, saves you time, worry and money. In some chains, you have the added advantage of knowing what the standards are all the way. The insistence on uniform standards of comfort, cleanliness and amenities is more common in motel than in hotel chains. (Easy to understand when you realize that most hotel chains are formed by simply buying up older, established hotels, while most motel chains have control of their units from start to finish.) However, individuality can be one of the great charms of a hotel. Some travelers prefer independent motels and hotels because they are more likely to reflect the genuine character of the surrounding area. There are several aids to planning available in this sphere. *The Hotel and Motel Redbook,* published annually by the American Hotel and Motel Association, 888 Seventh Avenue, New York City, N.Y. 10019, covers the entire world and sells for around $16.00. *Hotel and Travel Index,* published quarterly by Ziff-Davis, sells for about $20. These are probably best consulted at your travel agent's office. On a more modest scale, the AAA supplies, *to its members only,* regional *Tour Books* that list those establishments recommended by the Association.

Because the single biggest expense of your whole trip is lodging, you may well be discouraged and angry at the prices of some hotel and motel rooms, particularly when you know you are paying for things you neither need nor want, such as a heated swimming pool, wall-to-wall carpeting, a huge color TV set, two huge double beds for only two people, meeting rooms, a cocktail lounge, maybe even a putting green. Nationwide, motel prices for two people now average $37 a night;

hotel prices run from $35 to $85, with the average around $52. This explains the recent rapid spread of a number of budget motel chains whose rates average $17.50 for a single and $21 for a double, an obvious advantage.

The main national motel chains are Holiday Inn, Howard Johnson's; Quality Courts, Ramada Inns, Sheraton Motor Inns, and TraveLodge. Alongside the style that these places represent, however, are others, less luxurious and less costly, at which rates run about one-half those of the bigger, "more luxurious" ones. Here are the main ones operating in the South: Budget Host Inns, PO Box 25092 Fort Worth, Texas 76116; Days Inns of America, Inc., 2751 Buford Highway, Northeast, Atlanta 1, Georgia 30324 (various toll-free numbers); Downtowner Motor Inns, 202 Union Street, Memphis, Tenn., call 800) 238-6161; Family Inns of America, P.O. Box 2191, Knoxville, Tennessee 37901; Friendship Inns International, 739 South Fourth, West, Salt Lake City, Utah 84101, call 800) 453-4511; Motel 6, 1888 Century Park East, Suite 1900, Los Angeles, Cal. 90067; Scottish Inns of America, 104 Bridgewater Road, Knoxville, Tenn. 37919, call 800) 251-1962; Econo Travel Motor Hotel Corp., 20 Kroger Executive Center, P.O. Box 12188, Norfolk, Va. 23502, call 800) 446-6900; Red Roof Inns, 500 South Fourth Street, P.O. Box 283, Columbus, Ohio 43216; Thrift Inns Ltds., P.O. Box 6160, Newport News, Virginia 23606; Scottish Inns of America, 104 Bridgewater Road, Knoxville, Tennessee 37919. These chains all publish free directories of their member motels. The Save More Club, Inc., 1100 South Trail, P.O. Box 2493, Sarasota, Fla. 33578, is a national membership organization (fee $15) to provide discounts (usually 10%) at hotels, motels, restaurants, theme parks, car rentals, etc., all over the country.

Prices in the budget chains are fairly uniform, but this is not the case in chains such as Ramada, Quality, Holiday Inns, Howard Johnson's, and TraveLodge. Their prices vary widely by region, location, and season. Among the national non-budget chains the most expensive are Hilton, Marriott, and Sheraton; the middle range includes Holiday Inns, Howard Johnson, Quality Inns, and Trave-Lodge; and the least expensive are usually Best Western, Ramada, and Rodeway (mainly in the South).

HOTEL AND MOTEL CATEGORIES

Hotels and motels in all the Fodor guidebooks to the U.S.A. are divided into five categories, arranged by price.

Although the names of the various hotel and motel categories are standard throughout this series, the prices listed under each category may vary from area to area. This variation is meant to reflect local price standards, and take into account the fact that what might be considered a *moderate* price in a large urban area might be quite expensive in a rural region. In every case, however, the dollar ranges for each category are clearly stated before each listing of establishments.

Our ratings are flexible and subject to change. We should also like to point out that many fine hotels and motels had to be omitted for lack of space.

Super Deluxe: This category is reserved for only a few hotels. In addition to giving the visitor all the amenities discussed under the deluxe category (below), the super deluxe hotel has a special atmosphere of glamor, good taste, and dignity and it will probably be a favored meeting spot of local society. In short, super deluxe means the tops.

Deluxe: The minimum facilities must include bath and shower in all rooms, valet and laundry service, suites available, a well-appointed restaurant and a bar (where local law permits), room service, TV and telephone in room, air conditioning and heat, pleasing decor, and an atmosphere of luxury, calm and elegance. There should be ample and personalized service. In a deluxe *motel,* there may be less service rendered by employees and more by machine (such as refrigerators and ice-making machines in your room), but there should be a minimum of do-it-yourself in a truly deluxe establishment.

Expensive: All rooms must have bath or shower, valet and laundry service, restaurant and bar (local law permitting), limited room service, TV and telephone in room, heat and air conditioning, pleasing decor. Although decor may be as good as that in deluxe establishments, hotels and motels in this category are frequently designed for commercial travelers or for families in a hurry and are somewhat impersonal in terms of service. Valet and laundry service will probably be lacking; the units will be outstanding primarily for their convenient location and functional character, not for their attractive or comfortable qualities.

Moderate: Each room should have an attached bath or shower. There should be a restaurant *or* coffee shop, TV available, telephone in room, heat and air conditioning, relatively convenient location, clean and comfortable rooms and public rooms. *Motels* in this category may not have attached bath or shower, may not have a restaurant or coffee shop (though one is usually nearby), and may have no public rooms.

Inexpensive: Nearby bath or shower, telephone available, clean rooms are the minimum.

Free parking is assumed at all motels and motor hotels; you must pay for parking at most city hotels, though certain establishments have free parking, frequently for occupants of higher-than-minimum-rate rooms. *Baby sitter* lists are always available in good hotels and motels, and *cribs* for the children are always on hand—sometimes at no cost, but more frequently at a cost of $1 or $2. The cost of a *cot* in your room, to supplement the beds, will be around $3 per night, but moving an *extra single bed* into a room will cost around $7 in better hotels and motels.

Senior citizens may in some cases receive special discounts on lodgings. The Days Inn chain offers various discounts to anyone 55 or older. Holiday Inns give a discount to members of the NRTA (write to National Retired Teachers Association, Membership Division, 406 Grand Ave., Ojai, California 93023) and the AARP (write to American Association of Retired Persons, Membership Division, 215 Long Beach Blvd., Long Beach, California 90802). The amounts and availability of such discounts change, so it is well to check their current status with either your organization or with the hotel chain. The *National Council of Senior Citizens,* 1511 K Street NW, Washington DC 20005, works especially to develop low-cost travel possibilities for its members.

The closest thing America has to Europe's bed-and-breakfast is the private houses that go by the various names of tourist home, guest home, or guest house. These are often large, still fairly elegant old homes in quiet residential or semiresidential parts of larger towns or along secondary roads and the main streets of small towns and resorts. Styles and standards vary widely, of course; generally, private baths are less common and rates are pleasingly low. In many small towns such guest houses are excellent examples of the best a region has to offer of its own special atmosphere. Each one will be different, so that their advantage is precisely the opposite of that "no surprise" uniformity which motel chains pride themselves on. Few, if any, guest houses have heated pools, wall-to-wall carpeting, or exposed styrofoam-wooden beams in the bar. Few if any even have bars. What you do get, in addition to economy, is the personal flavor of a family atmosphere in a private home. In popular tourist areas, state or local tourist information offices or chambers of commerce usually have lists of homes that let out spare rooms to paying guests, and such a listing usually means that the places on it have been inspected and meet some reliable standard of cleanliness, comfort, and reasonable pricing.

In larger towns and cities a good bet for clean, plain, reliable lodging is a YMCA or YWCA. These buildings are usually centrally located, and their rates tend to run to less than half of those of hotels. Nonmembers are welcome, but may pay slightly more than members. A few very large Ys may have accommodations for couples but usually sexes are segregated. Decor is spartan and the cafeteria fare plain and wholesome, but a definite advantage is the use of the building's pool, gym, reading room, information services, and other facilities. For a directory, write to National Council of the YMCA, 291 Broadway, New York, N.Y. 10007; and the National Board of the YWCA, 600 Lexington Avenue, New York, N.Y. 10022.

 DINING OUT. The Chesapeake Bay area has a rich culinary tradition. *Baltimore* is famous for its seafood, notably oysters and crab cakes. And Chesapeake Bay yields over 40 species of fish including grey trout, sea trout, bluefish, black and channel bass, white and yellow perch, rock shad, herring (also taken in the Potomac), catfish, sea robin, flounder, and menhaden.

Maryland in general is known for its fried chicken, terrapin soup, terrapin stew (use butter and sherry), steamed hard-shell crabs, and beaten biscuits; but along the *Eastern Shore* you will encounter the towns of Bivalve, Md. and Oyster, Va. as well as the villages of Oystershell, and Shell-town, and the "Seafood Capital of the World," Crisfield, Md., much of which is built on a huge mound of oyster shells. Finer distinctions arise; you may attend a crab "feast" but an oyster "roast." The *Delmarva Peninsula* also produces melons, tomatoes, and potatoes; these last (with the skillful addition of milk, butter, eggs, sugar, lemon, cinnamon and nutmeg) are made into White Potato Pie, another regional specialty.

Virginia is another land of plenty overflowing with ham, spoonbread, fried chicken, crabs, and beef, if not milk and honey. It is said that a good *Tidewater* cook knows at least 20 ways to prepare a crab; and Crab *Norfolk,* seasoned with vinegar, salt, red and black pepper and baked en casserole, is but one of them. Nearby *Hampton* considers itself the Seafood Capital of Virginia (the world title being already taken, as noted above). At *Smithfield,* on the Pagan River, hogs are allowed to roam free in the fields until autumn and then are let into the peanut fields to fatten. It is the peanuts and the special method of curing that give the dark-red Smithfield hams their distinctive flavor. The state is also noted for Black Angus beef.

For evening dining, the best advice is to make reservations whenever possible. Most hotels and farm-vacation places have set dining hours. For motel-stayers, life is simpler if the motel has a restaurant. If it hasn't, try to stay at one that is near a restaurant.

Some restaurants are fussy about customers' dress, particularly in the evening. For women, pants and pants suits are now almost universally acceptable. For men, the tie and jacket remains the standard, but turtleneck sweaters are becoming more and more common. Shorts are almost always frowned on for both men and women. Standards of dress are becoming progressively more relaxed, so a neatly dressed customer will usually experience no problem. If in doubt about accepted dress at a particular establishment, call ahead. Roadside stands, turnpike restaurants and cafeterias have no fixed standards of dress. If you're traveling with children, find out if a restaurant has a children's menu and commensurate prices (many do).

When figuring the tip on your check, base it on the total charges for the meal, not on the grand total, if that total includes a sales tax. Don't tip on tax.

The restaurants mentioned in this volume which are located in large metropolitan areas are categorized by type of cuisine: French, Chinese, Armenian, etc., with restaurants of a general nature listed as American-International. Restaurants in less populous areas are divided into price categories as follows: *super deluxe, deluxe, expensive, moderate,* and *inexpensive.* As a general rule, expect restaurants in metropolitan areas to be higher in price, but many restaurants that feature foreign cuisine are surprisingly inexpensive. Limitations of space make it impossible to include every establishment, so we have listed those which we recommend as the best within each price range.

RESTAURANT CATEGORIES

Although the names of the various restaurant categories are standard throughout this series, the prices listed under each category may vary from area to area. This variation is meant to reflect local price standards, and take into account the fact that what might be considered a *moderate* price in a large urban area might be quite expensive in a rural region. In every case, however, the dollar ranges for each category are clearly stated before each listing of establishments.

Super Deluxe: This category indicates an outstanding restaurant which is lavishly decorated, must have a superb wine list, excellent service, immaculate kitchens, and a large, well-trained staff.

Deluxe: Many a fine restaurant around the country falls into this category. It will have its own well-deserved reputation for excellence, perhaps a house specialty or two for which it is famous, and an atmosphere of elegance, attentive service, and unique decor. It will have a good wine list where the law permits and will be considered one of the best in town by the inhabitants.

Expensive: In addition to the expected dishes, it will offer one or two house specialties, wine list, and cocktails (where law permits), air conditioning (unless locale makes it unnecessary), a general reputation for very good food and an adequate staff, an elegant decor and appropriately dressed clientele.

Moderate: Cocktails and/or beer where the law permits, air conditioning (locale not precluding), clean kitchen, adequate staff, better-than-average service. General reputation for good, wholesome food.

Inexpensive: The bargain place in town, it is clean, even if plain. It will have air conditioning (when necessary), tables (not a counter), clean kitchen and attempt to provide adequate service.

 SUMMER SPORTS. *Swimming* is excellent in the many lakes as well as along the golden beaches that edge much of this area (over 10,000 miles of ocean shoreline). *Water skiing* (equipment may be rented in many places) abounds on lakes and in sheltered salt-water areas (the *Masters Water Ski Tournament* is held annually at Pine Mountain, Georgia). *Skin- and scuba-divers* explore the fantasies not only of the salt-water world, but also of lakes and numerous outsize springs.

Tennis and golf are played virtually everywhere. *Shelling* is extremely popular on Gulf beaches; and *rockhounds* are particularly partial to northern Georgia. All forms of *boating* are highly popular throughout the region, as are races and boating *regattas;* and sailing ranks high in some areas (the *Gulf Yachting Races* are held in July at Gulfport, Miss.).

Fresh-water fishermen angle for bass, shad, perch, snook, etc., in the region's rivers, for trout, crappie, bream, muskie, walleye, catfish, bluegill, etc., in the many lakes and streams. Experts go after muskellunge in Georgia's Blue Ridge Reservoir. Fishermen will find *surf casting* in a number of areas, and fishing from piers and bridges lures literally millions at some seasons. Salt-water anglers go out after amberjack, cavalla, bluefish, king mackerel, grouper, red snapper, sea trout, etc., flats fishermen after the wily bonefish. Big-game fishermen go forth to do battle with tarpon, tuna, marlin, sailfish, etc. Vacationers will find tarpon and other big-game fishing tournaments in many areas. Everything from rowboats to cruisers is available for hire or charter almost everywhere.

Spectators flock to thoroughbred and harness races, to greyhound races, stock-car races.

To make certain you don't miss any of the exciting sports events in the areas where you are vacationing, read the local newspapers as you go along.

WINTER SPORTS. On the whole, the climate in this region is so mild numerous sports may be enjoyed year-round. *Spectator sports* include rodeos, stock-car races, football (including Bowl games on Jan. 1st), greyhound racing, harness and thoroughbred racing, fast and fabulous *jai alai* games at frontons in half a dozen Florida cities. Many of the big-league *baseball* teams hold their spring training in Florida communities. *Horse shows* are held in various areas; and *polo* is big in Florida and South Carolina (Aiken is called the Polo Capital of the South) during the first four months of each year. Both the *Masters Golf Tournament* in mid-April and the *Women's Titleholders Tournament* in mid-April draw large numbers of spectators to Augusta, Ga. Other important spectator events include the *races* held during February and March at the Daytona International Speedway and the *International Grand Prix Sports Car Race* at Sebring in March.

The range of *participant sports* is high, wide, and handsome. *Swimming* in midwinter is enjoyable only in the most southerly areas, as are *water skiing and skin- and scuba-diving.* But *boating* of all types is enjoyed throughout the area on a year-round basis, as is *golf.* *Horseback riding* and *skeet* and *trapshooting* are popular. *Hunters* trek out for deer, quail, grouse, goose, boar, turkey, rabbit, squirrel (open seasons vary within states, sometimes within areas). Exceptional waterfowl shooting is found along the Mississippi flyway.

Anglers angle for bass, perch, snook, etc., in the many rivers of this region, while lake and stream fishermen bait their hooks for bass, bream, crappie, trout, muskie, walleye, bluegill, and catfish. Piers and bridges are liberally sprinkled with casters throughout the winter; while out on the briny catches consist of amberjack, dolphin, king mackerel, cavalla, bluefish, grouper, sea trout, pompano, etc. Fishermen will find charter boats available in almost every area. Big-game fish here include tarpon, tuna, marlin, and sailfish. Bonefishing in the shallows has its many devotees, as does surf fishing.

ROUGHING IT. More, and improved, camping facilities are springing up each year across the country, in national parks, national forests, state parks, in private camping areas, and trailer parks, which by now have become national institutions. Farm vacations continue to gain adherents, especially among families with children. Some accommodations are quite deluxe, some extremely simple. For a directory of farms which take vacationers (including details of rates, accommodations, dates, etc.), write to *Adventure Guides, Inc.,* 36 East 57 Street, New York, N.Y. 10022 for their 224-page book *Country Vacations U.S.A.*

Because of the great size of the United States and the distances involved, youth hostels have not developed in this country the way they have in Europe and Japan. In the entire 3½ million square miles of the U.S. there are upwards of 160 youth hostels, and because they are, in any case, designed primarily for people who are traveling under their own power, usually hiking or bicycling, rather than by car or commercial transportation, they tend to be away from towns and cities and in rural areas, near scenic spots. In the U.S. they are most frequent and practical in compact areas like New England. Although their members are mainly younger people, there is no age limit. You must be a member to use youth hostels; write to *American Youth Hostel Association, Inc.,* National Campus, Delaplane, Virginia 22025. A copy of the Hostel Guide and Handbook will be included in your membership. Accommodations are simple, dormitories are segregated by sex, common rooms and kitchen are shared, and everyone helps with the cleanup.

Useful Addresses: National Parks Service, U.S. Dept. of the Interior, Washington, D.C. 20240; *National Forest Service,* U.S. Dept. of Agriculture, Wash., D.C., 20250. For information on state parks, write *State Parks Dept., State Office Building,* in the capital of the state in which you are interested. Exact addresses of such agencies are given separately in the *Practical Information* section for each state in this book.

The *National Campers & Hikers Assoc.,* Box 451, Orange, New Jersey, 07051, is an informal organization of camping enthusiasts. *American Camping Assoc., Inc.,* Bradford Woods, Martinsville, Indiana, 46151 is a commercial camping organization. Headquarters of the *Appalachian Mountain Club* is 5 Joy St., Boston, Mass., 02108. Also *Kampgrounds of America, Inc.,* PO Box 30558, Billings, Montana 59114.

 TIPPING. Tipping is supposed to be a personal thing, your way of expressing your appreciation of someone who has taken pleasure and pride in giving you attentive, efficient, and personal service. Because standards of personal service in the United States are highly uneven, you should, when you get genuinely good service, feel secure in rewarding it, and when you feel that the service you got was slovenly, indifferent, or surly, don't hesitate to show this by the size, or withholding, of your tip. Remember that in many places the help are paid very little and depend on tips for the better part of their income. This is supposed to give them incentive to serve you well. These days, the going rate for tipping on *restaurant* service is 15% on the amount *before* taxes. Tipping at counters is not universal, but many people leave at least 25¢ and 10% if it's anything over that. For *bellboys,* 25¢ per bag is usual. However, if you load him down with all manner of bags, hatboxes, cameras, coats, etc., you might consider giving an extra quarter or two. For one-night stays in most *hotels* and *motels,* you leave nothing. But if you stay longer, at the end of your stay leave the maid $1-$1.25 per day, or $5 per person per week for multiple occupancy. If you are staying at an *American Plan* hostelry (meals included), $1.50 per day per person for the waiter or waitress is considered sufficient, and is left at the end of your stay. If you have been surrounded by an army of servants (one bringing relishes, another rolls, etc.), add a few extra dollars and give the lump sum to the captain or *maître d'hôtel* when you leave, asking him to allocate it.

For the many other services you may encounter in a big hotel or resort, figure roughly as follows: doorman, 25¢ for taxi handling, 50¢ for help with baggage; bellhop, 25¢ per bag, more if you load him down with extras; parking attendant, 50¢; bartender, 15%; room service, 10-15% of that bill; laundry or valet service, 15%; pool attendant, 50¢ per day; snackbar waiter at pool, beach, or golf club, 50¢ per person for food and 15% of the beverage check; locker attendant, 50¢ per person per day, or $2.50 per week; golf caddies, $1-$2 per bag, or 15% of the greens fee for an 18-hole course, or $3 on a free course; masseurs and masseuses 20%; barbers, 50¢; shoeshine attendants, 25¢; hairdressers, $1; manicurists, 50¢.

Transportation: Give 25¢ for any taxi fare under $1 and 15% for any above; however, drivers in New York, Las Vegas, and other major resorts *expect* 20%. Limousine service, 20%. Car rental agencies, nothing. Bus porters are tipped 25¢ per bag, drivers nothing. On charters and package tours, conductors and drivers usually get $5-$10 per day from the group as a whole, but be sure to ask whether this has already been figured into the package cost. On short local sightseeing runs, the driverguide may get 25¢ per person, more if you think he has been especially helpful or personable. Airport bus drivers, nothing. Redcaps, in resort areas, 35¢ per suitcase, elsewhere, 25¢. Tipping at curbside check-in is unofficial, but same as above. On the plane, no tipping.

Railroads suggest you leave 10-15% per meal for dining car waiters, but the steward who seats you is not tipped. Sleeping-car porters get about $1 per person per night. The 25¢ or 35¢ you pay a railway station baggage porter is not a tip but the set fee that he must hand in at the end of the day along with the ticket stubs he has used. Therefore his tip is anything you give him above that, 25-50¢ per bag, depending on how heavy your luggage is.

 HINTS TO HANDICAPPED TRAVELERS. Two important sources of information are the books: *Travel Ability,* by Lois Reamy, published by Macmillan; and *Access to the World: A Travel Guide for the Handicapped,* by Louise Weiss, published by Chatham Square Press, Inc., 401 Broadway, New York, N.Y. 10013. *Rehabilitation International,* 20 West 40 Street, New York, N.Y. 10018 publishes a 16-page International Directory of Access Guides, actually a bibliography of some 275 individual manuals of access possibilities at travel facilities all over the U.S. and Canada, plus three European countries. Two other publications which give valuable information about motels, hotels, and restaurants (rating them, telling about steps, table heights, door widths, etc.) are *Where Turning Wheels Stop,* published by Paralyzed Veterans of America, 3636 16th St., N.W., Washington, D.C. 20010, and *The Wheelchair Traveler,* by Douglas R. Annand, Ball Hill Road, Milford, NH 03055. Many of the nation's national parks have special facilities for the handicapped. These are described in *National Park Guide for the Handicapped,* available from the U.S. Government Printing Office, Washington, D.C. 20402. TWA publishes a free 12-page pamphlet entitled *Consumer Information about Air Travel for the Handicapped* to explain available special arrangements and how to get them. A central source of free information is the *Travel Information Center, Moss Rehabilitation Hospital,* 12th Street and Tabor Road, Philadelphia, Pa. 19141. And you may also get information from the *Easter Seal Society for Crippled Children and Adults,* Director of Education and Information Service, 2023 West Ogden Ave., Chicago, Illinois 60612.

ALABAMA

Promise of Field and Factory

BY
CALEB PIRTLE

Caleb Pirtle, formerly Travel Editor of Southern Living Magazine, *has become one of the South's most eloquent and amusing spokesmen.*

Birmingham, Alabama's largest city, with a population of over 300,-000, is a good base, despite its industrialization, for touring the state. Though long known as the "Pittsburgh of the South," Birmingham's busy, modern look has rising cultural overtones. Its symbol, however, remains a giant statue of Vulcan, readily seen if you approach the city from the south on US 31. Presiding over a beautiful countryside, this towering monument stands mounted atop a pedestal 124 feet high. Cast in the Birmingham locale, the fifty-five-foot iron statue, created by Giuseppe Moretti, made its first public appearance at the 1904 St. Louis "Louisiana Purchase Exposition." Thousands come to view this exceptional sight yearly, a monument to the memory of the 19th-century artist. You can take a glass-enclosed elevator to the observation deck at the base of the statue for a breathtaking view of Birmingham and surrounding Jones Valley.

Near Birmingham and Bessemer is the Tannehill State Park, where you can enjoy camping, fishing and hiking along the Cahaba River, as well as view the old Tannehill Iron Furnaces, standing today as mute evidence of the fiery raid which destroyed them in the closing days of the War Between the States. There are several hiking trails in the park,

Points of Interest
(Birmingham)

1) Alabama Theater
2) Art Museum
3) Birmingham Green
4) City Hall
5) Civic Center
6) Engineering Building (U. of Alabama)
7) Greater Birmingham Arts Alliance
8) Liberty National Building
9) Medical Center (U. of Alabama)

10) Miss Liberty
11) Municipal Auditorium
12) Red Mountain Museum
13) St. Paul's Cathedral
14) School of Dentistry (U. of Alabama)
15) Sloss Furnace
16) Southern Research Institute
17) Vulcan Statue

including the Tannehill Scout Trail, which is 10.5 miles and takes an average of five to six hours to complete.

Find your way to 331 Cotton Avenue SW, and you can visit Arlington Antebellum Home, an eight-room, two-story dwelling built in 1842 by William S. Mudd. It is a half-timber structure which used the property's own trees and incorporated the nails, beams, and bricks hand-fashioned by local slaves. It has over six landscaped acres for a scenic background and brims with original furniture of the 1800's: French, English, and American in design. Arlington was constructed thirty years prior to the founding of Birmingham in what was then Elyton, the seat of Jefferson County. Owned over the past century and a quarter by the Mudd, Whitney, DeBardeleben and Munger families, the house was purchased in 1953 by the city. It has a Civil War Museum.

Birmingham's Museum of Art is worthy of inclusion on your city tour. You will be able to view numerous Old World paintings and a compendium of art objects from Palestine. Also on display is a great assortment of bronzes and silver together with standard museum fare.

Your small fry will enjoy a visit to the Jimmy Morgan Zoo at 2630 Cahaba Road SW on US 280, where they can visit an aviary, a serpentarium and the large variety of hoofed creatures housed there.

Nearby in the wooded areas of beautiful Lane Park are Birmingham's Botanical and Japanese Gardens.

For a different look at Birmingham, visit the Red Mountain Museum. Here you'll find geological displays from the area, and you can take a walking tour along one side of the Red Mountain Cut, where the center of a mountain was torn away, revealing thousands of years of geological history in its layers.

Birmingham is noted for its beautiful displays of roses and dogwood, and if you visit the steel city during the height of the season, late April and early May, get the latest information from the chamber of commerce regarding location of the best blooms.

Environs of Birmingham

If you're in Birmingham during the spring, be sure to take in the city's Festival of Arts, which has skyrocketed to national prominence. Each festive day is packed with entertaining and informative activities—concerts, dramas, operas, ballets top off outstanding exhibits of painting, sculpture, and crafts. Each year the festival salutes a different country.

Also located in Birmingham, on the south side, is the University of Alabama Medical Center. The rapidly growing, multi-million-dollar complex covers more than sixty blocks and contains more than sixty health service facilities. It is considered one of the leading medical centers in the South, where patients come from all over the world for open heart surgery. It also has the only diabetes hospital in the world. Nearby is Southern Research Institute, where important cancer research is under way.

To begin a northern circle tour from Birmingham, follow US 78 northwest to Jasper. Nearby is Smith Lake, covering 21,000 acres, with 500 miles of wooded shoreline, formed by the Lewis Smith dam. At Jasper change to State 5 (also State 4 in this section), and proceed to the town named Natural Bridge. Nearby is Alabama's natural bridge. Slowly

ALABAMA

eroded by the perpetual abrasion of the stream, the sandstone fell away, leaving two large arches, one 148 feet long and 33 feet wide. Nearby, just outside of Hodges, is Rock Bridge Canyon with a major hiking trail that winds for about two miles through tunnels and unusual rock formations. Ball rock, Alabama's largest, is a huge hunk of sandstone rising 285 feet above the canyon.

Tuscumbia is the birthplace and early home of Helen Keller. "Ivy Green," built by her grandfather in 1820, is still there. Typically southern in architecture, its large square rooms have individual fireplaces. An office where the plantation books were kept was built in the yard near the house, and later a dressing room and porch were added. When Captain Keller brought his bride home, the ex-office-turned-residence was furnished for them. Here Helen Keller, a normal child, was born on June 27, 1880. Two years later, typhoid fever tragically deprived the little girl of both sight and sound, beginning the greatest drama in Ivy Green's long history. The story of how she overcame her handicaps has been an inspiration to millions the world over.

Much the same now as it was then, the many significant places and things—Whistle Path, the pump, her personal effects—have been kept intact for the visitor. Her story is retold each summer when William Gibson's play "The Miracle Worker" is staged at her birthplace.

Tuscumbia once was the site of an eighteenth-century Chickasaw town. During the 1830's, a canal was built around Muscle Shoals in the Tennessee River to aid navigation, and the first railroad west to the Allegheny Mountains was built from Tuscumbia to the boat landing. In Tuscumbia's Legion Park is the Big Spring. The copious flow of water attracted the Indians who located there and later it became the home of the first white settlers.

Sheffield (like Florence) can be reached easily from Tuscumbia. It's the principal railroad and industrial center of the Muscle Shoals areas. Your chief interest, however, will be the Wilson Dam, five miles northeast on State 133. Part of its powerhouse and an overlook are open free to the public. Its great bulk—4,500 feet in length, 137 feet in height and 101 feet thick at the base—creates Wilson Lake. The resulting miles of available shoreline make it a popular area for vacation activities, with the emphasis, of course, on aquatics.

Florence—third of the Tri-Cities—was settled in 1779 and has a population of 31,650. Florence was the birthplace of William C. Handy, famous Negro composer of "St. Louis Blues," and his home on W. Mobile St. has undergone restoration. Also in Florence is the largest Indian mound in the Tennessee River Valley, rising upward forty-two feet. The temple, which once stood atop the mound, was used for Indian ceremonials honoring the sun god. A modern museum, tracing the movement of prehistoric Indians through Northern Alabama, has been opened at the base of the mound. The city's other major attraction is restored Pope's Tavern, an early-day stagecoach inn. It was here that Andrew Jackson stopped for a night on his way to the battle of New Orleans.

Eighteen miles east of Florence on US 72, turn off on State 101 and, four miles south, you will reach Wheeler Dam, named for "Fighting Joe" Wheeler who served as a Confederate cavalry commander and with the

U.S. during the Spanish-American War. Behind Wheeler Dam is Wheeler Lake on the Tennessee River. Another of the TVA dams, Wheeler backs the river up for seventy-four miles. Today Joe Wheeler State Park, opened on the north bank of the Tennessee River, offers an eighteen-hole championship golf course, a beach front swimming area, 116 campsites, a marina with 120 slips, a lavish 75-room resort hotel and restaurant. There are also a fishing pagoda, tennis courts, riding trails, biking and nature trails, and cottages.

Continuing south on State 101, you junction with Alternate US 72 which runs south of the lake. Heading east on 72A, it's a short drive to Decatur, a flourishing, industrial area thriving as a result of the TVA. Founded in 1820, it was later the scene of so many Civil War battles that when peace was declared all but five buildings had been reduced to rubble. In Decatur, Point Mallard, named for the ducks that come each winter to the adjacent Wheeler National Wildlife Refuge, is a family park, complete with the nation's first wave pool. Although Decatur is three hundred miles from the nearest ocean, its olympic-size pool provides three-foot-high waves just like the seashore. The 749-acre park also provides a 175-site campground, picnic facilities, and biking and hiking trails. There are an eighteen-hole championship golf course, paddle boats for use on the Tennessee River, and a playground for children.

Continuing east six miles on US 72A, you come to Mooresville. The first town incorporated in the state, it has a post office that still uses wooden call boxes of the last century, and still radiates a feeling of the early 1800's.

From cotton field to the moon might be a good description of your next stop—Huntsville, which likes to call itself "The Space Capital of the Universe."

Before Wernher von Braun and his space experts arrived on the scene, the city was a sleepy cotton town with a population hovering around 16,000. Today, a little over a decade later, Huntsville has a population of more than 135,000 and is one of the fastest growing cities in the country.

Most of the fantastic growth is due to the emergence of the Alabama Space and Rocket Center, located at Redstone Arsenal, just southwest off US 231.

Some of the most important experimental work in man's conquest of space has taken place here, and arrayed just inside the center and dominating the skyline are gleaming white models of numerous rockets.

The sprawling space flight center, set up at Redstone Arsenal in 1960, is also the home of the Army Missile Command and the Army's Missile and Munitions Center and School.

In the Space Orientation Center at Marshall, the history of rocketry and space exploration is recounted through the use of exhibits "from the early Chinese fire arrows to the V-2 rocket." Also on display is the Mercury capsule piloted by Commander Walter M. Schirra, Jr., on this country's third manned flight in 1962. You can also see exhibits illustrating the National Aeronautics and Space Administration's method for conducting a lunar landing, and an exhibit showing the late Lieutenant Colonel Edward H. White's "space walk."

To meet its fantastic boom, Huntsville now has under way several multi-million-dollar urban renewal projects which will give the old downtown section a completely new look. Already built are the city's gleaming new city hall, civic center, and probably the most modern and up-to-date courthouse in the South.

But the old still remains with such structures as the First National Bank, Alabama's oldest bank, on the downtown square, still standing. Rows of cotton may be seen too, planted along the city's traffic-laden Memorial Parkway, where numerous motels, restaurants, and shopping centers have sprung up practically overnight. All of the town's old textile mills have closed their doors, but farsighted leaders saw that they were put to good use. The offices of a number of space-oriented firms are now housed in one of the old cotton plants which was reconverted and is now known as the "Huntsville Industrial Center."

The city's research park, located near the University of Alabama at Huntsville campus, northwest of the city off US 231, also is a must for the tourist.

Huntsville's link to the past is Twickenham, a twelve-block, 300-structure district recently added to the National Register of Historic Places. In the area, 159 buildings are said to have historic and architectural significance, and twelve are listed in the Historic American Buildings Survey of 1935. Twickenham is the founding place of Huntsville and the cornerstone of Alabama.

Huntsville was the home of six Alabama governors, and is known for many beautiful old homes, located in the tree-shaded Twickenham District just a few blocks from downtown.

The Pope-Spragins Home, though not open to the public, was the abode of Confederate Secretary of War, LeRoy Pope Walker. It is noted for its classic portico—Mr. Walker for his command to bombard Fort Sumter.

Another TVA Creation

Guntersville, site of another huge TVA dam, is your next destination, via US 431. Originally an 18th century Indian village, Guntersville became a boomtown in the early 1820s with the coming of the steamboat and white settlers. Today it's just a sleepy Southern town, known mostly for its water recreation. Nearby Guntersville Dam and Lake provides 76 miles and 67,900 acres of fresh water for boating, fishing and swimming.

Two state parks are located near Guntersville. Buck's Pocket is 16 miles to the northeast via State 227 and county road 60. It has 55 campsites for tent or trailer, picnic facilities and 2,000 acres of rugged mountain scenery.

Lake Guntersville State Park, six miles northeast of Guntersville on State 227, features a luxury 100-room lodge, restaurants, 20 executive cottages, 16 lakeside cottages, swimming pool, 315-site campground, tennis, an 18-hole golf course, fishing and bicycles and canoes for rent.

Driving along State 79 north from Guntersville to Scottsboro, and then swinging northeast on US 72 headed for Bridgeport will roll you through some of Alabama's most mountainous terrain. Bridgeport is the gateway to the Russell Cave National Monument, which lies about eight miles northwest off US 72 via County 75 and 91. Originally a gift from the National Geographic Society, and now under strict supervision of the National Park Service Administration, the cave has a striking significance in that man has dwelled in it for some 8,650 years: a possible unparalleled continuity of cave life. The main cave area has been only partially opened; an immense, relatively unexplored cavern lies behind it. Near the Tennessee River where it passes the Cumberland Plateau, the Russell Cave National Monument takes up over three hundred acres. To gain added knowledge of how life was lived by prehistoric man, stop at the Visitors Center, and view the intriguing exhibits there.

Backtracking on US 72 a short distance to its junction with State 117, follow 117 to Hammondville. Five miles north are Sequoyah Caves, named for the unusual Indian who developed the Cherokee language in written form. Sequoyah Caves were probably inhabited about 500 B.C. and today, under private ownership, they may be explored daily.

Also near Hammondville—five miles east on State 117—is De Soto State Park, a 4,869-acre playground for outdoor-action devotees. Little River Canyon, said to be the deepest gorge east of the Rockies, runs twenty-seven miles within the park. A sixteen-mile road edges the canyon for scenic delights, and you may wish to view De Soto Falls which plunges 110 feet from a mile-long lake.

Within the state park, atop Lookout Mountain, is a 25-room lodge, 22 cabins (both chalet and rustic), restaurant, 82-site campground, hiking trails, fishing, bicycles for rent, and a country store. During May, the rhododendron and mountain laurel are abloom.

Out of Hammondville, you can take either US 11 or I-59 to Fort Payne. Will's Town, an Indian community where Sequoyah lived, is nearby but more magnetizing is Manitou Cave right in Fort Payne. The cavern's attractions include rooms twenty to sixty feet from floor to ceiling plus a rock-formed span. Take a sweater, as the cave has a steady fifty-degree temperature. If traveling with children be sure to visit Canyon Land Park. They will love the miniature train ride and the chair lift to the bottom of the canyon.

To resume your meandering, head down US 11 for Gadsden to see Noccalula Falls about five miles north of the city on State 7. Noccalula was the despondent daughter of an Indian chief who, according to legend, pressed on by a broken heart, hurled herself from a ledge ninety-five feet high atop Lookout Mountain. At this drop, the mountain has wept ever since. Now gaiety prevails at the site's barbecue pits and picnic tables.

Beside the falls is a pioneer village, made up from old cabins hauled in to Gadsden from the surrounding rural highlands. Tying them all together is one of the state's best preserved covered bridges.

Gadsden has erected a monument, at Broad and First, to another girl, Emma Sansom. It is a memorial to the young girl who, during the War Between the States, used her intimate knowledge of the area to help Confederate troops under the command of General Nathan Bedford Forrest to safety. This, in turn, enabled one of the men to give early warning that the Northern army was advancing on Rome, Georgia, thus insuring the safety of the town's inhabitants.

Before heading for Birmingham, you can take a side trip south, via US 431, to Anniston. The Church of St. Michael and All Angels and its bell tower, noted for its architectural beauty, is worth a visit. Of interest also is the Regar Memorial Museum of Natural History. Not too far from Anniston, at Fort McClellan, you can visit the Edith Nourse Rogers Museum, U.S. Women's Army Corps Center with permanent and temporary military exhibits. During the summer, all of Anniston is a stage at its annual Shakespeare Festival. Recently declared the State Theater of Alabama by the governor, this is the only professional resident repertory in the Southeast. Performances are given during July and August.

Traveling southwest from Gadsden toward Birmingham, two routes (US 11 and 411) lead to a junction with US 231. US 11 is the shorter. At US 231, proceed northwest toward Oneonta for a visit to the odd Horse Pens 40. On top of Chandler Mountain, they are between Oneonta and Ashville near where US highways 11 and 231 intersect. Named by John Hyatt, who climbed pathless Chandler Mountain in the 1870's, they are an unusual formation of rocks including a stone pen which he used as a corral. The "40" indicates the number of acres the rocky area comprises, and apparently Indians had also used them for penning horses. Today, little Horse Pens 40 has become a favored locale for art shows, Bluegrass Festivals, and folk fairs, focusing on the games and crafts from the past.

You can reach Cullman via US 231 to its junction with US 278, and then into town. Before you enjoy the city's nearby recreational areas, you might like to view the unusual Ave Maria Grotto, on the campus of St. Bernard College. Covering four acres, it consists of the handiwork of one Joseph Zoettl, a Benedictine lay brother, who for almost half a century labored over 150 diminutive duplicates of celebrated European and Middle Eastern cathedrals, shrines, and churches. They are masterpieces of stone and concrete and Brother Joseph even used marble, beads and jars during their construction. California missions, though not as striking, have been included. Beautiful gardens add spectacular luster to the attraction.

North of Cullman, six miles east on US 31, is Hurricane Creek Park. Among the many enticements—a nature trail of a mile and a half with a natural spiral staircase and stone sculptures wrought by the elements; waterfalls; swinging bridges. A small cable car can be used for rides out of a canyon which can also be viewed from an overlook. Picnic tables are provided.

Enroute to Birmingham, pull off at Warrior, a tiny town, if you'd like to roam through Rickwood Caverns State Park. They have an abundance of glittering stalagmites plus a lake. Camping facilities, picnic tables, a cafe and swimming pool are part of the cavern area's amenities.

South of Birmingham

For your swing south, take US 280 out of Birmingham to Childersburg.

Five miles east, via State 76, is DeSoto Caverns, the home of Kymulga Onyx Cave. The caverns, named for explorer Hernando DeSoto who trekked across the land that was to become Alabama, was believed by the Creek Indians to house fairies. These fairies, it was said, assisted the divine "Master of Breath" who gave the Indian life and let him live in the warmth of the sun, sustaining himself on corn. DeSoto is the oldest recorded cave in the United States, reported by an Indian Agent to President Washington in 1796.

Again moving south on US 280, you pass through Sylacauga, a town noted for its excellent marble. Two miles outside Sylacauga are the great quarries which have contributed their output to such buildings as the U.S. Supreme Court in Washington. Sylacauga, by the way, is at the western wedge of uniquely split Talladega National Forest.

From Sylacauga, stay on US 280 to Alexander City, springboard to the recreational complex of Martin Lake, formed by Martin Dam at Cherokee Bluffs. Wind Creek Park is another water wonderland just seven miles south of Alexander City on State 63. Open daily all year, it has nine acres of shoreline on Lake Martin, a marina, 1,400 acres of rolling hills, 400 campsites and a country store.

State 22 northeast from Alexander City leads to Newsite after 13 miles, and a short drive further, on State 49 south, puts you at the entrance to Horseshoe Bend National Military Park. A captain at the time, Andrew Jackson and his soldiers met the rebelling Red Stick (Upper Creek) Indians on March 27, 1814, in a short but bloody stand. The Battle of Horseshoe Bend ended the Creeks' power in the southeastern region and added territory comprising more than half of the present state of Alabama to the United States. It also started Jackson on the road that was to lead eventually to the White House.

You can tour the area by car.

Pick up State 49 again and, moving south, you'll rejoin US 280. Following the route, which dips southeast, you come to the twin cities of Opelika and Auburn. Auburn University's 2,105 acres are quite attractive and contain an agricultural experiment station. Though Opelika is also agricultural it has a number of well-known textile mills.

On to the Capital

Montgomery, Alabama's capital, should be your next goal. En route from Auburn on either I-85 or US 80, you may wish to divert briefly to Chewacla State Park, three miles southeast off US 29. Chewacla's 696 acres encompass a 26-acre lake popular with swimmers, as well as picnicking facilities, cottages, camping, riding trails and the like, all amid a valley as cragged as any below the Appalachians.

Another halt could be made en route to Montgomery at Tuskegee. Booker T. Washington founded Tuskegee Institute here in 1881. Part of the campus—1,800 acres—is the George Washington Carver Museum, among many buildings. At the museum, the African Negro's cultural enrichment of western civilization is illustrated through the use of dioramas while the history of the American Negro is vividly portrayed in the Chapel's stained-glass panes with religious genre folk songs as the theme. Washington was a leading researcher in agricultural chemistry, but he never took money for his discoveries. As a result, his fame was always greater than his fortune. His ambition was to teach people how to make fertile again that soil which overplanting with cotton had wasted away. And when the boll weevil ate out the cotton fields of 1910, he persuaded farmers to plant peanuts, then developed a staggering array of commercially practical synthetic products, using the shell as well as the nut, creating a new important industry.

Art and history behind them, hunters and fishermen may find more energetic enjoyment in nearby Tuskegee National Forest with its sizeable 10,777 acres.

Finally in Montgomery, you'll find a city of antebellum homes and, in some respects, an antebellum attitude, still proudly conscious of its deep Southern traditions: a heritage that emanates from every building and monument. Sacred, too, for Southerners, is the capitol edifice site where, on February 18, 1861, Jefferson Davis was sworn in as president of the Confederate provisional government. Later, the hope that there would be no Civil War was buried with the words—"Fire on Fort Sumter," the ominous orders from the capital of the Confederacy. Northerners are sometimes amused at Montgomery's long memory, but men here are as genuinely proud of their family's fight for independence as Bostonians are of theirs against the British, and jokes, on tour or just around town, are ill-placed.

Prime tour point is the historic State Capitol. Using the nation's capitol building as his inspiration, George Nichols is credited with this Alabama edifice, one of the Southland's most beautiful. Inside, the state's rich, historical background has been caught by an artist's brush in great, colorful murals. Conveniently across from the Capitol is the two-story First White House of the Confederacy. Built on Bibb Street, it is difficult to guess by looking at it that this handsome dwelling has been moved to a new setting. The capitol building is surrounded by other state office buildings including the Archives and History Building.

A reminder of the Union's eventual entry into Montgomery is Teague House, at High and South Perry street, noted since it was used by Northern General J. H. Wilson during Civil War days. St. John's Episcopal Church is another interesting structure. Built in 1855, it has a special gallery once set aside for slaves. Jefferson Davis also attended services there.

Most of Montgomery's outstanding historic homes are now in private hands or used by various establishments such as insurance firms or schools. Visits may be made, however, to the buildings not used for personal possession, and among the most important are the Lomax House, the Murphy Home, and the Seibel-Ball-Lanier Home, all built before 1860. The second, on the corner of Bibb and Coosa Streets, is an elaborate home built in 1851. During the Civil War the Union Army used it as headquarters. It now houses offices of the City Waterworks Board. Seibel-Ball-Lanier Home, 405 Adams St., an imposing Colonial house on a spacious, landscaped lawn, contains heirlooms, including carved marble mantels and ornate Regency mirror frames. Also restored and open to the public is the Old North Hull Historic District, which includes a tavern, church, log cabin, grange hall, doctor's office, and 1850's townhouse.

Eight miles north of Montgomery on US 231 are the lovely Jasmine Hill Gardens. Statues and fountains stud the flowering formal grounds, and green pines are prominent. Programs in performing arts are given in an amphitheatre during the summer months.

Montgomery does have modernity, most notable is its large Garrett Coliseum, its Museum of Fine Arts, and Maxwell Air Force Base. It was Wilbur Wright himself who founded the airfield but its name was bestowed in 1922 in honor of Lieutenant William C. Maxwell who was killed during the Philippine insurrections. Annual events that pack the Coliseum include the Southeastern Livestock Exposition and Rodeo in mid-March, and the South Alabama Fair in mid-October.

The W.A. Gayle Planetarium is interesting for adults and children alike. It has education programs for children, films and lectures. You can also buy astronomy and space science items.

Selma and Environs

Leaving Montgomery, you can ease out of the Civil War reminders surrounding you and drive seventeen miles northeast on US 231 to Wetumpka. Via State 9 just two miles south and then some three miles west on State 11, you encounter the site of Fort Toulouse State Monument. This marks the locale of a French fort erected in 1714 and successfully stormed by the British in 1763 and held by them until Revolution's end dictated surrender. Also close to Wetumpka is Lake Jordon, four miles north on State 11, a recreation region particularly popular with fishermen. Twenty-five miles north via US 31 is Clanton and ten miles further is Lake Lay for more outdoor activity, plus a possible free tour of Lay Dam's hydroelectric plant.

After such side trips you could return to Montgomery and take a fast trip to Selma, high above the Alabama River. It was the scene of frequent bombardment during the Civil War. But despite the ensuing destruction many architecturally attractive homes lend the town an aura of antebellum life even today. Sturdivant Hall, built in 1852, is among those with a neo-classic air. Reconditioned to its original state, the handsome mansion, designed by a relative of Robert E. Lee, is open to the public.

Twelve miles from Selma, southwest off State 22, is Cahaba, the state's first established capital. Now a moss-covered crumbling ruin is all that remains.

Much livelier is Paul M. Grist State Park, seventeen miles north of Selma and four miles northwest of State 22. This 1,080-acre playland has a primitive camping area for visitors who wish to stay overnight. Also available are opportunities to swim, fish and hike along wooded trails.

Continuing north on State 22 and 139, you come to Brierfield, site of Brierfield Ironworks Park, where the outdoor drama *Brighthope* by Kermit Hunter is performed June through August.

Moving west on US 80 from Selma, you can make a side trip on State 5 at Browns, turning north to visit the town of Marion. It is very small and famed for three people of historical significance who have lived there: Francis Marion, the "Swamp Fox," for whom it was named; Sam Houston who took for his bride a young woman who lived there—in fact, the wedding ceremony took place at her Green Street home, and Civil War teacher Nicola Marshall, who created both the uniform and the flag for the Southern Confederacy. A large segment of the small population (under 4,000) is made up of cadets who are enrolled in the Marion Institute, established twenty-nine years prior to the Civil War, and Judson College, Alabama's only non-coeducational institution of higher learning.

Returning to US 80 via either State 5 or 183 to Uniontown, drive on to Demopolis. Despite its name, with its proletarian implications, it was French aristocrats—officers and courtiers—who colonized the government-given lands in the early 1800's. Straight from soft European court life, they struggled here vainly for three years and fell before the task. The land itself, with perfect growing soil, was waiting for tillage, which came with the advent of heartier native settlers. Responsive to their touch, great cotton plantations grew and with them, vast fortunes. Left behind as a testimonial to these times are many magnificent mansions. Among these is beautiful Gaineswood. Purchased by the state, it is open for tours.

Highlight: Tuscaloosa

Retracing your tour eight miles on US 80, you pass through Prairie-ville to track State 69 north to Greensboro. Here, Magnolia Grove, the ancestral home of Rear Admiral Richmond P. Hobson, is the main attraction. Hobson drew fame as the hero of the action that sank the *Merrimac* in Santiago Harbor to bottle up the enemy fleet in June, 1888, during the Spanish-American War. You can visit his home, representative of the 1800's.

Twenty-one miles to the north via State 69, you encounter a different facet of Alabama history at Moundville. It is Mound State Monument, a 325-acre park surrounded by forty Indian ceremonial hills ranging up to fifty-eight feet high. In the wings of the museum, excavated Indian burials are housed. The park graphically reveals how the Indian mound builders once lived, worked and worshipped. Nature trails by the river and picnic facilities add to the pleasantness of this site.

Sixteen miles north on State 69 is Tuscaloosa, home of the University of Alabama. Beginning in 1836, Tuscaloosa was the state capital for ten years until a collapsed cotton market instigated the government's move to Montgomery. The Civil War took its toll too but antebellum homes are nonetheless in evidence—at least a trio of them on the University of Alabama campus. Two merit special attention: The Gorgas House, dating from 1829, honors by name Dr. William C. Gorgas, whose work in Panama triumphed over yellow fever. With Neo-Grecian architecture, the second of the pair is the 1840 President's mansion.

Filling the air of the campus with music both day and night are the bells of the Denny Chimes. From a carillon tower hymns are played and time is marked by the quarter hour. Named for Dr. George H. Denny, a onetime President and Chancellor of the University, the chimes are especially lovely.

At the university, a marker for students that fought Tuscaloosa invaders during the Civil War is located near the "Little Round House," once used as a sentry box. Smith Hall contains a Museum of Natural History.

From Tuscaloosa, you can return to Birmingham via US 11 and portions of I-20 and I-59. En route, pause at Vance. Just off US 11 lie the Bama Rock Gardens. Prehistoric Indian artifacts and rock houses are among some unusual natural formations.

Pioneer and Recreation Spots

Dedicated explorers will want to set off on another circle tour from Montgomery. This one would begin by heading southeast on US 82 through Union Springs to Eufaula on the banks of the Chattahoochee River. In Eufaula is the famous "tree that owns itself." This oft-used phrase emanates from the fact that in 1936 the city commission deeded the land on which the tree stands to the tree itself. No legal challenge has ensued. Some locals feel that Eufaula is in for a boating boom due to formation of Walter F. George Lake by the same-name dam about twenty-five miles south, and that this will enrich the town as a springboard site. At any rate, you can reach the dam by following US 431 to Abbeville and there following State 10 to the structure on the Alabama-Georgia line.

If you pass through Eufaula in the spring, be sure to inquire about its Spring Pilgrimage of old homes. Most notable of these is the beautiful Shorter mansion.

Following this side trip, get back on US 431 and continue south to Dothan, a southeast Alabama trade center. In the 1880's when it was founded, it was a rough-and-tumble town that made mincemeat of any mild-mannered marshals but today, reasonably calmed by the benefits of its peanut production, life is much as elsewhere. Each October, Dothan is the scene of the National Peanut Festival, which adds pork to the annual playtime with a greased-pig contest as well as parades and similar festival adjuncts.

A drive up U.S. 231 to Troy brings you to the Pike Pioneer Museum, located three miles north of the city. It recreates a 19th century way of life through reconstructed buildings and antique furnishings.

Following State highways 87 and 167 south, you arrive at Enterprise, a town that has, in gratitude, erected a monument to an insect. That pest is the boll weevil, and Enterprise is delighted that it so ravaged its cotton that the town changed over to the production and processing of peanuts with a resultant surge of prosperity. Peanut butter plants are, in fact, the town's dominant structures.

Continuing west on US 84, you pass through Opp and Andalusia mainly to get to Conecuh National Forest's scenic splendors via US 29 and State 55. Alternatively, you could take State 88 south sixteen miles of Andalusia to Open Pond Recreational Area for leisure along the shores of its fifty-acre lake.

Evergreen, thirty-three miles west of Andalusia, is the map mark from which to swing southeast on State 29 for six miles to the Jay Villa plantation, site of the boyhood home of William Barrett Travis. On the grounds of this 135-year-old estate, Travis, one of the Alamo's heroes, played. It is not open to the public, but you can view from the outside the log cabin where young Travis lived while the plantation home was being built.

Near the little town of Belleville, ten miles west of Evergreen, the first clash of the Creek Indian War of 1813-14 occurred at Burnt Corn Creek.

Returning to Montgomery via US 31 or I-65, you go through Greenville, correctly dubbed The Camellia City. An antebellum mansion, White Columns, stands at nearby Camden on State 10. From there, you can get back to Montgomery either by returning to US 31 at Greenville or by taking State 21 from Camden directly to the capital.

Mobile, the Garden City

Deep-Alabama Mobile is another hub for sightseeing tours. This busy port city overlaps past and present on the western bank of the Mobile

River at the top of Mobile Bay. Despite a raking by Hurricane Frederick in 1979, old mansions, grillwork balconies and lovely gardens abound, and belie the madness of the city's annual Mardi Gras for ten days preceding Shrove Tuesday. Its industrial endeavors are typified by the Alabama State Docks, capable of berthing some thirty ships at one time.

Fort Conde was the name the French gave the site in 1711, around which blossomed the first white settlement within what is now Alabama. For eight years it was the capital of the French colonial empire and stayed under their control after New Orleans became government headquarters, or until 1763.

Mobile today is noted for its tree-lined boulevards fanning out from Bienville Square at the center of the city. Many firms in town are in buildings dating prior to the Civil War, and the streets lead through flower-gardened residential sections.

At 350 Oakleigh Place and Savannah Street stands Oakleigh, built between 1833 and 1838. A half-timber house, Oakleigh is a splendid example of the period. Towering oak trees outside; fine furniture pieces inside. Owner James W. Roper was also its architect and today there is a museum on the lower floor.

Admiral Raphael Semmes is remembered as a Mobile resident, and for his fame during the Civil War, with a statue downtown and preservation of his house at 802 Government Street, given him by a grateful Confederacy.

Most highly publicized of gardens in the Mobile area is Bellingrath. This 800-acre spread is twenty miles south of town on US 90 and then Bellingrath Road, in the hamlet of Theodore. A river, the Ile-aux-Oies, laces through some sixty-five acres of gardens and forest, and Bellingrath's owners claim to have counted 250,000 azalea plantings comprised of two hundred different varieties.

Thousands of showy flowering shrubs and bushes are beautifully placed. Guides are on hand throughout the gardened vastness to assist or explain but a free map lets you plan your own flower-fringed strolls along paths as you will. Industrialist Walter D. Bellingrath began the nucleus of the noted section in 1917 when he and his wife bought a large tract as a hunting preserve. Their travels, however, prompted them to create, instead, a garden shrine rivaling some of the well-planned properties they had seen abroad. The Bellingrath-Morse Foundation has supervised the management of the gardens ever since his demise. Mrs. Bellingrath died in 1943, and their home, in the middle of the garden grandeur, is magnificently furnished, with objets d'art of all kinds and fine, old glassware.

In downtown Mobile, as a contrast to so many gardens, is the $2.2 million restoration of 18th century Fort Conde, whose remains were discovered when construction began on the I-10 interchange. I-10 now runs through a tunnel under the fort. A village of unique shops is located around the fort. Also downtown is the thirty-five-story First National Bank building, Alabama's tallest structure.

Also of interest are the Phoenix Fire Museum on 203 S. Claiborne St., and the Mobile Art Gallery, Langan Park.

If you plan your visit to Mobile for February and March you will be in the right place to participate in the famed Azalea Trail Festival. Along

Mobile's streets and in and around the city the Trail twines for thirty-five well-marked miles, showing off azaleas at their best. Scores of special events celebrate the yearly blossoming, from concerts to art exhibits and, of course, crowning of a queen—in this case, America's Junior Miss.

Don't let the fun, frolic and touring of the Azalea Trail Festival exhaust you, however, as there are still a couple or so side trips you should make from Mobile for full appreciation of Alabama's attractions.

Rewarding Side Trips

To reach Alabama's seashore area, take US 90 east through the Bankhead Tunnel that cuts beneath Mobile Bay. Then turn south on either US 98 or State 59. The latter is the only way to reach Pleasure Island, a thirty-mile region for romping along the Gulf of Mexico. It was a peninsula until the Intra-Coastal Waterway Canal cut across the land.

Before reaching Pleasure Island, though, you pay a call aboard the U.S.S. *Alabama.* She's berthed alongside a four-lane highway of the U.S.S. Alabama Memorial Park, created by dredging up enough of the bottom of Mobile Bay to spread out seventy-five acres. Public subscription saved the ship from being scrapped ignominiously after her heroic World War II service, which ranged from Scapa Flow to the South Pacific.

Indian Mounds and Industry

Other activity is underway at Gulf State Park, two miles east of Gulf Shores on State 182. Amid those 6,000 acres are a beach-front lodge with 144 rooms, restaurant, swimming pool, cabins, 468-site campground, two freshwater lakes large enough for skiing, canoes, sailboats, fishing boats, tennis, bicycles, a beach pavilion, and an 18-hole golf course. A white sand beach is lapped by the Gulf for two and a half miles, and a freshwater lake lures boaters. Pick your season: the park is open all year.

On the western end of the island is Fort Morgan, centerpiece of twenty-eight acres in a four-hundred-acre reservation, both under state control. With an extremely unique design, the construction of the fort began in the early nineteenth century. It was named after Daniel Morgan, an American Revolutionary hero. Both Confederate and Union relics and artifacts are housed in its museum.

Stone Age caves, Indian mounds, colorful caverns, antebellum homes, Space Centers, faded fortresses and rising resorts—such is the spectrum of sightseeing that greets the tourist in eye-opening Alabama.

PRACTICAL INFORMATION FOR ALABAMA

 FACTS AND FIGURES. In Choctaw Indian, *Alabama* means "vegetarian-gatherers" or "thicket-clearers." The state boasts two nicknames: the Cotton State and Yellowhammer State. Yellowhammer is also the state bird; camellia its flower; southern pine, its tree. Alabama's motto: *Audemus jura nostra defendere* ("We dare defend our rights"). "Alabama" is the state song.

Montgomery, the Confederacy's first capital, is the state capital. State population: approximately 3,500,000.

HOW TO GET THERE. *By air:* Birmingham may be reached on direct flights of U.S. Air, Delta, Eastern, Republic and United; Huntsville-Decatur on Republic and United; Mobile on Eastern, Pan American, Texas International, and Republic; Montgomery on Delta, and Republic; Anniston, Dothan, Gadsden and Tuscaloosa on Republic.

By car: I-59 runs from Chattanooga, Tenn., to Birmingham, Tuscaloosa; I-20 from Atlanta, Georgia, to Anniston and Birmingham; I-65 from Tenn. passes through Decatur, Cullman, Birmingham and Montgomery and terminates in Mobile; I-85 comes from Atlanta, via LaGrange, Georgia, to Auburn and Montgomery; I-10 from New Orleans to Biloxi, Miss., Mobile and Pensacola and Jacksonville, Florida.

By bus: Greyhound and Trailways have good service. In addition Capital Motor Lines, Colonial Trailways, Gulf Transport Co., and Ingram Bus Lines, Inc., come into the state.

By train: Amtrak trains go into Birmingham, Anniston, Eutaw, Livingston and Tuscaloosa.

HOW TO GET AROUND. *By air:* Local flights are provided by *Republic.*

By car: I-65 goes from the Tenn. state line to Mobile; US-80 crosses the state from the Georgia state line to the Mississippi state line; US 43 from the Tenn. state line through Florence, Tuscaloosa to Mobile.

Car rentals: Hertz, Avis, National, Econo Car, Budget Rent-A-Car and Dixie Drive-It-Yourself, Thrifty, Sears, and American International.

By bus: Greyhound, Basden Transportation, Thrasher Transportation, and Trailways operate.

By train: Amtrak.

TOURIST INFORMATION SERVICES. There are numerous sources of tourist information in Alabama. Among them are: Alabama Bureau of Publicity and Information, State Highway Bldg., Montgomery 36130; Alabama State Parks, State Administrative Bldg., Montgomery 36130; Alabama Travel Council, 660 Adams Ave., Montgomery 36130; Forest Supervisor, U.S. Forest Service, P.O. Box 40, Montgomery for detailed information on recreational facilities in national forests. Alabama Department of Conservation and Natural Resources, Information and Education Section, 64 N. Union St., Montgomery 36130, for fishing, hunting and camping. All local Chambers of Commerce. Alabama Mountain Lakes Association, P.O. Box 2222, Decatur 36501; DeKalb County Tourist Association, P.O. Box 316, Fort Payne 35967; Greater Birmingham Convention & Visitors Bureau, Suite 940, First Alabama Bank Building, Birmingham 35203; Gulf Shores Tourist Association, Gulf Shores 36542; Mobile Tourist Information Mobile Chamber of Commerce, P. O. Box 2187, Mobile 36601; Tallacoosa Highland Lakes Association, Rte. 1, P.O. Box 128, Sterrett 35147; Historic Chattahoochee Commission, P.O. Box 33, Eufaula 36027. For toll-free information from out-of-state, (except Alaska, Hawaii), call 1-800-633-5761.

SEASONAL EVENTS. Because of its warmer climate, Alabama features outdoor events throughout the year. Some highlights are:

January. Mobile: Senior Bowl Football Game.

February. Mobile: Azalea Trail Festival, featuring 35 mi. of the beautiful blossoms, continuing into March; Mardi Gras. *Birmingham:* Camellia Show.

March. Fairhope: Arts and Crafts Week. *Mobile:* Tour of historic buildings. *Montgomery:* Southeastern Livestock Exposition and Rodeo. *Opp:* So. Alabama Rattlesnake Rodeo. *Selma:* Annual homes pilgrimage.

Spring. Birmingham: Festival of Arts.

April. Eufaula: Antebellum home pilgrimage. *Guntersville:* Civitan Horse Show. *Tuscaloosa:* Heritage Week Open House (mid-Apr.).

May. Birmingham: Annual sidewalk art show. *Eufaula:* Fresh Water Fishing Rodeo. *Ft. Payne:* Tours of homes (3rd weekend). *Mobile:* America's Junior Miss Pageant (usually early May). *May to Sept.: Talladega:* Alabama International Motor Speedway, car and motorcycle races.

June. Alexander City: Dixie Sailboat Regatta. *Tuscaloosa:* Charity horse show.

July. Bayou La Batre: near Mobile: Blessing of the Shrimp Fleet (1st Sun.). *Tuscumbia:* "The Miracle Worker," powerful drama depicting Helen Keller's heroic struggle with deafness and blindness. *Brierfield:* Outdoor drama "Brighthope," depicting the birth of Alabama coal and iron industries (early July–early Aug.) *Anniston:* Alabama Shakespeare Festival (early July–mid-Aug.).

September, Florence: North Alabama State Fair. *Montgomery:* National Championship Sports Car Race. *Selma:* Horse show (late Sept.); Central Alabama Fair (last week).

October. Birmingham: Alabama State Fair. *Dothan:* National Peanut Festival. *Mobile:* Greater Gulf State Fair. *Montgomery:* South Alabama Fair. Folk Festival and Bluegrass Festival, *Horse Pens 40.*

November. Montgomery: Southeastern Championship Horse Show.

December. Birmingham: Botanical Gardens Christmas Show. *Talladega:* state's biggest Christmas parade.

On the first Mon. and preceding weekend of every month you can witness "Barter Day" on Court House Sq. in *Scottsboro.*

Year-round (except January): Greyhounds race at Greentrack in *Eutaw* and at Mobile Greyhound Park.

 NATIONAL PARKS AND FORESTS. Oldest of Alabama's four National Forests is the *William B. Bankhead,* established in 1913, located in the northwestern part of the state. A wilderness area with hiking trails has been preserved and set up at *Bee Branch. Talladega National Forest* consists of two divisions—the *Oakmulgee,* located in the west-central part of the state, and the *Talladega* in the northeast part. In east-central Alabama is the *Tuskegee National Forest,* while *Conecuh Forest* lies on the Alabama-Florida state line.

There are various recreational facilities at 17 different locations. In the *Bankhead Forest,* the most complete facilities are provided at *Brushy Lake, Corinth* and *Sipsey River* recreational areas. There are two major areas in the *Conecuh Forest* located at *Blue* and *Open ponds.* In the *Talladega Forest,* Payne Lake, Lake Chinnabee, and Coleman Lake are the most complete. Additional facilities are being installed at *Houston Lake* in *Bankhead Forest.*

Alabama's National Military Park—Horseshoe Bend. The 316-acre site commemorates General Andrew Jackson's victory over the Creek Indians in the battle on the banks of the Tallapoosa River in March, 1814. The resulting peace treaty opened 23 million acres of land to white settlement. A Visitors' Center features graphic displays depicting events causing the Creek War of 1813 to 1814, Indian life, and the course of the battle. It's located on Rte. 49 and US 280, 12 mi. N of Dadeville, and 80 mi. SE of Birmingham. Closed Christmas.

The state's *Russel Cave National Monument* is located eight miles northwest of Bridgeport off US 72 via county roads 75 and 91. Oldest known cave-homes in southeast, where Stone-Age men lived, are here. A Visitor's Center provides information and displays depicting life of those prehistoric and historic cave dwellers. Closed Christmas.

STATE PARKS. Alabama has 24 state parks all equipped for the handicapped: *Blue Springs; Buck's Pocket; Roland Cooper; Cheaha,* (highest point in Alabama); *Chewacla; De Soto, Little River Canyon* is the deepest gorge east of the Rockies, also has *De Soto Falls; Fort Morgan; Gulf; Joe Wheeler; Lake Guntersville; Monte Sano, Mound; Oak Mountain, Wind Creek; Bladon Springs; Chattahoochee; Chickasaw; Florala; Lake Lurleen; Lakepoint Resort; Paul M. Grist; Rickwood Caverns; Tannehill; First Creek;* and *Wind Creek.* There is camping and swimming at most. In addition *Gulf, Joe Wheeler* and *Lake Guntersville* also offer boating and fishing. Sun. open-air worship services at *Wind Creek.*

Family camping is possible in 13 of the parks. All provide picnic areas. Fishing tackle and rental boats are available from concessionaires at several parks.

In addition, Alabama has 23 managed, public, fishing lakes under the administration of the Department of Conservation. These lakes range in size from 32 to 250 acres. There's a daily fee of $1.50 per fisherman.

Anglers are required to have fishing licenses for Alabama waters. A seven-day, nonresident license costs $4.25. A nonresident annual license costs $10.25.

CAMPING OUT. Camping facilities for both those who enjoy living under canvas, and those who tow trailers are available in 13 state parks: *Blue Springs,* 6 miles E of Clio; *Buck's Pocket,* 2 miles N of Groveoak; *Roland Cooper,* 6 miles NE of Camden; *Cheha,* 17 miles N of Lineville; *DeSoto,* 8 miles NE of Fort Payne; *Gulf,* 10 miles S of Foley; *Lake Guntersville,* 6 miles NE of Guntersville; *Lakepoint Resort,* 7 miles NE of Eufaula; *Lake Lurleen,* 12 miles NW of Tuscaloosa; *Oak Mountain,* 15 miles S of Birmingham; *Tannehill,* 12 miles SW of Bessemer; *Rickwood,* 4 miles N of Warrior; and *Wind Creek,* 7 miles SE of Alexander City. The number of campsites with hookups ranges from 50 at Blue Springs to 468 at Gulf State. Family cottages are available at Cheha, DeSoto, Joe Wheeler, Lake Guntersville, Oak Mountain, Roland Cooper, Chewacla and Monte Sano State Parks. Camping fees vary from park to park, ranging from $3 to $5 for tents, and $3.50 to $5 for trailers. A waterfront site at Gulf State Park is $1 extra. Maximum occupancy is 8 persons per site. Two-week limit on stays.

Brushy Lake, 15 mi. S of Moulton, 10 tent and camping sites; *Corinth Recreation Area* (open 4/1 to 10/31), 4 mi. E of Double Springs, 64; *Lake Chinnabee,* 10 mi. S of Oxford, 14; *Taska,* 2 mi. E of Tuskegee, 6 for tents only; *Open Pond,* 15 mi. SW of Andalusia, 20; *Payne Lake,* 24 mi. W of Centreville, 46; *Pine Glen,* 2-½ mi. W of Heflin, 13; *Coleman Lake* (open 5/1 to 10/31), 8 mi. N of Heflin, 40. Fee is $2 per day.

TRAILER TIPS. Alabama's trailer laws are similar to those of other states. Maximum over-all length of trailer and car is 50 feet. For 24-hour travel, widths are limited to 8 feet. Trailers up to 12 feet wide and 12-½ feet high can be moved on the highways between sunrise and sunset.

Trailer camping facilities are found in state parks and in the national forests. In addition, there are a number of private trailer parks.

KOA has trailer facilities on Lake Eufaula ($7 per night for two, 75¢ ea. additional person, $1.50 electric hookup); *Montgomery* ($8 for two, $1 each additional person). Mobile: Two locations (At junction of I-10 and U.S. 90, $8.50 for two, $1 each additional person) (26 miles East of Mobile off I-10, $9 for two, $1.25 each additional person); *Valley Head,* adjacent to Sequoyah Caverns ($7 per night for two, $1 ea. additional person; a/c or electric heat $1.25 per day extra).

ALABAMA 33

Pell City/Riverside ($7.50 for two, $1 each additional person, a/c or electric heat $1.25 extra).

MUSEUMS AND GALLERIES. *Birmingham: Arlington Antebellum Home and Civil War Museum.* 331 Cotton Ave. SW. Built 1822. Gift shop. *Gulf Shores: Fort Morgan Museum.* Free. *Tuskegee: Tuskegee George Washington Carver Museum,* on campus of Tuskegee Institute. *Huntsville:* The Burritt Museum, built in the shape of a Maltese cross, contains works of local artists, historical articles. *Jacksonville:* Doctor Francis Medical Museum. *Montgomery:* Tumbling Waters Museum of Flags, 131 S. Perry St.

Art: *Birmingham: Museum of Art.* 2000 8th Ave., N. Modern as well as classical paintings. Free; *the Greater Birmingham Arts Alliance,* 2114 First Avenue North. Changing exhibits of area artists. Free. *Mobile: Mobile Art Gallery,* Langan Park. Free. *Montgomery: Museum of Fine Arts,* 440 S. McDonough St. Free.

Special Interest: *Anniston: Regar Museum of Natural History,* 1411 Gurnee. Features bird material—present-day and extinct birds in natural settings—and an excellent bird-egg exhibit. Free. *Birmingham:* Red Mountain Museum, 2230 15th Ave. S., Geological displays. Free. *Fort McClellan: Edith Nourse Rogers Museum,* U.S. Women's Army Corps Center, Permanent and temporary military exhibits. Mon. to Fri. Free. *Mobile: Bellingrath Home,* in Theodore. Open daily. *Phoenix Fire Museum,* 203 S. Claiborne. Free. *Tuscaloosa: Museum of Natural History,* Smith Hall, U. of Ala. campus. Free. *Tuscumbia: Ivy Green,* 300 W. North Commons. Helen Keller's birthplace. "The Miracle Worker" performed on Fri. and Sat., July & Aug.

Other: *Florence: Indian Mound Museum, Pope's Tavern, W.C. Handy Home. Old Tavern* in Tuscaloosa, a restored stagecoach stop in Alabama's old capital.

HISTORIC SITES. The state was once heavily populated by Indian tribes. Famous battles of Indian wars and the Civil War are commemorated in many historic sites. Today, near *Atmore,* is Creek community, which the Indians retained through treaty with Andrew Jackson after the Battle of Horseshoe Bend. They live here on farms they own themselves. *Confederate Museum. Dadeville: Horseshoe Bend National Military Park,* Rte. 1, nr. Alexander City. Site of General Jackson's 1814 defeat of Creek Indians. Visitors' Center. Free.

Gulf Shores: Fort Morgan, twin fort defending the entrance to Mobile Bay, captured by Union forces during Mobile Bay campaign. *Civil War Museum.* Free. *Mobile: Oakleigh Home,* 350 Oakleigh Pl. *Monterey Home,* 1553 Monterey Place. *Fort Conde,* S Royal St. *Montgomery: First White House of Confederacy,* Washington & Union Sts., displays personal furnishings of Jefferson Davis and his family, preserved since their brief residency there over 100 years ago. *Capitol Bldg.* Free. *North Hull Historic District. Teague House* (State Chamber of Commerce Bldg.) Closed holidays. Free.

Moundville: 16 mi. S of Tuscaloosa on Rte. 69. State's largest ground of prehistoric *Indian mounds.* Also museum. *Selma: Sturdivant Hall. Tuscaloosa: Gorgas Home,* on U. of Ala. campus. Donations.

TOURS. The *Gray Line Tours,* part of a nation-wide system, offers a variety of package tours to Mobile's historic points of interest and famous gardens. Office is located in the Sheraton Inn on Government Street.

INDUSTRIAL TOURS. You can make a variety of industrial in-plant tours in Alabama at the following cities: *Albertville:* Reeves Rubber, Inc. (rubber floor tiles); *Anniston:* Alabama Pipe Co.; *Birmingham:* U.S. Pipe & Foundry Co.; *Coosa Pines:* Kimberly-Clark Corp.; *Decatur:* Autolite Corp. of Alabama (electrical hardware), Minnesota Mining & Manufacturing Co. (textile treating compounds, plastics and rubber); *Elba:* Dorsey Trailers Inc. (truck trailers, livestock vans); *Gadsden:* Republic Steel Corp.; *Opelika:* Textile plants and mills of West Point-Pepperell, Inc.; *Prattville:* Continental Gin Co. (cotton ginning machinery); *Sheffield:* Reynolds Metal Co. (aluminum).

SPECIAL INTEREST TOURS. *DeSoto Caverns,* nr. Childersburg. *Manitou Cave,* off US 11, Fort Payne. *Natural Bridge,* nr. Haleyville. *Alabama Space & Rocket Center.* On Rte. 20, Huntsville. Bus tour through the Space Flight Center. Closed Christmas. *NASA Bus Tour.* Space and Rocket Center Exhibits. *Horse Pens 40,* nr. Oneonta. *Sequoyah Cave Valley Head. Rickwood Caverns,* Warrior, nr. Birmingham. *St. Michael and All Angels Church,* 18th St. & Cobb Ave. Anniston. *Lay Dam,* Rte. 145, Clanton. Tour of hydroelectric generating plant. Free. *Ave Maria Grotto,* off US 278, on campus of St. Bernard College, nr. Cullman. Features 150 carved replicas of great religious buildings. *Wilson Dam,* Power House and Overlook, on Rte. 133, Sheffield. Free.

GARDENS. The French, who came as colonists, brought to Alabama their architecture and their traditional azalea gardens. Mobile is the azalea center of the state, and houses Alabama's most famous gardens. Best known is *Bellingrath,* featuring hundreds of thousands of azaleas and magnificent displays of many other flowers. Located in Theodore, 20 mi. S of Mobile via US 90, on Bellingrath Road. Also, *Bellingrath Home. The Botanical & Japanese Gardens,* 2612 Lane Park Rd., Birmingham. Dawn to dusk. Free. *The Jasmine Hill Gardens,* Montgomery. Attractive garden with statuary. *Dismals Wonder Gardens,* Phil Campbell. *Bama Scenic Rock Gardens,* Vance.

MUSIC. The Mobile Symphony and Civic Music Association presents six concerts and two recitals each season. The season extends from Oct. to April.

NIGHTCLUBS. *Birmingham: The Cane Break* at 1926 Fourth Ave. remains the city's traditional place to go after dark. However, a new night club scene has developed in Birmingham, along the cobblestone Streets of Morris Avenue. Located in old, but refurbished warehouses, are such clubs as the *Old Town Music Hall* and *Gatsby's.* Also popular are *Grundy's Music Room,* 208 23rd St. N.; and *The Polaris Lounge* in the Birmingham Hyatt House. The Library in the Sheraton-Mountainbrook features pianist Larry Russo and his band. *Montgomery: Wrangler's Club,* 113 S. Jackson, featuring country music. Western attire encouraged but not essential. Closed Sun. *Mobile: Chez Paree,* located in St. Francis Motel, US 90, 3 mi. W. Open six nights, closed Sun. Continuous live entertainment; *Club Oasis,* 3405 Moffat Road. Open daily. Live music, Wed. to Sun.; *Club Manor,* 3260 Halls Mill Road. Open daily. No rock 'n roll music.

DRINKING LAWS. Liquor is sold by the drink in licensed hotels, restaurants, and clubs in the state. It is sold in miniatures (1/10 pint bottles) and 1-½ pints in restaurants and cocktail lounges, which also sell beer. Beer is sold for both on- and off-premises consumption. Liquor is also sold in state stores.

No Sun. sales. Minimum age limit: 19 years. The state has some "dry" counties, but most of the metropolitan areas are "wet."

 SPORTS. Whether you're an armchair athlete or an active participant, you will find ample opportunity to satisfy your sports taste in Alabama. Due to its geographic location, there's little difference between summer and winter activities.

For the active man or woman, there are ample opportunities. *Fishing,* of course, is an important sport as a result of the numerous *fresh water rivers* and *lakes,* plus the *Gulf of Mexico* for *saltwater angling.* Anglers must have a license. Nonresident, sports licenses cost $4.25 for seven days; annual $10.25. The state has an open season the year round with no size limitation, but there are daily limits for various species.

With an abundance of water; *boating* is popular. Rental boats can be obtained in many state parks, and from marinas and fish camps located both on fresh and salt water.

Swimming and *water-skiing* are popular in some state parks, in many lakes and in the Gulf of Mexico.

Golf: Point Mallard G.C., Decatur, a public course with 10 water holes; *Jetport G.C.,* Huntsville, a municipal course with practice range; *Lakewood G.C.,* Point Clear, an excellent, tree-lined resort course; *Langan Park G.C.,* Mobile, a fine municipal course; *Isle Dauphine C.C.,* Dauphin Island, a private tough course with sand dunes, water; *Pine Harbor Champions C.C.,* Pell City, open to members and guests of the motel; *Alabama International C.C.,* Talladega, two tree-lined Robert Trent Jones courses; *Still Waters G.C.,* Dadeville, a private course with tight fairways; and *Olympia Spa & C.C.,* Dothan, a resort course with rolling fairways and several water holes; *Point Aquarias,* a first-class resort near Birmingham, also offers an 18-hole championship golf course, as well as tennis.

Hunting is excellent, exact dates for various types of hunting can be obtained from the *Alabama Department of Conservation, Game and Fish Division,* Montgomery. Nonresident hunting licenses cost $50 annually for all game and $15 for small game. A 5-day license for all game is $25 and for small game $10.

 SPECTATOR SPORTS. If you like to watch rock 'em and sock 'em, *big-time football,* you have a full menu. The University of Alabama and Auburn University are rated among the top teams in the nation each year, and play heavy schedules dotted with intersectional games. Many of these are played in *Birmingham's Legion Field Stadium.* Seating 70,000, it is the largest stadium in the Southeast other than the Orange and Sugar Bowls. In addition, Alabama has two famous post-season games. The Hall of Fame Bowl in Birmingham in December, and the Senior Bowl Game, held each January in Mobile. Birmingham now has professional *hockey*—The Bulls of the World Hockey League, with games in the new sports arena of the city's civic center.

Basketball thrills, too, are available via the college teams. *Horse shows* are held in *Guntersville, Anniston* and *Athens* during the late spring and early summer.

Water enthusiasts can watch *sailing regattas* and both *inboard and outboard races. Alexander City* stages the *Dixie Sailboat Regatta* in June. *Gulf Shores* stages an *Outboard Regatta. Guntersville* stages the *Dixie Cup hydroplane regatta* in August. For other races and regattas on Mobile Bay and lakes throughout Alabama, check local papers.

Although you're a long way from the wild and woolly West, you can watch *bronc riders* and other *rodeo acts. Montgomery* stages a *rodeo* in Mar. in connection with the *Southeastern Livestock Exposition. Opp* has the *South Alabama Rattlesnake Rodeo* in Mar. *Athens* is the site of the *state championship rodeo* in Aug., and you find other less publicized rodeos scattered throughout the state.

Action also at the *Alabama Intern. Motor Speedway,* featuring the famed *Winston 400* in May, Talladega.

WHAT TO DO WITH THE CHILDREN. Many of Alabama's attractions will appeal to the varied interests of children. Here are some of those most likely to win the applause of the younger generation. *Birmingham: Birmingham Zoo,* 2630 Cahaba Rd., on US 280. It features 11 major exhibit areas and a wide array of animals housed in ultramodern facilities, and miniature train.

Bridgeport: Russell Cave National Monument features caves where primitive men lived as long ago as 6000 B.C.—their oldest known home in the Southeast. These caves were still used as dwelling places up to about 1650 A.D. Located 8 mi. NW of Bridgeport off US 72 via country roads 75 and 91.

Fort Payne: Canyon Land Park. Miniature train, ferris wheel, chair lift to the bottom of the canyon. *Manitou Cave,* off US 11. *Huntsville: Alabama Space & Rocket Center.* NASA bus tours.

Mobile: Bellingrath Gardens, one of the most famous gardens in the South. Located 20 mi. S in Theodore, via US 90 and Bellingrath Rd. *Bellingrath Home U.S.S. Alabama,* Battleship Parkway.

Montgomery: W. A. Gayle Planetarium, 1010 Forest Ave. Lectures, films, varied showtimes. *Tuscaloosa: Museum of Natural History,* on campus of the U. of Ala. Indian artifacts and geology exhibit. *Tuscumbia: Ivy Green,* birthplace of Helen Keller. *Ave Maria Grotto* at St. Bernard College. *Dismals Wonder Garden* at Phil Campbell.

RECOMMENDED READING. A few good books include: *History of Montgomery with Pictures; Remember Mobile,* by Caldwell Delaney; *Story of Mobile,* by Caldwell Delaney; *Colonial Mobile,* by Peter Joseph Hamilton; *Mansions of Alabama,* by Ralph Hammond; and *History of Alabama,* by Albert James Pickett.

HOTELS AND MOTELS. Most of the motels and hotels in Alabama, especially those along the Gulf Coast, boast swimming pools and various other forms of indoor and outdoor recreational facilities. Listings are in order of price category. Price categories, i.e., *Expensive:* $22-$32; *Moderate:* $16-$22; *Inexpensive:* $10-$16. For a more complete explanation of hotel and motel categories see *Facts at Your Fingertips* at the front of this volume.

Albertville

King's Inn Motor Hotel. *Moderate.* Air-conditioned rooms on 2 levels. Pool. Restaurant adj. Coffee makers in rms. Lighted tennis courts.

Alexander City

Horseshoe Bend. *Moderate.* On 280 Bypass, 1-½ mi. SW. Comfortable, attractive rooms. Pool, restaurant. Pets allowed.

Bob White Motel. *Inexpensive.* Small. Pool. Restaurant nr.

Anniston

Ramada Inn. *Expensive.* Airport courtesy car. Well operated. Pool, color TV. Pets allowed.

Downtowner. *Moderate.* Appealing. Restaurant, pool. Airport courtesy car.

Holiday Inn. *Moderate.* Pool. Courtesy airport transportation. Pets accepted.

Days Inn. *Inexpensive.* One of fine chain. Pool, play area, gift shop, gas station. *Tasty World* restaurant. Pets.

Heart of Anniston. *Inexpensive.* TV, cafe; apartments available.

Van Thomas Motel. *Inexpensive.* Pleasant rooms. Air conditioning, TV, pool. Pets permitted.

Auburn

Days Inn. *Moderate.* One of chain, with restaurant and playground.

Heart of Auburn Motel. *Moderate.* A medium-sized motel near the University. Attractively furnished with restaurant and room service. Pool, pets allowed.

Holiday Inn. *Moderate.* Airport courtesy car. Nice rooms, some studios. Pool. Pets accepted.

Birmingham

Birmingham Airport Motel. *Expensive.* Opposite air terminal. A large 3-story sound-proof motel with connecting units and day rates available. Restaurant, cocktail lounge. Free parking.

Hilton Inn. *Expensive.* 260 Goodwin Crest Dr. Restaurant, lounge with a view of downtown. Airport courtesy car.

Hyatt House. *Expensive.* 901 21st St. N. Hugo's is one of the city's finest restaurants. Lounge.

Plaza Hotel South. *Expensive.* Fine restaurant, outstanding lounge for dancing.

Sheraton Motor Inn. *Expensive.* 300 N. 10th St. Large. Restaurant, entertainment, dancing. Pool. Free parking.

Sheraton-Mountain Brook. *Expensive.* Restaurant. Swimming pool. Lounge with live entertainment.

Tara House. *Expensive.* 2800 20th St. S. Restaurant, lounge with fine entertainment, some of the best in the city.

Holiday Inn. *Moderate.* Six locations. All have restaurant, pools and allow pets. **20th Place:** 420 20th St. S. **East:** 7941 Crestwood Blvd.; **South:** 1548 Montgomery Hwy. Nicely located. Entertainment, dancing. Coffee in rms. **West:** 1089 9th Ave. S.W., Bessemer. **Civic Center:** 2230 10th Ave. N. Pool (heated). **Airport:** 500 10th Ave. N.

Motel Birmingham. *Moderate.* 7905 Crestwood Blvd. Pleasant rooms; some family units and efficiencies. Coffee makers in rms. Restaurant nr. Pool, play area. Library.

Passport Inn. *Moderate.* 8th Ave. S. at 11th St. Swimming pool. Restaurant, convenient to the campus of the University of Alabama in Birmingham.

Primeway Inn. *Moderate.* 195 W. Oxmoor Rd. All facilities.

Ramada Inn. *Moderate.* Four locations: 1535 Montgomery Hwy., 5216 Airport Hwy., 616 Decatur Hwy., and Tuscaloosa Hwy. in Bessemer. Pleasant location and rooms. Restaurant, entertainment, dancing. Pool.

Southern Motor Inn. *Moderate.* 1313 3rd Ave. N. All facilities.

Econo Travel. *Inexpensive.* 103 Green Springs Hwy. Cafe adjacent.

Boaz

Holiday Inn. *Moderate.* Pleasant. Pool (heated). Pets accepted.

Cullman

Anderson Motel. *Expensive.* Pool, restaurant, coffee shop.

Holiday Inn. *Moderate.* Indoor pool (heated). Free airport transportation. Pets allowed.

Decatur

Decatur Inn. *Expensive.* Very attractive rooms. Restaurant. Huge pool. Pets permitted. Airport courtesy car.

Holiday Inn. *Expensive.* Two floors. Some studios. Restaurant. Pets allowed.

Ramada Inn. *Expensive.* Pleasant rooms. Airport courtesy car. Pool, putting green. Pets.

Nitefall. *Moderate.* Pool, playground, cafe next door.

Red Carpet Inn. *Moderate.* Pool (heated). Restaurant. Pets accepted.

Dothan

Holiday Inn. *Moderate.* Free airport transportation. Appealing rooms. Pool. Pets permitted.

Motel Leon. *Moderate.* 1621 E. Main St. Restaurant.

Olympia Spa and Country Club. *Moderate.* U.S. 231 S. Restaurant. Golf.

Quality Inn Carousel. *Moderate.* Ross Circle. Pleasant. Some studios. Restaurant, bar. Pool.

Ramada Inn. *Moderate.* Airport courtesy car. Very nice rooms, some studios. Restaurant, bar. Pool (heated).

Sheraton Motor Inn. *Moderate.* All rooms with color TV. Dining room, lounge. Pool.

Days Inn. *Inexpensive.* Pool, restaurant.

Heart of Dothan. *Inexpensive.* 314 N. Foster St.

Eufaula

Holiday Inn. *Moderate.* Two locations. Restaurant. Pool. Pets allowed. Airport courtesy car.

Lake Eufaula Motor Lodge. *Inexpensive.* Coffee in room. Pool. Cafe opposite.

Florence

Howard Johnson's Motor Lodge. *Expensive.* Very nice. Restaurant, room service. Pool. Airport courtesy car.

Florence TraveLodge. *Moderate.* Attractive units. Air conditioning, TV, restaurant. Pool (heated). Wheelchair ramps.

Tourway Inn. *Moderate.* Medium-size motel with restaurant next door.

Florence-Muscle Shoals

Holiday Inn. *Expensive.* Airport courtesy car. Color TV. Restaurant. Huge pool. Pets permitted.

Fort Payne

Best Western. *Moderate.* Restaurant, pool, airport courtesy car.

Holiday Inn. *Moderate.* Good accommodations. Restaurant. Pool. Airport courtesy car.

Gadsden

Holiday Inn. *Expensive.* Airport courtesy bus. Attractive rooms; some studios. Restaurant. Pool. Pets allowed.

Ramada Inn. *Expensive.* Restaurant, pool, pets accepted.

Redwood Inn. *Moderate.* A 2-story facility with some kitchens, pool. Cafe next door.

Greenville

Holiday Inn. *Moderate.* Well managed; appealing rooms. Restaurant. Pool. Pets accepted.

Gulf Shores

Holiday Inn. *Expensive.* Beach front. Multi-stories. Restaurant, bar, dancing, entertainment. Pool. Seasonal rates.

Lighthouse. *Expensive.* Small motel with some cottages. Overlooks Gulf.

Robinson's Riverside. *Moderate.* Quiet, comfortable motel. Some efficiencies and family units. TV, air conditioning. Restaurant 5 mi. Coffee in rooms. Playground and outdoor games. Fishing pier on Bon Secour River, boats available.

Guntersville

Holiday Lodge. *Moderate.* Small motel near golf course. Pool.

Val-Monte Motor Hotel. *Moderate.* 3-½ mi. S, 1 mi. E off US 431. A medium-sized resort motel. Large rooms and living-bedroom suites, efficiencies, kitchenettes. Restaurant, room service. Pools, playground, lawn games, putting green, 18-hole golf course, 9-hole, par-3 course lighted for night play; yacht basin, fishing, water-skiing. Seasonal rates.

Huntsville

Best Western Sands Motor Hotel. *Expensive.* 2700 Memorial Pkwy. Multi-storied. Large tastefully decorated motel. Restaurant, room service. Pool (heated).

Carriage Inn. *Expensive.* 3811 University Dr. Very appealing rooms, some with balcony. Restaurant, entertainment, dancing. Airport courtesy car. Pool. Pets allowed.

Hilton Inn. *Expensive.* 401 Williams Ave. at Freedom Plaza. Restaurant, pool. Pets accepted. Airport courtesy car.

Holiday Inn. *Expensive.* 3810 University Dr. Airport courtesy car. Handsome rooms. Pool (heated). Pets accepted.

Ramada Inn. *Expensive.* 3502 Memorial Pkwy S. Appealing rooms. Restaurant. Pool.

Sheraton Motor Inn. *Expensive.* 4404 University Dr. Large and comfortable. Specialty restaurant, entertainment, dancing. Pool.

Skycenter Hotel. *Expensive.* At airport. Large, attractive. Some studios. Restaurant, entertainment, dancing. Golf, pool (heated). Free parking.

Howard Johnson's. *Moderate.* 2524 Memorial Pkwy. N. Some rooms with terraces. Restaurant. Pool. Pets allowed.

Kings' Inn Motor Hotel. *Moderate.* 1220 N. Memorial Pkwy. A large, very attractive motel. Restaurant, room service. Pool.

Tourway Inn. *Moderate.* 1304 Memorial Pkwy. N. Nice rooms; some studios. Coffee makers in rooms. Pool.

Jasper

Holiday Inn. *Moderate.* Nice. Some suites. Restaurant. Pools. Pets accepted.

Mobile

Best Western Admiral Semmes Motor Hotel. *Expensive.* 250 Government St. Large nicely decorated downtown operation. Some suites. Restaurant, room service, bar. Pool (heated).

Holiday Inn. *Expensive.* Three locations: 3339 Government Blvd., 255 Church St., 850 S. Beltline Hwy. Restaurant, pool. Accept pets. Airport courtesy car. Entertainment.

Howard Johnson's. *Expensive.* 3132 Government Blvd. Appealing rooms, some with terraces. Pool (heated). Restaurant, room service.

Malaga Inn. *Expensive.* 359 Church St. Excellent restaurant. Pool. In restored buildings with a courtyard.

Quality Inn. *Expensive.* 3650 Airport Blvd. Airport courtesy car. Nice rooms. Restaurant, bar. Pool. Pets allowed.

Ramada Inn. *Expensive.* Two locations: 600 S. Beltline Hwy., and 1705 Dauphin Island Pkwy. Attractively furnished; some studios. Restaurant, room service. Pools.

Days Inn. *Moderate.* I-65 & US 90. Member of popular chain. Pool, play area, gift shop, gas station. Pets. Tasty World restaurant.

Taylor Motel. *Inexpensive.* 2598 Government Blvd. Comfortable rooms. Pool. Restaurant nr. Coffee makers in rooms.

Town House Motor Hotel. *Inexpensive.* 1061 Government St. Nice rooms & grounds. Restaurant, bar, room service. Pool.

Montgomery

Governor's House Motel. *Expensive.* 2705 E. Southern Blvd. Attractive rooms, many overlooking pool-patio area; some studios. Sauna, golf. Restaurant, bar, dancing. Airport courtesy car.

Howard Johnson's. *Expensive.* Two locations. Both have some rooms with balconies. Restaurant, bar, coffee makers in rooms. Pool. Accept pets. 1110 Eastern Bypass and 995 W. South Blvd.

Quality Inn Diplomat. *Expensive.* Medium-size motel with restaurant and entertainment.

Ramada Inn. *Expensive.* Two locations: 1355 Eastery Bypass, and 4243 Ramada Drive at I-65. Pleasant rooms. Airport courtesy car. Restaurant, dancing, entertainment. Pool (heated). Pets permitted.

Days Inn. *Moderate.* Two locations. 1150 W. South Blvd. and S. Bypass & I-65. A good buy. Pool, play area, gift shop, gas station. Pets. Tasty World restaurant.

Holiday Inn. *Moderate.* Three locations. All have restaurant, pool and accept pets. **East:** I-85 & US 231. Entertainment. Airport courtesy car. **Midtown:** 924 Madison Ave. Some studios. Dancing, entertainment. **Southwest:** 4231 Mobile Hwy. (US 31). Airport courtesy car.

Sheraton Motor Inn. *Moderate.* 1100 W. South Blvd. Airport courtesy car. Multi-story. Restaurant, dancing, entertainment. Pool. Pets allowed.

Motel 6. *Inexpensive.* Pool. Cafe adjacent.

Town Plaza Motor Hotel. *Inexpensive.* 743 Madison Ave. Two blocks from state capitol. Coffee in rooms.

Opelika

Holiday Inn. *Moderate.* Comfortable, attractive rooms. Air conditioning, TV. Restaurant, coffee makers in rooms. Pool, large grounds.

Days Inn. *Inexpensive.* Restaurant, pool.

Travelers Inn. *Inexpensive.* Medium-size 2-story motel with restaurant. Pool.

Ozark

Holiday Inn. *Expensive.* Some studios. Restaurant, bar, coffee makers in rooms. Entertainment. Airport courtesy car. Pool. Pets allowed.

Candlelight Motel. *Inexpensive.* Restaurant, swimming pool.

Point Clear

Grand Hotel. *Expensive.* Large resort hotel with wide choice of accommodations —cottages, cabanas, suites, studio rooms—on Mobile Bay. TV in most rooms. Dining rooms, bar. Social program. Tennis, golf privileges, pool, beach, dock, rental boats & motors, fishing, water-skiing. With advance notice, trains and planes met. Seasonal rates, MAP and EP.

Selma

Holiday Inn. *Moderate.* Airport courtesy car. Restaurant, bar. Pool (heated). Pets allowed.

Plantation Inn. *Moderate.* Hwy. 80 E. Small motel. Restaurant, pool, pets accepted.

Selma Motel. *Inexpensive.* Nice rooms. Restaurant. Coffee makers in rooms. Pool. Pets allowed.

Tuscaloosa

Holiday Inn. *Expensive.* Two locations: 2 miles N. on 82 bypass, and 3-½ miles S. at junction of 82 bypass, I–20 and I–59. Both have restaurant, pool and accept pets.

Days Inn. *Moderate.* 3600 McFarland Blvd. E. One of fine chain, pool, playground.

Ramada Inn. *Moderate.* Two locations: downtown, and Skyland Blvd. Nice rooms. Restaurant. Pool.

Sheraton. *Moderate.* 4810 Skyland Blvd. Restaurant. Free newspapers delivered at door.

YOUTH HOSTELS. Mobile: *YMCA,* 61 S. Conception St.; *YWCA,* 1060 Government St. Montgomery *YMCA's* are: *Central Branch,* 761 S. Perry St.; *East Montgomery Branch,* 3407 Pelzer Ave.; and *Cleveland Ave. Branch,* 1202 Cleveland Ave.

DINING OUT in Alabama leads one toward trying traditional Southern dishes, including Southern fried chicken, ham steak with red gravy, and chicken pan pie. You'll soon discover that virtually everything is accompanied by at least a side-dish of the ubiquitous grits. Along the Gulf Coast, you can try creole specialties, so be sure to ask for Gulf flounder, shrimp, and other special seafoods and gumbos. In river towns or nearby, you might try catfish caught fresh from the Tennessee River. For other worthwhile restaurants, re-check our hotel listings. Restaurants are in order of price category. Price categories and ranges for a complete meal are as follows: *Expensive:* $9.50 and up; *Moderate:* $6.50–$9; *Inexpensive:* $3.50–$6. For a more complete explanation of restaurant categories see *Facts at Your Fingertips* at the front of this volume.

Albertville

The King's Restaurant. *Moderate.* Specialty, steaks and seafood. Closed Christmas Day.

Food Basket. *Inexpensive.* 301 Martlin. Steaks and seafood served here. Closed Thanksgiving and Christmas.

Alexander City

Horseshoe Bend Restaurant. *Moderate.* A daily buffet with large selection of items.

Anniston

Annistonian. *Moderate.* Specialty: steaks, seafood.

House of Chen. *Moderate.* Chinese cuisine.

Mikado. *Moderate.* Japanese-style restaurant.

Auburn

The Golden Dragon. *Inexpensive.* Specialty: Chinese food. Closed Mon.

Gridiron. *Moderate.* Specialties: prime ribs, steak.

BIRMINGHAM

EDITOR'S CHOICES

Rating restaurants is, at best, a subjective business, and obviously a matter of personal taste. It is therefore, difficult to call a restaurant "the best" and hope to get unanimous agreement. The restaurants listed below are our choices of the best eating places in Birmingham, and the places we would choose if we were visiting the city.

HUGO'S ROTISSERIE   French Cuisine
The dining room, set atop the 14-story Hyatt House, is candlelit and elegant. The menu is ambitious, and the service first-rate. Dancing. *Expensive.* 21st Street N.

MICHAEL'S SIRLOIN ROOM   American/International

Top-notch steaks, seafood and "kabobs" serve as the best part of the menu. The atmosphere is subdued, and the food delicious. *Expensive.* 431 20th Street S.

SUMO   Japanese

Japanese hibachi-style cooking at table, with an all-Japanese staff. Food preparation is a show in itself. *Expensive.* 7767 Eastwood Mall.

LEO'S   American

Specializing in fresh seafood, this restaurant has a relaxed atmosphere in which patrons are comfortable in casual dress. *Moderate.* 401 1st Street S.

LLOYD'S   American/Southern

Casual atmosphere, regionally popular. Specialty is barbecue, but limited other dishes available. *Inexpensive.* 5301 Hwy. 280 S.

Other recommended restaurants:

The Coalyard. *Expensive.* 312 20th St. Specialty: steaks.

Gulas. *Expensive.* 7401 Atlanta Hwy. A varied menu specializing in steaks and chops. Live music and dancing.

The Cabana. *Moderate.* Hwy 31 S. at junction of State 149. Quiches, salads, sandwiches, in pleasant plant-filled atmosphere.

Cathay Inn. *Moderate.* 1926 29th Ave. S., Homewood. Specializes in Chinese cuisine, Mandarin and Szechuan.

Joy Young. *Moderate.* Brookwood Shopping Plaza. Restaurant with Chinese motif, specializing in Chinese and American food, 18 different menu selections. Open daily for lunch and dinner.

La Paree. *Moderate.* 2013 5th Ave. N. Specializes in lamb kebob, seafood and steak. Liquor served. Music.

Lovoy's. *Moderate.* 420 Green Springs Hwy. Italian food. Closed Sun.

Paul's Lamplighter. *Moderate.* At Ramada Inn South Motel. Serves all meals in nice atmosphere. Children's portions.

Rossi's. *Moderate.* 427 S. 20th. The emphasis is on Italian cooking.

Sarris. *Moderate.* 600 N. 31st St. Seafood with a Greek flavor. Lunch is cafeteria style. Ten blocks from Civic Center.

Mathews Cafeteria. *Inexpensive.* Formerly Britlings, at 2711 Culver Rd. in Mountain Brook Village.

Steve Leontis Smokehouse. *Inexpensive.* 2731 8th Ave. South. Barbeque deluxe with the spotlight on ribs.

Cullman

All Steak Restaurant. *Inexpensive.* As you'd expect, steak is emphasized here, aged and in large portions, but they also offer seafood and chicken, plus rolls and pastries baked on the premises. Sun. buffet lunch. Children's portions.

Holiday Inn. *Inexpensive.* Attractive dining room, overlooking an enclosed pool, provide relaxed dining. Buffet is featured.

Decatur

Lyon's Dining Room. *Moderate.* Specialty: steaks.

Gibson's. *Inexpensive.* Specialty is barbecue, but the Brunswick stew is popular also.

Dothan

The Conestoga. *Moderate.* Dinners only; specialty is steak.

King's Inn. *Moderate.* Popular locally. Dinners only. Children's portions. Entertainment. Closed Sun.

Eufaula

The Chewella Restaurant. *Inexpensive.* Steaks a specialty.

Town Terrace. *Inexpensive.* Specialty: steaks.

Florence

Dale's. *Moderate.* Steak served in pleasant atmosphere. Dinners only. Children's portions. Closed Sun.

Lakeview Inn Restaurant. *Moderate.* Regional specialties, sandwiches. Children's portions.

Starkey's Cafeteria. *Inexpensive.* An inviting atmosphere in which to enjoy Southern fried chicken. Dinners. Children's portions.

Gadsden

The Embers. *Moderate.* Specializes in seafood and delicious home baking.

Greenville

Wyatt's Restaurant. *Moderate.* General menu, casual atmosphere.

Alabama Grill. *Inexpensive.* Steaks a specialty. Closed Sun.

Gulf Shores

MeMe's. *Expensive.* Seafood is the specialty. Evening reservations requested. Closed Mon.

Gulf Shores State Park Lodge. *Moderate.* Steaks and seafood are the specialties.

Shrimp Boat Restaurant. *Moderate.* Specializes in fresh Creole-style seafood, with children's plates available.

Guntersville

Reid's. *Inexpensive.* Specialty is catfish, with fresh vegetables in season, and home baked desserts.

Val Monte. *Inexpensive.* Seafood and steaks.

Huntsville

Rib Cellar. *Expensive.* Well-prepared beef and lobster specialties. You can dance here, too. Dinners only.

T.P. Crockmier's. *Moderate.* Serves lunch and dinner. Specialty is seafood, with own baking.

Michael's. *Inexpensive.* Specializes in steak, with own baking. Serves all meals.

Jasper

White Way Restaurant. *Moderate.* Steaks and seafood. Check days closed.

S&F Restaurant. *Inexpensive.* Features general menu.

Mobile

Bernard's. *Expensive.* 407 Conti St. Steak and seafood, offered in French creole style. Pleasant decor.

Gaslite Square. *Expensive.* 271 Azalea Road. Steaks and seafood with live entertainment in an adjoining lounge. Lunch and dinner.

The Pillars. *Expensive.* In old home, specializing in steaks and seafood.

Constantine's. *Moderate.* 1500 Government St. An outstanding restaurant for gourmet dishes, both Continental and American. Emphasis is on seafood preparations with shrimp, oysters or crab. All meals served.

Eight Kings. *Moderate.* 3209 Airport Blvd. Fine European cuisine. Gracious atmosphere. Bar. Also informal Pub and inexpensive sandwich shop.

Malaga Inn. *Moderate.* 359 Church St. French/American menu. Lump crabmeat *pestalozie* and *escalopes de veau au purmesane* are specialties.

Wintzell's Oyster House. *Moderate.* 605 Dauphin St. If you like oysters, this is the place to find the best, prepared any way you want them, "fried, stewed or nude". Informal atmosphere and friendly service. Children's portions.

Morrison's. *Inexpensive.* 3282 Springdale Plaza. A regional chain of outstanding cafeterias, with good food, attractively displayed and served. A favorite for family dining. Children's portions.

Montgomery

Rotunda. *Expensive.* In Governor's House Motel. Specialties are beef, pastries; music to dine by.

Elite. *Moderate.* 129 Montgomery St. A Montgomery tradition. Specialties: Trout amandine, oysters and shrimp Athenean. Open breakfast, lunch and dinner.

La Chateau. *Moderate.* I-85 at Perry Hill Rd. One of chain. Specializes in steaks.

Riviera. *Moderate.* 3085 Mobile Hwy. Good varied selection. Entertainment, dancing. Chef-owned. Closed Sun.

Sahara Restaurant. *Moderate.* 511 Edgemont. Music and pleasant decor provide a relaxing atmosphere in which to enjoy beef and seafood specialties. Children's portions. Closed Sun.

Morrison's. *Inexpensive.* 150 Lee St. Good food, attractively displayed. Children's portions. Open for lunch and dinner.

Oneonta

Little Joe's. *Inexpensive.* Family style meals.

Round The Clock. *Inexpensive.* Delicious, buffet-style lunch and dinner.

Opelika

Original Andy's. *Inexpensive.* Steak and seafood.

White Columns. *Inexpensive.* 915 Ave. B. In old home, specializes in steaks and seafood. Buffet daily.

Point Clear

Grand Hotel Restaurant. *Moderate.* Specialty: steaks and seafood in the heart of a 4-star resort.

Yardarm. *Moderate.* Seafood.

Baron's. *Inexpensive.* Steaks and seafood. Closed Mon.

Selma

Costa's. *Expensive.* 1629 W. Highland Ave. Gourmet dining with American-Greek cuisine. Fresh seafood three times a week.

Mangolds. *Moderate.* Seafood and steaks.

Tuscaloosa

The Lamplighter. *Moderate.* An inviting dining-out spot, charmingly decorated in a theme of the past. The menu items are today's favorites, however, including charcoal-broiled steak and seafood. Children's portions.

Nick's. *Moderate.* Two locations. Small and cozy. A hideaway for steaks. Bar with restaurant.

Morrison's. *Inexpensive.* The usual good food and pleasant environment, in this regional chain cafeteria. Open for lunch and dinner.

Piccadilly Cafeteria. *Inexpensive.* One of regional chain. Features own baking.

FLORIDA

Where the Sun Spends the Winter

BY
FLORENCE LEMKOWITZ

Florence Lemkowitz, former travel editor of the Hartford, Connecticut, Times, is a freelance writer whose articles appear in a number of magazines and newspapers.

Exploring Miami and Miami Beach

Miami Beach has almost everything else of a livelier nature, however, and among these are visitors. Millions come to this little (7.2 square miles of land) island which lies just three miles across Biscayne Bay from mainland Miami. There is a permanent population of over 90,000, but the city can accommodate three times this many visitors. One-fourth of the hotels in Florida are situated here in a slender strip of architectural virtuosity.

Whereas the municipal limits show Miami Beach bounded on the south by Government Cut (the channel to Miami's port) and on the north by 88th Street, in truth the beach and the hotels extend northward more than a hundred more blocks. Surfside and Bal Harbour, plus some bayside towns, are immediately adjacent on the north, then comes the county's Haulover Park with a public beach and a marina, and then the oceanfront motels—fancy, gaudy, pretty, monstrous, prim, ostentatious —side by side in a battle for attention almost all the way to the county line.

Points of Interest (Miami)

1) Antique Arms Museum
2) Bass Museum of Art
3) Bayfront Park
4) Biscayne Kennel Club
5) City Convention Complex
6) Dinner Key Auditorium
7) Fairchild Tropical Gardens
8) Flagler Monument
9) Hialeah Park Race Course
10) Hotel Fontainebleau Hilton
11) Jai-Alai Fronton
12) Japanese Gardens
13) Lincoln Road Mall
14) Lowe Gallery
15) Marine Stadium
16) Miamarina
17) Miami Bayfront Auditorium
18) Miami Beach Auditorium & Convention Center
19) Miami Beach Garden Center & Conservatory
20) Miami Beach Ocean Front Auditorium
21) Museum of Science & Natural History, Planetarium
22) North Shore Open Space Park
23) Omni International Hotel
24) Orange Bowl
25) Parrot Jungle
26) Planet Ocean
27) Seaquarium
28) South Florida History Museum
29) Tropical Park Race Course
30) University of Miami
31) Vizcaya Art Museum
32) Wax Museum
33) Zoo and Miniature Railroad

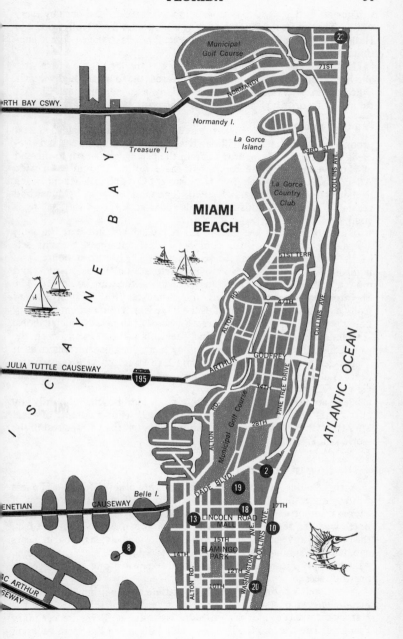

RTH BAY CSWY.

Municipal
Golf Course

71ST

NORMANDY

Normandy I.

Treasure I.

La Gorce
Island

63RD ST

La Gorce
Country
Club

B
I
S
C
A
Y
N
E

B
A
Y

**MIAMI
BEACH**

COLLINS AVE.

51ST TERR

ALTON RD

47TH

ARTHUR

GODFREY

JULIA TUTTLE CAUSEWAY

195

34TH

PINE TREE DRIVE

COLLINS AVE.

ATLANTIC OCEAN

ALTON RD

Municipal Golf Course

28TH

2

19

Belle I.

ENETIAN CAUSEWAY

DADE BLVD.

18

17TH

13 LINCOLN ROAD
MALL

10

WASHINGTON AVE.

COLLINS AVE.

8

15TH

FLAMINGO
PARK

12TH

ALTON RD.

12TH

C ARTHUR
SEWAY

10TH

20

The entire string, top to bottom, should be seen at least once by every . visitor. The tour can start at the top by taking A1A from Hollywood and Hallandale, where it will be noted that such hotels as the *Diplomat* continue the fashion with vigor and decor.

Haulover Park, just south of motel row, is the largest along the strip and has beachside picnicking facilities. Across the four-lane highway, via a pedestrian underpass, is a large parking area and marina. Charter fishing craft, drift boat fishing, and sightseeing boat trips are available here.

A new beach, stretching as wide as 300-feet, is Miami Beach's newest production tabbed at $64-million. It all begins at 80th Street and proceeds north to Bal Harbour, and from the fishing pier north to the end of Haulover Park. When completed, there will be 10½ miles of wide Atlantic oceanfront beach from Government Cut at South Miami Beach to the northern end of Haulover Park. The sand is topped by dunes and sea oats. New bicycling paths have also been added. And the shelling is good, too.

A high bridge over the inlet to the bay takes you into Bal Harbour, a strictly zoned, plush little compound where neatness, building setbacks, and lawn maintenance seem supreme. Apartment houses and hotels of the fashionably expensive variety are on the oceanfront, and more apartments of the same rating are across the wide boulevard. The Sheraton Bal Harbour (formerly the Americana) at 97th Street and Collins Avenue, will be the first of the large, convention-oriented luxury hotels you will see. Across the street are some of the area's fancier shops.

Collins Avenue, for the next ninety-seven blocks, is Miami Beach, the resort, in all its variety. Broken only by block-long oceanfront parks at 71st Street, 65th Street, 46th Street, and 23rd Street, plus the really better beaches along Ocean Drive in the low-rent district of South Beach, the view is of hotels.

There are plenty of economical hotels in Miami Beach, but hardly any cheap ones. Most are new since World War II. (For a number of years after the war, Miami Beach built more new hotels than all the rest of the world combined.)

The Row of Splendor

Across Collins Avenue from these hotels are other hotels, but of a less flamboyant caste. They do not have the ocean front. It is a matter of supreme importance to many visitors that they stay at an oceanfront hotel, whether or not they ever go near the ocean, and whether, in fact, the hotel has any actual beach remaining, erosion being a problem. Years ago, it was a similar mark of distinction to stay at "This Year's" hotel, which simply meant the fanciest, most expensive one built since the previous season.

New hotels continue to go up from time to time, but in truth, the *Fontainebleau,* on one thousand feet of beachfront that was once the Harvey Firestone estate, has settled the issue. In late 1978, the legendary Fontainebleau became the Fontainebleau Hilton, a 1200-room vacation paradise. More than $15-million was spent to refurbish and improve the splendid resort. The old cabana club, torn down for an unobstructed view of the Atlantic, was replaced by a gorgeous freeform swimming pool with natural waterfalls, water slides, Grotto Bar. A lagoon, hot jacuzzi springs, an aquarium, lavish gardens and alfreso restaurants are adjacent. Along with new, rich decor, there are new boutiques, lively lounges, and a dramatic 22-foot glass dome in the lobby ceiling to let the sun shine in.

The newest and most elaborate hotels and apartments stretch northward from the *Fontainebleau Hilton,* at 44th Street and Collins Avenue, but the "older" hostelries south to Lincoln Road are still luxury hotels by any definition of the word.

South of Lincoln Road are the first-built, generally smaller hotels which offer good location and the same sun—plus a superior beach—at economy rates.

Hotel rooms, sand, and water do not a vacation make, of course—at least, not a Miami Beach vacation. The island is maintained like a garden to foster that euphoria which tends to make people want to stay a little longer. A million plants and flowers a year are grown in the city nursery to maintain elaborate displays along Alton Road, Pine Tree Drive, and the eight-block-long Lincoln Road Mall. The open-air mall has 180 stores along artistically decorated walkways decorated with luxuriant plants, shrubs, semi-tropical flowers and fountains. It was designed for strolling among the gardens en route to the boutiques, but an electric tram can also take you from one end of the traffic-free mall to the other. There are no "dead" times—flowers and shrubs are transferred to the viewing beds when they're in bloom, taken out and replaced by others as the blossoms fade. The three golf courses and two-hundred acres of recreational parks get similar attention. You shouldn't pick the flowers, of course—sometimes the city's justly proud gardeners volunteer to sit up all night and guard a particularly tempting display.

Entertainment Galore

The nightlife is considerable—everything from elaborately costumed showgirl reviews, to name-act comedians and singers, to impromptu amateur acts by the patrons of small bars. The big shows are in the big hotels, and the entertainment bill is big, too. Estimates of the cost of live performers run up to $10 million a year; an individual act may cost $25,000 a week and it is said one big name drew $60,000 for a week's work. Almost all the big oceanfront hotels have a cocktail lounge, supper club and late-night disco.

Some big names may be expected during the winter season. Depending on your appetite—and thirst—the tab for a table of four will run over $150 for dinner when one of the names is there to entertain.

Concerts by the Miami Beach Symphony and touring groups are also held in the Miami Beach Auditorium, plus an occasional championship boxing match.

Much of the lure of Miami Beach consists of other divertissements on the mainland. Causeways connect the two in six places, from north to south at 163rd Street, 125th Street, 79th Street, 36th Street, 15th Street, and 13th Street. All street numbers are for the mainland side; Miami Beach street numbers differ.

The Julia Tuttle Causeway at 36th Street (41st Street on the Beach) offers quick access to Miami and connects with the city's expressway system, while MacArthur Causeway, exiting at 15th Street in Miami, jogs south to the lower end of Miami Beach. MacArthur, Tuttle, and the 79th Street Causeways are free; the Venetian Causeway at 15th Street and Broad Causeway at 125th Street have a small toll charge.

MacArthur Causeway was the first, and offers a bit of sightseeing as a bonus. It's bounded on the south by the channel to Miami's new seaport, which stretches for more than a mile parallel and across the channel from the Causeway; while on the north are symmetrical, man-made islands with fine homes and yachts "parked" in front. Al Capone lived here for a spell, on Palm Island.

Watson Island, near the west end of the Causeway, was the mooring spot for the Goodyear blimp, now moored at Pompano Beach. Helicopter and seaplane services are still available here. Just across the roadway in a small bayside city park is an authentic Japanese teahouse and garden. A Tokyo industrialist visited Miami some years ago and was so pleased with the place that he began sending gifts back to the city. He started with several hundred wild orchid trees, then a 300-year-old stone lantern, then an eight-ton statue of Hotei, Japanese god of good fortune. The teahouse was built in Japan, taken apart and shipped over, along with Japanese carpenters to put it back together. It's a delightful little spot—and free.

Just over the final bridge and on Miami's mainland, stretching north to the Venetian Causeway, is the *Miami Herald* building, which is one of the most modern newspaper plants in the world. Uniformed guides conduct tours daily both morning and afternoon.

Getting around in Miami by automobile is fairly simple, but can run into a lot of mileage. The street numbering system begins at Miami Avenue and Flagler Street, and is divided into quadrants from that point—i.e. northeast, northwest, southeast, and southwest. Streets run north and south, as do terraces. The avenues and places run east and west. There are sufficient exceptions to befuddle anyone, however; Coral Gables has its own system of Spanish named avenues and the like, which only a map and diligence can fathom. And Hialeah uses streets and avenues, but of a different and perplexing orientation. Everywhere else, overridding municipal borders, the basic system prevails generally—to 215th Street on the north, 360th Street on the south, and 217th Avenue on the west. If you want to get to Northwest South River Drive, or Southwest North River Drive, however, it's perhaps best to take a cab.

Downtown Miami

Biscayne Boulevard is the city's best-known thoroughfare and runs north and south. Since it is also US 1, it will wend you to Key West or Canada if you stick with it, but, in the main, it is the city's downtown "show" street. Stately royal palms line its eight traffic lanes, divided by four parking lanes, between Southeast First Street and Northeast Fifth Street. On the west are tall hotels and office buildings; on the east is Bayfront Park, sixty-two acres of tropical flora, statues, pools, shaded benches and walkways. On the north end of the park is the city's auditorium—where visitors can pick up a bale of information from the publicity office—and an access road to the Dodge Island three-hundred-acre seaport. Cruise ships leave daily from ultra-modern $40-million

Port of Miami for the most fascinating Caribbean ports. You can also catch a luxury liner to Mexico or Central America.

A stroll about a bit will reveal some 21,000 well-kept plants, plus annuals in flower beds as the seasons change. At the south end of the park is the bandshell, where open-air concerts (free) are held and just north, at the foot of Flagler Street, is the Miami Public Library. Between the two is a plaque marking the spot where, in 1933, a crazed assassin tried to kill Franklin D. Roosevelt but mortally wounded Chicago's Mayor Anton Cermak instead.

Along the boulevard in the northern corner of the park is the Torch of Friendship, signifying Miami's ties with neighboring Latin republics. There is also a plaque memorializing President John F. Kennedy, and the official national seals, in bronze, of most Latin American nations. Colorful flags of the nations wave from atop the curved native stone wall with a gas-fed perpetual flame as the centerpiece. Regrettably, the Torch of Friendship is the place various groups usually gather to protest whenever they are displeased with the action of either the United States or any other nation—or with another faction of same.

In Miami, the Old Havana before Castro, has been reborn. It is called "Little Havana," not surprisingly, an exciting area of excellent restaurants, nightclubs, and shops. For the English-speaking visitor it provides the flavor and feel of a foreign country. Although there are several large sections of Miami in which Cubans are the dominant population, "Little Havana" is that region around S.W. 8th Street and W. Flagler Street where most of Miami's Cubans work and live.

Little Havana is no hybrid; it's a completely Cuban world. A familiar sign in store windows is: "English Spoken Here." English or Spanish, communication is easy in the hundreds of open front cafes, restaurants, oyster bars, bookstores, tobacco shops, and groceries. About all that is missing from Old Havana are the cries of lottery ticket vendors and the covered arcades.

Some famous Old Havana spots have established Miami counterparts —the Floridita where Ernest Hemingway used to drink daiquiris, the Zaragozana seafood restaurant, founded in 1832, was transported to Miami and emerged as two extravagant nightclubs, the *Flamenco* and the *Les Violins*.

Prices in Little Havana can be ridiculously low for good Cuban dishes in some of the smaller niches to downright expensive in such places as the two supper clubs just mentioned. There are also excellent Cuban-Chinese restaurants in the area.

Unfortunately, Little Havana is not as much fun as it used to be. Since boatloads of refugees from Cuba (and from other islands) arrived in 1980, there has been strife among the prosperous, older citizens and the impoverished arrivals. In addition, the 1980 Liberty City riots didn't help the situation. Just be careful on the streets and don't walk alone at night or park in a deserted lot.

Close to downtown, at Northwest Third Street and 14th Avenue, is the Orange Bowl, where the Miami Dophins and University of Miami Hurricanes play their games. It's simpler to park downtown and take a special bus or cab on game days, for parking facilities are limited.

Also close in—only some twenty blocks south of Flagler Street via Brickell Avenue, US 1—is the Rickenbacker Causeway which for a quarter will pass a car from the hurly-burly city to a very reasonable facsimile of a South Sea island. Key Biscayne, the ultimate destination, was a coconut plantation for long before the postwar causeway was built and is a favorite of movie-makers for its tropical lushness. Parts of *Guadalcanal Diary* and *They Were Expendable* were filmed here.

Even the causeway itself is a park of sorts, providing wide parking areas adjacent to the four-lane road and handy swimming, boating and waterskiing areas.

Of Keys, Parks and Villas

The first real island reached will be Virginia Key, which in addition to a palm-fringed beach, offers the Seaquarium, a commercial attraction with an elaborate collection of sea life, including trained porpoises and seals, colorful reef fishes, sharks, barracuda, turtles, and the like. It's open until dark, and there's a monorail passenger car which circles the entire area. The monorail ride can be taken without paying to enter the Seaquarium itself, but you'll miss the real show in the viewing tanks and the like. Bird Island, which is part of the Seaquarium, was designated as a wildlife sanctuary by the Audubon Society in summer '78.

Also on Rickenbacker Causeway is Planet Ocean, the new $6-million attraction dedicated to exploring and explaining the mysteries of the seas. Visitors are encouraged to push buttons and activate exhibits with special effects, board a submarine and an iceberg, and explore 100 space-age exhibits or view the panoramic, multi-media shows.

Nearby is Miami's Marine Stadium, a modern, $2 million concrete structure providing 6,500 armchair seats for the viewing of powerboat racing. Most popular use of the stadium, however, has been for early evening concerts of light music, the orchestra being situated on a barge in front of the grandstand. Acoustics are good, and the low admission for all has resulted in full-house attendance for each concert since they began in the summer of 1965. For the same fee private boats cluster around the barge, and many bring a picnic supper in order to arrive early and gain a good position. Special buses from the downtown area make it simpler for those who wish to escape the post-concert traffic tie-ups. Summer and winter series of concerts are usually held on Friday or Saturday nights, weather permitting.

A New State Park

A bridge connects Virginia Key to Key Biscayne, which is, by all odds, the area's favorite recreation spot. The northern half of the 4½-mile long island is county-owned Crandon Park, which offers a marina, 2½ miles of uncluttered beach, landscaped parking areas, barbecue pits.

The middle third of the island consists of privately owned homes, apartments, and hotels. In 1967, the State of Florida opened the southern third—Cape Florida—as a state park. Once a haven for pirates and shipwreckers who lured sailing craft onto the reefs with false signals, the Cape also is the site of the aforementioned lighthouse attacked by Indians, not to mention by federal gunboats during the Civil War.

Life on Key Biscayne changed a bit when former President Nixon became a resident, after vacationing there for many years. Demonstrations and protests were common fare when the President visited his villa, but strategically placed guardhouses at either end of the *cul de sac* street prevented such rowdies from disturbing the executive tranquility. The guardhouses also prevented a steady parade of sightseers hoping for a glimpse of the Nixon clan.

You'll have to retrace your route back to the mainland, but it won't cost anything to exit. Just a few blocks south (follow the signs) is another county facility, Villa Vizcaya, the former home of James Deering of the International Harvester fortune. Deering collected art works abroad for twenty years before beginning work in 1912 on what is, in reality, an Italian Renaissance palace. With up to one thousand craftsmen working, it took five years to complete the sixty-nine-room main palace and formal gardens. The latter cover ten acres with clipped hedges, fountains, reflecting pools, and statuary in seven separate garden areas. As a breakwater, offshore from the steps leading to Biscayne Bay, there is a stone version of Cleopatra's barge.

Inside the mansion, architects were faced with the problem of designing rooms to accommodate a frescoed ceiling here, a sideboard from a fifteenth-century Italian church there, or the tapestry that hung in Robert Browning's villa in Asolo, Italy, which the poet described in his "Childe Roland to the Dark Tower Came."

What it all cost, Deering didn't say, but estimates range up to $10 million hard, pre-World War I, pre-income tax dollars. A hundred million couldn't duplicate it today. You can see it all and enjoy what is now the Dade County Art Museum.

Across South Miami Avenue from the Vizcaya entrance is the Museum of Science, on original Vizcaya grounds. The Space Transit Planetarium at the east end of the museum aims to make every viewer feel like an astronaut; visitors blast off and go on a reeling simulated space ride. A sixty-five-foot dome makes it the third largest planetarium in the country.

Coconut Grove isn't a town anymore, but it was one before and in fact until Miami, it is alleged, pulled a sneaky annexation one summer while a lot of residents were vacationing out of town. But Coconut Grove is still a different place; part Greenwich Village and part Sausalito, with overtones of Tahiti. To reach it, go south on Miami Ave., which becomes Bayshore Drive.

It is arty hereabouts. There are some fine painters in residence, so it follows that bad painters will be here too in the hopes that buyers may know and buy what they like, even if it isn't good. There may be more ovens employed in the baking of ceramics than bread; perhaps more guitars are carried about than are really played, but it is not all sham. There is good theatre at the Coconut Grove Playhouse, where pre-Broadway bugs are worked out of the script, or touring companies perform.

The village atmosphere is conducive to shopping and dining. Besides a handful of smaller art galleries, the large Grove House next to the theater offers a wide range of *objets d'art*—all for sale. Prices are not out of hand. A good way to look around is on a bicycle. You can rent one in the Grove, and there are bicycle paths to adjacent Coral Gables and down to Matheson Hammock, another pleasant county park with nature trails and a swimming lagoon.

Residential Gables

To get to Coral Gables city hall, go west from US 1 on Southwest 12th Street. It will jog a little here and there, and become Coral Way. At 37th Avenue, you enter Coral Gables. Stick with it as you drive through a business area of shops and stores on a wide boulevard (this is Miracle Mile), and at the end of this section, dead ahead, will be the Spanish-towered and columned city hall. Inside they'll give you a map and notes for the self-guided tour.

Using the two, you can follow a series of self-guided tour signs on the street that will hit all the high spots for twenty rambling miles. With luck and close attention, you'll always know where you are.

Markers and the notes explain the what and wherefore about such as the Venetian Pool, the University of Miami, the villages (little compounds of homes in Dutch, French, and Chinese architecture), the plazas, and entranceways.

Coral Gables is not a tourist attraction, but rather an example of what can be done to keep a city's tone and appearance the way most of the residents want it. Every street was planned and plotted before a lick of work was done when it all began in the early '20's. George Merrick, the founder, wanted a certain sort of city for pleasant living, and he got it. Now as always, every new building must be approved by a board of architects and erected according to a strict zoning code. There are no billboards, no cemeteries, no trailer parks, and the only industry allowed must be clean, smokeless, and within a designated area. For most Americans, Coral Gables is something different.

For a guided group tour, including the history of Coconut Grove and Coral Gables, contact The Villagers, a non-profit organization dedicated to preservation and restoration. Tour includes downtown Miami. Call (305) 667-4246 or 595-1146, or write Marlies Tindall, The Villagers, Inc., 4900 Biltmore Dr., Coral Gables 33146.

Sports Paradise

The agenda of spectator sports in the whole Miami area is practically endless. Powerboat and sailboat races are weekly events, stock car racing, boxing, wrestling, baseball (both minor league variety and major league spring training games), tennis tournaments, basketball, soccer, major golf tournaments and the pari-mutuel sports of horse racing, dog racing, and jai alai abound.

Greyhound racing continues the year around at one or more of the area's four tracks. Summer racing has been added to the thoroughbred horse racing scene in the Miami area with the completion of Calder Race Course. An air-conditioned grandstand and clubhouse prevents heat prostration among overexcited bettors. The Calder season runs for 132 days (May through November). Hialeah Park, March through mid-April, and Gulfstream Park, mid-January to March, just across the county line to the north, provide horse racing in the winter season. Tropical Park is run at the Calder Race Course, mid-Nov. to mid-Jan.

Summer or winter, Hialeah is a showplace worth seeing, and hundreds of thousands tour the elaborate racing plant each year with not a horse in sight. Forty groundskeepers keep things pretty, including some 1,200 stately royal palms and 95,000 other plants and flowers. The track is open to visitors and there's a tram ride around the 209 acres. The four hundred pink flamingoes nesting on the infield lake are free to leave whenever they want, incidentally, but nowhere else can they depend on a daily supply of free shrimp.

PRACTICAL INFORMATION FOR MIAMI AND MIAMI BEACH

HOW TO GET THERE. *By air:* You can reach Miami on direct flights from all major U.S. cities via American, Air Florida, Braniff, Delta, Eastern, Pan Am, US Air, Ozark, Piedmont, Republic, Northwest Orient, TWA, United. Most of these airlines serve Miami from various cities within the state, since deregulation. Air Florida, an all-jet airline, is always adding service between the state's most important cities and other U.S. and foreign destinations.

Air Canada, Delta and Eastern have direct flights from Montreal; Eastern from Ottawa; Air Canada or Eastern from Toronto. There are connecting flights from Calgary, Edmonton, Halifax, Hamilton and Vancouver, via Air Canada, CP Air, Eastern Provincial, Nordair or Western.

By train: Amtrak has regular service. Even before streamlining by Amtrak, the *Seaboard Coast Line,* a Miami to New York run, was one of the last truly luxury trips by train still available in the U.S. Now it is even better. Coach fare is cheaper than by air; sleepers are much more expensive. Approximately a 24-hr. journey.

By car: From the northeast I-95 (almost complete now except for a confusing detour near Vero Beach) is your fastest route; A1A the beautiful, leisurely way.

By bus: Trailways or Greyhound will get you there.

By boat: The Intracoastal Waterway parallels the coastline and runs 349 mi. from Jacksonville to Miami.

HOW TO GET AROUND. Take the airport limousine to your hotel, if it is a major one. You will save about $4-5 on the trip. *Taxis* charge $1 for the first mi.; 20¢ for each additional 1/6th mi. Taxi rates will get another hike in 1982, making Miami one of most expensive taxi cities. Renting a car is your best bet, but be prepared for heavy traffic and high tariffs.

TOURIST INFORMATION. Metro Dade County Dept. of Tourism, 234 W. Flagler St., Miami 33130. City of Miami Beach Tourist Development Authority, 555 17th St., Miami Beach 33139.

SEASONAL EVENTS. *January:* New Year's Day, *Orange Bowl Classic football game. International Travel Camping Show,* Miami.

February: Doral Open Golf Tournament, late Feb. to early Mar., at Doral Country Club. *Sidewalk Art Show,* Coral Gables. More than 200 artists participate. Feb. 15 to 17. *Spring training for Baltimore Orioles* begins Feb. 15. *Vizcaya Art Show,* on grounds of old Deering estate, 3251 S. Miami Ave. Last Sun. in Feb.

March: Lipton Cup Sailing Race, early Mar. *Exhibition games of the Baltimore Orioles,* mid-Mar. to Apr. *Museum of Science's Annual Around the World Fair* at Tropical Park Race Track.

June: Poinciana Festival, early June.

July: Fourth of July Parade, Key Biscayne, old-fashioned parade, featuring floats, marching units, and bicycles. *Bowling Tournament of the Americas,* Miami. Amateur bowling champions from nations of the Western hemisphere vie for top honors. July 8 to 14.

November: Jr. Tennis Championships, Coral Gables, for youngsters 8 to 12, regarded as tune-up for Jr. Orange Bowl Tennis Tournament.

December: Orange Bowl Festival, one of the nation's most celebrated festival and sporting events. King Orange Jamboree Parade highlights New Year's Eve in downtown Miami, terminating with the football classic on New Year's Day. *Junior Orange Bowl* activities in nearby Coral Gables round out spectacular events of the colorful Orange Bowl festival. *Orange Blossom Classic.* Florida A & M University meets an outstanding selected opponent in an annual football duel in the Orange Bowl Stadium Early Dec.

 MUSEUMS AND GALLERIES. Historical: *Cape Florida State Recreation Area,* 1200 S. Crandon Blvd., Key Biscayne. Seminole history. Restored Cape Florida Lighthouse. *Historical Museum of Southern Florida,* 3280 S. Miami Ave., Miami, Maintained by nonprofit Historical Association of South Florida. Free. Closed Christmas.

Art: *Bass Museum of Art,* 2100 Collins Ave., Miami Beach. The John and Johanna Bass collection of paintings; sculpture; vestments and tapestries. Free. Closed Sun. & holidays. *Bacardi Art Gallery,* 2100 Biscayne Blvd. Exhibitions by local, national, and international artists. Free. *Grove House.* Gallery, market place, and school featuring Florida arts and crafts. Wkdays 10 to 5. *Lowe Art Museum,* 1301 Miller Dr., Coral Gables. Becoming one of the finer galleries in the South. Free. Closed New Year's, Thanksgiving and Christmas. *Metropolitan Museum and Art Center,* two branches, 7867 N. Kendall Dr. and 12400 NE 8th Ave., both Miami. Soon to move into Coral Gables' famed old Biltmore Hotel, which is being restored. Heart of the Miami art establishment. Free. Closed Fri. *Miami Museum of Modern Art,* 381 Northeast 20th St., Miami. Daily. Closed July, Aug. and holidays. *Monastery Cloister of Saint Bernard,* 16711 W. Dixie Hwy., North Miami Beach. Built in Segovia, Spain, in 1141, it was disassembled and brought to the U.S.

Special Interest: Museum of Science, 3280 S. Miami Ave., Miami. Children can clamber around reconstructions of prehistoric monsters. Museum has extensive displays of Florida wildlife. Free Planetarium is adjacent to the Museum of Science. Afternoon and evening show daily. Weekly programs in Spanish. Programs changed every 5 to 6 wks. Closed Christmas. *Holbrook Antique Arms and Gun Museum,* 12953 Biscayne Blvd., North Miami. South's largest display of militaria. Closed holidays. *Planet Ocean,* 3979 Rickenbacker Causeway, near Key Biscayne. An International Oceanographic Foundation $6-million showcase for "exploring" the mysteries of the seas. Visitors can climb into a submarine or upon Florida's only iceberg. More than 100 exhibits with special effects, including a new Weather Machine. Open daily.

Others: Miami Wax Museum, 13899 Biscayne Blvd., Miami. From Columbus to the astronauts in life-size wax sculptures. *International Design Center,* North Miami Ave. at 42nd St., Miami. A grouping of art centers that offer revealing glimpses of interior design and the technical construction of architectural and decorating innovations. Only building of its kind, they say, in the world. Full reference system, changing programs on "Centre State" which aim to dramatize the newest work of the finest designers.

 HISTORIC SITES. *Vizcaya,* Dade County Art Museum, 3251 S. Miami Ave., Miami. An Italian palace, created by an American millionaire with a Hollywood imagination continues to be one of Miami's main attractions. Added to the $9 million worth of magnificence is a new Sound and Light show. Check ahead for schedule.

TOURS. *Nightclub tours: Leblang Tours,* 216 71st St., Miami Beach; *Grayline tours,* 587-8080 or see the bell captain at your hotel.

By boat: The Island Queen makes a 2-hr. Great Circle Cruise of Biscayne Bay from Pier 5 at Bayfront Park in Miami. See Vizcaya and the millionaire estates.

By air: Cruise a fine camera height in a *helicopter* from Gold Coast Helicopters, 1501 Biscayne Blvd. or 3000 Interama Blvd., or try *glider-sightseeing* from the Miami Gliderport, operating from Nov. to May and located on Krome Ave. and S.W. 162nd St. Flying instructions, also some air tours from Gene Simmons of Dar-Sim Aviation.

Everglades by airboat. Along the Tamiami Trail, on US 41 about 17 mi. W of downtown Miami, airboat operators will whisk you off on small craft with aircraft motors and guarded propellers. These were developed for fishing and hunting forays into the remote wilderness areas. Four to twelve persons can pile aboard and the normal sightseeing tour has only a nominal fee—perhaps $1.25 for adults and 50¢ for children.

Other tours: American Sightseeing Tours offers one-day and extended tours to Disney World, shuttle service, group sightseeing, special tours, school charters and race track service. 1000 N.W. LeJeune Rd. Call 633-0281, 448-1711 or 445-0098. *Burnside-Ott,* at the Opa Locka Airport, offers air tours with professional pilots and late-model aircraft. Call 685-5111. *Grayline* offers boat and bus tours to the Seaquarium, Parrot Jungle, the Palm Beaches or Ocean World in Fort Lauderdale. *Nikko Gold Coast Cruises* offers good variety; call 945-5461. Do check at hotel desk, as new sightseeing cruises are added (or disbanded) each season.

INDUSTRIAL TOURS: The *Miami Herald Publishing Co.,* 1 Herald Plaza. Tours Mon. to Fri. *Bertram Yacht Corp.,* 3663 N.W. 21st St. Fiberglass boats, 20-38 ft. Tours.

 GARDENS. The Cloud Forest, part of the Miami Beach Garden Center and Conservatory (a rapidly building horticultural complex), is operated without admission charge by the city. On Washington Ave. 2 blocks N of Lincoln Road Mall (follow in to the west). The air inside the dome is changed very frequently, but it's so hot no visitor can stay too long. The Cloud Forest plants thrive in a droopy-hot atmosphere like that in the backwaters of the Amazon. This is a compact display with many rarities. The conservatory was recently gifted with one of the world's larger orchid collections. Closed Christmas.

Fairchild Tropical Gardens, 10901 Old Cutler Rd., Miami, always open from sunrise to sunset and the "largest tropical botanical garden in America," holds the Fairchiid Ramble in early Dec. It's a benefit bargain hunt with unimaginable goods—bobcat skin, a 90-year-old baby buggy, a Japanese party set that cost the lady who gave the party $2,500. The garden itself, founded by a tax attorney, is spread out on 83 acres south of Matheson Hammock Park. Leave US 1 at S.W. 112th St. and take a short jog on S.W. 57th Ave. before turning left on Old Cutler Road. Admission charge.

Other horticultural things to see: the *Miami Flower Show* is in mid-Mar. Women who go to the *Orchid Jungle,* 25 mi. S of Miami, receive an orchid as a gift. *Garden of Our Lord,* St. James Lutheran Church, 110 Phonetia, Coral Gables, with many exotic plants mentioned in the Bible. *Japanese Garden,* Watson Park, on the MacArthur Causeway, which features statue of Hotei, arbor, teahouse, stone lanterns, pagoda, ornate main gate, rock gardens, and waterfall lagoon. Free. *Redland Fruit and Spice Park,* 35 mi. SW of Miami, Homestead. Intersection of Coconut Palm Dr. (SW 248th St.) & Redland Rd. (187th Ave.). A 20-acre tropical showplace featuring fruit, nut, and spice-producing plants from around the world. Guided tours. Free. Lost Islands at the Miami Seaquarium has more than 100 varieties of palms, breadfruit trees, exotic plants in a jungle setting. In 1978, it was designated a Wildlife Sanctuary by the Tropical Audubon Society. Seabirds and migratory birds feed here. Between Miami and Key Biscayne.

MUSIC. The *Opera Guild of Greater Miami* books important stars from the Continent, the Met, and elsewhere. Its seasonal openings bring out a socially conscious, conspicuously gowned and furred crowd. Rehearsals are year round, the chorus members are paid just as the stars are. The company keeps engagements as far off as Fort Lauderdale. Family operas are booked as late as spring and make a memorable musical occasion. A number of leading families lend their support to the Opera Guild. Call 854-1643 for up-to-date information. The Company usually appears at Dade Auditorium and Miami Beach Auditorium.

Miami is proud of the *Greater Miami Philharmonic,* which is now housed in Gusman Hall, formerly the old ornate Olympia Theatre in the heart of downtown. There is a year-round series of concerts. For information and tickets go to performing hall at 174 Flagler Street.

Miami Beach also has a symphony, with a season extended into the warmer months with a *Summer Pops series.* Barnett Breeskin directs both the winter symphony and the summer program. The Miami Beach auditorium box office at 1700 Washington Ave. will provide current information.

The *Youth Symphony of South Florida,* the *Chamber Music Society in Greater Miami,* the *Miami Little Orchestra* and dozens of other groups are active in the resort area. The Miami Herald is a good source for information on current performances. *Marine Stadium,* just off Rickenbacker Causeway, Virginia Key, has a summer music series, with the audience listening from boats as well as from the grandstand.

STAGE AND REVUES. The Greater Miami area cannot yet compete with New York in legitimate theater, but it is doing quite well in its own right. Visitors who love theater will find a variety of excellent productions.

Coconut Grove Playhouse, 3500 Main Hwy., Coconut Grove, a chief outpost of the Broadway theater, plays major hits with major casts. Fine full-cast productions draw top society from throughout Greater Miami and, in winter, from around the U.S. Aesthetically and technically, the theater itself is an improvement on many of Broadway's more famous houses, with fine seats, good acoustics, excellent restaurant service attached, and an upstairs art gallery. Coconut Grove, really a corner of Miami, is a semi-art colony with millionaires and artists living in close proximity.

The Miami Beach Theatre of the Performing Arts is a promising new addition to the South Florida stage scene. Its musicals in a $6 million new house especially fill the seats. 1700 Washington Ave.

The *Ring Theater,* Univ. of Miami, offers presentations of such high quality they could compare with Broadway performances.

The *Player's Repertory Theatre,* 3280 S. Miami Ave., uses the stage facilities of the Museum of Science, which have been converted to its uses. It is probably the most up and coming theater in the area, already offering season subscriptions. Its amateur and professional talent productions usually are of high quality.

The *Merry-Go-Round Playhouse and Drama Studio,* 235 Alcazar, Coral Gables, has continuous *Children's Theater;* also presents amateur Shakespeare and contemporary plays.

North Miami Playhouse, 1603 N.E. 123rd St., North Miami, presents both legitimate and children's theater, Sat. matinees.

Cinema Theatre, Washington Ave., Miami Beach, presents great stars of the Jewish theater in winter.

Public Trust Theater Company, 3356 Virginia St., Coconut Grove, upstairs in the old post office building. Good selection of plays drawing on top local talent.

Parker Playhouse, Fort Lauderdale was created by Zev Buffman, former owner of the Coconut Grove Playhouse (he's now with the new Miami Beach Theatre of the Performing Arts) and run on the same principles. Most shows appearing at Coconut Grove go to the Parker next stop.

At the *Sunrise Theater,* West Commercial Blvd. and 95th St. in Sunrise, top celebrities such as Frank Sinatra are booked.

 BARS. In Miami Beach, many of the cocktail lounges could swallow the nightclubs of other cities twice over and have room for more. The nightclubs, in turn, are larger than theaters in many cases. Most bars mentioned here are among the swinging spots rather than tiny hideaways where a man can find room to talk to himself. Everyone comes to see and be seen in the window-walled lobby-bar in the new *Omni International Hotel,* at 16th St. and Biscayne Blvd. Luxuriously comfortable seats, lots of greenery, and splashing fountains enhance the scene. No extra charge for the daily splendiferous sunset. The *Marco Polo Swinger Lounge* (Marco Polo Hotel), Collins Ave. at 192nd Ave. has a good live show. In the magnificently redecorated Fontainebleau Hilton, there's a variety of unusual bars, including the *Grotto Bar,* where a 17-foot-high waterfall cascades outside the window; *Coconut Willie's* for papaya daiquiris; *Pizzaz Pizzaz* for beer and wine. *Cye's Rivergate,* 444 Brickell Avenue, downtown Miami, is a popular rendezvous. *Tuttle's,* Biscayne Blvd. just off Julia Tuttle Causeway, is the newest "in" place (located in Charter Club condominium). The Silver Sands Motel, at 301 Ocean Drive in Key Biscayne, has its *Sandbar.* The bar in the *Sonesta Beach Hotel and Tennis Resort* is a popular rendezvous for Key Biscayne visitors, too. These are merely representative. Though local laws may keep them from putting signs on the street, most of the larger hotel and motel operations have pleasantly run bars which are open to the public.

DRINKING LAWS. In The Miami area, the swingers can get service until very late (or early) in the day—see *Bars* section.

 NIGHTCLUBS. The headliners, who can make more money per minute by appearing in a nightclub than most people make in a week, have really only one complaint: they say that New York doesn't have the number of big dates for the top acts that are available in Miami Beach. Christmas season—really, Christmas Eve itself—marks the annual opening of the great star parade. Veterans and comparatively new entries—so long as they bear a famous name and have whipped up what is reputed to be a headline act—are brought on here. To "fill the big room"—for the rooms can be very big—tends to be an ultimate test of personal stardom.

On Miami Beach most of the important nightclubs are located in resort hotels. Most of the hotel nightclubs have developed a style—they go for revues, for smash action, or for intimacy. Prices often range from expensive to staggering but the cost can be softened up by paying a very nominal fee for a nightclub tour.

In Miami the most lavish, and the wildest, night spots are the Cuban supper clubs. The best are *Les Violins* and *Les Folies,* both on Biscayne Blvd. They're not cheap, of course, but the prices won't stagger you, as per the average Miami Beach lollapalooza. But money spent in a Cuban nightclub is never regretted—when the Cubans do a nightclub show, they tear off a good one. And the food is usually excellent. Manolo Godinez, who owns Les Folies, is a showman Flo Ziegfeld style. His classy Las Vegas revues spotlight extravagantly costumed girls, a real Rolls Royce driven on stage, gold cages hoisting dancers to the ceilings, free-flowing waterfalls and rainstorms on stage, and a full-sized ice rink. Fantastic! The *Little Havana* clubs of SW 8th Street (Calle Ocho) have proliferated in recent years and count many Anglos as appreciative regulars. Lively combos entertain for listening and dancing in the *Sonesta Beach Hotel and Tennis Resort* on Ocean Drive, Key Biscayne.

SPORTS. Because of the semi-tropical climate there is no division of sports activities into summer or winter in the greater Miami area. Instead, we will list them alphabetically.

Bicycling: There are about 120 mi. of well-marked secondary routes adjoining thoroughfares for safe, scenic cycling. Greynolds Park is a good starting point in the north part of the Miami area—bike paths wind through picnic grounds, around a lake with boat rides and fishing. Coconut Grove has excellent bike paths, winding through the oldest and most historic section of Miami. Route maps are provided by local chambers of commerce, the Coral Gables Community Development Dept. and Miami-Metro Dept. of Publicity and Tourism. Numerous shops offer loaners; bicycles can be included in some auto rental arrangements.

Boating: Miami has berthing for over 4,000 boats and takes anything up to a 180-ft. yacht. Miamarina is the city's newest and most modern marine facility with all the downtown advantages. It offers 178 slips for pleasure craft and space for 30 commercial craft, such as charger and sightseeing boats. There are circuit voyages out of Miami through the Keys. Fort Myers and Okeechobee Waterway. As for distance on the Intracoastal Waterway, Jacksonville to Miami is a 349-mi. trip; and it's 158 mi. inside the Keys from Miami to Key West. Competitive boating includes a speed classic at the Marine Stadium on Rickenbacker Causeway and, in mid-Jan., a 9-hr. endurance race. There's an 807-mi. race from Miami to Montego Bay and races from St. Petersburg to Fort Lauderdale and Miami to Cat Cay in late Feb. The Lipton Cup yacht race is considered by yachtsmen to be a warmup for the great Miami-Nassau race—both are held in Mar. The new Miami Beach Marina (south of Fifth St.) claims to be the largest marina in the southeastern U.S.

Fishing: Deep-sea fishing: You can charter boats for trolling, drift-fishing or bottom fishing. Charter boats vary in cost from about $80 for a half day to around $150 for a full day. Since they carry up to six persons, you can share the costs of the charter. The deep blue of the Gulfstream is their beat for the big gamefish, marlin, sail, wahoo, dolphin and tuna. Key Largo, south of Miami in Florida Keys, is great sport-fishing haunt. There are about 200 licensed fishing guides to take you to the Upper Keys and into the flats of Florida Bay.

Pier Fishing: Try your luck at Haulover Pier in Haulover Beach Park, north of Bal Harbour on A1A; Sunny Isles Pier, 167th St. and Collins Ave; Pier Park, Ocean Dr. and First St., Miami Beach; Children's Pier, adjacent to City Hall; Dinner Key, Miami.

Freshwater fishing: Most famous freshwater fishing in Greater Miami is the Tamiami Canal, extending from west edge of Miami along US 41. The canal is 50 ft. wide, 50 mi. long with plenty of parking and fishing spots along the banks. A freshwater fishing license is necessary. Skiffs and hired guides are available along the Tamiami Trail for trips into the Everglades. The Miami Herald's Metropolitan Miami Fishing Tournament, one of the world's largest, runs each year from mid-Dec. to mid-Apr. Despite the skill and knowledge of local anglers, a majority of the average annual 50,000 entries of fish contesting for citations and trophies are made by visitors from all parts of the world.

Golf: The greater Miami area has over 45 golf courses. Green fees are much less expensive on summer wkdays at most 18-hole municipal courses. Many courses offer reduced "twilight" rates, which go into effect daily between 3 P.M. and 6 P.M., depending on the season.

The *Doral C.C.,* Miami, is outstanding. Other excellent courses are: *Le Jeune G.C.,* with gently rolling terrain; *North Dade G. & C.C.,* nicely landscaped with palm trees. *C.C. of Miami,* a fine resort course; *Miami Lakes Inn & C.C.,* a challenging course; *King's Bay Yacht & C.C.,* a challenging, scenic course open to members and hotel guests; *Fontainebleau Hilton C.C.,* a Mark Mahannah course with seven lakes, rolling fairways (all in Miami). Also: *Miami Shores C.C.,* Miami Shores, for members and their guests only; *Miami Springs G. & C.C.,*

FLORIDA 65

Miami Springs, former site of the Miami Open; *Bay Shore Municipal,* Miami Beach, a municipal course with rolling fairways, mounds and lakes; *Key Biscayne G.C.,* Key Biscayne, a unique Robert Von Hagge course, with tough tests; *Palmetto G.C.,* So. Miami, a municipal course with 13 water holes; *Biltmore G.C.,* Coral Gables, a municipal course, with some tricky water holes; and *Normandy Shores G.C.,* Miami Beach, on the Isle of Normandy in Biscayne Bay.

Ice Skating: The Polar Palace in Miami, at 3685 N.W. 36th St.

Shelling: This is a passionate pastime for many. Dredging for Miami Beach's new wide beach from Government Cut to the northern end of Haulover Park uncovered a bonanza of shells, starting at 80th St. and northward. Coral and sand beaches along the Keys are good spots, or you may acquire, painlessly, cheaply and unwetly a fine collection at the shops everywhere.

Water sports: Water-skiing schools, jumps, and towing services are located along beaches and causeways. *Skiing* lessons consist of approximately three 1-hr. sessions. Boats with tow equipment and fuel can be rented. *Surfing* is a practiced art in Florida, although the local surfers are a frustrated lot—the waves are seldom large enough. However they do their best at Haulover Beach Park and South Miami Beach, where there are special areas reserved for surfers. There are miles of sand beaches for *swimming:* Crandon Park and Cape Florida State Park on Key Biscayne; Haulover Beach on Collins Ave., north of Bal Harbour; Lummus Park on Miami Beach; Matheson Hammock, 2 mi. south of Miami on Old Cutler Rd; Tahiti Beach in South Miami, are among the many choice spots. Another favorite swimming spot is the Venetian Municipal Pool, 2701 DeSoto Blvd., formed from the coral quarry which is mined to build the city. The pool is reminiscent of a Venetian palazzo, with shady porticos, loggias and towers.

A number of local firms specialize in *scuba* and skin-diving instructions and excursions to sunken hulls, reefs and underwater gardens. Fowey Rocks Light area, just south of Key Biscayne, is among the best for *underwater photography.* Persons renting scuba diving equipment must have a card certifying that they are licensed divers. Other fine locations are Haulover, Elbow Light, Pacific Light, Carysfort Light and John Pennekamp State Park. Skin divers should observe State Conservation laws regarding crawfish (Florida lobster) and other regulations on *spearfishing.* Crawfish may not be taken by spearing. There are no special restrictions on the use of spearguns in Dade and Broward Counties, but it is prohibited in Pennekamp Park and within one mile of US1 in the lower keys. Diver flags are required. *Windsurfing* is the new rage and most big resort hotels have rentals and schools on their beaches.

 SPECTATOR SPORTS. *Baseball:* One of the first things sports-minded Florida visitors are interested in (especially if they're late vacationers) is the baseball training camps. In Miami, the Baltimore Orioles work out at the Miami Stadium, 2301 N.W. 10th Ave., beginning Feb. 15, with exhibition games starting Mar. 15. *Football:* The Miami Dolphins, under Coach Don Shula, won their first World Championship in 1973 and repeated in 1974. They play in the Orange Bowl, as do the Univ. of Miami Hurricanes.

Racing: There are 3 horse racing tracks and 1 harness racing track in South Florida. Hialeah Park, 4 E. 25th St., also features an aquarium, rare birds, flamingos, English carriages, riding regalia, snacks and souvenirs. You can take a tram ride. Gulfstream Park Race Track, US 1, Hallandale, is open mid-Jan. to Mar. Miami's Calder Race Course, N.W. 27th Ave. at 210th St., has two seasons: May to Nov. All three tracks are within easy reach of Miami and Miami Beach. While meets are in progress, buses run directly to horse and greyhound racing facilities. Special buses from Miami Beach to Pompano Beach for harness racing at Tourist Attractions, mid-Dec. to early April. The races may be watched from a terraced dining room in the spectacular 7-story grandstand. Dog racing (greyhounds, of course), a Florida staple, at Miami Beach Kennel Club, 1 So. Collins;

Biscayne, 320 N.W. 115th St.; West Flagler, 300 N.W. 37th Ave.; Investment Corp. of South Florida Track in Hollywood.

Jai-alai: A dangerous combination of handball, tennis and lacrosse, jai-alai requires great nerve, endurance and savvy—and lends itself to betting. The sport derives from Spain and 17th-century Basques. Players use a pelota (virgin-rubber ball covered with goatskin) and a cesta (curved basket of imported reed) which straps to the wrist. At push *Dania Jai-Alai,* you may view the game directly or on closed circuit TV. Dec. To Apr. *Miami Fronton,* 3500 N.W. 37th Ave. is also served by bus from Miami Beach.

WHAT TO DO WITH THE CHILDREN. A number of sea zoos have been created in Florida. The largest and most famous is the *Miami Seaquarium* located beyond the Rickenbacker Causeway (follow US 1 to the sign with the circling shark), south of downtown. It has been there 18 years, and it is often so crowded that daddies should be prepared to hold the youngest on their shoulders for the show in the porpoise tank. But there are also the shark show, the killer whale show, the penguin-seal-pelican show (for this you sit in an inclining grandstand), and the show down below in the great tank when the divers vacuum the bottom and feed the ocean's biggest captive. The Seaquarium also includes Lost Islands, a bird sanctuary in a jungle-like setting.

Serpentarium, US 1, 126th St. and Dixie Hwy., South Miami. Cobras and other snakes, tortoises, crocodiles, galapagos, iguanas. Cobra venom extraction. *Parrot Jungle,* 11000 S.W. 57th Ave. White cockatoo named Butch has been in with all the big shots. He kissed Winston Churchill. Birds perform all kinds of tricks. Winding trails through natural hammock to Flamingo Park.

Planet Ocean is sort of an Expo of the Seas. Educational portrayal of mankind's dependence upon the oceans, but highly entertaining for kids and adults alike. On Key Biscayne just before Seaquarium. For details call 361-2186.

Monkey Jungle, about 20 mi. s. of Miami on US 1, features monkeys cavorting without being caged. Visitors are in the cage instead! New *Metrozoo,* 12400 S.W. 152nd St., Miami, features animals roaming in natural habitat. No fences or cages.

The "Just Us Kids" program at the Sonesta Beach Hotel and Tennis Club offers daily clubhouse activities, and visits to nearby attractions, along with exclusive lunchpails and T-shirts. Specially-trained counselors are in charge at this Key Biscayne showplace.

A colorful two-story carousel is part of the whirl of fun in Treasure Island, part of the 10.5-acre hotel/shopping complex of the Omni International Hotel on Miami's Biscayne Blvd. at 16th St. The family entertainment center, one level below the lobby via the glass-bubble elevator, features games, a carousel, fortune tellers, pirates from Robert Louis Stevenson's famous adventures, etc.

HOTELS AND MOTELS. The hotels of Miami Beach seem almost like one continuous city. The Flabbergast Hotels, as they have been called, are the prototypes of much of the resort architecture around the world.

What the hotels charge varies widely, coming to a peak in mid-December, January, February. The labels attached here have meaning mostly as a way of establishing one or another as a bit more expensive than its neighbor. Many modestly rated establishments are the equal in comfort and location of those that—usually because of a later construction date—have a higher standard price.

The lowest rates are in the summer, which usually begins in May and continues until Nov. 1. This is the period for bargain hunters, when you can acquire pleasing and even sumptuous accommodations for about $20 a day per person.

We have listed hotels and motels alphabetically in categories determined by double, in-season rates: *Deluxe,* from $80; *Expensive,* from $50; *Moderate,* from

$40; *Inexpensive,* from $25. For a more complete explanation of hotel and motel categories see *Facts at Your Fingertips* at the front of this volume.

Miami

Coconut Grove Hotel. *Deluxe.* 2649 S. Bayshore Drive. Pool, tennis, marina, saunas, swanky *Horatios* restaurant on 20th floor, garden, Bar with dancing, entertainment. Strong Florida flavor in modern garden setting.

Costa Del Sol Golf & Racquet Club. *Deluxe.* Adjacent to Doral Country Club (N.W. 36th St. Exit). Two and 3 bedroom split-level villas. Restaurant, cocktail lounge. Mediterranean atmosphere. Daily, weekly, monthly, yearly rates.

David William Apartment Hotel. *Deluxe.* 700 Baltimore Way. A favorite with actors appearing at Coconut Grove Playhouse. Rooftop pool. Solarium-gymnasium. *Chez Vendome* and *700 Club* gourmet restaurants.

Doral Country Club. *Deluxe.* 4400 N.W. 87th Ave. Elegant resort hotel that is almost a city in itself. Pools, play areas (with supervision during major holidays), tennis, golf, water sports, boating. Restaurant, cocktail lounge. Dancing, entertainment. MAP, golf pkg. rates avail.

Dupont Plaza. *Deluxe.* 300 Biscayne Blvd. Way. Pools, sauna, golf avail. Some kitchen units. Dining room, bar.

Harbor Island Spa. *Deluxe.* More than just a place for overweights seeking slimness. Special "finishing school" plan for teen-age girls in summer. Pools, sauna. Full sports program. Tennis pro. Fishing, boating. Social director, planned entertainment, dancing. Dining room, set ups. Closed Sept., Oct. 7900 Harbor Island.

Hotel Inter-Continental Miami. *Deluxe.* 801 S. Bayshore Dr. Pools, sauna, play area. Marina. Golf, tennis avail. Fine restaurant, bar. Kitchen units avail. (May go condominium in 1982.)

The Hotel Mutiny at Sailboat Bay. *Deluxe.* 2951 S. Bayshore Dr. Closest to Coconut Grove business district, with sweeping view of Dinner Key Marina. Exotic fantasy décor in each room.

Omni International Hotel. *Deluxe.* Biscayne Blvd. at 16th St. Outstanding resort-in-city complex, with swimming pool, whirlpool, health club, sauna. Four lighted tennis courts. Variety of restaurants, lounges, entertainment, dancing. Lower level has international shopping-restaurant-entertainment area.

Sonesta Beach Hotel and Tennis Club. *Deluxe.* 350 Ocean Dr., Key Biscayne. Beachside pool. Bicycles, sailboats available. "Just Us Kids" program. Four unusual restaurants, bar. MPA avail., also fam. rates summers. Eight special villas for vacationing royally.

Miami Airways. *Expensive.* 5055 N.W. 36th St., Miami Springs. Pool. Restaurant, dining room, bar, entertainment. Opp. International Airport.

Miami International Airport. *Expensive.* In terminal at N.W. 20th St. & Le Jeune Rd. Restaurant, bar. Rooms are soundproof, available for day use.

Miami Marriott Hotel and Racquet Club. *Expensive.* 1201 Le Jeune Rd. Restaurants, bars, dancing, entertainment. Tennis, lawn games. Pool. Golf avail.

Miami Springs Villas & Kings Inn. *Expensive.* Olympic pool, sauna. Restaurants, bars with entertainment. Lawn games; golf avail.

Sheraton River House. *Expensive.* At Miami International Airport (3900 NW 21st St.), opposite terminal entrance. Overlooks Miami River. Three lounges, gourmet restaurant (Daphne's), lighted tennis courts, boat docking. Heated pool; health club.

Holiday Inn. *Moderate to Expensive.* At 10 locations, Miami and Miami Beach areas: **Holiday Inn Central,** I-95, 79th St.; **Holiday Inn Civic Center-Airport East,** N.W. 12th Ave. (East-West Expressway); **Holiday Inn-Golden Glades,** 148 N.W. 167th St., North Miami; **Holiday Inn-International Airport** (one mi. n. of terminal entrance), Miami Springs; **Holiday Inn Airport Lakes** (about 3 mi. from entrance), 1101 N.W. 57th Ave.; **Holiday Inn at Calder Race Course,** 21485 N.W. 27th Ave.; **Holiday Inn of Coral Gables-Downtown,** 2051 LeJeune Rd.; **Holiday Inn of Coral Gables South,** 1350 S. Dixie Hwy.; **Holiday Inn-Surfside,** 8701 Collins Ave. at 87th St.; **Holiday Inn-Miami Beach-22nd St,** 2201 Collins Ave. (oceanfront).

Columbus Hotel. *Moderate.* 312 N.E. 1 St. Pleasant rooms. Restaurant, bar. Friendly management.

Howard Johnson Key Biscayne (formerly Quality Inn). *Moderate.* 798 Crandon Blvd. All efficiency units. No restaurant so far, but conv. to restaurants. More Howard Johnson's: **HJ's Motor Lodge-Downtown,** 1100 Biscayne Blvd.; **HJ's Motor Lodge Plaza,** 200 S.E. 2nd Ave.; **HJ's Motor Lodge-Airport,** 1980 N.W. Le Jeune Rd.; **HJ's Motor Lodge-Airport West,** N.W. 36th St. (4 mi. from airport); **HJ's Motor Lodge-Broad Causeway,** 12210 Biscayne Blvd., North Miami, **HJ's Motor Lodge,** 4000 Alton Rd.

Miami Airport Inn (Best Western). *Moderate.* 1550 N.W. Le Jeune Rd., 1 block S of International Airport. Color TV. Pool (heated). Famous **Les Jardins** restaurant. Bar, dancing in season. Free airport transportation.

Miami Lakes Inn & Country Club. *Moderate.* N.W. 154th St. Pool. Restaurants. Bar, entertainment, dancing. Golf, tennis.

Ramada Inn. *Moderate.* 2 locations: Airport: LeJeune Rd. to 25th St. Heated pool, dining room, cocktail lounge, entertainment. Also 7250 N.W. 11th St., about 5 miles from airport. Pool, sauna, restaurant, cocktail lounge.

Riviera Court. *Moderate.* 5100 Riviera Dr. (US 1) Coral Gables. 30 rooms, 14 efficiencies. Pool, patio. Opposite University of Miami. Nr. restaurants.

Town and Country. *Moderate.* 600 Coral Way. Heated pool. Attractive efficiency apartments. Garden setting. Across the street from public golf course.

University Inn (Quality Inn). *Moderate.* 1390 S. Dixie Hwy. Most convenient to the University of Miami's Coral Gables campus.

Vagabond (A Red Carpet Inn). *Moderate.* 17301 Biscayne Blvd. Pool. Restaurant, cocktail lounge, entertainment. Play area.

Miami Beach

Sheraton Bal Harbour (formerly Americana). *Deluxe.* 9701 Collins Ave., Bal Harbour. One of the leading resort hotels in Florida. Their biggest pool is not olympic, it's "lagoon-sized." Private beach. Golf and tennis privileges; lawn games, special children's programs; social director. Restaurants, nightclubs, dancing, entertainment. Tropical gardens and 2-story terrarium in lobby add an extra touch of glamour. MAP, suites avail.

Carillon. *Deluxe.* 6801 Collins Ave. Glamorous hotel, with many big name stars appearing yr-round. Teen-age program; golf, tennis privileges. Private beach, pools, sauna. Restaurants, nightclub. Fam. rates, EP, suites avail.

Deauville. *Deluxe.* 6701 Collins Ave. Free sightseeing cruises are part of many luxury services offered. Pools, sauna, private beach. Golf, tennis privileges. Restaurants, nightclubs. EP avail.

Doral-on-the-Ocean. *Deluxe.* 4833 Collins Ave. Stunning high-rise, decorated like a Fellini set. Shares sports facilities with Doral Country Club & Hotel, and cosponsors Florida's biggest golf tournament. Pool, beach; 4 18-hole, 1 9-hole golf courses; tennis, baseball. Restaurants, nightclub, dancing, entertainment. MAP, suites avail.

Eden Roc. *Deluxe.* 4525 Collins Ave. Large, attractively furnished rooms. Pool, private beach. Golf, tennis, boating, water sports. Restaurants, nightclub features name talent nightly. Penthouse suites, EP avail.

Fontainebleau Hilton. *Deluxe.* 4441 Collins Ave. Something of a legend. Vast resort hotel with multitude of accommodations ranging from single rooms, to plush suites. The standard by which flamboyant hotels are measured. Pools, cabanas, private beach. Golf, tennis, boating. Restaurants, boutiques, cocktail lounges, nightclubs, disco. Newly redecorated and refurbished. Waterfalls, grottos and free-form swimming pool cover over 15,000 acres.

Ivanhoe. *Deluxe.* 10175 Collins Ave., Bal Harbour. Pool, sauna, cabanas; private beach. Golf, tennis privileges; lawn games. Restaurants, bars; dancing, entertainment in season. MAP, kitchen units avail.

Konover Hotel. *Deluxe.* 5445 Collins Ave. A grand oceanfront resort. Pool, wading pool, health club, theaters. Rooms with small refrigerators. Coffee shop, gourmet restaurant, cocktail lounge, entertainment, dancing.

Montmarte Hotel. *Very Expensive.* 4775 Collins Ave. *Eden Roc* and *Fontainebleau Hilton* are neighbors. Refrigerators in rooms. Three pools, children's activities. Coffee shop, dining room, cocktail lounge, nightclub.

Algiers Hotel. *Expensive.* 2555 Collins Ave. Beach, game room, health club. Restaurant, cocktail lounge, dancing, entertainment.

Aztec Resort Motel. *Expensive.* 15901 Collins Ave. Pools, game room. Restaurant, bar, dancing, entertainment. MAP, kitchen units avail. Informal. Popular with French-Canadian tourists.

Barcelona Hotel. *Expensive.* 4343 Collins Ave. Pools, beach, health club. Pets. Restaurant, cocktail lounge, dancing, entertainment. Refurbished, glamorous hotel of the 50s.

Beau Rivage Hotel (Best Western). *Expensive.* 9955 Collins Ave., Bal Harbour. Pools, beach, lawn games; golf & tennis privileges. Restaurants, cocktail lounge, dancing, entertainment. Solarium, sauna. Lively resort atmosphere. Children's & teen's program, many activities. Kitchen apts., MAP avail.

Colonial Inn. *Expensive.* 18101 Collins Ave. Pools, beach, game area. Supervised children's, teens' program. Restaurants, bars, dancing, entertainment. Very well-maintained and well-managed. Convenient to shopping. MAP, kitchen units avail.

Di Lido. *Expensive.* 155 Lincoln Rd. Pools, private beach. Special program for teen-agers. Restaurants, bars, dancing and entertainment. Popular with older tourists. MAP, penthouse suites avail.

Marco Polo Resort Motel. *Expensive.* 192nd St. & Collins Ave. Pools. Supervised program for children, teens. Golf & tennis nr. Casual and informal, for the young at heart. Restaurant, bar; dancing, entertainment. Lower level shopping arcade. Very lively atmosphere.

Pan American. *Expensive.* 17875 Collins Ave. Pool, play area, private beach. Restaurants. Kitchen units avail. Tasteful decor, very well-maintained. Friendly service. You get money's worth here.

Sans Souci. *Expensive.* 3101 Collins Ave. Pool, private beach. Golf, tennis nr. Game room. Restaurant, bar, night-club. Newly refurbished—great appearance! Very attentive service.

Seville. *Expensive.* 2901 Collins Ave. Pools, cabanas, private beach. Restaurants, bar. Game room. Nightclub with entertainment nightly. MAP avail.

Sherry Frontenac. *Expensive.* 6565 Collins Ave. Pool, cabana club, private beach. Supervised children's program during holidays, summer. Game room. Restaurants, bars, dancing, entertainment. MAP avail.

Singapore Resort Motel. *Expensive.* Oceanfront at 96th St. Private beach, big pools, sundecks. Golf, tennis. Coffee shop, dining room, cocktail lounge. Cooperative packages with *Aztec Resort Motel* at 159th St.

Twelve Ceasars Resort Motel. *Expensive.* 9449 Collins Ave. Pool, beach, boating, fishing, game area. Restaurant, bar, dancing, entertainment. Pets. MAP, kitchen units avail.

Versailles. *Expensive.* 3425 Collins Ave. Pool, cabana club, private beach. Pets. Supervised children's program during holidays, summer. Restaurants, bar, dancing, entertainment. Was a fancy hotel in the 1950's. MAP avail.

Sheraton Beach Resort. *Moderate to Expensive.* 19400 Collins Ave. On 21 acres, including two sides of road. Resort hotel with pool, beach, boating, fishing, tennis, game area. New Lobster Shack restaurant with seafood menu and fruit bar, open-hearth cooking in Klein Richards restaurant. Bar. Kitchen units, fam. rates avail.

Alujo Motel (formerly Hawaiian Inn). *Moderate.* 17601 Collins Ave. Large 2-story motel. Pools, beach, boating, game area. Supervised children's program. Restaurant specializes in luaus. Bar, dancing, entertainment. New steak house; disco. Cheerful, informal atmosphere. Family favorite. MAP avail.

Castaways Beach and Tennis Club. *Moderate.* 16375 Collins Ave. Pools, beach, boating, game area. Pets. Restaurant, bar, dancing, entertainment. Also hydrotherapy pool. Special French-Canadian night club. Lively atmosphere. MAP avail.

Chateau Resort Motel (Best Western). *Moderate.* 19115 Collins Ave. Pools, beach, boating, game area. Restaurants, bar, dancing, entertainment in season. MAP avail.

Chez Paree. *Moderate.* 17475 Collins Ave. Pools, beach, game area. Golf nr. Restaurant. Kitchen units avail. Very friendly, casual atmosphere.

Desert Inn & Motel. *Moderate.* 17201 Collins Ave. Pools, beach, game area. Restaurant, bar, dancing, entertainment. AP, kitchen units avail. A French-Canadian favorite.

Golden Nugget. *Moderate.* 18555 Collins Ave. Pool, beach, game area. Restaurants, bar; entertainment in season. MAP. Kitchen units avail. Very pleasant for family vacations.

Moulin Rouge Resort Motel (Quality Inn). *Moderate.* 280 Arthur Godfrey Rd. Pools, beach, boating, fishing. Restaurant. Pets. Kitchen units avail.

Ocean Roc Resort Motel. *Moderate.* 1955 Collins Ave. Very pleasant. Spacious rooms with balconies (formerly a Holiday Inn). Tennis, heated pool, pool for children. Beach-view dining room, cocktail bar. Good value for families.

Sahara Resort Motel (Best Western). *Moderate.* 18335 Collins Ave. Resort motel with pool, beach, boating, game area. Restaurant, bar, entertainment in season. MAP avail.

St. Moritz Hotel and Motel. *Moderate.* 1565 Collins Ave. Pool, beach, game area. Restaurant open in season. Attracts older clientele—old fashioned hotel. MAP avail.

Sea Breeze. *Moderate to Inexpensive.* 16151 Collins Ave. New ownership; attractive nautical Scandinavian decor. New air-conditioning in carpeted rooms. Renovated pool, sundeck. On older part of beach, but terrific bargain.

Suez Resort Motel. *Moderate.* 18215 Collins Ave. Pools, beach, game area. Restaurant, bar, dancing entertainment. Better maintained than most 1950's hotels on beach. Bright yellow-orange exterior. Lively disco, lounge. Tennis. Another French-Canadian favorite. AP avail.

Wakiki Resort Motel. *Moderate to Inexpensive.* 18801 Collins Ave. Near restaurants, shopping, amusements. Comfortable, neat rooms. Casual family atmosphere. Tennis courts. Lively, with groups of Canadian vacationers. Pools, beach, game area. Restaurant, bar, dancing, entertainment. Kitchen units avail.

Canadian Horizon Hotel & Lodge (Formerly Blue Horizon Hotel). *Inexpensive.* 8925 Collins Ave. Pools, beach, play area. Restaurant, bar. Efficiency rooms with kitchenettes available.

Caravan Motel. *Inexpensive.* 19101 Collins Ave. Pets. Pool, beach, boating. Restaurant, bar. Patronized by French-Canadians. Fam. rates, kitchen units avail.

Pier House Inn. *Inexpensive.* 17451 Collins Ave. Formerly a Holiday Inn. Family games, heated pool on rooftop. (Views into the lobby from underwater portholes in pool.) Coffee Shop. Nr. restaurants.

Sea Isle Hotel. *Inexpensive.* 3001 Collins Ave. Pool, beach, game area. Restaurant, bar, dancing, entertainment. Interesting art-deco high-rise. About $500,000 spent for refurbishing. Attentive management, friendly staff. American and kosher cuisine. In good shape for a grand dame hotel. Nightly social program. Lower level has shops. MAP avail.

DINING OUT. Of the several thousand places to dine in Miami and Miami Beach, the range is from gourmet restaurants to economical cafeterias, from hotels to sandwich shops. Some of the Cuban restaurants in Miami are among the finest anywhere, and offer dishes you won't find elsewhere. Stroll along "Calle Oche" (S.W. 8th St.) and order a many-layered meat-cheese-vegetable salad on crispy Cuban bread; refreshing "batidos" (fruit shakes); rich bean soups and South American specialties; hot, strong coffee and luscious pastry at a sidewalk café. The area offers a full range of foreign restaurants, with entrees running the gamut from sea foods to roast beef, turkey or steaks and lavish feasts.

Florida lobster, or crawfish, is a big favorite in these parts. You can dine on succulent Everglades froglegs, pompano or conch chowder. Stone crabs are a native south Florida delicacy, and fresh shellfish, lobsters and oysters are flown in daily. Tangy key lime pie is the dessert.

Restaurants are listed alphabetically by cuisine and price category. Dinner in an *expensive* restaurant will run approximately $15 and higher for one (without drinks, tip, tax); in a *moderate* restaurant from $10 to $15; in an inexpensive restaurant, from $5 to $10. Cafeterias and hamburger houses fall into the inexpensive category, with an adequate dinner selection costing perhaps $3 to $5. A la carte selections will of course be more expensive. For a more complete explanation of restaurant categories see *Facts at Your Fingertips* at the front of this volume.

EDITOR'S CHOICES

Rating restaurants is, at best, a subjective business, and obviously a matter of personal taste. It is, therefore, difficult to call a restaurant "the best," and hope to get unanimous agreement. The restaurants listed below are our choices of the best eating places in the Greater Miami area, and the places we would choose if we were visiting this area.

CAFE CHAUVERON French Cuisine
New York City's loss was Miami's gain. Roger Chauveron pulled up stakes and moved his world famous establishment to a lovely waterside location, and if anything, the new restaurant stands out even more now than before. The diversity of the menu is enormous, and all dishes are cooked to order. There is real artistry at work here, and this restaurant ranks with the finest in the entire country. 9561 East Bay Harbor Drive (Bay Harbour Island, Maimi Beach). *Deluxe.*

THE HASTA Steak & Seafood
The gathering place for celebrities of sports, theater, films and politics, and even former President Nixon was a frequent booth-holder. There are two dining areas, plus a Wine Cellar Lounge for entertainment. Red and gold dominates the decor, accented by fine paintings and fresh flowers. Fine food, well prepared, particularly the French dishes and the seafood, with top-notch service. 2665 S.W. 37th Ave. (Miami). *Deluxe.*

FAMOUS Steak House
What's truly "famous" is the preparation of the mostly Jewish and Romanian specialties. Try the *gefulte* fish and beef flanken. Very friendly atmosphere belies the plush red velvet and crystal. A landmark for the many visitors who glory in this style of cooking. 671 Washington Ave. (Miami Beach). *Expensive.*

WORDS TO THE WISE
A Few Useful Travel Hints

Whether you are on holiday or have important business to do, after a flight through several time zones give your body's clock a chance to catch up. It is easy to underestimate the effects of jet-lag.

Don't carry all your cash, travellers' checks, passport etc. in the same place, spread them around a bit – and never carry your wallet in your hip pocket.

Experienced travellers travel light. Don't forget that the hand luggage you carry with you onto the plane is a vital part of your travel equipment. Make sure you have your essentials in it, not in your other baggage.

With strikes and the cost of excess baggage always in the background, you would be sensible when flying not to take more than you could comfortably carry yourself – in a pinch.

Don't leave already exposed film in your pockets or in any hand luggage while passing through airport X-ray machines. The process can sometimes fog the film and you may find a whole trip's photographs ruined. Put the film on one side while passing through.

Never make long-distance phone calls from your hotel room without checking first on the likely price. Some hotels have been known to mark up the cost of a call as much as 200%.

Several airlines will provide a cardboard carrying box for any loose items you might arrive clutching at the checking-in desk. It saves leaving a trail of last-minute purchases all the way to the plane.

You would be amazed the amount of free information that you can get from National Tourist Offices to help you plan your trip – all the way from brochures to movies.

Put a tag with your name and address on it *inside* your suitcase as well as outside. It will greatly help identification if the case goes astray.

Never leave valuables in your hotel room – put them in the hotel safe.

PLACE FOR STEAK
Steak House

The name says it all, and it is wise to go with the house specialty. It is a fine piece of beef. The "house" salad dressing is also very good, and the cheesecake is truly special. Harbor Lounge often features fine jazz combos. 335 79th St. Causeway (Miami Beach). *Expensive.*

THE GARDEN AT HARRISON SQUARE (OR FOOD AMONG THE FLOWERS.)
Continental/American

Fresh flowers, antiques and David Harrison's artistry create a beautiful setting in a less than beautiful part of old Miami; memorable dishes from Danish chefs, especially the seafoods and salads. Closed Sundays. 21 N.E. 36th Street. *Deluxe.*

MARCELLA'S CUCINA MIA
Italian Cuisine

The dining area is a simulated Roman grotto, complete with white-washed walls and tiny niches filled with Italian bric-a-brac. There's no menu, but a nine-course meal is served every night at a fixed price. It includes literally everything. Very pleasant atmosphere that is friendly above all. Food is first rate. Reservations are a must. 13800 West Dixie Highway (North Miami). *Expensive.*

COURT OF TWO DRAGONS
Japanese/Chinese

Choice of exotic Japanese and Chinese gourmet cuisines. A feast for the eyes and taste-buds. Japanese dining room is simply beautiful. Chinese dining room has romantic, canopied booths with beaded curtains. Overlooking Japanese garden in Sonesta Beach Hotel, Key Biscayne. *Expensive.*

EL BATURRO
Cuban/Spanish

It is no surprise that a fine Latin American/Spanish restaurant should exist in this center of Cuban expatriates, and this is the place. Interesting items dot an extensive menu, and the specialties are the paella and the sauteed red snapper. Music is live. 2322 N.W. 7th St. (Miami). *Moderate.*

PORT OF CALL
Seafood

The owners are fishermen themselves, and it is partially their own catch that graces the tables. The decor is nautical in the extreme, and the entire dining area is festooned with ship's rigging, nets, running lights, and mooring lines. The bouillabaise is something special. 14411 Biscayne Blvd. (Miami). *Expensive.*

TAURUS STEAK HOUSE
Steak House

Located in scenic Coconut Grove, near the Playhouse, it is popular with theatergoers and just plain diners alike. Steaks are the prime attraction, and there is also a popular cocktail lounge. 3540 Main Highway (Miami). *Expensive.*

JOE'S STONE CRAB
Seafood

Stone crabs cooked to order. Dinner only. Expect a crowd, but it is well worth the wait. Closed when stone crabs not in season (May-Sept.). 227 Biscayne St. *Expensive.*

Other recommended restaurants:

Miami

American International

Chez Vendome. *Expensive.* David William Hotel, 700 Biltmore Way. Fine French cuisine in elegant surroundings. Strolling musicians serenade diners. Piano bar.

The Depot. *Expensive.* 5830 S. Dixie Hwy., (US 1 South). Elaborate railroad décor, including a dine-inside reproduction of Henry Flagler's swanky dining car. Award-winning specialties, prime rib, seafood. Menu printed on replica of Florida East Coast Railway timetable. Limo service and helicopter from airport but make arrangements in advance. Closed Mondays.

King Arthur's Court. *Expensive.* Miami Springs Hotel, 500 Deer Run, Miami Springs. Pleasant old English atmosphere. Music. Fine, well-aged beef and stone crabs are their specialty. Closed Labor Day, Christmas Eve. Jacket required.

Maison. *Expensive.* In Omni International Hotel. Gourmet menu is changed monthly in this classy restaurant. Prix fixe. Dinner only. Closed Mon. The Terrace and Poolside serve breakfast, lunch, and dinner, if you would rather be informal.

Prince Hamlet. *Expensive.* 8301 Biscayne Blvd. Scandinavian food in a chalet-like atmosphere. The salmon is a treat and they have a wide selection of other dishes.

Les Violins. *Moderate to Expensive.* 1751 Biscayne Blvd. Dinner and show are a terrific combination. Lunch was served with entertainment this past season, so check on this good bargain.

Country Store. *Moderate.* 2880 Florida Ave., Coconut Grove. Several dining rooms decorated with antiques and quasi-antiques collected by the owners on trips to Europe. Special luncheon menu. Good selection of seafoods, chicken Kiev, flaming shish kebab.

Green Dolphin. *Moderate.* At Miamarina, in downtown Miami. Filet mignon, skewered shrimp and beef, and a variety of fish dishes, plus a lovely view of the city's night skyline.

Grentner's for Steak. *Moderate.* 5859 S.W. 73rd St., S. Miami. Unblemished reputation for top beef. Businessmen's luncheons; early-bird dinner specials.

Gypsy's Pub. *Moderate.* 7400 Bird Rd. Pepper steak, veal a la fancaise, veal Cordon Bleu. Piano bar and fireplace add to cozy atmosphere.

Les Jardins. *Moderate to Expensive.* 1546 N.W. LeJeune Rd. At Miami Airport Inn. French garden ambience. Lobster soufflé is excellent. Fine wines. Moderately priced lunches, but expensive dinners. Worth the price. Dancing in the lounge. Reservations at night, also jackets for men.

Jamaican Pub. *Moderate.* 320 Crandon Blvd., Key Biscayne. A fantasy of tropical plants, relaxed dining. Open for lunch, dinner.

My Apartment. *Moderate.* Miami Springs Hotel. Filet mignon served at "cook-it-yourself" tables. Jacket required. 6 to midnight. Closed Sun.

94th Aero Squadron. *Moderate.* 1395 N.W. 57th Ave. Nr. Miami International Airport. World War I aviation memorabilia décor is unusual. Supersize margaritas. Bird of Paradise salad, quiche, steaks on varied menu. Lunch, dinner. Very popular.

Piccadilly Hearth. *Moderate.* 35 N.E. 40th St. A glamorous pub located on Decorator's Row. Excellent Continental fare.

Bill & Ted's Tavern. *Inexpensive.* 5757 S.W. 68th St. Longtime favorite with U. of Miami fraternity boys. Good hamburgers.

Biscayne Cafeteria. *Inexpensive.* 1917 Biscayne Blvd. Usual cafeteria fare. Be prepared for a wait during the winter season.

Gallagher's. *Inexpensive.* 12605 Biscayne Blvd. Open-hearth cooking. Children's portions.

Hofbrau Bar. *Inexpensive.* 172 Giralda. Tasty sandwiches, lots of atmosphere.

International House of Pancakes. *Inexpensive.* 8110 Biscayne Blvd. Main dishes, sandwiches and lots of pancakes. Open 24 hours.

Sally Russell's Part I. *Inexpensive.* 68 W. Flagler. Downtown opposite the Dade County Courthouse. A varied menu of meat and fish. Red snapper is a good choice. Open for lunch and dinner.

Italian

Casa Santino. *Expensive.* 10999 Biscayne Blvd. Italian specialties include saltimbocea alla Romana and Lobster Santino. Fine wine list. Bar, piano bar with vocalist. Closed Thanksgiving.

Raimondo. *Expensive.* 201 N.W. 79th St. Try the zuppa di pesce alla Peppino or stuffed veal Dante. Special orders only by advance notice. Intimate. Closed New Year's, Easter, Thanksgiving, Christmas. No credit cards.

Valenti's. *Moderate.* 9101 S. Dixie Hwy. Comfortable atmosphere, with delicious breadsticks, 2 salads. Open for lunch, dinner. Not to be missed if you like Italian food.

Sorrento. *Inexpensive.* 3059 S.W. 8th St. You don't have to be Cuban to have a restaurant on "Calle Ocho." Family-owned, casual. Lunch, dinner. The Florentine chicken is a favorite.

Latin American

Juanito's Centro Vasco. *Moderate.* 2235 S.W. 8th St. Charming and intimate. Among the Spanish specialties, seafood à la Basque is a favorite.

Minerva Spanish Restaurant. *Moderate.* 265 N.E. wnd St. Convenient location downtown. Popular long before Cuban refugees arrived. Lunch, dinner.

La Tasca. *Moderate.* 2741 W. Flagler. Another longtime favorite. Paella Valenciana and red snapper Cataloman rate raves. Nr. Dade County Auditorium.

Oscar's. *Moderate.* 901 S.W. 8th St. Delicious black bean soup, Colombian stews. Dance off any calories in Oscar's Latin Disco—open until dawn.

Oriental

Japanese Steak House. *Expensive.* Miami Springs Hotel. Patterned after Misono Steak House in Tokyo. Specially built tables with stoves in center turn out superior steak with Japanese vegetables. Chopsticks are the order, although forks are furnished upon request.

Tiger Tiger Teahouse. *Moderate.* 5716 S. Dixie Hwy. Mandarin, Shanghai and Mongolian dishes. Jin jo shrimp and cashew chicken are specialties.

Polynesian

Rusty Pelican. *Expensive.* Off Rickenbacker Causeway, nr. Key Biscayne. Very atmospheric. Open hearth cooking. Succulent Polynesian spareribs.

Miami Beach

American International

Embers. *Expensive.* 245 22nd St. Settle for duckling, stone crabs and homemade pastries. Jacket & tie for dinner.

Fishery. *Expensive.* Sheraton Beach Motel. Local seafood in nautical setting overlooking ocean. Children's portions.

The Forge. *Expensive.* 432 Arthur Godfrey Rd. Prime ribs & steak in an intimate 1890's room. Ornately decorated. Extensive wine list (1,000 choices!) Dinner only. Disco entertainment until dawn in lounge.

La Belle Epoque. *Expensive.* 1045 95th St. Bay Harbor Island. Romantic setting in Garden Room with waterfall. Terrace dining also. Turbot en courte and chicken Josephine among nicely prepared dishes. Soft piano music. Reservations. Dinner only.

Vinton's Town House. *Expensive.* 116 Alhambra Circle. The town house is La Palma, reputed to be oldest hotel in Coral Gables. Luncheon menu highlights omelets. Favorites such as beef, lamb, chicken at night prepared with continental accent.

Kaleidoscope. *Moderate to Expensive.* 3112 Commodore Plaza, Coconut Grove. At least 20 entrées on interesting menu. Delicious crepes filled with King crabmeat. Delightful garden patio atmosphere.

Mike Gordon Seafood Restaurant. *Moderate to Expensive.* On Biscayne Bay at 79th St. Causeway. Serving New England-style seafood for over 30 years, and local fish, too. Try the red snapper.

Newport Pub. *Moderate.* 167th St. and Collins Ave. Steak, chicken, ribs and seafood in pleasant, informal surroundings.

Old Key West Fishing Village. *Moderate.* 18288 Collins Ave. Lots of atmosphere. Casual, friendly. Dinner only.

Post & Paddock. *Moderate.* Bay Harbor Hotel. Continental cuisine in a mecca for prominent sports figures and writers.

Roney Pub. *Moderate.* 23rd St. and Collins Ave. Same management as *Newport.* Very generous servings of roast beef.

Coco's. *Inexpensive.* 9700 Collins Ave. Bal Harbour. In classy shopping area. Delightful salads, soups, sandwiches, omelets, and super hamburger Americain. Luscious desserts, good house wines.

French

Le Parisien. *Deluxe.* 474 Arthur Godfrey Rd. Authentic French cuisine. National award winner with sole meuniere, frogs' legs provencale, among many specialties. Closed Sun., early fall. Reservations required.

Henri's. *Expensive.* In Konover Hotel. 5445 Collins Ave. Dining and dancing to a continental orchestra. Good scallopini of veal Française, salade Henri, Peach Melba. Dinner only.

Italian

Gatti's Restaurant. *Moderate.* 1427 West Ave. Continental food with Northern Italian accent. Chicken a la tetrazzini a specialty. Closed Mon. and May 1 to Nov. 1.

Picciolo. *Moderate to Inexpensive.* 136 Collins Ave. Extensive menu featuring seafood and Italian specialties. Home-made ice cream.

Jewish

Wolfie. *Moderate.* 2 locations; 2038 Collins Ave.; 195 Lincoln Rd. Stuffed cabbage, cheesecake, corned beef, smoked whitefish.

Bagel Nosh. *Inexpensive.* 2 locations. 12480 Biscayne Blvd. N. Miami; 10175 S. Dixie Hwy. US 1 S. Breakfast, lunch, dinner and snacks until the wee hours.

Pumpernik's. *Inexpensive.* 6700 Collins Ave. Hearty deli sandwiches, smoked fish, complete lunches, dinners. Open every day.

Rascal House. *Inexpensive.* 17190 Collins Ave. "Wolfie" Cohen, creator of the Wolfie delicatessen restaurants satisfies thousands daily with overstuffed sandwiches and hearty full-course meals. From breakfast to a pre-dawn feast.

Middle East

Middle East Restaurant. *Moderate.* 1764 Coral Way. Pass the pita while enjoying the gyrations of the in-house exotic dancer. Shish-kebab dinners, too.

Omar's Tent. *Moderate.* 534 Arthur Godfrey Rd. Fantastic pastries. Try the beef or lamb shish kebab and other delicacies of Middle East. Bar serves only wine, beer. Closed Mon.

Natural Foods

The Garden. *Inexpensive.* 17 Westward Dr., Miami Springs. Excellent vegetable soup, stuffed clams, shrimp tempura, broiled locally caught fish sauced with lemon and herbs. Mixed vegetable salads, just-squeezed fruit and vegetable drinks.

The Spiral. *Inexpensive.* 380 Andalusia Ave. Coral Gables. Only foods free of preservatives and naturally seasoned are served. Tempting desserts sweetened with honey, maple syrup.

Oriental

Benihana of Tokyo Steak House. *Expensive.* 1665 N. E. 79 St. Causeway. Japanese décor. Steak, chicken, seafood dramatically prepared by chef at hibachi table. Cocktails, lunch, dinner.

Christine Lee's Gaslight. *Expensive.* 18401 Collins Ave. In Thunderbird Motel. Lobster Cantonese in a subtle sauce is among the 36 Chinese entrées. Or compromise and order sliced broiled sirloin garnished with Chinese vegetables. A Mandarin Feast for 4 diners is memorable. Exotic décor. Cocktails. Dinner only. A live combo entertains nightly.

Yangtze. *Expensive.* 280 41st St. Inside Moulin Rouge Hotel. Popular for cuisine from the different Chinese provinces.

Dragon World. *Moderate.* 192nd St. and Collins Ave. At Marco Polo Hotel. Well-prepared Chinese favorites for lunch and dinner every day of the week.

Exploring Florida

US 1, forerunner of the superhighway which first made possible a motor trip from the Canadian border to the tip of Key West, resumes its dreams of glory as it crosses the St. Marys River and enters northeast Florida. Suddenly the road is wide and handsome—if not very high—and seems to rush through the piney woods toward Jacksonville, forty miles away.

Jacksonville, although surrounded by historical and recreational high spots, makes no pretense at being a typical Florida resort. Rather, industry and business are the city's forté, and in addition to seaport-related trade and the Navy's carrier base at nearby Mayport, it is a center for regional headquarters of national firms. The city does make a good base for tours to nearby beaches and historic sites, however, unless one prefers seaside accommodations.

Jacksonville's downtown district is situated in a bend of the St. Johns River, where the river turns eastward to join the Atlantic, some ten miles away. A network of expressways makes entry and egress simple in almost any direction.

A rewarding one-day adventure, including time for ocean bathing, can be had by examining the area and coast northeast of Jacksonville—an unlikely looking spot for history but one that has seen French-Spanish scuffling over squatters' rights in the New World, a pirate fleet, a flamboyant slave-runner, a short-lived "Republic of Florida," and capture of the strip of land by the United States Navy from its "Mexican" ruler.

From Jacksonville, either US 17 or Interstate 95, north, will take you to Heckscher Drive, just across the Trout River from downtown Jacksonville. Turn right onto Heckscher, stopping at the free Jacksonville Zoo if the children demand, then continue along the north bank of the St. Johns to Fort George.

Fort George Island's most colorful resident perhaps was Zephaniah Kingsley, a squat little Scotch slave trader who picked the island as headquarters for his business because it was still Spanish territory and he expected the United States to forbid slave imports. The U.S.A. did just that in 1807, but Kingsley was already in action. He had expanded his operation into a combination plantation and training school for slaves by the time the U.S.A. acquired Florida from Spain in 1821. His activities then became illegal, of course, but more profitable as well.

Kingsley married the daughter of an African East Coast king, and she—as Ma'm Anna—oversaw the training of the slaves. Her full name was Anna Madegigine Jai, and she remained Kingsley's favorite despite his propensity for spotting other comely companions among the slave cargo.

The Kingsley plantation buildings are preserved in a state historical memorial and may be seen by taking a paved but unnumbered road from Fort George. The trip takes only a few minutes.

Heckscher Drive continues from Fort George to Little Talbot Island State Park, directly on the ocean, and here's the first chance for that swim. (There'll be another at Fernandina Beach.) On the island, your road becomes A1A and continues north, ending temporarily at Nassau Sound where a ferry will take you across to Amelia Island, named for Princess Amelia, sister of England's George II, by Oglethorpe in 1735.

At the north end of Amelia Island is Fernandina, named for Don Domingo Fernandez, who was given a huge tract of land by the Spanish government in 1783, when Florida was returned to Spain by the English after the success of the American Revolution. Spain had ceded Florida to England in 1763, and during the Revolution Florida remained loyal to the crown. Many loyalists from the colonies in the north fled to Amelia Island, eventually making a total of 16,000. All but a handful emigrated to the Bahamas, West Indies, and Nova Scotia when American independence came and the territory was ceded back to Spain by England.

Just across the American border, Fernandina became a haven for pirates, smugglers, and hijackers, and Highway A1A along the length of the island is called "The Buccaneer Trail."

The Republic of Florida

Shortly before the War of 1812, a band of two hundred Americans crossed the St. Marys from Georgia and captured Spain's Fort San Carlos, north of Fernandina, proclaiming a "Republic of Florida." The action had the actual support of the U.S. government, but failed after President Madison yielded to strong objections from the English and Spanish ministers. Spain regained possession, but weakened by an impending war with Napoleon, could do little to prevent the island from being usurped by one adventurer after another.

Gregor McGregor, another Scotsman, arrived with five ships and accepted the surrender of the Spanish in 1817, but left again when other Spaniards in Florida joined forces to do battle. Then Jared Irwin, a former Pennsylvania Congressman took over, recruited some help from the pirates who populated the port, and routed the Spanish again. But another pirate, Luis Aury, arrived with a superior force and claimed the island. He did allow Irwin to remain as "adjutant general," however. Aury, who had been governor of Texas under Mexican rule, raised the Mexican flag and declared the island "annexed" to the Republic of Mexico. The United States moved to break up such free-lance government when it sent the navy in and took possession "in trust" for Spain. Four years later, in 1821, the United States had all of Florida.

After all that, it would seem Amelia Island was past the point of fortification, but work began in 1847 on Fort Clinch, named after Gen. Duncan Lamont Clinch. However, the fort was neither finished nor equipped by the time the Civil War broke out and the Confederates, who quickly moved in, had to try to finish the job. The Third Florida Volunteers occupied the fort until 1862 when a strong Union Army force approached. The Northern forces kept Fort Clinch throughout the rest of the war.

Used briefly during the Spanish-American war, the fort was almost abandoned; but after being acquired by the city of Fernandina and the State for a park in 1935, it was used again during World War II for radar and Coast Guard details.

Today, the fort makes a pleasant sightseeing and picnicking spot. There are trails and camping areas, a lodge and a boat ramp. South of the Fort, at Fernandina Beach, is one of the finest bathing beaches anywhere, some fourteen miles long. At times, cars may be driven over the packed sands, depending on the tides.

To return to Jacksonville, you can either retrace your route, or, for a faster trip, take State 200 east to Yulee, then US 17 south to the city. Another option is to return south on A1A to catch the ferry that crosses the St. Johns to Jacksonville Beach on the south shore of the river.

South of Jacksonville

Inland, the St. Johns River wends its way north (one of the few anywhere to do so), offering a freshwater fishing paradise more than eighty miles long. US 17, south, skirts the western shore of the river and its by-product of lakes for much of the way. Along the route are some once-fashionable and still colorful resort towns. Green Cove Springs, for instance, was the stopping place for President Grover Cleveland back in the late 1880's when steamers from Charleston and Savannah came up the St. Johns to the spa. J. C. Penney of the chain stores and Gail Borden, condensed milk mogul, were regulars.

Palatka, twenty-seven more miles south, was also a popular tourist resort right after the Civil War, and one of the fancy hotels put its imagination to work Madison Avenue-style by listing on its menu "adolescent chicken."

The fisherman's route can be followed all the way to De Land, a pleasant college town (Stetson University) another fifty miles or so south, or a fairly quick connecting trip back to US 1 or A1A and the coast can be made at several points.

But for general touring the first southern step should perhaps better take care of Fort Caroline, just east of Jacksonville. The national monument is also on the way to St. Augustine, if you take the Jacksonville Expressway east out of the city to State 10 and follow the markers to the

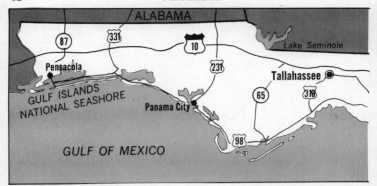

fort, directly across the river from the first day's northshore trip to Fort George.

The actual site of the original fort no longer exists, having been washed away after the river channel was deepened in the late nineteenth century. But the National Park Service has reconstructed the walls of the triangular fort, following a sketch by Jacques LeMoyne, artist and mapmaker for the Huguenot colony. On an overlook 110 feet above the river stands the Ribaut monument.

Returning to State 10, head east again to reach the ocean beaches, then turn south on A1A. Jacksonville Beach has thousands of guest accommodations, and, along with coastal cities southward for two hundred miles, actually it is more a summer resort for inland Southerners than a winter warming spot for chilled Northerners. The chill can be felt here, too, in the winter months.

A few miles of semicommercial congestion gives way to a relatively sparse assortment of beach houses and dunes south of Jacksonville Beach. First, though, there is the Ponte Vedra Club, a plush resort and inn, plus oceanfront cottages and a challenging but fine golf course. The beach here, offering excellent surf swimming, was once mined for titanium and other minerals, but the state legislature eventually halted the digging by declaring the beach a public highway.

Oldest City

An abrupt right turn, and A1A rejoins the mainland. Just as abruptly, you are in St. Augustine, the nation's oldest city, with history dripping from every overhanging balcony. For this, you'll need some time . . . and a guide book, for volumes have been done about this antique treasure without fully covering the subject. Recommended is *St. Augustine's Historical Heritage,* a publication of the St. Augustine Historical Society. There are numerous illustrations, an excellent map, and a well-written text. Try the information center on San Marco Ave. as you near the city gates.

St. Augustine celebrated its 400th anniversary in 1964, but its fifth century should prove a lively one without getting too far away from the pageantry of the past. In midsummer a festival called Days of Spain has inhabitants out sword fighting (rather bloodlessly) in the streets. Along St. Geroge St.—in the evening—musicians and dancers cast spells. The *New York Times* has said that St. George St. "is losing all resemblance

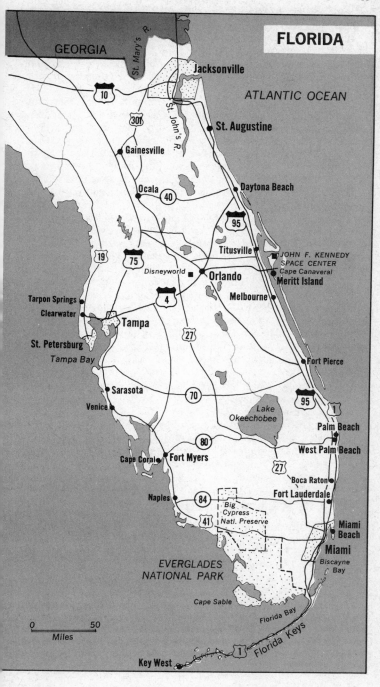

FLORIDA

GEORGIA

St. Mary's R.

Jacksonville

ATLANTIC OCEAN

10

301

St. John's R.

St. Augustine

Gainesville

Ocala

40

Daytona Beach

95

Titusville

JOHN F. KENNEDY
SPACE CENTER
Cape Canaveral

19

75

Disneyworld

Orlando

Meritt Island

4

Melbourne

Tarpon Springs

Clearwater

Tampa

27

St. Petersburg

Tampa Bay

Fort Pierce

Sarasota

70

95

Venice

Lake
Okeechobee

1

Palm Beach

80

West Palm Beach

Cape Coral

Fort Myers

27

Boca Raton

Naples

84

Fort Lauderdale

41

Big
Cypress
Natl. Preserve

Miami
Beach

Miami

EVERGLADES
NATIONAL PARK

Biscayne
Bay

Cape Sable

Florida Bay

0   50

Miles

1

Florida Keys

Key West

to a modern street." That's about right. No light poles—lanterns from
Seville light the way.

Another drama, with the traditional cast of thousands, can run con-
currently in your mind as you walk (or ride in horse-drawn surreys)
through the narrow streets, seeing a tiny stone cottage here, an elaborate
cathedral there, a massive stone fortress yonder . . . and all old, but each
from a different layer of history:

From the First Spanish period, the mission of Nombre de Dios, founded on the same day as the city when Father Francisco Lopez Mendoza
Grajales stepped ashore with Don Pedro Menendez de Aviles and
became the first parish priest of a nation-to-be. And at the mission, the
Shrine of Nuestra Senora de la Leche, a tiny jewel of a chapel, coquina
rock covered with ivy, as appealingly antique as any Old World shrine
anywhere but actually built in 1918, following the design of the original.

Or The Cathedral of St. Augustine—from the second Spanish period
—completed in 1797, restored after a fire in 1887; the Llambias House—
English period—once owned by T. Llambias who was a member of the
Minorcan colony brought to Florida by Dr. Andrew Turnbull to settle
a grant at what he called New Smyrna, seventy miles south. Today, the
house is called the Prince Murat House, after Napoleon Bonaparte's
nephew who lived there. Ralph Waldo Emerson was a guest in 1827.

And the St. Francis Inn, once known as the Dummitt House, headquarters for Civil War spies, before that a jail just after Florida became
a U.S. territory, before that a barracks for English soldiers . . . and before
that the first church of the Franciscans, in 1577.

So it is an old town. With an Old Jail, an Oldest House, Oldest
Schoolhouse, Oldest Store . . . and quite rightly for Florida, the oldest
alligator exhibition, at the St. Augustine Alligator Farm founded in
1893.

But some new things, too. New motels, new attractions with a wide
spectrum of taste displayed in both.

Among the new might be considered Castillo de San Marcos, the
quadrangular, moated fortress just opposite the old city gates, for the
Castillo isn't finished yet. It has been a national monument since 1924,
and it now is being improved by restoration of some of the inside rooms
together with the reconstruction of the Cubo Line, the ancient town wall
which extended from the Castillo to the San Sebastian River.

Some 19th-Century Grandeur

St. Augustine is also the homesite of the fabled Ponce de Leon Hotel.
(Unfortunately, it is now closed.) Built by Henry Flagler in 1889 to house
the nation's rich and famous as they helped him, and his railroad,
establish St. Augustine as a *ne plus ultra* winter resort, it was a wondrous place.

South from St. Augustine into the newer Florida. Route A1A is the
more scenic, and after a splash of modernity and neon along St. Augustine Beach, there's a souvenir reminder of the old city again, fourteen
miles south at Matanzas Inlet. It was here that Menendez caught up with
Jean Ribaut's hapless French fleet, which had sailed out of Fort Caroline
to attack the Spanish, only to be caught in a hurricane while Don Pedro
wiped out the fort by land assault. Helpless on the sands, the four

hundred French were slaughtered in the cruel fashion of that time to give the inlet its name, Matanzas (slaughter).

The stone fort, built at the inlet in 1742 to protect the inland waterway approach to St. Augustine, is a national monument and a park ranger will give you information during the daily visiting hours of 8:30 A.M. to 5:00 P.M.

The Ormond-Daytona Complex

Only a couple of miles south is Marineland of Florida, a commercial, interesting attraction presenting displays of marine specimens, porpoise acts, a performing whale, and below-the-water viewing ports of the ocean's creatures, some bizarre, some brilliantly colored. There are two restaurants (the Dolphin Room, overlooking the ocean, is more expensive) and a cocktail lounge.

Half an hour more on A1A will put you in the first of the major tourist-oriented resorts on this route—the Ormond Beach-Daytona Beach complex, geared almost totally to entertainment of the fun-seeking tourists. If the automobile isn't king here, it is at least the royal godfather.

From Daytona Beach, it is sixty miles to Cape Canaveral directly down the coast along US 1, or it is sixty miles to Orlando, a bustling but attractive interior city which can be reached quickly by car via Interstate Highway 4, which cuts all the way across the state to St. Petersburg.

You may wish to sample some of Florida's inland lake country. Interstate 4 skirts past the towns of De Land and Sanford, but you will see some rich citrus and farm land, dotted by lakes. This is a ridge section dividing the state: the watershed flows north through the St. Johns; south by the Kissimmee River to Lake Okeechobee and the Everglades.

Around Orlando

Orlando was settled, after the Seminole Wars, by former volunteers who decided to stay with the land after the withdrawal of the regular army. Later, new blood was added by English settlers who bought land from the state and railroad interests for as little as $1 an acre. They came to grow citrus, but they also brought a way of life with them, and many built tennis courts and played cricket. They had organized a polo team by 1884. In 1975, Orlando celebrated its 100th birthday.

More than half the citrus growers abandoned their groves after a devastating freeze hit the trees in 1895, but many remained to rebuild or to take up new occupations. For many years Orlando, with its well-ordered beauty, was a favorite winter vacation and retirement center for middle-aged or older people who found its climate, location, and atmosphere "just right."

Today, Orlando is having a hard time retaining that old atmosphere. As soon as the Space Age began, a booster was ignited under the city. Cape Canaveral is only sixty-five miles away, and Orlando qualifies as the nearest—or only—semilarge city within handy distance. Some 3,000 people a day commute to the Cape, and more than 4,000 work at the Glenn L. Martin Company's twenty-two-building plant on the outskirts.

Because of its location amidst the state's main and best highways, Orlando is an excellent hub for one-day touring in almost any direction.

Lake Apopka

Lockhart

OCOEE RD.

SILVER STAR RD.

Pine Hills

PLANT ST.

Winter Garden

50

Orlando

FLORIDA'S TURNPIKE

535

Lake Down

4

Lake Butler

ORANGE BLOSSOM TRAIL

L. Hancock

535

L. Tibet Butler

REAMS RD.

L. Sheen

Sand L.

CONNECTOR

BEE LINE

Sea World of Florida

Stars Hall of Fame

WALT DISNEY WORLD

FLORIDA'S TURNPIKE

Buena Vista Village

Gatorland Zoo

Walt Disney World Entrance

192

4

530

Kissimmee

Walt Disney World

(A hotel/motel explosion since Disney World has added 20,000 new rooms.)

Twenty miles south, for instance, on four-laned US 17, is Kissimmee, still a cow town although the cowboys aren't as visible as they were ten years ago, when more of them wore the Florida version of cowpunchers' togs: wide-brimmed hat, dungarees, plaid shirt, and boots. The real fancy duds never did go here. This was cow country a hundred years ago, and by 1870 Kissimmee's bars were set up to serve a thirsty but hurried cowboy a drink while he still was on his horse.

These days bars do get their share of cowboys, but they'll have to thread their way through the city slickers. Perhaps things have toned down a little bit because one of the big ranchers these days (300,000 acres) is the Mormon Church.

Things are undeniably lively, however, at least twice a year—in late February and on the Fourth of July—when the Silver Spurs rodeos are held. Some Saturday nights in between are rather sprightly, too.

Of course anyone who is in the Orlando area will want to visit Walt Disney's Magic Kingdom, which is as much a part of the Space Age as Cape Canaveral. You can spend a day or a week and still not see everything the Magic Kingdom has to offer, but since Disney World opened, the average visitor has spent nearly nine hours. Located on US 192, just west of Interstate 4, Walt Disney World offers golf, boating, swimming, camping, hiking, waterskiing, horseback riding, canoeing, and night life as well as the thrills and excitements of the theme park. About a five-minute drive away, the almost 200 acres of Sea World also entice the visitor. Shamu, the star killer-whale, performs with porpoises, penguins, and mermaids. The Japanese Village, Hawaiian Village, water-ski shows with Batman and Wonder Woman, and the Atlantis Theater all add to the excitement.

North of Orlando, within an hour's time, via US 441 to Eustis, then State 19, is the outdoorsman's jackpot: Ocala National Forest. There are thirty-one varied recreation areas within the forest's 362,000 acres of lakes and rolling hills, offering swimming, camping, trailer sites, fishing, and scenery by the mile.

In fact, there are sixty-five miles without a stoplight on State 19, which offers a north-south "vistaway" all the way from Palatka, north of the forest. Another state road, 40, is east-west and crosses 19 in the middle of the forest.

Two favorite spots in the forest are Alexander Springs, near the southern entrance, and Juniper Springs, near the crossroads. Alexander Springs bubble up a torrent of 76 million gallons of 74-degree water every day of the year, and there's a white sand beach, picnic area, refreshments, a bathhouse, boats for rent, nature trails and nearby camping and trailer sites, equipped with electricity, water, and sewers.

Juniper Springs offers the same, basically, but in addition there's a thirteen-mile (downstream) canoe rental trip available. One can just laze along, drifting through a subtropical forest, until reaching a waterway park back beside State 19. The Forest Service people take the canoe back by trailer.

Whenever you're ready, the return to Orlando can be made by taking either State 40 or 42 east to US 17, then south to get back on Interstate 4.

The final leg of the northeast-Florida tour takes you back to a history-laden coastline, but this time the history is only years old, instead of centuries, and could be as current as today's breakfast.

Missile Land

Cape Kennedy, the Merritt Island moon-launch site, Patrick Air Force Base Missile Test Center—all the jumping-off places for our epochal strides into space—are aligned along a forty-mile strip of until recently deserted sandpits. Mainland villages just a few years ago—Titusville on the north, Melbourne on the south, Cocoa in the center—pulsated with the excitement of heart-stopping suspense as giant, flame-spitting cylinders carried live men to the moon.

From Orlando, for instance, State 50, east, will take you twenty four-laned miles to a junction: south of State 520 for Cocoa and Cocoa Beach, or straight ahead on 50 for Titusville.

If there's no blast-off scheduled, you can tour Cape Kennedy, the main launching area for the Atlantic Missile Range and the place from which astronauts are shot into space, and/or NASA's moon-launch area on Merritt Island. The only authorized guided tours of the Kennedy Space Center and Cape Kennedy are NASA Tours, operated by TWA and conducted by Greyhound. Tours depart regularly throughout the day from the Visitors Information Center from 8 A.M. until two hours before sunset. However, due to operational activity at the space center, the tours are subject to change. Because the VAB (Vertical Assembly Building) has been closed for future missile operations, everything is now concentrated in the Visitors Information Center, where all is free, including a series of fascinating movies. The NASA Tours are operating, too, of course. Handicapped persons may ask, a week in advance, for a guide at no extra charge to take them on the tour in their own car.

On Sundays you can drive your own car around Cape Kennedy and the space center, at no charge. During 1978, there were some new restrictions for the Sunday only self-drive tours, due to the activity of the Space Shuttle program. It did not affect the NASA Tours or the Visitors Center. You can check ahead with Patrick Air Force Base, or from anywhere in Florida, you can call this toll-free number for information: (800) 432-2153. It operates 24 hours a day and also has information about upcoming launches from the Space Center.

Before you leave the Cocoa Beach-Sebastian Inlet area and you like to fish, anglers report that fishing is "the hottest" here in the coldest months. Best surf-fishing includes bluefish and redfish. Or you can troll offshore for dolphin, king mackerel and sailfish. From the piers, you can fish for snook, flounder, whiting. Fishermen-in-the-know claim this is "the saltwater trout capital of the world."

In whatever manner you choose to visit this historic site, be sure to stop at the Visitors Information Center, located at the space center, six miles east of US 1, south of Titusville, which has splendid free exhibits, movies and detailed lectures on the space program.

For those who can't take the weekend tours, there's a display of missiles at Patrick Air Force Base, reached by A1A just south of Cocoa Beach. And near the south gate of Cape Kennedy are thirty rockets that help make up the Air Force Space Museum.

Gold Coast Beaches

The first faint reflections of South Florida's Gold Coast show up slowly, then in a tumbling cascade as you proceed south from Melbourne along the south central coast. Included in the 120-mile strip to the Broward County line, just south of Addison Mizner's storied Boca Raton, are brand new oceanfront resorts, older fishing villages only barely retaining their quaintness, the great millionaires' playground of Palm Beach with its brawnier big brother, West Palm Beach, and a skinny megalopolis of side-by-seaside municipalities made up of motels, restaurants, shuffleboard courts and the almost unending beach.

But more, too. Giant jet engines are built at Pratt & Whitney's sprawling plant inland from West Palm Beach. The nation's winter vegetables spring from the rich black muckland surrounding Lake Okeechobee. Sugar mills send giant stacks upward to process tens of thousands of tons of cane daily. And the cowboys are Indians on the Brighton Reservation ranch.

Stick with A1A south from Melbourne for a relaxing drive. On the east will be the rolling surf of the Atlantic; on the west the Indian River. Pelican Island, a National wildlife refuge established by President Theodore Roosevelt in 1903, is washed over daily by the tides in the river, but thousands of pelicans are hatched here annually.

Sports fishing and agriculture offer both substance and diversion in the towns of Vero Beach, Fort Pierce, and Stuart. This is Indian River citrus country, yielding some of the state's tastiest oranges and grapefruit. Citrus packing houses are open for visitors from October through May. With luck, in one of the three towns you may be able to locate a glass of fresh orange juice, rather than the frozen concentrate sort.

But there'll be no trouble finding a place to fish. Offshore, the sailfish is much sought after—and found—by charter craft, while bay waters provide snook, channel bass, pompano, and sea trout. Freshwater catches are numerous and weighty in the St. Lucie River, which joins the ocean at Stuart.

Bridges and piers offer the pedestrian angler his chance, and Fort Pierce provides especially constructed balconies on either side of the bridge spanning the Indian River.

On the ocean at Vero Beach stands the well-nigh unbelievable Driftwood Inn, a rambling, unpainted conglomeration that has been variously described as "Florida's Most Fabulous Hostelry," and "The Junkpile by the Sea" in national publications. The late Waldo Sexton, owner, architect and scavenger, furnished the place with an unbelievable array of cast-offs, pickups, float-ins, and exotic bric-a-brac from everywhere. Sexton bought much of the leftover furnishings Addison Mizner had brought over from Europe for Palm Beach mansions, getting the discount price when the boom's bust halted construction. And he added to the collection thirty years later when many of the Palm Beach mansions that had been built were razed to escape taxes.

And at Jensen Beach, a tiny tongue of land between the St. Lucie and Indian River just east of Stuart, there's Frances Langford's Outrigger restaurant, plus villas and a yacht basin. You may remember Frances as the blond singer who spent a lot of World War II and the Korean War entertaining troops around the world.

The yacht basin, in case you're interested, can handle any craft up to 120 feet long. New in 1978, the luxurious Indian River Plantation Resort flaunts a challenging 18-hole golf course and 11 tennis courts, beautiful villas and restaurants. If you catch a fish, the chef will prepare it for free for your lunch or dinner in the Porch restaurant.

Directly east of Jensen Beach is Hutchinson Island, with protected beaches which offer the spectator sport of watching giant sea turtles, usually loggerheads, come ashore during the summer months to lay their eggs. Weighing up to two hundred pounds, the mother-to-be waddles up on the beach, usually at night, and starts digging a hole in the sand. Her flippers scoop out sand as far as she can reach, then she begins laying the eggs—pingpong ball sized. Her eyes begin to water as the count increases—she may lay up to 150—and some see the giant tears as indications of pain. Others suspect the digging has gotten sand in her eyes. She waddles back to the sea after covering the eggs, which hatch into baby turtles if they're lucky.

The turtles don't mind human witnesses, but turtle eggs are considered a delicacy by some and there are fines of $200 or more for disturbing the nests. Raccoons, however, have no respect for the law and devour up to ninety percent of the eggs. At the House of Refuge museum on Hutchinson Island a sea turtle hatchery rescues the eggs and protects them until birth. Green turtles, much desired for green turtle soup, once were numerous here, but diminished as human appetites grew. Now the nursery imports infant green turtles from Costa Rica in an effort to reestablish the species in this area.

The House of Refuge, however, wasn't originally established for the protection of turtles, but to give aid to shipwrecked sailors.

The Elliott Museum, nearby, is devoted to the evolution of wheeled vehicles and to examples of business shops near the turn of the century. During 1955, Perry Como attracted attention to Jupiter by signing off his broadcasts with, "Good-night, folks. I'm going home to a little bit of Heaven called Jupiter, Florida."

Superstar Burt Reynolds opened the Burt Reynolds Dinner Theater in Jupiter, his hometown, early 1979 and that, too, is attracting national attention.

Upper-Crust Palm Beach

The change won't be noticeable for a spell, but, after you cross the St. Lucie inlet proceeding south, you are in a very ritzy neighborhood. So ritzy, in fact, that the part-time residents of the Hobe Sound colony over on Jupiter Island consider Palm Beach a bit "gaudy."

Don't bother taking a look, for Hobe Sound likes privacy. You can't see anything except high shrubs hiding estates. Roads, parks and even a post office have been fought off in the pursuit of nontourism.

It's more neighborly on Jupiter's south end, where the fishy Loxahatchee River snakes past the 106-year-old red brick Jupiter lighthouse.

South into Palm Beach Country on A1A there's a nice view from atop an oceanside dune near Juno Beach.

Mr. Flagler's Dream Come True

To get to Palm Beach, you go to West Palm Beach, and that's just the way Henry Flagler wanted it. Palm Beach is an island, with Lake Worth giving it stylish distance from the mainland. Flagler saw the island in 1893, some fifteen years after a Spanish bark loaded with coconuts and wine went aground and broke up. The coconuts floated up on the beach, as did the wine-soaked crew, and before long the island had a new profile, with graceful coconut fronds undulating in the sea breezes.

Flagler could envision a great resort, but as usual he didn't dwell long with a mere vision. Work began on the Royal Poinciana Hotel, with the best of everything, naturally.

The best was good enough for Philadelphia's Wideners, Stotesburys, and Wanamakers, who were early samplers, and spurred by such social acceptance Palm Beach was on its way, via Flagler's railroad, of course.

So was West Palm Beach, the town Flagler built for his "help," who would build and run the resort. There was no bridge connection with the eighteen-mile-long island back then, and for years no automobiles were allowed in Palm Beach.

Many of the great mansions—for example Mrs. E. L. Stotesbury's El Mirasol and Mrs. Horace Dodge's Playa Reinta—are gone now, victims of another age . . . and another tax scale. But the Via Mizner remains: a tiny, Old World shopping alley with some of the world's most fashionable—and expensive—goods. And the Everglades Club is still there (members only). And up on North County Road, behind a high wall, is the oceanfront villa where a young John Kennedy frolicked on the beach . . . and where he spent the last weekend of his life as President of the United States.

West Palm Beach, the city Flagler built for his help, has helped itself as well, and now is comfortably supported by a three-way economy: tourism, agriculture, and industry. Pratt & Whitney's research and development center is a bit outside the city limits, it's true, but the impact is felt in downtown dollars. Minneapolis Honeywell, International Telephone and Telegraph, and RCA are closer in and near the airport.

The weather helps the resort trade perhaps a bit more here in winter, for the warming Gulf Stream comes closer to shore than at any other mainland Florida point. There are diversions aplenty: greyhound racing, polo, jai alai, fishing, a number of important boat races.

West Palm Beach may also be said to have the closest thing to casino gambling—the Lucayan Beach casino at Freeport in the Bahamas is directly east and only minutes away from the West Palm airport.

The area lacks not for cultural pursuits, either. West Palm's Norton Gallery has an almost priceless collection of jades, plus current and permanent art works. In Palm Beach, the Royal Poinciana Playhouse offers direct-from-Broadway legitimate theatre during the winter season, and the Society of the Four Arts with a garden entrance on Royal Palm Way has an art gallery, library, and film theatre. This, too, during the winter only.

Strung together south of West Palm Beach, each with a mainland

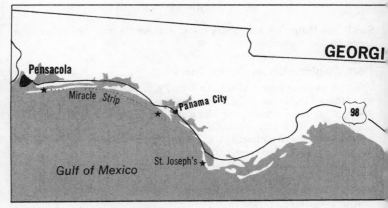

business section and an offshore island beachfront, are the towns of Lake Worth, Lantana, Boynton Beach, and Delray Beach. All have everything Palm Beach has, except perhaps the ratio of millionaires and the flossy history.

Boca Raton, however, is next in line and has had plenty of both. Although the name came from a Spanish phrase, *boca de ratones*, meaning mouth of the sharp-pointed rocks, it is more generally agreed that Boca Raton means rat's mouth. And that sounds a lot better than some of the things investors were saying about it after the mid-'10's boom went blooey (among them, according to resort historian Cleveland Amory, was "Beaucoup Rotten").

The top-rated polo players in the United States play every Sunday, January through April, in Boca Raton. The only other polo teams with higher-rated men in the world are the Argentines. Prince Phillip's team in England is in the same class, but the fact is, the boys from Boca Raton have beaten the Prince's best on their own field. Polo is growing rapidly as a spectator sport, but still preserves vestiges of its aristocratic origins. Most of the players are members of old and still very wealthy families who can afford a stable of ponies. (Each player must have six ponies just to play one game.) And be careful when you order two cold ones as you are sitting in the bleachers—the vendor sells splits of champagne as well as beer.

The Lake of Plenty

From pâté and champagne to meat and potatoes—not to mention sugar, beans, corn, lettuce, celery, and twenty-six other vegetables—it's only about an hour's drive into the rich Lake Okeechobee area. From West Palm Beach, US 98 and 441 will deliver you into Belle Glade on the southeastern corner of the 730-square-mile lake, second largest fresh water body wholly within the United States.

It's worth the trip, especially during the winter growing season. More than 30,000 railroad carloads of vegetables are shipped each season from Belle Glade to frosty but hungry Northerners—and occasionally, Californians. In addition, there are lush grasslands by the hundreds of thousands of acres to support a growing cattle industry, including the Brighton Seminole Indian Reservation's 35,000 acres which will eventually field a herd of 44,000 cattle.

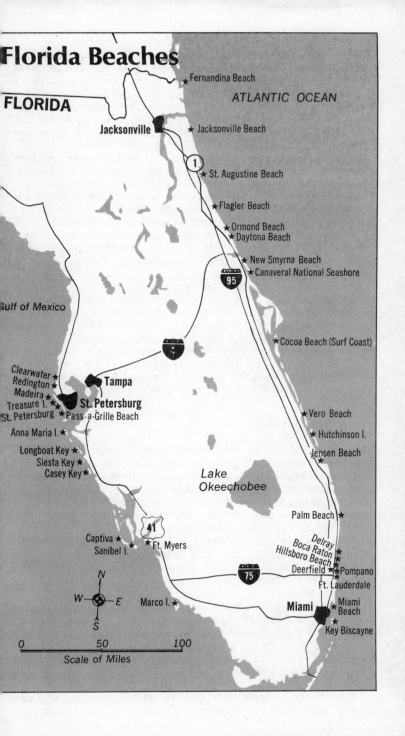

The secret of this whole area's success is the lake, which really was more of a swamp until the Herbert Hoover Dike was built along the southern edge beginning in 1930. The sixty-six-mile-long dike, plus a network of canals and pumping stations, make possible the water control that is the key to agricultural success. It also makes possible a cross-state canal from Stuart on the East Coast to Fort Myers on the West Coast. Belle Glade, Clewiston, Pahokee, South Bay, and the other towns around the edge are actually often below the level of the lake's waters.

Sports fishing is a primary diversion, and the lake, although rarely more than six or eight feet deep, is a contender for the best-fishing-in-America title. Guides and boats are available.

There has been a vast increase in the amount of sugar production in this area since 1959, when Castro came to power in Cuba, but the state had its first commercial sugar operation in 1767 at the Minorcan colony in New Smyrna. Present sugar operations in the Lake Okeechobee region began about 1923, and today there are eleven sugar mills serving a cane growing area of almost a quarter of a million acres. Half a million tons of sugar are produced each year.

During the November-April harvesting season, free tours are conducted at the Sugar House of the U.S. Sugar Corp. in Clewiston. As the oldest and largest sugar firm, U.S.S.C. laid out the town of Clewiston with an eye to spaciousness. And it also built and operates the Clewiston Inn, which has a dependably good hotel and restaurant. After all, that's where the company's executives stay when they come to town.

To return to the coast and your first glimpse of the golden tip of Florida, you can return to West Palm Beach on US 441, or angle south on US 27, then branch off east on State 84 to Fort Lauderdale.

The Golden Tip

Fort Lauderdale is not the Venice of America, despite its occasional use of this Chamber of Commerce slogan. Venice should be so lucky.

There are inland waterways—165 miles of them—but they connect areas of subdued prosperity rather than decaying grandeur. Here there are no waterlogged tenements, but manicured fingers of land, spread to let the warm blue waters lick along bulkheaded back yards.

The fortunate residents—some with an old automobile out front and a rowboat in back, others with two cars and a yacht—are pretty well-equipped to go anywhere they want. Many already have, for Fort Lauderdale is the home of a colony of the world's wealthy who have traveled near and far and have decided that this is a congenial place for their retirement years.

In Florida, a man of vision is one who turns out to be right sooner or later. Many dreamy developers who put in wide, concrete sidewalks through scrub pine woods to accommodate the "proposed" shopping center are long forgotten, for only the sidewalks ever came. But Fort Lauderdale's men of vision somehow saw that the city should have lots of clear, uncluttered beach and that there should be protected waters for the yachts.

In the case of the beach, the acquisitive city commissioners, who kept adding little chunks until there were six miles of it, were proved right when adjacent communities allowed hotels, motels, restaurants, and what-have-you directly on the oceanfront, shutting off public access.

Once, there seemed plenty of beach to go around, and the concessions to attract hotels and business may have seemed sensible, perhaps even visionary. But now, of course, Fort Lauderdale has been proved right and profits greatly because the hotels, apartments, shops, and the like are across a wide boulevard from the public's sands.

From US 1, you can get to where the boys were for several springtimes during the college vacation madness by taking one of three routes. On the north is Sunrise Boulevard, which connects with oceanfront A1A at the south edge of Birch Park; in the center is Las Olas Boulevard, and on the south S.E. 17th Street, which becomes Brook Memorial Causeway.

East Las Olas offers a fashionable shopping and browsing area from Federal Highway to 12th Avenue. Resort clothing is sold in branch stores of firms that operate in the summer in other resorts such as Nantucket and Blowing Rock. Grillwork, shutters, and a restrained use of signs give a pleasant air and there's even a French-style sidewalk cafe. Galleries, a museum, ballet studio, and plush furnishings shops add to the cultural effect.

Other noteworthy shopping areas are on North Federal Highway near Oakland Park Blvd. (which also will take you to the beach and a sumptuous hotel and high-rise apartment area) and a large, modern shopping center on Sunrise Blvd.

The 17th Street Causeway on the south offers a good view of Port Everglades, which is a port of call for many cruise ships as well as freighters. Alongside this causeway is Pier 66, an elaborate marina, restaurant-motel complex, and, just as the beachfront is reached, there is the world-famed (among yachtsman, anyway) Bahia Mar Marina.

After exploring Miami, head south to the Everglades National Park, some of the world's most productive farm land and the Florida Keys.

Bus tours are conducted both to the park and to Key West, and the Audubon Society conducts one- and two-day trips through parts of both, starting in Miami. If you prefer to drive, you can take old reliable US 1 south from Miami some twenty-five miles to Florida City and turn west on State 27. Ten more miles will put you at the Everglades Park entrance, connecting with the park's thirty-seven-mile road which ends at Flamingo at the southern tip of the park.

Tip: You can avoid much US 1 congestion in Miami by taking Old Cutler Road south until it rejoins US 1. Turn east from US 1 at LeJeune Road, which is 42nd Avenue, and keep going. You can stop at Fairchild Tropical Gardens along the way and browse among the nation's largest collection of tropical plants. An estate area of fine homes and vegetable farming areas are also along the route.

The Everglades

The beauty of Everglades National Park escapes some people, but it wouldn't if they'd shift mental gears and slow down enough to really look at it. There are more than two thousand square miles in the park, making it the nation's third largest. At first, there seems a sameness, a monotony to the landscape. But the sameness isn't actual. There are

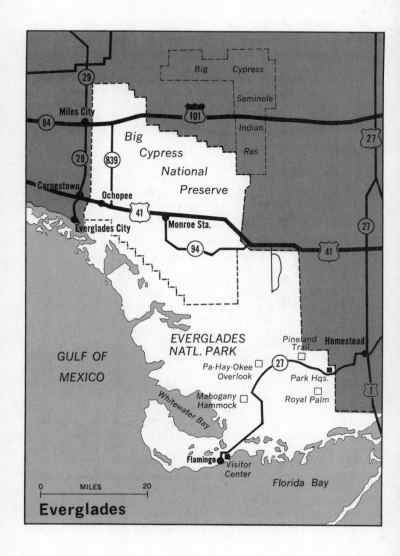

Everglades

subtle blendings of plant and animal life in cycles that began, ended, and began again thousands of years ago.

Near the park entrance, at the Royal Palm Hammock visitors' center, Park Rangers can tell you what to look for as you progress—and can show you what is there through exhibits and color movies. But the vastness, the variety, the shadings do not appear in miniature representations. You can only see them in their larger-than-life actuality.

Branching off from the main road are various viewing areas and trails which sample the complexity of the Everglades. Pa-hay-okee overlook is elevated to give you the perspective of a sea-of-grass panorama stretching endless miles. Gumbo Limbo trail leads you through a tropical density where you can see only a few feet through the dark foliage. At Taylor Slough, alligators, water birds, ducks, turtles, otter, deer, panther, black bear, and bobcats congregate. You will see some of them. The *Anhinga Trail* is a boardwalk which reaches out over a slough, in which the visitor can observe the everyday life and death drama of the glades.

About the time you have become convinced that you are near the outer limits of anthropoid civilization, that only you, the road, and your strange vehicle remain as outcroppings of the nonnatural universe, you will reach Flamingo and the surprising world of martinis and steaks and air conditioning.

Flamingo has a lodge, a dining room for two hundred, shops, a drug store, a marina, rental boats, groceries, gas, tires, oil, and all the accoutrements you suspected were far behind you. From here you can go on to see more of the park—and there is much more to see than you have, to this point—but from here you go by boat. And with a guide, of necessity. Morning and evening excursion boat tours can accommodate the mildly curious; those with their own or rented craft may join the Saturday Ranger-conducted boat-a-cades which ramble along for sixty-five mile tours.

There are picnic and camping areas at Flamingo and Long Pine Key. The Flamingo campsites hold 60 mobile homes and 171 tents or trailers, at a charge of about $2 per car. A small store sells groceries, fishing supplies, and sundries. Long Pine Key has 108 camp units, each including a picnic table, cookout grill, and a paved strip for trailer or tent, with drinking fountains and comfort stations close by. The charge is about $1 per car. You can fish all year here and do pretty well. You won't even need a license for saltwater fishing. But no hunting of any kind at any time. (You may, of course, defend yourself against the mosquitoes, but they are the hunters in this case.)

A long, furious, not-always-low-keyed controversy has surrounded the "flood control project" in the park. The project has cost in the hundreds of millions and, according to conservationist and naturalist opponents, controls flooding only in a minor way. They consider it land reclamation in disguise; a publicly subsidized move, benefiting landowners and real estate men. They have raised fears that loss of water, without replenishment, could destroy the park and hurt tourism.

Unless you're traveling by boat, return to Florida City, US 1, and the turnoff point to the Florida Keys by the same way you went.

South from Florida City on US 1, the first twenty-mile leg of the journey to the Florida Keys may be considered the dreariest segment of landscape anywhere. There's nought but swampy grasslands on either side as far as the eye can see. Then come little ponds to help a bit, then a bay and the beginnings of civilization again. The last short hop over Jewfish Creek bridge puts you on Key Largo, northernmost and largest of all the keys.

To Key West

Curving southwestward in a one-hundred-mile scimitar are the keys, strung like a necklace along the highway that went to sea. The highway, of course, came by train more or less, because it follows the fabulous Flagler's route to Key West for much of the way and uses most the railroad's original bridges.

The terrible killer hurricane that swept the keys on Labor Day in 1935 signaled the end for rail service to Key West—and to Cuba—but opened the way for the highway that carries many times more people than any railroad ever could.

There are forty-two bridges linking the keys, some little more than one hundred feet in length, several a mile or more, and one seven miles long. The scenery is almost all seascape, but among the world's most spectacular. This is the saltwater fisherman's happy hunting grounds, offering a choice of bonefish on the shallow flats or tarpon in Florida Bay and the Gulf of Mexico, plus the Gulf Stream's sporty smorgasbord.

Despite the plentitude of ocean, however, this is not beach and bathing territory; there are few beaches, except where they have been pumped up by man, and the water is shallow and surfless generally. Sharp coral rock discourages wading.

There are resort areas of every stripe along the way—from plush to primitive—plus a few commercial attractions and some, but only some, really good restaurants. Seafood is, naturally, a frequent specialty of the house, and green turtle steak, conch chowder, stone crabs, and Key lime pie are regional items worthy of being searched out. When ordering Key lime pie, be sure that it is yellow in color, not green. Real Key lime pie is yellow, and only establishments with no aesthetic sense will serve the artificial, dyed green variety.

Guides and boats are plentiful all along the keys, but spearfishing is allowed only along the southern portion of the route from Long Key to Key West. Skindiving, of course, is great sport the whole route, but perhaps at its very best near the beginning on Key Largo.

Stretching twenty-one miles parallel to Key Largo, and three and a half miles wide, is the John Pennekamp Coral Reef State Park, the nation's first continental underseas park, named for the associate editor of the *Miami Herald,* who had much to do with the park's establishment, plus that of Everglades National Park.

Glass-bottom boats embark from the park's 2,100-acre land base for viewing the only living coral reef along the Atlantic Coast. The crystal-clear water allows clear views to sixty-foot depths of the forty-one varieties of coral in colorful, flowerlike formations, with here and there the hulks of old sailing wrecks. Reef fish, giant turtles, barracuda, and sharks add an accent. A better view is possible, certainly, for those with diving equipment, but the glass-bottom views will suffice for most.

The park's headquarters on Key Largo also affords overnight camping facilities, boat docks and launching areas, trails through natural woods, and a bathing lagoon. An entrance fee is charged.

Along the way south you can stop and browse along the shore for driftwood, old bottles, or just a closer look at the busy marine life.

Eventually, you'll reach Key West, an old and different town with an air of its own. There are nearly 30,000 individualists living here, each proudly proclaiming himself a "Conch" (pronounced Conk), even though he may have moved in only last month. The original Conchs trace to Cockney English settlers in the Bahamas, their descendants moving to Key West in the early 1800's as marine salvagers and fishermen. Stir in some native Bahamians, a large portion of Cubans, some Yankee sailing men, and Virginia merchants and you have the basic blend.

In the 1830's, this mixture was assessed as the richest per capita citizenry in the United States. But a hundred years later, the depression left it perhaps the poorest. Eighty percent of the population was on relief. A state agency was created to bring the city back to life via tourism, and out-of-work artists and writers were set to work changing the town's appearance and image. One administrator decreed that all men should wear shorts, to appear picturesque for the tourists' benefit. All seemed to be going well until the '35 hurricane cut the umbilical to the mainland. Only World War II and the U.S. Navy really brought economic stability, although completion of the highway permitted postwar growth.

Today, the city's colorful past, it's every-man-for-himself architecture and some big names have made another blend that pulls the tourism in.

The best way to see Key West is via the Conch Tour Train, a tram affair which rambles some fourteen miles in a 1½-hr. viewing of such sites as Harry Truman's Little White House, Ernest Hemingway's home, Audubon House, the turtle kraals, the shrimp fleet, art centers, and all the seeable attractions.

Audubon House was the Geiger House when the artist stayed there in 1831-32 while sketching Keys birdlife. It's been restored and contains some of Audubon's work, plus a mixture of furnishings much like the original owner salvaged from shipwrecks.

Ernest Hemingway lived in Key West during much of his most productive writing period, working on *Green Hills of Africa, To Have and Have Not, Snows of Kilimanjaro,* and *For Whom the Bell Tolls.* Hemingway was attracted by the old (1851) house's grillwork. He furnished it heavily with Spanish antiques and rebuilt the kitchen to put all the appliances several inches higher and thus handier for him whenever he wanted to whip up a specialty.

A wealthy couple bought the house in 1961, intending to make it their home, but as they discovered more and more artifacts and Hemingway memorabilia they decided instead to make it a museum.

The town's atmosphere seems to stimulate writers. Tennessee Williams, John Dos Passos, and Robert Frost also worked here.

West of Key West in the Dry Tortugas is Fort Jefferson National Monument, an early venture in defense spending that never really defended anything. After almost twenty years of building with forty million bricks (at $1 each for the shipping alone), the massive fort never fired any of its 243 big guns. Nor did any foe test the five-foot-thick walls. The fort did manage to serve as a prison for Dr. Samuel Mudd after Lincoln's assassination.

The return to mainland Florida again is simple—US 1 north. And if you plan to continue the tour west across Florida on the Tamiami Trail, you can miss metropolitan Miami traffic by switching to US 27 at Florida City, then turn west on US 41.

The Tamiami Trail connects Miami with Tampa, sweeping through Everglades country for one hundred miles to the West Coast at Naples, then angling northward, generally inland from the "quiet coast" of Florida. The section from Miami to Naples, however, is more specifically known as "The Trail." It was built at a cost of $13 million during five hard years of the mid-'20's and changed the face and future of South Florida. What had been a two-day roundabout excursion became a two-hour jaunt, thanks to The Trail.

There is also a two-lane toll road from US 27 west of Fort Lauderdale to Naples, completed in 1967, but it is referred to as Alligator Alley by Miamians jealous of the intrusion on the Trail's place in history.

Along the Tamiami Trail

Aside from its purely transportational aspects, The Trail has long served as a recreational access route, both in reaching the West Coast beaches at Marco and Naples, and in supplying one of the world's longest fishing holes. The Tamiami Canal, which parallels the road on the north, was dug to supply fill for the roadbed and automatically presented prime freshwater fishing grounds the length of the route.

Here, too, are the Seminole villages—or at least the villages you are permitted to see. Most of them along The Trail are semitourist attractions, ranging in scope from a couple of elevated huts, called *chickees,* to an elaborate restaurant-marine-souvenir shop-filling station complex, erected via a government loan. Airboat rides are offered, and are exhilarating once one gets over the shock of skimming along over an inch or two of water or perhaps only some damp sawgrass.

Another thirty-five miles brings you to State 29 and a choice: to the south are Everglades City, a planned metropolis that didn't pan out, but which does offer the renowned Rod and Gun Club which has been host to several U.S. Presidents; and the village of Chokoloskee on a tiny island off shore. Smallwood's Store, a rustic former Indian trading post, is worth seeing.

Access to the western portion of Everglades Park is by boat from Everglades City. Birdwatchers will want to see this section, which includes Duck Rock, home of some 75,000 white ibis during the summer months.

Turn north on State 29 and you will reach the town of Immokalee, then Corkscrew Swamp Sanctuary, the National Audubon Society's six-thousand-acre preserve which features thousands of rare birds, elevated walkways through the heart of a jungle, and giant bald cypress trees seven hundred years old and 130 feet high. The Sanctuary also can be reached via State 846 north of Naples, if you prefer.

The third choice can keep you on The Trail to Naples, Naples isn't the end of The Trail, but it's the culmination of the tour of Florida's tip.

Long a favorite with wealthy folks, Naples' aesthetic raw material has been pretty well protected. There's a seven-mile white sand beach, and a continuing fight to uphold strict zoning laws. The town's success in this matter may be measured by the fact that many longtime Miamians vacation in Naples and find it offers refined relief from the hurly-burly of bigtime resortery. With several dozen part-time resident millionaires, Naples has a sufficiency of smart shops. There are six golf courses. Sunset watching and beach strolling are the favorite "active" sports hereabouts except for the truly wild and woolly Swamp Buggy Races in November and February.

Another eight miles up US 41 is the turnoff point for Sanibel and Captiva Islands, which are the seashell fancier's idea of paradise because of the supply of left-handed welks, spiny periwinkles, large cockles, and coquina. Sanibel, connected to Captiva on the north end by a small bridge, was considered the ultimate in tropical splendor mixed with blessed privacy when only a ferry gave access to the mainland at Punta Rassa, but a toll causeway now makes the 3½-mile trip simple and quick. The $3 roundtrip toll, a concession to islanders who didn't want so many visitors after all, keeps the traffic down. The beaches are fine, accommodations range from simple but comfortable to the epitome of resort luxury.

Fort Myers is next, a pleasant city on the broad Caloosahatchee River and Thomas Alva Edison's choice for a winter home site. You can reach both via McGregor Blvd. from Punta Rassa. Edison had the home prefabricated in Maine, shipped it down by schooner, and used it well for fifty years. Now a museum, it's just as Edison left it, with such ahead-of-his-time Edison touches as an intercom system and automatic lights in the closets. His laboratory is intact, and you may note that they don't make light bulbs any more the way Edison did—some of his have been burning twelve hours a day ever since he made them.

Fort Myers also is bracketed by two of the large, complete-city housing developments designed to attract retirees. Some residents are tickled pink with their new life, others can't get used to the change. Any who are thinking about buying a retirement home of this sort may wish to browse around and talk to the residents. Cape Coral is east of town, across the river. Lehigh Acres is west on State 82. And north on State 41 is Port Charlotte.

As US 41 bends westward to skitter along the Gulf Coast again, you may detect a subtle quickening, a feeling that something is going on up ahead. Indeed, lots of things are, for you approach Sarasota and its outrigger keys which extend north to south for thirty-five miles, and with all this casual living frontier there is also culture.

Culture-happy

Sarasota—and the term is used loosely to apply to the mainland and its companions north and south, plus Siesta Key, Lido Key, and Longboat Key—seems to be the place with a little something, or everything, extra. More space, more beach, more to see and do in more comfort and in a most scintillating atmosphere.

Whatever the combination, it's pulled in a lot of people who could live and work almost anywhere, yet they chose this place.

An early one was John Ringling, the circus magnate, who enriched the community and state with his collection of art, his mansion, and his appreciation of the stimulating good things of life. The John and Mabel Ringling Museum of Art, owned and operated by the state, contains one of the nation's outstanding collections of Baroque and Renaissance paintings, the Rubens collection being America's finest. Contemporary and modern art also are on display. New galleries opened early in 1967.

Near the museum is the state-acquired Asolo Theater, a magnificent eighteenth-century interior from the castle at Asolo, Italy, which is in almost constant use for appropriate presentations—opera, concerts, and an eight-month season of plays.

The grandiloquent Ringling mansion on Sarasota Bay, and Ringling Museum of the Circus, also are part of the overall museums, which may be entered separately or with a combination ticket for all.

The culture doesn't linger in the past, however. Such outstanding architects as Paul Rudolph and Victor Lundy have contributed greatly with churches, homes, shops, and schools, and I. M. Pei designed buildings for the Oxford-like New College, which had Dr. Arnold Toynbee on the faculty for the first handpicked class of ninety-four scholars.

Among the well-known writers who have worked here are the late MacKinlay Kantor, and John D. MacDonald. The well-known names in the artists' colony range from cartoonist V. T. Hamlin, organizer of *Alley Oop,* to Ben Stahl, Syd Solomon, and Philip Guston.

The intellectual life is contagious, of course. Little theater groups, art schools, concerts, and art shows permeate all strata of the population. And everybody shares the "regular" niceties of sun, beaches, fishing, golf, tennis, patio socializing, and the like. But a little bit more, this being Sarasota.

Bradenton is contiguous to Sarasota on the north, and you'll be into it without knowing you've left Sarasota. There's a little difference, but county and municipal lines spawn competing chambers of commerce promoting the same thing. Bradenton has its own offshore key, too, but this one's an island—Anna Maria—instead of a key. The terms are always interchangeable, of course. And in fact, Longboat Key, one of Sarasota's claims, extends well into Manatee County and the Bradenton sphere. A bridge connects Longboat to Anna Maria if you want to stick with the beach route.

At the mouth of the Manatee River, five miles west of Bradenton, is De Soto National Memorial Park and the spot whence de Soto began his ill-fated trek all over the south. Just across the river on US 41 or 301, turn east for a couple of miles to reach the Gamble Mansion, a plantation-style antebellum museum. Judah P. Benjamin, Confederate Secretary of State, hid out here briefly after the South lost the war and eventually made it to England where he became a successful barrister.

The Sunshine Skyway

Either 41 or 301 will take you to Tampa, but for a spectacular view and a quick entry into St. Petersburg and that burgeoning resort area, it's best to switch to US 19 north, just outside Palmetto. This will take you across the fifteen-mile Sunshine Skyway (Toll: $1 per car) and save some forty-five miles. The Skyway is part causeway and part bridge

St. Petersburg–Tampa Area

Points of Interest

St. Petersburg
1) Bayfront Center
2) Big Pier 60
3) Bounty Exhibit
4) County Fairgrounds
5) Derby Lane (dog racing)
6) Jack Russell Stadium
7) Kalb Park
8) London Wax Museum
9) Museum of Fine Arts
10) Payson Field (baseball)
11) Sunken Gardens
12) The Pier
13) Tiki Gardens

Tampa
14) Al Lopez Field (baseball)
15) Greyhound Track
16) Jai Alai Fronton
17) Municipal Beach
18) Shrimp Fleet
19) Tampa Stadium
20) University of South Florida
21) University of Tampa

spanning Tampa Bay and replacing the old Bee-Line Ferry. High spot, in more ways than one, is the high-level main Skyway Bridge, four miles long and rising the equivalent of fifteen stories above the water. Although ocean freighters cruised underneath with plenty of room to spare, in 1980, a phosphate freighter slammed into the southbound span of the Skyway during a rainstorm and knocked a large chunk of the bridge into the water. Thirty-five persons, driving over the span, lost their lives. So far, there has been no decision about how to rebuild the lost portion. However, traffic is not impaired between Sarasota and St. Petersburg; it's all one-lane each way, via the causeway, and just takes more time. The destroyed part of the bridge has become a sightseeing attraction.

You enter St. Petersburg from the south, this way, and it doesn't look like an old resort town, for old people. It isn't, really, but the part that is is clustered in a semicircle with the radius point at the Municipal Pier and Central Ave. Rambling hotels and frame, gingerbread decorated two-story homes along quiet brick streets, shaded by giant oaks, mark the original retirees' compound. If you're coming down from the north, I-75 will take you directly into St. Petersburg.

The ocean beaches north of Mullet Key (turn west onto State 699 if returning from Mullet Key) are known collectively as the Pinellas Sun-coast, consisting of the eight Gulf of Mexico communities: Clearwater Beach, Dunedin, Holiday Isles, Madeira Beach, St. Pete Beach, St. Petersburg, Tarpon Springs, Treasure Island. The Holiday Isles include Redington Beach, Indian Rocks Beach and other small Gulf communities. All told, there are twenty-eight miles of beach—and beachfront accommodations ranging from luxury hotels and apartments to weathered frame beach houses that may be rented by the week or month.

St. Pete is connected to the mainland by Corey Causeway (free) and is a favorite place to stay, shop, and dine. Waterfront restaurants, chartered fishing boats, rental sailboats, and the wide expanse of sandy beach attract sun-seekers all the year-round. Serious shell-hunters comb the beach as early as 6 A.M.

Clearwater Beach connects with Clearwater, on the mainland, via Garden Memorial Causeway. Clearwater has a fine marina and a large sport-fishing fleet. As with St. Petersburg and Tampa, its major league spring training games help make it popular with baseball fans.

From Clearwater, a choice: south on US Alternate 19 you can reach downtown St. Petersburg, sampling en route the modern suburbs; west on State 60 will feed you into the north part of Tampa across the Courtney Campbell Causeway; or north on Alternate 19 gets you to Tarpon Springs, a mere fifteen miles away. En route, is Innisbrook Golf and Tennis Resort, considered one of the best in the country. A long, winding lane leads to the 900-acres of landscaped gardens, three championship golf courses, tennis courts, and the vacation villas.

Tampa is now Florida's third largest city, with such industries as breweries and cigar factories, plus a busy deep-water port.

Busch Gardens, a public relations whim of the Anheuser-Busch ownership, is a man-planted tropical garden with one of the world's largest aviaries. Hundreds of colorful birds and animals live among the 150,000 trees, plants, and lakes on 300-acres. You can tour the Dark Continent complete with Moroccan Village, Claw Island, the Congo, Stanleyville,

Serengeti Plain, etc. The beer is on the house. Recent additions are "Timbuktu," on seven acres of the "Dark Continent," and "Adventure Island," the ultimate in water parks, with surf-tipped pools, white sand beach, etc.

Drive north on 40th Street to Temple Terrace Highway, then west, to reach Busch Gardens. And, if you like, a few more blocks north on 30th Street to the Schlitz Brewery for a tour and complimentary brew.

On the way to, or returning from, Busch Gardens via 40th Street, a turn west onto Broadway will yield a sample of Ybor City and the Latin Quarter of Tampa. It's pronounced "E-Boe" City by folks hereabouts and offers Spanish architecture and some of the nation's best Spanish restaurants. Tampa has picked up mightily in recent years, and now has a $4½ million convention center and streamlined traffic system.

Mr. Plant's fine hotel still sits in the middle of town, just across the Lafayette Street Bridge, but now it's the University of Tampa. The thirteen Moorish minarets on this interpretation of the original Alhambra make it hard to miss. There's a museum in the south wing of the main building, and nearby on the well-kept grounds is the De Soto Oak, whereunder de Soto supposedly bargained with the Indians.

The city's biggest day of the year is the second Monday of February. School is out for Gasparilla Day, a festival keyed to the "capture" of Tampa by a modern "Jose Gaspar" and his crew of one-day buccaneers as they cruise up Hillsborough Bay in a flag-bedecked pirate-type ship to accept the city's surrender. The original Jose Gaspar supposedly buried some of his treasure in the area, although there's much dispute from some quarters that he ever existed at all. No matter, the excitement of Gasparilla Day is real. Best spot for watching is along Bayshore Blvd.

Winter Haven can be reached quickly from either Lakeland (via US 92) or Bartow (via US 17) and should. Not only because it's another pleasant, lake-dotted town with all the amenities, but because from Winter Haven it is only five miles to Cypress Gardens. Drivers needn't worry about the road number—plenty of signs direct the way.

Perhaps as much as any place in Florida, Cypress Gardens proves what imagination, promotion, and a pliant Mother Nature can do. What was once only a swamp well off the beaten track now has its own track, very well beaten by up to eight thousand tourists a day, and the swamp has been nurtured, prodded, drained, elevated, and manicured into 164 acres of botanical flamboyance, accented by pretty girls. In 1980, Cypress Gardens attracted 1,366,000 visitors, making it Florida's fifth largest attraction.

The amateur photographer may not be king here, but he will feel like one—even after the film is developed. Expert professionals give the proper camera settings for every shot, and it's very hard to take a bad picture under these circumstances. There's even a special grandstand for the picture takers (it costs a little extra to get in it).

But the gardens cannot be overshadowed—or perhaps oversplashed—once you're on the scene. Lagoons, moss-hung cypress, bougainvillea, banks of azaleas, and rare and exotic plants from around the world combine to present a series of "vistas" along the winding walkways and waterways (electric boats, a little extra charge). Millions were spent for new attractions in 1980, including Living Legends of the South and a walk-through aquarium.

Entrepreneur Dick Pope, who started it all and has kept it going and growing for over forty years, with the assistance now of his son, Dick Jr., has even managed to make the parking lot outside into something different with a spiral "Palm Bowl" arrangement.

Anyone within reasonable distance should try to see Cypress Gardens —and bring the camera.

An Area of Sundry Attractions

Leaving Cypress Gardens, tourists may take State 540 east, cross US 27, continuing west on 540, and should be prepared for a surprise. Here, tucked away beside a little lake smack in the center of Florida is what appears to be a miniature European castle. This is Chalet Suzanne, which offers one of Florida's dining adventures. A big splurge is recommended for those who have the time and money.

There are also thirty guest rooms, furnished with an intriguing collection of antiques from throughout the world.

Lake Wales and the Bok Tower are only four miles south of Chalet Suzanne, by US 27.

Edward Bok, wealthy editor of the *Ladies Home Journal* and a Pulitzer Prize winner in 1920, established Mountain Lake Sanctuary on the slope of Iron Mountain (324 feet above sea level, the highest point in peninsular Florida) as a refuge for birds and man, as well as a proper setting for the carillon tower that now serves as his memorial. Lovely gardens surround the 205-foot tower, and there are "blinds" for visitors to observe or photograph the birdlife. A pool reflects the image of the tower, and carillon concerts are given several times weekly. There is no access for tourists to the tower's top. Serenity is the attraction.

Near the entrance to the Sanctuary is Spook Hill, a Lake Wales city street (5th Street at North Avenue) on which one may park, release the brakes and have the illusion that the car is rolling uphill.

Lake Wales is also the scene, from early February to mid-April, of the Black Hills Passion Play, presented four times a week in a 3,500-seat amphitheater with a stage more than one hundred yards wide. In 1977, the performers celebrated the 25th year of this annual event. Along with the fine cast of actors, a flock of 30 sheep, lambs, and two camels participate.

Thirty miles south of Lake Wales—again by US 27 or Alternate 27—is Sebring, famous for its annual twelve-hour speed and endurance sports car races, held in March. Located in the citrus belt, with its lemon, lime and avocado groves, visitors are welcome at the Sebring Packing Co. from October to May. Otherwise, Sebring is just a quiet spot for fishing, hunting, golf and outdoor pursuits. The nearby Highlands Hammock State Park has catwalks into a cypress swamp area, as well as a guided tour and small museum.

For variety, it's suggested that, if the trip south to Sebring from Lake Wales was on US 27, the return north should be via Alternate 27. Some nice panoramas present themselves, and at Babson Park, named for himself by economist Roger Babson when he bought the town of Crooked Lake in 1923, is Webber College. Webber, founded at Wellesley, Mass., by Mrs. Babson to teach rich young ladies how to take care of money, has a branch here. In 1959, the Babson Park branch began admitting males—day students only—perhaps to teach rich young men how to protect themselves from rich young ladies.

North Central Florida

The drive northward into the state's varied north central section can be that rare thing in this motorized age: simply a pleasant drive without too much traffic and with an interesting countryside unrolling past the windows. On US 27 north—this will be through the heart of the citrus area with trees of all sizes stretching to the horizon in exact lines like the dots on a sheet of graph paper—there are rolling hills, with little lakes in the valleys, and giant propellers sticking up above the groves to stir up chill air when frost threatens, or smudge pots to generate a layer of warm smoke over the tender trees. You are also in real cattle country, po'dner, between Lake Wales and Okeechobee at Yeehaw Junction. If you like to ride 'em, cowboy, and feast on delicious grub, a vacation is fun at River Ranch on 50,000 acres. A million-acre cattle ranch, the Kicco, was here long ago. Cookouts, square dancing, and rodeos are part of guest activities.

Just north of the town of Clermont is one of the state's two Citrus Towers (the other is at Lake Placid, also on US 27, fifteen miles south of Sebring). On a hill of 340 feet elevation, the Clermont tower rises an additional 226 feet to an observation platform reached in less than a minute by elevator. The view is spectacular, an expansion of what may be seen from ground level with hundreds of lakes and two thousand square miles of citrus land spreading in all directions. Admission is charged to the tower.

There are, of course, other excellent viewing routes north. If the swing into the interior of the state isn't taken, US 19 north from St. Petersburg offers a near-coastal route and access to Weeki Wachee and Homosassa Springs, two of the state's twenty-seven major producers of crystal clear waters. Accommodations and underwater viewing of freshwater fish— and freshlooking girls—are available at both. From Tampa, US 41 wends north through interesting lake and river country, with dependably excellent fishing and camping facilities. Rainbow Springs is near Dunnellon on this route.

A few miles north of Clermont, the Sunshine State Parkway offers superhighway connections to Wildwood. There is a toll for the approximately twenty miles, but then a connection with Interstate 75 at Wildwood for a rapid arrival at the Ocala interchange. An option is to stick with US 27 to Leesburg, in the middle of the bass fishing country. US 27 and 441 join here for a divided-highway approach to Ocala.

Southern Wild West

Ocala is in the middle of what used to be called rural Florida, but now it's pastoral. And in the pastures are some very high-class thoroughbred horses who live in $75,000 barns. All this is relatively recent—the biggest boost came when a locally bred dandy named Needles won the Kentucky Derby in 1956—but it all adds up to an additional tourist attraction for Ocala's already well-endowed bill of fare.

Other winners followed Needles, such as Carry Back with the 1961 Derby and Preakness, and Hail to All in the 1965 Belmont, but these are results, not causes, of the Florida horse farm boom.

The real and original causes are basic: limestone water, rolling hills and grassy knolls, the things Kentucky offered earlier in the game. Ocala adds the clement climate, and the mere presence of good horses brings others, breeding being a consideration.

As usual, the horsemen go first class, riding on a nationwide amalgamation of $2 tickets, with which the bettor pays all bills. The result is some 150 thoroughbred farms worth more than $20 million, and all kept parklike with white fences, green grass, and old oaks. Most of the farms welcome visitors, but the hours vary. However, in mid-Ocala, at the Chamber of Commerce, are free maps showing the location and hours for most of the showplaces.

Ocala was the stage for the beginning of the Seminole War in 1835 when Wiley Thompson, an Indian agent, called a meeting to explain just how the government was going to ship the Seminoles west to the Indian Territory. The Seminoles demurred with vigor, and Thompson cut off the sale of guns and ammunition. This upset Osceola, who said, in the more temperate parts of his little speech, "I will make the white man red with blood, and then blacken him in the sun and rain . . . and the buzzard shall live upon his flesh."

Some months after the Ocala confrontation, Osceola and his companions killed a Mikasuki chief who had been selling cattle to the white men, then scattered the chief's presumably ill-gotten profits to the winds. In December, two months later, Jumper and Alligator, allies of Osceola, ambushed and massacred Major Francis Dade and one hundred officers and men near Bushnell. On the same day Osceola appeared at Fort King to the north, two miles east of Ocala, and killed the Indian agent, Thompson, and an Army lieutenant. After that day the war was on in earnest.

It sometimes sounds like it's still on in this neighborhood, for only a mile or so away, on what is now State 40 east of Ocala, is an elaborate attraction called "Six Gun Territory," where shoot-outs in the street continue on schedule all day.

Six Gun Territory is a manufactured version of an old Western town, with some forty buildings and a wood-burning locomotive and train, which hauls the customers in at the rate of two thousand an hour. There is a Palace Saloon, naturally, and cancan dancers, wild Western Indians (but no wild Eastern Indians, like Osceola), an O.K. Corral, general store and the like, plus such anachronisms as a cafeteria, photo shop, coffee house, and a movie house showing only the oldest available films.

Just why a Western frontier town should be sitting here in the middle of Florida does not have an answer, except that the ownership started getting rich with the same sort of thing up in North Carolina.

Nearby, just a mile or so east on State 40 (again, it's unlikely anyone will miss seeing the signs), is Silver Springs and a veritable shopping center of attractions—all at a price, of course.

Silver Springs itself attracts close to two million visitors a year, and a complete motel and restaurant industry has been built up in the area to accommodate the viewers.

Glass-bottom boat guides describe the wondrous sights, starting with the main spring, a cavern twelve feet high, sixty-five feet long and sixty feet below the surface, from which gush 650 million gallons of beautifully clear water every day. This would keep such cities as New York well-supplied, unless perhaps a political water commissioner was in charge.

The trip continues over fourteen other springs or groups of springs, all colorfully named, plus visits to pools where friendly, or hungry, fish come up to nibble from the fingers of passengers. A viewing station eight feet below the surface offers a good chance for photographers at the trip's end.

Other attractions, with additional admittance charges, include the Jungle Cruise, a deer ranch with more than three hundred tame deer from around the world (the kids like to feed them), Ross Allen's Reptile Institute for those who are interested, an Early American Museum, and a Prince of Peace Memorial with religious themes in a series of small chapels containing dioramas illustrating the life of Christ. New arrivals are four one-year old, 450-pound zebras to keep about 700 other animals company in the natural settings. Wild Waters, opened in Spring '78, is an exciting $1 million, 10-acre attraction of flumes and surf-crested pools that is sure to bring more gold into Silver Springs.

Certainly there is enough going on here to keep everyone occupied the minimum of six hours the management recommends.

Another recommendation is that State 40 be pursued just three more miles east, where one can find sanctuary in the Ocala National Forest. The noncommercial springs and attractions here are noted in the tour of northeast Florida.

The gauntlet must be rerun returning to Ocala, but the thirty-five miles north to Gainesville from there is pleasant or fast, depending on the route. Interstate 75 is quickest, but bypasses almost everything inhabited and presents little to attract the eye. US 441, however, threads through some Old South towns and villages that possess a genteel charm. Especially is this so in the spring, which begins in early March hereabouts. Banks of azaleas, dogwoods, the fresh green leaves of oaks, sweetgum, and camphor trees make all this seem a thousand miles from the stereotype Florida of palms, sand and sunglasses.

Back to the Old South

Just north of Lake City on US 41, at White Springs, is the Stephen Foster Memorial on the Suwannee River. Carillon recitals from the two-hundred-foot tower feature the composer's work four times daily. Foster never even saw the Suwannee, of course, picking the name for its beauty. As it happened, he picked a good one—the rambling Suwannee, from the Georgia line to the Gulf, is a beautiful stream, and the 243-acre park at the Memorial sets it off well. The Florida Folk Festival, with two thousand or more folk dancers, singers, craftsmen and tale tellers, is held during the first week in May each year. A "Jeannie With the Light Brown Hair" contest is held in February, with Florida lasses of both beauty and musical talent competing for a scholarship.

Less than twenty miles east of Lake City, on US 90, is the Olustee Battlefield Memorial, where the only significant Florida battle of the Civil War occurred. A museum there has displays of the action, plus newspaper accounts of the battle, in which the Confederates entrenched east of Lake City.

The way west from Lake City on US 90 reveals a change in the terrain: instead of flat pinelands, the surroundings become rolling red clay hills, giant live oaks and other hardwoods taking over from the pines. Live oaks were once a national resource, and much of the area here was held in reserve by the government for use in building wooden naval ships. Timber cutters hereabouts were called "Live Oakers" by Audubon in the 1830's, but, when the area was opened to homesteading in the late nineteenth century, much of the forest was destroyed during land clearing.

There's a town of Live Oak on the route; a picture-pretty version of the sleepy Southern village, moss hanging from the giant trees along shady streets. This area now is cattle country, but it has also long been a producer of bright leaf tobacco.

West of Live Oak, the meandering Suwannee is encountered, and at its juncture with the Withlacoochee River (there's another Withlacoochee River farther south) is Suwannee River State Park. There are old Confederate earthworks near a picnic area, fresh springs, and nature trails. Overnight camping is allowed.

The farther west a traveler ventures along US 90, the deeper into the Old South he finds himself. There are such towns as Madison, founded by South Carolina planters in 1838 when Sea Island cotton was grown here. This was a Confederate stronghold during the Civil War, and the news of secession brought bonfires and speeches, bell ringing, and Southern songs.

Then there's Monticello, with a courthouse modeled after Thomas Jefferson's home, elaborate plantations, and the remains of even more elaborate ones. The town's school, built with slave labor in 1852, was integrated—calmly—in 1965.

Tallahassee, the Capital

West again, on US 90, ahead is Tallahassee, the state's capital some 650 miles from Key West. And beyond Tallahassee, more than two hundred more miles of another, and different, Florida.

Tallahassee (the name means Old Fields in Apalachee Indian talk) has one of the state's most spectacular floral extravaganzas at Maclay State Park, formerly Killearn Gardens, about five miles north of town on US 319. Given to the state by Mrs. Alfred Maclay in 1953, the gardens are maintained by the state and are open from October 15 to June 15. Spring is probably the best time to visit. There are 308 acres of garden and recreation area with pools, formal arrangements of flowers bracketed by blooming trees, a walled garden, and a Camellia Walk flanked by twelve-foot-high camellias. Adjacent in the recreation area are picnic shelters with grills, swimming, and a boat ramp.

Near the airport is the Tallahassee Junior Museum's Pioneer Village, which presents typical farm buildings and implements of Northwest Florida farm life, circa 1880. The kids will like this, and older folks will enjoy the country store's stock of 19th-century goods.

South on Rte. 61, you can enjoy Wakulla Springs, with its glass-bottomed boats and refuge wildlife, and St. Marks, with its state museum. A turnoff a few miles south of Tallahassee takes you the short distance to the site of the Battle of Natural Bridge, where Confederate soldiers, bolstered by boys from the West Florida Seminary in Tallahassee, repulsed a Union march in 1865 to maintain Tallahassee's record as the only Confederate capital east of the Mississippi never captured by Union troops.

Westward from Tallahassee, remain with US 90, being especially careful at Chattahoochee lest you drift over the adjacent state line into Georgia. The mile-long Jim Woodruff dam creates Lake Seminole here, and you will have access to excellent lakeside facilities at Three Rivers State Park, a mile north of the town of Sneads, a few minutes farther along. Set your watches back an hour after passing westward through Chattahoochee, for you'll be in the Central Time Zone.

The Miracle Strip

Just to prove to yourself that Florida has at least a little bit of everything, stick with US 90 the twenty-four miles to Marianna, then swing off to the north three miles on State 167 to reach Florida Caverns State Park. This must be one of the few cave complexes anywhere with its own golf course, but rest assured the golf course is outside the cave. A hook or slice is trouble enough without stalactites adding some funny bounces.

The caverns, with well-lighted underground tours, are not the whole show; the aforementioned golf course—a 9-holer modeled after St. Andrews Golf Course—picnic and camping areas, and nature trails fill out the bill.

But to get on with it, best start southward to reach Florida's greatest expanse of beach, one hundred miles extending from Apalachicola to Pensacola and modestly termed the Miracle Strip.

Nine miles west of Marianna on US 90, turn south on US 231 for a fifty-five-mile straight shot into Panama City. This is summer resort country, with excellent reason, and out-of-state visitors to the area make it among the state's most popular. The figures are a bit misleading, however, for Alabamans and Georgians can make the trip every weekend, and lots do.

Some come in the winter, too, for although the temperature runs five to ten degrees below that of South Florida, the rates for good accommodations take a deeper dip.

In truth, there is not only more beach to spread the throng, but there is better beach along the Miracle Strip: it's pure white sand, quartz variety, and the offshore formation provides a good surf.

Panama City qualifies as a sort of Southern Atlantic City, complete with roller coaster and convention hall, but the fishing is better than Jersey's. The city claims as its share twenty-three miles of beach, a portion of it in St. Andrews State Park, with a 450-foot fishing pier to help pedestrian anglers get out there with the bigger ones. Sports fishing of all types is a big attraction, and the city's $7 million marina is home port for a considerable fleet of charter craft.

US 98 is the east-west coastal route, and in truth the Miracle Strip extends eastward of Panama City all the way to Port St. Joe and Apalachicola. The latter towns, however, haven't joined the cooperative promotion efforts of Panama City, Fort Walton Beach and Pensacola, and are chopped off the end of maps you may pick up in the area.

It's a bit quieter, therefore, to the east, but Port St. Joe is there all right, and in fact has been for a long spell: the state's first constitutional convention was held there. Apalachicola is also there, twenty miles east of Port St. Joe, and perhaps it deserves a complimentary visit from grateful tourists if for no better reason than that this is where air conditioning got its start.

Dr. John Gorrie built an ice-making machine here in 1845 and used it to cool the rooms of fever-stricken patients, but he was never able to raise enough cash to get the invention into production. He died in 1885, four years after securing a patent, and is one of the few Floridians to be honored in Washington's Statuary Hall.

Oysters, shrimp, and other seafoods are also an Apalachicola industry, but couldn't be if ice were still floated in, ensconced in sawdust, by ship.

Nearby Apalachicola National Forest is prime hunting land, and there are supervised black bear hunts during September and October. The area is also easily reached from Tallahassee.

But back to the Miracle Strip. Westward from Panama City via US 98 there remain some relatively unpopulated seashore vistas, by Florida standards at least, but you will have little trouble finding accommodations almost anywhere along the route.

Fort Walton Beach is approximately midway between Panama City and Pensacola and has staked out twenty-five miles of the beach. The town itself is built on and around a huge Indian temple mound, which has yielded important artifacts that trace American Indian culture back for ten thousand years.

In the center of town is a museum displaying some of the pottery, tools, and idols found here, although many earlier discoveries are on display at the Peabody Museum in Boston. There is also a diorama illustrating how the area may have looked five hundred years ago.

Inland from Fort Walton Beach is Eglin Air Force Base, which serves as a proving ground for both planes and weapons and where a climatic hangar tests equipment for use in arctic conditions. This is where Jimmy Doolittle's men trained for the raid on Tokyo. The base's huge proving grounds cover eight hundred square miles, but a large part of the land is a game preserve, and managed hunts for deer and turkey are held. There are conducted tours of the base.

Another marine aquarium, the Gulfarium, with leaping porpoises and the like, is on the beach where US 98 resumes its westward trek to Pensacola.

Anchors Aweigh

The last city in the state of Florida and on this tour, Pensacola was almost the first, historically. Don Tristan de Luna and an expedition of 1,500 landed here in 1559—six years before the founding of St. Augustine—and called the place Santa Maria. A storm destroyed de Luna's fleet two years later, however, and the settlement was abandoned.

Pensacola Beach has been a postwar bonanza; before 1945 Santa Rosa Island and its fifty-five miles of virgin beach were held undeveloped by the government. Now, with good causeway connections and with Fort

Pickens State Park on the western tip overlooking the channel entrance to Pensacola, tourism has joined the city's economic standbys.

Driving from Fort Walton Beach on US 98, you can cross over to Santa Rosa Island on State 399 at Navarre and continue to Fort Pickens. This is another one of those brick salesman's dreams which never really saw much action. The Confederates, who held Pensacola, ordered the Federals to surrender Fort Pickens in 1862 or face the consequences. The Federals said no, so the Rebels said they didn't want the danged thing anyway. Like Fort Jefferson in the Dry Tortugas, it wound up as a sort of prison. Geronimo was among those jailed here.

To reach Pensacola itself, take State 399 to US 98 and enter the city via a four-lane bridge. The downtown area offers a few historic sites, among them the Plaza Ferdinand VII at Palafox and Ferdinand streets, where Spanish headquarters were situated; the Panton trading post at Barcelona and Main streets; and Old Christ Church, now City Museum.

The Naval Air Station (take Garden St. to Navy Blvd. from downtown) has its own attractions in a blend of new and old. Free Navy buses take you on tours of the station, plus visits to Fort San Carlos and Fort Barrancas.

Included are visits to the Naval Aviation Museum, Sherman Field, home of the Blue Angels, a precision flying team, the giant aircraft carrier U.S.S. *Lexington* (on holidays you can go aboard), and the Old Pensacola lighthouse, built in 1825 and still working.

Each summer, Pensacola erupts in what it calls the Fiesta of Five Flags. Auxiliary events such as fishing tournaments begin as early as April, but the parades, fancy-dress balls, coronation, a reenactment of Don Tristan de Luna's landing, and a treasure hunt are concentrated in a single week in June.

PRACTICAL INFORMATION FOR FLORIDA

FACTS AND FIGURES. Florida takes its name from the Spanish *Pascua florida*, referring to the Easter Feast of Flowers. Its nicknames are Everglades State, Land of Flowers and Sunshine State. The state flower is the orange blossom; the state tree, the sabal palm; the state bird, the mockingbird. "In God We Trust" is the state motto. Stephen Foster's "Swannee River" is the state song.

Tallahassee is the state capital. State population is over 8,425,000.

Miles of excellent white beaches border Florida's long Atlantic and Gulf of Mexico coastlines, and the seaside plus a mild climate have combined to make the state one of the nation's leading resort areas, with tourism the state's major industry. Most of Florida is flat coastal lowlands, with only a few low hills in the center of the state. Next to its beaches, Florida's most notable natural scenery is in the wild swamps of the vast Everglades National Park at the state's southern tip. The mild climate that attracts tourists also makes it possible for Florida to be the nation's leading producer of citrus fruit and some vegetables, and food processing is the state's leading manufacturing industry.

The famous Florida climate is also noted for being considerably wet, especially in late summer and early fall.

HOW TO GET THERE. *By air:* Ozark, Piedmont, American, US Air, serve Gainesville, Jacksonville, Orlando, Panama City, Sarasota-Bradenton, Tallahassee, Tampa-St. Petersburg-Clearwater, Titusville, and West Palm Beach, depending on your point of origin. Air Florida, the all-jet inter-state carrier, has regular schedules to most of the important cities. Pan Am flies non-stop to Mexico City from Tampa/St. Petersburg/Clearwater; Pan Am also flies to Frankfurt and Paris from Tampa/St. Petersburg/Clearwater. Laker Skytrain inaugurated Tampa-London service in 1980.

Air Canada, Delta, Eastern fly from major cities in Canada to Florida's major airports, where you can connect easily to your destination within the state.

By train: Amtrak has service to Orlando, Winter Haven, Tampa, St. Petersburg, W. Palm Beach, Ft. Lauderdale and Hollywood. You might want to look into the popular "Week of Wheels" package, which includes use of a car.

By car: The speedy way to penetrate to the main East Coast resort area and Central Florida from the northeast is I-95. Not yet completed, in some parts you will have to use US 301, 15 and 17, which will slow you down somewhat. The beautiful, leisurely way is A1A. The frustrating, stoplight way is US 1. If going to the west coast from the northeast, take I-95 to Daytona Beach, then I-4 through Orlando to Tampa and I-275 to St. Petersburg.

Car rentals are possible in all major cities.

By bus: Trailways and Greyhound provide good service.

HOW TO GET AROUND. *By air:* Delta, Eastern, Pan Am,, TWA, U.S. Air, Braniff, Ozark, North Central, Piedmont, Air Florida or Commuter Airlines serve Daytona Beach, Eglin A.F. Base, Ft. Lauderdale, Ft. Myers, Gainesville, Lakeland, Melbourne, Ocala, Pensacola, Tampa/St. Petersburg/Clearwater, Sarasota/Bradenton, Jacksonville, Key West and other airports within the state. With deregulation, new routes are constantly added and more airlines fly in.

By car: Major routes, some still being perfected are: I-4 from Daytona Beach, on the eastern seaboard, to St. Petersburg, on the Gulf Coast; I-10 from Jacksonville to Alabama line projection. US 301 diverges from US 1 at Callahan, strikes off through Starke, Ocala, Wildwood, Dade City, passes Tampa, to Sarasota. State 60 goes cross-state from Clearwater, on the Gulf Coast, to Vero Beach, on the Atlantic Coast, taking Clearwater-Tampa Bay traffic. State 84 (Alligator Alley) is a toll shortcut from the lower west coast to the Ft. Lauderdale area—access 6 mi. east of Naples, running across the Everglades to US 27 at Andytown.

By boat: The intracoastal Waterway parallels the coastline and runs 349 mi. from Jacksonville to Miami. It is 8 ft. deep in the shallower southern portions. Canals abound, connecting to the ocean. Write: Florida Dept. of Natural Resources for *Florida Boating.*

By bus: In addition to Greyhound and Trailways, Gulf Coast Motor Lines offers service within the state.

TOURIST INFORMATION. Florida makes it easy for the tourist to get information with a proliferation of welcome stations for the motorist, a superbly equipped boaters' station at Fernandina Beach and tourist conscious airlines, which are geared up to answer all sorts of questions.

Welcome stations, dispensing information, are located on US 17, a few miles north of Yulee; at the junction of US 1, 301 and 23 at Hilliard; at Pensacola on US 90; Campbellton-Jennings on I-75; Havana on US 27; and on the Suncoast at 688 between Tampa and St. Petersburg.

Florida Development Commission, 107 W. Gaines St., Tallahassee, 32304; Florida Department of Natural Resources, Rm. 664, Larson Bldg., Tallahassee, 32304.

Pinellas Suncoast Tourist Development Suite 228, St. Petersburg/Clearwater Airport, Clearwater, 33520.

Visitor Information Center, 10 Castillo Dr., St. Augustine, 32084.

Marine Welcome Station, Fernandina Beach, is at the entrance to the Intracoastal Waterway.

 SEASONAL EVENTS. *January: Epiphany (Greek Cross Day),* Tarpon Springs; Epiphany rites begin with elaborate services at St. Nicholas Greek Orthodox Church, followed by a colorful "Diving for the cross" ceremony. *American Bowl Football Game,* Tampa, North-South all-star college seniors. *International Kite Flyoff,* Sarasota. *Old Island Days,* Key West; city pays tribute to its colorful past with elaborate celebration. Late Jan. through Feb. *Southwest Florida Championship Rodeo,* Fort Myers; parade, rodeo, horse show, gymkhana, dance, barbecue, and rodeo queen contest.

February: Old Island Days, Key West; city pays tribute to its colorful past with elaborate celebration. *Flagler Museum Open House,* Palm Beach. *Speed Weeks,* Daytona Beach; two full weeks of speed fare are offered at Daytona International Speedway. *National Sprints,* Tampa, spring car racing at Florida State Fair. *Edison Pageant of Light,* Fort Myers. *Ybor City Pirate Fiesta Days* (Gasparilla), Tampa; Tampa's Latin Quarter, Ybor City, has own special participation in the Gasparilla celebration. *Gasparilla Pirate Invasion,* Tampa; founded in 1904, Gasparilla has become one of Florida's most elaborate pageants. *Swamp Buggy Races,* Naples. *Black Hills Passion Play,* Lake Wales; reconstructs dramatic events of the seven last days in the life of Christ, mid-Feb. through Apr.

March: Bach Festival, Winter Park; unique musical experience attracts music lovers from around the country. *Daytona Motorcycle Classic,* Daytona Beach, *Gatornationals,* Gainesville; national record holders and former national champions in drag racing gather for top-ranked competition. *Sidewalk Art Festival,* Winter Park. *Antique Car Show,* Tarpon Springs. *Winter Lightning Championships,* St. Petersburg; small sailcraft compete in annual regatta hosted by St. Petersburg Yacht Club. *Fun 'n' Sun Festival,* Clearwater; State Pram Regatta and National Records Power Boat Race, Pancake Festival, State Baton Twirling Contest.

April: Delray Affair, Delray Beach; sidewalks turned into a showplace for arts, crafts, flowers, and produce. *King Neptune Frolics,* Sarasota; landing of King Neptune, Queen Athena, and Y Mystic Krewe, fish fry, water-ski show, art displays, boat parade, tennis tournaments, horse show, sports car rally, and children's parade. *Blessing of the Fleet,* St. Augustine; traditionally held on Palm Sunday, the ceremony of blessing shrimp boats and power craft is held at the Yacht Pier on Matanzas Bay.

May: Eight Flag Shrimp Boat Races, Fernandina Beach, only race of its kind in Florida. *Cypress Gardens Festival,* Cypress Gardens; Florida State Delta Wing Kite Championships, Aquarama Pool Shows, sky diving demonstrations, and fashion shows. *Sunfish Regatta,* Cypress Gardens, *Dunnellon Art Show,* Dunnellon. *Blessing of the Fleet,* Destin; each year on Ascension Day (40 days after Easter), this picturesque fishing village on Florida's Miracle Strip presents its Blessing of the Fleet ceremony. *New College Music Festival,* Sarasota. South's only music festival of its kind; among nation's top forty. World-famous artists perform. Six public concerts from beginning of May through mid-June.

June: West Florida Rodeo, Pensacola. All the ride-'em-cowboy events plus western musical groups to entertain. *Fiesta of Five Flags,* Pensacola. Reenactment of 1559 landing of Don Tristan de Luna and Spanish colonists. Concerts, parades, sports activities. *Sea Turtle Watch,* Jensen Beach. Ancient sea turtles deposit eggs on beach. *Florida Theatre Festival,* Daytona Beach; full program of seminars and entertainment, open to the public. *Classic Car Meet,* Cypress Gardens; some 100 classic and antique cars are on display, wknds. *"Cross and Sword,"* St. Augustine; outdoor drama by Pulitzer Prize winner Paul Green, Florida's official state play is based on the founding of St. Augustine by Pedro Menendez de Aviles in 1565, late June to Sept. *All-American Water Ski Championships,* Cypress Gardens. *Miss Florida Pageant,* Orlando; Florida's most beautiful and talented young women vie for the title of Miss Florida and the opportunity to represent state in Miss America Pageant in Atlantic City. *Jefferson County Watermelon Festival,* Monticello; Watermelon Queen Contest, parade and watermelon eating and seed-spitting contests.

July: Pirate Days, Treasure Island; pirates' arrival on beach, boat races, pancake day, sand castle contest, children's party, movies on beach, and fireworks. *Dixie Frolics,* Daytona Beach; Miss Daytona Beach Pageant, fireworks on beach, and Hound Dog Derby at kennel club. *International Moon Walk Festival,* Space Coast; county-wide celebration is presented on anniversary date of the crew's landing on moon. Special guests are NASA astronauts and show business celebrities; events are scheduled in Titusville, Melbourne, Cocoa Beach and other cities. *Rough Riders Day,* Tampa. Action takes place in Ybor Square to re-enact Teddy Roosevelt's 1898 departure for Cuba and the Spanish-American War. Parade, dancing in the streets.

August: Days in Spain Festival, St. Augustine. *Fun Day,* Wasau. Small northwest Florida town has day-long old-fashioned bullfrog races, possum auction, gopher races, cornpone baking, hog-calling, mule-rides, horse-wagon rides. *Fishathon,* St. Petersburg. Fishing event for boys and girls 12 years of age and younger. Cane poles and fishing gear provided—also cookies and cold drinks. Annually for over 30 years.

September: National Delta Wing Kite Championships, Cypress Gardens. *Labor Day Regatta,* Jacksonville. *Labor Day Regatta,* Sarasota, series of sailboat races. *World Championship Series Point Meet,* Gainesville; drag race competitors from throughout the nation compete for points and cash prizes.

October: Western Roundup, Pensacola; six-guns and shoot-outs, stagecoaches, can-can girls, Indian ceremonies and dances; TV and movie personalities are special guests. *World Finals Drag Race Championship,* Lakeland; national champions in drag racing gather at Lakeland International Raceway for the International Hot Rod Association's most prestigious race, the World Finals. *Rattlesnake Roundup and International Gopher Race,* San Antonio; bounties are paid on all rattlesnakes brought in during the Sept. 2 to Oct. 20 roundup, and prizes are awarded for both the heaviest and the largest number; activities include hourly snake shows, demonstrations of venom milking, first aid exhibitions, chicken dinner, pottery exhibit and appearance of former Indian Chief Osceola and family. The Gopher (Land Turtle) Races are presented in heat, semi-finals and International Championship run. *World's Chicken Pluckin' Championship,* Spring Hill. Miss Drumstick contest, performances by Masaryktown Czechoslovakian dancers, "chicken concertos," "plucking" concerts. Previous festival pluckin' records in *Guinness Book of World Records.* This small community northwest of Tampa is one of nation's leading poultry centers.

November: Exposition of Steam, Fort Lauderdale; Gold Coast Railroad presents interesting examples of the bygone era of steam. *Antique Car Meet,* Ormond Beach. *"Turkey Trot" Drag Races,* Gainesville; draws contestants from throughout the Southeast. *Walt Disney World Golf Classic,* national team championship featuring world's leading pro golfers paired in contest for $200,000 prize.

December: Tangerine Bowl, Orlando; holiday bowl game for two top football teams from small colleges. *Christmas Boat Parade,* Pompano Beach, *Gator Bowl Festival,* Jacksonville; the Gator Bowl football game, basketball tournament, boating regatta, and President's Ball. *Mt. Dora Christmas Regatta,* Mount Dora. Illuminated boats cruise along Lake Dora. *Candlelight Processional,* Lake Buena

Vista. Disney World Christmas extravaganza on Main St. U.S.A. from Cinderella Castle to Town Square, 800-voice choir carrying lighted candles. *Illuminated Christmas Boatacade,* Madeira Beach.

 NATIONAL PARKS. Warren F. Hamilton, former superintendent of *Everglades National Park,* said. "There is a subtle charm to the area unlike anything else in this country." Alligators, orchids, and stilt-walking birds are subtle? Well, it is subtle in the sense that the 'Glades' larger self creeps up on you like a wind rising rising. Only as your eyes become accustomed to the seeming sameness do you begin to glimpse the world within. Its grasslands, jungle hammocks, and mangrove forests bemuse the first-time visitor. To begin to *see,* in the Everglades, is to enjoy an unfolding more vital and strange than the opening of a great flower. Motorists en route to Flamingo, the civilized takeoff point for most ventures, have a better chance to understand all their journeys in the 'Glades if they are first briefed at the park entrance by a ranger.

When you get there, forget your first impression that nothing is moving in that great sawgrass marsh and look again for otter, bobcat, black bear, panther, whitetail deer, and 230 species of birds. Hammocks (small jungle islands which dot the 'Glades) are their natural habitat. The Park Service has established some elevated boardwalks so the visitor may peer down into the hammock itself. Here in their natural state are the tropical mixtures of orchids, mosses, and ferns imitated in the city gardens. No visitor, the rangers say, has been bitten by a poisonous snake, for the snakes mostly stay clear of inhabited sections. The Shark Valley Loop Road, south of the Tamiami Trail and the newest gateway to the park, provides a look at alligators, which sluggishly con the tourists for pretzels. An observation ramp over Shark Valley shows the Everglades nakedly to the eye from 35 feet up. Traveling speed on the Loop Road is 25 miles an hour; it has 21 stopping points, each with exhibits indicating the rocks, plants, animal and bird life to be found there.

The Visitor Center at Flamingo has a large dining room, cocktail lounge, a good-size motel, and a U.S. post office. The facilities include a large marina with dockside electric power, launching ramps for private boats, campgrounds, picnic areas, service station. Boats can be hired for fishing or sightseeing; there are also houseboat rentals and canoe trips into huge rookeries. Ranger naturalist lectures and excursions are free. Campsites continue to expand, with a growing corps of outdoor types springing up in the U.S. Admission to Everglades National Park is $2 per car and 50¢ on foot. Fees for campsites are $2 per car on improved sites and $1 on unimproved sites.

For *Apalachicola National Forest,* Tallahassee can be your take-off point. Silver Lake, one of the forest's chief attractions, is just 8 mi. W on Rte. 20 and three mi. S on Rte. 260. Many lakes and rivers lie in an extensive upper state area running to more than 500,000 acres. At Silver Lake, camping with tent or trailer is possible, and electrical and water connections are available for trailers—along with laundry, sewage, drinking water, and toilet facilities. Hitchcock Lake, 17 mi. N of Carrabelle and approached first on Rte. 67 and then a mile and a half east on Forest Service Road 125-B, has camping, with all the trimmings. Camel and Wright lakes are other main attractions. Wright Lake is two mi. S of Sumatra on Rte. 65 with a turn west for a mile and a half on Forest Service Road 101. Camel Lake is 5 mi. S of Bristol and Rte. 20, on Rtes. 67 and 379 and Forest Service Road 108.

In *Ocala National Forest,* private hunting and fishing camps mingle with a rather untamed semitropical wilderness managed by the Forestry Service. Canoe trips down Juniper Springs provide an exciting look at the inside of the forest. The recreation area at Alexander Springs has drawn attention of late from those who describe the camping glories of the state. What can you see here? If you know your way, there are glimpses of wild hog, alligator, otter, deer, even panther and bear.

In the springs, water temperature is 74 degrees most days of the year, and a wide, white sand beach lures the bather. A paddlewheeler makes scenic trips down Spring Creek. Head for the Alexander Springs area on State 445. It's 48 mi. from Ocala, or 45 mi. from US 1 at Daytona Beach. Marjorie Kinnan Rawlings' much-read book, *The Yearling,* was set in the Big Scrub, which gives the forest its native character. The *Big Scrub Hunt Camp* is located at a junction of Forest Service roads 88 and 73, 12 mi. S of Central Tower and Rte. 40. Pens for hunting dogs are here, and a meat storage house for those who come in with game. Halfmoon Lake Campground, 20 mi. W of Astor on State 40 (south one and a quarter miles on Forest Service Road 79), sits on a large lake in a beautiful oak hammock. It has boat launching facilities.

In *Osceola National Forest,* the chief attraction is a 2,000-acre natural lake. To reach Ocean Pond go two and a half miles north of US 90 at Olustee. Lake City is also in the vicinity of the forest, which runs to 157,000 flattish acres. Hunters head for the nearby Osceola Game Management Area, where a special permit is required. Ocean Pond has 24 camping and picnicking units, and a boat dock with launching ramp.

Fort de Soto National Memorial Park is a prime 900-acre picnicking area near St. Petersburg. It has smooth roads and consists of five islands with white beaches, well dispersed picnic tables and charcoal grills. You can approach by boat. Take excursion craft from St. Petersburg, or drive in by toll causeway (65 cents total) from US 19 near Sunshine Parkway. Near the fort itself, at the southwest end, fishermen can cast from a 1,000-foot pier. Another long pier overlooks Tampa Bay. Fine facilities for tenters at St. Christopher Key. Units also are being developed on St. Jean Key.

Gulf Islands National Seashore, almost 76,000 acres, stretches from Destin all the way to Ship Island near Gulfport, Mississippi. Excellent beachfront camping, or by Fort Pickens. Admission fee to the Fort Pickens area. Ranger programs scheduled. For details, write to Gulf Islands National Seashore, P. O. Box 100, Gulf Breeze 32561.

Canaveral National Seashore, encompassing 57,000 acres, is located north of the Kennedy Space Center. The Visitor Center is open every day from 7:30 A.M. to 7:30 P.M. Beautiful beaches for swimming; excellent fishing.

 STATE PARKS. Despite the often justified concern that Florida is rapidly becoming overdeveloped, there are many areas which remain in a natural condition. Happily, many of those areas shall remain so permanently, as state parks. Parks that offer recreational and camping facilities have a 25¢ entrance fee, with additional fees for camping sites. The parks in the following list are easy to get to and have ample facilities for making visitors comfortable. In some of them, deeper exploration is available for the more adventuresome.

Anastasia is 3 mi. S of St. Augustine on A1A. 1,035 acres with facilities for camping, picnicking, boating, nature trails, skin diving and scuba diving.

Caladesi Island State Park, offshore Dunedin. Swimming, boating, fishing, skin diving, scuba diving, picnicking, 60-ft. observation tower.

Bill Baggs Cape Florida State Park, on the southern tip of Key Biscayne, historic *Cape Florida Lighthouse,* all sports and picnicking.

Collier-Seminole State Park is 12 mi. NE of Marco where Big Cypress Swamp joins the Everglades. Historically, the last refuge of Seminole Indians. Picnicking, boating, ramp, fishing, camping, and nature trails.

Falling Waters State Recreation Area is a 154-acre park 3 mi. S. of Chipley off Rte. 77A. Picnicking, camping, swimming, nature trails.

Faver-Dykes State Park, 752 acres of woodlands and marsh. Picnicking, camping, fishing, boat ramp, boating, and hiking. 15 mi. S. of St. Augustine.

Florida Caverns State Park, 3 mi. N of Marianna. Picnicking, camping, boating, swimming, skin diving and scuba diving, fishing, concession, nature trails, and youth camping area.

Fort Clinch State Park has museum exhibits, nature trails. On State A1A at Fernandina Beach; 1,086 acres, with picnicking, fishing barbecue pits, tent and trailer camps, recreation lodge. Union Army-uniformed Park Rangers staff garrison in Living History exhibit.

Fort Gadsden State Historic Site, south of Sumatra on State 65, has 78 acres cut with nature trails. Picnicking facilities and historical and recreational spots.

Mike Roess Gold Head Branch State Park has vacation cabins and barbecue pits with 1,338 acres of recreational park. 6 mi. NE of Keystone Heights on State 21. Fishing, boating, rentals, ramps, water skiing, swimming, skin diving and scuba diving, picnicking, concession, camping.

Highlands Hammock State Park is 6 mi. W of Sebring off US 98. Has 3,800 acres, including picnicking, fireplaces, shelters, concession, camping, nature trails.

Hillsborough River State Park is accented by a swinging bridge which spans the river. Picnicking, concession, camping, boating, rentals, skin diving and scuba diving, fishing. 6 mi. SW of Zephyrhills.

Hontoon Island State Park, 1,060-acre park 6 mi. W of De Land, accessible only by boat. Tent camping only, picnicking, cottages for rent, observation tower, boating, nature trails, marina, concession, boat rentals, fishing.

Ichetucknee Springs State Park, 16 mi. NW of High Springs, Rte, 47N, 238W from Fort White. 2,241 acres, borders the Ichetucknee River. Especially popular for tubing, swimming, skin diving and scuba diving. Picnicking, fishing and boating. 8:30 to sundown.

John Pennekamp Coral Reef State Park is the first underwater park in the United States. 3 mi. NE of Key Largo. Part of only living coral reef formations in North America. It is a mecca for skin divers. Picnicking, swimming, fishing, marina, boat rentals, launching facilities, nature trails, concession and camping.

Jonathan Dickinson State Park is 3 mi. N of Jupiter on US 1 and has 8,923 acres. Picnicking, camping, concession shelters, playground equipment, cabins, swimming, fishing, boating, rentals, ramps, nature trails, bicycle rentals, horseback riding, guided tours.

Little Talbot Island State Park, 17 mi. E of Jacksonville on A1A. 2,500-acre island park with picnicking, swimming, museum, fishing, boating, sand dunes, bathhouse, playgrounds, concession, camping, thick forest, skin diving and scuba diving, and youth camping area.

Long Key State Recreation Area is 291 acres of island in the Florida Keys. Camping, picnicking, swimming, fishing, boating, skin diving and scuba diving, playground equipment, youth camping area and concession. Located on Long Key at Layington.

Manatee Springs State Park. 8 mi. W of Chiefland on Rte. 320. 1,799-acre site with camping, picnicking, concessions, swimming, skin diving, scuba diving, boat ramp, rentals, fishing, nature trails.

Myakka River State Park, nationally noted for variety and quantity of birds, 17 mi. SE of Sarasota, 28,875 acres. Picnicking, concession, fishing, boat rentals, cabins, camping, nature trails, nature museums, and backpacking trail.

Ochlockonee River State Park, 4 mi. N of Panacea. Heavily wooded land, with swimming, boating, picnicking, fishing, and camping.

O'Leno State Park, 9 mi. N of High Springs on US 41, has 1,717 acres. Picnicking, camping, swimming, skin diving and scuba diving, fishing, boating, well-equipped group camp, and nature trails.

Pepper Park State Park, E of Fort Pierce on State A1A. 32 acres of white sand beach with footbridge across the Indian River to 958-acre Jack Island. Picnicking, swimming, fishing, boating, skin diving and scuba diving, concession, guided tours. Museum of local history.

St. Andrews State Recreation Area has 1,022 acres, 3 mi. E of Panama City Beach. Camping, picnicking, concession, swimming, skin diving and scuba diving, fishing, boating, ramp, dock, museum exhibits.

St. Joseph Peninsula State Park has one of most beautiful beaches in Florida. 20 mi. W of Port St. Joe. Camping, swimming, fishing, boating, skin diving and scuba diving, picnicking, concession, playground equipment, boat rentals.

Suwannee River State Park has 1,838 acres of scenic, historical and recreation sites. 13 mi. W of Live Oak on US 90. Camping, picnicking, stoves, concession, fishing, boating, ramps, swimming, youth camping area, and nature trail.

Tomoka State Park, 2 mi. N of Ormond Beach, is an archeological park on 915 acres of land with scenic historical interest. Camping, picnicking, concession, shelters, playground, fishing, launching ramp, dock, nature trails and museum with exhibits.

Torreya State Park, on State 20, 4 mi. E of Blountstown. Confederate gun pits, old river boat landing. Fishing, picnicking, concession, barbecue pits, camping, and nature trails.

Wekiwa Springs State Park, E of Apopka on State 436. Picnicking, nature trails, fishing, swimming, boating, skin diving and scuba diving.

Wiggins Pass. 6 mi. S of Bonita Springs. Picnicking, swimming, saltwater fishing, boating.

 CAMPING OUT. Florida is a year-round affair, although the best times are winter (except in cold spells) and spring. Mosquitoes and rain are most likely to intrude in spring, summer or early fall. Florida state parks permit camping for $4 per day ($5 for parks in the Florida Keys only) on a 2-wk. permit issued by the park superintendent, for up to and including four people in one family. Additional campers using the site will be charged $1 per person (maximum persons per site is eight). Exceptions will be made for families with minor children. Fees for extra cars at a campsite are $1 nightly. More than 2600 campsites are available, with no additional charge for fishing, swimming, picnicking or boat ramps. Campsites may be reserved by telephone only directly to the parks. Many camp areas in the national forests permit 3-wk. stays; fees vary.

 TRAILER TIPS. Here are just a few of the more elaborate sites available across the state:

Guernsey City. A mobile waterfront community at Tampa on the sandy beaches of Old Tampa Bay. 4851 Gandy Blvd. (write for brochure). *El Rancho Village.* At Bradenton. It's one of the larger Florida parks. Citrus trees and concrete patios. Door-to-door mail delivery. Beaches and fishing nearby. Adults only and no pets. Rte. 301 and Cortez Road. Write for color brochure. *Mobilemanor Inn.* They want the retired ("adults only") for this park at 2866 Okeechobee Road in West Palm Beach. Ten-minute drive to the ocean. Served by city buses. Fishing and boating on lake. Pool. One block to shopping center. Dog-racing, jai alai, baseball nearby.

Sarasota Mobile Home Park. In their air-conditioned auditorium, year-round dances. Free movies, too. Game nights. Big layout of shuffleboard courts. Calls itself "One of America's finest and oldest trailer parks." US 301 at Laurel St. *Shangri-La.* Dramatic pool under a tremendous screened enclosure. Putting green for golfers and lawn croquet. Mail at the door, sodded lawns, city water. On the West Coast, it's between Largo and Clearwater. *Crystal Bay Mobile Estates.* Between Clearwater and Tarpon Springs. Pool and marina (applications taken for membership in Crystal Bay Yacht Club). Recreation hall and shuffleboard courts. Reached on A19. 5 min. drive to Gulf fishing. *Whispering Creek Village.* At Fort Pierce on US 1 and Airport Road. Pool and party cook-out facilities with city sewer service, private phones, modern laundry, barber shop, hobby rooms, library lounge. *Colonial Acres.* Pool and putting green, recreation hall, planned activities. Barbecue and picnic area, twice weekly garbage collection, mail at the door, street lights. 9674 NW 10th Ave., Miami. *Rainbow Isles.* Pompano Beach waterfront setting at 751 S. Federal Hwy. Over a hundred spaces on the water. Patios and paved roads, city water, putting green, pool, luggage storage, free lawn maintenance. *Bay Pines Park.* Three private lakes stocked for fishing in a St. Petersburg setting at 1005 Bay Pines Blvd. A19. Tall pines and oaks surround the trailer spaces. Lots for the largest. Recreation hall, planned fun, near beaches. "Largest adult park in Florida," they claim, with over 400 occupied lots and still expanding.

 HOT SPRINGS. A year-round 87 degrees is the constant temperature of *Warm Mineral Springs,* 12 mi. below Venice on US 41. No hotter springs exist in Florida. Approximately 10 million gallons flow daily. The Warm Mineral Springs Inn has 29 units plus nearby cottages. It usually has a brisk business of arthritis victims testing the waters. The Inn is inexpensive.

For sightseeing purposes, the cooler springs of Florida are unmatched in the nation, and many have been developed as tourist attractions.

Some places to go: *Silver Springs,* near Ocala on State 40. Its daily discharge is 834 million gallons. It's a famous resort, sought after by the outdoor-minded. *Rainbow Springs,* near Dunnellon on US 41, has a larger flow than any limestone spring in the U.S. and possibly the world (659 million gallons). Underwater glimpses here from submarine boats at exotic marine growths and browsing fish. *Homosassa Springs,* on US 19, and *Salt Springs,* 28 mi. E of Ocala on 19, both have saltwater fish swimming in them. Observatory portholes view directly on mangrove snapper, sea trout, snook, channel bass, sheepshead at Homosassa. It's called "Nature's Fish Bowl." In *Ocala National Forest,* campers go to *Juniper Springs,* off Rte. 40; *Silver Gleen,* on State 19; *Alexander Springs,* 14 mi. from Umatilla on State 19 and 445. "A virtual Eden" says the State Development Commission of Alexander Springs. Below Tallahassee at *Natural Bridge,* springs bubble in a river that appears and disappears. More remote springs (you boat in or have to go by winding, unpaved road) are *Cypress Springs* near Vernon, and *Ichatucknee Springs* near Hildreth on State 47 and State 238. A principal attraction: *Ponce De Leon Springs,* 8 mi. N of De Land, reached on US 17, at the town of DeLeon Springs.

 MUSEUMS AND GALLERIES. *Historical: Pensacola Historical Museum.* 405 S. Adams St. Housed in 1832 Old Christ Church. Closed Mon. Free.

St. Petersburg: Haas Museum & Grace S. Turner House & Village, 3511 2nd Ave. Antiques. Closed Mon., Sept.

Tallahassee: The capitol building, *Division of Archives, History & Records Management,* 401 Gaines St. Archeological history museum.

Tampa: Tampa Municipal Museum, in the south wing of the U. of Tampa's main building. Mon. to Sat. Closed Aug. Free.

Art: Daytona Beach: Museum of Arts and Sciences, 1040 Museum Blvd. Cuban paintings, F. Batista collection; U.S., Caribbean, and Central American fine and decorative arts. Closed nat'l. holidays. Free. Charge for planetarium.

Fort Lauderdale: Fort Lauderdale Museum of the Arts, 426 East Las Olas Blvd. Emphasis on American and European graphics of the 19th and 20th centuries. Southwestern American Indian ceramics and basketry, and collection of Japanese *Inro* and *Netsuke.* Special exhibitions Sept. to July. Closed Mon. and August. Free.

Gainesville: University Gallery, U. of Florida, S.W. 13th St. and 4th Ave. Study collection contains historic and contemporary prints and Oriental (India) paintings and small sculptures. Closed Sat., holidays and Sept. Free.

122   FLORIDA

Florida State Museum on U. of Florida campus has outstanding historical exhibits and Mayan walk-through palace.
Jacksonville: Cummer Gallery of Art, 829 Riverside Ave. Western European art from 6th century B.C. to present. Free. Closed Mon. & nat'l. holidays; *Jacksonville Art Museum,* 4106 Blvd. Center Dr. Emphasis on 20th-century works by living artists and pre-Columbian art. Free. Closed Aug. and legal holidays.
Orlando: Loch Haven Art Center, Inc., 2416 North Mills Ave. Small collection 20th-century American paintings, graphics. Closed Mon. and holidays. Free.
Palm Beach: The Society of the Four Arts. Four Arts Plaza. Special exhibitions and performing arts events. Closed Sat. Botanic gardens: open all year. Free.
Pensacola: Pensacola Art Association, 407 S. Jefferson St. Graphics and regional paintings. Closed Mon. and nat'l holidays. Free.
St. Augustine: Pan American Building, 97 St. George St. Art gallery with South American paintings, sculptures and artifacts.
St. Petersburg: Museum of Fine Arts, 255 Beach Dr. N. 9 galleries, including 3 authentic English and French period rooms. Closed Mon., July. *Dali Museum,* opening 1982, at 1000 Third St. So., will house extensive privately owned collection.
Tallahassee: Florida State University Art Gallery, Fine Arts Bldg. Temporary exhibitions of collections and special exhibitions. Free. Closed school holidays: *Le Moyne Art Gallery,* N. Gadsden St. Free.
Tampa: Florida Center for the Arts, U. of S. Fla., 4202 E. Fowler Ave. 25 art exhibitions presented annually. Free. Closed university holidays.
West Palm Beach: Norton Gallery, 1451 S. Olive Ave. Chinese jades and many collections. Free.
Winter Park: Morse Gallery of Art., Holt Ave., Rollins College. American and European art, glass, stained glass windows. Free. Closed holidays and school vacation.

 HISTORIC SITES. *Apalachicola: John Gorrie State Historic Memorial,* Ave. D & 6 St. Features exhibits of early local history. *Bradenton: DeSoto National Memorial,* 75th St. Free. *Bushnell: Dade Battlefield State Historic Site,* on US 301. Site of infamous Dade Massacre in 1836, which touched off Second Seminole War. Monuments mark the battlefield, museum contains exhibits and artifacts of the battle. 80-acre recreational site. Admission 25¢. *Cedar Key: Cedar Key State Memorial.* State 24. 19 acres of scenic and historical sights, including the St. Clair Whitman Museum. *Crystal River: Crystal River State Archeological Site,* off US 19, 98. One of the most spectacular and important pre-Columbian Indian sites in Florida. Museum houses Indian artifacts. *Ellenton: Gamble Mansion State Museum,* US 301, 4 mi. NE of Bradenton. *Fort Myers: Edison Home Museum,* 2341 McGregor Blvd. First prefabricated home built in Maine and brought to Florida by boat, housing Edison's inventions. *Homasassa Springs: Yulee Sugar Mill State Historic Site.* 5 mi. W of US 19 on State 490. Part of sugar-making machinery built by David Levy Yulee, Florida's first U.S. Senator and Confederate leader. Free. *Jacksonville: Fort Caroline National Memorial,* 12713 Ft. Caroline Rd. Free.

Key West: Audubon House, Whitehead & Greene Sts. Close to the Coast Guard Station, almost as far south as you can go. *New Smyrna Beach: New Smyrna State Historic Site,* 1 mi. W on Rte. 44. Remains of a large sugar mill destroyed by Indians during Seminole War. Free.

Olustee: Olustee Battlefield State Historic Site Museum, off US 90, 2 mi. E. *Port St. Joe: Constitution Historic Memorial.* On US 98. 12 acres of historical and scenic sights, museum exhibits.

Rattlesnake Island: Fort Matanzas National Monument, 14 mi. S of St. Augustine. Free.

St. Augustine: All of St. Augustine is, in fact, one enormous historic site, with the early days of American development written indelibly in crumbling or reconstructed stone. The Visitor Information Center has a free Visitor's Guide to help you decide which of dozens of historical buildings you want to see. The *Historic St. Augustine Preservation Board* has strip tickets to all the historic buildings. *Castillo de San Marcos,* located on site of an original Spanish fort. *St. Petersburg: Madira Bickel Mound.* 10-acre historic memorial located at Terra Cela Island off US 41 S of St. Petersburg. *Tallahassee: Natural Bridge State Historic Site* marks spot where Confederate forces repulsed a Federal force to prevent capture of the state capitol. Free. *Prince & Princess Mural Home of Bellevue.* Wknds.

 TOURS. *Gray Line Tours* and *American Sightseeing Bus Tours* operate all over the state. Seven of their most popular tours are Walt Disney World, Sea World, Kennedy Space Center, Cypress Gardens, Busch Gardens, Silver Springs, St. Augustine. Gray Line also conducts tours of major cities in the state, such as Miami, Fort Lauderdale, St. Petersburg, Tampa, and special tours to attractions within the cities. Tours of varying lengths (3½ hrs. to one day).

Florida Parlor Car Tours offers a seven-day Circle Tour from Jacksonville, which visits Silver Springs, Weeki Wachee Springs, St. Petersburg, Cypress Gardens, the Everglades, Miami Beach, Miami, Parrot Jungle, Key West, Fort Lauderdale, Walt Disney World, Marineland and St. Augustine among other places. *Tauck Tours,* departing from Jacksonville, has a similar nine-day Florida Circle Tour. *Greyhound, Continental,* and *Trailways* all offer special tours from cities around the country to various Florida locations and attractions. Greyhound also operates a good many local tours.

By Boat: The *Captain Anderson* features two-hour narrated cruises of the St. Pete Beach area, daily at 2 p.m. (except Sun.). Sunset dinner-dance cruises sail out at 7 p.m. and return at 10 p.m. Private charters available, too. Behind Dolphin Shopping Village on St. Petersburg Beach. From mid-Oct. to mid-May. The *Steven Thomas,* a sleek new yacht, sails from St. Petersburg's waterfront (near HMS *Bounty*) for two sightseeing cruises daily in season. Snack bar, soft drinks.

St. Augustine's sightseeing cruise takes 1½ hr., leaves from Municipal Yacht Pier, Avenida Menendez. In *Titusville* boat tours leave from Westlands Marina daily. *Winter Park* has a narrated tour of the canals and lakes to view estates, azaleas, Rollins College, etc. There's also a 2-hr. narrated cruise on the *Commodore II* leaving from Bill King's Marina in Marathon, Oct. to May and July to Labor Day. And at *Homosassa Springs,* US 19, there is a scenic boat trip.

Glass-bottom boats will open a whole new world. Silver Springs, Wakulla Springs.

You can rent a river cruiser on pontoons from *Sun Line Leisure* in Deland. The fleet of 30 cruisers is available for the St. Johns River trip, which can go as far north as Jacksonville, about 130 nautical miles. Information at *Sun Line Leisure,* P.O. Box 3349, Deland 32720.

Key Largo has a 2-hr. boat trip to the coral reefs daily if the weather is good and *Key West* a 2-hr. reef cruise on the *Fireball* from the Gulf to the ocean daily, if clear, except for one week in May and in Oct.

Il Cristo Degli Abissi (Christ of the Abysses), a 9-ft. bronze replica of an Italian statue, can be glimpsed by sightseers who take a glass-bottom boat tour of the *John Pennekamp Coral Reef State Park.* Skeletons of old ships lie here with tropical fish swimming among them. The remarkably visible reef has 40 kinds of coral and is 21 mi. long. The trip lasts 2½ hrs.; leaves three times daily. Those who are willing to take the underwater tour can hire diving equipment on the spot—tank with air, masks, fins, snorkel.

Jungle Queen cruises, leaving from Fort Lauderdale's huge and beautiful Bahia Mar Yacht Basin, has two sailings daily. The Jungle Queen passes Venetian Isles, winds through Fort Lauderdale, takes in exotic gardens, tropical bird grounds, alligator wrestling, Seminoles and their chickees, Dania Waterway, Broward International Airport, Hollywood, Intracoastal Waterway, Port Everglades and

Stranahan River. From mid-Jan. to May there are also dinner cruises with entertainment. The *Paddlewheel Queen* leaves from 1 blk. S. of Oakland Park Beach Bridge on daytime and evening dinner cruises.

Everglades Jungles Cruises leaves from City Yacht Basin, Fort Myers, for a 3-hr. trip up Caloosakachee River to Everglades. Birds, rookeries, wild orchids and alligators can be seen. No cruises in Sept. or on Mon. from May to Aug. and Nov. to Christmas.

If you have the time, take a *Shanty Boat Cruise* on the *Lazy Bones* from Caloosakatchee River into Everglades. There's time allotted to explore by swamp buggy and air boat and to visit heron and egret rookeries. Departs on Mon. from Orange River Dock, Nov. to Apr. and July, returns Fri. No children under 16. For reservations write Rte. 29, Box 434, Fort Myers 33905, or tel. 694-3401.

At *Myakka River State Park,* on State 72, 17 mi. E of Sarasota, you can see an exciting variety of wildlife.

Island and Casino Tours. Cruise ships leave daily from Dodge Island port in Miami, and Port Everglades in Fort Lauderdale. The casinos at Freeport and Paradise Island are the favored destinations. Island life lures non-gamblers, also, to Nassau, and colorful Caribbean ports.

By train. When you hit the Florida Keys, you can take the *Conch Train Tour,* which is narrated. Fort Lauderdale has three train tours: *Voyager Train* leaves from Bahia Mar Yacht Basin for an 18-mi., 1½ hr. trip through the city, daily. There is also from the same location a Safari Tour, 25 mi., daily. The *Gold Coast Railroad,* 811 S.W. 34th St., offers a steam train tour Sun. The fee includes inspection of an armored car used by Presidents Roosevelt, Truman and Eisenhower, and a museum car with railroading souvenirs. *St. Augustine's* sightseeing train trip offers a 24-hr. ticket, stop-off privileges, and pkg. tours. The regular 7-mi., 1-hr. narrated trip leaves 3 Cordova St. daily, except Christmas, every quarter hr.

 SPECIAL INTEREST TOURS. *Wild life tours* can be arranged during the winter season into remote areas where the eagles and egrets fly. Contact the Audubon Center of Greater West Palm Beach Chamber of Commerce. Naturalist guides take nature tours through Okefenokee, Dry Tortugas and other spots.

The Florida traveler becomes a *bird watcher* in spite of himself. Tall water birds grace the canals and the lower coast has cowbirds among the sea cows. Only here and in Alaska can you see the bald eagle with his treetop nest. You'll see them in the Kissimmee River Valley, Everglades National Park and Ocala National Forest. At Myakka River State Park, 17 mi. E of Sarasota, a 30-ft.-high observation tower offers a glimpse of a great water bird rookery. Six miles of the road is in too bad shape for cars, you'll have to go by bus. An evening train tour leaves Tues. to Sat. at 7:30 (8:30 in summer). The frigate bird exists in great concentration on Bird and Kitchell keys, near Fort Myers. Southeast of Fort Myers a great nesting colony of wood storks inhabits Corkscrew Swamp at Immokalee. The pelican, celebrated for his beak, actually is most astounding in his diving habits. You can see his amazingly funny slop-plop into the water at Pelican Island, 15 mi. N of Vero Beach in the Indian River, where up to 3,500 pelicans hatch annually. Access is by boat only. The Cape Kennedy area has been called the best bird-watching territory in the country—and not for its "iron birds," either: *Suncoast Seabird Sanctuary.* Ralph Heath has received national fame for his tender, loving care to sick and injured land and seabirds. Open 7 days a week during daylight hours. Free. 18328 Gulf Blvd., Indian Shores, near St. Pete Beach.

Turtle watching: Female sea turtles come shoreward on a July night to lay their eggs in the sand. Local newspapers keep track, and can tell you which nights to stake yourself out on the shoreline. Mother digs a hole and lays up to 300 eggs in 45 min. She is jittery beforehand, but is not easily disturbed once she's embarked on egglaying. Try Jensen Beach in Martin County.

GARDENS. Garden visiting in Florida is nothing like tulip time in the Netherlands. Enter a noted garden in this state (there are many, for its very name means "flowers"), and you will often find you have come not to a garden but a garden-jungle. Considerable commercial competition has been exerted by tropical planters trying to outdo each other. At Cape Coral a Mount Rushmore in miniature has taken shape in the gardens created for a pathway known as the *Avenue of Roses.* Many growers, not geared up to make sculptured mountains within their jungles, simply strive for the closest possible imitation of the more spectacular aspect of the tropical and subtropical forests.

One of the first to be seized with a desire to realize a true tropic garden was the inventor, Thomas A. Edison. Edison's Tropic Gardens, open to the public, are located within the laboratory he left at his winter home at Fort Myers. This botanical garden ("one of the most complete in America") must be much as he pictured it when he first began to plant. The two-inch banyan tree brought him from India in 1925 by Harvey Firestone is now more than 250 feet around the trunk. Edison found the materials of invention growing right out of the ground. The swimming pool he built in 1900 was reinforced with the same material he used for electric-light filaments—bamboo. It was a natural stand of bamboo that helped attract him to Fort Myers. His swimming pool has no leak as yet. The artesian well which fills it also supplies the underground irrigation for the gardens. Visit Edison Tropical Gardens.

Edison had the jump on most of those who now capitalize on Florida's rare propensity to throw up lush gardens on a quick schedule. But fabulous gardens abound. Here are a few of them:

Bok Singing Tower, southeast of Cypress Gardens, houses one of the world's largest carillons. The 205-foot tower is made of coquina stone and marble, surrounded by sub-tropical gardens and nature trails.

Busch Gardens— yes, they owe everything to Anheuser Busch and to Adolphus Busch, August A. Busch, Sr., and Adolphus Busch, III. Showmanship with birds mingles with a concentration of 150,000 trees and shrubs. Each fall 50,000 annuals are planted. No other Florida garden hands out a brochure that says, "Relax in the Hospitality House and enjoy the world's finest beers. With our compliments, of course." A monorail passes through "African veldt inhabited by hippos, rhinos, waterbuck, and wildebeest." As Horace Sutton says: "The drinking man's Disneyland." 3000 Busch Blvd., Tampa.

In the *Caribbean Gardens* at *Naples* winding paths take the visitor through an ordered jungle interspliced with lagoons. Waterbirds in great numbers; and there are several bird shows daily.

Cypress Gardens, east of Lakeland, a world-famous attraction of tropical plants and flowers, and water-ski shows of champions and aqua maids.

Marie Selby Botanical Gardens, opened in Sarasota in 1975, created for scientific research. Offers guided tours, lectures and botanical courses. Includes stroll through the Selby house, built in 1920s, and display greenhouse.

Merritt Island Tropical Nursery was called by Logan Owen, Jr., "a kind of United Nations of Tropical plants that grow naturally on the island plus scores of tropical and semitropical specimens from most of the countries in the torrid zone." Prospective purchasers only are invited to tour. Between the missile firing range at Cape Kennedy and the mainland.

Sarasota Jungle Gardens, highly accessible, is at 3701 Bay Shore Road, just off US 41. Cactus as well as tropical plantings grow along the jungle lake. Flamingos, swans, and other waterbirds flash in the sun-streaked waters.

Maclay State Gardens, 51½ mi. N of Tallahassee, planted as a private estate garden, has one of the South's finest azalea and camellia collections. The original Aunt Jettyu Camellia—125 yrs. old—blooms there. Lake Hall picnic area is adjacent; open year round. Swimming, skin diving and scuba diving, boating, fishing, picnicking and concession. Open 9 to sunset all year.

Sunken Gardens. 1825 Fourth St. N. Georgeous tropical gardens with thousands of flowers, plants, and trees from all over the world. Orchid Arbor. Walk-through aviary of colorful exotic and native birds. King of Kings exhibit.

Tiki Gardens, Indian Rocks Beach (nr. St. Pete Beach), features a Polynesian Adventure Trail, a Mangrove Jungle Walk and a thicket of shops, as well as a pleasant restaurant with views of birds, beasts and fish while dining.

Washington Oaks State Gardens was originally a Spanish land grant to Bautesta Don Juan Ferreira in 1815. Nature museum, picnicking, nature trails and fishing. Three mi. S of Marineland. *Botanic Gardens* at the Society of the Four Arts, Palm Beach, is open daily. Free.

 MUSIC. Among the many orchestras in the Sunshine State are the *Florida Symphony* (Orlando), *Fort Lauderdale Symphony, Hollywood Philharmonic, Jacksonville Symphony, Pensacola Symphony. Central Florida Community Orchestra* (Winter Park), *Palm Beach Symphony, Lakeland Symphony Orchestra.* All are active throughout the winter season, and a number give pops concerts in late spring and summer. The *Florida Gulf Coast Symphony Orchestra* performs regularly at McKay Auditorium, Tampa, Nov. to late Apr. and at Bayfront Auditorium, St. Petersburg, early Nov. to early May.

The *Asolo Opera Co.,* Sarasota, offers opera in English mid-Jan. to mid-Feb. Also in Sarasota, *Van Wezel Performing Arts Hall,* 777 N. Tamiami Trail, offers a varied program Sept. to June.

Outstanding annual musical events in Florida include the *Florida Folk Festival* at White Springs in early May, when over 2,000 performers present choral and dance works; *Winter Park's Bach Festival* (mid-Feb.); *Stephen Foster Week,* White Springs (mid-Jan.); *New College Summer Music Festival,* Sarasota, wkends in June. *Hollywood's Seven Lively Arts Festival* (mid-Feb.) offers everything from classic drama to jazz concerts.

 STAGE AND REVUES. Popular plays are presented in winter at the *Royal Poinciana Playhouse,* Palm Beach. From early Feb. to mid-Apr. the *Black Hills Passion Play* can be seen at the Passion Play Amphitheater, nr. Lake Wales. Sarasota offers an 8-month season of plays at *Asolo Theater,* a gem of an Italian 18th-century theater. (Mid-Feb. to Aug., nightly except Mon.; matinees Tues., Wed., Sat.) The *Players* is a Sarasota community theater group with nightly performances mid-Oct to mid-May at 838 N. Tamiami Trail. *Daytona Playhouse,* 100 Jessamine Blvd., presents drama, comedy and musicals in late Oct. to early June, as well as a musical in Aug. *Lake Worth's Playhouse* and *Lakeland's Theatre-in-the-Round* at Florida Southern College, schedule regular performances in winter. Broadway musicals and plays are presented at *Parker Playhouse,* Fort Lauderdale, late Dec. to mid-Apr. Mon. to Sat.; matinees on Wed., Sat. The *Sunrise Music Theater,* near Fort Lauderdale, has booked such superstars as Frank Sinatra. Now a National Historic Landmark, the ornate *Tampa Theater,* downtown Tampa, features live entertainment and film festivals. St. Petersburg's *Bayfront Center* offers an interesting program of Broadway plays, ice-skating revues, and personal appearances by entertainment celebrities.

 CASINOS. The closest casino to Florida is in the Bahamas. Extralegal card games are common in south Florida, but powerful factions continue to defeat those who would make gambling go the Nevada way. The procasino element hasn't overcome the objections of Florida governors from nonresort counties; nor has it been able to sway objecting caterers, who fear the wrong kind of visitor. Palm Beach and West Palm Beach (as well as Miami and Miami Beach) have become, therefore, prime jumping-off spots for visitors lured by the promise of close action with a pair of dice. But there are also roulette and slot machines. The well-spoken, very young British croupiers are a pleasure to watch. At *Paradise Island,* across the causeway from Nassau, is another large casino.

NIGHTCLUBS. Resort area night life includes very high, and very low, quality clubs. Nearly all of those listed here will mean an expensive evening. But claims of "No Cover —No Minimum" don't necessarily mean a cheap evening. Know about cost before you order. A continuous effort is made to eliminate the B-girl from south Florida but the clubs are forever changing hands. There are clubs for the dignified and for the sport. In the more expensive nightclubs, a small card will often make a simple statement of minimum-per-person for dinner and drinks. It can be as much as $10, and good-sized tips are expected.

Some top south Florida nightspots:

Cafe Cristal at the Diplomat Hotel in Hollywood puts the most conspicuous names in American show business on its schedule. Besides guests from the hotel complex itself, the audience is likely to include guests from Palm Beach downward and Key West upward. Some come by yacht—why not? The Diplomat also has *The Tack Room,* a cocktail lounge, and *Les Ambassadeurs,* the dining room.

Mai Kai. A restaurant-nightspot between Pompano and Fort Lauderdale on US 1, where Miami Beach or Palm Beach visitors often drop in on a fun-excursion. Most perfectly realized of all the Polynesian places, its exterior architecture stuns the eye with torches, palms, wooden idols, exotic plants, small pools, thatched roofs, winding trails, and dugouts all blended into something that Polynesia itself has never seen.

The *Columbia* restaurant in Ybor City (Tampa) presents flamenco shows in a red velvet and crystal ambiente, and the Spanish food is delicious.

The *Monster,* a branch of the Fire Island, New York, disco, isn't exactly a nightclub, but the colorful patrons are fun to watch. It's part of the Key West dusk-to-dawn scene.

Most hotels in Florida have live music in the cocktail lounge or dining room, either to listen to or for dancing.

BARS. Heartland in Palm Beach is Worth Avenue, and *TaBoo* is where the action is. The elegant bars in *The Breakers* are relaxing. *Sloppy Joe's* and *Captain Tony's* in Key West are hangouts of the old city's artists, writers, fishermen and assorted bohemians. Although everyone mistakenly thinks it was Sloppy Joe's, Captain Tony's was Ernest Hemingway's favorite watering hole back in the 1930s when he lived in Key West. In the resort area, it's not a bad idea to stick close to the bars in the well-established hotel or motel where you're stopping. If they're run as a subsidiary service, they're generally run well. The management holds them to a standard. St. Pete Beach and the adjoining Holiday Isles are dotted with waterfront bars, some with small discos. Most of the bars offer Happy Hour drinks, two for the price of one, with hors d'oeuvres. Just about every seaside community has a window-walled bar for drinking in the view with the martinis. Some, like *Pier 66* in Fort Lauderdale and the *Hiltons* on Clearwater Beach and St. Pete Beach, offer penthouse-seascapes.

DRINKING LAWS. City and county establish their own closing times for bars and nightclubs where liquor is sold. It's not unusual in the resort area to find establishments with licenses good until 4 or 5 A.M. In Fort Lauderdale city bars are open until 2; some in the county are open till 4. In the Miami area, the swingers can get service later yet (see Bars). Package liquor stores, common throughout the area, are under control of State Beverage Commission. Supermarkets can't sell wine 'til past 1 o'clock on Sundays. Under recent legislation, Florida now grants adult privileges to 18-year-olds.

SPORTS. The state's subtropical climate makes sports possible throughout the year. For that reason, they are listed alphabetically here, and not grouped by season. Florida is high on participant sports—fishing, hunting, tennis, even boccie—and takes a nibble from the national sports scene, too. It is the great winter training ground for big league baseball. Snow sports aren't the style, although ice skating is a growing summer sport, and Bradenton throws an artificial blizzard every year (orange-colored snow). Skiers, in *conquistador* costumes, compete for the Florida State Skiing Championship, in mid-March. In addition, there are sports exotica for the tourist and the gambler—jai alai, polo, racing with dogs, horses, sulkies. And the state pleases the playboy set with some of the world's great sailing and powerboat events. Shuffleboard is everywhere, including perhaps, your motel. St. Petersburg's Mirror Lake Park has the world's largest shuffleboard court.

Boating: Florida beckons insistently to touring, sporting, and competing boatsmen. There are 8,426 miles of tidal shoreline, thousands of navigable lakes and rivers. South Florida has so many canals that babies must learn to swim as soon as they learn to walk—or live in constant danger. Under the out-of-state reciprocity system, Florida grants full recognition to valid registration certificates and numbers from other states for 90 days. Those staying longer must register their vessels with the county tax collector. You'll find ramps and berthing easily, but to be totally prepared write the Florida Department of Natural Resources, Crown Bldg., Tallahassee for a boating directory. This gives route maps, lists marine facilities, and tells where all ramps are located.

Tested trips include the circuit voyage—out of Miami to the Florida Keys, then northward to Fort Myers and across the state, via the Okeechobee Waterway, and down to Miami again. It has become a popular odyssey for the local and out-of-state boater. Your course depends on boat size. Larger yachts, after running south-ward to the Keys, go on to Islamorada before heading north via Nine-Mile, Oxfoot, and Schooner banks on the outside passage. The light-draft outboard, and many sterndrive craft, can go into Florida Bay; entry is by Jewfish Creek, via the Boggies. Aim for Naples going north. A 200-mi. sail from White Springs to the Gulf of Mexico takes 3 days, offers camping spots at Suwannee River State Park, near Live Oak, and Manatee Springs State Park, near Chiefland. "The most beautiful boating mile" in Florida, claimed Grantland Rice, is the *Dora Canal*. It is part of a trip starting on the St. John's River, leading into the Oklawaha, and taking you (via the Haines Creek lock and another canal lock) to *Lake Apopka*. Miamians have great weekends island hopping along Islandia keys, an area which may become a national park. You'll find a 93-acre park at Elliott Key, where the pirate Black Caesar roamed. Look out for brownish colored water. It usually indicates a flat or exposed reef.

Distances on the *Intracoastal Waterway:* Jacksonville to Miami is a 349-mi. trip, with a marked channel depth of 12 feet to Fort Pierce, and 8 ft. from that point south to Miami. On the two charted routes, it's 158 mi. inside the Keys from Miami to Key West (limited to five-foot draft), and 152 mi. by way of Hawk Channel, on a buoyed passage between the outermost reefs and the Keys (limited to 10-ft. draft). Pensacola to St. Marks is 259 mi. with a 12-ft. depth-marked channel through protected harbors and the inland canal to Carrabelle (from Carrabelle, one route is across the Gulf and Apalachee Bay; the other through Crooked and Ochlockonee Rivers—channel depth limited to 3 ft.)

Distances on *main water routes.* On *Okeechobee Waterway,* it's 135 mi. from St. Lucie Inlet, near Stuart, across the State to Fort Myers. From below Welaka, where the Oklawaha flows into the St. John, it's 52 mi. upstream to dramatic Silver Springs. From Kissimmee to Lake Okeechobee, on the Kissimmee Waterway (via lakes Tohopekaliga, Cypress, and Hatchineha) it's 137 mi. You must, for the latter voyage, check locally for directions and the condition of the waterway—it leads across one of the state's least explored areas. It's 107-plus mi. from Apalachicola to Jim Woodruff Lock and Dam at Chattahoochee, traveling the 9-ft. channel from your takeoff on the *Apachicola River.*

Canoeists claim to paddle Florida's most unvisited waters and not suffer a mosquito bite—that's when beautiful tourists have lured all the mosquitoes to the resort cities. Take Rte. 445 to the *Alexander Springs* recreational area, in *Ocala National Forest.* The Alexander Springs canoe trail is one way, runs 6½ mi., and takes you through startling forest tunnels that open suddenly on broad shallows. A trip on the *Silver River* offers shades of early Tarzan movies. The Dept. of Natural Resources has designated 17 rivers as canoe trails. They will supply a booklet listing locations and length.

The so-called shantyboat or houseboat can be a thing of glory these days. It provides something different for the trailerite who thinks he ought to be on water or the boater who wants the comforts of land. Houseboat operations can be found at Naples and Fort Myers and on the St. Johns River.

Marinas throughout the state offer information for the boater. On the Amena River, at Fernandina Beach, is a marine welcome station: a two-story octagonal building, with yacht and outboard parking space. It dispenses charts, maps and weather information.

Fishing: The question isn't where—because it's everywhere. Only shy Florida cities fail to claim fame as fishing capitals of one sort or another. Most deserve these self-conferred titles. You'll hear that tarpon have sometimes finned so thickly across the Boca Grande Pass, their bodies were like a bridge. There's great sport everywhere—but you need to know the habits of the fish you're after. No license needed for saltwater, but a freshwater license is necessary. You have the choice of fishing in canals, lakes, rivers, by ocean pier, or by ocean-going yacht. Canal fishing can provide a dinner; deep-sea fishing the fury and ecstasy Ernest Hemingway experienced to write *The Old Man and the Sea.*

Freshwater equipment may be used in saltwater, but must be cleaned afterwards to prevent corrosion. If you're able, buy big gear after arrival, when you know what you want to catch. Tackle shops are everywhere.

For saltwater quarry: Try for tarpon May to July anywhere, except for upper east coast. Sailfish, which make handsome mounts, are good prey winter and spring anywhere, and even in summer. Snook, a favorite of the fishing writers, are scattered in winter but go for the passes and tidal rivers in spring and summer. Try for snook and tarpon all along the Florida Keys bridges, and near Stuart on the east coast. Pompano and dolphin are supreme among the catchable-eatables. Other excellent eaters are: bass, flounder, bluefish, cobia, Nassau and red grouper, king and Spanish mackerel, mullet, porgies, red and yellowtail snapper, and wahoo.

For freshwater quarry: Ocean-running fish like snook, mangrove snapper, channel bass, sheepshead and tarpon turn up in freshwater as well. There are about 40 strictly freshwater species. Day's bag limits: 10 black bass; 15 chain pickerel; 50 panfish—bream, perch and red-finned pike individually or in aggregate; 6 sunshine bass; 6 striped bass (min. length 15 inches). Total possession limit: Two days's bag limit after first day of fishing. There are also special bag limits on certain lakes and rivers. For complete fresh and saltwater rules write: Game and Fresh Water Fish Commission, Tallahassee, Fla., 32304. The really big bass are in Lake Rosalie, Lake George, Cypress Lake, Talsa Apopka, Orange Lake, the St. Johns River, and the Withlacoochee.

Spearfishing: Legal in saltwater except in the Pennekamp Coral Reef State Park, Collier County, that part of Monroe County from Long Key north to the Dade County line, and the immediate area of the following: all public bathing beaches; commercial or public fishing piers; bridge catwalks; jetties. It is illegal to spearfish in fresh water or for freshwater fish in brackish water except for rough fish in special areas designated by the Game and Fresh Water Fish Commission.

Water Sports: With aquatic adventurers abounding, Florida keeps pace, with water-ski schools, skindiving shops and surfing-supply houses. Dozens of local restrictions exist on where and when water skiers may be towed, and many areas are off limits to divers (too dangerous), so inquiries should always be made.

The *surfing* craze has created thousands of surfers and filled the beaches with wahinis and beach bunnies (surfing girls and nonsurfing girlfriends), but the Florida waves are rarely conducive to first-class sport. Mobile surfers spend hours, going from Miami to Fort Pierce, and higher, seeking the best water. Cocoa Beach is a favored spot. *Windsurfing,* an international sport, has caught on quickly on St. Pete Beach and Clearwater Beach, complete with schools for novices and rental boats. *Parasailing* is a fun sport on St. Pete Beach.

Lobster diving. Use only your hands—it's a state law. Spears and hooks aren't allowed, skin divers wear a mask, swim fins, cotton gloves, possibly a snorkel, to go after the lobsters. They're found at any depth from three feet on. In daylight, the lobster hides but can be spotted under logs or rocks by his antennae. Grabbed, the antennae break off; so the diver must get a grip on the front body shell. First he twists, then he pulls. Watch out for the moray eel, barracuda, and the black, pincushiony sea urchin.

Shelling: Even before Marco Island became the object of massive real estate development, in the Florida manner, it was considered excellent shell-hunting. Many tourists become passionate shellers the minute they hold the hard little cowries, shaped like disembodied jaws, and shining with colors no jewel can match. Other shellers become hooked by a visit to one of the tightly packed seashell novelty houses which dot the major highways. In these shops, you may painlessly, cheaply, and unwetly acquire a fine seashell collection, lacking only the *Canus gloria-maris Chemnitz,* the Glory-of-the-Seas, worth $1,200-per specimen. Many shellers frown on buying. They collect their own, some specializing in minute specimens. Some go into the Everglades to find fossilized shells from other eons (you can also find brilliant tree snails in the Everglades).

The sheller is best advised to search for specimens after a storm, when high tides have delivered new batches to the beaches. Still the champion shelling spot in Florida (and one of the world's better stalking grounds) is *Sanibel Island,* west of Fort Myers Beach and approached by ferry. It has the secluded tang of the South Seas. So does little Captiva Island, which neighbors it. A free shell fair at Sanibel Community House is held in early Mar. The excellent Branaham Shell Collection is part of the Shell Factory in North Ft. Myers. Other places: Coral and sand beaches along the Florida Keys down to Key West are good spots; so is the Cape Sable area—it has to be approached by boat. . . . Shellers also go to the beaches north and south of Naples; to the Sarasota area, including Longboat Key and Anna Maria Island; to beaches west of Bonita Springs; to Tarpon Springs, Clearwater, Pass-a-Grille Beach, and Cedar Key. The St. Petersburg Club offers the Smithsonian Award for year's top shell find.

Golf: Florida is a golfer's paradise, with some of the finest courses in the U.S. The *Seminole G.C.,* North Palm Beach, ranks among the best. *Pine Tree G.C.,* Delray Beach, is Florida's toughest. Some others: *PGC National G.C.,* Palm Beach Gardens, *Bay Hill Club,* Orlando; *Innisbrook G. & C.C.,* Tarpon Springs; *Disney World G.C.,* Lake Buena Vista. The three extraordinary courses at the Innisbrook Golf and Tennis Resort are among the finest in the state.

Other courses are located in: Jacksonville, Ponte Vedra Beach, Tallahassee, Pensacola, St. Augustine, New Smyrna Beach, Daytona Beach, Ormond Beach, Cocoa Beach, Titusville, two in Vero Beach, Ft. Pierce, Stuart, Port St. Lucie, Tequesta, Lost Tree Village, No. Palm Beach, four in W. Palm Beach, Palm Beach, Royal Palm Beach, two in Lake Worth, Lantana, two in Boynton Beach, two in Delray Beach, six in Boca Raton, Coral Springs, four in Pompano Beach, Plantation, Lauderhill, seven in Ft. Lauderdale, six in Hollywood, Homestead, Biscayne Village, No. Key Largo, Marco Island, four in Naples, Rotonda West, four in Ft. Myers, Cape Coral, two in Lehigh Acres, Englewood, two in Punta Gorda, Port Charlotte, No. Port Charlotte, two in Venice, Captiva Island, six in Sarasota, Palma Sola, Sun City, Lake Placid, two in Sebring, three in Clearwater, five in Tampa, Leesburg, several in St. Petersburg, Dunedin, Clearwater, two in Orlando, Sanford, Howey-in-the-Hills, Crystal River, Wildwood, Ocala and two in Panama City Beach.

Hunting: Hunting seasons are: deer, Nov. 13-Jan. 23 in northwest region, Nov. 13-Jan. 9 in northeast, central, south and Everglades; turkey, Nov. 13-Jan. 23 in northwest, Nov. 13-Jan. 9 in northeast, central south and Everglades; quail and squirrel, Nov. 13-March 6 in northwest, Nov. 13-Feb. 27 in other regions. Rabbit, no closed season. Statewide seasons for turkey gobblers, wildhog, and bear are more complicated. Best go get Game and Fresh Water Fish Commission's book of rules. Also, use that publication to check for sizes and hunting methods allowed, as well as those species that are protected. Florida has many species that are on endangered and threatened lists.

A sport on the upsweep here is hunting with bow and arrow. Archery season, statewide, is from Sept. 4 through Sept. 26. Legal game are deer of either sex, other than fawn; bear (in Baker and Columbia counties and on Tyndall AFB in Bay County); turkey (except in northwest region); quail, squirrel, rabbit, and wild hog. No open season in Broward or Dade counties or certain parts of Palm Beach, Hendry, Collier and Monroe counties.

Milder prey for the hunter include woodcock and snipe, ducks and doves, coots and geese. There's a forty-day season on ducks, geese and coots. It starts in late November and goes into early January. West Coast Florida is a natural flyway for ducks; and wild fowl, in general, are plentiful.

Riding: Florida's version of the Old West is Davie, 18 mi. W of Fort Lauderdale; a horse breeding area where cowboys abound and kids ride bareback through the center of town. Near St. Petersburg, there are some good riding stables in Seminole. River Ranch Resort in central Florida attracts dude-ranch vacationers.

SPECTATOR SPORTS. *Baseball:* Late vacationers can see some early baseball at the training camp cities, where major leaguers repair their rusty throwing arms. The Washington Senators tried Florida in 1888, and most teams since have followed suit. Two hundred exhibition games start mid-Mar. and continue for a month. Seventeen of 20 major league teams train on the lower coast—Winter Haven built a $300,000 stadium to catch a defector, the Boston Red Sox. The Houston Astros have a super, five-diamonds, $800,000 training complex at Cocoa. Bradenton's million-dollar stadium (for the Pittsburgh Pirates) has a winged canopy roof extending far out over the center seating section. *Home Bases:* Atlanta Braves, at West Palm Beach; Chicago White Sox at Sarasota; Cincinnati Reds at Tampa; Detroit Tigers at Lakeland; Kansas City Royals at Fort Myers; L.A. Dodgers at Vero Beach; Minnesota Twins at Orlando; St. Louis Cardinals and New York Mets at St. Petersburg; New York Yankees at Fort Lauderdale; Phillies at Clearwater; Twins Farm Teams at Melbourne; Texas Rangers at Pompano Beach; Baltimore Orioles at Miami; Montreal Expos at Daytona Beach. Toronto Blue Jays at Dunedin. During Spring training, some exciting major-league games are played at the $3.5-million Al Lang Stadium near the bay in St. Petersburg. Or at Payson Field, not far from downtown St. Pete, you can watch the baseball stars play for free, while they train.

Car racing: The once famous 12-hr. endurance race at Sebring in Mar. is no longer held. There are still races to be run in Sebring in Mar., but they are a far cry from the good old Grand Prix days. The Feb. Daytona 500 has attracted as many as 82,000 spectators. Short and long stock car events precede the 500. Drag and sports car races are held at Lakeland International Raceway. Auto races in Tampa, Mar. to Nov. Stock car races at W. Palm Beach, Feb. to Nov. Refer to Sports pages of St. Petersburg Times for schedule at Sunshine Speedway.

Dog racing: Slick greyhounds are champion performers at the no-children emporiums. At Daytona the dog track is close by the International Speedway. Other greyhound tracks are: St. Petersburg Kennel Club (Derby Lane); Sanford-Orlando Kennel Club at Winter Park; Orange Park Kennel Club at Jacksonville; The Jacksonville Kennel Club; Bonita Springs Track; Associated Outdoor Clubs at Tampa; Investment Corp. of Palm Beach, West Palm Beach; Jefferson County Kennel Club, Monticello; Keys Racing Assoc., Key West; Pensacola Greyhound Racing; Hollywood Dog Track; Ebro Dog Track, Panama City; Sarasota Kennel Club.

Boat racing: powerboat racing is off to a zippy start in Jan. Several top events are scheduled as adjuncts to the Orange Bowl festivities. In early Feb. the bluewater racing season spawns a series of famed events, grouped under the Southern Ocean Racing Conference. There are an 807-mi. race from Miami to Montego Bay and races from St. Petersburg to Venice, St. Petersburg to Fort Lauderdale and Miami to Cat Cay (late Feb.) In late Feb. or early March is the Orange Cup Regatta on Lakeland's Lake Hollingsworth, where more than 100 limited hydroplane world speed records have been set, along with dozens of world skiing and ski-jumping records.

Horse racing: Tampa has mid-winter racing at Florida Downs, Jan. to Mar. No children. Gulfstream Park in Hallandale runs mid-Jan. to Mar. Post time 1:15 daily except Sun. No children. There are two harness tracks in the state: Tourist Attractions at Pompano Beach, with races nightly except Sun. at 8, mid-Dec. to mid-Apr. Seminole Park, in Casselberry, runs mid-Apr. to Sept. There is quarter horse racing at Gator Down Racing, Pompano, June to Sept. In Hollywood the Calder Race Course has thoroughbred racing from May to mid-Nov.

Jai Alai is played at Dania, Daytona Beach, Tampa, W. Palm Beach, Winter Park, Ocala, Fort Pierce, Fern Park, Melbourne.

Hydroplane races are held at Lakeland in Mar., also on Lake Maggiore, St. Petersburg, in Feb. and Aug.

Water-ski shows are given in Sarasota from Jan. to Mar. on Sun. afternoons.

Polo: The sport of princes is pursued and gaining popularity as a spectator sport in Boca Raton, where games are played every Sun., Jan. to Apr. Polo is also played in the Gulfstream Polo Field, West Palm Beach. Also, games at the new West Palm Beach Polo Club Resort complex.

SHOPPING. A famous shopping street in Florida is Worth Avenue in *Palm Beach,* where Bonwit Teller, Saks and Elizabeth Arden mingle with shops as exclusive if not as nationally known. Worth Avenue's Spanish architecture, with its many arcades, alleyways, balconies, stairways, and nooks and crannies create a pleasant and relaxing European atmosphere.

In *Palm Beach,* the *Salon Francaise* was just a chink in an alleyway a few years go. Now Mrs. Douglas Dillon supposedly drives down from the nation's capital to shop there. It's at 2 Via Mizner. . . . Next door is *Dita* Naylor-Leyland's children's shop. *Lilly Pulitzer* ("The fabulous," said the former *New York Herald-Tribune*) is at 11 Via Mizner. . . . The *Congo Shop* at 333 Worth Avenue is remarkable for leather goods. . . . You can drive home in style after a stopoff at *Taylor Imported Motors, Inc.,* at 1314 S. Dixie in Palm Beach. Dealers in Rolls-

Royce, Bentley, Jaguar, Ferrari, they have one of the country's more stunning collections of treasuries-on-wheels. . . . Florida has roadside stands everywhere specializing in products from the *orange groves.* A super-deluxe box (as packers call it) may cost as much as $24.50. That will be over a bushel and a half of oranges, grapefruit, pecan halves, candied fruits, coconut patties. To buy oranges, sample first. Quality varies. . . . Among the outstanding places to shop in St. Petersburg are downtown Beach Drive (elegant shops!), Tyrone Mall, Pinellas Park Mall; Clearwater Mall, Countryside Mall, Clearwater. *St. Armand's Key,* off Sarasota, has the beautiful and diverse *St. Armands Shopping Circle,* with over 100 individually owned and operated shops, services, restaurants, representing styles, architecture and exotic goods from around the world. Lake Buena Vista's *Shopping Village,* situated among trees and flowers on the banks of the Buena Vista Lagoon, offers 29 cedar-shingled shops and four restaurants. This Walt Disney World adjunct features such things as Toys Fantastique, European toys for children of any age; Posh Pets, with exotic animals such as albino skunks, besides the usual dogs and cats; and Port of Entry, with fashions, furniture and other goods from around the world. Of course, there are many shell shops in the resort areas, but the Shell Shop near Ft. Myers is certainly the largest. Even if you don't care for shells, you're sure to get "hooked" after a visit here. The *Old Marine Market Place* at Tin City in Naples is unusual, with 40 boutiques, craft and gift shops, snack bars, and the *Riverwalk Fish and Ale House.* Also in Naples, art galleries and shops line Fifth Avenue and on South Third Street, courtyards (Old Naples).

 WHAT TO DO WITH THE CHILDREN. Marine shows are popular with children and their parents. One of the most developed sea shows is at *Marineland* of Florida, 18 mi. S. of St. Augustine. Six performances daily. The *Gulfarium,* E of US 98 on Okaloosa Island, nr. Fort Walton Beach, has fish and scuba diving shows in their reef tank; trained porpoises in the main tank. *Miami's Seaquarium* has a shark channel, killer whales, porpoise and sea lion shows. A monorail circles the 60-acre garden. At *Flipper's Sea School* in Marathon you can see the porpoises at their lessons daily from 10 to 4.

The *Theater of the Sea,* in Islamorada, offers hr-long "bottomless" boat tours in addition to trained porpoise shows and the aquarium. You can also take a charter boat to visit underwater coral gardens and the wreck of a Spanish galleon, or take a 2-hr. glass-bottomed boat ride from Chesapeake Dock to view the reefs.

There's lots to see at Tarpon Spring's sponge docks. *Spongeorama,* 510 Dodecanese Blvd., gives sponge-diving exhibitions, shows movies and exhibits about the sponge industry.

On the other side of the nature-lover's coin are animal refuges. Tiny key deer, 25 in. high, can be photographed at the *National Key Deer Refuge* off Rte. 940 on Big Pine Key. Tame deer may be fed at *International Deer Ranch,* Silver Springs. The visitor is caged, the monkey free at *Monkey Jungle,* 3 mi. W of US 1 in Goulds, 20 mi. S of Coral Gables. In Tarpon Springs, visit *Noell's Ark Chimpanzee Farm* or the *Tarpon Zoo,* US 19, which supplies South American animals for medical research. Closed holidays. The *Jacksonville Municipal Zoo,* on Trout River off N. Main St., features animals and birds from many countries, with moated islands for bears and lions. Miniature railroad. Free.

Over 100 lions and other African wild animals roam at large in *Lion Country Safari,* on US 98 in West Palm Beach. You can rent an explanatory tape and tape recorder. "African Safari" at Caribbean Gardens in Naples is a 200-acre tropical garden with exotic birds, waterfowl, chimp shows and a lion and tiger training school. *Sarasota Jungle Gardens* has an awesome number of tropical plants in wild jungle and formal gardens, exotic birds, chimp acts and bird shows. 3701 Bayshore Rd. There's a bird walk, guided boat tours, a sundown train trip to a bird rookery and native wildlife at Myakka River State Park, 17 mi. E of Sarasota. *St. Augustine's Alligator Farms,* on Anastasia Island, has been in operation for over 75 years, features alligator wrestling, zoo of Florida wildlife. *Gatorland Zoo,* Kissimmee, features alligators, crocodiles, giant tortoises, zebras. Train ride.

Costumed Indians make dolls, do beadwork and make baskets at *Seminole Okalee Indian Village,* 6073 Sterling Rd., West Hollywood. There's an arts & crafts center, small zoo and alligator wrestling. Closed early Sept. to late Nov., Christmas and Easter. The Seminole Indian Reservation is on State 721, W. of Brighton. Exhibits at *Temple Mound and Museum,* US 98, Fort Walton Beach, tell story of Indian culture, religion.

Circus buffs will have a hey-day at the *Ringling Museums,* a complex of 4 bldgs. on 68 acres on US 41, 3 mi. N of Sarasota. The circus museum covers circus history from ancient Rome to the present day; with collections of handbills, posters, costumes, wagons, etc. The Ringling Residence is a fabulous Venetian Gothic building; the Museum of Art has both a fine collection of contemporary work and a renowned collection of baroque art; the Asolo Theater is a reassembled Venetian theater. Venice is winter quarters for *Ringling Bros.-Barnum & Bailey,* with a rehearsal hall and arena on Airport Ave. *Circus World* (at Haines City), near all the other fantasy worlds in Orlando, is fun for everyone. Kids and parents can walk the tightrope, swing from a trapeze, or perhaps be painted up like a clown. Panoramic screens bring circus life right to you. Older children who are movie and TV fans will enjoy *Stars Hall of Fame,* with lifesize, lifelike statues of the most famous celebrities in their best-known settings, such as *The Wizard of Oz.* Outdoor pavilion has footprints and fingerprints (even an earprint) of well-known headliners. Multi-vision movie features what show biz is all about.

One of Florida's major attractions is *Cape Kennedy.* The Visitor Center is on NASA Causeway nr. Titusville. There are lectures (Mon. to Fri.) and films (daily); except Christmas or morning of manned space launching.

There's no doubt at all that the kids will love *Walt Disney World.* The "Magic Kingdom" is divided into 6 sections: *Fantasyland,* with Cinderella Castle, Mickey Mouse revue and Captain Nemo subs; *Main St. USA*—a study in nostalgia; *Tomorrowland,* preview of the future; *Adventureland* with jungle cruises, tiki birds; *Frontierland,* a recreation of the Old West; *Liberty Square* with colonial shops, Hall of Presidents and a haunted house. There are motels, camping sites, tours, special package tours. The attractions are open daily. Write Disney World, Lake Buena Vista, Fla. 32830 for brochures. *River Country,* water-oriented adventure, located in Fort Wilderness campground. Contains two large flume slides 260 feet and 160 feet long into Old Swimming Hole. Also, you can plunge some rapids on inner tubes. There is a heated pool, nature walk, and play park. *Sea World,* only a few minutes' drive away, almost upstages Mickey Mouse with Shamu, the performing killer-whale, and his all-star cast of porpoises, penguins, and mermaids. On beautiful landscaped acres, Sea World also has Japanese and Hawaiian Villages, water-ski shows, Atlantis Theater with star performers, observation tower, and restaurants.

Weeki Wachee Spring features underwater ballet by "mermaids" in a specially designed auditorium 16 ft. below the surface. A narrated boat cruise makes regular trips down the Weeki Wachee River. There's also an Exotic Trained Bird Show with macaws and cockatoos skating, playing cards and doing other unbird-like tricks. The Springs are 12 mi. W of Brooksville at the jct. of Rte. 50 & US 19.

Cypress Gardens, in Winter Haven, has water skiing, aquarama shows, boat tours of the canals and exquisite gardens. Garden is open daily from sunrise to sunset. The walkthrough aquarium and Living Legends of the South are just two of the new attractions added to Cypress Gardens in 1979.

Six Gun Territory, Silver Springs, is a recreation of an Old West Frontier town. Steam train, gondolas, rides, gunfights, Indian dances add to the fun. Daily June to Labor Day. Rides and shows are included in fee. *Petticoat Junction,* 10 mi. W of Panama City at Long Beach Resort, also features cowboy & Indian fights, steam engine rides. Mar. to Labor Day. Free. In Key Biscayne, *Crandon Park* has a beach, amusement park, miniature train ride. Small fee for rides. *Pirate's World* at E. Sheritan St., Dania, is an amusement park with rides, exhibits, concerts. Children love to explore the Dark Continent at Busch Gardens, Tampa, complete with African animals grazing on the Serengeti Plain, a Moroccan Village, the Congo Jungle Cruise, an exciting Python ride, Stanleyville, and bazaars. Monorails, a sky-ride, and a Nairobi-style railroad take visitors around the vast, garden-bordered acres. In '79 and '80, Busch Gardens opened new *Timbuktu* on seven acres and *Adventure Island* (the ultimate "water world").

Also of interest to the pirate-adventure lover is *Pirate Treasure Ship,* 100 Margaret St., Key West. This is a full-sized Spanish galleon with booty collection and tours explaining pirate life. And in St. Petersburg, adjoining Municipal Pier, is MGM's replica of *The Bounty,* the mutiny ship. Best free attraction is *Suncoast Seabird Sanctuary,* Indian Shores, near St. Petersburg. Open 7 days, 9 A.M. to dark. Over 500 seabirds of 40 species, most recuperating from injuries and free to fly away after rehabilitation.

There are many museums which will interest children. Among them: *South Florida Museum & Bishop Planetarium,* 201 10th St. W., Bradenton. *Museum of Sunken Treasure,* 8625 Astronaut Blvd., Cape Canaveral. Closed New Year's, Christmas. *Children's Museum,* Jacksonville, 1025 Gulf Life Dr. Ecology, wild life, Timaqua Indians. Planetarium shows. Closed Sept. and major holidays. *John Young Museum and Planetarium,* 810 E. Rollins Ave., Orlando. Free. Planetarium shows Wed., Thurs., Sat., Sun.

The *Museum of Yesterday's Toys,* 52 St. George St., St. Augustine, displays over 1500 dolls, other toys and accessories. Guided tour of house, garden. Free. *Oldest Store Museum* in St. Augustine carries turn-of-the-century merchandise. The *Zorayda Castle,* 83 King St., St. Augustine, was inspired by the Alhambra in Spain. Daily mid-June to Aug. Kids will also appreciate the *Ripley's Believe It or Not Museum,* 19 San Marco Ave. In Winter Haven, the *Museum of Old Dolls and Toys* at 1530 6th St. displays 3-century-old dolls, mechanical banks. Sarasota's *Bellm's Cars & Music of Yesterday,* 5500 N. Tamiami Trail, has antique cars, mechanical music boxes.

Tallahassee's Junior Museum, 3945 Museum Dr., is a restoration of a pioneer farm with blacksmith shop, farm house, smokehouse, etc.; 4 museum bldgs, nature trails. Closed Easter, Thanksgiving, Dec. 23-New Year's Day. In Tampa, the *Junior Museum* features Seminole Indian culture, and a man in space display. Mid-Sept. to July. Free.

Newest fun things to do are the water worlds—winding flumes filled with flowing water, and then a plunge into the pool below. *Walt Disney World* has a Wet 'n' Wild watersport theme-park in River Country. There's the *Zoom Flume* in Panama City; *Water Boggan* in Pompano Beach; *Hawaiian Slip Waterslide* in Kissimmee; and *Okaloosa County Water Slide* in Fort Walton Beach. Silver Springs set aside 10 acres and a cool million to construct an aquatic park, *Wild Waters,* with a 180-foot pool, almost four-foot-high waves, playpools, and three flumes.

Also new is *Alligator Safari* in Kissimmee, an animal jungle compound; *Ross Allen Wildlife Park* in Fort Myers (near the huge Shell Shop); *'Gator Jungle* in Plant City.

 INDIANS. If you know the Indian tongues well enough, you can learn a good deal about Florida simply by reading the names on the map. Oklawaha means "muddy or boggy," Palatka—"fording place," and Seminole (the name of the Florida tribe)—"wild man" or "runaway."

Outside influence on the tribes, as well as tribal influence on Florida, is detectable everywhere. At Boca Raton, in the chapel at *St. Andrew's Episcopal School for*

Boys, the altar mural by Mary Osceola shows the Holy Family as Seminoles. (At Christmas, the Seminoles celebrate "Big Safe Day," as they like to call it.) The menfolk wear blue jeans these days and are abandoning the dugout for the airboat. They have automobile license plates—but special ones, for tribe members alone. Intermarried in the past with escaped Negro slaves and now put under a magnifying glass by those who would see them as they were, they contrive to be Seminoles still. Some of the spots where you can find traces of the tribe, both ancient and as their not-so-modern selves, are: The *Okalee Village* at Dania, a Seminole reservation; the *Indian Temple Mound* at Fort Walton Beach; the *Southeast Museum of the North American Indian,* at Marathon; the *Musa Isle Indian Village,* at Miami; the *Indian Burial Mound* at St. Augustine; the *Seminole Indian Village,* at Silver Springs; the *Tiger* and *Osceola Seminole Indian camps* on the Tamiami Trail. Ancient Florida, with artifacts from the Creek Indians of 200 B.C., is represented in the new *Indian Mound Museum* at Crystal River. It is situated on an 18-acre tract in western Citrus County.

When the Spanish came, four tribes, numbering perhaps 10,000, inhabited Florida. The Calusa in the southwest, the Tequesta on the east coast, the Timucuan in central and northeast Florida, and the semicivilized leading tribe, the Apalachee in the northwest. The Seminoles, runaways from the Creek tribes of Georgia, became important in the mid-18th century. They were forced to flee to the Everglades after Osceola fought, and lost, the Second Seminole War. (That war was declared over in 1938 when the Seminoles and the U.S. signed a truce.) Reduced to 208 tribe members in 1880, the Seminoles had quadrupled by the early 1950's. A council of five holds judicial power on the reservations; the *Green Corn Dance* (the first day after the first new moon of the vernal equinox) is their day of decision. *Bulow Plantation,* the wilderness kingdom where John Bulow defied the Mosquito Roarers and sided with the Seminoles during the Seminole War, is an extensive ruin and memorial. It is near St. Augustine, southeast of Bunnell on Old Dixie Highway—and it has boating and picnicking facilities.

Tours at Miami run to the exhibition village—the sights at Silver Springs are similar. The Dania Reservation is very accessible, but *Big Cypress* is far larger and more interesting. Deepwater alligator wrestling, most typical exhibition, is practiced at Okalee Village—reached via State 7. The arts and crafts shop at the village has carvings and brilliantly patterned skirts.

The *Miccosukee,* their chickees lining the Tamiami Trail between Naples and Miami, cling most firmly to the old ways. (The chickee is a thatched hut made from palmetto and cypress poles, with a sapling platform for sleeping.) These Trail Indians headquarter at Forty Mile Bent, and have a school and an Episcopal mission. The *Cow Creek Tribe,* at Brighton Reservation, is building a herd of mixed-stock Brahma cattle. The Bureau of Indian Affairs recently lent the Miccosukees over $100,000 to establish a service station-restaurant between Naples and Miami on the Trail. It is run by the Indians themselves and decorated with murals depicting their strange detainment in the Everglades.

In spite of these ventures, the Florida Indians remain shy and remote; it is said "they speak quietly . . . walk lightly . . . never raise their voices . . . even the children are not noisy."

HOTELS AND MOTELS. A Florida vacation means "which hotel" more than a sojourn in any other state, for your entire schedule of activities in the Sunshine State will probably revolve around where you stay. If you want active sports, you will want one kind of hotel; if you prefer to lounge on the beach, you will prefer another. Rule of thumb on prices: the farther from the ocean, the cheaper the room. Good buys can be found up and down US 1 on the east coast. Prices, of course, are always subject to change, but categories generally remain constant. In many locations, offseason prices are as much as 50 per cent cheaper, making an expensive hotel a summer bargain.

We have listed hotels and motels alphabetically in categories determined by double, in-season rates: *Deluxe,* from $50 up; *Expensive,* $35; *Moderate,* $25; *Inexpensive,* under $25. For a more complete explanation of hotel and motel categories see *Facts at Your Fingertips* at the front of this volume.

Amelia Island

Amelia Island Plantation. *Deluxe.* On A1A. Luxurious oceanfront resort with main hotel, private villas (some with own pools). Four miles of white-sand beach, 90-foot pool. Beach club, tennis center, championship golf course. Observation deck atop 50-foot sand dune. Restaurants, shops, marinas. Half-hour drive from Jacksonville Airport. Nr. Fernandina Beach airport.

Apalachicola

A number of motels and cabins, some with kitchenettes, can be found along US 98 and in East Apalachicola. *Apalach Motel, Rancho Court and Gibson Hotel. Moderate.* Each has cabins and a restaurant. *Bay City Lodge and Restaurants. Sportsman's Lodge. Inexpensive.*

Apopka

Lake Page Motel. *Inexpensive.* On South Orange Blossom Trail. 9 units, several with kitchen. Pets.

Auburndale

Chandler's Rainbow Drive Motel. *Inexpensive.* Cottages on lake. Beach, fishing, boats. Restaurant nr.

Bartow

El Jon Motel. 1460 E. Main St. *Moderate.* Pool (heated), 18-hole golf. Restaurant nr.

Belle Glade

Days Inn. *Inexpensive.* US 27 and Fl 80. Pool, restaurant. 121 rms., one suite. Nr. Lake Okeechobee, 2nd largest freshwater lake in U.S. 47 mi. to West Palm Beach.

Boca Grande

Gasparilla Inn & Cottages. *Deluxe.* Pool, private beach within walking distance. Games, rec. room, fishing. Golf, tennis. Dining room, bar. MAP. Area famous for tarpon fishing.

Boca Raton

Boca Raton Hotel. *Deluxe.* One of the most celebrated Gold Coast hotels. Rambling palace with villas avail. Golf courses, skeet & trap shooting, yacht dock, splendid beach, cabana club. Shopping arcade. Olympic-size pools (heated). Polo in season. Even a brokerage office! Fabulous Boco Beach Club opened 1981.

Bridge Hotel. *Deluxe.* On Intracoastal Waterway. New, 1977. 150 rooms. Top of the Bridge Restaurant and Supper Club.

Holiday Inn. *Expensive.* SR 808. Nr. beach and Florida Atlantic Univ. Pool (heated). Restaurant, bar.

Best Western University Inn. *Moderate.* 2700 N. Federal Hwy. Pool (heated). Beach 2 mi. away. Restaurant, bar. Fam. rates, kitchenettes avail.

Bokeelia

Useppa Island Club. *Deluxe.* Island hideaway with landing strip. You can jet into Tampa, take Florida air taxi to this tarpon-rich location. Launch transportation from Boca Grande or Bokeelia. Full sporting facilities. Off the coast of Captiva/Sanibel Islands.

Boynton Beach

Best Western Sage-N-Sand Motel. *Moderate.* US 1 S. Pool (heated), beach 1 mi. away. Play area. Coffee shop; wine & beer. Restaurant nr. Free tennis and golf 2½ mi.

Farmer in the Dell. *Moderate.* 2821 S. Federal Hwy. Pool, sauna. Kitchen units. Pets.

Bradenton-Bradenton Beach

Resort 66 Motel. *Expensive.* 6600 Gulf Dr. Holmes Beach. Pool (heated). Coffee shop. Private beach. Barbecue area. 15 mi. from Bradenton.

Smugglers Cove. *Expensive.* 1501 Gulf Dr. N. Beachfront. On Gulf of Mexico and Sarasota Bay. Boat and fishing dock. Heated pool. Tennis privileges. Rooms, apartments, studio efficiencies.

Aquarius Motel. *Moderate.* 105 39th St. Holmes Beach. On white sand beach. Heated pool, shuffleboard. Playground, fishing pier one block away. Efficiency apartments.

Harbor Lights Motel. *Moderate.* 1301 Gulf Dr. Private beach, heated pool. Picnic area. Fishing dock on bay. Kitchenette available.

Hoosier Manor Motel. *Moderate.* 1405 14th St. Walking distance to downtown, shops, restaurants. Picnic area. Game room, shuffleboard court. Efficiencies, cottages available. Continental breakfast included.

Days Inn. *Inexpensive.* US 41 and FL 301. A good operation. Pool, play area, gift shop, gas station. Popular *Tasty World* restaurant. Pets. Beaches 10 mi. Airport 7 mi.

Cape Coral

Country Club Inn. *Expensive.* 4003 Palmtree Blvd. Pool (heated), sauna. Pets. Restaurants, bar, entertainment, dancing. Golf, tennis.

Colonial Resort. *Inexpensive.* Pets. Free coffee & rolls in motel units. Restaurant nr. Lawn games, free transportation to bus terminal. Kitchen units avail.

Nautilus Inn. *Inexpensive.* Pool; golf nr. Pets. Restaurant, bar, entertainment, dancing. Free airport transportation.

Captiva

South Seas Plantation. *Deluxe.* Lovely 1856 plantation, with private beach, heated pool, restaurants, bars, entertainment. Golf, marina, Steve Colgate's Offshore Sailing School, 16 tennis courts, Greg Parker Tennis School. Villa-style suites.

Cedar Key

Faraway Inn. *Moderate.* A very special fishing spot, catering to fishermen and honeymooners. Special hunting, fishing pkg. Free champagne for honeymooners.

Island Inn. *Moderate.* Favorite rendezvous for art colony. Bohemian atmosphere. Friendly bar is a famous landmark. Quaint rooms.

Clearwater

Belleview Biltmore. *Deluxe.* Resort hotel on 625 acres. Olympic-sized pool (heated). Two championship golf courses, tennis, play area. Supervised children's program during vacations. Cabana club on gulf, private beach. On Intracoastal Waterway. EP avail. World's largest occupied frame structure, built by millionaire Henry Bradley Plant. On National Registry of Historic Places and Monuments. Closed summer.

Ramada Inn. *Moderate.* US 19 across from beautiful Countryside Mall. Very good Aspen restaurant; lively cocktail lounge. Friendly management.

Days Inn. *Inexpensive.* US 19 and M.E. Coachman. Well-kept. Pool, play area, gift shop, gas station. *Tasty World* restaurant. Pets.

Clearwater Beach

Hilton Inn. *Deluxe.* Pool (heated), tennis, play area, fishing, boating. Skin diving instruction avail. Golf nr. Restaurant, bar, live entertainment in window-walled penthouse.

Sheraton Sand Key. *Deluxe.* 1160 Gulf Blvd. 390 waterview rooms. On beautiful beach. Pool, tennis, recreation room. Restaurant, penthouse Sky Lounge with nightly entertainment.

Aegean Sands Resort Motel. *Expensive.* 421 Gulfview Blvd. S. Opposite beach. Heated pool. Kitchenettes, efficiencies avail.

Caribbean Gulf. *Expensive.* 430 S. Gulfview Blvd. Lively resort hotel on Gulf of Mexico. Bar, disco, Calico Jack's restaurant, entertainment nightly.

Franzman Patio Apartments and Motel. *Expensive.* 17 Somerset St. Garden patio directly on white sand beach. Rooms, efficiencies, 1- and 2-bedroom apartments.

Gulfview Inn. *Expensive.* 504 Gulfview Blvd. S. Refrigerators, coffee-makers in every room. Heated pool, fishing dock. Direct access to beach.

Clermont

John Newcombe's Tennis Resort. *Expensive.* On US 27. Everything to keep tennis buffs happy, including "Newk" himself when he visits. Pool, game area. Tennis courts, of course. Restaurant, cocktail lounge.

Howard Johnson's. *Moderate.* Fla. Tpke. and US 27 (exit 85). 8 mi N. of Clermont, 14 mi. S. of Leesburg. Pool, playground. Coin laundry. Citrus Tower, 6 mi. Water-skiing, golf, 8 mi. Restaurant, cocktail lounge. Accommodations for handicapped. Nr. Disney World, Sea World (easy drive).

Sky Line Motel. *Inexpensive.* 190 Hwy. 27, Rt. 2. Pool, sundeck, shuffleboard. Across highway from Citrus Tower, Florida's highest point for vistas of $700 million worth of citrus acreage, hills, lakes. Tower includes amusements, boutiques, post office, restaurant.

Cocoa

Howard Johnson's. *Moderate.* 860 N. Cocoa Blvd. Pool. Pets. Restaurant (24 hr.).

Days Inn. *Inexpensive.* I-95 and Hwy. 524. Nr. beach, zoo, Kennedy Space Center, shopping. *Tasty World* restaurant.

Cocoa Beach

Atlantis Beach Lodge. *Expensive.* 900 N. Atlantic Ave. 410 feet of beach, surf. 2 pools. Snack bar, restaurant, cocktail lounge, entertainment, dancing.

Holiday Inn. *Expensive.* 1300 N. Atlantic Ave. Olympic-sized pool, play area, beach. Pets. Restaurant, bar, entertainment, dancing.

Howard Johnson's. *Moderate.* 2080 N. Atlantic Ave. Pool, private beach approached by walkway, play area. Restaurant, bar, dancing.

Bal-Ray Resort Motel. *Inexpensive.* 400 N. Atlantic. 2-bedroom cottages, motel rooms. On ocean. Nr. restaurants, shops.

Crystal River

Plantation Inn and Golf Resort. *Moderate.* Just off US 19. Special vacation packages. PGA golf course, newly resurfaced tennis courts. Marina. Cocktail lounge. Dining rooms also open to public. Fishing and scuba diving arranged. Social programs.

Cypress Gardens

Cypress Gardens Motel. *Inexpensive-Moderate.* Between US 17 and US 27, east of Winter Haven. 160 rooms, adjoining the famous water-ski show and floral attraction. Owners renovated at a cost of a half-million dollars.

Daytona Beach

Daytona Hilton. *DeLuxe.* 2637 Atlantic Ave. Luxurious oceanfront resort and convention center. All rooms with bar, refrigerator. Pool, tennis courts, putting green, games. Exercise room, sauna. Boutiques, beauty salons. 5 mins. from golf course, charter boats. Rooftop restaurant, cocktail lounge. Also *Sunroom Café* and *Islander Lounge.*

Best Western Aku Tiki. *Expensive.* 2225 S. Atlantic Ave. Pool (heated), play area. Restaurant, bar, dancing, entertainment.

Beachcomber Oceanfront Inn. *Expensive.* 2000 N. Atlantic Ave. Pool (heated). Play area. Kitchen units, wkly rates avail. Restaurant, cocktail lounge.

Treasure Island Inn. *Expensive.* 2025 S. Atlantic Shores, Oceanfront. Rooms, efficiencies, penthouses. 2 pools, Game room, putting green, shuffleboard. *Billy Boone's Tavern, Barefoot Bar, Galley Restaurant.* Entertainment.

El Caribe Motel. *Moderate.* 2125 S. Atlantic Ave. Has addition of 50 units with king-size and queen-size beds. Kitchenettes avail. Game room, gift shop, small meeting room. Window-walled *Garden Room* on 4th floor with ocean and river views. Coffee and home-made doughnuts served every morning in Garden Room. Pool, sundeck.

Neptune Inn. *Inexpensive.* 2655 S. Atlantic Ave. On the beach. Some rooms with balconies. One room for the handicapped. Pool, game room. Pets allowed. Children under 12 free in parents' rooms.

De Land

Chimney Corner Motel. *Inexpensive.* 1727 South Blvd. Pool, with closed circuit TV viewing. Pets. Restaurant. Opp. Stetson Univ.

Save Inn-Deland. *Inexpensive.* I-4 & SR 44. Excellent bargain at this fast-expanding southern chain. Pool, playground, game rooms. 2 double beds in each room. Save More Club members get good discounts on participating hotels, motels, resorts, theme parks, etc. throughout U.S. and Canada.

Delray Beach

The Barrington. *Deluxe.* 1775 S. Ocean Blvd. Pool (heated), beach. Kitchen apartments in 2-story hotel. Restaurant nr.

Talbot House. *Deluxe.* 125 N. Ocean Blvd. Resort hotel with kitchen units. Pool (heated), beach, play area. Restaurant nr. Closed May–Oct.

Wright by the Sea. *Deluxe.* 1901 S. Ocean Blvd. Pool (heated), beach, play & barbecue area. Restaurant nr. Kitchen units avail. Closed June–Sept. 20.

Bermuda Inn. *Expensive.* 64 S. Ocean Blvd. Beach nr. Kitchen units avail. Pets. Restaurant.

Holiday Inn. *Expensive.* 2809 S. Ocean Blvd. Pool (heated), beach, play area. Restaurant, bar.

Destin

Hawaiki. *Deluxe.* Hwy. 98E. Nine-story hotel on beach. Balconies facing Gulf. Pool, wading pool. Beautiful revolving roof dining room and cocktail lounge.

Sandestin Resort Inn (formerly a Sheraton). *Expensive.* On Florida Gulf. Championship golf course, nine tennis courts. Fishing in Choctawhatchee Bay or Gulf of Mexico. Two pools. Private half-mile beach. Restaurants, lounge with entertainment. Limo service available from Destin/FWB private airport (6 mi.) and Okaloosa County Airport (25 mi.). Bus station within 18 mi.

Florida Girl Motel. *Moderate.* At Destin Harbor. Homey atmosphere. Gulf view. 16 units, 2 cottages. Party boat *New Florida Girl* and *Capt. Dave's Seafood Restaurant* adjacent. Monthly rates in season.

Disney World (Lake Buena Vista)

(See also Kissimmee (5 min. from gate), Orlando, Clermont, St. Cloud and Altamonte Spring.)

Buena Vista Palace. *Deluxe.* On lake's shore. Completion scheduled late 1982. 27-story, 825-room hotel will be central Florida's tallest. Views of EPCOT Center at Walt Disney World from balconies. Rooftop restaurant, casual restaurants, lounges. A beautiful total resort.

Contemporary Resort. *Deluxe.* In Disney World, right on monorail stop. Lakeside, beach, marina. Canoes, water-skiing. 2 heated pools, wading pool. Health club, sauna. Playground, game room, supervised children's activities. Lighted tennis courts, bicycles, golf, horseback riding. Gorgeous vistas from several dining rooms, cocktail lounges. Nightly entertainment, dancing. 24-hour snack bar.

Polynesian Village Resort Hotel. *Deluxe.* In Disney World. On lake. Exotic South Seas-style, tropical gardens, lagoons. Beach, marina. Heated pool, wading pool, playground. Supervised children's programs. Same sports as Contemporary Resort. Sauna. Boutiques, beauty shop. Luxurious suites. Coffee Shop, restaurant, cocktail lounge with entertainment.

Treehouse Villas. *Deluxe.* Walt Disney World Resort Community Shopping Village nrby. The 60 hideaways are nestled among trees at the 17th fairway of golf course. Beautiful views from picture windows. Completely equipped kitchen, dining-living room (2 bedrooms have 2 bathrooms). Nr. 7 restaurants, including *Empress Lilly Riverboat.* Nr. *Village Lounge.* Shuttlebus to Disney World's Vacation Kingdom.

Everglades

Flamingo Inn. *Moderate.* Pool, play area. Bicycles avail. Great bird watching in park.

Rod and Gun Club Lodge. *Moderate.* Presidents have stayed here! Great for hard-core fishermen. Chef will grill your catch. Charter boat and skiff fleet. Dock. Pool; golf nearby.

Captain's Lodge. *Inexpensive* to *Moderate.* At western water gateway to Everglades National Park. 16 motel rooms, 44 1-bedroom apartments. 7 2-bedroom apartments. Full-service marina.

Fort Lauderdale

Bahama Hotel. *Deluxe.* 401 N. Atlantic Blvd. Oceanfront. Pool (heated), play area. Golf nr. Restaurant in season. Bar, entertainment in season, dancing.

Bahia Mar Hotel. *Deluxe.* 801 Seabreeze Blvd. At Bahia Mar Yachting Center. Pool (heated), play area, yachting, fishing. Golf nr. 2 dining rooms, coffee shop, lounge. Also *Patricia Murphy's Candlelight Restaurant.*

Fort Lauderdale Marriott Hotel and Marina. *Deluxe.* Overlooking Intracoastal Waterway. Outstanding new resort complex. Pool, whirlpool, sauna, tennis. Excellent Riverwatch restaurant. Vacation packages for one day or longer.

Bali Hai Polynesian Resort Apartments. *Expensive.* 149 Isle of Venice. Hotel rooms with refrigerators, 1- and 2-bedroom apartments, large efficiencies. Heated pool, putting green, games. Barbecue grills, fishing dock, sundeck. Nr. restaurants, shopping.

Quality Inn American. *Moderate.* 1055 N. Federal Hwy. Pool (heated). Restaurant, bar, entertainment.

Twin Sails Oceanfront Motel. *Moderate.* 2016 N. Atlantic Blvd. On the ocean, private beach. Rooms, efficiencies, apartments. Daily, weekly, monthly rates.

Spindrift Motel. *Moderate.* 2501 N. Ocean Blvd. A1A. About 150 yards from beach. All rooms have refrigerators, also efficiencies and 1-bedroom apartments with fully equipped electric kitchens. Coin laundry. Large heated pool. Sundeck, shuffleboard courts. Barbecue area with gas grills. On city bus line.

Gateway Motel. *Inexpensive.* 1117 N. Federal Hwy. US 1. Rooms, efficiency apartments. Heated pool. Shuffleboard. Lake fishing in back of motel. 5 min. to beach.

Idle Hour Motel and Apartments. *Inexpensive.* 3300 N.E. 27th St. About 200 yards to beach. Heated pool, garden patios. Shuffleboard. Units with all-electric kitchens available. Walk to Galt Ocean Mile for restaurants, shops.

Fort Myers

Ramada Inn. *Expensive.* 2220 W. First St. Pool, playground. Within 10 min. of airport. Accommodations for handicapped. Free local telephone calls. Restaurant, cocktail lounge, entertainment. Nr. Thomas Edison home.

Fort Myers Rodeway Inn. *Inexpensive.* 4811 Cleveland Ave. Heated pool. Roman baths available. Restaurant, lounge.

Fort Myers Beach

Island Towers. *Deluxe.* 4900 Estero Blvd. Pool (heated), play area. Kitchen apts. Overlooking gulf.

Caribbean Court. *Expensive.* Pool (heated), fishing pier, beach. Pets. 7600 Estero Blvd. Restaurant nr. Cook-out facilities.

Kahlua Inn. *Expensive.* 4950 Estero Blvd. Pool (heated), play area. Restaurant nr. Beachfront. Coin laundry.

Sandpiper Gulf Resort. *Expensive.* 5550 Estero Blvd. Pool (heated), play area. Beach. Restaurant nr. Kitchen apts. with private patios or balconies.

Fort Pierce

Sandpiper Bay Resort. *Expensive.* Two heated pools, golf courses, tennis courts, boating. Luxurious resort at nearby Port St. Lucie.

Best Western. *Moderate.* 2601 S. US 1. Pleasant hotel, 6 mi. E of Sunshine Pkwy. and I-95. Golf, restaurant nearby.

Holiday Inn Oceanfront (formerly Ramada Inn-Oceanside). *Moderate.* 2600 N. A1A. Beachfront, Pool. Tennis courts. Arrangements also with private beach and tennis club. Golf 15 min. away. 3 meeting rooms. 4 mi. to downtown. 5 mi. to airport, courtesy car. Sea Oats Restaurant with ocean view; live entertainment in Teaser's cocktail lounge. Gazebo dining, too.

Bamboo Court Motel. *Inexpensive.* Pool, play area. Cook-out area. Restaurant nr.

Fort Walton Beach

Aloha Village. *Deluxe.* 860 Scallop Court. Pools. Restaurant. Free airport transportation.

Coronado. *Expensive.* On "Miracle Strip." Pool (heated), play area, beach. Restaurant, bar. Kitchen units avail.

Howard Johnson's. *Moderate.* On US 98. Pool (heated), beach, play area. Fishing pier, dock. Restaurant, bar, entertainment, dancing.

Sheraton Marina Motor Inn. *Moderate.* Pool, fishing, boating. Pets. Restaurant, bar, dancing, entertainment. Fam. rates avail.

Blue Horizon. *Inexpensive.* Pool, play area, beach. Restaurant nr. Picnic area.

FLORIDA

Gainesville

Gainesville Hilton. *Expensive.* 2900 S.W. 13th St. 208 Mediterranean-style rooms overlooking lake. Heated pool, recreation area. Adjacent to University of Florida. Restaurant, lounge, nightclub.

Howard Johnson's. *Moderate.* 2 locations. 2830 N.W. 13th St, I-75 and State Rd. 26. Both have outdoor pools, restaurant, lounge.

Plantation Inn. *Moderate.* 1901 S.W. 13th Ave. Pool. Restaurant, *Mardi Gras Lounge* with shows.

Best Western Ponderosa Lodge. *Inexpensive.* I 75 and SR 121. Cozy. Pool. 36 rooms.

Days Inn. *Inexpensive.* 6901 N.W. 8th Ave. One of popular chain. Pool, play area, gift shop. *Tasty World* restaurant.

Haines City

Grenelefe. *Deluxe.* This Radison Resort may be difficult to find at first, but it is worth the search for this vacation hideaway. One- and two-bedroom fully-furnished suites with patio or balcony. Championship golf, two heated pools, fishing, playground, tennis. Dining room, coffee shop, cocktails. On acres of landscaped gardens, 6 mi. E of US 27 on SR 544. Convenient to Cypress Gardens, Circus World, Sea World, and Disney World.

Hallandale

Sunaqua. *Deluxe.* 1945 S. Ocean Dr. Pool, play area, dock. Restaurant. Cook-out facilities. Kitchen units avail.

Hallandale Beach TraveLodge. *Moderate.* Pool (heated), play area, beach. Restaurant with piano bar, dancing.

Hialeah

Holiday Inn. *Moderate.* Pool. Pets. Restaurant, bar, dancing, entertainment. Free airport transportation.

Hillsboro Beach

Barefoot Mailman. *Expensive.* 1061 Hillsboro Mile, just north of Pompano Beach. Newly decorated rooms. Docking facilities on Intracoastal Waterway. 18-hole golf course. Sundeck. Private 4-mile beach. Gourmet Mary Celeste dining room. Transportation to and from Ft. Lauderdale Airport.

Hollywood

Attaché. *Deluxe.* 2711 S. Ocean Dr. Resort hotel with beach. Pools. Golf, tennis. Play area. Supervised program for children, teen-agers. Restaurant, bars, dancing, entertainment.

Diplomat. *Deluxe.* Resort hotel on 600 acres. Pools (heated), beach, Golf, tennis. Play area. Supervised children's program. Coffee shop, dining room. Bars with name entertainment, dancing. Excellent service.

Homosassa Springs

Riverside Villas Resort Motel. *Moderate.* Pool. Tennis, fishing, boating. Golf nr. Kitchen units, wkly rates avail. Homosassa River views.

Sheraton-Homosassa Springs Inn. *Moderate.* Overlooks Pepper Creek. At US 19 and 98. Heated pool. Tennis, playground. Restaurant, cocktail lounge. Entertainment.

Indian Shores

Holiday Villas III. *Moderate.* 18610 Gulf Blvd., near St. Pete Beach and Clearwater. On beautiful beach. One- and two-bedroom apartments with kitchens, living rooms. Rent by day, week, month. Near restaurants, shopping, fishing. Friendly, attentive management.

Islamorada

Cheeca Lodge. *Deluxe.* US 1. 25-acre resort with 1,100-foot ocean beach, 525-foot illuminated fishing pier, par-3 nine-hole golf course. Once a rich man's hideaway; now a year-round resort.

Jacksonville

Jacksonville Hilton. *Deluxe.* 565 S. Main St. Pool (heated), play area, marina. Restaurant, bars, entertainment. Overlooks city, river.

Sheraton St. Johns Place. *Deluxe to Expensive.* 825 Hendricks Ave. Overlooking river. $20-million, 350-room hotel, opened late 1980. Pool, tennis courts, two restaurants, lounges with entertainment.

Best Western Foxfire Inn. *Moderate.* 9150 Baymeadows Rd. Convenient to downtown, beaches, sightseeing. Pool. Tennis, 18-hole par golf course. Oyster bar, gourmet restaurant, nightly entertainment. Airport limo service.

Quality Inn-Skycenter. *Moderate.* Conveniently located at Jacksonville Intl. Airport. Pool, restaurant, lounge, fish-stocked lake.

Admiral Benbow Inn. *Inexpensive.* 820 Dunn Ave. Pool (heated), play area. Pets. Restaurant, bar, dancing. Free airport transportation.

Days Inn. *Inexpensive.* I-95 & State 102, Airport Rd.; Cagle Rd. & University Ave. Many family efficiency suites; 5929 Ramona Blvd. Pool, play area, gift shop, gas station and *Tasty World* restaurant at all addresses. Pets allowed.

Jacksonville Beach

Howard Johnson's. *Expensive.* 151 N. 1st St. On the beach. Pool, whirlpools. Game room. Coin laundry. Tennis, Golf, fishing nearby. Accommodations for handicapped. 24-hr. restaurant, cocktail lounge.

Sheraton Resort Inn. *Moderate.* Oceanfront, S. 1st St. 10 mi. from I-95. Pool, volleyball, croquet. Golf, tennis nearby. Yellow Pelican Restaurant, *J.C. Hillary's Lounge.* Entertainment nightly.

Key Biscayne

Key Biscayne Hotel & Villas. *Deluxe.* Pool (heated). On private beach, with Sunfish avail. Tennis, play area. Supervised children's program in summer & holidays. Restaurant, bars, dancing.

Sonesta Beach Hotel & Tennis Club. *Deluxe.* Resort hotel on private beach. Luxurious villas also available. Pool (heated), play area, tennis, sailing & bicycles avail. Supervised children's program in summer, vacation period. Restaurants, bars, entertainment, dancing. MAP avail., fam. rates avail. in summer.

Key Colony. *Expensive.* Pool (heated), private beach. Tennis, play area. Cookout facilities. Restaurant nr. Golf.

Royal Biscayne. *Expensive.* Pools (heated), beach, tennis, sailing, scuba diving, play area. Restaurants, bar. Kitchen units, fam. rates avail.

Key Largo

Holiday Inn. *Moderate.* US 1. Pool, marina, tennis. Kennel. Restaurant, bar.

Howard Johnson's. *Moderate.* Gulf-front, 2-story motel. Pool (heated). Restaurant, bar. Suites, studio rooms avail.

Key West

Howard Johnson's. *Deluxe.* US 1. 3031 N. Roosevelt Blvd. Pool. Nr. sport fishing, scuba, snorkeling. Also nr. conch sightseeing train, boutiques, Oldtown. Beach, 5 min. shopping mall, 2 movie theaters across street. Cocktail lounge.

Marriott's Casa Marina Resort. *Deluxe.* Formerly the palatial Casa Marina Hotel, built by Henry Flagler in 1920. Declared an Historical Structure. Popular with celebrities in the '30s and '40s. Refurbished and expanded to 250 rooms, 200-seat restaurant, 150-seat cocktail lounge, cabana bar, pool, tennis courts, gym. About 1,000 feet of Atlantic beachfront. On 6.5 acres.

Pier House and Beach Club. *Deluxe.* Harborfront in picturesque old section of town. A landmark. Everybody meets here. Fortune spent in 1980–81 on improvements, refurbishing. Balconies, patios. Some efficiencies. Boating, waterskiing arranged. Interesting restaurant.

Quality Inn. *Expensive.* 3850 N. Roosevelt Blvd. one mi. from airport. Conch tour train on premises. Pool. Game area, nature walk on 4 landscaped acres. Free in-room movies. Nr. fishing. Suites, kitchenettes avail. Coffee shop, dining room, cocktail lounge. Social activities and children's program.

Sugar Loaf Lodge. *Moderate.* Pool, play area. Tennis. Marina, airstrip near. Restaurant, bar. Kitchen units avail. (On Sugarloaf Key, about 17 mi. from Key West.)

Days Inn. *Inexpensive to Moderate.* Suites, too. Kennel.

Kissimmee

Orlando Hyatt Hotel World. *Deluxe.* 6375 Space Coast Parkway. Resort world with 8 pools, playgrounds, 3 lighted tennis courts. Shuttle to Disney World. 960 rooms! 1.3 mile-free Fit-Trail jogging course on property with 12 "exercise stations," basketball courts, "electric" game room. Helicopter rides. Exhibit hall, convention facilities. Coffee Shop, *Limey Jim* dining room, cocktail lounge, entertainment.

Hilton Inn Gateway. *Expensive to Deluxe.* 7470 Space Coast Pkwy. Only 1 mile from Disney World. 360 rooms with 2 queen-sized beds in each, 3 studios, 10 suites. Covered garden terrace dining area, 2 pools, 18-hole par 54 putting course. Playground, coin laundry. Game room. Boutiques. Convention facilities. Restaurant, cocktail lounge, entertainment. (see listing for 2 Hilton Inns, Orlando).

Holiday Inn. *Expensive.* Two locations. East: 5678 Space Coast Pkwy. West: 7300 Space Coast Pkwy. Both with pool, wading pool, playground, tennis, coffee shop, restaurant, cocktail lounge, entertainment.

Rodeway Inn at Disney World. *Expensive.* 2795 State Rd. 545 S. One mi. west of Disney World entrance. Heated pool, playground. Coin-operated laundry. Restaurant, cocktail lounge. Game room.

Colonial Motor Lodge. *Moderate.* 1815 Vine St. Apartments avail. with kitchens. 2 pools. Nr. restaurant. Pets.

Days Inn. *Moderate.* 4 locations: 5820 Spacecoast Pkwy., 5840 Spacecoast Pkwy., 7980 Spacecoast Pkwy. US 441 and Sunshine Pkwy. St. Cloud. Spacecoast Parkway inns are a couple of mins. from Disney World. All have pools, restaurant, playground. (see listing of 6 Days Inns under "Orlando," Altamonte Springs, Clermont, Sanford).

Kissimmee Red Carpet Inn. *Inexpensive.* 2009 W. Vine St. 120 rooms. Heated pool, sundeck. Family game room, playground. Dining room, cocktail lounge. Nr. tennis, golf.

Lake City

Best Western Travelers Inn Motel. *Moderate.* 13 mi. S of Lake City on US 41-441 at Junct. of I-75. Pool. Tubing on Ichetucknee River 15 min. away. Restaurant nr. University of Florida (Gainesville) about 30 mi.

Howard Johnson's. *Inexpensive.* I-75 & US 90. Pool, play area. Golf nr. Pets. Restaurant. Nr. tubing, hunting.

Quality Inn. *Inexpensive.* Pool, play area. Pets. Restaurant, bar entertainment, dancing on wknds.

Lakeland

Holiday Inn. *Moderate.* 3 locations with usual amenities: Wheeler St.; **North:** 910 E. Memorial Blvd.; **South:** 3405 S. Florida Ave.

Lakeland Hilton Inn. *Moderate.* I-4 and US Hwy. 98. One of the city's newest. Spanish-style structure has 40-by-50-foot L-shaped swimming pool, sun terrace and play area. Covered promenade connects dining room, lounge and meeting room. 5 mi. from Lakeland Civic Center. One mi. from 18-hole golf course.

Days Inn. *Inexpensive.* On I-4 and US 98 (3223 N US 98). Usual good value at this chain. About 40 mi. from Disney World, 35 mi. from Busch Gardens.

Lake Wales

Chalet Suzanne Resort Inn. *Deluxe.* Pool (heated), play area. Fine restaurant. Kitchen units, cottages avail. Each room is decorated differently with objets d'art from around the world. Arab dhow moored in lake.

River Ranch Resort. *Moderate.* Route 1, Box 400. Hayrides, cookouts, square dances, rodeos, and dude-ranch diversions. Check to see if still open before you go.

Howard Johnson's. *Inexpensive.* US Rt. 27 N. Pool, play area, fishing, boats. Private freshwater lake. Restaurant open 24 hrs.

Emerald Motel. *Inpensive.* Pool. Pets. Restaurant nr. (Superior Motels chain.)

Lake Worth

Martinique Motor Lodge. *Inexpensive.* Free coffee & morning rolls in season. Restaurant nr.

Holiday House. *Inexpensive.* Pool, beach nr., play area. Kitchen units avail. Restaurant nr.

Marathon

Sombrero Reef Club (formerly Bill King's Sombrero Resort). *Expensive.* Pool (heated), sauna. Restaurant, bar, dancing, entertainment occasionally. Fishing, boat ramp. Cook-out facilities. Free airport transport. Kitchen units, cottages avail.

Buccaneer Lodge. *Moderate.* US 1. Private beach, lagoon, pools. Tennis, fishing, boat ramp. Restaurant, cocktail lounge, entertainment.

Faro Blanco Marine Resort. *Moderate.* Salt-water pool. Play area. Golf, tennis nr. Dock, charter boats avail. Cook-out facilities. Kitchen units avail.

Marco

Port of the Islands (formerly Remuda Ranch). *Expensive.* Route 41. On Gulf of Mexico. Newly refurbished Southern-style resort with outstanding, relaxed decor. Y-shaped pool, six lighted tennis courts, marina with charter boats, landing strip. Own airline (Royal Airways) for charter to Miami (75 mi. away) or other points. About 250 rooms. 16 mi. from Marco Island.

Marineland

Marineland Quality Inn. *Inexpensive.* Pool (heated). Beach, pools, marina. Tennis, putting green. Rest. cocktails. Free return passes to Marineland exhibit.

Melbourne

Holiday Inn Melbourne Oceanfront. *Expensive.* New in 1979. Colossal swimming pool dramatically includes part of lobby area. Three tiered restaurant with seascapes. Beautiful supper club. $5-million showcase.

Ramada Inn. *Moderate to Expensive.* 964 S. Harbor City Blvd. Pool, 2 mi. to beach. Restaurant, cocktail lounge, accommodations for handicapped.

Naples

Beach Club Hotel. *Deluxe.* 851 Gulf Shore Blvd. Pool (heated), beach, golf, tennis. Play area. Free airport transportation. Golf pkg., EP, kitchen units avail.

Best Western Beach & Tennis Club. *Deluxe.* Hickory Blvd., Bonita Beach (at Naples). 7 mi. Gulf beach. 10 clay tennis courts. Fishing, boating, family recreation center.

Cove Inn. *Deluxe.* Pool (heated), play area. Boats avail. Golf nr. Kitchen units avail. Restaurant, bar. Free transportation to bus terminal, golf.

La Playa Beach and Racquet Club. *Deluxe.* 9891 Gulfshore Blvd. Beautiful 5-mile white sand beach. Heated pool. Fishing. Nr. golf. Penthouse suites available. Gourmet restaurant, lounge.

Sheraton Edgewater Beach Inn. *Deluxe.* Gulfshore Blvd. Pool (heated), play area. Golf nr. Private beach. Kitchen units, fam. rates avail. Free transp. to terminals. Swank, statue-decorated entrance; small, attractive lobby.

Best Western Buccaneer Inn (formerly Buccaneer Red Carpet). *Moderate.* U.S. 41 N. Heated pools with garden area. Pretty view from rooms. Very well-maintained.

Naples Motor Lodge. *Moderate.* 250 9th St. Heated pool. 5 min. from beach. Nr. fishing pier, fishing boats, golf.

New Smyrna Beach

Best Western Islander Beach Lodge. *Moderate.* 1601 S. Atlantic Ave. Heated pool, playground, restaurant, lounge. Wading pool, putting green. Indoor whirlpool, sauna. Miniature golf.

Smyrna Motel. *Inexpensive.* 1050 N. Dixie Freeway. Play area. Restaurant nr. Pets.

Ocala

Quality Inn Town and Country. *Moderate.* 3330 S. Pine Ave. 1 mi. south of Ocala. Heated pool. Restaurant. Poolside dining. Putting green. Game area, game room. Cocktail lounge.

Sheraton-Ocala Motor Inn. *Moderate.* Pool, play area. Restaurant, bar, dancing, entertainment wknds.

Days Inn. *Inexpensive.* I-75 and FL 40. Usual good standards. Pool, play area, gift shop, gas station. Pets. *Tasty World* restaurant.

Orlando

Orlando Marriott Hotel. *Deluxe.* 6700 Sand Lake Rd. (formerly Sheraton Olympic Villas). A multimillion-dollar renovation encompassing 652 rooms, 264 full kitchen suites. 11 separate 2-story buildings on 35 acres. 2 Olympic heated pools, 6 lighted tennis courts with pro, 2 playgrounds, putting green, miniature golf, shuffleboard. Golf courses nearby. Restaurants, live disco, cocktail lounges, snackbar gazebo. 24-hr. coffee shop. Boutiques, pro shop. Big convention facilities.

Sheraton-Twin Towers Hotel. *Deluxe.* 5780 Major Blvd. Suites avail. Heated pool, whirlpool, Sauna, gymnasium. Shuttle to Disney World. Restaurant, coffee shop, cocktail lounge, entertainment.

Best Western World Inn. *Expensive.* I-4 and 33rd St. About 14 mi. to Disney World, Sea World. Heated Olympic pool, playground. Small pets. (*Deluxe* Best Western World Inn at Lake Buena Vista.)

Colonial Plaza Motor Inn. *Expensive.* 2801 E. Colonial Dr. Nr. U.S. Naval Training Center. Suites, kitchenettes available. Heated pool, therapeutic pools. Nr. golf, restaurants. *Wooden Nickel* cocktail lounge.

Gold Key Inn. *Expensive.* 7100 S. Orange Blossom Trail. Heated pool, tennis arranged. Putting greens. Suites, also. Popular *Picadilly Restaurant* and cocktail lounge.

Hilton Inn-Florida Center. *Expensive.* 7400 International Dr. 285 rooms, sev. suites, kitchenettes. 2 pools (covered, outdoor). Coffee shop, restaurant, cocktail lounge.

Holiday Inn Disney World Airport. *Expensive.* 7900 S. Orange Blossom Trail. Pool, wading pool. Restaurant, cocktail lounge. Pets allowed.

Holiday Inn at 6 other greater Orlando locations, all with resort amenities: **Holiday Inn-Altamonte Springs** (short distance from Worlds); **Holiday Inn-**

International Dr. (largest and most attractive); **Holiday Inn-Lee Road; Holiday Inn-Midtown; Holiday Inn-South; Holiday Inn-Orlando West.**

Sheraton World. *Expensive.* 10100 Intl. Dr., next door to Sea World. Beautiful resort complex; heated pool, restaurants, cocktail lounge with entertainment. Wading pool, miniature golf. Two lighted tennis courts. Shuttle to Disney World.

Howard Johnson's Motor Lodge. *Moderate to Expensive.* Seven of 12 locations, each with full amenities of this reputable chain: **Sea World:** State 528 at I-4; **Airport:** 8820 S. Orange Blossom Trail; **Downtown:** 304 W. Colonial Dr.; **Florida Center:** Kirkman Rd.; **North:** 603 Lee Rd.; **South:** 4201 S. Orange Blossom Trail; **West:** 2014 W. Colonial Dr.

Sheraton Orlando Jetport Inn. *Moderate to Expensive.* Convenient to airport. 9301 S. Orange Blossom Trail. Heated pool, popular restaurant, lively lounge.

Ramada Inn. *Moderate.* 3 locations. West Highway 50. Pool, wading pool, playground. Lighted tennis. Shuttle for Disney World, Stars Hall of Fame, Mystery Fun House, Wet and Wild. Gift shop. Restaurant, cocktail lounge. Also at 4919 West Colonial Dr.; 8700 S. Orange Blossom. Accommodations for handicapped at two—not at Colonial Dr.

Red Carpet Inn O'Wizard. *Moderate.* 6301 International Dr. Heated pool, wading pool, playground. Wet and Wild flume attraction across the street. Coffee shop, restaurant, cocktail lounge. Nr. golf, shops.

La Quinta Motor Inn. *Inexpensive to Moderate.* Located next to Quality Inn High Q 5825 International Dr. Heated pool, wading pool. 2-story Spanish inn style. Good for families on a budget—rooms accommodate up to 6 persons. Restaurant adjacent to Quality Inn's La Trattoria.

Davis Bros. Motor Lodge. *Inexpensive.* 6603 International Dr. Heated pool, wading pool. Cafeteria. (Also Davis Bros. Motor Lodges and Cafeterias in Ocala, Ormond Beach, Bartow.)

Ormond Beach

Ellinor Village Vacation Resort. *Deluxe.* Villas include fully equipped kitchens, bedrooms, living room, dining area, bathrooms. 1, 2, 3 or 4 bedroom villas.

Days Inn (formerly Sheraton Daytona Beach Motor Inn). *Expensive.* Pool (heated), play area, beach. Golf and tennis nr. Kitchen units. All the amenities of this top-rated, family-oriented chain.

Biltmore Beach Lodge. *Moderate.* 187 S. Atlantic Ave. (A1A) Pool (heated), play area, golf nr. Beachfront, restaurant, lounge.

Palm Beach

Brazilian Court Hotel. *Deluxe.* 300 Brazilian Ave. TV on request. Fine restaurant, bar. Breakfast free. AP avail. Closed Apr. to mid-Dec.

Breakers Hotel. *Deluxe.* Large, elegant resort hotel on private beach with cabana club. Pool (heated), golf, tennis, riding. Social director, planned activities. Dancing, entertainment. Restaurant, bars. MAP Feb., Mar.; EP June to Sept.; AP palace of the Flagler family.)

Colony. *Deluxe.* 155 Hammon Ave. Pool (heated), sauna. Golf nr. Restaurant, bar, dancing. Closed late Apr. to Thanksgiving.

Best Western Palm Beach Hawaiian. *Expensive.* 3550 S. Ocean Blvd. Private beach, pool (heated). Restaurant, cocktail lounge, entertainment. Nr. Worth Ave. shopping.

Holiday Inn. *Expensive.* 2770-2830 S. Ocean Blvd. Pools, sauna, play area, beach, tennis. Restaurant, bar, dancing. Kitchen units avail. A resort complex.

Howard Johnson's. *Expensive.* 2870 S. County Rd. Pool (heated), beach. Pets. Restaurant, bar. Exceptionally attractive balconied rooms.

Palm Beach Hampton. *Expensive.* 3080 S. Ocean Blvd. On Private beach, with play area. Kitchen units. No children under 12. Closed May 1–Oct. 1.

Pensacola

Ramada Inn. *Expensive.* 6550 Pensacola Blvd. Suites available. Pool, playground. Restaurant, lounge.

Best Western Seville Inn. *Moderate.* 223 E. Garden St. Indoor, outdoor pools. Children under 18 free. 2 blks. from historic Seville Sq. Beaches 5 mi.

Holiday Inn. *Moderate.* 3 locations, each with pool, play area: 19 mi. E. on State 399; **Gulf Breeze South:** US 98; **North:** US 29.

Howard Johnson's. *Inexpensive.* Two 7051 Pensacola Blvd. **Beach:** 14 Via de Luna. *Expensive.*

Pompano Beach

Beachcomber Hotel & Villas. *Deluxe.* 1200 S. Ocean Blvd. Resort style motel with private beach. Pools (heated), play area. Free golf off-season. Restaurant, bar, music. Kitchen units avail.

Best Western Sea Garden Resort. *Deluxe.* 615 N. Ocean Blvd. Beautiful tropical gardens, oceanfront. Rooms, efficiencies apartments. 2 pools (heated), putting green. Tennis arrangements. Restaurant, lounge.

Yardarm Inn. *Deluxe.* On Hillsboro Inlet. No daily room rate less than $100. Only for 322 wealthy guests! Three gourmet restaurants, saunas, marina. 24-hour room service, too.

Lighthouse Cove. *Expensive.* 406 N. Ocean Blvd. Pools, golf, tennis, beach, supervised play. Restaurant, bar. Kitchen units avail.

Ponte Vedra Beach

Ponte Vedra Club. *Expensive to Deluxe.* Old-fashioned southern style resort; one of four oldest in state. New wings, of course, with all comforts. Main inn and villas; VIP suites. One of top 50 tennis clubs. (Elaborate Racquet Club). 36-hole golf course with lagoon. Three swimming pools. Excellent restaurant, cocktail lounge. Entertainment. 20 mi. s. of Jacksonville and 20 mi. n. of St. Augustine.

Port St. Lucie

Sandpiper Bay Resort. *Moderate to Expensive.* On banks of St. Lucie river (just off U.S. 1). Award-winning resort on 1,000 acres. 11 tennis courts, tennis clinic; 45 holes championship golf. Marina with powerboats, sailboats. Terrific restaurant, coffee shop, lounges. All accommodations are attractive suites. Vacation packages.

Riviera Beach

Hilton Inn. *Deluxe.* 3800 N. Ocean Dr. Pool (heated), private beach. Tennis, sauna, children's pool, play area. Restaurant, bar, entertainment, dancing. Kitchen units avail. Golf privileges.

Seaspray Best Western. *Expensive.* 123 Ocean Ave. Pool (heated), play area, beach. Restaurant, bar, entertainment, dancing in season. Barbecue facilities. Kitchen units avail.

Sheraton Ocean Inn. *Expensive.* 3200 N. Ocean Dr. Attractive oceanfront resort. Heated pool. Restaurant; cocktail lounge with entertainment. Some suites.

Tahiti on the Ocean. *Expensive.* 3920 N. Ocean Dr. Pools (heated), private beach. Cook-out facilities. Restaurant nr. Kitchen units avail. Picnic grills and tables. Nine-hole putting green; playground.

St. Augustine

Ponce de Leon Lodge & Country Club. *Expensive.* Resort style motel on 350 acres. Pool (heated), play area, golf, tennis. Restaurant, bar, entertainment, dancing Sat. MAP, suites avail.

Best Western Inn. *Moderate.* Jct. I-95 and FL 16. Pool, wading pool. Play area. Cocktail lounge.

Holiday Inn. *Moderate.* 2 of 3 locations, each with pool, restaurant, bar, dancing, entertainment in season: I-95 at State 16; US 1, 1300 Ponce de Leon Blvd.

Best Western Spanish Quarter Inn. *Inexpensive.* 6 Castillo Dr. Pool. Across from Chamber of Commerce info.

Candyland Red Carpet Inn. *Inexpensive.* I-95 and FL. 16. Pleasant 2-story motel. Pool. Pets. Restaurant.

St. Augustine Beach

Holiday Inn By The Sea. *Expensive.* On SR A1A. Beachfront. Pool. Tennis arranged. Some kitchenettes. Restaurant, cocktail lounge, entertainment.

La Fiesta Motor Lodge. *Moderate.* Pool, play area, private beach. Coffee shop.

Sea Shore Motel. *Inexpensive.* A1A at 12th St. Kitchenettes, weekly rates avail. Convenient to restaurant, laundromat.

St. Pete Beach Area

Don CeSar Beach Resort Hotel. *Deluxe.* 3400 Gulf Blvd. A big, pink towered and turreted Spanish-style villa in the grand manner, completely modernized. 300 rooms, suites, penthouses. Private beach, tennis, health club, playground. Restaurants, lounge, entertainment. Boutique shops, ice-cream parlor. Designated a National Historic Landmark.

Breckenridge Resort Hotel. *Expensive.* 5700 Gulf Blvd. Gulf-front large rooms, some efficiencies. Heated pool. Dining patio. Popular restaurant, live entertainment.

Dolphin Resort. *Expensive.* 4900 Gulf Blvd. On long stretch of beach. Heated pool, play area. Kitchen units avail. Restaurant, cocktail lounge, entertainment, dancing.

Normandy Beach Resort. *Expensive.* 5606 Gulf Blvd. On beautiful white sand beach. Small, friendly, family-oriented resort. Garden apartments, efficiencies. Children's supervised activities. Large heated pool. Coin laundry.

St. Petersburg Beach Hilton Inn. *Expensive.* 5250 Gulf Blvd. Unusual octagonally shaped tower on beach. Outside glass bubble elevator to revolving rooftop restaurant and cocktail lounge. Polynesian specialties. Entertainment. Coffee shop, boutique.

Schrafft's Sandpiper Resort Inn. *Expensive.* 6000 Gulf Blvd. Three penthouse apartments, lanai suites, balconied rooms. Kitchen units avail. Heated pool and patio, children's pool, new glass-enclosed, climate-controlled pool with sundeck. Supervised children's programs. Tennis, private beach. Gift shops. Snack shop. *Brown Derby* restaurant and *Luv Pub* nr. entrance.

Howard Johnson's Motor Lodge. *Moderate.* 6100 Gulf Blvd. Beachfront, heated pool, restaurant.

Odyssey Gulf Resort. *Moderate.* 5400 Gulf Blvd. Pleasant, small resort with comfortable efficiency units, garden apartments, heated pool, wading pool. Right on wide, white sand beach. Coin laundry. Pets. Coffee shop. Inter-resort children's supervised activities. Nice for families.

St. Petersburg

Bayfront Concourse (formerly Hilton). *Expensive.* 333 First St. on Bayfront. Extensively refurbished. Lobby bar, Greenhouse restaurant, New Playboy Bunny Club opened mid-1981; bring your Playboy Club keys, members! Convention-oriented. Nr. Municipal Marina, sightseeing attractions, shopping.

Sheraton-St. Petersburg Marina & Tennis Club. *Expensive.* 6800 34th St. At Sunshine Skyway bridge entrance. Pools, play area. Marina, fishing. Restaurant, cocktail lounge, entertainment. Kitchen units avail.

Albermarle Hotel. *Moderate.* 145 Third Ave. N.E. Family-owned for over 40 years. Public rooms furnished with gorgeous antiques. Elegant atmosphere. Heated pool. TV in lounge. Social program. Dining room. Open winter season only.

Lamp Post Inn. (Best Western). *Inexpensive.* 1200 34th St. N. In-room coffee. Pool, restaurant, cocktail lounge, entertainment. Gulf beaches 10 min. Nr. Sunken Gardens, Bayfront.

Quality Inn (formerly Save Inn). *Inexpensive.* I-275 and 54th Ave. N. A budget bargain. Pool, play area, game room. Very good restaurant; cocktail lounge.

Sanford

Best Western Sanford Inn. *Moderate.* I-4 and Hwy. 46. Heated pool. *Jungle Joe's* restaurant, lounge. Auto Train, 3 min. Disney World, 35 min.

Slumberland Court. *Inexpensive to Moderate.* 2611 Orlando Dr. Motel kitchenette units, too. Weekly rates avail.

Sanibel Island

Casa Ybel. *Deluxe.* Villa-style accommodations on site of island's first resort. Interval-ownership plan also. Excellent restaurant. Outstanding beach.

Island Inn. *Deluxe.* Pool (heated), beach, play area, tennis. Dining room with box lunches avail. MAP, fam. rates, kitchen units avail.

Best Western Shell Harbor Inn. *Deluxe.* Pool (heated), beach, dock. Free in-room coffee. Kitchen units avail. Cook-out facilities. Tennis. Golf nr.

Song of the Sea. *Deluxe.* Pool (heated), beach, boats avail., play area. All accommodations (studios to apartments) have fully equipped kitchen, screened balcony. Cook-out facilities. Restaurant nr.

Sundial Beach Hotel. *Deluxe.* 1246 Gulf Dr. Heated pool. Gulf front villas. Putting green, tennis courts, bikes. Shuttle to Sanibel Inn restaurant.

West Wind Inn. *Moderate.* Gulf Dr. Pool (heated), play area, beach, tennis. Restaurant nr. Kitchen units avail.

Sarasota

Best Western Aku Tiki Inn. *Deluxe.* 1854 Ben Franklin Dr. On beautiful Lido Beach. Heated pool, sundeck. Restaurant, cocktail lounge, beach bar.

Colony Beach & Tennis Club. *Deluxe.* 1620 Gulf of Mexico Dr. Longboat Key. National headquarters for U.S. Professional Tennis Association (over 21 championship courts and stadium court). Pool (heated), beach, tennis, play area. Restaurant, bar, dancing, entertainment.

Far Horizons. *Deluxe.* 2401 Gulf of Mexico Dr., Longboat Key. Pool (heated). Golf, tennis, play area. Beach with thatched cabanas. Kitchen units, suites avail. Closed Labor Day–Oct. 1.

Longboat Key Hilton. *Deluxe.* 4711 Gulf of Mexico Dr. Luxurious beachfront resort. Heated pool, tennis. Scuba, sailboats avail. *Banyan Tree* and *Pineapple Place* restaurants, *Tree House* cocktail lounge, entertainment.

Sarasota Hyatt House Hotel. *Deluxe.* 1000 Blvd. of the Arts. Four lighted tennis courts, marina, pool. Gourmet restaurants, cocktail lounge. Near Van Wezel Hall and Asolo Theatre.

Sheraton Sandcastle. *Deluxe.* 1540 Ben Franklin Dr. Lido Beach. Restaurant, cocktail lounge. Pool (heated); beach with thatched shelters. Golf nr. Sprawling resort complex with variety of accommodations.

Azure Tides Hotel. *Expensive.* 1330 Ben Franklin Dr. Lido Beach. Pool (heated), beach, fishing, play area. Restaurant, bar. Kitchen units avail.

Buccaneer Inn. *Expensive.* 595 Dream Island Rd. at Yacht Harbor. Longboat Key. Pool (heated), beach nr., boating, fishing, tennis, play area. Restaurant, bar, entertainment. Kitchen units avail.

Coquina on the Beach. *Expensive.* 1008 Ben Franklin Dr. Pool (heated), beach, boating, fishing, play area. Restaurant nr. Kitchen apts. avail.

Ramada Inn. *Expensive.* 6545 N. Tamiami Trail. Pool (heated), play area. Thatched shelters on beach. Golf nr. Kitchen units avail. Restaurant, bar, dancing in season.

Red Carpet Inn-Hawaiian Villa. *Moderate.* 8150 N. Tamiami Trail. Heated pool. Dining room, nightclub.

Best Western Royal Palms. *Inexpensive.* 1701 N. Tamiami Trail. Pool (heated), play area. Restaurant.

Days Inn Sarasota. *Inexpensive.* 4900 N. Tamiami Trail (Hwy. 41). New, $2 million two-story, 122-room inn. On five-acre site nr. Sarasota-Bradenton Airport. *Daybreak* restaurant, pool.

Stuart

Indian River Plantation Resort. *Deluxe.* On 195 acres on southern end of Hutchinson Island. Beachfront on Atlantic Ocean. 120 villa-style accommodations in two 4-story lodges. Each with private balcony overlooking beach. Fully equipped kitchens in all 1- and 2-bedroom apartments. 2 swimming pools, 11 Har-Tru tennis courts, 18-hole executive golf course, bicycle paths. Tom Falkenburg, Director of Tennis; PGA member Bob Erickson, Golf Pro. Sailboat rentals, charter fishing nearby. Direct access to beach via boardwalks, sand dunes. Porch Restaurant, cozy, relaxed. Open from early breakfast to late dinner. Hotel guests who catch fish may have them prepared and served. Small conference center.

Tallahassee

Tallahassee Hilton. *Moderate.* 101 S. Adams St. Pool (heated). Pets. Restaurant, bar, entertainment, dancing. Golf & tennis nr.

Tallahassee Motor Hotel. (Master Hosts-Red Carpet Inn). *Moderate.* 1630 N. Monroe St. Playground. Restaurant. Rooms for handicapped.

Tampa

Host International Hotel. *Deluxe.* In Tampa's showcase International Airport. Luxurious rooms. Special Executives' Sixth Floor, with complimentary cocktails, champagne, and European services. Lobby Seafood Bar, cocktail lounge with backgammon games, pool, disco, coffee shop, revolving CK's penthouse restaurant.

Bar Harbor Inn. *Expensive.* 7700 Courtney Campbell Causeway. Heated pool. Small beach, rental sailboats. Playground. Restaurant, entertainment.

Tampa Marriott. *Expensive.* 100 N. Westshore Blvd. Opened early summer, 1981. Indoor-outdoor pool, hydrotherapy pool, saunas, exercise center. Game room. Restaurants, lounges. Two plush suites. 23 special executive rooms (300 rooms in all).

Hall of Fame Inn. *Moderate–Expensive.* 2222 N. Westshore Blvd. Tampa Bay Bucs headquarters. Pool, lighted tennis courts; golf extra. Very popular dining room and cocktail lounge with entertainment.

Admiral Benbow Inn. *Moderate.* 1200 N. Westshore Blvd. Heated pools, sauna. Dining room, cocktails, lively entertainment. Meeting rooms. Nr. airport entrance.

Tampa Hilton. *Moderate.* 200 Ashley Dr. $2-million refurbishing work in 1981. New Ashley's restaurant; Coco Hut bar at pool area and lanai deck. Special executive floor. Beautiful river views. Rooms have balconies.

Days Inn. *Inexpensive.* 3 locations. 2901 E. Busch Blvd. nr. Busch Gardens; I-75 (701 E. Fletcher Ave.); E Tampa at I-4 and FL 579N.

Howard Johnson's. *Inexpensive.* 2 locations, with pool, restaurant: **Airport:** 702 West Shore Blvd.; **North:** 720 E. Fowler Ave. At the E. Fowler motor lodge, guests can pick their own fruit (it's free!) in season from the citrus grove with 19 different trees.

156 **FLORIDA**

Tarpon Springs

Innisbrook Golf and Tennis Resort. *Deluxe.* US 19. 900 landscaped acres. Villas, lodges. Top-rated championship golf courses. Golf pro, tennis pro. 5 heated pools. Clubhouse dining rooms. Fishing, boating, biking. Wildlife sanctuary. Children's program. Special package rates. Entertainment nightly. Guests can pick oranges, grapefruit from private groves. Deluxe Australian Tennis Institute opened June, 1981. Great summer bargain: family of four, about $13 each per day!

Tierra Verde

Tierra Verde Hotel Yacht and Tennis Club. *Deluxe.* Opened late 1977, after being completely refurbished. Las Brisas casual restaurant. *Le Jazz Hot* cocktail lounge with entertainment; *Le Club* for romantic dining and dancing to live orchestra on special nights of week and weekend. Coffee shop. Huge swimming pool.

Titusville

Best Western First National Inn. *Inexpensive.* I-95 & Fl 50. Pool. Prime Rib restaurant. Entertainment nightly. 15 mi. to Playalinda Beach. Cape Kennedy Space Center, 9 mi. Disney World, Sea World, etc. 50 min.

Holiday Inn. *Inexpensive.* Pool (heated), play area. Restaurant, bar. Free in-room coffee.

Vero Beach

The Breakers. *Moderate.* Pool, play area, private beach. Morning coffee & rolls free. Restaurant nr. Kitchen units avail.

Reef Resort Motel. *Moderate.* Pool (heated). Pets. Restaurant, bar, dancing, entertainment. On ocean with private beach.

Sheraton Regency Resort Motel. *Moderate.* SR A1A. Oceanfront. Beach, indoor and outdoor heated pools. Pets. Restaurant, lounge with entertainment.

Best Western Landmark. *Inexpensive.* US 1 at 17th St. Heated pool. Restaurant nr. Pet dep. required.

Wesley Chapel

Saddlebrook. *Expensive to Deluxe.* New golf and tennis resort, about half-hour from Tampa Intl. Airport. Beautifully appointed suites, patios or balconies (villa style). *Little Club* restaurant, lounges. On 400 acres, surrounded by southern woodlands. Pools, six tennis courts, 18-hole championship golf course. Beauty salon, barber shop. 40 suites completed; 300 total by end of 1982.

West Palm Beach

Palm Beach Polo and Country Club. *Deluxe.* 13198 Forest Hill Blvd. On over a thousand acres. Golf, tennis and equestrian-polo villages with swimming pools. 18-hole championship golf course, 19 tennis courts (9 illuminated); polo fields, stables. Restaurants, lounges. About 15 mi. from beach and Palm Beach.

Howard Johnson's. *Expensive.* I-95 at Okeechobee Blvd. Pool, restaurant, bar. Accommodations for handicapped.

Ramada Inn. *Expensive.* Pool (heated). Free in-room coffee. Restaurant, bar, entertainment, dancing. Free airport transportation. Tennis. Golf.

Friendship Inn Lake Shore Court. *Moderate.* Pool (heated). Dock with charter boats avail. Play area. Free morning coffee & rolls. Outdoor grill. Restaurant nr.

Holiday Inn. *Moderate.* 100 Datura St. Pool, sauna. Pets. Restaurant, bar. Overlooking Lake Worth on Intracoastal Waterway.

Sheraton Inn-West Palm Beach. *Moderate.* Six-story inn with restaurant, pool (heated). Golf opposite; tennis nr.

Parkview Motor Lodge. *Inexpensive.* 4710 Dixie Hwy. Friendly, family-owned. Neat, quiet rooms. Nr. beaches, golf, shopping. Lion Country. Palm Beach International Airport 5 mins.

Winter Haven

Ranch House. *Moderate.* Pool (heated), play area. Boating, fishing, swimming in Lake Ina. Kitchen units avail.

Banyan Beach Motel. *Inexpensive.* Pool (heated). Pets. Dock, boats, fishing.

Best Western Landmark. *Inexpensive.* At US 17. Pool (heated), sauna. Restaurant, bar. Kitchen units avail. Shuffleboard. Nr. Cypress Gardens, Singing Tower. Disneyworld 25 mi.

• Winter Park

Alabama Hotel. *Moderate.* 800 Palmer Ave. Built in the 1920s, typical of resort of that era. Nostalgia has been preserved. Now open all yr. Rates for overnight or all winter. Public dining room.

Holiday Inn North. *Moderate.* Pool (heated). Pets. Restaurant.

Langford Resort Hotel. *Moderate.* Pool (heated), play area. Handsomely decorated restaurant, bar, dancing, entertainment. Kitchen units avail.

Best Western Mt. Vernon Motor Lodge. *Moderate.* Pool. Pets. Restaurant, bar.

 DINING OUT. Eating your way across Florida may not be good for the waistline—or the budget—but what fun you can have hopping a boat to *Cap's Place* in Lighthouse Point for turtle steak and hearts of palm salad, as well as a little history about rum-running days or the time Winston Churchill sampled Cap's cooking during a secret wartime conference! Or maybe the treat will be an old-fashioned farm feed at *Branch Ranch,* just off I-4 between Lakeland and Tampa. Or how about watching the shrimp boats come home as you dine in Florida's southernmost fish house, the A and B Lobster House in Key West? It's all mighty fine fare, and it's hard to find a city without at least one superior eating place. Restaurant categories reflect the cost of a medium-priced dinner at each establishment. Included are hors d'oeuvres or soup, entree and dessert. Not included are drinks, tax and tip. Price ranges for Florida are *Expensive:* $9.50 and higher, *Moderate:* $5.50 to $9 and *Inexpensive:* below $5. For a more complete explanation of restaurant categories see *Facts at Your Fingertips* at the front of this volume.

Boynton Beach

Bernard's. *Expensive.* 1730 N. Federal Hwy. Worth the splurge. Price of entree includes seafood coquille or soup du jour, fresh bread, unusual vegetable platter, salad, coffee and dessert! Wine, no liquor. Gorgeous gardens. Reservations required.

Busch's. *Moderate.* Alaskan King Crab a specialty. Entertainment.

Bradenton

Piccirilli's Italian Restaurant. *Expensive.* 2½ mi. n. of Sarasota-Bradenton Airport on U.S. 41. 6713 14th St. W. Pillared villa in garden setting. Gourmet Italian specialties, also chops, brochette, steaks, seafood. Dinner only.

Pete Reynard's. *Moderate.* 5325 Marina Dr. Fisherman's platter, roast duckling, steak & prime ribs. Music. The revolving dining room overlooks bay. Beautiful cocktail lounge. Arrive by car or boat (turn in at Inland Waterway Marker 62 and follow markers.) Lunch, dinner.

Pewter Mug Steak House. *Moderate.* 108 44th Ave. E. (Cortez Rd.). Just off U.S. 41. Famous for steaks, 2 lb. prime rib, lobster tails, crab legs, teriyaki chicken. Big salad bar and imported cheese dressings included. Classy, beamed ceiling atmosphere. Cocktail lounge. Dinner only. Another Pewter Mug in Venice, 1485 So Tamiami Trail.

The Pier. *Moderate.* Foot of 12th St. downtown. On historic Bradenton Memorial Pier, overlooking Manatee River. Key West 1920s nostalgia décor. Menu includes prawns-on-a-skewer, swordfish steak, beef. Double cocktail Happy Hour, lunch, dinner.

Cape Coral

Cape Coral. *Expensive.* Country Club Inn. Nicely-prepared continental dishes. Dancing & entertainment nightly in bar. Closed Mon.

Willy's. *Inexpensive.* German-American specialties, beer & wine. Closed Sun.

Clearwater

(Attractive Clearwater Mall and Countryside Mall, both US Hwy 19, have excellent snack shops, small restaurants.)

Siple's Garden Seat. *Expensive.* Prime ribs, roast duckling, steak, shrimp. Music. Overlooks garden and bay.

Kapok Tree Inn. *Moderate.* 923 McMullen Booth Rd. Palatial estate named for 100-year-old tree. Gardens and fountains inspired by Villa d'Este near Rome. Seating for 1,700 in resplendent dining rooms. Long wait for tables, so stroll through the gardens.

94th Aero Squadron. *Moderate.* Near St. Pete-Clearwater Airport. Normandy farmhouse on landscaped acres. World War I nostalgia theme. Lunch, dinner, late and light supper. Bar with theater showing old movies, if you have to wait for tables. Adjoins Boatyard (designed as old fishing village) with *Crab Cooker* restaurant—seafood grilled over mesquite wood fire.

Tio Pepe's. *Moderate.* 2930 Gulf-to-Bay Blvd. Spanish-villa atmosphere. Baked shrimps with almonds the specialty. Lunch and dinner.

Morrison's Cafeteria. *Inexpensive.* 1315 Cleveland. Roast beef, shrimp, homemade soup.

Clearwater Beach

Pelican. *Expensive.* Seafood, delicious baked goods. Stuffed shrimp a specialty. Closed Mon., late-Aug. to early-Sept.

Heilman's Beachcomber. *Expensive.* Steak, skillet-fried chicken, fresh seafood. Music.

Flagship. *Inexpensive.* 20 Island Way. Seafood platters and fish are specialties. Cocktails, too. Lunch, dinner. Artistically decorated.

Cocoa

Dixie. *Moderate.* Forrest Ave. Their Greek salad is renowned. Dancing. Closes only for Christmas.

Neptune Restaurant. *Moderate.* Forrest Ave. Seafood, shrimp, pastries. Children's portions. Closed Sun., hol.

Dell's Café des Crepes. *Inexpensive.* 210 Brevard Av. Cocoa Village. A tempting variety of crepes served in French sidewalk café ambience.

Cocoa Beach

Bernard's Surf. *Expensive.* S. Atlantic Ave. Fresh seafood, steak. Candlelit dining. Children's portions. A family restaurant for 30 years. If you dare, try whale meat or alligator steak.

Pelican Point Inn. *Expensive.* 2200 S. Orlando Ave. On scenic Banana River. Unusual turf and surf combinations. Own fishing fleet to catch seafood. Baked rock shrimp stuffed with crabmeat a winner. Delicious quail, steaks. Terrific Salad Bar, corn fritters. Don't miss dining here!

Carriage House Restaurant. *Moderate.* 136 Fifth Ave. Beach side of 192 Causeway. New York-style lunches, dinners. Delicious homemade cheesecake. Sun. brunch with free champagne. Cl. Mon.

Alma's Pizza and Italian Restaurant. *Inexpensive.* 306 N. Orlando Ave. Special pasta dinners. Take-out, too. Cocktail lounge.

Mousetrap. *Inexpensive.* On A1A. At Polaris Motel. Lunch, dinner, cocktail Happy Hour with hors d'oeuvres table. Sun. dinner only. Dancing, entertainment. Known for beef and salad bar dinners.

Willard's Landing and Rusty Steamer. *Inexpensive.* 1300 N. Atlantic Ave. At Holiday Inn. Luncheon buffet under $3. Grandma Peavy's Round-the-World Buffet every night, under $5. Half-price for children. Happy Hour cocktails half-price with free nibblers.

Dania

Le Cordon Bleu. *Expensive.* French cuisine, wine and brandy cellars. Frogs' legs a specialty plus Belgian dishes. Patronized by many celebrities. Over 40 years of distinguished dining. Reservations advised. Closed summers.

Daytona Beach

Anchor Inn. *Moderate.* Seafood and steak cooked to order.

Bali Restaurant. *Moderate.* Shish kebab a specialty.

160   FLORIDA

Chez Bruchez. *Moderate.* 304 Seabreeze Blvd. Try the roast filet nivernaise or frogs' legs provencale. French or American food. Attentive service. Beer, wine. Chef-owned. Everything is extra special.

Anchor Inn. *Inexpensive.* 608 W. Dunlawton Ave. at Port Orange Shopping Center. Not easy to find but well worth the search. Chef-owned. Delicious Florida seafood dishes (chicken and steak for landlubbers). Children's plates. Beer, wine.

Morrison's. *Inexpensive.* 200 N. Ridgewood. You can always count on this excellent chain for good food at low prices. Take-out service, too.

Deerfield Beach

Riverview Restaurant. *Expensive.* E. Riverview Rd., end of Intracoastal Bridge. Rustic atmosphere, old pine and cypress packing house. with Intracoastal Waterway view makes this a favorite among locals. Boaters can tie up at restaurant dock.

Pal's Captain's Table. *Expensive.* All the best from the sea. Baking done on premises.

Marsha's Blue Danube. *Moderate.* 949 S. Federal Hwy. Hungarian-accented dishes (goulash, veal paprika, wiener schnitzel and Blue Danube chicken). Lunch, dinner.

De Land

Amber Inn. *Moderate.* 225 W. New York Ave. In old landmark hotel, the Putnam. Unusual dishes, excellent salad bar. Old South atmosphere.

Old Spanish Sugar Mill. *Moderate.* At Ponce de Leon Springs park, near De Land. Restored historic building, housing The Grill and Griddle House. Diners prepare especially ground flour pancakes on electric griddle and steaks on charcoal grill at the table. Food is piping hot and just the way you like it.

Delray Beach

Arcade Tap Room. *Expensive.* 411 E. Atlantic. Cozy bar, with celebrity photos. Daily special. Closed Sun.; July. Dancing.

Dolphin Bay. *Expensive.* 244 Venetian Dr. On intracoastal Waterway. Elegant arches lead to classy dining room. Lunch, dinner, cocktails.

Le Petit Chalet. *Expensive.* 2515 N. Federal Hwy. Tres chic, intimate dining. Snails en croute, lobster soufflé, chicken Josephine among specialties.

Patio Delray. *Expensive.* 714 E. Atlantic Ave. Steak, chops and king crab. Pianist, patio dining. Lunch, dinner, Sun. brunches.

Del Golfo's. *Inexpensive.* 320 N. Federal Hwy. Family-style, friendly, informal. Great spaghetti, hot bread, crisp salads. Inexpensive wines, too.

Dunedin

Bon Appetit. *Moderate to Expensive.* On scenic Marina. Superbly-prepared seafood, veal, beef, chicken. Delicious cocktails, fine wines. Classy service. Music in lounge. Beautiful seascapes from window walls. Breakfast, lunch, dinner.

Fernandina Beach

The Sandbar. *Moderate.* A beach roadhouse serving seafood in a fun way, like roasted oysters on a tin tray, shrimp on a towel. Overlooking Amelia River at Fernandina Beach.

Palace Saloon. *Inexpensive.* Florida's oldest (1878). Historic antiques on display. Player piano, copper still, artistic murals. Famous spicy boiled shrimp with hot tomato sauce only food served. Great drinks, especially the 22-ounce Pirate's Punch.

Fort Lauderdale

Charcoal Pit. *Expensive.* 825 E. Sunrise Blvd. Open only for dinner. Excellent wine list. Lovely patio-garden setting.

Dante's. *Expensive.* 2871 N. Federal Hwy. Dover sole chablis and veal cordon bleu recommended. Great charcoal-broiled beef. Dressy atmosphere. Reservations suggested.

La Corrida. *Expensive.* 3536 N. Federal Hwy. Paella Valencia and other gourmet specialties are prepared tableside in a luxurious, Spanish setting. Romantic, intimate. Atop *Brave Bull* restaurant.

La Ferme. *Expensive.* 1601 E. Sunrise Blvd. Rated as one of the top French restaurants in Fort Lauderdale. Excellent food; simple décor.

Le Cafe de Paris. *Expensive.* 715 Los Olas Blvd. Small, with intimate atmosphere. Fine French cuisine for over 10 yrs.

The Caves. *Moderate to Expensive.* 2205 N. Federal Hwy. (US 1). Cave men and cave girls in leopard skin togas serve in romantic, black plush caves. (Caves for non-smokers also.) Steaks, Alaskan king crab legs, snapper Dijon and other entrées served with soup, rice pilaf and selections from the Sterling Silver Salad Bar. Even a fur bar with stalactites in the lounge! Dinner only.

Cafe de Geneve. *Moderate.* Authentic Swiss fondues. Frog legs top the 24 dinner choices. Casual, friendly. Lunch, too.

Creighton's. *Moderate.* 2670 Sunrise Blvd. Nr. Sunrise Shopping Center. Likes to be known for its apple pie and large menu. On Intracoastal Waterway, with outdoor dining areas. Docking facilities. A showplace of objets d'art ($1,500,000 worth).

Golden Spike Restaurant. *Moderate.* 6000 N. Federal Hwy. Lunch in the Mug Cellar is different, surrounded by tagged antiques, curios in this replica of an 1800 baggage room. Upstairs, there's Gold Rush atmosphere, candlelight and a continental menu.

Hacienda Del Rio. *Moderate.* 2525 N. Federal Hwy. Muy bueno with lots of Mexican atmosphere and real Mexican cuisine. Lunch, dinner. Guitarists at night.

New River Storehouse. *Moderate.* Part of Marina Bay hotel resort. Looks like dockside warehouse, but dining is elegant. Try the rock shrimp and "Tropical Pye." Dinner only.

94th Aero Squadron. *Moderate.* At Executive Airport. World War I flying aces are honored in this unusual theme restaurant. Oversize Margaritas. Good steaks, brochette, quiche. Very popular and crowded.

Patricia Murphy's Candlelight Restaurant. *Moderate.* In Bahia Mar Yachting Center. Intracoastal Waterway views. Lunch, dinner, cocktails.

Fast Eddie's. *Inexpensive to Moderate.* 535 N. Andrews Ave. Patio bar, waterfall and lots of tropical foliage. Open-face sandwiches, hamburgers, salad plates are luncheon specials. Charcoal your own steaks for dinner on the open hearth (save $2 for grilling it yourself). Good salad bar, too.

Lauder-Deli. *Inexpensive.* Hearty delicatessen sandwiches and other combinations. Breakfast, business luncheon specials, dinner. Nr. airport.

The Loft. *Inexpensive.* 5460 N. State Rd. 7 (441). In Plaza Central Shopping Center. Country barn décor with fresh from the gristmill bread. Delicious homemade soups and antipasto bar. Home-y menu of beef, chicken, seafood. Dinner only.

Fort Myers—Fort Myers Beach

Pate's Restaurant and Bar. *Expensive.* Broadway and Second. Downtown. Old-fashioned mansion tastefully decorated with antiques of historical Florida. French-accented menu served in dining room or garden. Dinner only. Entertainment nightly in adjoining, attractive cocktail lounge.

Ye Olde Holmes House. *Expensive.* 2500 Eastero Rd. Creative chef highlights 10-page menu with fresh seafood casserole, wild rice stuffed pheasant, chateaubriand. Two salad bars. Cocktails. Fancy coffees. Dinner only.

Pete Miranda's Barge. *Moderate to Expensive.* 2024 West First St. Downtown. Scenic river views. Fish and seafood highlight the varied menu. Seafood marinara and spaghetti a favorite. Also shad roe, frogs' legs, steaks. Flaming coffees, desserts. Cocktails, wine, beer. Lunch, dinner. Sunday dinner only. Entertainment nightly in *Poop Deck Lounge.*

Pelican Restaurant. *Inexpensive to Moderate.* 3040 Estero Blvd. Own boats to catch delicious fish. Seafood combination plate is excellent. Charcoal grilled steaks, also. Cozy with nautical antique décor. Gulf views. Lunch, dinner. At Pelican Hotel and Cottages, a local landmark.

Gainesville

The Prime Rib Restaurant. *Expensive.* 2900 S.W. 13th St. At Hilton. Gourmet dishes created at table-side. Chateaubriand, Steak Diane, baked stuffed shrimp, prime rib, Maine lobsters. Good wine list. Dinner only. Reservations suggested.

Plantation Inn. *Moderate to Expensive.* 1901 S.W. 13th St. Old New Orleans ambience. Beef, seafood specialties. Happy Hour with entertainment, half-price drinks, free hors d'oeuvres. *Mardi Gras Lounge* adjacent.

Sovereign Restaurant. *Moderate.* 12 S.E. 2nd Ave. Old carriage house converted to New Orleans-style restaurant with courtyard patio. Continental cuisine.

Culpepper's. *Inexpensive.* W. University Ave. and 34th St. Very casual. Nightly specials include shrimp fry, all you can eat. Country cooking. Children's menu.

Down to Earth. *Inexpensive.* 625 W. University Av. Natural foods breakfast house. Pancakes, herb omelets, huevos rancheros, freshly squeezed juices, etc.

Islamorada

Conch. *Moderate.* Good eating, specializing in seafood, conch chowder, stone crabs, steak. Player piano. Bar.

Green Turtle Inn. *Moderate.* Highly recommended for chowder, turtle steak, rum pie and Key lime pie. Entertainment.

Lazy Dolphin. *Moderate.* Nicely prepared local seafood dishes. Don't miss the luscious Grasshopper Pie. Special plates for children.

Jacksonville

Sandy's Steer Room. *Moderate.* 1780 W. Beaver St. Quality beef, seafood. Closed Sun.

Stricklands. *Moderate.* Mayport, near Jacksonville. Rustic fishing-village atmosphere. On banks of St. Johns river. Just-caught red snapper, sheepshead, flounder, bass, shad, sea trout, and seafood. Seating for over 300.

Patti's East. *Moderate.* 7300 Beach Blvd. Italian and American food. Try the *chicken à parmigiana.* Beer, wine.

Jensen Beach

Frances Langford's Outrigger Restaurant. *Moderate.* Polynesian decor and cuisine. Shrimp with "outrigger sauce" is a winner. Pert Miss Langford was one of the top pop-singers of the 1940s.

Key Largo

Marker 88. *Moderate.* Federal Hwy. Beachfront at "Marker 88," nr. Plantation Key. Interesting, creative menu. Lots of atmosphere. Dinner only. Very popular. Reservations necessary.

Key West

A & B Lobster House. *Moderate.* Casual atmosphere in America's southernmost fish house. Bay views vie with conch chowder and turtle steak for attention.

Pigeon House Patio. *Moderate.* 303 Whitehead St. Charming, historical restaurant. Real Key West-Bahamian cuisine (conch fritters, bollos, piquant seafood).

Half Shell Raw Bar. *Inexpensive.* Old Duval St. Where the locals go for real hot conch chowder, just-shucked oysters, and draft beer. Oyster-eating records are made here!

Kissimmee

Buenaventura Lakes Country Club. *Moderate.* Boggy Creek Rd. 301 Buenaventura Blvd. Steaks, seafood, varied menu. Good Strawberry Margaritas and Daiquiris. Lunch, dinner. Cocktail lounge. Club open to public.

Mrs. Mac's Restaurant. *Moderate.* 122 E. Broadway. Chicken, steaks, homemade pie—family fare in family style.

Lakeland

Foxfire Inn. *Moderate.* Oyster bar, prime ribs. Dancing, entertainment wkdays. Closed Sun.

Talk of the Town. *Inexpensive to Moderate.* Turn-of-the-century theme. Costumed waiters, waitresses. Excellent salad bar and onion soup with lunch, dinner.

Varied menu from chopped steak to lobster tails. Strawberry shortcake dessert is special. Talk of the Towns also in Clearwater, Orlando, Winter Haven.

Lake Buena Vista

Walt Disney World Village (at Lake Buena Vista) has good eating establishments among the 30 boutiques. Everything from freshly shucked oysters in a waterfront lounge *(Cap'n Jack's Oyster Bar)*, *Heidelberger's Deli* and *Lite Bite* for sandwiches, *Village Restaurant* for complete meals, and the *Empress Lilly* for elegant dining.

Empress Lilly Riverboat Restaurant. *Moderate—Expensive.* At Walt Disney World Shopping Village. Gourmet seven-course meals in The Empress Room. Fisherman's Deck and Steerman's Quarters for seafood and steaks. Baton Rouge Lounge is a good-time show bar.

Great Ceremonial House. Papeete Bay Veranda. *Moderate to Expensive.* In Polynesian Resort Hotel. South Seas lagoon and garden artistic atmosphere. Breakfast buffet, lunch buffet, dinner. Children's prices for breakfast, lunch. Oriental-influenced dishes for enjoyable exotica. Nightly entertainment in *Captain Cook's Hideaway Lounge.* Reservations essential for dinner.

Madeira Beach

Peter Pan Inn (formerly Kapok Tree). *Moderate.* 5001 Duhme Rd. Acropolis-style statuary, lavish gardens, and lagoons. Ornate dining rooms, but low prices.

Santa Madeira. *Moderate.* On Intracoastal Waterway near Madeira Shopping Mall. This specially-built Spanish galleon is captained by the expert Brown Derby restaurant franchise. Varied menu of seafood, beef, chicken. Salad bar. Nautical decor with some real artifacts. Long wait to get aboard during tourist season.

Captain's Galley. *Inexpensive.* Near Madeira Shopping Mall. Broiled grouper a specialty. Excellent strip steaks. Cozy dining room with water views. A longtime favorite with locals, the small restaurant is busy with the "overflow" from the nearby Santa Madeira restaurant.

Naples

The Chef's Garden. *Expensive.* 1300 Third St. S. Selected as one of Top Ten Florida restaurants by *Florida Trend* magazine. Features creative interpretations of continental cuisine in both indoor and outdoor setting. Extensive wine list.

Mirabelle. *Expensive.* On Gulf. Imaginative, gourmet menu. Terrific almond fried shrimp! Great roast beef. Tempting desserts; flaming coffees.

St. George and the Dragon. *Moderate.* Fifth Ave. S. Beef is the specialty, but there are many other selections on the menu, conch chowder and red snapper among them. Setting is amidst nautical memorabilia.

Ocala

1890 Beef House. *Moderate.* 917 E. Silver Springs Blvd. Prime ribs, Southern fried chicken, steaks. Hearty sandwiches, too. Converted turn-of-the-century residence. Closed Sun.

Orlando

Maison & Jardin. *Expensive.* 430 S. Wymore Rd. Altamonte Springs, near Orlando. Beautiful garden-surrounded villa. Prize-winning continental and American dishes. Romantic dining.

Piccadilly. *Expensive.* 7100 S. Orange Blossom Trail. Just like being in London with prime ribs and Yorkshire pudding, shrimp in beer batter, kidney pie. All this and French pastries, too.

Gary's Duck Inn. *Moderate.* 3974 S. Orange Blossom Trail. Good place for French-fried jumbo shrimp.

Lili Marlene's Aviators' Pub and Restaurant. *Moderate.* Church St. Station complex. Turn-of-century nostalgia, with oak paneling, brass fans, stained-glass windows. Delicious wiener schnitzel, creole gumbo, stone crab claws, coffee praline parfait, fresh-baked cheesecake.

Purple Porpoise. *Moderate.* Downtown Maitland, near Orlando. Famous for salad bar and delicious, fresh seafood.

Willoughby's. *Moderate.* 3911 E. Colonial Dr. English pub atmosphere. Cocktails, lunch, dinner.

The Spaghetti Factory. *Inexpensive to Moderate.* 109 W. Pine St. A "Pasta Palace," housed in old automobile warehouse; renovations cost over $250,000. Noodles, spaghetti, every type of pasta made before your eyes. Imported machinery cost over $40,000! Sauces galore. Lunch, dinner.

Palm Beach

Petite Marmite. *Very Expensive.* 309 Worth Ave. Definitely worth the big splurge for lunch or dinner. Excellent service. Reservations necessary. Extremely well-dressed clientele.

Capriccio. *Expensive.* 336 Royal Poinciana Plaza. Opp. Playhouse. Fine dining in an elegant setting. Mostly Italian and French specialties. Long wine list. Lunch, dinner.

Chez Guide. *Expensive.* 251 Royal Palm Way. Tropical rattan and floral décor but the menu is strictly European. Superb flaming dishes. Reservations. Lunch, dinner.

La Seine. *Expensive.* In the classy Palm Beach Towers, 44 Coconut Row. Walk down one flight. Continental menu from appetizers to dessert. Specialty is sweetbreads. Good wine list. Lunch, dinner.

Bentley's. *Expensive.* N. Palm Beach (730 US Hwy 1). Romantic candlelight, stained-glass windows, terraced gardens. Well-prepared veal, steak, duckling, chicken, fish. Lunch, dinner, Sun. brunch.

Ta-Boo. *Expensive.* 221 Worth Ave. Celebrity rendezvous for over 30 years. Imaginative décor with tropical fruit lights! Seafood, steaks, cannelloni, veal piccata are menu favorites. Lunch, dinner, Sun. brunch. Dancing nightly in lounge.

Testa's. *Expensive.* 221 Royal Poinciana Way. Family-owned for over 50 years. Varied menu, principally Italian specialties, seafood. Sidewalk cafe, patio dining and tropical orchid greenhouse.

Dutch Treat. *Inexpensive.* 412 S. County Rd. Home-y atmosphere for breakfast, lunch and dinner before 5 P.M.

Palmetto

Pelican Point Sea Hut. *Moderate.* Snead Island Rd., or arrive by boat at Pelican Point Marina. Southern fishing village decor in secluded atmosphere. Very casual at lunch. Delicious fish, shellfish—steak, too. Crab is a specialty. Nr. Bradenton, Sarasota.

Panama City and Panama City Beach

Angelo's Steak Pit. *Expensive.* Hickory broiled ribs, steak, chicken. Apple pie is delicious. Children's portions. Longhorn saloon.

Boar's Head Restaurant and Tavern. *Expensive.* 17290 W. 98A. Medieval English atmosphere with lanterns, beams, armored knight displays. Hearty servings. Prime ribs, Yorkshire pudding, steaks, seafood, chicken. Super salad bar. Irish-style coffee in 20-ounce goblet. Live entertainment, generous drinks in cozy tavern. Dinner only from 4 P.M.

Foxfire Restaurant and Tavern. *Moderate to Expensive.* 4500 W. Hwy. 98. Red Fox Room with $4.95 entrees including salad bar (snapper, stuffed shrimp, barbecued ribs, etc.). *Torch Room* with gourmet dining. Special cocktails in souvenir glasses. Entertainment. Dinner only.

The Hearty House. *Inexpensive to Moderate.* 3210 Thomas Dr. Delicious locally caught catfish, jumbo shrimp. Apalachicola oysters, Panamanian seviche appetizer, extra special. Steaks, too. Cocktails, wine, beer. Lunch and "to go" for fishermen. First call for breakfast 4:30 A.M.! 7 days a week. At the lagoon.

The Treasure Ship. *Inexpensive to Expensive.* Treasure Island Marina. 3605 Thomas Dr. 17th-century, 3-masted sailing galleon 200 feet tall. 4 decks of restaurants, gift shop, game room, wharf with raw bar, sandwiches, cocktails. Second deck main dining room. *Pirate's Pleasure* ice cream parlor third deck, *Top of Ship* for elegant dining. The *Brig* disco. Open 5:30 A.M. to 2 A.M.! No charge to board. *Top of Ship* dinner reservations (904) 234-8881.

Pensacola

Bartels Restaurant & Winery. *Moderate.* 120 S. First St. Fried chicken, seafood, steak and home-made wines. Bar, with dancing Wed. to Sat. Closed Sun.

Apple Annie's Courtyard, Coppersmith Galley, Lili Marlene's World War One Pub, Oyster Bar, Rosie O'Grady's, Phineas Phogg's Disco. *Inexpensive.* Seville Quarter. Imaginative casual restaurants in historical, restored Spanish square. Phineas Phogg's took two years to plan, 15 months to construct. High point is 6-foot-high copper-brass balloon with gondola. (Also see *Orlando* listings.)

Plant City

Branch Ranch. *Moderate.* This restaurant, which grew out of Mrs. Branch's inviting a few friends to dinner, is worth the drive from Tampa—or anywhere. Serves chicken, ham, chicken-ham combination. Vegetable dinner has chicken pot pie as side dish. Everything is home grown. Antique shop upstairs.

Lani Purcell's 1776 Restaurant and Lounge. *Moderate.* Interstate 4 at SR 39 (12 mi. E. of Tampa). Gulf shrimp, Apalachicola oysters among appetizer selection. Florida frog legs, steak, Maine lobster, combination seafood platter, good salad bar. Senior Citizens' menu. Children's menu. Entertainment, dancing nightly. Open 7 days. Consecutively voted Number One Holiday Restaurant in the world.

Pompano Beach

Cap's Place. *Expensive.* Turtle steaks, Florida lobster tails, broiled catch-of-the day, hearts-of-palm salad. Roosevelt and Churchill dined here. Across from Intracoastal Waterway. Park at Lighthouse Point Marina on 28th Court, flip light switch on dock, and shuttle boat-taxi will come to fetch you. Dinner only.

Gentleman Jim's. *Moderate.* Lighthouse Point. Cheese soup, salads, beef and seafood are the attractions. Comfortable atmosphere.

Norris Catfish Restaurant. *Moderate.* Casual restaurant offering all you can eat of fried catfish.

Perry's. *Inexpensive.* Greek specialties. Early bird specials and lunches are real bargains. Go early or be prepared for a crowd.

Sarasota

L'Auberge du Bon Vivant. *Expensive.* 7003 Gulf of Mexico Dr. Long Boat Key. Currently an "in" place for dinner. Two couples own it; the men are chefs, the wives, hostesses. Coquille St. Jacques Sauce Mornay just one of the gourmet selections. Good wines and beers. Less than 100 seats, so reservations necessary. Dinner only.

Buccaneer Inn. *Expensive.* Buccaneer Inn, 595 Dream Island Rd. Pirate theme in relaxed atmosphere. Charbroiled beef. Bar. Arrive by car or boat.

Cafe L'Europe. *Expensive.* St. Armand' Circle. Flower-filled, continental ambiance in Sarasota's perpetual prize-winning restaurant. Crepes, duck l'orange, and international specialties. Lunch, dinner.

Columbia Restaurant. *Moderate.* St. Armand's Circle. Excellent Spanish and American dishes. Same family as famous Columbia in Tampa.

The Sawmill Inn Restaurant. *Moderate.* 33 Crossroads Shopping Center. Imaginative, attractive rustic setting. Delicious food, everything from soup and sandwiches to great steaks, Veal Cordon Bleu and seafood. Lunch, dinner. Dinner only Sat., Sun. Cocktail lounge, entertainment.

Shannon's Way. *Inexpensive.* 3904 Tamiami Trail. Home-style soups and hearty fare. Everything under $5 except steaks. Colorful decor. No Blarney, but owners claim longest bar in state. Guitar music at night.

Oyster Bar. *Inexpensive.* 7250 S. Tamiami Trail. Always good seafood at very low prices in this popular chain. King crab salad a favorite, also seafood platters. Lunch, dinner, cocktails.

St. Augustine

Chimes. *Moderate.* Old atmosphere, roast lamb, broiled snapper. Overlooking Matanzas Bay. Childrens portions.

Corner House. *Moderate.* Delicious Spanish bean soup, tantalizing desserts featured. Intimate dining area

St. Petersburg

Peter's Place. *Deluxe.* 208 Beach Dr. downtown. Bayfront continental café. Exquisite crystal, linens. Imaginative entrées: Roquefort quiche, Pork loin with brandied pineapple, Bananas Foster. Prix fixe dinner about $22 per person (wines, tax, tip extra). Open Tues.–Sat., dinner only.

Isla del Sol Club House. *Expensive.* 5000 Sun Blvd. On the Bayway. Part of Isla del Sol Golf and Racquet Club complex. Varied dinner menu of steaks, seafood, continental dishes. Cocktails. Lunch, moderate, featuring crepes, sandwiches, salads, prime ribs, seafood.

PierSide. *Moderate.* On fourth floor of showplace. Five-story, unique inverted pyramid building on downtown St. Petersburg's waterfront. Wonderful views from window walls. Seafood specialties, but varied menu. Cocktail lounge.

Seaman's Cove. *Moderate.* U.S. 19 at Maximo Moorings Marina. Scenic waterfront dining at yacht-lined harbor. Shrimp scampi the specialty. Varied menu. Window-walled dining room.

Sea Ketch. *Moderate.* 800 Bay Pines Blvd. No. Beautiful bay views from window walls. Superlong bar. Almond shrimp a specialty. Same management as Fish House. Lunch, dinner.

Athenian Gardens. *Inexpensive.* 2066 Tyrone Blvd. Crossroads Shopping Center. Friendly Greek atmosphere for souvlaki, shish kebab, moussaka, stuffed grape leaves and famous gyro sandwich. Delicious Greek salads and soups. Lunch, dinner. Beer, wine.

Aunt Hattie's. *Inexpensive.* 625 1st St. S. (Next door to *Uncle Ed's* for sandwiches, salads, beers.) Chicken & dumplings, seafood. Victorian decor. Childrens plates.

Tampa

Bern's Steak House. *Expensive.* 1208 S. Howard Ave. Serves superb steaks. 1100 wines on hand, raises own vegetables in organic garden, ages own cheeses, roasts own coffee. Food cooked to order. Chef-owned. Entertainment.

Columbia Restaurant. *Expensive.* In Ybor City, Tampa's famous Latin Quarter. Winner of *Holiday* magazine's award for excellence. Spanish and American cuisine. Exciting floorshows nightly except Sun., plus strolling musicians.

CK's. *Expensive.* Atop Host International Hotel, high over Tampa International Airport. CK was a legendary aviator of unusual exploits, but the delicious specialties in this revolving glass-walled penthouse are for real. Prize-winning menu. Bar. Impressive vistas.

Crawdaddy's. *Moderate to Expensive.* 2500 Rocky Pt. Rd. Old fish-house atmosphere. Unique décor, including old-fashioned bloomers in bar-discotheque. 7 levels for dining, with Tampa Bay vistas. Lobster Whisky, Rum Runner Steak, all unusual entrées. Huge margaritas. Lunch, dinner, late supper.

Old Swiss House. *Moderate.* 3610 E. Busch Blvd. Cheese fondue, other Swiss, continental dishes. Terrace overlooks gardens. Just outside admission gate for Busch Gardens.

Prime Time. *Moderate to Expensive.* 222 S. Dale Mabry. Prime ribs, steaks, seafood specialties. Deluxe Appetizer Bar with caviar, crab legs, smoked salmon, almost 50 items. Cocktail lounge. Dinner only.

Mullet Inn. *Inexpensive.* 6415 Courtney Campbell Causeway. Casual place for Suncoast's smoked mullet. Unusual smoked shrimp.

Oyster Shanty. *Inexpensive.* 5421 W. Hillsborough SR 80. Real atmosphere with newspapers over plastic tableclothes for enjoying steamed crabs (all you can eat), shrimp steamed in beer, steamed clams, smoked mullet. Seafood combination plates, salads, chowders, desserts. Smoked chicken. Beer, wine. Lunch, dinner.

Tarpon Springs

Louis Pappas Riverside Restaurant. *Moderate.* On the sponge docks. Flavorful Greek and American foods. Chef's salads and fish delicacies. Bar. Family-owned for more than half a century.

Shrimp Boat. *Inexpensive.* 530 Athens St. Happy Greek taverna with lively music nightly. Greek home-style special daily for lunch and dinner. Terrific salad bar in shrimp boat replica. Also shrimp broiled, fried, boiled (you-peel-it). Wine, beer.

Tierra Verde

The Good Times. *Moderate.* 1130 Pinellas Bayway, Tierra Verde. Rostbraten Esterhazy, Veal Roast Florentine, roast duckling, old-fashioned soups, and steaks are popular. Delicious desserts. Lunch, dinner, but check ahead for special serving hours. About 20 min. drive from St. Petersburg en route to DeSoto Park.

Titusville

Sand Point Inn. *Moderate.* 801 Marina Rd. 30 mi N. of Titusville. Seafood specialties in an attractive weathered-wood building, jutting out over Indian River. Owned by Ponce Seafoods, own fishing fleet. Rock shrimp, scallops, quail, steaks, salad boat are great! Worth a special trip.

Treasure Island

French Connection. *Expensive.* 9610 Gulf Blvd. Very elegant; international menu. Flaming coffees the grand finale. Host-owners Marinette and Andre deKoster always there with Southern hospitality. Seascapes from window walls. Lovely cocktail lounge; entertainment. Open for lunch in season.

Vero Beach

Ocean Grill. *Moderate.* Sexton Plaza. Seafood, prime ribs & steak in rustic atmosphere. Dinner by candlelight. Unusual antique collections, bucket bar. Sensational sandwiches, salads for lunch. Beautiful beach vistas. Restaurants built by the late Waldo Sexton, famous for the Driftwood Inn.

Wellburn

Stephen Foster Colonial Inn. *Moderate.* At the gate of the Foster Memorial. Beer only.

West Palm Beach

Frederic's Steak House. *Moderate.* 1930 N. Dixie Hwy. Shrimp scampi, roast beef. Bar, entertainment.

New England Oyster House. *Moderate.* Seafood, Maine lobster. Buffet lunch. Children's portions.

Winter Haven

Christy's Sundown Restaurant. *Moderate.* Ave. K and 3rd St. W. Neat, attractive dining room, varied selection, featuring charcoal steaks and seafoods. Cocktail lounge. Entertainment nightly. On US 17 S.

Coach Light Buffet. *Inexpensive.* All you care to eat at lunch and dinner "groaning boards," including Friday night seafood buffet. Also soup, salad, and beverage specials for calorie-counters. 2601 Havendale Blvd.

Winter Park

Beef & Bottle. *Expensive.* 358 Park Ave. N. Sizzling steaks, tender prime rib, broiled lobster satisfy the inner man.

Dummy's Wharf. *Expensive.* 665 N. Orlando Ave. New England lobsters and seafood, also prime ribs for landlubbers. Dancing, too.

Villa Nova. *Moderate.* 2 dining rooms, extensive continental cuisine. Dancing nightly. Cocktail lounge & bar. An award-winner.

GEORGIA

Pacesetter of the New South

BY
CAROLYN CARTER

Carolyn Carter, a native Georgian, was a staff writer and photographer for The Atlanta Journal and Constitution Sunday Magazine. *She now is a freelance writer specializing in travel.*

Revolving lounges atop two hotels in Atlanta provide a view from which you can *almost* see the city grow. New buildings are springing up at every compass point; old ones are being removed to make way for progress. A few years ago the Atlanta newspapers published a photograph of the skyline in the early '60's—another, of the same spot in the '70's. Two entirely different cities.

Atlanta is running ahead, pacing the South, just as she has since early Reconstruction days following the Civil War when most of her residences and businesses were devastated, but she came up with a determination to win—and she has.

Scarlett O'Hara said: "Atlanta is full of pushy people." Pushy, ambitious, determined—whatever the word—Atlanta had a winning combination which came through and is still excelling.

Much of the charm of legendary southern hospitality is tenaciously guarded, cherished. New tides of energy are surging everywhere, but the past remains as real as the present and will continue to color the future.

Businessmen regard the Georgia capital as a "national city" and its economic influence goes far beyond regional confines. The business community is aggressive, competitive. More than 400 of the Fortune 500 companies have headquarters or offices here. Atlanta is growing rapidly. Unemployment is half the national average. Bank deposits are well above average for cities of like size. Five Points (Decatur, Peachtree and Marietta Streets) is known as the heart of Atlanta's financial business district. The Peachtree Center Complex consists of a modern living center renowned for its architectural uniqueness. It includes office buildings, the country's second largest merchandise mart, and several new hotels. Headquarters for the Sixth Federal Reserve District are in Atlanta. Hartsfield Atlanta International Airport is the largest passenger terminal in the world. The Atlanta State Farmer's Market, ten miles south on I-75, is a large wholesale fresh fruit and vegetable distribution center.

Cultural leaders say the renaissance of art throughout the nation is nowhere more truly reflected than in Atlanta. Everything termed "cultural" has a way of thriving in the Georgia city. Visitors find rich treasures of music, drama and visual arts for their enjoyment and edification. The $13-million Atlanta Memorial Arts Center offers something for everyone interested in the arts: the High Museum of Art (including a collection of Old Masters), the Atlanta School of Art, the Atlanta Symphony Orchestra under Robert Shaw's direction, the Alliance Theater and a children's theater.

Atlanta also supports a diversity of repertory drama and musical theater and books many of the major national road attractions in theater, opera, ballet and concert soloists. Noteworthy literary shrines are those connected with Joel Chandler Harris and *Uncle Remus,* and with Margaret Mitchell and *Gone with the Wind.*

The Atlanta Civic Center is an auditorium complex for conventions and music events. The Center contains a 70,000-square-foot exhibit hall, as well as a 4,600-seat auditorium where the Metropolitan Opera plays.

The Georgia World Congress Center, adjacent to the giant Omni megastructure, contains facilities for national and international meetings. It has a 2,000-seat auditorium, meeting rooms, and the largest single room of its kind on one level in the United States (350,000 square feet).

The Cyclorama, famous three-dimensional panoramic painting of the Battle of Atlanta located at Grant Park, is now being restored. (To be reopened mid-1982.) The Swan House (Atlanta Historical Society, 3099 Andrews Dr. NW) has an interesting collection of mementos from Georgia's past housed in the former Edward H. Inman residence. Adjacent is the Tullie Smith farmhouse which looks essentially as it did in 1840's. Georgia's governor resides in a new mansion located at 391 West Paces Ferry Road, a show place, opened for tourists several times each week.

Six Flags Over Georgia, a family entertainment park, covers 331 acres, has over 100 attractions, rides and live shows—all for one admission price. Rides include the Dahlonega runaway mine train, the log flume and the Jean Ribaut riverboat adventure. The park has sections, one for each of the six flags which have flown over Georgia—French, Spanish, English, Confederacy, United States and Georgia. The world's largest roller coaster was installed in 1973 in a newly opened area devoted to a "turn of the century" theme. Newest ride is the Great Gasp, a daring parachute jump that feels like a 40-foot freefall before the wind catches you and opens your chute. Then you slowly descend to a perfect landing 30 stories below.

Underground Atlanta, a four-block area, has original cobblestone streets and store fronts dating to the late 1800's. Restaurants, night spots, specialty shops operate on varying individual hours. Zero Mile Post, erected 1850, marks birthplace of Atlanta.

The Toy Museum of Atlanta (2800 Peachtree Rd.) has a rare collection of antique dolls and doll houses, model trains, boats, soldiers—13 rooms.

Atlanta Botanical Garden, Piedmont Park at the Prado, is located on 63 rolling acres dedicated to educating people about plants and plant culture.

The Bank Museum, in the Federal Reserve Building, displays Dahlonega gold coins, other rare coins, and has exhibits explaining how money is made.

Archives, 330 Capitol Avenue, houses history of the State of Georgia; research, displays, exhibits.

A visit to the Martin Luther King, Jr., District should begin at the Information Center, 413 Auburn Avenue N.E., and include his birthplace, tomb, and the church where Dr. King pastored.

The Center for Puppetry Arts, 1404 Spring St., N.W., has exhibits, shows, lectures, classes, workshops.

Stone Mountain

Stone Mountain, the world's largest mass of exposed granite, is surrounded by a 3,200-acre park that attracts nearly 4 million persons each year. A massive Confederate carving features General Robert E. Lee with General Stonewall Jackson and Confederacy President Jefferson Davis. Lee's likeness is 138 feet from the top of his head to his horse's hoof. His face measures twenty-one feet, his nose, five feet. The stars on his collar are bigger than dishpans and the sword, measuring fifty-eight feet in length and four feet in width, weighs one hundred tons. The giant granite dome, which rises 650 feet above the surrounding plain, stands about twenty miles east of downtown Atlanta and is visible from the top of many of the city's larger buildings. A cable-car lift rises from the base of the mountain to the summit 2,600 feet distant. Two glass-enclosed cars, each carrying fifty passengers, afford a superb view. A replica of the famous Civil War locomotive, "The General," pulls vintage coaches along a railroad that circles the base of the mountain. The seven-mile ride gives an idea of how massive the granite giant really is. A Memorial Building contains a museum featuring Sherman's famous "March to the Sea," depicted in a sixty-foot relief map. Magnolia Hall, an authentic antebellum plantation, was moved from its original site at Dickey, Ga., carefully furnished and restored. There is a game ranch, an antique automobile museum, a steamboat operating on an adjoining lake, a marina, a carillon with concerts daily, fishing, horseback riding, golf and camping.

ATLANTA
DOWNTOWN

Points of Interest (Atlanta)

1) Atlanta Historical Society
2) Atlanta Stadium
3) City Hall
4) Civic Center
5) Coach House Restaurant
6) Cyclorama
7) Emory University School of Dentistry
8) Exhibition Hall
9) Fox Theater
10) Georgia Institute of Technology
11) Georgia State College
12) Georgia World Congress Center
13) High Museum of Art
14) Historic Lamp Post
15) Martin Luther King grave
16) Memorial Arts Center
17) Merchandise Mart
18) Municipal Auditorium
19) Omni Hotel and Megastructure
20) Peachtree Plaza Hotel
21) Realto Theater
22) Regency-Hiatt Hotel
23) State Capitol
24) Underground Atlanta

Fifth Avenue South

Fashion-conscious shoppers deem Peachtree Street the Fifth Avenue of the South. Added to Georgia-based stores that have been style pacers for almost a century are many leading fashion firms from other parts of America that have opened Atlanta branches in suburban shopping developments. Strollers along the avenue which Margaret Mitchell popularized through her novel are noted for their beauty and their chic attire.

Whether you want souvenirs from the Civil War Period, an antique from Vining's, an emerald from Tiffany's or furs from Sak's, Atlanta has some.

Educators consider Atlanta a mecca. In the area there are nineteen degree-granting institutions of higher learning, twenty-four business schools, ten vocational training schools, six two-year schools equivalent to junior colleges, and over 400 elementary and high schools.

Architecturally Atlanta is a city to see because of its famous residential area and its vast assortment of downtown office buildings.

As a sports center, Atlanta has an $18-million, 58,000-seat stadium, home of the Braves baseball and Falcons football teams. Its $17-million, 17,000-seat coliseum, the Omni, is home of the Hawks basketball and Chiefs soccer teams. Atlanta International Raceway, I-75 at Hampton, a 1½-mile oval track, has two Grand National race events annually, plus Indy car races, motorcross and other motor sports.

There's golfing for every handicap in the city that produced one of the greatest golfers, Bobby Jones. The country's largest lawn tennis association is in Atlanta, and racquet ball is moving in significantly.

A short distance from Atlanta is sprawling Lake Lanier, a paradise for water sportsmen. The 1200-acre family recreation resort area includes: an island for picnics, a white sand beach, bathhouses, golf course, rental houseboat fleet, rental sailboats, kyaks, canoes, pontoons, catamarans, paddle boats, fishing, trout ponds, riding stables, boat launching ramps, mini-golf course, and a 430-foot water slide.

The annual July 4 Peachtree Road Race attracts 12,000 runners at the starting line for the six-mile run.

The state capitol, its dome plated with gold leaf from Dahlonega, Ga., contains a Hall of Fame consisting of famous Georgians and a State Museum of Science and Industry. Both are open to the public. Tours are available on request. The museum contains Indian artifacts, rock minerals and industrial products.

Fernbank Science Center houses the third largest planetarium in the world. Performances change frequently and are accompanied by music ranging from Chopin to the Beatles. The center includes one of the largest observatories housed within a major city, a seventy-acre virgin forest, a "see and touch" museum as well as an electron microscope lab, a meteorological lab and supporting service areas. The planetarium, forest and observatory are open to the public year round.

Annual events include the Atlanta Dogwood Festival each spring, the Peach Bowl (football) late in December, the Atlanta Arts Festival at Piedmont Park each May, the Atlanta Golf Classic at the Atlanta Country Club in early June or late May. Two events at the Atlanta International Raceway south of Atlanta are the "Atlanta 500" in the spring and the "Dixie 500" in late summer.

PRACTICAL INFORMATION FOR ATLANTA

HOW TO GET THERE. *By air:* Atlantic Southeast, Bahamasair, Braniff, British Caledonian, Delta, Eastern, Frontier, KLM, Lufthansa, Ozark, Northwest, Piedmont, Republic, Sabena, and Southeastern Commuter.
By Car: I-85, I-75, and I-20 will all get you to Atlanta.
By train: Atlanta may be reached by Amtrak with passenger service between New Orleans and Washington, D.C.
By bus: Greyhound, Trailways and several other companies come into Atlanta.

HOW TO GET AROUND. *By air:* Delta, Eastern, Piedmont, and Republic serve cities within the state.
By car: I-75 comes in from the northwest and goes south through Atlanta; I-85 from the northeast and also continues south through the city; I-20 runs across the city east to west; I-285 comes in from the north, cuts across I-75, I-20 and I-85 and continues east.
By bus: The Metropolitan Rapid Transit Authority operates the bus system in Atlanta and the suburbs. The fare is 50¢, transfers free. Maps may be obtained from the Chamber of Commerce, 34 Broad St. MARTA is building a 57-mile train system. The first phase opened in 1979. Fare 50¢.
Especially for the handicapped: Airports in Atlanta, Savannah, Columbus and Augusta have special accommodations for the handicapped, with parking areas designated for users of wheelchairs, and ramps and special restrooms. The Georgia Welcome Centers have similar facilities.

MUSEUMS. *Georgia Dept. of Archives and History,* 330 Capitol Ave. SE. Displays, exhibits. History of Georgia depicted in lovely stained-glass windows. *Cyclorama* is huge canvas depicting 1864 Battle of Atlanta. Now being refurbished. To reopen mid-1982. *Swan House,* 3099 Andrews Dr. NW. Period rms. on first floor. *Governor's Mansion,* 391 W. Paces Ferry Rd. Federal furnishings in elegant home. Free. *Emory Museum.* Bishop's Hall, Emory Univ., S. Oxford Rd. NE in Druid Hills. Far Eastern, African, Near Eastern, American Indian artifacts. Closed school vacations.
Art. *High Museum of Art,* in Memorial Arts Center, 1280 Peachtree St. NE. Free. Contains Western art from early Renaissance to present.
Special Interest. *Georgia State Museum of Science and Industry,* 4th fl. State Capitol Bldg. Displays, dioramas. Free. *Fernbank Science Center,* 156 Heaton Park NE. Observatory, exhibit hall, forest & reference library. Third largest planetarium in the nation. Open daily.

HISTORIC SITES. *Wren's Nest,* 1050 Gordon St. SW. Home of Joel Chandler Harris, creator of Uncle Remus stories. Mon. to Sat. *Dr. Martin Luther King, Jr.* is entombed beside the Ebenezer Baptist Church, 413 Auburn Ave. NE. *Zero Mile Post,* nr. Decatur St. under Central Ave. Bridge, marks the southwestern terminus of the Western & Atlantic Railroad, and is the "birthplace" of the City of Atlanta.

TOURS. *By bus:* Tours range from 3 to 5 hours and include downtown, Georgia Tech, Peachtree St., Lenox Square, Emory University, Cyclorama, Druid Hills, State Capitol, Stone Mountain, Underground Atlanta. Operators are American Sightseeing, Gray Lines, Arnel, Tour Gals, Atlanta Convention Planners, Presenting Atlanta Tours, and Guidelines.

MUSIC. The *Atlanta Symphony Orchestra* brings in many guest artists and guest conductors during its annual concert series from around Nov. 1 to Apr. Supplementing the symphony are the top stars—popular and classical— brought to Atlanta, Columbus, Savannah, Augusta, Macon and Athens by Famous Artists, and the classical attractions booked by the civic-minded *Atlanta Music Club,* which formed the symphony more than fifty years ago.

STAGE AND REVUES. *Theatre of the Stars* presents its summer season at Civic Center Auditorium, winter season at Peachtree Playhouse, 1150 Peachtree St. NE. *Academy Theatre,* 581 Peachtree St. N.E., presents dramas and musicals year round. *Alliance Theatre Company,* in Memorial Arts Center, professional productions mid-Jan. to mid-May. *Barn Dinner Theatre,* 1690 Terrell Mill Rd., Marietta, off Hwy. 41.

NIGHTCLUBS. The *Windjammer* and *Harbor House Lounge* at the Marriott are always lively, and the *Club Atlantis* at the Regency offers top-name entertainment. *Dante's Down the Hatch,* in Underground Atlanta. Lounge specialty is strawberry frozen daiquiri. *Houlihan's,* Lenox Square.

Discos: *Another World,* Courtland and Harris streets; *Burt's Place* in the Omni; *Clarence Foster's,* 1915 Peachtree Rd; *Century Center Hotel Lounges; Club 2001 V.I.P.,* 2581 Piedmont Rd. N.E.; *Jeryl's,* 2101 Powers Ferry Road NW. *Limelight,* 3330 Piedmont Rd. N.E.

SHOPPING. *Rich's,* the South's largest store, has downtown stores of six stories and four stories, which cover two city blocks. A full-line department store, with restaurants, cafeterias, coffee shop. A genuine tourist attraction. *Neiman Marcus* has a branch at Lenox Square. *Phipps Plaza,* across from Lenox Square on Peachtree and Lenox, has branches of *Lord & Taylor, Saks Fifth Avenue, Tiffany's, I. Miller* and *Mark Cross. Perimeter Mall* (I-285 and Ashford Dunwoody Rd.), *Northlake Mall* (I-285 and La Vista Rd.), Park Aire in Sandy Springs (corner Roswell Rd. and Johnson Ferry) and Southlake (near Airport), are new shopping centers, each containing fine specialty shops. Other fine stores: *Leon Frohsin.* A smart shop for business, party clothing, furs. Peachtree Center, just beyond Davison's and at Lenox Square, 3393 Peachtree Rd. NE. *J. P. Allen.* Moderate to higher-priced women's apparel. Beauty salon. 215 Peachtree NE, 3393 Peachtree Rd. NE. *Muse's.* Moderate to higher-priced men's fashions, notions. 52 Peachtree NW, 630 Peachtree NE, 3393 Peachtree Rd. NE, at Lenox Square. *Spencer's, Ltd.* Exclusive men's store features British imports only. 693 Peachtree St. NE. *Maier & Berkele.* Exclusive, long-established jewelry store. 173 Peachtree St. NE, 3225 Peachtree Rd. NE, and 122 Clairmont Ave., Decatur. *Atlanta Galleries.* Widest selection of antiques in city, specializing in furniture. Auctions. 2050 Hill Ave., N.W. *Atlanta State Farmers Market,* 146 acres, is delightful. You can pick up home canned pickles, relishes and preserves as well as fresh fruits and vegetables, hen-house eggs, smoke-house meats.

HOTELS AND MOTELS. Atlanta's accommodations should prove pleasant for even the most discriminating traveler, and cover a wide, diverse range. Listings are in order of price category. Based on double occupancy without meals in the peak season the ranges are as follows: *Deluxe:* $79 to $97; *Expensive:* $54 to $78; *Moderate:* $32 to $53; *Inexpensive:* $14 to $31. For a more complete explanation of hotel and motel categories see *Facts at Your Fingertips* at the front of this volume.

Atlanta Hilton. *Deluxe.* 255 Courtland St. at Harris St. Largest hotel in the southeast (1250 rooms) and spanking-new (opened in 1976). Its 29 stories include a spectacular rooftop restaurant with an adjoining nightclub: *Nickolai's,* a combination of old-world Imperial decor and modern pop and rock music. At lobby level are other restaurants and lounges: *Casablanca, Cafe de la Paix, Acapulco Bar, Cafe di Rome* and *Trader Vic's.* Four tennis courts, swimming pool, sauna, health club—and a jogging track!

Peachtree Plaza. *Deluxe.* Peachtree at International Blvd. World's tallest hotel (70 stories), opened in 1975. A truly breathtaking hotel: seven-story atrium lobby with half-acre lake, greenery, tapestries, live birds, sculpture. Spectacular *Sun Dial,* a three-level revolving restaurant and cocktail lounge, is atop the hotel; *Terrace Room,* multi-level dining room, has waterfall 100 feet long; *Cafe Express* is a mirrored coffee shop; *Sidewalk Cafe* serves luncheon of rib roast, salad, vegetable, fresh-baked bread. Swimming pool, sun deck, health club.

Hyatt Regency Atlanta. *Expensive* to *Deluxe.* 265 Peachtree St. NE. 1,000 rooms. In-rm. movies avail. Pool. Restaurants, bars, revolving Polaris dining rm. and bar atop roof with panoramic view. Spectacular 23-story atrium is heart of this splendid hotel.

Colony Square. *Expensive.* Peachtree and 14th St. There are 500 rooms, three restaurants and a cocktail lounge. The *Venetian Room* has big-name entertainment nightly. The *Coromandel* may become one of Atlanta's finest French restaurants, the *Fairmont Crown,* 27 stories up, has brunch, lunch, dinner and dancing. The decor of the entire hotel has been chosen with great originality.

Atlanta Airport Hilton. *Expensive.* 1031 Virginia Ave. (350 rooms).

Atlanta Mariott Hotel. *Expensive.* (763 rooms) Courtland & International. Excellent, lavishly hotel with in-rm. movies avail. Pool, golf & tennis nr. Saunas, health clubs. Restaurant, bar, dancing, entertainment.

Capitol Airport Inn. *Expensive.* (300 rooms) 1200 Virginia Ave.

Dunfey Atlanta Hotel. *Expensive.* (400 rooms) I-75 at Howell Mill Rd. Pool. Pets. Restaurant, bar, dancing, entertainment.

Master Hosts Inn. *Expensive.* (100 rooms) 2375 Delk Rd.

Northlake Hilton Inn. *Expensive.* 4156 La Vista Rd., Tucker. Pool. Restaurant, bar, dancing, entertainment.

Radisson Inn. *Expensive.* (400 rooms) I-285 at Chamblee Dunwoody Rd.

Red Carpet Inn. *Expensive.* Two locations: I-85 at Chamblee-Tucker Rd. (148 rooms); I-75 south of I-285 (170 rooms).

Riviera Hyatt House. *Expensive.* 1630 Peachtree St. NW. Pool, tennis. In-rm. movies avail. Restaurant, bar, dancing, entertainment.

Travelodge at Executive Park. *Expensive.* I-85 at N. Druid Hills exit. Pool. Restaurant, bar, dancing, entertainment. Free airport transportation.

White House Motor Inn. *Expensive.* (9219 rooms) 70 Houston St. NE.

GEORGIA 179

Holiday Inn. *Moderate to Expensive.* Four locations, each with pool, kennel, restaurant, bar. **Airport,** 1380 Virginia Ave., **Downtown,** 175 Piedmont Ave., NE.; **East,** 4300 Snapfinger Wood Dr., Decatur; **I-85,** 1944 Piedmont Circle NE.

Admiral Benbow Inn. *Moderate.* 1470 Spring St. NW; (190 rooms); Airport, 1419 Virginia Ave. (253 rooms); I-285 and Buford Hwy. (250 rooms). Pool, with poolside service. Restaurant, bar, entertainment, dancing.

Atlanta American Motor Hotel. *Moderate.* (350 rooms) Spring & International Blvd. Pool. Restaurant, bar, dancing, entertainment. In-rm. movies avail.

Atlanta Central TraveLodge. *Moderate.* (70 rooms) 311 Courtland St. NW. Pool (heated). Restaurant nr.

Stadium Hotel. *Moderate.* 450 Capitol St. SE. 410 rooms. Pool. Restaurants, bar, entertainment.

Ladha Continental Hotel. *Moderate:* (302 rooms) 100 10th St. NW.

Guest Quarters. *Moderate.* 7000 Roswell Rd NW. Kitchen units. Pool. Pets permitted.

Holiday Inn. *Moderate.* Five in this category, with pool, play area, restaurant: **I-75:** 6288 Old Drive Hwy, Jonesboro; **Northeast:** 4422 Northeast Expwy, Doraville; **Northwest:** 1810 Howell Mill Rd. NW; **6 Flags West:** 4225 Fulton Industrial Blvd.; **South:** Hapeville.

Howard Johnson's. *Moderate.* Five locations, each with pool, restaurant: **Airport:** 1377 Virginia Ave. East Point; **Northeast:** 2090 N. Druid Hills Rd.; **Northwest:** 1701 Northside Dr. NW; **Sandy Springs:** 5793 Roswell Rd. NW; **South:** 759 Washington St. SW.

Mark Inn. *Moderate.* Three of nine total: with pool, restaurant, bar: 5021 Old National Hwy.; **Six Flags:** 200 Six Flags Rd.; **West:** 4430 Frederick Dr.

Ramada Inn. *Moderate.* Three of 6 locations, each with pool, restaurant: **Airport:** 845 N. Central Ave. Hapeville. Bar, dancing, entertainment; **Six Flags:** 305 Industrial Circle. Bar, dancing, entertainment; **Stockbridge:** 3509 Hwy. 138, Stockbridge.

Sheraton. *Moderate.* Seven locations: **Sheraton Atlanta** (501 rooms) 590 West Peachtree; **Sheraton Biltmore** (654 rooms) 817 West Peachtree; **Airport** (362 rooms) 1325 Virginia Ave., Hapeville; **Emory** (113 rooms) 1641 Clifton Rd.; **Northlake Inn:** (164 rooms) 2180 Northlake Pkwy; **Olympic Motor Inn:** at I-285 N. Peachtree exit; **Winchester Inn:** 1200 Winchester Pkwy. Smyrna. Pool, restaurant, bar.

Carlton. *Inexpensive.* 6610 S. Expwy., Jonesboro. Pets welcome. Restaurant nr.

Days Lodges. *Inexpensive.* Six locations: I-75 south; I-85 at Clairmont; I-285 and Old Dixie Highway; Buford Hwy. & Beverly Hills Dr; Buford & Old Stone Mtn. Rd; Shallowford Rd. Each has pool, play area, pets welcome, restaurant.

DINING OUT in Atlanta can mean the usual fine fare to be found in most large American cities, but it can also mean good Southern cooking—often in re-created rural surroundings. Restaurants price categories are as follows: *Deluxe,* $15 and up; *Expensive,* $10-15; *Moderate,* $6-10; *Inexpensive,* under $6, for a complete dinner, excluding drinks. A la carte meals will bring the tab up. For a more complete explanation of restaurant categories see *Facts at Your Fingertips* at the front of this volume.

EDITOR'S CHOICES

Rating restaurants is, at best, a subjective business, and obviously a matter of personal taste. It is, therefore, difficult to call a restaurant "the best" and hope to get unanimous agreement. The restaurants listed below are our choices of the best eating places in Atlanta, and the places we would choose if we were visiting the city.

MIDNIGHT SUN　　　　　　　　　　　　　Scandinavian/Continental
An alert and intelligent staff and unusual and tasteful decor are combined with excellent food. Scandinavian standards are offered, together with a number of interesting continental dishes. There is also fine steak and lobster for more conservative palates. 235 Peachtree St. N.E. (Peachtree Center South) *Deluxe.*

BRENNAN'S　　　　　　　　　　　　　　　　　　　Creole
You can merely close your eyes and transport yourself to New Orleans' Commander's Palace. The sumptuous Creole dishes of that Garden District landmark have been imported intact to Atlanta, and if you long for crabmeat Imperial or crayfish Etouffe, they are yours to command. The flaming desserts are guaranteed to light a fire in any appetite. 103 West Paces Ferry Road, N.W. *Expensive.*

AUNT FANNY'S CABIN　　　　　　　　　　　　　　Southern Cooking
Dining room is created inside a genuine former slave's cabin, and the fare is first class southern specialties with an emphasis on traditional recipes. The cooking and the atmosphere are marvelously merged, and the experience is more than just a good meal. Virginia ham and fried chicken are "musts". Bring your own liquor. 2155 Campbell Rd. (Smyrna). Dinner only, except for Sunday lunch at 1 P.M. *Moderate.*

ABBEY　　　　　　　　　　　　　　　　　　　French
Located in a converted church, with waiters in monks' robes and a harpist in the choir loft. Pheasant is a specialty. Entertainment. 163 Piedmont Ave. Dinner only. Open every day. *Expensive.*

Other recommended restaurants:

Ambassador. *Expensive.* 3850 Roswell Rd. N.E. Steak, seafood and New Orleans specialties. Drinks. Dancing, entertainment.

Anthony's. *Expensive.* 3109 Piedmont Rd. N.E. French specialties. A la carte dinner topped off with delicious macaroon pie. Drinks. Located in a restored 18th-century plantation house.

Dante's Down the Hatch. *Moderate.* 84 Old Pryor St. S.W., Underground Atlanta. Located in building used as hospital during Civil War, later as candy factory. Specialties: cheese trays, fondue; jazz. Lunch and dinner only.

The French Restaurant. *Expensive.* One Omni International. Garden atmosphere, entertainment nightly Mon.-Sat.

Ichiban Japanese Steak House. *Expensive.* 151 Ellis St. N.E. Tabletop cooking: teppan-yaki steak, chicken. Music.

Lickskillet Farm. *Expensive.* Old Roswell Road (Alpharetta). A limited menu offers simple but elegant entrees that make the half-hour drive from midtown worthwhile.

The Mansion. *Expensive.* 179 Ponce de Leon Ave., Built in 1885, this is all that remains of a 400-acre tract. Specialties: red snapper a la careme, filet Aida. Lunch and dinner.

Nikolai's Roof. *Expensive.* Atop Atlanta Hilton Hotel. Floor to ceiling wine vault and outstanding bill of fare. Reservations required.

Bugatti. *Moderate to Expensive.* Omni International Hotel. Specialties from Northern Italy as well as American and Continental fine foods. Italian Sunday brunch.

Coach and Six. *Moderate.* 1776 Peachtree Rd. NW. Steaks, chops, seafood and veal.

Gene and Gabe's. *Moderate.* 1578 Piedmont Ave. N.E. Veal is the prime attraction (scaloppina al marsala is irresistible), and the spices are lightly applied.

Herren's. *Moderate.* 84 Luckie St. N.W. Long-established restaurant with its own art gallery. Excellent American cuisine, exemplary service.

Journey's End. *Moderate.* Powers Ferry Rd. at Lockheed-Dobbins AFB exit, I-75, Marietta. International cuisine.

The Peasant Uptown. *Moderate.* 3200 Peachtree Rd. NE, in Phipps Plaza. French country cuisine.

Pittypat's Porch. *Expensive.* 25 Cain St. N.W. in Peachtree Center. Excellent southern specialties (ham, quail, venison). Home baking. Entertainment.

The Pleasant Peasant. *Moderate.* 555 Peachtree St. N.E. Built in 1800's as an ice-cream parlor. Country French cuisine and lavish desserts. Dinner only.

The Sandpiper. *Moderate.* 2960 Piedmont Rd. NE. Sandwiches, salads, omelettes at lunch. Steak Oscar, bouillabaisse, among dinner dishes.

Swan Coach House. *Moderate.* 3130 Slaton Drive N.W. Salad plates, cheese straws. Lunch only. Closed Sundays.

Sidney's Just South. *Moderate.* 4225 Roswell Rd. NE. Downhome continental cuisine with a country Jewish flavor.

The Varsity. *Inexpensive.* 61 North Ave. N.W. Large fast-food drive-in next to Georgia Tech. Chili dog, frosted orange, onion rings. Lunch and dinner.

Tapas Restaurant. *Moderate.* 3130 Piedmont Rd NE. Delicacies from around the world.

Davis Bros. Cafeteria. *Inexpensive.* Roast beef and fried chicken. Forest Pkwy at I-75. Eleven other locations in the area.

Mary Mac's Tearoom. *Inexpensive.* 224 Ponce de Leon Ave. NE. Southern cooking.

Morrison's. *Inexpensive.* 1025 Virginia Ave., Hapeville. Attractive cafeteria with background music. Fish amandine and roast beef are specialties. Children's portions. Eight other locations in the area.

S. & W. *Inexpensive.* 189 Peachtree St. N.E. Pleasant cafeteria, with southern cooking, own baking. The fried chicken merits attention.

Exploring Georgia

Georgia has "Visitor Information Centers" at every major entry into the state, and all these facilities are staffed by friendly, knowledgeable receptionists who are happy to assist travelers with current information, and are eager to suggest various tours through the state. All centers, except the one at the Atlanta Airport, have park-like areas with landscaping and picnic tables. At appropriate times of the year cotton may be found growing in the yard.

Receptionists suggest events and fun places to visit while in Georgia. They tell how to travel the most picturesque or the most expeditious route—as you choose—and they tell what to see and do at your chosen points of visitation. Information available includes the latest materials on golfing, hunting, fishing, camping, state and national parks, big league sports, special events, conventions, historical sites, scenic and guided tours, mountains and lakes, Golden Isles and other beaches and family fun attractions.

The Centers are located near Savannah on I-95 for tourists entering from South Carolina; Lavonia, I-85, one-half mile Southwest of the South Carolina line; Sylvania, US 301, one-half mile Southwest of the South Carolina line; Augusta I-20, one-half mile west of the South Carolina line; Columbus, intersection of US 280 and 27 for motorists coming into Georgia from Alabama; Ringgold, I-75, two miles south of the Tennessee line; Valdosta, I-75, two miles north of the Florida line, I-95 near Kingsland, just north of Florida line; on I-85 near West Point and on I-20 near Tallapoosa for motorists coming from Alabama; at Plains on US 280; and at the Atlanta airport.

A stop at one of these Centers immediately upon arrival in Georgia can make your trip more meaningful, more enjoyable. Suggested routes are many, and the following are typical:

Colonial Georgia Route

Colonial Georgia route will take you along US 17 and portions of I-95 through Savannah, Midway, Darien, Brunswick and the Golden Isles, Kingsland and St. Marys.

GEORGIA

0   50
Scale of Miles

TENNESSEE

APPALACHIANS   NORTH   CAROLINA

SOUTH
CAROLINA

Dalton
75
19
23
L. Sidney
Lanier
85
Rome
Allatoona
L.
Cartersville
Marietta
Athens
Clark Hill
Lake
20
285
78
20
College
Park
Atlanta
20
Augusta
West
Point
L.
Newnan
75
Lake
Sinclair
Savannah R.
La Grange
185
80
Macon
Dublin
319
85
16
16
Columbus
Americus
Altamaha R.
Savannah
19
75
341
95
82
Albany
Tifton
441
Moultrie
Waycross
Brunswick
Lake
Seminole
Okefenokee
Swamp
Cumberland I
Natl.
Seashore
Thomasville
Valdosta
St. Mary's R.
FLORIDA
ATLANTIC

ALABAMA

Chattahoochee R.

OCEAN

Savannah

Points of Interest

1) City Hall
2) Civic Center
3) Forsythe Park
4) Grayson Stadium
5) Old Historic Buildings
6) U.S. Custom House

In 1732, General James E. Oglethorpe brought his English colonists and settled the area named for his king, George II. An awareness of history, an appreciation for its preservation and perpetuation is everywhere evident.

Downtown Savannah remains essentially as General Oglethorpe planned it. For monuments, go to Johnson Square with its monument to Nathanael Greene; Wright Square, which contains a boulder honoring Indian Tomo-Chi-Chi, the Yamacraw Indian chief who befriended Oglethorpe's colonists; and Chippewa Square with its monument to Oglethorpe created by Daniel Chester French, designer of the Lincoln Memorial in Washington.

Historic houses include Owen-Thomas, designed by William Jay in 1818-19 and considered one of the purest examples of Regency architecture in America; Davenport House (1820), an excellent example of Georgian architecture; Telfair Academy of Arts and Sciences, site of the royal governor's mansion; Green-Meldrim Home, headquarters of General Sherman during his Savannah occupation and the birthplace of Juliette Gordon Low, founder of Girl Scouts. Savannah has 1,100 structures termed worthy of preservation. More than 90% of them have been saved and refurbished in the last 15 years. A 1-square-mile section of Victorian homes adjacent to Forsyth Park is being surveyed for restoration. Included are about 400 homes.

Other sights include the Ships of the Sea Museum; Factor's Walk Military Museum; Old Cotton Exchange Building and Walk, a nineteenth century meeting place for cotton merchants and center of commerce; Washington Guns, presented to Chatham Artillery by George Washington; Trustees' Garden, America's first experimental garden; Forsyth Park, especially in the spring when azaleas and flowering trees bloom.

Marked tours of historical and scenic areas of the city are designed for do-it-yourself touring, but two bus companies have daily sightseeing trips originating at motels, hotels, and the Chamber of Commerce. Bike tours are marked also.

Five forts may be visited in the Savannah area: Fort Jackson, Fort Wayne, Fort Screven on Tybee Island, Fort McAllister, ten miles east of Richmond Hill off US 17, and Fort Pulaski, east of Savannah, now operated by the National Park Service. Built from 1829 to 1849, Pulaski was Robert E. Lee's first engineering assignment after graduation from West Point.

Savannah was the center of a struggle for power during the Revolutionary War, most of which it spent under English occupation. Count Casimir Pulaski, the great Polish patriot, gave his life during an attempt to retake it. Today Pulaski is honored along with Sargeant William Jasper, an Irish-American warrior who lost his life in the same battle. The city regained its important role as a center for export to Europe and served as a supply center for the Confederacy during the Civil War until the fall of Fort Pulaski in 1862. Fort Pulaski, a monumental engineering feat, guarded the city from the sea from a perch overlooking the Savannah River, while Fort McAllister, a huge earthwork fortress, defended the south. Surviving seven attacks by the Union Navy, Fort McAllister finally fell to Sherman on his march to the sea. In evacuating the city in the face of Sherman's advance, Confederate General Hardee spared the city the battering and burning Sherman had given Atlanta.

Savannahians observe Georgia Day each year on February 12, the anniversary of Oglethorpe's establishment of the Colony. Other annual events are a tour of homes and gardens late in March; a St. Patrick's Day Parade; the Savannah Arts Festival early in April; Designers Showcase in April, when local architects, decorators, landscape designers re-do a home; Garden Tour in April; Night in Old Savannah in spring; Blessing of the Fleet in June.

South from Savannah is Midway with its beautiful old church dominating the view from the highway. The church was erected in 1792. The old slave gallery and high pulpit remain unchanged. From its congregation that never numbered more than 150 came two signers of the Declaration of Independence, two Revolutionary generals, and a U.S. Senator. The church and historic cemetery may be visited at any time. Keys are available free at a nearby service station. The Midway Museum next to the church, is an Historic Site. The museum is built in raised-cottage style and displays furniture, artifacts, documents from early eighteenth to mid-nineteenth century.

Darien, a colonial Georgia town, has Fort King George, southernmost outpost in 1721 and an important Spanish site prior to that time. A museum depicts various periods of occupation by Indians, Spanish and English.

The route continues through Georgia's pine belt, producer of vast naval stores. Brunswick, a busy port, is noted for its shrimp. Fleets operating off the coast bring in as much as ten million pounds annually.

The Lanier Oak, just north of the town, is a living tribute to Georgia's most famed poet, Sidney Lanier, who immortalized the area in his epic, "The Marshes of Glynn." (The Marshes of Glynn are the largest salt marshes on the American east coast. An overlook park in Brunswick gives a fine view of their ever-changing beauty.) Plaques mark the tree under which he is said to have been inspired to write many poems. Another famous tree, giant Lover's Oak in downtown Brunswick, is believed to be nine hundred years old, measures thirteen feet in diameter three feet from the ground, at which point it branches into ten limbs, each measuring from twelve to thirty inches in diameter. Gulf and inland fishing as well as tours of the area are popular.

Brunswick is the gateway to Georgia's Golden Isles. Sea Island is home of the world-famed Cloister, a year-round vacation complex of luxurious privately owned cottages, flower-bordered streets that run the entire north-south length of the island, a beach club, miles of flawless sand beach for beach walking or bathing. Classic cuisine is featured in the hotel dining areas.

St. Simons is the largest of the islands. Here is Fort Frederica National Monument from which Oglethorpe's troops marched off to defeat the Spanish at the Battle of Bloody Marsh. Foundations of the old settlement have been recreated as they were in the early 1700's. Christ Church is the historic frame building where John and Charles Wesley, the founders of Methodism, preached to Indians and settlers. The current structure was built in 1884 upon the site where they preached.

St. Simons Lighthouse was rebuilt in 1871. The lighthouse has been made into a museum. Ruins of Retreat Plantation may be visited on St. Simons; now a frontispiece for the Sea Island Golf Club. Hotels, motels and cottages along the excellent beaches are available at rates varying from luxury to economy.

Jekyll, now state-owned, once was a favorite for such millionaires as J. P. Morgan, William Rockefeller, William Vanderbilt and Joseph Pulitzer. The entire ocean side is beach, 9½ miles long. Rockefeller's twenty-five-room "cottage" is a museum. Faith Chapel, a small interdenominational church of English design, was one of the original buildings. The island's facilities are extensive. Many conventions are held each year and a permanent colony of several thousand persons reside on the island, many of them retirees. Georgia purchased the property in 1948 and developed it as a year-round vacation area. Four noted golf courses are located on the island—two of championship lengths and one a nine-hole seaside links designed after the sand dune courses of Scotland.

South from Jekyll and off the main route at Kingsland is Crooked River State Park, the only inland park in Georgia with saltwater fishing. Santa Maria Mission has outstanding tabby ruins. At the southernmost point is the old sea town of St. Mary's with its Presbyterian Church, one of the state's oldest.

South to the Wilderness

Entering Georgia on US 301 from South Carolina, motorists are greeted at the state's first tourist information center. Available here are free literature, free directions and free picnic areas.

The nearest town is Sylvania. Ten miles east is Brier Creek Battle Site, and breastworks from this Revolutionary War battle are still visible. Dell House is the only remaining structure in once- busy Jacksonborough, six miles north.

An interesting side junket may be made to Waynesboro (north on State 24), then to Millen (south on US 25) into 301 at Statesboro. Waynesboro, named for General "Mad Anthony" Wayne, once was a part of the plantation belt. About five miles away is Shell Bluff, an unusual geological formation. Here, high above the Savannah River, are many giant oyster fossils twelve to fifteen inches long. The bed is said to have been formed when the coastal plains of Georgia were submerged beneath the sea.

Located near Millen is a $70,000 fish palace—an aquarium that displays freshwater game and fish native to the area, a few specimens of tropical fish, turtles, eels and alligators. A special feature is a fat, pink-eyed catfish.

On State 17 is Jones Plantation at Birdsville considered to be the oldest plantation in Georgia lived in continuously by the family who built it. The rambling, romantic house was built in the 1780's. It is open to tourists by appointment.

North of Statesboro on a country road at Clito is Marsh Hunting Preserve, one of Georgia's many privately owned quail preserves where managed hunts may be arranged.

The route continues through agricultural areas, planted timbers and fields of peanuts and tobacco. Statesboro is trading center for naval stores and farm products.

Cake baking is major tourist attraction at Claxton where more than six millions pounds of quality fruit cakes are produced each year. Signs along US 301 invite motorists to visit the plant (three miles off the main route). As many as 150 to 200 cars stop each day.

A country-wide rattlesnake roundup is held each year in mid-March in Claxton. Contestants vie for the honor of catching the most rattlesnakes as well as the largest.

Giant oak trees shade the streets of Jesup, another agricultural town. Chief products are livestock, corn, cotton, timber, naval stores and milled lumber. The Lovers' Oak, one of the state's oldest, has a spread of 150 feet. The Altamaha River nearby offers excellent water activities including fishing, water-skiing and swimming. Cherokee Lake is approximately two miles northwest of US 301.

Driving through the piney woods and wiregrass section motorists next reach Nahunta. A frequent sight along the highway are giant log trucks enroute to sawmills.

Folkston is one of two eastern entrances to the famed Okefenokee Swamp. Visitors may enjoy the quiet natural surroundings on boat tours of the primitive wilderness area or visit a center where flora and fauna are explained in exhibits. An observation tower and many bird walks and nature trails are featured. There are boat tours, canoe liveries and special waterways where visitors are permitted without guides.

Westward twenty-three miles is Waycross and the entrance to the Okefenokee Swamp Park, which features wildlife shows, boat trips (ten-mile, two-hour guided boat trips or all-day excursions by advance reservations). There is an Interpretative Center, an Ecology Center and Pioneer Island exhibits. Visitors may even pick orchids as they stroll paths that pierce the almost forbidding growth of moss-strewn live oak, long leaf pine, hammocks, sweet gum, red bay, magnolia, water oak, hardwoods, and hollies of incredible size. The swamp is the headwater of both the Suwannee River and the St. Mary's, and Stephen Foster State Park, on State 177 north of Fargo, pays tribute to the famed composer. Because of the genuine peril from alligators and more than a dozen varieties of snakes, as well as the danger of becoming lost, no visitor is permitted in the park after dark. The park is open daily 8 A.M. to sunset. The area has the Waycross State Forest Game Management Area consisting of 37,500 acres of timberland. Hunters may take deer, rabbits or squirrels. Hunting is regulated by the Department of Natural Resources.

Annual events include a Forest Festival at Laura Walker State Park in early May; Okefenokee Holidays in late November, Fall Festival in mid-October and the Water Lily Festival in early June, all at Okefenokee Swamp Park; Haunted House, a Jaycee project in an old school house in Waycross in October.

The Satilla River Canoe Trail, about three miles north on US 82, begins its 149-mile trip to Woodbine, Ga. There are campsites, boat ramps, fish camps along the trail.

A Tour of Historic Houses

Entering Georgia from South Carolina via I-20, US 25 or US 1, Augusta looms up as the industrial giant of the Savannah River. A thriving textile city, its industry also includes the nearby Savannah River Project of the Atomic Energy Commission and the multi-purpose Clark Hill Dam located twenty miles upriver.

Golfing is king at Augusta where the Masters Tournament is played each spring. Former President Dwight Eisenhower had a cottage adjoining the course.

St. Paul's Episcopal Church, founded in 1735 and rebuilt four times, is a historic must-see. Its rear door to the river afforded escape for many officials during the Revolutionary War when the fort was the capital of Georgia.

Another landmark is Meadow Garden, which was a part-time residence of George Walton, one of the Georgia signers of the Declaration of Independence. It is a curious house that George Washington and Marquis de Lafayette visited, now a museum operated by the Daughters of the American Revolution. The Harris-Pearson-Walker House (pre-1750) is the oldest house in town. Thirteen American patriots were hanged in the house by a British officer during the Revolution.

The Augusta National Clubhouse was the antebellum home of P. J. Berckmans, a noted experimental horticulturist from Belgium who planted the avenue of magnolias leading up to the clubhouse. The Gertrude Herbert Institute of Art, a three-story frame built in 1818, is a showcase for local and nationally famous artists. The Signers' Monument is dedicated to the Georgia signers of the Declaration of Independence—George Walton, Lyman Hall and Button Gwinnett.

The route from Augusta is via US 278 or I-20 to the Crawfordville turnoff. At Crawfordville is the home of Confederacy Vice-president Alexander H. Stephens and a state park named for him. His home, Liberty Hall, is focal point of the shrine and a museum displays mementoes relating to Stephens and the Confederacy.

Continue north on State 47 to Washington, a gracious old city dating from the late eighteenth century and untouched by Civil War destruction. A list of forty antebellum homes dating back to 1790 is obtainable from the Chamber of Commerce. It is possible to visit a few homes from time to time. Many are open during the spring home tour. The Washington-Wilkes Historical Museum is a rambling eighteen-room building dating back to 1835. Thirteen doors open to the outside. Displays are Civil War relics.

From Washington take State 17 north to Elberton, the greatest monument-granite quarrying area in America. Free tours of granite quarries and plants in the area are available.

Continue north on State 77 to Hartwell, a light manufacturing city and site of Hart State Park, a day use area with picnic facilities, bike trails and points of historical interest. The Hartwell Reservoir, built for flood control and power generation, has as its by-product recreation—boating, camping, water sports.

The route then leads through an agricultural area with many cattle, cotton and chicken farms. Textile and garment manufacturers, pulpwood and poultry-processing plants may be viewed at Commerce.

Athens is home of the first chartered state university. It also is distinguished for its antebellum homes, where Greek porticoes with pediments and impressive Doric columns make up the dominant architectural theme. The romantic tradition of the Deep South lives amid early boxwood gardens, oaks and elms grown stately with age, and white-blossomed magnolias.

Points of interest at the University include the Georgia Arch, main entrance, placed in 1856; Demosthenian Hall completed in 1824, home of the university's first literary society; the Chapel, completed in 1832, has large painting of interior of St. Peter's in Rome; Phi Kappa Hall, 1836; Old College, a three-story red brick structure of post-Colonial design, completed in 1805 and modeled after Connecticut Hall at Yale.

Athens-of-Old Tours begin at 280 E. Dougherty St., in a federal style house built in 1820, which serves as Athens Welcome Center—considered the city's oldest surviving residence. Information on do-it-yourself tours of over 50 local historic sites. See the science center, Art Museum and the only double-barreled cannon in existence. The cannon was designed to fire two balls simultaneously, but failed because the chain linking them spoiled the trajectory and accuracy. In Watkinsville, on US 129 and 441, is the Eagle Tavern, a former stagecoach stop and store.

Madison is the town Sherman refused to burn. When Federal forces marching from Atlanta approached Madison, U.S. Senator Joshua Hill, who did not vote for secession, rode out to meet General Sherman whom he had known in Washington. Sherman favored Hill's plea that the city be by-passed. Some damage was done to the town, however, when General Slocum's troops came through. During this raid a silver service was taken from the Presbyterian church. After the war, General Slocum returned it, and today the service is still treasured and used.

Historic homes abound in Madison, a city chartered in 1809 and located on an old stagecoach road. Owner-maintained antebellum homes may be seen by visitors with the use of a map-keyed brochure. There are tours of homes and gardens in December and spring.

In Eatonton there's a monument to a rabbit. This town, where Joel Chandler Harris lived as a boy, has a statue of Br'er Rabbit, the famous character of Uncle Remus tales.

Rock Eagle 4-H Center is the world's largest youth camp of its kind. The Rock Eagle effigy is a huge rock formation made from milky quartz. The Indian-made effigy measures 102 feet from head to tail and 120 feet from wing tip to wing tip.

Milledgeville has the old State Capitol used from 1807 to 1867, now rebuilt and a part of the Georgia Military College. The Old Governor's Mansion served as the home of ten Georgia governors for some forty years. Built in 1838, the mansion is a superb example of Greek Revival architecture. It was restored in 1967.

Macon, a picturesque blend of Old South culture and New South progress, is six miles from the geographical center of the state. Modern settlement dates from 1806 when the Federal government established Fort Benjamin Hawkins on the east side of the Ocmulgee River. A reproduction of the original structure has been erected on the site and is open Sunday afternoons.

Ocmulgee National Monument traces the evolution of the Southeastern Indian cultures from 8000 B.C. to the present in one of the South's largest archeological museums.

The world's first college chartered to grant degrees to women, Wesleyan, is located in Macon.

Notable houses are the Hay House, a twenty-four-room antebellum villa of Italian Renaissance style, and the Old Cannonball House, a Greek Revival built in 1853 and struck by a cannonball during the Federal attack on Macon in 1864. The Grand Opera House has the largest stage in the United States. Mark Smith Planetarium is housed at Macon Museum of Arts and Sciences.

Shunpike to Cherokee Nation

The Dixie Highway from Chattanooga to Atlanta (US 41) winds through the green Appalachian Valley, heart of the Cherokee nation until 1838. Shunpikers entering Georgia from Tennessee on I-75 may obtain routing from the Visitor Center at Ringgold. The Dixie Highway closely follows the route taken in 1864 by General William T. Sherman in his Dalton-to-Atlanta campaign, but few marks of the devastation of war remain. In their stead are evidences of the fresh, productive energies of this vibrant section. Dalton is the carpet capital of the world and easily earned the title since there are more than 160 carpet mills in the town.

From Dalton take US 76 to Spring Place and Chatsworth. Spring Place is location of the Vann House, an outstanding example of Cherokee Indian wealth and culture. Built in 1804 by James Vann, the house features hand carving inside and out. Bricks for the house were made on Vann's plantation, and hinges were produced in his own blacksmith shop.

At Chatsworth is Fort Mountain State Park. This park derives its name from an ancient fortification, the ruins of which stand on the high point of the mountain. Speculation regarding its origin includes reference to Spanish conquistadors hunting gold, twelfth-century Welsh adventurers and to the "moon-eyed people," mysterious white tribesmen.

From Spring Place take State 225 back into US 41/I-75 at Calhoun, old-time center of the Cherokee nation. Named for John C. Calhoun, the town has bedspread factories and cotton mills. A memorial arch and statue pay tribute to Sequoyah, the Dutch-Cherokee who gave the Cherokees their alphabet, which was used to publish their own newspaper, the *Cherokee Phoenix*. In happier days, the Cherokees set up a government in the area patterned after the U.S. Government. New Echota, three miles northeast on State 225, served as the capital of the Cherokee Indian Nation from 1825 to 1838. A thriving community of stores, homes, a print shop, and government buildings comprised the original settlement. The nation prospered until a treaty banned the Cherokees from the state. It was ruled unconstitutional by the U.S. Supreme Court, but President Andrew Jackson's defiance of the court forced the Cherokees to abandon their lands and set off for Oklahoma on the infamous "Trail of Tears." The village has been partially restored.

South from Calhoun by I-75 or US 41 is Cartersville, an exceptionally rich and varied mineral community with many workers engaged in mining and processing limestone, talc, manganese, barite, potash, ochre, shale, bauxite, cement and slate.

Etowah Indian Mounds, three miles south on marked route, are the most significant Indian settlement in the Etowah Valley. The burial grounds and copper, shell and stone relics from a village that thrived here two thousand years ago may be seen. The museum has artifacts and displays.

Nearby is Lake Allatoona, a vast federal flood control project on the Etowah River. The lake provides numerous recreation areas including campsites, fishing, sand beaches, swimming, boating and water-skiing.

Lowry Covered Bridge (or Euharlee Creek Bridge) is six miles west via State 113 and two miles north on the county road to Euharlee. The bridge was constructed in 1886 after high water swept a previous one downstream. It is one span wide, 116 feet long and of town lattice design. Numbers still legible on the bridge timbers indicate that such structures often were assembled in a nearby field to assure perfect fit, then rebuilt over the stream.

Scenery Plus Civil War

Rock City, atop Lookout Mountain on the Georgia side, is within sight of Interstates 24, 59, and 75. It has ageless rock formations, a sweeping panoramic view of the Appalachians and colorful flowers and foliage. Youngsters delight to the artistry of Fairyland Caverns and Mother Goose Village.

Continue to Chickamauga and Chattanooga National Military Park on US 27, the scene of a Confederate victory during the Civil War. A Union victory at the Battle of Chattanooga, however, shattered the South's hopes of winning the war. The oldest and largest of the national military parks, this one commemorates the heroic soldiers of both North and South. The park features an eight-mile driving tour, restored Brotherton House, specific battlelines, museum and numerous state monuments erected in memory of the state troops that fought in the battle. The park is operated by National Park Service and it's free.

Cloudland Canyon, off State 143, near Rising Fawn, covers 1,699 acres and is part of the old Cherokee Indian territory. According to legend, there is a secret and fabulously rich lead mine in the vicinity. When the first white settlers built a trading post here, the Indians were able, with just a few hours notice, to deliver lead to the settlers to make bullets. The Indians never revealed the location of their mine and it has never been found.

Rome is located on US 27 and 411. Like its Italian namesake, it is located on seven hills, from which it exerts a dominant industrial influence over the fertile Coosa Valley. A prominent statue of the Capitoline Wolf nursing Romulus and Remus is a famous gift from the Italian city. Rome is the seat of diversified industry—more than one hundred manufacturers turn out items ranging from textiles to chemicals.

The Chieftains was the home of John Ridge, Chief of the Cherokees, and was the scene of the U.S.-Cherokee Treaty that removed the Cherokees to Oklahoma. It is open to visitors. Oak Hill, north on US 27, was the gracious home of Miss Martha Berry, founder of Berry Schools. Miss Berry once traveled by horse and buggy to teach young people in the north Georgia mountains. The campus includes 30,000 acres of Berry-owned fields and forest, and it now has a senior college. Martha Berry Museum and Art Gallery exhibits Berry memorabilia, and it has a court of honor, a small theatre and art gallery. Rome was also the home of Ellen Axson, the first Mrs. Woodrow Wilson. She is buried in Myrtle Hill Cemetery on Broad Street.

Take US 441 to Cartersville, back onto US 41, and then to Kennesaw Mountain where a national Battlefield Park is located. Commemorated is the Battle of Kennesaw Mountain, decisive during the Civil War. The museum has slide presentations and exhibits, eighteen miles of hiking trails, picnic facilities. Kennesaw, known for many years as Big Shanty (for the still of the same name), was scene of the first major engagement in the Dalton-Atlanta campaign. The mountain has an altitude of 1,809 feet; the park covers three thousand acres.

Lockheed-Marietta Aircraft and Dobbins Air Force Base are near. Lockheed has seventy-eight acres under one roof with much work space underground as a result of World War II when the plant, then making Bell bombers, was bomb-proofed. The highway passes Marietta National Cemetery, twenty-four acres of lavishly landscaped grounds containing the graves of more than ten thousand Union soldiers and many veterans of other wars. Large oaks, magnolias, hollies, evergreen shrubs and a profusion of rose bushes surround the mansion-like main building over-looking the cemetery from atop a hill. A Confederate Cemetery lies about a half-mile from the Marietta city square. It has about three thousand slabs, most of them nameless.

From Marietta turn east eleven miles to Roswell on Ga. 120, a community gradually being enveloped by the suburban Atlanta complex. This town was laid out in 1835 by Roswell King, a Connecticut banker who managed the Pierce Butler plantation on St. Simons Island, almost 350 miles to the south. Envisioning a mountain retreat for himself and his friends from the summer heat of the Sea Islands, Mr. King set up about a dozen homes in the community. One of his neighbors, Martha Bulloch, married the senior Theodore Roosevelt there in 1835. One of their sons was the future president; another was the father of Eleanor Roosevelt. Barrington Hall, built by the town's founder in 1842, housed Union troops during the Civil War. Fourteen Doric columns and wide-planked floors are outstanding features, along with original antique furniture. It is shown by special arrangement. Roswell has a number of privately owned antebellum homes that visitors may see while driving through the town. Mimosa Hall (1846) is Greek Temple style. A tour of homes and gardens is scheduled each spring.

Mountains Where There's Gold

Georgia has mountains (one almost a mile high) and some with gold. In fact the expression "Thar's gold in them thar hills" originated at Dahlonega, site of America's first gold rush.

If you enter Georgia from South Carolina over I-85, a Visitor Center at Lavonia can direct you. Or you may choose a few days in the mountains following a stay in Atlanta.

Starting at the Lavonia Center, the first stop should be at Toccoa, which was on the stage coach routes of old. Traveler's Rest, six miles east on US 123, served as a plantation house, tavern, trading post and post office. It has authentic furnishings. One of Georgia's remaining relics of the road.

Toccoa Falls is two miles northeast off State 17 on grounds of Toccoa Falls Institute. The drop is 186 feet. Lake Yonah, a Georgia Power Company facility, eight miles north on State 184, is one of Georgia's most beautiful remote, uncrowded mountain lakes.

Tallulah Gorge on US 23 is believed to be the oldest natural gorge in North America. It is one and a half miles long and reaches a maximum depth of two thousand feet. There are five waterfalls in the bottom of the gorge; however, the main water supply has been diverted for hydroelectricity. A 1,100-foot cable, used by Karl Wallenda in his historic tightwire walk across the gorge, spans the chasm. A thirty-minute movie explaining the erection of the cable, the daring walk and two famous headstands by Wallenda can be seen daily during the summer at Tallulah Point. A nature trail follows a portion of the gorge's rim. There is also an overlook.

A Mountaineer Festival is held in Clayton each year honoring the contributions of mountain folk to the American way of life. Events include buck and square dancing, a wood cutting contest, greased pole climbing, horse show, and baby contest.

The Bartram Trail attracts hikers who visit this area. Quaker naturalist William Bartram first blazed this route over 200 years ago. Midpoint of the trail (which extends about 40 miles) is 3 miles east of Clayton at Warwoman Dell.

Rabun Bald Mountain has a trail to an elevation of 4,663 feet and offers a panoramic view of the surrounding Chattahoochee National Forest.

In the downtown area of Cornelia, there is a Big Red Apple monument honoring the area's major crop. A Memorial Tower one mile from downtown has a fire observation station at the summit of Tower mountain, a memorial to men of the Forest Service killed in World War II.

Over 100,000 visitors go to Hiawassee each year for the Mountain Fair which lasts for ten days. This is an old-fashioned country fair with a wondrous variety of exhibits including quilting parties, wood carving, soap and hominy making, and "hawg rifle" shoots. There are no commercial exhibits but many special events.

Andy's Trout Farm near Dillard offers rainbow trout fishing that doesn't require a license. Sky Valley Ski Area, northeast of Dillard on State 246, has excellent snow-skiing facilities including beginner, intermediate and expert slopes. Equipment is available for rent or purchase. A lodge and double chair lift are also available.

Brasstown Bald, south of Blairsville via US 129 and 19, then east via State 180 to State 66, is the highest point in Georgia—4,784 feet. A visitors center is open May 1 to October 31.

Richard Russell Scenic Highway extends fourteen miles through the state's most beautiful mountain areas. The Appalachian Trail crosses the road at Tessnatee Gap, highest point on the highway. Elevations range from 1,600 feet to almost 3,000 feet.

Camping facilities are extensive throughout the mountain area. One at Lake Winfield Scott covers twenty-six acres in the Chattahoochee National Forest. Another is located at Track Rock where rock hounds delight in several soapstone boulders bearing many carved figures of unknown origin. According to Cherokee legends, the petroglyphs had been placed here by an earlier people before the first Cherokee entered the region. There are camp sites in Vogel State Park where (legend has it) fabulous treasures were buried and bloody battles fought between Creek and Cherokee Indians. The southernmost point of the Appalachian Trail is nearby.

Architecture is the key to the charm of Helen, an Alpine-type village. The buildings, redesigned in recent years to add appeal to visitors, feature gingerbread trim and face paintings. Unique shops, stone streets, and a picturesque setting make this Bavarian town a "must" for visitors to Georgia.

Anna Ruby Falls is one of the most beautiful waterfalls in the area, one and a half miles north of Unicoi Recreational Experiment Station. A covered bridge three miles north of Helen on Ga. 255 at Stovall Mill, is a seventy-five-year-old, forty-foot span across Chickamauga Creek.

Cleveland has a Fall Leaf Festival each year during the October peak of the season. Events take place in the downtown area, dominated by the Old White County Court House, built from 1857-59 and in continuous use until 1965. It now houses a local historical society.

Dahlonega's courthouse dominates the town square also. It is a museum and commemorates the exciting era when the nation's first major gold rush took place here in 1828, bringing scores of prospectors into the area. A branch of the United States Mint was located here in 1838, and more than $6 million of Georgia gold was coined during the twenty-three-year life of the mint. Crisson's Gold Mine, three miles north of the city on Wimpy Mill Road, has gold-panning and picnicking from April to November. Blackburn Park, five miles south on State 9E, is a site of early gold discovery. There are a nature museum, archery range and gold mine.

Steele's Covered Bridge (1897), eighty-four feet long, is near Dawsonville.

Lake Sidney Lanier, with a 540-mile shore line, extends around Gainesville, Cumming, Buford; it is the most visited U.S. Corps of Engineer impoundment in the United States. Fishing, boating, waterskiing are available.

Road Atlanta, ten miles south of Gainesville off State 53, is an SCAA-sanctioned road course for Grand Prix road racing.

Fountains, Flowers, FDR

The Columbus Visitor Center, located on US 27, is the first spot tourists from Alabama visit when they enter Georgia. Attendants suggest tours around Columbus, to Callaway Gardens, Roosevelt's home at Warm Springs, and through Pine Mountain areas into Atlanta.

"Fountain City" is an appropriate description for Columbus because fountains can be found in public parks, at office buildings, or gracing lawns in residential areas. The Springer Opera House is a restored Victorian theater where Edwin Booth and Franklin D. Roosevelt appeared. Performances are from mid-September to late May. Columbus has a Museum of Arts and Crafts where Yuchi Indian materials, paintings, a children's museum and prehistoric Indian artifacts are housed.

At the Fort Benning Infantry Museum the evolution of the Infantry is traced from the French and Indian War to the present. Fort Benning is the Free World's largest infantry training center, covering 282 square miles of varied terrain. An open reservation, it welcomes visitors.

Confederate navy ships are displayed at a museum on US 27. Included are the hull of the iron-clad *Muscogee*. The Ladies' Defender Cannon is displayed here, too. It was made from brass articles donated by the women of Columbus during the Civil War. Ladies gave up brass beds, cooking utensils, jewelry and door knobs to be made into this unusual field artillery piece.

A heritage tour of historic points is scheduled regularly. It originates at the Georgia Visitor Center, US 27, and lasts for two hours, visiting four house museums and the Springer Opera House.

Pine Mountain is home of the famed Callaway Gardens, a 2,500-acre resort noted for its wildflowers of the Southern Appalachians. There are miles of scenic drives, walking trails and display greenhouses, sixty-three holes of golf, a 175-acre fishing lake, horseback riding, quail hunting on a 1,000-acre preserve and skeet and trap shooting. From April through September a mile-long beach is open with rides for the entire family. The Florida State University Circus performs throughout summer, and a children's recreation program is provided free for children staying in motel or cabins.

Now managed by the nonprofit Callaway Foundation, the Gardens are engaged in a constant improvement program, in which as many as 75,000 plants may be planted in a single year. Pathways wind through banks of azaleas, rhododendrons, camellias, gardenias, boxwoods, hollies and magnolias. Grapes from the Gardens' arbors go into Pine Mountain muscadine sauces and jellies, sold at the Country Store and served in the Gardens' restaurants. The store features stone-ground corn meal, hickory smoked hams, guinea hens, banana nut breads and locally produced condiments.

Across the road from the Country Store is the entrance to Franklin D. Roosevelt State Park, established in honor of the wartime President who died at nearby Warm Springs. President Roosevelt chose the Pine Mountain area for his home because of the curative qualities of the mineral waters at Warm Springs and because of the peaceful atmosphere. A spot called Dowdell's Knob, on the mountain road from Callaway's to Warm Springs, was visited often by the President when he drove around the Georgia countryside. Mr. Roosevelt went to Warm Springs in 1924 for treatment of his infantile paralysis. He built a modest white frame house where he died in 1945. The Little White House has been operated as a shrine for thirty years and remains just as President Roosevelt left it. The furnishings are spartan. Displayed is the unfinished portrait of him that was being painted when he was fatally stricken. Native stones and flags line the walkway leading from a memorial fountain to the museum. A twelve-minute movie is shown.

In La Grange is Bellevue, home of U.S. Senator Benjamin H. Hill who acquired it in 1853. He was arrested in this home by Federal forces. On a more festive occasion, Jefferson Davis was entertained here. It is open Tuesday–Sunday. A Callaway Memorial tower is also located in La Grange. It is patterned after the famous Campanile of St. Mark's Square in Venice, Italy, and was built in 1929 as a tribute to the memory of Fuller Callaway, Sr.

Newnan was named for General Daniel Newnan of War of 1812 fame. It is a center of manufacturing and peach orchards. The town is noted for its springtime beauty when great clouds of purple wisteria, clusters of multi-colored tulips and banks of golden daffodils burst forth in its many gardens. Three red brick buildings on College Street served as a hospital for Confederate and Union soldiers. Buena Vista, an elegant old home of double porches and massive white columns, served as local headquarters for Confederate General Joe Wheeler. Antebellum homes are found throughout the city. Although privately owned, they may be seen on a driving tour of residential areas.

Power's Crossroads Country Fair and Arts Festival is held early each September about ten miles west on State 34.

A glimpse of Georgia's agricultural cash register is afforded motorists who come into the state from Florida via I-75, then shunpike over US 82 from Tifton to Georgetown near the Alabama line.

Turpentine is a major industry, and miles of pine forests may be seen from all sections. Hunting is excellent in acres of low-lying timberland. Deer, quail, dove, rabbit and squirrel hunting is regulated by state laws.

Crescent House is the garden center of Valdosta, built in 1898 with a ballroom that seats three hundred. The Withlacoochee River Canoe Trail starts two miles west for a fifty-five-mile journey south. Valfestiva Festival of the Arts takes place each April.

Take I-75 to Tifton, one of the state's leading tobacco markets. Farmers sell more than nine million pounds of tobacco at this market in a typical year. Visitors are welcomed at the sales in July and August. Soil is king in Tift county. Vegetable plants from this section are sent to major markets throughout the United States. Pecans are prominent, and bees raised here are shipped to apple orchards as far north as Canada in order to increase the fruit yield. The Abraham Baldwin Agricultural College is adjacent to the Coastal Plains Experiment Station where farmers and students study better methods of producing beef cattle, hogs, grasses and legumes, blueberries and muscadine grapes. The Georgia Agrirama off I-75 at Tifton is a living historical museum depicting a rural community of the 1800s. Over 25 authentic restorations—gristmill, sawmill, cotton gin, farmhouse, rural village.

The route is hewn from planted timberlands; it runs alongside tobacco fields and through peach and pecan orchards. Motorists see the money crops, which gained prominence as Georgians phased out the one-crop cotton economy.

Albany and Andersonville

US 82 leads through Sylvester to Albany, Georgia's newest metropolitan area. This brisk town was settled by Nelson Tift (for whom Tifton was named), a Connecticut Yankee who laid out the broad palm-bordered avenues which dominate the city today. During the slavery period, Albany was a leading cotton market with the Flint River serving as a major artery of transportation. Now it is the paper-shell pecan capital of the world with orchards of 700,000 trees, covering more than 60,000 acres.

Four miles south is Radium Springs, the largest natural spring in the state, maintaining a constant temperature of 68 degrees.

Albany also has excellent quail shooting with several preserves offering hunting privileges by prior arrangement. Chehaw Wild Animal Park on Ga. 99 off US 19 bypass is a 100-acre preserve where exotic animals roam free in their natural habitats, separated from visitors who stroll along protective trails and elevated walkways. Banks-Haley Museum, on Slappey Boulevard, is home of the Southwest Georgia Art Association. Exhibits change monthly. Thronateeska Museum, Heritage Plaza, is housed in a 1910 train depot and includes the McIntosh Indian collection of arrowheads and artifacts.

Andersonville National Historic Site is on State 49, north from Americus. A Confederate military prison was established here in 1864 and used for fourteen months. Many states have placed monuments. West of Americus on US 280 is Plains, the home of President Jimmy Carter and a center of Georgia's peanut country.

Westville is a recreated, functioning rural village of 1850 just a half-mile from Lumpkin. Authentic buildings were moved to the site, restored and furnished. Working craftsmen demonstrate the skills of yesteryear. In the town of Lumpkin, on the square, is Bedingfield Inn, a restored 1836 stagecoach inn that also served as a family residence. It is furnished with authentic period appointments. Providence Canyon State Park is Georgia's "Little Grand Canyon." The central basin of this octopus-shaped cavern covers more than three thousand acres, and the chasm is some three hundred feet wide and two hundred feet deep. Erosion began almost a century ago. Red clay, blue marl, shell and a yellow clay have crumbled away, and the giant erosion, having eaten into a layer of chalk, seems as insatiable as ever. Trees, leaning outward and awry, cling precariously to the steep walls. Small islands rise from the bottom of the vast fissure, and on these a few small pines struggle to survive.

Turn south on US 27 to Cuthbert, located on a fertile plateau between the Flint and Chattahoochee rivers. It was one of the earliest settlements in this area after the Lower Creek Indians were expelled. Many antebellum houses of the Classic Revival design may be seen, including: the McWilliams house with pedimented porch and square columns in center of the front; Key house, one story with colonnade on front only; Toombs house (1850), one of the first two-frame houses in town; McDonald house with its immense McDonald pecan tree, said to have been started from a Texas seedling nut planted in 1846.

Continue south on US 27 to Blakely and the Kolomoki Indian Mounds. Archeologists are still searching this key village of the ancient Mound-builders of Georgia. Two museums display their findings, but the huge burial mounds, built over five thousand years ago, are the most intriguing aspect of the old village. The Mounds are in a State Park where swimming, family camping and fishing are available.

There's a flagpole on the Court House Square, the last of the Confederate ones, erected in 1861; and there's a monument to the peanut, which serves as a constant reminder of the product's importance to this area's economy.

Next is Bainbridge where the fisherman, camper and swimmer may enjoy the bounty of sprawling Lake Seminole at Seminole State Park.

Take US 84 east from Bainbridge to Cairo (pronounced Kay-ro), a city bathed year round with blossoms. The fields around Cairo yield more cane sugar than any other area in the United States, and the spring-flowering tung tree is tapped for extensive supplies of tung oil used in paints, varnishes and as a dyeing agent. A huge pickle plant is one of the town's chief attractions.

If there is any modern parallel to the image of sprawling Southern plantations shaded by magnolias and sweet with the scent of many flowers, it would have to be Thomasville, Georgia's home of the roses. A Rose Festival takes place each April, and the Rose Test Gardens are one of twenty-five such gardens in the United States used for experimenting with development of new types of roses. The Test Gardens are open from mid-April to mid-November.

The most imposing single attraction of the town is the Big Oak, a sprawling live oak almost three hundred years old that has attained a magnificent spread of 155 feet; it is 65 feet high and the trunk is 22 feet in circumference.

Out beyond Pine Tree Boulevard are the great plantations maintained as winter retreats by many of America's leading industrialists, including former Secretary of the Treasury George M. Humphrey, a frequent host of former President and Mrs. Dwight Eisenhower and one of a long line of plantation owners with ties to the late Mark Hanna of Cleveland. A demonstration of the political power that made Hanna a formidable foe or ally is evident in the fact that William McKinley was his guest at Thomasville's Mark Hanna house when McKinley was nominated for the presidency.

There are many plantations in the area. The most noted is probably "Greenwood," the 140,000-acre quail hunting preserve maintained by Mr. and Mrs. John Hay (Jock) Whitney. The main house was constructed of heavy, hand-hewn timbers cut from the estate in 1835, and the architect personally carved an immense magnolia blossom and laurel wreaths on the front gable. Magnolias grace the lawn and Lady Banksha yellow roses surround the balconies in the spring.

Hedges of Cherokee roses border the highway alongside the large Dutch Colonial, Melrose, one of three plantations bought by the Hanna family, and now owned by Hanna's daughter. Plantation buildings are painted to match the hard, coral-colored clay and white oyster shell roads, and the elegant home boasts a swimming pool, motion picture theater, and a collection of antique cars. Ichauway Plantation, Pebble Hill (another Hanna estate), Hickory Grove, Pine Bloom, and Iris Court are other standouts among the thirty great plantations. Alas, they can only be seen from outside, and the great quail hunting is by invitation only.

PRACTICAL INFORMATION FOR GEORGIA

FACTS AND FIGURES. Georgia was named for King George II of England. It has a long string of mostly less august nicknames: Buzzard State; Cracker State; Goober State; Peach State; Empire State of the South. The state flower is the Cherokee rose; the state tree, the live oak; the state bird, the brown thrasher. "Wisdom, Justice, Moderation" is the state motto. "Georgia on My Mind" the state song.

Atlanta, the state's biggest city and the leading business center of the Southeast, is the state capital. Population of the state is over 5 million.

The furthermost reaches of Georgia are the string of offshore island resorts in the Atlantic, among them the tiny and fashionable Sea Island. From its Atlantic coastline, a flat coastal plain of swamps, pine forests and gracious old antebellum towns like Savannah, the land rises to the low hills of the central Piedmont district and in the north to the mountains and lake region of the southern reaches of the Appalachians. Georgia's economy has progressed since the '30's, when cotton reigned as the state's single crop and major source of income. Industrialization and agricultural diversification have brought great improvements in the state's finances.

HOW TO GET THERE. *By air:* Atlanta may be reached on direct flights of: Braniff, Delta, Eastern, Northwest, Piedmont, Republic, TWA, and United airlines. Delta and Atlantis have direct flights to Augusta; Delta and Atlantic SE to Macon; Delta to Savannah; Delta and Atlantic SE to Columbus; Republic to Albany, Moultrie and Valdosta.

By car: I-95 enters Savannah from South Carolina and continues along the east coast south to Florida. I-85 comes in from Anderson, South Carolina, continues to Atlanta, then goes southwest to Alabama. I-75 enters Georgia from Tennessee, goes through Atlanta and continues south to Florida. I-20 comes into Augusta from Aiken, South Carolina, west to Atlanta and on to Alabama. US 84 enters from Dothan, Alabama, and goes east to Bainbridge, Valdosta and Waycross. US 441 comes in from North Carolina, goes south through Athens and Dublin to Florida. I-16 extends from Macon to Savannah; I-185 connects Columbus with I-85 a short distance out of Lagrange.

By train: Amtrak serves Atlanta from New Orleans, Washington, and New York, and Savannah and Brunswick from Florida and the east.

By bus: Greyhound and Trailways.

HOW TO GET AROUND. *By air:* Delta, Eastern, Piedmont and Republic serve cities within the state.

By car: I-95 goes from Savannah south to the Florida state line; I-16 runs from Savannah northwest to Macon; I-20 goes from Augusta west to Atlanta and on to Alabama; I-85 comes in from South Carolina, proceeds southwest to Atlanta, La Grange and continues to Alabama; I-75 enters from Tennessee, goes south to Atlanta, southeast to Macon and Valdosta and continues south to Florida; US 84 comes in from Alabama and goes east to Bainbridge, Valdosta and Waycross; US 441 enters from North Carolina, goes south to Athens and Dublin and on to Florida. I-16 extends from Macon to Savannah; I-185 connects Columbus with I-85 a short distance out of Lagrange.

Car rental: You will find Avis, Hertz, National and Budget rental offices throughout Georgia.

By bus: Southeastern Motor Lines, Inc., services cities within the state, in addition to Greyhound and Trailways.

By train: Amtrak has trains to Atlanta, Savannah, Thalman, Waycross and Valdosta.

Tennessee line; Sylvania—US 301, ¼ mi. SW of South Carolina line; Valdosta—I-75, 2 mi. N of Florida line; Augusta—I-20, ½ mi. W of South Carolina line, I-95 at Kingsland; I-85 at West Point; Atlanta—Atlanta Airport.

Additional information: Game & Fish, Dept. of Natural Resources, 270 Washington St. S.W., Atlanta 30334; Division of State Parks and Historic Sites, 270 Washington St., S.W., Atlanta 30334; Ga. Chamber of Commerce, Commerce Bldg., Atlanta 30334; Tourist Division, Georgia Dept. of Industry and Trade, P.O. Box 1776, Atlanta 30301; U.S. Forest Service, Box 1437, Gainesville 30501 (camping areas).

 SEASONAL EVENTS. Many Georgia cities take advantage of the natural beauty of dogwood, peach, camellia and azalea blossoms in the spring to showcase their finer homes. Augusta and Savannah sponsor camellia shows in January, early February. Home and garden tours are held in Augusta, Columbus, Washington, Newnan, Madison, St. Simons and Savannah in March and April. Thomasville's Rose Festival is held in April.

Summer: Georgia Mountain Fair draws over a hundred thousand visitors to view the quiltmaking, woodcarvings, soap making, hog rifle shoots. 10 days, early Aug. Watermelon Festival in Cordele; frequent watermelon cuttings at Agrirama, Tifton. Buggy Days in Barnesville; Mule Day at Cairo and Dahlonega.

Fall: In this traditional time for harvest fairs, Lawrenceville has an Apple-Picking Rodeo, Stone Mountain, a Yellow-Daisy Festival; Helen, an Oktoberfest. *Powers Crossroads Country Fair & Arts Festival,* in early Sept., is the South's largest arts & crafts festival fair. *Dahlonega's Gold Rush Days* features country music, costumed citizens, pioneer floats, mule races. 3 days, Oct.

Winter: Several towns have Christmas celebrations: In Pine Mountains, Callaway Gardens has a 3-wk. Christmas program. Fitzgerald's civic clubs decorate the town parks with modern and traditional decorations. Westville has special Christmas events.

 NATIONAL FORESTS. Georgia has two national forests, the *Chattahoochee* and the *Oconee.* The Chattahoochee National Forest covers 687,000 acres in northern Georgia, and the Oconee comprises more than 100,000 acres in the central part of the state. Both contribute substantially to the state's timber production and share their wealth of natural, unspoiled, preserved beauty with vacationer and tourist alike. There are scenic hiking trails, mountain streams and lake fishing and ample camping facilities. The Chattahoochee has 31 recreation areas; the Oconee, four. For information about admission permits, write to U.S. Forestry Service, P.O. Box 1437, Gainesville.

 STATE PARKS. Georgia's State park system contains parks distributed throughout the state. Facilities vary from simple picnicking areas to highly developed recreation and overnight accommodations for families.

Georgia has been divided into seven areas to add thrust and to unify tourism programs. State parks in each sector tend to meld historic and geographic identities.

In the Big A (Atlanta) sector are Chattahoochee River State Park near Atlanta, Indian Springs at Indian Springs, John Tanner at Carrollton, Sweetwater Creek at Lithia Springs, Panola Mountain, and Franklin D. Roosevelt State Park at Pine Mountain.

The Classic South has Alexander H. Stephens at Crawfordsville, Bobby Brown at Elberton, Elijah Clark at Lincolnton, Fort Yargo at Winder, George L. Smith II at Twin City, Hard Labor Creek at Rutledge, Magnolia Springs at Millen, Mistletoe at Appling, Watson Mill Bridge at Comer, and Will-a-Way (especially for handicapped persons) at Winder.

Three parks are in the Heart of Georgia region: High Falls at Jackson, Little Ocmulgee at McRae, Hamburg at Mitchell.

The Colonial Coast has Crooked River at Kingsland, General Coffee at Nicholls, Laura S. Walker at Waycross, Richmond Hill at Richmond Hill, Skidaway Island at Savannah, and Stephen C. Foster at Fargo.

The Northeast Georgia Mountains have Amicalola Falls at Dawsonville, Black Rock Mountain at Mountain City, Hart at Hartwell, Moccasin Creek at Clarkesville, Tugaloo at Lavonia, Unicoi at Helen, Victoria Bryant at Royston, and Vogel at Blairsville.

In Pioneer Territory (the northwest) are Cloudland Canyon at Rising Fawn, Fort Mountain at Chatsworth, James H. Floyd at Summerville, and Red Top Mountain at Cartersville.

Plains Country has George T. Bagby at Georgetown, Georgia Veterans Memorial at Cordele, Kolomoki Mounds at Blakely, Providence Canyon at Lumpkin, Reed Bingham at Adel, and Seminole at Donaldsonville.

All state parks are open year round. Many provide rental cottages and/or mobile homes. Campgrounds open at 7 A.M. and close at 10 P.M. No reservations accepted. Rental cottages and mobile homes are completely furnished, including linens and blankets. All reservations for cottages and mobile homes must be made through the superintendent of the park you wish to visit.

There are regulation golf courses in three of the parks—Victoria Bryant, Hard Labor Creek and Little Ocmulgee. One—Georgia Veterans Memorial—has an airplane landing strip. "Dream Boat" rentals are available at Vogel, Franklin D. Roosevelt, Indian Springs, and Georgia Veterans. There are tennis courts at Georgia Veterans and Little Ocmulgee.

For additional information and descriptive folders listing all parks and their facilities, write State Parks, Department of Natural Resources, 270 Washington St. S.W., Atlanta 30334.

 CAMPING OUT. The U.S. Forest Service, U.S. Corps of Engineers, State Parks Commission and private owners operate many campgrounds. Campers in state parks are served on a first-come basis, and must obtain a permit from the park superintendent before setting up. Campsites for recreation vehicles cost $6 per night; tent and pop-up trailers, $5. The State Parks Dept., 270 Washington St., Atlanta 30334 and Georgia Campground Owners Assoc., P.O. Box 5487, Columbus 31902 have pamphlets, maps.

 MUSEUMS AND GALLERIES. Historical: *Thronateeska Heritage Museum* in Albany has a permanent collection of Indian artifacts; changing nature, science, history & art exhibits. *Augusta Museum,* 540 Telfair St., has archeological, historical, natural science exhibitions, is open Tues. to Sun. *Harris-Pearson-Walker House,* 1822 Broad St., Augusta, is the site of a Revolutionary War battle. Eighteenth-century furnishings, Indian artifacts, Revolutionary relics. Tues. to Sun. Closed major holidays. *Midway Museum,* on US 17, commemorates the Midway Society, descendants of Puritans who came to Georgia as missionaries to the Indians in 1752. Period rooms, records, historical library. Tues. to Sun. *Salzburger Museum,* 6 miles from Rincon off Ga. 21 on Savannah River, commemorates 18th Century settlement of Salzburgers.

In Columbus is the *Confederate Naval Museum,* 101 4th St., May to Oct., Tues. to Sun. The *U.S. Army Infantry Museum* has exhibits covering the French & Indian War to present. Tues. to Sun. *Chattahoochee Promenade* is an outdoor historical museum developed during the National Bicentennial. Fitzgerald has the

Blue and Gray Museum, with Civil War momentos; open Wed. and Sun. by appointment. A memorial museum to Jefferson Davis is north of Irvinville on a country road. Savannah's *Factor's Walk Military Museum,* 222 Factor's Walk, houses Civil War mementos. In Washington, *Wilkes Historical Museum,* 308 E. Robert Toombs Ave., displays Confederate records, antebellum furnishings. Closed major holidays. In Valdosta, the *Children's Museum,* N. Patterson St., displays 40 exhibits relating to science and history plus five color slide presentations. In Jefferson, the *Crawford W. Long Museum* sits on the site where Dr. Long performed the first operation using ether.

Art: *Georgia Museum of Art,* on campus of U. of Ga., Athens, has permanent Holbrook and Kress collections. Closed August & part of Sept., academic and legal holidays. Free. *Augusta Museum,* Old Richmond Academy Bldg., 504 Telfair St., built 1802. History, Art, Military, Archeology and Natural Science collection. Free. The *Columbus Museum of Arts and Crafts,* 1251 Wynnton Rd., offers changing exhibits as well as Indian collection. Regional contemporary art, as well as scientific exhibitions, are on display at the *Macon Museum of Arts and Science and Planetarium,* 4182 Forsyth Rd. Closed major holidays. *Telfair Academy of Arts & Sciences,* 121 Barnard St., Savannah, was established in 1875, and its main bldg. was designed by William Jay. Fourteen galleries display paintings from eighteenth century to present.

If you're fascinated by Indian history and culture, you'll want to spend a lot of time at *New Echota* nr. Calhoun. The restoration of a 220-acre site includes *Worcester House,* original home of a missionary to the Cherokee nation, *Print Shop, Courthouse, Vann Tavern,* all furnished authentically. Closed major holidays. Be sure to see the Indian museum in *Kolomoki Mounds State Park* near Blakely. Eighteen exhibits interpret artifacts and culture of moundbuilders. *Etowah Mounds Archaeological Area,* 3 mi. S of Carterville, also has a museum. Closed major holidays. Nr. Eatonton is a 10-ft. high mound of milky quartz called Rock Eagle, shaped like an outstretched bird with a 120-ft. wingspread, created approx. 6,000 yrs. ago. At *Indian Springs State Park* is the home of Creek Indian chief William McIntosh. Ten thousand yrs. of Indian settlement are reviewed at *Ocmulgee National Monument* nr. Macon. The museum is open daily. Cherokee history can be further studied at *Chieftain Museum.* 100 Chatillon Rd., Rome. Feb. to mid-Nov.

Special Interest: *Science Center,* U. of Ga., Athens, has 6-ft. relief globe of the world, planetarium, and 24" reflector telescope. *Crawford W. Long Medical Museum,* US 129, in Jefferson, commemorates the first use of sulphuric ether as an anesthetic. Diorama, exhibits. *Savannah Science Museum,* 4405 Paulsen St., Savannah, has habitat groups of plant & animals; salt water & tidal aquariums, regional animals and planetarium lectures. Closed major holidays.

Others: *Dahlonega Courthouse Gold Museum* with exhibits from this country's first gold rush. *Uncle Remus Museum,* in Turner Park, Eatonton, has dioramas of 12 Uncle Remus stories, slave cabins, mementos. *Jekyll Island Museum,* 329 Riverview Dr., Jekyll Island, displays Edwardian Era (1901-10) furnishings. *Ships of the Sea Museum,* 503 E. River St., Savannah, displays ship models depicting the history of this early American port.

 HISTORIC SITES. Most famous—or infamous—is undoubtedly *Andersonville National Historical Site,* a Confederate prison where many Union soldiers died of exposure, hunger and inadequate medical care. On the grounds are Providence Spring, Sundial Monument commemorating Clara Barton's work, and adjoining, Andersonville National Cemetery. Rte. 49, 11 mi. NE of Americus. Free. One of the fiercest battles of the Civil War was fought at *Chickamauga,* nr. the Tennessee border. Part of Chickamauga and Chattanooga National Military Park is in Georgia, the rest in Tennessee. Visitor Center, on US 27, is open daily. Closed Christmas. At *Kennesaw Mountain National Battlefield*

Park, US 41, 2 mi. N of Marietta, the Visitor Center has exhibits and a self-guided walking tour. *Fort Pulaski,* 15 mi. E of Savannah off US 80, was built during colonial days, demolished, rebuilt again 1829-47. It was captured and manned by Union forces, serving effectively in the blockade of the South. *Fort Frederica,* 12 mi. NE of Brunswick on St. Simons Island, was planned by James Oglethorpe in 1734. It was destroyed by fire in 1758, and the town abandoned soon after.

Fort McAllister, 17 mi. S of Savannah, off US 17 on the banks of the Ogeechee River, an earthen fortification withstood heavy naval ordinance during the Civil War. *Fort King George* at Darien, constructed in 1721 to protect against Spanish and French aggression, was first settlement in what is now Georgia.

Among the houses restored and maintained as State Historic Sites are *Eagle Tavern,* 8 mi. S of Athens on US 129 at Watkinsville; Chief Vann House at Spring Place; Jarrell Plantation near Macon; Lapham-Patterson House at Thomasville; Midway Museum, *Meadow Garden,* 1320 Nelson St., Augusta, was restored by the state DAR; *"Liberty Hall,"* home of Alexander H. Stephens at Crawfordsville.

Traveler's Rest, 6 mi. NE of Toccoa, off US 123, is a restored plantation house & stagecoach inn. *Callaway Plantation,* W of Washington on US 78, has restored houses, hewn log kitchen with utensils, craft demonstrations, working farm. The *Little White House,* Warm Springs, is preserved as it was during Pres. Franklin D. Roosevelt's occupancy. Museum, free movie.

FAMOUS LIBRARIES. *Margaret Mitchell Library,* adj. to original Fayetteville Academy, between Rte. 85 and Lee St. in Fayetteville, has over 14,000 author autographed books, and an extensive Civil War reference collection.

TOURS. *Columbus:* Two-hour *Heritage Tour* leaves from Georgia Visitor Information Center, Victory Dr., covers 5 historic houses and Springer Opera House. *Athens, Macon, Madison, Savannah, Fort Gaines,* and *Sparta* offer do-it-yourself maps of historic sites. *Thomasville* Chamber of Commerce sponsors tours of plantations, historic homes and gardens of the immediate area, daily. Tours of *Okefenokee,* ranging from 2-hr. trips to 8-hr. trip into the interior, are available at the Suwannee Canal Recreation Area, 7 mi. SW of Folkston. Electric boat tours at Okefenokee Swamp Park, Waycross.

A number of sightseeing companies provide several tours of Atlanta and the surrounding areas.

GARDENS. The *All-America Rose Test Garden,* 1840 Smith Ave., Thomasville, is open to visitors from Apr. 15 to Nov. 15 daily except Sun. morning. *Callaway Gardens* at Pine Mountain, US 27, offers miles of scenic drives and walking trails through wildflower and cultivated gardens and flowering shrub displays. The Green House exhibits native and tropical flower arrangements. *Founder's Memorial Garden,* Babcock Dr. and Lumpkin St., Athens, is the site of the first garden club in the country. *Garden Center,* 598 Telfair St., Augusta. *National Camellia Society Headquarters,* Massee Lane Farms, 5 miles south of Ft. Valley on Ga. 49. *Trustee's Garden,* East Broad near Bay St., Savannah, America's first public experimental garden.

MUSIC. Macon's annual *country music festival* is held early in April. *Carillon* concerts at 12 & 4 daily, Sun. 1, 3, 5, June to Sept. at Stone Mountain. Augusta's *symphony season* is active in both fall and spring.

STAGE AND REVUES. *Barn Dinner Theatre,* 1690 Terrell Mill Rd., SE. Marietta (436-6262), provides gourmet buffet dinner, professional plays in unique setting. Macon's *Little Theater,* 4220 Forsyth Rd., presents musicals every summer. Write Box 7171, Macon 31204, or call 477-3341, for schedule. Albany's *Little Theater,* Pine Ave., presents four plays annually in restored, pre-Civil War home. *Springer Opera House,* Columbus, is a restored Victorian theater, with museum, tours, performances year round. Box 1622, Columbus 31902 for schedule. Jekyll Island has a music theater in summer.

DRINKING LAWS. Min. age is 19. Liquor stores are generally open from 8 A.M. to 11:30 P.M. daily except Sun. and election days. You can buy a drink during the same hours. State law prohibits the purchase of more than two quarts of liquor at a time. It is far easier to buy package liquor or beer and wine in those towns allowing it than to buy it by the drink.

SUMMER SPORTS. The active outdoorsman thrives in Georgia in the summer. Actually he can pursue his interests almost all of the year. Water-skiing, fishing, swimming and sailing are the chief participant activities in summer. Golfing is good all year. Atlanta International Raceway's summer schedule of stock and big car races, Callaway Gardens' Masters Water Ski Tournament and the Augusta National's Masters' Golf Tournament are the big ones. The Atlanta Braves play major league baseball at the 50,000-seat Atlanta Stadium.

Fishing: The fisherman can find a challenge in many mountain lakes and streams as well as at Lake Lanier, above Atlanta, and Lake Allatoona, just south of Lanier. Clark Hill, Hartwell, and Savannah Bluff reservoirs near Augusta are fished extensively for bass, trout, crappie and other varieties. Bait, tackle and fishing boats are readily available in all areas. Lake Seminole near Blakely, West Point Lake, and Lake Sinclair near Macon offer anglers many challenges. Bass are particularly plentiful in these areas.

Golf: Since the first Scottish immigrants introduced the sport to the state at Darien in 1736, Georgians have taken their golf seriously. Mild temperatures and layouts ranging from the gently rolling greens of north Georgia to the windswept seaside courses of *Jekyll* and *St. Simons Island* permit golfing almost the year round. Private airstrips at Callaway Gardens and Jekyll-St. Simons have made golfing weekends a standard diversion for big city businessmen. There are 104 public courses and a host of private ones, the most famous of which is the *Augusta National,* home of the Masters Tournament and rated in the first ten of America's 100 greatest golf courses. Peachtree Golf Club, Atlanta, ranks among the fourth 10; Atlanta County Club and Sea Island Golf Club, St. Simons Island, among the second fifty. *Atlanta,* home of legendary Grand Slam Champion Bobby Jones, has a trio of excellent public courses.

WINTER SPORTS. *Skiing.* Georgia's newest winter spot is found at *Sky Valley Ski Area,* northeast from Dillard on Rte. 246. Facilities include beginner, intermediate and expert slopes. Equipment is available for rent or purchase. A lodge and a double chair lift are also available. It is open daily during the season.

Hunting: Game is abundant in the vast woodlands and includes quail, ruffled grouse, rabbit, 'coons, foxes, deer, 'possums and an occasional brown bear or wild boar. The twenty-two public preserves range from federal wildlife areas to small quail fields stocked and operated by farmers. Dogs, guides, transportation and dressing of game are available at moderate fees. Overnight facilities are available or may be arranged.

SPECTATOR SPORTS: The *Atlanta Falcons* brought professional football to football-mad Georgians. They play in the Atlanta Stadium and bring a special extra to gridiron enthusiasts, who ardently follow the *Yellow Jackets* from Georgia Tech and the *Bulldogs* from the University of Georgia. Atlanta now has professional basketball, soccer and ice hockey as well. The *Hawks,* of the NBA, the *Flames,* of the NHL, and the Chiefs (soccer) play in the city's new multi-million dollar coliseum—the Omni.

WHAT TO DO WITH THE CHILDREN. Pan for gold with the kids at Crisson's, 3 mi. N of Dahlonega on Wimpy Rd., Apr. 12-Nov. 7. *Fairyland Caverns* and *Mother Goose Village* is open daily yr. round at Rock City. *Big Shanty Museum,* Kennesaw, see "The General," famous Civil War locomotive; *Ocmulgee National Indian Monument,* Macon, is site of Georgia's first Indian settlement; at *Chehaw Wildlife Park,* Albany, see animals face to face, including jaguar and ant-eater; Visit Okefenokee Swamp, at Waycross. *Stone Mountain Park,* 16 mi. E of Atlanta on US 78, is a 3,800-acre recreation park with game ranch, antebellum plantation, skylift, lots more. Combination ticket available. *Six Flags over Georgia,* on I-20 outside of Atlanta, is an amusement park with six distinctive areas representing periods of Georgia's history. Rides, live entertainment. *Atlanta Zoo,* in Grant Park, southeast Atlanta, is the largest zoo in the state.

HOTELS AND MOTELS in Georgia run the gamut from the deluxe resort on Sea Island to the inexpensive, but attractive, motels found along many of the state's major highways. Accommodations are listed according to price categories, based on double occupancy in the peak season, without meals: *Expensive* $42 to $56; *Moderate:* $22 to $40; *Inexpensive:* $14 to $21. For a more complete explanation of hotel and motel categories see *Facts at Your Fingertips* at the front of this volume.

Adel

Adel Motor Lodge. *Moderate.* 1102 W. Fourth St.

Quality Inn of Adel. *Moderate.* I-75 at Moultrie Exit.

Davis Bros. Motor Lodge. *Inexpensive.* Pool, play area. Restaurant. Pets.

Albany

Downtowner. *Moderate.* 732 Oglethorpe Blvd. (220 rooms). Pool. Pets. Restaurant, bar, dancing, entertainment. Rms. have refrigerators, snack dispensers.

Holiday Inn. *Moderate.* Pool. Pets. Restaurant, bar. Free airport transportation.

Quality Inn. *Moderate.* 2 locations, each with pool: **Merry Acres:** 1500 Dawson Rd. Restaurant, bar; **Town House:** 701 Oglethorpe Blvd. Cafeteria across street.

Ramada Inn. *Moderate.* 2505 N. Slappey Blvd. (118 rooms). Pool. Restaurant, bar, dancing, entertainment.

Sheraton Motor Inn. *Moderate.* 999 E. Oglethorpe Expw. (150 rooms). Pool (heated), pets. Restaurant, bar, dancing, entertainment.

Oglethorpe Motel. *Inexpensive.* 941 Oglethorpe Ave. 34 rooms.

Americus

Americus. *Moderate.* US 19S. Pool, restaurant near.

Best Western. *Moderate.* US 19S. Pool, restaurant.

Eight Inn. *Inexpensive.* US 19S.

Athens

Downtowner Motor Inn. *Moderate.* 1198 S. Milledge Ave. Pool. Restaurant, bar.

Sheraton History Village Inn. *Moderate.* (113 rooms) 295 East Dougherty St.

Holiday Inn Downtown. *Moderate.* (191 rooms) 2 restaurants, 3 bars. Broad at Hull St. Pets. Restaurant, bar. Nr. Univ. of Georgia.

Howard Johnson's. *Moderate.* 2465 W. Broad. Pool. Restaurant. Fam. rates avail.

Bulldog Inn. *Inexpensive.* US 441N. Pool. Pets. Restaurant nr.

Augusta

Augusta Hilton. *Expensive.* (216 rooms) 640 Broad St.

Continental Airport Hotel. *Moderate.* (92 rooms) Bush Field on State 56, opp. airport terminal. Pool, sauna, play area. Pets. Free in-rm. coffee. Restaurants, bars, entertainment, dancing. Golf nr.

Heart of Augusta. *Moderate.* 954 5th St. Pool. Restaurant nr. Morning rolls & coffee free. Pets.

Holiday Inn. *Moderate.* (175 rooms) 1602 Ft. Gordon Hwy. (US 1, 78). ¼ mi. W of US 25. Pools. Restaurant, bar, entertainment, dancing. Terminals transportation avail. **Holiday Inn Augusta** at 1075 Stevens Creek Rd.

Horne's Motor Lodge. *Moderate.* (143 rooms) 1520 Ft. Gordon Hwy. at jct. US 1, 25, 78, 278. Pool. Golf nr. Restaurant, bar. Terminals transportation avail.

Howard Johnson's Motor Lodge. *Moderate.* (61 rooms) 1238 Ft. Gordon Hwy. Pool. Golf nr. Restaurant, bar with dancing Wed. to Sat. Pets.

Oasis Motor Hotel. *Moderate.* 1370 Ft. Gordon Hwy. Pool (heated), sauna, play area. Restaurant, bar, dancing.

Quality Inn. *Moderate.* 3 locations, each with pool: **Miles:** 2077 Old Savannah Rd. Restaurant; **Embassy Towers:** 444 Broad St. Restaurant; **Warrick.** 441 Broad St. Bar, entertainment.

Ramada Inn. *Moderate.* Ft. Gordon Hwy. & Molly Pond Rd. Pool, play area. Restaurants, bar, entertainment, dancing. Free airport transportation. Pets.

Thunderbird Inn. *Moderate.* (121 rooms) 919 15th St. Pool. Restaurant, bar, entertainment.

Econo-Travel. *Inexpensive.* Ft. Gordon Hwy. at Molly Pond Rd. Pleasant, unpretentious. Member of chain. Restaurant nr. Free coffee.

Bainbridge

Holiday Inn. *Moderate.* Hwys. 27 and 84. (80 rooms). Pets. Restaurant, bar.

Bainbridge. *Inexpensive.* 710 Scott St. Pool. Restaurant.

Palmer. *Inexpensive.* Hwy. 27S. Pool, play area. Restaurant.

Blakely

Quail. *Inexpensive.* US 27 downtown. Free in-rm. coffee. Restaurant nr. Pets.

Brunswick

Holiday Inn. *Moderate.* 2 locations I-95 at US 341; 2307 Gloucester St., each with pool, restaurant, bar, dancing & entertainment.

Howard Johnson's. *Moderate.* 341 at I-95. Pool, play area. Restaurant, bar. Pets.

Quality Inn. *Moderate.* 2 locations: Palms, and on I-95 at 490 New Jesup Hwy. each with pool, restaurant nr.

Ramada Inn. *Moderate.* 2 locations: East at 3241 Glynn Ave.; and I-95, each with pool, play area, restaurant, bar, dancing and entertainment.

Days Inn. *Inexpensive.* I-95 at US 341

Oak Park Inn. *Inexpensive.* 3104 Glynn Ave.

Oleander Motel. *Inexpensive.* 2700 Glynn Ave.

Calhoun

Ace Motel. *Moderate.* I-75, exit 130.

Duffy's Motel North. *Moderate.* I-75 at Resaca Exit 132.

Big 5 Motor Inn. *Inexpensive.* I-75 at Rt. 5, Red Bud Rd.

Cartersville
Howard Johnson Motor Lodge. *Moderate.* I-75 and 411.

Quality Inn. *Moderate.* (86 rooms) US 41 S.

Ramada Inn. *Moderate.* I-75 and 411.

Chatsworth

Adco Motel. *Inexpensive.* Pool. Pets. Restaurant.

Chief Vann Motel. *Inexpensive.* Pool. Restaurant nr.

Colonial Pines. *Inexpensive.* Pool. Restaurant nr.

Claxton
Mae's Motel. *Inexpensive.* 111 N. Grady St.

Clayton

Heart of Rabun. *Moderate.* Pool (heated). Restaurant. Fam. rates avail.

Dillard Motor Lodge. *Moderate.* Main Street. Pool nearby. Rooms have mountain views from private patios. Free-in-room coffee. Seasonal rates available.

Cleveland

Gateway Inn. *Moderate.* (30 rooms). Pool (heated). Pets. Restaurant.

Columbus
Camellia Motel. *Moderate.* 2339 Fort Benning Road.

Heart of Columbus. *Moderate.* (65 rooms) 1024 4th Ave. Pets. Restaurant.

Holiday Inn. *Moderate.* Two locations: **Airport,** (173 rooms), 2800 Manchester Expwy; **Columbus South** (172 rooms), 3170 Victory Dr. Pool, play area. Pets. Restaurant, bar.

Quality Inn of Columbus. *Moderate.* (180 rooms) 1011 4th Ave. Pool (heated). Restaurant, bar, dancing, entertainment. Pets.

Sheraton-Ralston Inn. *Moderate.* (156 rooms). Pool (heated). Pets. Restaurant.

Motel 6. *Inexpensive.* Pool (heated). Small fee for TV. 24-hr. coffee shop.

Commerce

Holiday Inn. *Moderate.* Pool, play area. Kennel. Restaurant.

Quality Inn-Davis Bros. *Moderate.* Pool (heated), play area. Cafeteria open for bkfst, lunch, dinner.

Bulldog Inn. *Moderate.* Pool. Pets. Restaurant.

Days Inn. *Inexpensive.* Pool, play area. Pets. Restaurant.

Parkham. *Inexpensive.* Pool, play area. Restaurant.

Cordele
Colonial Inn. *Moderate.* Pool. Cafeteria. Pets.

Colonial Inn West. *Moderate.* Pool, play area. Pets. Restaurant. Golf nr.

Holiday Inn. *Moderate.* (200 rooms) I-75. Pool (heated), play area. Pets. Restaurant. Golf nr.

Ramada Inn. *Moderate.* (102 rooms) I-75 and US 280. Pool. Pets. Restaurant; beer & wine served in taproom, dancing. Free airport transportation. Golf nr.

Days Inn. *Inexpensive.* Pool, play area. Restaurant.

Hi-Lite Motel. *Inexpensive.* Hwy. 280 E.

Perlis Truckstop and Wenona Motel. *Inexpensive.* I-75 Wenona Exit.

Dalton

Best Western. *Moderate.* 2306 Chattanooga Rd. Pool. Pets. Restaurant.

Convoy Inn Motel. *Moderate.* I-75 at Carbondale Rd.

Davis Bros. *Moderate.* Pool, play area. Pets. Free morning coffee & rolls. Restaurant.

Holiday Inn. *Moderate.* I-75 and Walnut Ave. (200 rooms). Pool. Pets. Restaurant, serving beer & wine only.

Howard Johnson's Motor Lodge. *Moderate.* 2007 Chattanooga Rd. Pool. Restaurant. Free airport transportation. Pets.

Lee's Inn. *Moderate.* 2201 Chattanooga Rd. (103 rooms). Pool. Restaurant, serving beer & wine. Pets limited.

Quality Inn. *Moderate.* I-75 and Ga. Hwy. 3.

Knight's Inn. *Inexpensive.* 2208 Chattanooga Rd.

Passport Inn. *Inexpensive.* 1519 Walnut Ave.

Rodeway Inn. *Inexpensive.* 1518 W. Walnut Ave.

Dillard

Dillard House. *Moderate.* Restaurant specializes in homegrown vegetables.

Dillard Motel. *Moderate.* Mountain view. Restaurant. Seasonal rates.

Eastman

Stuckey's Carriage Inn. *Moderate.* US 23 and 341 (40 rooms). Pool, play area. Restaurant. Pets.

Folkston

Howard Johnson Motor Lodge. *Moderate.* Pool, play area. Restaurant.

Folkston Motel. *Moderate.* Pool, play area, fishing. Golf nr. Restaurant.

Quality Inn. *Moderate.* Tahiti, Hwys. 1, 23 and 301 S. Pool, play area, restaurant.

Forsyth

Best Western Inn. *Moderate.* I-75 and Ga 42.

Davis Bros. *Moderate.* Pool (heated). Complimentary morning coffee & rolls. Restaurant. Pets.

Holiday Inn. *Moderate.* I-75 and Juliette Rd. (120 rooms). Pool (heated), play area. Pets. Restaurant, serving beer.

Howard Johnson's. *Moderate.* Pool, play area. Restaurant. Pets.

Days Inn. *Inexpensive.* Pool, play area. Pets. Restaurant.

Days Lodge. *Inexpensive.* Pool, play area. Pets. Restaurant.

Economy Inn. *Inexpensive.* Pets. Restaurant nr. Simple, but comfortable.

Gainesville

Days Inn & Lodge. *Moderate.* Cafe. Pool. Pets.

Holiday Inn. *Moderate.* Pool (heated), play area; tennis & golf nr. Kennel. Restaurant, bar, entertainment. Free airport transportation.

Georgiana. *Inexpensive.* Pool. Restaurant. Fam. rates.

Hazelhurst

Esquire Inn. *Inexpensive.* (78 rooms) Hwy. 341 and 23.

Helen

Helendorf Inn. *Moderate.* (34 rooms) 305 Main St.

Unico. Lodge/Conference Center. *Moderate.* (60 rooms) Hwy. 356.

Jekyll Island

Buccaneer Motor Lodge. *Expensive.* (210 rooms) 85 Beachview Dr. Pool, play area. Golf & tennis nr. Restaurant, bar.

Holiday Inn Beach Resort. *Expensive.* 200 Beachview Dr.

Jekyll Island Hilton. *Expensive.* 975 Beachview Dr.

Sheraton-by-the-Sea. *Expensive.* (338 rooms) 1175 N. Beachview Dr.

Jekyll Estates Motel. *Moderate.* (35 rooms) 721 Beachview Dr.

Ladha Island Inn. *Moderate.* 60 Beachview Dr. S.

Wanderer. *Moderate.* 711 Beachview Dr.

Seafarer. *Moderate.* Pool, play area, beach opp. Pets. Restaurant nr.

Jesup

Holiday Inn. *Moderate.* Pool. Pets. Restaurant, bar. Free airport transportation.

Lake Lanier Islands

Stouffer's Pineisle Resort. *Expensive.* (256 rooms) Golf adjoining. Lake and boating.

Macon

Macon Hilton. *Expensive.* First and Walton Sts. Pools, restaurants, convention facilities.

Davis Bros. *Moderate.* Chambers Rd. I-475 at US 80. Pool. Cafe. Pets.

Holiday Inn. *Moderate.* 2 locations with all the amenities typical of this chain: **Warner Robins:** 2024 Watson Blvd. 7 mi. E of Warner Robins-Centerville exit; **West:** 4775 Chambers Rd. at Jct. of US 80 and I-75.

Howard Johnson's. *Moderate.* 2 locations each with pool, play area: **North:** 2566 Riverside Dr.; **West:** Romeiser Dr.

Quality Inn. *Moderate.* 2 locations: North at 2720 Riverside Dr.; South at I-75 and Hartley Bridge Rd.

Ramada Inn. *Moderate.* 2 locations, each with pool, restaurant, bar: 1440 Watson Blvd., dancing, entertainment; North 2400 Riverside Dr.

Courtesy Court. *Inexpensive.* 2240 Gray Hwy. Play area. Restaurant nr.

Marietta

Master Hosts Inn. *Expensive.* Pool. Pets. Restaurant, bar.

Ramada Inn. *Expensive.* Pool (heated). Restaurant, bar, dancing, entertainment.

Squire Inn. *Expensive.* Pool. Pets. Restaurant, bar.

Bon Air. *Moderate.* Pool, play area. Pets limited. Restaurant nr. Family & seasonal rates.

Holiday Inn. *Moderate.* Pool, play area. Kennel. Restaurant, bar, entertainment, dancing.

Pacemaker. *Moderate.* Pool. Pets limited. Restaurant, bar, dancing, entertainment.

Quality Inn-Marietta. *Moderate.* Pool, play area. Pets. Restaurant.

McDonough

Davis Brothers Motor Lodge. *Moderate.* I-75 and Ga. 155.

Holiday Inn. *Moderate.* Pool. Restaurant. Kennel.

Quality Inn Motel. *Moderate.* Pool. Restaurant. Kennels.

Candyland-Red Carpet Inn. *Inexpensive.* Pool. Restaurant.

Milledgeville

Downtown Motel. *Moderate.* 225 E. Hancock St. Pool. Pets. Cafe.

Holiday Inn. *Moderate.* Pool, play area. Pets. Restaurant, bar. 117 rooms.

8 Inn Motel. *Inexpensive.* Hwy. 441 N. Pool. Playground. Pets.

Newnan

Holiday Inn. *Moderate.* I-85 and US 29 (100 rooms). Pool (heated). Pets. Restaurant; bar, serving wine, beer.

Perry

Holiday Inn. *Moderate.* Pool, play area. Pets. Restaurant, serving beer, wine. Entertainment, dancing. Kennel.

Howard Johnson's. *Moderate.* Pool, play area. Golf nr. Restaurant. All rms. have patios or balconies. Pets.

New Perry Hotel and Motel. *Moderate.* 800 Main St. (56 rooms). Excellent dining room.

Quality Inn. *Moderate.* Pool, play area. Pets. Free airport transportation. Spacious, lovely grounds. I-75 and US 341 (77 rooms).

Bel-Aire. *Inexpensive.* Pool. Golf nr. Restaurant. Laundry facilities free. Free airport transportation. Pets limited.

Capri. *Inexpensive.* Pool, play area. Restaurant. Pets.

Travelers 8 Inn. *Inexpensive.* Pets. Restaurant nr.

Travel Host Motel. *Inexpensive.* 101 Marshallville Rd. Pool. Restaurant.

Pine Mountain

Callaway Gardens. *Expensive.* Pools, heated, play area. Kennel. Restaurant. Free admission to Gardens & facilities. AP, MAP, seasonal, pkg. rates avail. (365 rooms).

Callaway Cottages. *Moderate.* A family recreation park with kitchen cottages, supervised recreation program, entertainment, free admission to Gardens and its facilities. Fee for TV. Restaurant. Fam. rates only with 1-wk min., 2-wk max. in summer; S & D daily rates Sept. to June. No liquor on grounds. Free terminal transportation.

Richland

Kay-Lynn Kourt. *Inexpensive.* Pool, play area. Pets. Restaurant nr.

Rome

Holiday Inn. *Moderate.* Pool. Golf nr. Pets. Restaurant, bar. Fam. rates avail. 707 Turner McCall Blvd. (155 rooms).

Oak Hurst Motel. *Moderate.* 1201 Martha Berry Blvd.

Roman Inn. *Moderate.* Pool. Restaurant, bar. Pets.

Sheraton-President Inn. *Moderate.* Pool. Cafe. 840 Turner McCall Blvd. (106 rooms).

St. Simons Island

Sea Palms Golf & Racquet Club. *Expensive.* (150 rooms.) Frederica Rd. Resort hotel with kitchen units & villas. Pools (heated); supervised program for children. Golf, tennis, riding, fishing. Entertainment, dancing. Restaurant, bar. Free airport transportation. Seasonal rates.

King & Prince Beach Hotel. *Expensive.* Arnold Rd. (94 rooms). Resort hotel on ocean. Pool, play area. Golf, tennis, sailing. Restaurant, bar, entertainment, dancing. Cottage, seasonal rates avail.

Queen's Court. *Moderate.* 437 Kings Way. Pool. Free in-rm. coffee. Golf nr. Restaurant, bar.

Sea Gate Inn. *Moderate.* 1014 Ocean Blvd. (32 rooms). Pool, play area. Pets. Golf nr. Cook-out facilities. Restaurant nr. Kitchen units, seasonal rates avail.

Savannah

Sheraton Savannah Inn and Country Club. *Deluxe.* 612 Wilmington Island Rd. Resort hotel with villas & cottages on Wilmington River. Pool, sauna, play area. Golf, tennis, riding, hunting, fishing, boating, marina. Restaurant, bar, dancing, entertainment. Seasonal, family, golf pkg. rates avail. (208 rooms.)

De Soto Hilton. *Expensive.* Liberty & Bull St. Rooftop pool (heated). Golf nr. Free in-rm. coffee. Restaurant, bar. (250 rooms.)

Downtowner. *Moderate.* 201 Oglethorpe Ave. Pool. Restaurant, bar. Pets. (204 rooms.)

Quality Inn Heart of Savannah. *Moderate.* 300 W. Bay St. (53 rooms). Pool. Free morning coffee & rolls.

Holiday Inn. *Moderate.* 2 locations, each with pool, restaurant, bar: 121 W. Boundary St. just S of Talmadge Bridge; at Jct US 17 & I-95.

Howard Johnson's. *Moderate.* 2 locations, each with pool, restaurant: **Downtown:** 224 W. Boundary St. 232-4371; **West:** Rte. 204 at I-95. Bar. Golf nr.

Mary Lee Guest Accommodations. *Moderate.* 117 E. Jones St. Restored historic home. 3 guest suites.

Quality Motel. *Moderate.* At Travis Field. Pool. Restaurant, bar.

Ramada Inn. *Moderate.* 2 locations each with pool, restaurant, bar: 231 W. Boundary St.; US 17 at I-95.

Sheraton Oasis Village. *Moderate.* 1 Gateway Blvd., 15 mi. SW on GA 20 at I-95 Abercorn exit. Pool. Pets. Cafe.

Days Inn. *Inexpensive.* Mall Blvd. Pool, play area. Restaurant. Pets.

Savannah Beach

Ramada Inn. *Expensive.* Pool. Restaurant. Fam. rates.

Days Inn. *Inexpensive.* Pool. Pets. Kitchen units avail.

Tides Motel. *Inexpensive.* Tybee Island.

Sea Island

The Cloister. *Deluxe.* One of the most glamorous, exclusive resort hotels. On 5 mi. private beach. Pools (heated), play area. Supervised play, golf, tennis, riding, boating, fishing. Bar. Dancing, entertainment. AP. Seasonal rates. (237 rooms).

Statesboro

Bryant's Best Western. *Moderate.* Pool. Pets. Cafe.

Holiday Inn. *Moderate.* Pool. Golf nr. Restaurant, bar. Kitchen & studio units avail. Kennel.

Quality Motel. *Moderate.* At 2 locations, each with pool, restaurant, golf nr.: **Bryants:** 461 S. Main St.; **Downtown:** 109 N. Main St.

Crossroads. *Inexpensive.* Pool, play area. Pets. Good restaurant nr.

Stiles. *Inexpensive.* Pool, play area. Golf, fishing nr. Pets. Cook-out facilities.

Wilde's. *Inexpensive.* Pool. Restaurant nr.

Stone Mountain

Stone Mountain Inn. *Moderate.* (89 rooms). In state-owned family recreation area.

Sylvania

Quality Inn Paradise. *Moderate.* Pool, play area. Restaurant nr. Secluded, in 14-acre pecan grove. Pets.

South Manor Motel. *Inexpensive.* Pool. Restaurant.

Thomasville

Downtown Motor Inn. *Moderate.* Restaurant, bar.

Holiday Inn. *Moderate.* US 19 (140 rooms). Pool (heated), play area. Restaurant.

Days Inn. *Inexpensive.* (120 rooms). Pool, play area. Restaurant. Pets.

Tifton

Davis Bros. *Moderate.* Pool, play area. Morning coffee & rolls free. Fine cafeteria.

Quality Inn of Tifton. *Moderate.* I-75 at 2nd St. exit. Pool, play area. Free in-rm. coffee. Free airport transportation.

Ramada Inn. *Moderate.* (100 rooms) I-75 & US 82. Pool. Pets.

Thunderbird Motel. *Moderate.* I-75 at W. 2nd St. Pool (heated). Restaurant nr.

Days Inn. *Inexpensive.* Pool, play area. Restaurant. Pets.

Howard Johnson's. *Inexpensive.* I-75 at US 41. Pool, play area. Free airport transportation. Restaurant.

Town Terrace Motel. *Inexpensive.* 12th St. and N. Ridge Ave.

Toccoa

Sheraton Motor Inn. *Moderate.* (80 rooms) Hwy. 175. Pool. Restaurant. Fam. rates avail.

Valdosta

Best Western King of the Road. *Moderate.* (137 rooms). I-75 at Hwy 94. Pool, lounge, restaurant.

Holiday Inn. *Moderate.* Pools, play area. Pets. Restaurant, bars, dancing.

Howard Johnson's. *Moderate.* (88 rooms) 1330 St. Augustine Rd. Pool, play area. Restaurant. Pets.

Quality Inn. *Moderate.* 2 locations: north at 1209 St. Augustine Rd.; south at 1902 W. Hill Ave. Pool, play area, fishing, putting green. Restaurant, bar.

Sheraton Valdosta Motor Inn. *Moderate.* (75 rooms) I-75 and US 84. Pool, play area. Restaurant, bar. Free airport transportation.

Big 7. *Inexpensive.* Attractive rms. Pets. Restaurant nr.

Days Inn. *Inexpensive.* Pool. Pets. Restaurant.

El Carlo Motel. *Inexpensive.* 2525 N. Ashley St.

Holiday Terrace Motel. *Inexpensive.* 1620 N. Ashley St.

Jolly Inn. *Inexpensive.* Pool. Pets. Restaurant nr.

Waycross

Holiday Inn. *Moderate.* (103 rooms) 1725 Memorial Dr. Pool, play area, putting green. Pets. Restaurant, serving beer & wine.

Quality Motel Arcade. *Moderate.* Pool, play area. Golf, bowling nr. Pets. Free in-rm. coffee.

Pine Crest. *Moderate.* Pool, play area. Free morning coffee. Restaurant.

Palms Court. *Inexpensive.* Pool, play area. Golf nr. Restaurant nr. Pets.

Woodbine

Stardust Lodge. *Moderate.* Pool, play area. Pets. Restaurant nr.

 DINING OUT in Georgia can mean fine Southern-style foods in a rural atmosphere or charming plantation house, or sophisticated French cuisine in an elegant urban dining room. Many worthwhile restaurants may be found at the hotels we have listed. Our price categories are for a complete dinner: *Expensive* means a complete dinner may run over $15; *Moderate* will run about $10; *Inexpensive,* below $5. A la carte meals will, of course, bring the bill up. For a more complete explanation of restaurant categories see *Facts at Your Fingertips* at the front of this volume.

Athens

Farmer John's. *Inexpensive.* 1260 S. Milledge Ave. Smorgasbord lunch and dinner.

The Fountains. *Moderate.* 325 N. Milledge Ave. 1855 Italianate mansion specializes in Italian dishes.

Augusta

Town Tavern. *Moderate.* 17 7th St. Popular, attractive. Bar. Children's portions.

Wyld's Way House. *Inexpensive.* 1824 Wyld's Way. Built in 1802 as stagecoach lodge. Family style service.

Bainbridge

"Our" Tara. *Moderate.* Southern specialties. Homemade bread and ice cream. Children's portions.

Brunswick

The Deck. *Moderate.* Seafood, steak, chicken. Cocktails.

The Forks. *Inexpensive.* Homestyle cooking; seafood, steaks.

Clarkesville

Prade's. Hwy 197 N. Specializes in mountain trout, country ham. Closed winter months.

Clayton

Dillard House. *Inexpensive.* Fine family-style restaurant, serving fresh, homegrown vegetables, fruit, fried chicken, country style ham.

Columbus

Goetche's House. *Expensive.* Gourmet food and drink in historic home of restoration district.

Black Angus. *Moderate.* Steak, seafood. Luncheon buffet. Children's portions. Drinks.

Emmy's Schnitzel Haus. *Moderate.* Authentic German cuisine.

Morrison's Cafeteria. *Inexpensive.* In Cross Country Plaza Shopping Center.

Dahlonega

Smith House. *Inexpensive.* Old-fashioned mountain boarding house serves all-you-can-eat family style.

Helen

Sautee Inn. *Inexpensive.* Located in an old hotel that dates to turn of century.

GEORGIA
Macon

Len Berg's. *Moderate.* Centrally located in Post Office Alley, ½ blk off US 41. Well established, popular meeting place. Beer served only with evening meal.

St. Simons Island

Bennie's Red Barn. *Moderate.* Steak, seafood in rustic atmosphere. Drinks. Children's portions.

Emmeline and Hessie Seafood Restaurant. *Moderate.* St. Simons Causeway. Overlooks Intercoastal Waterway.

Savannah

The Pink House. *Expensive.* In one of city's oldest homes.

Johnny Harris Restaurant. *Moderate.* 1651 Victory Dr. A Savannah landmark. Open barbecue pit. Children's portions. Reservations wise for wkend.

Pirate's House. *Moderate.* 20 E. Broad at Bay St. in historic Trustee's Garden. 17 dining rms. serving regional specialties, Oysters Savannah among them.

The Shrimp Factory. *Moderate.* 313 E. River St. Converted Civil War warehouse. Specialty: pine bark stew and seafood.

Spanky's. *Moderate.* 317 E. River St. Stone walls constructed from ballast of 18th century sailing vessels. Pizza, chicken fingers, exotic drinks.

Tassey's Pier. *Moderate.* River Rd. Seafood in riverside marina. Maine lobster a favorite. Children's portions. Drinks.

Statesboro

Vandy's Barbecue. *Inexpensive.* Has served pit-cooked BBQ for over 50 years.

Tifton

Davis Bros. Cafeteria. *Inexpensive.* Modern, good food.

Valdosta

Davis Bros. Cafeteria. *Inexpensive.* Good food.

Waycross

Green Frog. *Inexpensive.* Good variety (steak, fried chicken and seafood) served family style. Children's portions. Beer.

KENTUCKY

Belles, Bourbon and Bluegrass

BETTY ELLISON

Betty Ellison is a native of Tennessee, now living in Lexington, Kentucky.
Before becoming a freelance writer she was chief travel writer for the
Commonwealth of Kentucky.

Fort Harrod, established in 1774, proved a haven for settlers pouring
into the West through the Cumberland Gap and the Wilderness Road,
and the tradition of the famed Kentucky hospitality began here. Others
who came down the Ohio River by flatboat also found safety from hostile
Indians and warmth from the chill of the trail.

Fort Harrod has been rebuilt again in Harrodsburg, on US 127 and
68. Authentic as to details, the wooden enclosure contains blockhouses,
cabins, even a log schoolhouse; it was here that Jane Cooms began the
first school in Kentucky. The rude buildings are stocked with handmade
utensils and farm implements and the hastily assembled furnishings of
the pioneer era. The fort replica makes up a portion of Old Fort Harrod
State Park in the center of Harrodsburg.

Other buildings in the park contain items that recall more of Kentucky's romantic past. The Lincoln Marriage Temple was designed to
represent an early nineteenth-century Kentucky church and shelters the
log cabin in which Abraham Lincoln's parents, Thomas Lincoln and
Nancy Hanks, were married on June 2, 1806. The one-room cabin was

removed from its original location in Washington County to the present site in 1911 by the Harrodsburg Historical Society.

The Mansion Museum, in a house built in 1830 by Major James Taylor, stands across from the Lincoln Marriage Temple in the park. In the Lincoln and Confederate rooms, the George Rogers Clark room and the Gun and Music rooms, it houses mementos associated with great periods in Kentucky history.

Fort Harrod's Pioneer Cemetery, older than any other burial ground west of the Alleghenies, contains the graves of more than five hundred early settlers. George Rogers Clark isn't among them, but his contribution to Kentucky's beginnings is honored by a monument at the entrance to Old Fort Harrod State Park. Clark planned his campaign to free the midwest from the British at Fort Harrod. It was from Fort Harrod that another Kentucky pioneer, Gabriel Jones, set forth to convince the Virginia House of Burgesses that they should include Kentucky as a part of their commonwealth.

Each summer the park amphitheater comes alive with an exciting outdoor drama, *The Legend of Daniel Boone*. Audiences witness the excitement, sorrows, struggles and joys that greeted Americans making the westward trek in the 1700's.

Harrodsburg Pioneer Red Arrow Tour (maps are available at the Mercer County Chamber of Commerce): The first ten points of interest can be seen at Old Fort Harrod State Park, the other thirty-nine from your auto. Some of these include Diamond Point and other homes that are considered some of the state's finest examples of Georgian and Greek Revival architecture. Once a girl's academy, Beaumont Inn is renowned for its good Kentucky food and for its hospitality. The Morgan Row Houses, said to be the oldest standing row houses used for a commercial purpose, are five distinct buildings that were once connected by first-floor passageways. They were built between 1807 and 1830 by Joseph Morgan, and they have been restored. They hold a museum, historical records and businesses.

Seven miles north of Harrodsburg on US 68 is the restored Shaker Colony of Pleasant Hill. The United Believers in Christ's Second Appearing founded their communal religious colony at Pleasant Hill in 1805 on the 140-acre Shawnee Run Farm. By 1820 the Shakers numbered more than five hundred members in their settlement, and had erected some twenty-five buildings, increased their acreage to 4,300 acres and constructed wharf and warehouse facilities on the Kentucky River.

One of the more lasting legacies bequeathed by the Shakers is the simplicity and honesty of design of their furniture and architecture. Micajah Burnett, an expert builder, with skilled stonecutters, brickmasons and woodcarvers, produced a "Georgian-Shaker" style that presents some of the finest examples of nineteenth-century construction in America.

In the mid-1850's the society began to decline. It's natural to suppose that the Shakers' strict practice of celibacy was to blame, though the Civil War and its ravages contributed to their demise. The last Shaker, Sister Mary Settles, died in 1923, marking the end of over one hundred years of the colony at Pleasant Hill. Now, the village of Shakertown at Pleasant Hill has been restored to its early nineteenth-century appearance, and it provides lodging and delicious Shaker food for travelers all year.

The First Seat of Government

South of Harrodsburg, still on US 127, is Danville, and here Kentucky acquired statehood in 1792, but it took nine stormy conventions before all details could be agreed on by the participants. Kentucky's first post office, courthouse, jail and meeting hall were erected to accommodate the conventions. Today, the original post office building stands in Constitution Square State Shrine on Danville's Main Street. Giant trees hover over the square which also includes reproductions of the courthouse, jail and meeting hall.

Danville was an early religious center of Kentucky. The ivy-covered Trinity Episcopal Church, built in 1830, still stands on Main Street; the parish register, begun in 1839 to record baptisms, marriages, confirmations and burials, is still in use today. The church is open to the public daily.

Other attractions in Danville include the Georgian home of Dr. Ephraim McDowell, open daily. On Christmas in 1809, Dr. McDowell performed the first successful ovariotomy in this country on Jane Todd Crawford, who had ridden sixty miles on horseback for removal of a tumor that weighed over twenty pounds. Mrs. Crawford lived to an old age. The house contains many period furnishings and a number of the doctor's personal items. Adjoining the house is a restored apothecary shop that has a collection of eighteenth- and nineteenth-century pharmacy equipment.

Dix Dam impounds the Dix River and forms Herrington Lake, near Danville. The lake, a favorite with both fishermen and boaters, lies between US 127 and 27.

West of Danville, on US 150, is Perryville, where the greatest military event in the history of Kentucky occurred on October 8, 1862, when nearly 100,000 Union and Confederate troops met in a battle lasting only from 2 P.M. until dark; there were over 6,000 casualties on both sides. Perryville Battlefield State Shrine has a museum with a diorama of the battle. The Historic Perryville Tour leaves from the Information Booth on Main Street four afternoons a week to visit the battlefield and other historical sites.

Horses, Horses, Horses

Kentucky's Interstates and parkways bring travelers near all of the commonwealth's scenic and historic attractions. The Bluegrass Parkway connects Kentucky's two north-south Interstates—I-75 southward from Covington and I-65 from Louisville. Heading west, Lexington is the first stop on the Bluegrass Parkway. In the Bluegrass Region around Lexington are more than 350 horse farms, and some are open to visitors. The best bet to see them is to take a ride with Bluegrass Tours, whose buses leave the office of the Greater Lexington Area Chamber of Commerce on North Broadway daily, from April through October.

Some seventy-five Kentucky farms raise standardbreds, the horses that are used in harness racing. Another breed one hears much about are the saddlebreds. Kentucky was the birthplace of the foundation sires of the

Lexington Horse Farms

(Lexington Map)

Horse Farms:

1) Almahurst
2) Belair
3) Brookdale
4) Bwamazon
5) Calumet
6) Castelton
7) Claiborne
8) Crestwood
9) Crimson King
10) Danada
11) Darby Dan
12) Dixiana/Domino Stud
13) Donerail
14) Dunreath
15) Elmendorf
16) Elmsmead
17) Fayette
18) Greentree Stud
19) Hamburg Place
20) Hurstland
21) King Ranch
22) Maine Chance
23) Mineola
24) Pin Oak
25) Poplar Hill
26) Spend Thrift
27) Steelway
28) Sycamore
29) Whitney
30)

American saddlebred horse; it is the home of the registry of the American Saddle Horse Breeders Association. The saddle horse is a product of necessity. In the early days of the trackless wilderness, horses were the only means of transportation for men and materials; the American pioneers needed a mount that was hardy, intelligent, sure-footed and possessed of comfortable gaits. The Kentucky Saddler, progenitor of today's saddle horse, met that need. Saddle horses reign supreme at such national shows as the World's Championship Horse Show at the Kentucky State Fair in Louisville during August, and the Junior League Horse Show (the world's largest outdoor horse show) in July in Lexington, at the Red Mile. Souvenirs of Wing Commander, a Kentucky horse who was eight times the World's Grand Champion; over two hundred equestrian paintings; trophies, saddles and harness, and numerous types of conveyances may be seen at the American Saddle Horse Museum at Spindletop, on the Iron Works Pike, open April to November.

From whatever direction you enter Kentucky's horse country, you'll recognize it by its miles of board fences, slave-built stone walls (without mortar), groves of stately trees, white-columned mansions and legions of horse barns. The farms are elaborate developments; many are open to visitors. A score of them are scattered around Lexington, almost in sight of the city. Among the best known are Spendthrift, Calumet, Claiborne, Darby Dan, Dixiana, Main Chance and King Ranch.

Among Lexington's most glamorous spectacles are the yearling sales at the Keeneland race track west of town on US 60. At these sales, in mid-July, the handsome animals are led into the track's flower-decked salesroom to stand in the spotlight while the bidding soars. The Fasig-Tipton sales take place in November at Fasig-Tipton Farm on Newtown Pike.

Also held in Lexington, the last week in September and the first week in October, is the ten-day Grand Circuit Meeting, Kentucky's most significant harness race. The event, sponsored by the Lexington Trots Breeders Association, takes place on Big Red Mile near the downtown section. This, the world's fastest trotting track, holds more records than all other harness tracks combined.

A very special tribute to the horse and his place in the state's history and economy is the lavish $27-million state-operated Kentucky Horse Park, which opened in September 1978. The complex, built on the site of the former Walnut Hall Stud Farm, features various equine events, and there are horseback and pony rides for visitors as well as rides in horsedrawn antique carriages. A model working farm includes displays of various types of shoe and harness, and there are attendants on hand to explain things and answer questions. There is a museum and a visitors' information center, where the short film *Thou Shalt Fly Without Wings* is not to be missed. Towering over all is the huge statue of the great Man O' War, whose grave has been moved here.

The Park also houses the Kentucky Equine Education Program, devoted to teaching the care and handling of horses to young people who hope to make a career in the field.

Besides priding itself as the Horse Center of America, Lexington also lays claim to being the world's largest looseleaf tobacco market. Between November and February tobacco auctions provide a fine spectator sport.

In the tobacco warehouses, rapid-fire auctioneers, like priests at a pagan ritual, intone their unintelligible chant as they move from one fragrant tobacco basket to another, surrounded by a crowd of attentive buyers. You'll find it fascinating to watch and listen to, even though you don't come away much wiser.

City of Culture

Some of Lexington's distinguished old homes are open to travelers. "Ashland," Henry Clay's estate, has a beautifully furnished twenty-room mansion, smoke-, carriage- and icehouses and a well-kept garden. "Ashland" is closed only on Christmas Day.

"Hopemont" was the home of both the famed Confederate raider, John Hunt Morgan, and the first millionaire in Kentucky, John Wesley Hunt, who built the house in 1814. Waveland State Shrine stands on land surveyed by Daniel Boone, and contains an extensive collection of items relating to early Kentucky life. Other Lexington attractions include the Man O' War statue in the Kentucky State Park; Headley Jewel Museum, Old Frankfort Pike, the only private collection of valuable bibelots open to the public; Guild Gallery, Euclid Avenue, the state's most complete display of works by Kentucky artists and craftsmen, and Old Morrison, the Greek Revival administration building at Transylvania University, designed by Gideon Shryock in 1833, which houses a Science Museum.

From the Lawrenceburg interchange, thirteen miles from Lexington on the Bluegrass Parkway, US 127 offers a delightful side trip. To the north lies Kentucky's capital, Frankfort, on the Kentucky River. In South Frankfort, a section that seceded from North Frankfort during a turbulent period in the city's history, stands the new State Capitol, erected in 1909. On its grounds is an unusual upright floral clock. The hands actually move, and as many as 20,000 live plants make up the clock face. A bronze statue of Abraham Lincoln, Kentucky's greatest native son, dominates the rotunda of the Capitol, which allegedly causes some unreconstructed Rebels to refuse to enter the building by the front door. A statue of Jefferson Davis, the President of the Confederacy and another native Kentuckian, stands on a lesser pedestal in a corner. One modern-day Kentuckian explains: "The Commonwealth is proud of him, too, but after all, he lost."

Sharing the same grounds as the Capitol is the Governor's Mansion, styled after the "Petit Trianon," Marie Antoinette's villa near the Palace of Versailles. Daily tours are conducted through the Capitol, and the first floor of the Governor's Mansion.

Liberty Hall, on Wilkinson Street, is the oldest historical house in the city that is open to the public. Built in 1796 by John Brown, one of Kentucky's first U.S. Senators—not the John Brown of Harpers Ferry— Liberty Hall has entertained six presidents and France's Prince Louis Philippe; and it has a "family ghost," reputed to be the friendly spirit of an elderly spinster, aunt of the first mistress of the house. This unfortunate lady came to Frankfort from New York City to live with her newly married niece, but the rigors of travel at the turn of the nineteenth century were too great and the aunt died shortly after her arrival. Today, according to the legend, her ghost still wanders the corridors of the mansion. Most of Liberty Hall's furnishings are original family items; the property is operated by the Colonial Dames. Another historical house, well known in Frankfort, is the Orlando Brown House at 202 Wilkinson St.

Back on the Bluegrass Parkway, head west to the Springfield exit. Six miles north of Springfield is the Lincoln Homestead State Park where Abraham Lincoln's paternal grandparents settled after coming to Kentucky from Virginia in the early 1780's. Lincoln's father, Thomas, grew up here, and Lincoln's grandfather, Captain Abraham Lincoln, who had served in the Revolutionary War, was killed here by hostile Indians. Log cabins with pioneer furnishings, among them several pieces made by Abe Lincoln's father, have been erected on the homestead site.

The Bourbon Capital

Bardstown, another twenty miles or so west of Springfield, is generally agreed to be one of the highlights of any visit to Kentucky. Second oldest community in the state (settled in 1778), it is cosmopolitan and filled with historic buildings, wide streets and fine trees. Among other distinctions, it proudly proclaims itself "The Bourbon Capital of the World." Fourteen distilleries are located in the small town of 4,800 and there are several more in the environs. An off-beat but fascinating place to visit is the Barton Museum of Whiskey History, operated by a distillery open seven days a week and free. In it is a rare collection of whiskey-making and drinking paraphernalia. The museum and a tour of the adjacent distilling plant make a good excursion. The plant tours are conducted weekdays only. Unfortunately, Kentucky law no longer permits the giving away of free samples on distillery tours.

A free Tourmobile makes scheduled tours of Bardstown, leaving from the Information Center on the Courthouse Square. On the itinerary is a visit to My Old Kentucky Home State Park, with its mansion, Federal Hill, which inspired Stephen Foster to compose the ballad, "My Old Kentucky Home." Built in 1795 by one of Kentucky's famous judges and United States Senators, John Rowan (a friend of Jefferson, Madison, Monroe and other Presidents), the mansion was occupied by the family until it was purchased with its grounds as a state park in 1922. Costumed hostesses give entertaining and educational lecture-tours of the handsome house which has been restored to its mid-nineteenth century elegance. Note the children's room upstairs, with its unusually wide crib and tin bathtub.

In the park's amphitheater, *The Stephen Foster Story,* an outdoor drama built around famous songs of the composer, is presented nightly (with Sunday matinees) from June to September. You can buy tickets for the unreserved seats on the day of the performance. The Bourbon Open Golf Tournament, under the sponsorship of the community's distilleries, is held on the park's golf course every spring on the second weekend in May. This is probably one of the few national golf tournaments in the country to be held on a single nine-hole golf course with a registration numbering over four hundred.

Other Bardstown tourist sights include the John Fitch Monument on Courthouse Square, dedicated to the man whom Bardstown calls "the first to invent the steamboat"; Wickland, a dignified Georgian mansion built in 1817 which was the birthplace of three governors—two of Kentucky and one of Louisiana—and which is filled with antique treasures; and the beautiful St. Joseph's Cathedral, the oldest Catholic cathedral west of the Allegheny Mountains, which was built in 1819. In the cathedral are paintings by Van Dyck, Murillo and artists from the studio of Rubens. These were given to the then Catholic Bishop in Bardstown by Prince Louis Philippe, later King of France, who visited the United States in the early nineteenth century and spent some time in Bardstown.

Twelve miles south of Bardstown is the Gethsemane Abbey, first Trappist monastery on the continent. Guided tours of the building and grounds are open only to men, but the gift shop, where a delicious monastery-made cheese is sold, is open to all.

From Bardstown it is about twenty-five miles south over US 31E to Hodgenville, where, three miles south of town, the Abraham Lincoln Birthplace National Historic Site is located. Here, at Sinking Spring Farm, Abraham Lincoln was born on Feb. 12, 1809. Fifty-six steps, one for each year of the martyred President's life, lead up to a granite memorial building overlooking the old spring. Inside is the log cabin that was the actual birthplace. A magnificent oak, an old boundary landmark when Lincoln was born, still grows nearby. The National Park Service also maintains a small museum building here, in which an excellent short film on Lincoln's early life in Kentucky is shown throughout the day.

In the Hodgenville area there is also another log cabin which is preserved as a reconstructed version of the home Lincoln lived in as a small boy. It stands by the roadside at Knob Creek, just a few miles from Sinking Spring, and it is the spot to which the family moved when Lincoln was four years old. "My earliest recollection is of the Knob Creek place," the President wrote in 1860. It was here that Lincoln and his sister first went to a "subscription" school. Each February a festive Lincoln Day Celebration is held.

In Elizabethtown, nine miles northwest of Hodgenville via Route 61, are several Lincoln family home sites: (1) the historic Helm Mansion—birthplace of Abraham Lincoln's brother-in-law, Confederate General Benjamin Hardin Helm; (2) the site of the mill and millrace which Thomas Lincoln supposedly built prior to his marriage, on Valley Creek just off 31W on Race Street; (3) the farm where Tom lived with his mother, sister and brother-in-law (follow Miles Street to the Battle Training Road and turn left); (4) on Main Street one block north of the courthouse, the site of the Patton home, where Thomas Lincoln was married to his second wife, Sarah Bush Johnston.

From Elizabethtown it is a short drive (less than fifty miles) back to Louisville over the Kentucky Turnpike. Or you can extend your tour to take in the recreation areas and scenery of western Kentucky, including a bit of cave exploration on the way.

The Caves of Kentucky

In the latter case it is about forty miles almost due south of Elizabethtown, part way by the Turnpike (I-65) and then on US 31W to Mammoth Cave National Park. It's worth remembering that there are many privately owned caves in this general area, each with its own special features which you may want to investigate, too. You are not actually inside the

Mammoth Cave

park, which is a Federal preserve, until you have passed the official signs of the U.S. Park Service.

Park headquarters are reached from the town of Cave City, which is on US 31W, by driving west ten miles over Route 70. The Visitor Center is the logical starting point for any of a half dozen different excursions into the eerie depths of the great cave. A program of slides and narration, lasting about fifteen minutes, is presented to help the visitor make a choice of tours. He is warned that all trips may be considered strenuous —even the shortest one, which runs three-quarters of a mile. This, called the Frozen Niagara trip, involves a descent of 250 feet by wooden stairs, but the effort is worth it. One feels a little like a modern-day Tom Sawyer as the cave passage ways narrow or widen during the tour and the dim glow of naked electric lights cast giant shadows on the sandstone, limestone and shale walls. Deep, seemingly bottomless pits, arched domes, an exquisite underground crystal-clear spring-fed lake and the draperies of limestone that constitute the Niagara Falls-like feature of this trip slowly come into view as the tour party winds onward into the depths.

About 150 miles of explored trails and passages in Mammoth Cave are open to the public. One notable excursion is an entire day's trip—it lasts seven hours—which takes you to the lowest depths of the cave at Echo River (360 feet down). At about 267 feet underground on this heroic trip, lunch is served in the cool, cool depths of the Snowball Dining Room, a chamber which takes its name from gypsum clusters that cover the ceiling. This section of Mammoth Cave has been attracting visitors since the middle 1800's. Among recently added improvements are stainless steel and tile counters to provide cafeteria service, an electric stove and refrigerators in the underground kitchen. On the menu are a complete box lunch, individual sandwiches, chili, soup, cakes and hot and cold drinks.

Rarely, the sympathetic and well-informed Park Service guides will tell you, will you have to crawl on any of the Cave excursions. You may have to tilt your head from time to time to avoid low ceilings, and the narrow Fat Man's Misery passage, the name of which is self-explanatory, may be a tight squeeze for some visitors. Elsewhere the passageways are enormous and both stalactites (the formations growing down from the ceilings) and stalagmites (cone-shaped columns growing up) can be seen. Interesting booklets on the Cave's history, issued by the National Park Service, are available at the Visitor Center.

Miss Green River carries 122 passengers on a scenic cruise of the Green River on the sixty-three-foot diesel-powered boat. One-hour trips are scheduled daily May through October. The park contains a hotel, motel lodge, cottages, dining room and recreational facilities.

Travel attractions in the Cave Country include Crystal Lake, Onyx Cave, which contains rare onyx formations and Indian burial grounds; House of Past Biblical Museum, with historical life-size scenes from the Bible; Huckleberry Hill, an unusual crafts center representing an Alpine village with Kentucky crafts and antiques; Jesse James Village and Skylift has train rides, a glass blowing shop, lake, campsites and a gift shop; Mammoth Cave Chair Lift and Guntown Mountain, a reproduction of frontier settlement, gunfights, shooting gallery, a haunted house and country store; Mammoth Cave Wax Museum, filled with scores of life-sized wax figures in historic settings; Vertigo, a house of illusion where waters appear to run uphill, and Wondering Woods, a family attraction with Harmony tower, Chapel Garden Galleries and Tranquil Valley Village—a reproduction of an early 1900's community. At Horse Cave on Route 218, east of I-65, you can visit Kentucky Caverns Park and Mammoth Onyx Cave.

The principal highway leading west from Mammoth Cave Park is US 68, the "Jefferson Davis Highway," which passes through Bowling Green, seat of Western Kentucky University. The Kentucky Building at the college contains a 16,000-volume library of Kentucky history and a museum of Indian and Moundbuilder artifacts as well as pioneer relics and antique furniture.

Across from the Kentucky Building, on top of College Hill, are about seventy-five feet of trenches that were once a part of a key position maintained by Confederate General Albert Sidney Johnston from September 1861 to February 1862, while Bowling Green was the Confederate capital of Kentucky.

Hobson Grove Park, on the north side of the Barren River, has 230 acres devoted to a recreational park with an eighteen-hole golf course.

Three miles west of Bowling Green is Beech Bend Park, a recreational complex with 6,500 camping sites, an amusement park, a covered mall, stock car racing, a dance pavilion, a free zoo and a general store.

Lost River Cave, two miles south of town, is said to have been a hideout of the James brothers, Frank and Jesse. Lost River itself disappears into the ground about three miles south of Bowling Green.

Twelve miles west of Bowling Green on US 68 is the restored Shaker colony of South Union. In 1807 the Shakers built the colony along the Gasper, Mud and Red rivers in Logan County. They brought with them innovative ideas and inventions in agriculture, construction, textiles, manufacturing and merchandising. They remained until 1922, the last western Shaker Society to disband.

The nine remaining South Union Believers sold over two thousand acres of rich farm land, as well as their buildings and furnishings, during a two-day sale. Each colonist was given a choice of $10,000 in cash or moving to the mother colony in New York. Two remained in the order, five stayed in Kentucky and William Bates and Lizzie Simmions were the recipients of the colony's only automobile, besides their cash, and drove off into the sunset of their lives.

Will and Lizzie would probably feel quite at home if they now could join a tour through the high, sparse rooms of the Centre House; much of the Shaker furnishings have been returned to the forty rooms. A four-story brick structure of Georgian design, Centre House is open from May 15 to October 1. Each July, Friends of the Shakers join to present the South Union Shaker Festival with several days of varied activities, and the story of early Shaker days is presented in a drama, *Shakertown Revisited*.

Lake Malone lies on the southern edge of Muhlenberg County, one of the principal coal-producing counties in the state. Here a handful of strip-mining (open-pit) companies dominate the industry in western Kentucky. Monstrous shovels are used to strip away the earth covering and expose the coal seams that lie near the surface of the ground.

Although an impressive sight, strip-mining despoils the landscape and in recent years has shocked the conscience of the state. In 1966 the Kentucky General Assembly enacted new regulations to help curb the erosion, stream pollution and flooding that has resulted from strip-mining operations in the past.

Nearby Russellville was the birthplace of Jim Bowie and the site of the famous Andrew Jackson-Charles Dickerson duel. At Russellville is the old Southern Bank of Kentucky, built around 1810, which Jesse and Frank James are said to have robbed of $10,000 in 1868. The Logan County Historical Society opens the building for tours. In the early fall an annual Tobacco Festival is held.

Again heading west on US 68, the visitor soon reaches the town of Fairview, with its 351-foot tower, said to be the world's largest concrete obelisk, honoring the birthplace of Jefferson Davis, President of the Confederacy. An elevator carries tourists to the top of the monument. It was built at a cost of $200,000, the sum raised by public subscription. Dedication ceremonies took place in 1924. Its appearance is very much like the Washington Monument. A twenty-two-acre park surrounds the obelisk.

Lake Country

Westward from Fairview and passing through Hopkinsville, it is a fifty-mile drive to western Kentucky's principal attraction, Kentucky Lake, one of the largest man-made lakes in the world. Created in 1944 by the impounding of the waters of the Tennessee River, this huge reservoir, whose southern extremity dangles over into Tennessee, has a shoreline more than 2,300 miles long.

In Kentucky its two major recreation spots are Kenlake State Park, on the west shore at the place where US 68 crosses the lake, and Kentucky Dam Village State Park, about twenty miles to the north at the huge Kentucky Dam. The lake's vacation fun includes all the water sports: sail and motorboating, water-skiing, swimming and fishing (runs of crappie, a popular fish with local anglers, are enormous during April). At both parks there are luxurious modern lodges, cottages and tent and trailer sites, boat docks, bathing beaches and facilities for riding, tennis and golf.

At Gilbertsville near Kentucky Dam is Kaintuck Territory, on US 641, a reproduction of a Kentucky frontier town of the 1880's spread over 167 acres. There are train rides, a saloon show and gunfight, chair lift, historical demonstrations and an exhibition of Kentucky long rifles. Kaintuck Territory is open from Memorial Day to Labor Day.

A Septemberfest is held annually at Kentucky Dam Village for square dance enthusiasts. "If you can walk, you can dance," these square dancers maintain, and dance they do, all around Kentucky Lake.

Car buffs will enjoy a visit to the Calvert Auto Museum on Route 95SW, with many vintage cars.

Another huge lake, Lake Barkley, has been formed by the impounding of the Cumberland River. It lies just east of Kentucky Lake. Lake Barkley State Resort Park, on the Little River embayment of Lake Barkley, has over 60,000 acres of water. Barkley Lodge hovers over the shore of Lake Barkley like a huge wooden bird, with wings extending out on either side. The central portion of one of the largest wooden structures built in the United States in recent years contains the lobby, dining room, a huge lounge, meeting rooms and a swimming pool that overlooks the lake. Each of the 120 rooms and four suites has an individual balcony that provides a breathtaking scene of the wooded shoreline and lake. Lake Barkley has the full range of recreational activities found at a resort park. This is such a popular resort park that it is a good idea to make reservations some time in advance.

Meantime, the Tennessee Valley Authority is developing the Land Between the Lakes as a major outdoor recreation and conservation area. The project is said to be the most ambitious of its kind in the United States. Between $32 and $35 million are being spent to preserve the natural features of the beautiful woodland while constructing new facilities for camping, boating, swimming and fishing. Lake Barkley, 118 miles long, is eventually to have five thousand family-unit campsites.

Any trip to western Kentucky should include a visit to Paducah, on a beautiful bend of the Ohio River, and one of the ports of call for the sternwheel paddleboat *Delta Queen*. Paducah, Kentucky's fifth largest city (pop. 35,000), is called the gateway to the Mississippi, which is just fifteen miles farther west. Though hunters and trappers established temporary camps at this spot as early as 1817, not until 1821 were the first log dwellings erected here. The early riverbank settlement catered to the occasional flatboats of settlers bound for the upper Mississippi and to trappers and hunters.

In the Civil War, General Ulysses S. Grant took possession of Paducah on Sept. 6, 1861. After the war Paducah became a railroad center, and by 1925 had developed the largest railroad repair shops in the world. For modern railroad buffs, Old No. 1518, last of the Illinois Central Steam locomotives, is preserved in the city's Barkley Park. The old engine, a relative newcomer to steam, was built in 1921 and retired in 1961. In Paducah is the home of former Vice President Alban W. Barkley. Here, too, is the final resting place of the humorist Irvin S. Cobb.

Paducah's city hall, designed by Edward Durrell Stone, is modeled after the American Embassy in India, and occupies a complete downtown block. Market House, S. 2 St. and Broadway, consists of the William Clark Museum with a collection of early Americana items and an art gallery.

For an interesting side trip drive thirty-three miles along US 60 from Paducah to Wickliffe for a tour of the Ancient Buried City. This is the remains of an ancient city of moundbuilders. Excavated mounds provide an insight into their living conditions and burial methods. Artifacts and pottery are on display.

Twenty-seven miles south of Paducah, on US 45, is Mayfield, which has the world's largest deposits of ball clay, used everywhere for ceramics and china. Also at Mayfield are the Wooldridge Monuments. Eccentric Henry G. Wooldridge designed sixteen statues of people, horses and dogs; had many of them cast in Europe; then placed in the Maplewood Cemetery just off US 45. Only one person is buried under any of the monuments, Henry G. Wooldridge.

Twenty miles south of Mayfield at the end of the Purchase Parkway is the town of Fulton. Here in the fall is held the International Banana

Festival, a celebration with a Latin American flavor. Fulton likes to regard itself as the "banana crossroads of the nation" because here bananas from Central America are re-iced and transshipped to cities all over the United States. A parade, a banana-pancake breakfast with "Miss America" as special guest, the nation's largest banana pudding and a bake-off contest of banana recipes are features of the festival, while parking meters all over town are decorated with bananas, which are free for the eating.

US 51 goes from Fulton to Columbus, where Columbus-Belmont Battlefield State Park is located. Here was the site of the northernmost fortification of the Confederate Army during the Civil War. A giant chain and huge anchor were stretched across the Mississippi River to stop Union ships. A portion of this chain and the anchor are on display in the park. A museum has a battle diorama, and there are hiking trails along old battlefield trenches.

Route 80 goes back east to Mayfield where the travelers can pick up the Purchase Parkway and twenty-one miles later be in Benton, where the sweet potato is king when everybody celebrates Tater Day. All sorts of items turn up on Tater Day to be swapped or traded; there's a bazaar and contests, and all proceeds go to charity.

Another event in Benton, begun in 1884, is the Big Singing Day in May. This is one of the few American music festivals using "shape" notes exclusively. Many ancient and unusual songs are performed.

For the return to central Kentucky, the quickest route back from Kentucky Lake is the Western Kentucky Parkway, a toll road that takes off from Princeton, about twenty miles east of Kentucky Dam. En route be sure to stop at Pennyrile Forest State Park in Madisonville (the turnoff is at Dawson Springs). The park is handsome and hospitable and you'll enjoy the regional food often served in the beautifully situated lodge on the banks of the park's fifty-five-acre lake. Some 15,000 acres of reclaimed forest make up the park and include the large Lake Beshear, which covers some 850 acres.

A side trip off the Parkway on US 41 leads north to Henderson, very much the town of John James Audubon, Kentucky's first great naturalist-artist. The John James Audubon Memorial Museum, in a state park of the same name, contains exhibits of original Audubon prints and memorabilia. The park also has a nature museum, a nine-mile and a three-mile Audubon Hiking Trail, a lake, golf, fishing and boat rentals. The cottages in the park are available from April to November.

The Audubon Raceway, on US 41, has harness racing in June, July, September and October. North of Henderson, also on US 41, is James C. Ellis Park and Race Track where thoroughbred racing is held from July to September. The track seats 10,000 along the nine furlong oval, and an air-conditioned clubhouse seats 1,000.

Owensboro is only thirty-five miles north from the Beaver Dam interchange of the Parkway, and here the traveler can see Glenmore's Little Museum, which tells the history of the distilling industry in the city; the Owensboro Area Museum with an art gallery, planetarium and collection of marine life; Festival of the Arts, in late September; the Governor's Cup Race of Unlimited Hydroplanes held on the Ohio River in downtown Owensboro each June; and at 2100 Frederica Street stands the largest sassafras tree in the world. Registered with the American Forestry Association, the tree is thought to be 250 to 300 years old, has a circumference of about sixteen feet and is over one hundred feet high, twice the height of an ordinary sassafras tree.

Farther east on the Parkway is the turnoff for Caneyville, north of which, twenty miles or so, is Rough River Dam State Park, a 9,234-acre preserve with a bathhouse and beach as well as facilities for boating, picnicking, camping, and a modern lodge.

Eventually the Parkway brings you to Elizabethtown, from where you can take the Kentucky Turnpike straight up to Louisville or follow the less direct US 31W northward and pause en route for a visit to Fort Knox, where all the gold is buried. More than $11 billion in pure gold bars is stored in the Fort Knox Bullion Depository; but you can't see it, and there are absolutely no free samples! Actually, Fort Knox is one of the biggest military installations in the United States, and was the site of two battles during the Civil War. It houses about 60,000 military personnel and is about thirty miles south of Louisville. Kentucky state officials are working on the Federal Government to put some gold bars on display. In the meantime, the Patton Museum, named for the fiery World War II tank commander, contains fascinating relics and military hardware that make a visit worthwhile. Admission is free.

Home of the Derby

In the colorful river city of Louisville is the *Belle of Louisville,* one of the last river sternwheelers. The *Belle* carries passengers on summer excursions from the new Riverfront Park, below the Galt House. There are also dancing cruises.

Industrial tours are available through such giant corporations as Berhaim Distilling Co., Brown-Forman Distillers, Brown & Williamson Tobacco Corporation, General Electric's Appliance Park, Hadley Pottery, and the Stitzel-Weller Distillery, Inc. Tour hours vary, and travelers should inquire at Founders Square, the Louisville Visitors Bureau, at Fifth and Walnut Streets.

Actors Theatre, headed by Jon Jory, has become one of the most successful professional resident theatres in America. It has moved into the renovated Bank of Louisville building, a designated National Historical Monument. Tours of the historic building are available during the season.

Churchill Downs is the home of the most exciting two minutes in sports, the Kentucky Derby, held each year on the first Saturday in May. The first Derby was held in 1875, and the Downs' familiar Edwardian spires are antique reminders of that era. Churchill Downs has some sixty racing days during the spring and fall seasons. The Kentucky Derby Museum, just inside the main entrance of Churchill Downs, depicts the colorful history of the Kentucky Derby and the horses and people who have made it famous. The museum is open all year.

Farmington, on Bardstown Road, was designed by Thomas Jefferson for the John Speed family and was built in 1810. It was here that Abraham Lincoln came to mend a broken heart during his courtship of Mary Todd, a Kentucky belle from Lexington. Lincoln was a friend of the Speed brothers; John Speed served in his cabinet as Attorney Gener-

Louisville

Points of Interest

1) Actors Theater
2) Calvary Cathedral
3) Cathedral of the Assumption
4) Catherine Spalding College
5) Christ Church Cathedral
6) City Hall
7) Convention Center
8) Fort Nelson Monument (site of Fort)
9) George Rogers Clark Memorial Bridge
10) Greyhound Bus Terminal
11) Louisville Gardens
12) Macauley Theater
13) Public Library
14) Riverfront Plaza Belvedere

al. The house has been restored and is furnished with many fine antiques originally in the home.

Ghost Town of the River, adjacent to Shawnee Park, combines a Western theme with twenty-five different family amusement rides. It is open May through Labor Day, and one ticket covers all rides and shows.

The Jefferson County Courthouse, designed in the 1850's by Gideon Shryock, contains a statue of Henry Clay by Joel T. Hart and one of Thomas Jefferson by Moses Ezeskill. The building is called a classic example of Greek Revival architecture.

Major events besides the Kentucky Derby are the steamboat race between the *Delta Queen* and the *Belle of Louisville;* the Pegasus Parade with more than two hundred units of horsemen, floats and marching bands; a large music show at the Kentucky Exposition Center made free to the public by the Phillip Morris Corporation; a coronation ball; bicycle race and balloon race; outdoor concerts and a fireworks pageant.

The Kentucky Railway Museum, on Upper River Road, contains the 1905 steam locomotive that pulled Teddy Roosevelt's campaign train, America's oldest streetcar, a French boxcar from World War I and much more railroad paraphernalia.

The Kentucky State Fair draws over a half million people during its ten-day run in late August. Held at the giant Kentucky Fair and Exhibition Center, this gala event includes a circus, carnival rides, a rodeo, performances of popular and country music stars; competition in arts, crafts, livestock and farm produce; and industrial displays. There is also the World Championship Horse Show for five- and three-gaited horses.

Locust Grove, on Blankenbaker Lane, was the last home of Louisville's founder, George Rogers Clark. The Georgian mansion was built around 1790, and has been restored by the Historic Homes Foundation. Included on the grounds are a smokehouse, log cabin and slave quarters.

Louisville Downs, on Poplar Level Road, is Louisville's only member of the Harness Tracks of America and was opened in 1966. Race meets are held in March-April and July-September. Parents may leave children in a supervised playground. The clubhouse serves gourmet food. Another race track, Miles Park on Cecil Avenue, features nighttime thoroughbred racing in June and July.

Rauch Memorial Planetarium, on the University of Louisville campus on Third Street, presents outstanding public programs on stars, constellations and outer space.

During the summer on Wednesday through Saturday nights, Shakespeare is performed in Louisville's Central Park.

The J. B. Speed Art Museum, on Third Street, is Kentucky's oldest and largest art museum. The Speed has permanent collections of paintings, sculpture, drawings, prints and decorative arts. There is the Satterwhite collection of Medieval and Renaissance art. Special exhibitions change monthly. You will find the Museum of Science and History at 743 S. 5th St.

Bones and Tobacco

To reach attractions in the central and eastern sections of Kentucky, Lexington makes a good starting point. From it excellent roads fan out north, south and eastward. The newly completed I-75, for example, leads straight north through plush, bluegrass pastures to Covington, on the Ohio, and Cincinnati, directly opposite on the river's north bank. About twenty miles south of Covington on this route is the turnoff for Big Bone Lick State Park, which lies just a few miles to the west on Route 338. Here fascinating paleontological diggings are now under way in an effort to unearth and further preserve the archeological history of the region. Along with such informative exhibits as a layered picture of the glacial action of the last 100,000 years, you'll find a display of bones of prehistoric mastodons and mammoths that have been found in the area. Many date back about 10,000 years.

Like Kentucky's other limited-access highways, I-75 is a great time-saver for visitors who want to cover a lot of ground. But leisurely travelers will find meandering roads more enjoyable. For one thing, the less modern highways let you get closer to the scenery. Two routes that run through Lexington—US 27 and 68—are excellent for sightseeing as well as driving. Both lead through the tobacco country, which yields Kentucky's chief agricultural crop.

The tobacco you see along these highways is most likely to be the tall leaves of white burley, one of the prime ingredients in the manufacture of cigarettes and smoking tobacco. Kentucky, which ranks first among the tobacco states in burley output, also grows all of the Green River dark, air-cured tobacco in the world. (This is used mainly for chewing tobacco.) Here, too, is grown over eighty percent of the entire world supply of Western, dark-fired leaf tobacco, which is used for snuff.

For a longer excursion out of Lexington, head eastward on I-64 to its junction with the Mountain State Parkway. Branch off on that toll road and continue eastward to Natural Bridge State Park, with its well-appointed Lodge. For those who do not want complete hotel facilities, cottages are available in the park.

Natural Bridge, a stone arch whose soft rock has been washed away by centuries of wind, rain and a prehistoric sea, gives the park its name. In this area there are twenty natural stone arches, and Rock Bridge is the only natural bridge in Kentucky under which a stream flows. From April to November a skylift takes visitors to the top of Natural Bridge. This park has one of the most complete recreation programs of any in the parks system. An island in the middle of a lake—Hoedown Island—is host to square dancers from early spring to late fall.

The Red River Gorge has long been the subject of a controversary between environmentalists and the Corps of Engineers, who want to build a dam for floor protection and water supply. A boulder-strewn area of rugged forest, streams, cliffs, overlooks, natural arches and rare plant life, the Red River Gorge is one of Kentucky's most breathtaking beauty spots. Nada Tunnel, Route 77 and 715, has an interesting feature: midway into the tunnel both the entrance and exit are seen as only small white dots.

From Campton, travelers can follow Route 15 to Hazard, and then Route 7 and 1103 to Lilley Cornett Woods, a remnant of one of the greatest prehistoric forests of all time—the Mixed Mesophytic—which reached its finest development in the Cumberland Mountains of eastern Kentucky. In the virgin timber portion of the woods, which contains 554 acres, are trees that have possibly reached four hundred years of age, or even more. Guided tours of the woods are available from April to September.

Legend of Jenny Wiley

Continuing east from the end of the Mountain Parkway, you come eventually to Jenny Wiley State Park at Prestonburg in the foothills of the Cumberland Mountains. A topnotch lodge, cottage and camping facilities, a beautiful white sandy beach on the shores of Lake Dewey and an Olympic-sized swimming pool make this park another good vacation spot. No matter what your pleasure may be—mountain-climbing, fishing, boating, water-skiing, horseback riding or golf—you'll find it here. There is even a skylift to take you to the top of one of the mountains. The scenery is dramatic. So is the legend of Jenny Wiley, for whom the park was named.

According to the local folklore, Jenny lived in the valley with her husband and three children. One night in 1787, the Wiley family's sleep was shattered by the blood-chilling screech of Shawnee and Cherokee marauders, who killed Jenny's husband and her two older children. Jenny, who was pregnant, and her youngest child, a baby in arms, were dragged off by the Indians. When the baby became a nuisance to the Indians, it was killed. Nine days of hard, fast travel to outwit pursuit followed.

Then the Indians paused on the Cherokee Fork of Big Blain Creek. In a cave Jenny Wiley bore her fourth child. This, too, was killed. The Indians went on, taking Jenny with them. Then one of the Cherokee chiefs of the dual band decided to add Jenny to his harem and purchased her from the Shawnee chief. Jenny was tied to a tree by the Cherokee. During the night a chill rain began to fall and, managing to twist free from the loosening rawhide thongs that bound her wrists to the tree, she escaped. Jenny Wiley lived until 1831, when she died at the age of seventy-one.

North from Jenny Wiley Park, mainly over scenic Route 201, you will come to Carter Caves State Park, one of Kentucky's newest (also reached directly from Lexington via I-64 and US 60). Added to all the usual park features are miniature golf, a nine-hole golf course and guided tours through the electrically lighted caves.

At the Grayson interchange of I-64, Route 1 goes to Greenbo Lake State Park, where the fieldstone arches of Jesse Stuart Lodge welcome guests. Wooden beams and a copper-hooded fireplace lend a warm atmosphere to the lobby, whose windows look out over the swimming pool and lake. Unusual features of the park include a one-room school and the ruins of a primitive iron furnace. Oldtown and Bennett's Mill covered bridge are still in use in Greenup County.

I-64 goes on to Ashland, via US 60 and 23, where Armco Steel Corporation operates one of the largest blast furnaces in the Western World and welcomes visitors for tours.

Also in Ashland is the region's famous "Traipsin' Woman," Jean Thomas, who heads up a unique event each June—the American Folksong Festival. It is held during the second week of the month and seeks to perpetuate the classic Appalachian folksongs which derive from Elizabethan sources. Costumed singers perform to the lilting music of zithers, dulcimers, lutes and the more familiar guitar in the three-day program.

Returning to Lexington via US 60 you pass through Mount Sterling, where the old Kentucky tradition of Court Day is still an annual event, attracting thousands. Marking the opening of the fall term of court, the day's activities include swapping (everything from household goods and hound dogs to Barlow knives and tall tales), visiting and trading.

One of the great recreational areas in Kentucky lies south of Lexington: Fort Boonesborough State Park, off I-75, the site where Daniel Boone built the first of his homestead forts in the wilderness 190 years ago. No trace of the old fort remains on this beautiful spot on the shores of the Kentucky River, but you will find ideal camping sites, a boat dock with complete rental service, and a luxury-style bathhouse beside the river's natural sandy beach. A small community on Route 388, the removed original settlement, is called Boonesboro. The park is Boonesborough, the old spelling of the name. It's interesting when looking at Daniel Boone's early records to note that he spelled it Boonsborough—without the "e"—because at that period in his career he was signing his name, Dan'l Boon.

Country Dances—Mountain Crafts

Just a mile west off I-75, five miles north of Richmond, is White Hall State Shrine, the former home of the anti-slavery advocate, Cassius Marcellus Clay (1810–1903). The forty-room Italianate mansion has been restored with much of the original furnishings and other items of the period. Clay, a cousin to Henry Clay, was the son of Green Clay, one of Kentucky's largest slave owners. This youngest son, who received the excellent education of a Southern planters' scion, fell under the master spell of William Lloyd Garrison while he was a student at Yale. Clay returned to Kentucky, established an antislavery newspaper, lectured far and wide on the evils of slavery and helped establish a college for all races at Berea. He is credited with making a stirring speech that swung the 1860 Republican Convention to Abraham Lincoln as the Party's presidential nominee. He served as Lincoln's minister to Russia, and he is credited with playing a major part in America's purchase of Alaska from Russia.

South of White Hall, twenty miles on I-75, is Berea (both the college and the town). Students at Berea are taught some of the traditional Appalachian crafts—weaving, woodworking, metalwork and broommaking—and they must pay their expenses. Boone Tavern, run by the college, specializes in the finest Kentucky foods, and at the same time trains students in hotel management. For four days in mid-May the Kentucky Guild of Artists' and Craftsmen's Fair is held at the College, in the Indian Fort Theatre. Berea's Appalachian Museum shows the dignity of the mountain people through displays of their art, crafts and lifestyle. Each summer the outdoor drama *Wilderness Road* tells about the mountaineers and their involvement with the Civil War. Be sure to visit the Art Department and Galleries. The Churchill Weavers, at Lorraine Court, will be of special interest to the ladies.

Fourteen miles south of Berea is the country music complex of Renfro Valley, where songs are still sung that have been handed down from

Elizabethan ballads. The country music show has been broadcast from
the Big Barn (which holds one thousand) each Saturday night continuously since 1939. A museum complex and country store recall interesting
items from yesteryear. Annual events of Renfro Valley are: an Old Time
Fiddler's Convention in July, a rodeo in August, an all-day singing
marathon in September and all-night singing in August. The Renfro
Valley Barn Dance has both reserved and general admission seats for the
Saturday night show.

Leaving I-75 at the Livingston exit, ten miles south of Renfro Valley,
the traveler will find Fort Sequoyah, a riverboat town with its own small
sternwheeler for trips on the Rockcastle River, gunfights on the streets
of an 1800's town, a saloon show and rides in the mule-drawn surreys.
Fort Sequoyah is located on US 25, which runs alongside I-75.

South to the Cumberland

On another trip out of Lexington, US 27 leads you almost directly
south to the Tennessee border. This route takes you to a beautiful scenic
region of the Daniel Boone National Forest. About ninety miles below
Lexington, on US 27, is General Burnside Island State Park, surrounded
by the waters of huge Lake Cumberland, which dominates the area
adjacent to the national forest. The park offers boating, fishing, golf, tent
and trailer camping, and picnicking.

You can turn off US 27 at Parkers Lake and head east on Route 90
to Cumberland Falls State Park, which can also be reached from Lexington south-bound on I-75, 19 miles from Corbin on US 25W. Here,
wandering in almost primeval glory through 1,098 acres of mountains,
forests and sheer-faced valleys, the Cumberland River spills over a rocky
ledge into a boulder-strewn gorge some sixty-eight feet below. These
beautiful falls are the largest east of the Rockies and south of Niagara.
They are 150 feet wide, and the torrent of water pouring over the ledge
strikes with such force that a perpetual mist hovers over the valley. One
of the sights created here is a hauntingly beautiful moonbow, the night-
time equivalent of a rainbow, that appears when the moon is full. The
only other moonbow is at Victoria Falls, in Africa. Also in the park is
Little Eagle Falls, a spot where a small mountain creek tumbles 125 feet
down a hill into the river below. The falls were considered sacred by the
early Indian tribes and many bitter and bloody battles were waged for
their possession.

If traveling with children you may want to visit Tombstone Junction,
by continuing south on 25W to Williamsburg.

This corner of the state is pioneer Kentucky, heralded in song and
legend that is solidly based in fact. East of Cumberland Falls State Park
there are a number of important and scenic historic sites, among them
Levi Jackson Wilderness Road State Park, near London, the Dr. Thomas
Walker State Shrine near Barbourville and Cumberland Gap National
Historical Park at Middlesboro, at the Virginia-Tennessee border point.

It was through Cumberland Gap that the first white men passed from
Virginia into Kentucky. They were Dr. Thomas Walker, a surveyor and
physician, and his party, who represented the Loyal Land Company of
Charlottesville, a Virginia enterprise with a grant of 800,000 acres in
Kentucky. Dr. Walker and his companions preceded Daniel Boone by

twenty years. A replica of the log cabin Walker built in 1750—the first white man's house in Kentucky—is in the Shrine at Barbourville.

It is at Barbourville, too, that the historical Daniel Boone Festival is held annually in mid-October. The festival, commemorating Boone's search for a route to the bluegrass, is quite a spectacle, with most of the townsfolk dressed in buckskins and carrying authentic flintlock rifles, and Cherokee Indians from the nearby North Carolina reservation on hand to reenact the treaty ceremony in which the white man first won privileges in this mountain country.

Also in this corner of Kentucky is the oldest of the state parks, Pine Mountain State Park, in the Kentucky Ridge State Forest at Pineville on US 25E. Here the rugged tourist is offered some challenging mountain hiking. All facilities from hotel-type lodge to cottages and camping sites are available, as are fishing, boating, golf, horseback riding and a complete recreational program for all ages. The Mountain Laurel Festival is held here the last weekend in May, at which time Kentucky's Mountain Laurel Queen is selected in the amphitheater at Laurel Cove. *The Book of Job,* a choral drama, is also staged in the amphitheater in late June, July and August.

Visit to a Coal Mine

The bleak coal mining towns of Appalachia also lie in this part of the state. Since many mines are now unprofitable and poverty is widespread, efforts are being made to help families trapped by the economic slump. One example is the tiny coal mining community of Blackey in Letcher County, which was on the verge of disappearing when an arts and crafts program was instituted. An international authority on hooked rugs was called in, and the ladies of Blackey were invited to submit rug designs that could be used in the project. The resulting "hound dog" rugs have become nationally famous and have given Blackey an economic shot in the arm.

From Pineville, Blackey is reached by driving east and north on US 119 to Cumberland, then heading westward over secondary state roads.

You can proceed northeast from Cumberland on US 119 to Pikeville and turn northwest on US 460 to Prestonburg, then 1½ mi. north on Route 304 to the Jenny Wiley State Park, with water sports, skylift rides and an amphitheater.

Most remote in all Kentucky is Breaks Interstate Park, on the Kentucky-Virginia border. Walk a little too far east in this park and you'll find yourself out of Kentucky and in Virginia. It lies seven miles east of Elkhorn City and consists of 1,880 acres of spectacular scenery on the Kentucky-Virginia line. The park, created in 1954, is operated by a six-man commission, three from each state. Through the years the region described as the Grand Canyon of the South has been known as "Breaks of the Sandy," "Breaks of the Cumberland," and more often just plain "Breaks." The name refers to the deep cleft cut by the Russell Fork River, a tributary of the Big Sandy River, through a sandstone uplift in the Cumberland Mountains.

Jumping-off point for Elkhorn City is Pikeville, which can be reached from Pineville and the Cumberland Gap area via US 119, or from Lexington and the east by way of meandering US 460.

PRACTICAL INFORMATION FOR KENTUCKY

 FACTS AND FIGURES. Kentucky translated from the Wyandot Indian word *Kah-ten-tah-teh* means "Land where we will live tomorrow" or "Land of Tomorrow." Kentucky is called the "Bluegrass State" because of the abundant growth of bluegrass on its rich limestone soil. Fields of bluegrass have a bluish-green hue during the spring. The state bird is the Kentucky cardinal; state tree, the Kentucky coffee tree; state flower, the goldenrod; state song, "My Old Kentucky Home," by Stephen C. Foster; state fish, Kentucky bass; state wild animal, the gray squirrel, and the state motto, "United We Stand, Divided We Fall."

Frankfort has been the capital of Kentucky since it became a state in 1792. Kentucky has an area of 40,395 square miles, and its population is 3,498,000 (1980 Census).

Kentucky is generally divided into four sections. The Western Waterlands is covered with those two giants of Kentucky waters, Kentucky Lake and Lake Barkley, which jointly hold more than 220,000 surface acres of water. The Ohio and Mississippi rivers form the border for this section of Kentucky.

Southcentral Kentucky includes the Cave Region, with the most famous of all caverns, Mammoth Cave. Five major lakes and some whitewater rivers are in this area.

Kentucky's most famous region is the Bluegrass, which reaches from the mountains to the Ohio River. When thoroughbreds are mentioned, the first thought is of sleek horses grazing in white-fenced pastures with a background of cross fences and colorful barns—a Kentucky landscape. There are more than 350 horse farms that surround Lexington.

The Eastern Highlands, once famous for mountain moonshine and feuding families, now includes the Daniel Boone National Forest resort parks and streams for both fishing and canoeing, shops selling original mountain crafts.

 HOW TO GET THERE. *By air:* Louisville can be reached from out of the state on direct flights of: U.S. Air, American, Delta, Eastern, Ozark, Piedmont and TWA; Lexington via: U.S. Air, Delta, Eastern and Piedmont. Cincinnati Airport is adjacent to Covington.

By car: Two major north/south interstates, I-75 and I-65, carry heavy traffic from the Ohio state line to the Georgia and Tennessee state lines. I-64 runs west/east from the West Virginia state line to the Illinois state line. US 41 enters the state in the north from Indiana and runs south to Tennessee.

By bus: In addition to Greyhound and Trailways, the ABC Coach Lines, Bowling Green-Hopkinsville Bus Co., Crown Transit, Gulf Transport Co., Illini-Swallow Lines, Inc., Lake Shore System, Short Way Lines and Southeastern States, Inc., operate into the state.

 HOW TO GET AROUND. *By air:* Delta, Ozark and Piedmont serve cities within the state.

By car: A network of interstate highways and state turnpikes and parkways make traveling in Kentucky a pleasure. Over 80% of Kentucky's planned 1,387 mi. of interstate highways and parkways is completed. From Princeton, in western Kentucky, it is possible to travel on four-lane highways all the way to the state's eastern border at Ashland. I-75 and I-65 run north/south and are connected by I-71 from Louisville to Cincinnati. I-24 is under construction. The interstate highways are integrated with nine equally modern state parkways.

Car rental: Avis and Hertz have rental offices in Frankfort, Lexington, Louisville and Paducah. In addition, Hertz has offices in Ashland, Bowling Green, Calvert City, Owensboro and Somerset.

By bus: Greyhound, Trailways, Bowling Green-Hopkinsville Bus Co., and Tennessee Trail Blazers.

 TOURIST INFORMATION SERVICES. Commonwealth of Kentucky, Dept. of Tourism, Fort Boone Plaza, Frankfort, Ky. 40601. Dept. of Fish & Wildlife Resources, Frankfort 40601. Lexington Area Chamber of Commerce, 239 N. Broadway, Lexington, Ky. 40508. Visitor's Bureau, Founders Square, Louisville, Ky. 40202.

 SEASONAL EVENTS. *February: Lincoln Day Celebration,* Hodgenville, weekend nearest Lincoln's Birthday. *April: Tater Day,* Benton (1st Mon. in April). *Mountain Folk Festival,* Berea. *May: Big Singing Day,* Benton. *Kentucky Guild of Artists' and Craftsmen's Fair,* Berea. *Kentucky Derby Festival,* 10-day celebration including Pegasus Parade, Steamboat race, Kentucky Derby, Louisville. *Mountain Laurel Festival* (end May), Pineville.

June: American Folksong Festival, at Grayson, near Ashland.

July: Jr. League Horse Show; Blue Grass Fair, Lexington. *Summer Festival,* Paducah. *Old Time Fiddlers' Convention,* Renfro Valley. *Shaker Festival,* South Union.

August: International Banana Festival, Fulton. *Kentucky State Fair; World's Championship Horse Show,* Louisville. *Rodeo and All-night Singing Marathon,* Renfro Valley.

September: Kaintuck Territory Septemberfest, Gilbertsville, *Grand Circuit Meet* (end Sept. to early Oct.), Lexington. *Salute to the Arts Festival,* Louisville. *Festival of the Arts,* Owensboro. *Kentucky Highlands Folk Festival,* Prestonburg. *All-day Singing Marathon,* Renfro Valley. *Tobacco Festival* (late Sept.) Russellville.

October: Daniel Boone Festival, Barbourville. *Court Day,* Mt. Sterling.

November: Blessing of the Hounds, Iroquois Hunt Club, Lexington.

 NATIONAL PARKS. Kentucky has two national parks, a national historic site and a national recreation area. *Cumberland Gap National Historic Park* near Middlesboro covers 20,170 acres at the juncture of Kentucky, Virginia and Tennessee. Hiking trails and the visitors' center remain open all year at Cumberland Gap, but camping, picnicking, fishing and planned recreation are only seasonal. Cumberland Gap, scene of the pioneer's early entry into not only Kentucky, but the entire West is located on US 25 just above the Kentucky-Tennessee line.

Mammoth Cave National Park, on Rte. 70, a few miles from the Cave City interchange of I-65, has 51,354 acres of wonders both above and below ground. Mammoth Cave has the world's longest connecting underground passage, and a number of cave tours explore these caverns. Cruises along the Green River are available. Housekeeping cottages are available only on a seasonal basis at Mammoth Cave. All other facilities—a lodge, dining room, camping, picnicking, hiking, tennis, fishing, a museum and gift shop—are open all year.

The *Abraham Lincoln Birthplace National Historic Site,* Hodgenville, on US 31E is about 10 miles from the juncture of the Western Kentucky Turnpike, I-65 and the Bluegrass Parkway via Rte. 61. A marble and granite monument covers the tiny log cabin where the 16th president was born in 1809. Leading up to the cabin are 56 steps, representing each year of Lincoln's life. Facilities here include a picnic area, hiking trails and the museum—all open year around.

Land Between the Lakes, a 170,000-acre wooded area between Kentucky Lake and Lake Barkley, was developed by TVA into a national recreation and conservation education area. It has three family campgrounds with over 700 sites, a herd of buffalo, a conservation center, iron furnace ruins, Empire Farm for youngsters to pet farm animals and see early farm equipment, 22 beaches and over 300 mi. of back-country trails. Camping, picnic areas, playgrounds, hiking trails, fishing and the museum are open all year on LBL, but planned recreation and the swimming beach are only seasonal.

Nearly 800,000 acres of eastern Kentucky are enclosed in the two units of the *Daniel Boone National Forest.* The main body of the forest reaches from the southern border of Kentucky almost to the Ohio River; it is crossed by the Cumberland, Rockcastle, Kentucky, Red and Licking Rivers. Numerous camping areas are maintained by the Forest Service. The Redbird Purchase unit of the forest lies to the east of the main body.

 STATE PARKS. Kentucky's system of resort, recreational and historical parks is among the finest in the nation, and more developments are planned. State parks in Kentucky cover around 40,000 acres, and there are 43 parks in the system plus an interstate park managed jointly by a commission from Kentucky and Virginia. Fifteen of these parks have the status of resorts (complete lodge and dining room facilities); most also have cottages and a wide range of recreation facilities. For complete information write to Dept. of Public Information, Capitol Annex, Frankfort, Ky. 40601.

 TRAILER TIPS. Because of the vast number of sites in Kentucky, we are listing only the State Parks which offer them. Unless otherwise indicated, all are open from Apr. to Oct., and the stay is limited to 14 days. Generally, tents and/or recreational vehicles use the same spaces. My Old Kentucky Home State Park; Fort Boonesborough State Park; Buckhorn Lake State Resort Park; Gen. Burnside State Park; Lake Barkley State Resort Park; Green River Lake State Park; Gen. Butler State Resort Park; Columbus-Belmont Battlefield State Park; Cumberland Falls State Resort Park; Pennyrile Forest State Resort Park; Lake Malone State Park; Breaks Interstate Park; Rough River Dam State Resort Park; Barren River Lake State Resort Park; Grayson Lake State Park; Greenbo Lake State Resort Park; Kenlake State Resort Park; John James Audubon State Park; Lake Cumberland State Resort Park; Levi Jackson Wilderness Road State Park; Mammoth Cave National Park (open all year); Carter Caves State Resort Park; Pine Mountain State Resort Park; Jenny Wiley State Resort Park; Natural Bridge State Resort Park; Big Bone Lick State Park.

A directory of campgrounds may be obtained from: Kentucky Dept. of Public Information, Frankfort, Ky. 40601.

 FARM VACATIONS AND GUEST RANCHES. Renfro Valley. *Brown's Vacation Farm,* Rte. 70. Farm vacations for families, hiking, horseback riding, fishing, hunting, picnics, hayrides, room and board.

 MUSEUMS AND GALLERIES. Historical. *Kentucky Library and Museum,* Western Kentucky University, Bowling Green. Closed University holidays. *Columbus-Belmont Battlefield State Park Museum.* Civil War relics. June to Aug. *Kentucky Historical Society Museum,* St. Clair St. & Broadway, Frankfort. *Harrodsburg Historical Society Museum,* located in one of the Morgan Row bldgs., S. Chiles St. June to Labor Day. Closed Mon. The *Filson Club*

Museum, 118 Breckenridge St., Louisville. Has portion of tree with Daniel Boone's initials on it. Closed Sat., and July to Sept.

Art: Though it is not a gallery, art lovers should not miss a visit to *St. Joseph's Proto-Cathedral,* Jct. US 31E and 62, Bardstown. The walls are resplendent with works of such masters as Van Dyke, Van Eyck, Rubens, Murillo; all gifts of Louis Philippe of France who visited the town in 1797. *Art Dept. Galleries,* Berea College, Berea. Mon. to Fri. Closed school holidays. *University of Kentucky Art Gallery,* Anthropology Museum, Lafferty Hall, Rm. 105 Fine Arts Bldg., early tools, furniture, photos, country store. Lexington. Closed summers. *Guild Gallery,* 811 Euclid Ave. Closed Sun. & July 4, Thanksgiving and Christmas. Free. *J. B. Speed Art Museum,* 2035 S. 3rd St., Louisville. Free. *Paducah Art Guild Gallery.* In Market House, S 2 St. & Broadway. Closed holidays.

Special Interest: *Barton Museum of Whiskey History,* Barton Rd., Bardstown. Free. *Appalachian Museum,* Berea College, Berea. Closed New Years and Christmas. *Wondering Woods,* reconstructed 1900's town, also is site of Chapel Garden Gallery, a museum of religious history, near Cave City. *Patton Museum of Cavalry and Armor,* in Fort Knox, 30 mi. SW of Louisville. Closed New Years and Christmas. *Shakertown,* at Pleasant Hill, Rte. 4., Harrodsburg. Village Museum, 27 historic bldgs. Center House Museum. *John James Audubon Memorial Museum,* Audubon State Park, Henderson. Personal memorabilia of John James Audubon. Closed Nov. to Mar.

In Lexington: *American Saddle Horse Museum,* Spindletop Farm, on Ironworks Pike. Closed Mon. & Nov. to Mar. *Headley Jewel Museum,* Old Frankfort Pike. Closed holidays. *Transylvania Museum,* 300 N. Broadway. Science museum housed in 1833 Greek Revival Bldg. (Old Morrison); by appointment. In Louisville: *Jos. Rauch Memorial Planetarium,* U. of Louisville, Belknap Campus. Shows: Sept. to July. Closed Aug. & national holidays. *Kentucky Railway Museum,* Upper River Rd. Closed Oct. to Apr. *Kentucky Derby Museum,* at Churchill Downs. Year round. *Museum of Natural History and Science,* 727 W. Main St. Over 194,000 traditional museum items, an atrium, costume collection and exhibits. Housed in 1878 cast-iron commercial bldg. on Nat. Reg. of Hist. Places. *Owensboro Area Museum,* 901 Frederica St., Owensboro. Closed Sat., Christmas and national holidays. *Wm. Clark Museum,* in Market Place. S. 2 St. & Broadway, Paducah. Mementoes of Irvin S. Cobb and Alben Barkley, Indian artifacts and an old-time drugstore. Closed holidays. *Shaker Museum,* Walnut St., South Union. Mid-May to mid-Oct. *Ancient Buried City,* Wickliffe. Archeology museum, 1,000-yr.-old botanical remains.

Others: *Mammoth Cave Wax Museum,* Rte. 70W, off I-65. *Calvert Auto Museum,* Rte. 95SW, Gilbertsville. May to Labor Day.

 HISTORIC SITES. *Abraham Lincoln Birthplace National Historic Site,* Rte. 1 Hodgenville. Birthplace cabin of Abraham Lincoln. Closed Christmas. Free. *Founders Square,* Fifth & Walnut Sts., Louisville. *Jefferson County Courthouse,* Jefferson St., Louisville. Statues of Henry Clay and Thomas Jefferson.

Historic Houses: *Federal Hill,* mansion immortalized by Stephen Foster's My Old Kentucky Home, in Bardstown, US 50E. *Wickland,* US 62, Bloomfield Rd., Bardstown. Home of 3 governors. Daily 9 to sundown. Closed Thanksgiving, Easter, Christmas. *McDowell House & Apothecary Shop,* 125-127 S. 2nd St., Danville. Collections: medical, herbarium, paintings, botany. *Lincoln Heritage House,* in Freeman Lake Park, Elizabethtown. *Liberty Hall Museum,* 218 Wilkinson, Frankfort. 1796-1801 Georgian house. Closed Mon. and national holidays. *Orlando Brown House,* 202 Wilkinson St., Frankfort. 1835 house and furnishings. Closed New Year's, July 4, and Christmas. *Old Fort Harrod Mansion Museum,* in Old Fort Harrod State Park, Harrodsburg. Historical museum housed in 1830 mansion. *Morgan Row,* 220 S. Chiles St., Harrodsburg. Oldest standing row houses used for a commercial purpose.

In Lexington: *The Henry Clay Memorial Foundation,* (Ashland), East Main St. & Sycamore Rd. Home of Henry Clay from 1811 until his death in 1852. *The Hunt-Morgan House* (Hopemont), Graetz Park 201 N. Mill St. 1814 Federalist mansion. *Waveland State Shrine,* Higbee Mill Pike, 1847 Greek Revival mansion built by Boone descendants.

In Louisville: *Farmington,* 3033 Bardstown Rd., designed by Thomas Jefferson. *Locust Grove,* 561 Blankenbaker Lane. Last home of General George Rogers Clark. *Brennan House,* 631 S. Fifth St., elegant Victorian mansion.

Historic Shrines and Monuments: A replica of the first pioneer-built log cabin stands in the *Dr. Thomas Walker State Shrine,* on Rte. 459 south of Barbourville. The original was built by Dr. Walker in 1750. *Constitution Square State Shrine,* US 127, Danville, was the site of nine conventions from 1784 to 1792. Here is the original post office and replicas of the courthouse, jail and meeting house. *Jefferson Davis Monument State Park,* Fairview. *Waveland State Shrine,* Higbee Mill Rd., Lexington, off US 27S, is a Greek Revival mansion built on land surveyed by Daniel Boone. Waveland has an extensive museum of early Kentucky life. Closed Mon., New Year's and Christmas. *Perryville Battlefield State Shrine,* Perryville. On US 150W. Site of Kentucky's bloodiest Civil War battle. Each October a reenactment of the battle is staged at the park. *White Hall State Shrine,* Richmond, Winchester-Boonesboro Interchange of I-75. Home of Cassius Marcellus Clay, Kentucky's great abolitionist who served as Abraham Lincoln's minister to Russia and helped accomplish America's purchase of Alaska. *Lincoln Homestead State Shrine,* Springfield. Park museum featuring the Francis Berry House, Lincoln Home, blacksmith shop. *William Whitley Home,* first brick house in Kentucky, US 150S, Stanford. William Whitley declared that horses should race counterclockwise on his oval race track, an innovation still followed on American tracks. *Old Mulkey Meeting House State Shrine,* on Rte. 1446 S. Tompkinsville, recalls the religious revivals that swept Kentucky in 1800.

TOURS. *By bus: Tourmobile,* Loretto Rd. provides free tours from the Information Center, Court Square, Bardstown, twice a day, from mid-June to Labor Day to all points of interest. For sightseeing in Louisville, bus tours leave from Founders Square Tues. to Sat.

By car: The *Red Line Auto Tour* is a marked auto course of 45 points of interest in Paducah. A brochure, map and description are available at the Chamber of Commerce.

By boat: At Mammoth Cave National Park, *Miss Green River Boat* has several 90-min. round trips daily from May to Oct. The *Belle of Louisville,* Riverfront Plaza, 4th & River, Louisville, has public cruises each Tues., Wed., Thurs., Sat. and Sun. Also Sat. night with orchestra for dancing at 8:30 p.m. At Fort Sequoyah, US 25 parallel to I-75. *Sternwheeler* trips on Rochester River. Memorial Day through Oct.

SPECIAL INTEREST TOURS. *Horse breeding farms:* Most of the thoroughbred horse farms known the world over are concentrated in the Lexington area of Kentucky. The following farms are usually open to the public and visitors are welcome to tour the grounds: *Dixiana Farm,* NE on Russell Cave Pike; *Walnut Hall Farm,* Newtown Pike, 6 mi. N of Lexington; *Greentree Stud,* at Elkhorn Creek; *Spendthrift Farm,* Iron Works Pike; *Darby Dan Farm,* 6 mi. NW on Old Frankfort Pike. You can tour the farms in your own automobile or by a bus tour conducted by Blue Grass Tours. Many other horse farms throughout the state welcome visitors. Arrangements should be made in advance. For free guide, "Kentucky—Where the Horses Are," write Kentucky Dept. of Tourism, Fort Boone Plaza, Frankfort, Ky. 40601.

Others: Natural Bridge State Resort Park, near Slade, has a *chairlift* ride, which offers a panorama of wilderness beauty and an easy way to the top of Natural Bridge.

Mammoth Onyx Cave, at Horse Cave, Ky. 1 hour tour of cave on 600-acre wildlife preserve. Year round daylight hrs. Tours depart from the Visitor Center at *Mammoth Cave National Park,* west of Cave City, for all trips through the cave. Prices and schedules vary; chairlift rides to Guntown Mountain.

Also near Cave City, on Rte. 70, off I-65, you can visit *Tranquil Valley Village,* Wondering Woods. Activities range from woodcarving to woolweaving and dyeing. Crafts and demonstrations, rides, musical entertainment. *Shakertown,* at Pleasant Hill, Ky., on US 58, 7 mi. NE of Harrodsburg. Authentic restoration of rural Shakertown community. Dining room open for all meals until 7:30 p.m. Year round.

Interesting life-sized monuments mark the burial place of Henry C. Wooldridge, eccentric horse trader and breeder. Maplewood Cemetery on US 45N, Mayfield.

Distilleries: Barton Distilling Co., Barton Rd., Bardstown; Whiskey History Museum at the same location. In Frankfort the *National Distillers Products Co.,* Glenn's Creek Rd. (Old Crow & Taylor plants), on Georgetown Rd. (Old Grandad Plant), both have tours Mon. to Fri.; *Schenley Distillers, Inc.,* Leestown Rd., Mon. to Fri. Near Loretto: Star Hill Distilling Co., where Malcer's Mark bourbon is made according to traditional methods, and you can watch the mash fermenting in great wooden barrels. In Louisville: *Bernheim Distillery Co.,* 1701 West Breckinridge, Mon. to Fri.; by appointment; *Brown-Forman Distillers Corp.,* 1908 Howard St. Mon. to Fri.; *Stitzel-Weller Distilleries, Inc.* (Old Fitzgerald Plant), Fitzgerald Rd., Mon. to Fri.; *Joseph E. Seagram & Sons, Inc.,* 7th St. Rd., Mon. to Fri.

MUSIC. At Benton, on the 4th Sun. in May, *Big Singing Day* features American music with many ancient and unusual songs. *Wondering Woods,* Tranquil Valley Village, nr. Cave City, Rte. 70, off I-65. Barbershop quartet performs Sun. afternoons, and features other musical groups throughout the summer. Here, too, the *Harmony Towers* present 15-min. carillon concerts several times daily.

In Danville, at the *Pioneer Playhouse* you can see Country Music Shows year round on Sat. From late June to Labor Day musicals and drama every night except Sun.

Taking its name from Kentuckian Bill Monroe and his Blue Grass boys, Kentucky is known for its contemporary folk music, called "bluegrass." You can hear good authentic bluegrass bands in Lexington. For authentic *Old-Time Fiddling,* visit Renfro Valley (50 mi. from Lexington).

You can hear the *Louisville Orchestra* and the *Kentucky Opera Association* at the Macauley's Theatre, 315 W. Broadway. The Louisville Orchestra presents a *Pop Concert* during the Kentucky Derby Festival at the Oxmoor Center.

STAGE AND REVUES. Summer in Kentucky marks the opening of outdoor dramas, which run from mid-June to Labor Day. These dramas include: "The Stephen Foster Story" at My Old Kentucky Home State Park in Bardstown, mid-June through Labor Day, performed nightly in the amphitheater, except Mon. at 8:30. There is a Sat. matinee at 3. In Berea, "Wilderness Road" is performed nightly except Sundays at 8:30 at the Indian Fort Theater from late June through Aug. "The Legend of Daniel Boone" is performed at Old Fort Harrod State Park, Harrodsburg. Mid-June to late Aug., nightly except Sun. at 8:30.

Topnotch Broadway musicals can be seen at the *Pioneer Playhouse* in Danville, mid-June to Labor Day. This playhouse offers dinner from 7 to 8:30, with curtain time at 9 nightly except Sunday. *Summer Music Theatre* at Jenny Wiley State Resort Park, Prestonburg. Mid-June to mid-Aug.

Louisville's Shakespeare in the Park, produced by the *Carriage House Players,* in Central Park, Louisville. Mid-July to mid-Aug. Wed. to Sat. 8:45. Free; and in Louisville also, the *Actors Theatre,* 316-320 W. Main St., has performances from Oct. to mid-May. Lexington's *Diners Playhouse* offers Broadway plays by top professional acting talent.

DRINKING LAWS. Liquor is available in Kentucky at package stores and by the drink at bars until midnight. No liquor is sold on Sundays and no liquor is served in any of the state parks. Age limit is 21 years.

SPORTS. *Boating:* Boat rentals are available at 19 state parks: Barren River Lake; Big Bone Lick; Buckhorn Lake; Carter Caves; Fort Boonesborough; General Butler; Greenbo Lake; Green River Lake; Jenny Wiley; John James Audubon; Kenlake; Kentucky Dam Village; Kincaid Lake; Lake Barkeley; Lake Cumberland; Lake Malone; Natural Bridge; Pennyrile Forest; and Rough River Dam. Ramp and docking facilities are available at all of the above, plus at every city along the Ohio River.

Fishing: A year-round visitors' delight in Kentucky because of the diversity in the temperature and physical character of the waters. They vary from 13 major man-made impoundments to 30 state-owned lakes and more than 13,000 mi. of fishable rivers and streams. Non-resident fishing licenses: annual $14, 15-day $5.50, 3-day $4.

Hunting: Includes squirrels, rabbits, quail, grouse, doves and deer. An annual non-resident hunting license $35; extra $10.50 for deer tags. 3-day non-resident hunting license, good for small game only, $12.50. For seasons and other information, contact Dept. of Wildlife Resources, Frankfort. *Primitive weapons hunting* area includes an 8,000-acre site in the Daniel Boone National Forest in Bath and Menifee counties. Only longbows, crossbows, or muzzle-loading rifles may be used. 118 of the state's 120 counties open for archery hunting for deer each Oct.

Golf: There are 120 9-hole and 80 18-hole courses in the state. Golfing is available at 14 state parks.

Water Sports: For *boating, swimming, water-skiing* and *fishing* visit any of the following state parks: Kenlake, Kentucky Dam Village, Land Between the Lakes, Rough River Dam Resort and the Natural Bridge.

SPECTATOR SPORTS. *Horse Racing:* All over the world the word "Kentucky" has come to mean horses. From Jan. to Dec. there is some form of horse racing in Kentucky. There is thoroughbred, harness and steeplechase racing almost every week in the year. Racetracks include: *Churchill Downs,* home of the famous Kentucky Derby; *Commonwealth Race Course,* thoroughbreds, Jan. & mid-June to mid-July, and *Louisville Downs,* harness-trotting, mid-July to late Sept., in Louisville. *Latonia Race Course,* 440 Price Pike, Florence, has thoroughbred and harness racing. *Midwest Harness Raceway* has harness racing May-July and Sept.-Nov., and *James C. Ellis Park,* thoroughbred racing from July to Sept. 1, both in Henderson. The *Red Mile* has harness racing; thoroughbred racing at *Keeneland Race Course;* steeplechasing at the *Kentucky State Horse Park,* all Lexington. Almost every weekend from March to November there is a horse show somewhere in the state.

Kentucky State Horse Park, 7 mi. N of Lexington on Iron Works Pike, has visitors' information center with film, museum, steeplechase course, dressage arena, polo field, show jumping ring, cross-country course and a half-mile dirt track with an infield for rodeo exhibitions and saddlehorse shows. Visitors may ride horses or ponies and in horsedrawn carriages. Cafeteria, picnic area, campground. Free general admission; tickets to special attractions are sold in books and can be used on different days. Horseback and carriage rides are extra.

Stock car racing at Fairgrounds Motor Speedway. Louisville, Mar.-Sept. *Hydroplane Regatta* on the Ohio River, at Owensboro, one week in June. *Steamboat race* featuring the *Belle of Louisville* and the *Delta Queen,* during the Kentucky Derby Festival in Louisville.

SHOPPING. The Bluegrass state has fine handcraft products. They range from distinctively styled furniture, rugs and pottery to fine carvings and novelty items. Many state park gift shops stock a wide variety of handcrafts. While touring the state, you might look for these workshops, where visitors are always welcome. *Churchill Weavers,* Lorraine Ct., Berea. Open daily. The small town of *Blackey* is known for its hooked rugs.

Village craft and gift shops display a number of reproduction Shaker wares and furniture, as well as handmade Kentucky articles, at Pleasant Hill, *Shakertown,* Rte. 4, Harrodsburg. Open 9 A.M. daily.

Bybee Pottery, on Rte. 52E, Richmond; and the *Hadley Pottery,* 1570 Story Ave., Louisville, are both makers of distinctive dinnerware.

Coffeetrees Gallery and Gift Shop, 501 River City Mall, 2nd floor of Stewart's Dept. Store, has fine selections of traditional and contemporary crafts. Every item in this beautiful shop is handmade in Kentucky.

Rebecca-Ruth Candy is famous for chocolates flavored with Kentucky bourbon, available throughout the state.

WHAT TO DO WITH THE CHILDREN. *Forgotten Past,* Rte. 9, Benton has go-cart, horseback and miniature train rides. May 15 to Sept. 1. All children are natural born spelunkers so don't miss a visit to *Mammoth Cave National Park,* 10 mi. W of Cave City on Rte. 70. Other smaller caves are also located through the state. Also near Cave City is *Wondering Woods* and *Tranquil Valley Village,* Route 70 off I-65. 150 acres of forest. Boys especially will enjoy a visit to the *Patton Museum of Cavalry and Armor* at Fort Knox. Free. *Kaintuck Territory,* on US 642 SW, Gilbertsville, is an authentic 1880 town; entertainment, petting zoo. Memorial Day to Labor Day. Children would be sure to find the many *horse farms* surrounding the Lexington area of great interest. In Louisville: *Kentucky Railroad Museum* will prove a delightful stop for the young railroad buffs. May to Sept. *Louisville Zoological Gardens,* 1100 Trevilian Way, special section where petting animals is encouraged. *Ghost Town on the River,* 203 S. Western Pkwy. One admission price covers all entertainment, rides, picnic area and parking. An exciting excursion on the picturesque steamboat *Belle of Louisville* will also delight the small fry. Cruises leave at 2 P.M. daily except Mon., Memorial Day through Labor Day, from Riverfront Plaza, 4th & River. *Tombstone Junction* is a reconstructed western town at Williamsburg, US 25W and Rte. 90, where the children can enjoy the steam train ride. Closed mid-Oct. to mid-Apr.

HOTELS AND MOTELS. Finding a place to stay in Kentucky is not difficult, as the state has an abundance of fine hotels and motels. It also has state-operated accommodations at several state parks, and these are noted for their attractiveness and comfort.

Accommodations are listed according to price categories, based on double occupancy in the peak season, without meals, i.e.: *Expensive:* $35 and up; *Moderate:* $25 to $35; *Inexpensive:* under $25. Most hotels in the Louisville area charge higher rates during Kentucky Derby week in May. For a more complete explanation of hotel categories see *Facts at Your Fingertips* at the front of this volume.

Ashland

Holiday Inn. *Expensive.* US 52E, Grandview Ave., Ironton, O. Courtesy airport transportation. Restaurant, bar, entertainment. Pool (heated), sauna, gym. Kennel.

Queen. *Inexpensive to Moderate.* 3020 Winchester Ave. Some family units. Pets allowed. Restaurant.

Bardstown

Holiday Inn. *Moderate.* 31E South and Bluegrass Pkwy. Courtesy airport transportation. Restaurant, entertainment. Pool (heated). Kennel.

Old Kentucky Home Motel. *Moderate.* 414 W. Stephen Foster Ave. Coffee maker in room; restaurant nr. Pool, putting green. Some pets. Seasonal rates.

Best Western General Nelson. *Inexpensive.* 411 W. Stephen Foster Ave. Restaurant, coffee shop. Pool, play area. Seasonal rates. Pets allowed.

Bardstown-Parkview Motel. *Inexpensive to Moderate.* 418 E. Stephen Foster Ave. Pool, play area, restaurant. Seasonal rates. Some pets permitted.

Benton

Shamrock Motel. *Inexpensive.* 806 Main St. Some efficiencies. Coffee makers in room. Pets permitted.

Berea

Boone Tavern Hotel. *Moderate.* Berea College campus, US 25 and KY 21. Operated by Berea College and staffed mainly by students. Charming. Restaurant serves regional food. No tipping. Pets accepted.

Holiday Motel. *Inexpensive.* Jct. KY 21 and I-75. Nice decor. Pool. Restaurant nr. Seasonal rates.

Mountain View Motel. *Inexpensive.* Jct. KY 21 and I-75. Pleasant rooms and round-the-clock restaurant. Pool. Pets allowed.

Prince Royal Motel. *Inexpensive.* E. of Jct. I-75 and KY 21. Appealing rooms. Pool. Restaurant. Seasonal rates.

Econo-Travel Motor Hotel. *Inexpensive.* ½ mi. W. on KY 21 at jct. I-75. Color TV, pets. Restaurant near.

Bowling Green

Holiday Inn-Expressway. *Expensive.* Jct. US 231 and I-65. Usual good standards. Pool, play area. Kennel.

Holiday Inn-Midtown. *Expensive.* US 31 W bypass. Courtesy airport transportation. Pool. Entertainment. Kennel.

Ramada Inn. *Expensive.* 3929 Scottsville Rd. Appealing rooms. Restaurant, coffee shop. Pool (heated), play area. Pets permitted.

Red Carpet Inn. *Expensive.* Old Scottsville Rd., Greenwood Int. off I-65. Restaurant, coffee shop, lounge with live entertainment. Pool. Pets accepted.

Best Western Continental Inn. *Moderate.* 411 W. Stephen Foster Ave. Dependable branch of international system. Restaurant, pool (heated). Some pets allowed.

AAA Budget 8 Town Towers. *Inexpensive.* 1 mi. NE. on 31W bypass. Pool, restaurant, room service, bar with entertainment. Free airport bus.

Cardinal. *Inexpensive.* 1310 US 31W bypass. Suitable for families. Restaurant nr. Play area, pool. Some pets allowed.

Day's Inn. *Inexpensive.* I-65 and US 31. Good value. Pool, play area, gas station, gift shop. Tasty World Restaurant. Pets allowed.

3 Penny Inn. *Inexpensive.* 3 mi. E. on 231, ½ blk. E. I-65. Cafe nearby, pets accepted.

Western Hills. *Inexpensive.* 1½ mi. S. at jct. 68, 231, KY 80. Single and family units. Restaurant nr. Play area, pool. Some pets accepted.

Buckhorn

Buckhorn Lodge. *Moderate.* In Buckhorn Lake State Resort Park, off Rte. 28. Handsome rooms overlook lake. Restaurant. Pool (seasonal). Park facilities: fishing, boating (year round), miniature golf, tennis (seasonal). Open May-Oct.

Burnside

7 Gables Motel. *Moderate–Inexpensive.* On US 27. Good selection of rooms. Restaurant. Coffee makers in rooms. Play area, pool. Pets allowed. Open May-mid-Nov.

Cadiz

Lake Barkley Lodge. *Moderate.* In Lake Barkley State Resort Park. Beautiful large lakefront inn; also a few family cottages and efficiency units. Restaurant. Pool (heated) in season. Park facilities: fishing, boating, tennis year round, riding available. Wheelchair units. State operated. Open year round. Seasonal rates.

Carrollton

Gen. Butler Lodge. *Moderate.* In Gen. Butler State Resort Park on US 42. Distinguished lodge and cottages. Restaurant. Some entertainment. Pool (heated), game room. Park facilities: fishing, tennis, golf (year round); beach, boating, miniature golf, pedal boats (seasonal). Pets under control accepted in cottages. State operated. Open year round. Seasonal rates.

Cave City

Holiday Inn. *Moderate.* I-65 and KY 90. Free airport transportation. Restaurant. Pool (heated), 9-hole par-3 golf course adj. Kennel. Seasonal rates.

Best Western Kentucky Inn. *Inexpensive to Moderate.* ¾ mi. W. on KY 70, 90. Restaurant nr. Olympic pool (heated). Seasonal rates.

Quality Inn. *Inexpensive to Moderate.* I-65 and KY 90, 70. Restaurant, coffee shop. Pool (heated), game room, play area, 9-hole golf nr. Seasonal rates.

Ramada Inn. *Inexpensive to Moderate.* I-65 and KY 70. Nicely furnished. Restaurant. Pool (heated). Seasonal rates.

Cave City Motel. *Inexpensive.* ½ mi. NE. on US 31W. Small. Restaurant nr. Play area, pool (heated), tennis. Some pets allowed. Seasonal rates.

Corbin

Howard Johnson's. *Moderate to Expensive.* US 25W at jct. I-75. Usual high standard. Restaurant. Pool (heated), pets allowed.

Dupont Lodge. *Moderate.* In Cumberland Falls State Resort Park. Lodge, cottages and efficiency cottages. Restaurant. Entertainment. Pool (seasonal), game room. Park facilities: fishing (year round); riding (seasonal). Pets under control allowed. State operated; lodge open year round; cottages only mid-Apr. through Oct.

Holiday Inn. *Moderate.* Jct. I-75 and US 25W. Pleasant location. Restaurant. Pool, play area. Kennel.

Quality Inn. *Moderate.* I-75 and US 25E. Restaurant. Pool (heated). Lawn games. Pets allowed.

Days Inn. *Inexpensive.* I-75 and US 25W. One of a chain. Quality at bargain rates. Pool, play area, gas station, gift shop, Cafeteria. Pets allowed.

Covington

Drawbridge Motor Inn. *Expensive.* Jct. I-71, I-75. Spacious rooms, indoor and outdoor pools, barber and beauty shops, over 20 convention and meeting rooms. Several fine restaurants. Various sports, theaters, amusement park, zoo, etc. within a 30-mile radius.

Quality Inn-Riverview. *Expensive.* 666 Fifth St. High rise with elevator. Good selection of rooms. Restaurant with panoramic view, entertainment, coffee shop. Heated pool.

Holiday Inn-Riverfront. *Moderate to Expensive.* 600 W. 3rd. St. Multi-story. Restaurant, entertainment. Pool (heated). Kennel.

Danville

Holiday Inn. *Moderate to Expensive.* Jct. Danville Bypass and US 127S. Newer chain member. Restaurant. Pool (heated), play area. Kennel.

Dawson Springs

Pennyrile Lodge. *Moderate.* In Pennyrile Forest State Resort Park on US 62. Lodge and cottages. Restaurant. Pool (seasonal), game room. Park facilities: fishing (year round), boating, miniature golf, 9-hole golf, riding, beach, pedal boats (seasonal). Pets under control allowed in cottages. State operated. Open Memorial Day-Labor Day.

Elizabethtown

Holiday Inn. *Moderate.* I-65 and US 62. **North.** Jct. US & I-65. Restaurant, entertainment. Pool (heated). Kennel.

Best Western Cardinal. *Inexpensive.* 642 E. Dixie Hwy. Attractive rooms. Restaurant, coffee shop. Pool (heated), play area. Pets allowed.

Days Inn. *Inexpensive.* I-65 and US 62. Branch of popular chain. Pool, play area.

Lincoln Trail Motel. *Inexpensive.* 905 N. Mulberry St. Restaurant; coffee makers in rooms. Pool. Some pets allowed. Seasonal rates.

Motel 6. *Inexpensive.* I-65 and US 62. Pool. Cafe nearby.

Erlanger

Howard Johnson's South. *Moderate to Expensive.* 630 Commonwealth Ave. 24-hr. cafe, bar with entertainment, pool. Free airport bus. Steam bath in some rooms.

Falls of Rough

Rough River Lodge. *Inexpensive to Moderate.* In Rough River Dam State Resort Park on Rte. 79. Pool (seasonal). Park facilities: fishing, boating (year round), beach, golf, miniature golf, riding, tennis (seasonal). Open Apr.–Oct.

Florence

Holiday Inn. *Moderate to Expensive.* 2100 Dixie Hwy. Courtesy airport transportation. Restaurant, entertainment. Pool. Kennel.

Ramada Inn South. *Moderate.* I-75 and US 42. Restaurant, entertainment. Some studios. Pool (heated), sauna. Pets allowed.

Wildwood Motor Inn. *Inexpensive.* 7809 Dixie Hwy. A good selection of nice rooms. Restaurant.

Frankfort

Holiday Inn. *Moderate.* 1 mi. W. of downtown. Some studio rooms. Restaurant, entertainment. Pool. Seasonal rates.

Quality Inn. *Inexpensive to Moderate.* 635 Versailles Rd. Restaurant, coffee shop, bar. Pool. Pets accepted.

Days Inn. *Inexpensive.* I-64 and US 127S. Good value. Tasty World Restaurant. Pool, playground.

TraveLodge. *Inexpensive.* 711 E. Main St. Nice rooms. Restaurant. Pool. Seasonal rates.

Fulton

Holiday Inn. *Moderate.* US 51 at Purchase Pkwy. Courtesy airport transportation. Some suites. Restaurant, pub. Pool (heated), play area. Kennel.

Kingsway Motel. *Inexpensive.* 806 Highland Dr. Restaurant nr. Pets allowed. A good bargain. Pool, play area.

Gilbertsville

Holiday Inn. *Expensive.* US 62 at I-24. Courtesy airport transportation. Restaurant. Pools. 9-hole golf course, play area. Water skiing. Near Kentucky Lake Dam and State Park. Kennel. Seasonal rates.

Ken-Bar Resort. *Moderate.* On US 641. Lakefront, attractive. Some efficiencies. Dining room, coffee shop. Coffee maker in rooms. Pools, fishing, sauna, tennis; riding available. Seasonal rates.

Kentucky Dam Village. *Moderate.* In Kentucky Dam Village State Resort Park, off US 62, 641. Beautifully situated at northern top of the lake. Lodge and family efficiency cottages. Restaurant. Pool (seasonal), game room. Park facilities: fishing, boating, tennis, golf (year round); beach, water-skiing, riding, miniature golf (seasonal). State operated. Open year round.

Greenup

Greenbo Lake Lodge. *Moderate.* In Greenbo Lake State Resort Park on Rte. 1. Attractive rooms with patio or balcony. Restaurant. Pool (seasonal), game room. Park facilities: fishing, boating (year round); beach, pedal boats, miniature golf (seasonal). Pets allowed. State operated. Lower rates Nov.–Mar.

Hardin

Kenlake. *Moderate.* In Kenlake State Resort Park. Lodge and family cottages overlooking bay. Restaurant. Game room. Heated pool (seasonal). Park facilities: fishing, boating (year round), beach, water-skiing, riding, tennis, golf (seasonal). Pets allowed in cottages. State operated. Lower rates Sept.–May.

Harrodsburg

Beaumont Inn. *Moderate to Expensive.* 638 Beaumont Dr. Historic inn, period furniture. Closed Dec. through Feb. Pool. Dining room. MAP available.

Shakertown at Pleasant Hill. *Moderate to Expensive.* At Shakertown, Rte. 4. Many on-the-spot attractions. Authentic 19th-century farm village & period furnishings. Some family units. Restaurant serves all meals. Tasty regional food.

Bright Leaf Motel. *Moderate.* 2 mi. S. on US 127. Pool, golf course, health spa. Restaurant nearby.

Stone Manor Motel. *Inexpensive.* 774 S. College. Nice rooms. Restaurant.

Henderson

Ramada Inn. *Expensive.* 2044 US 41N. Candlelite Dining Room, Quail & Ale Lounge, live entertainment. Pool.

Holiday Inn. *Moderate to Expensive.* 2030 US 41N. Convenient to race tracks. Restaurant, bar with entertainment. Pool. Kennel.

Kentucky Terrace Motel. *Moderate.* 2820 US 41N. Nice grounds. Restaurant. Pets allowed. Pool, play area.

Hodgenville

Lincoln Memorial Motel. *Inexpensive.* US 31E at KY 61. Pool (heated), play area. Restaurant nr. Some pets accepted. Seasonal rates.

Hopkinsville

Holiday Inn. *Moderate.* 2916 Ft. Campbell Blvd. Some studios. Restaurant, bar. Pool. Kennel.

Chesmotel. *Inexpensive.* 2625 Ft. Campbell Blvd. Good for families. Pool, play area. Restaurant nr. Pets allowed.

Colonial Motel. *Inexpensive.* 320 N. Main St. Small comfortable rooms. Restaurant. Pets.

Iv'ry Tower Inn. *Inexpensive.* 2700 Ft. Campbell Blvd. Cheerful rooms. Restaurant, bar, entertainment. Pool (heated), play area, sun deck. Some pets accepted.

Horse Cave

Horse Cave Motel. *Inexpensive.* 319 S. Dixie Hwy. Nice rooms. Restaurant nr. Pool, play area. Seasonal rates. Some pets accepted.

Rodeway Inn. *Inexpensive.* KY 218 at I-65. 24-hr. cafe. Pool.

Jamestown

New Lure Lodge. *Moderate.* In Lake Cumberland State Resort Park on US 127. Fine accommodations in lakefront lodge or family efficiency cottages. Restaurant. Three pools (seasonal). Park facilities: fishing, boating, tennis (year round); golf, miniature golf (seasonal). Pets must be under control. Game room. State operated. Open year round. Seasonal rates.

Pinehurst Lodge. *Inexpensive.* 1 mi. S. on 127. Motel, cottages, some kitchens. Cafe nearby. Pool.

Lexington

Hyatt Regency Lexington. *Expensive.* 400 W. Vine St., at Lexington Center. Downtown. 366-room hotel opened in 1977. Suites available. 3-level enclosed shopping mall, Rupp sports arena and convention center are all connected structurally. Restaurants.

Hilton Inn. *Expensive.* 1938 Stanton Way. Coffee shop, dining room, bar, entertainment, dancing. Pool.

Holiday Inn-North. *Expensive.* Jct. I-75 & Newtown Pike. Restaurant, bar, entertainment. Pool. Pets allowed.

Hospitality Motor Inn. *Expensive.* 2143 N. Broadway. One of chain. Courtesy airport transportation. Nice decor, spacious rooms. Round-the-clock restaurant, bar, entertainment. Pool (heated), sauna, putting green, games. Pets allowed.

Ramada Inn. *Expensive.* 2 locations. Restaurant, bar, entertainment, pets allowed: 232 New Circle Rd., N.W. Courtesy airport transportation; 525 Waller Ave.

Sheraton Inn. *Moderate to Expensive.* I-75, Athens-Boonesboro Rd. 24-hr. restaurant, lounge, pool.

Campbell House. *Moderate to Expensive.* 1375 Harrodsburg Rd. Nice surroundings and decor. Suites available. Restaurant. Pool (heated). Some pets permitted.

Continental Inn. *Moderate to Expensive.* 801 New Circle Rd. Some rooms with terraces or balconies, refrigerators. Deluxe suites available. Dining room, coffee shop, bar, dancing. Pool (heated). Pets accepted.

Holiday Inn. East: 826 Circle Rd. *Moderate.* Restaurant, bar, entertainment. Pool. Pets allowed.

Howard Johnson's. *Moderate.* Two locations. Pool, restaurant, entertainment, pets allowed at both. Some rooms with balcony or terrace. **North:** 1987 N. Broadway. Courtesy airport transportation. **South:** 2280 Nicholasville Rd.

Quality Inn Northwest. *Moderate.* 1050 Newtown Pike. Usual high standard. Restaurant, bar, entertainment. Pool, play area.

Springs Motel. *Inexpensive to Moderate.* 2020 So. Broadway. Some family and efficiency units. Well maintained. Pool (heated). Dining room, lounge, entertainment. Pets allowed.

Airport Motor Inn. *Inexpensive.* Versailles Rd. Coffee maker in rooms; restaurant nr. Pool. Some pets allowed.

Best Western Catalina Motel. *Inexpensive.* 208 New Circle Rd. On hill. Pleasant rooms. Restaurant, bar. Pool (heated). Seasonal rates. Pets allowed.

London

Harvest Inn. *Inexpensive.* Ky. 80 & I75. Convenient to Renfro Valley, Laurel Lake, Cumberland Falls. Steam rooms, restaurant.

Ramada Inn. *Moderate.* 1705 W. 5th St. Dining room, pool, wading pool. Color TV. In-room movies.

Louisville

(Most rates are higher and 3-day min. stay required during Kentucky Derby week).

Breckenridge Inn. *Expensive.* 2800 Breckenridge Lane. Fairly new. Courtesy airport transportation. Pools, health center, tennis, putting green. Restaurant, bar, entertainment.

Executive Inn. *Expensive.* Freedom Way & Phillips Lane. Courtesy airport transportation. Handsomely decorated. Pools (heated), health center, putting green, play area. Restaurant, bar, entertainment. Shops.

Executive West. *Expensive.* Freedom Way at Fairgrounds. Pool, restaurant, bar with entertainment and dancing.

Galt House. *Expensive.* 4th St. & River Rd. High rise with view, suites and two rooftop revolving dining rooms. Entertainment. Health club. Pools, tennis, lawn games, recreation room. Free parking.

Hilton Inn. *Expensive.* 700 Riverside Dr., Jeffersonville, IN. Restful riverside atmosphere, yet downtown Louisville is only 2 minutes away. Most of the 194 rooms provide a beautiful view of the Ohio River and Louisville skyline. Two restaurants, lounge. Racquetball, indoor tennis; WaveTek, Water-Boggan nearby.

Hyatt Regency Louisville. *Expensive.* 320 W. Jefferson. Handsome new 393-room motor inn has heated indoor pool, tennis courts. Fine dining room, lounge, entertainment; and dancing nightly except Sun. Barber and beauty shops.

Louisville TraveLodge. *Expensive.* 401 S. 2 St. Three-story bldg. with elevator. Restaurant, entertainment.

Marriott Inn. *Expensive.* 505 Marriott Dr., Clarksville, IN. Posh 366-room motor inn has resort atmosphere, offers indoor, outdoor pools, indoor, outdoor tennis, miniature golf, health spa, playground, picnic tables, grills. Entertainment, dancing, dinner theater.

Ramada Inn. *Expensive.* 9700 Bluegrass Pkwy. Courtesy airport transportation. Handsomely appointed rooms; suites available. Restaurant, bar, entertainment. Pools (heated), sauna, tennis, putting green. Pets allowed.

Ramada Inn Airport. *Expensive.* 1465 Gardiner Lane. Facing lake. Charming rooms, studios & suites. Restaurant, entertainment. Pool (heated), health center. Some pets accepted.

Rodeway Inn. *Expensive.* 101 E. Jefferson St. Courtesy airport car. Multi-story. Very pleasant rooms & suites. Restaurant, bar, entertainment. Pool (heated). Free parking. Pets accepted.

Sheraton Inn-East. *Expensive.* 9608 Blairwood Blvd. Some studios & suites. Restaurant, bar, entertainment. Pool (Heated).

Stouffers Louisville Inn. *Expensive.* 120 W. Broadway. Twelve-story complex. Handsomely appointed rooms & suites. Pool (heated). Free parking. Restaurant, bar. Some pets permitted.

Holiday Inn. *Moderate to Expensive.* Nine locations in area. All have heated pools & allow pets. Most have entertainment and studios. 1) **Midtown:** 200 E. Liberty St. 2) **Southeast:** 3255 Bardstown Rd. 3) **Central:** Newburg Rd. 4) **Shiveley-SW:** 4110 Dixie Hwy. 5) **Brownsboro NE:** 4805 Brownsboro Rd. 6) **South:** 3317 Fern Valley Rd. No studios. 7) **East:** 1125 Hurstbourne Lane. 8) **Rivermont:** I-71 & Zorn Ave. Coffee maker in rooms. 9) **North:** 342 Eastern Blvd., Clarksville.

Admiral Benbow. *Moderate.* 3315 Bardstown Rd. Courtesy airport transportation. Some studios and suites. Coffee maker in rooms. Restaurant, entertainment.

Howard Johnson's-Downtown. *Moderate.* 100 E. Jefferson St. Multi-story. Courtesy airport transportation. Some studios. Restaurant, bar, pool. Pets.

Howard Johnson's-St. Matthews. *Moderate.* 4621 Shelbyville Rd. Some rooms with terrace or balcony. Restaurant, bar. Pool, play area. Pets permitted.

Best Western Middletown Manor. *Inexpensive.* 12010 Shelbyville Rd., Middletown. Nice rooms & grounds. Pools, tennis, putting green. Restaurant near.

Thrifty Dutchman. *Inexpensive.* Two Locations: 460 Auburn Ave., Clarksville, IN; 3357 Fern Valley Rd. Pool. Restaurant nearby. Some pets allowed.

Lucas

Barren River Lake Lodge. *Moderate.* In Barren River Lake Resort Park on Rte. 31E. Attractive lodge rooms & family efficiency cottages. Restaurant. Game room, pool (in season), tennis. Park facilities: fishing year round, boating, beach, 9-hole golf, riding (seasonal). Pets allowed in cottages. State operated. Open year round.

Madisonville

Ramada Inn. *Expensive.* US 41A bypass at Providence exit. Attractive decor. Restaurant, coffee shop. Pets allowed. Huge pool (heated), sauna, play area.

Madisonville TraveLodge. *Moderate.* Pennyrile Pkwy. Appealing rooms. Restaurant. Pool. Pets accepted.

Downtowner. *Inexpensive.* 320 E. Ct. Center St. Some family units. Restaurant. Pets allowed.

Mammoth Cave National Park

Mammoth Cave Hotel. *Moderate.* KY 70, 10 mi. W. US 31, I-65. Hotel, motel and cottages. Restaurant, camp store, gift and craft shop. Family rates available.

Mayfield

Holiday Inn. *Moderate.* Jackson Purchase Pkwy. Nice rooms; some studios. Restaurant. Pool (heated), play area. Kennel.

Mid-Towner Motel. *Inexpensive.* 512 E. Broadway. Choice of room, studios or efficiencies. Restaurant nr. Coffee maker in rooms.

Middlesboro

Best Western Downtown Motor Lodge. *Moderate.* 1623 E. Cumberland Ave. Pleasant rooms. Olympic pool. Restaurant nr.

Natural Bridge State Resort Park

Hemlock Lodge. *Moderate.* On Rte. 11. Motel rooms & efficiency cottages operated by State. Restaurant. Pool, play area. Pets allowed. Seasonal rates.

Olive Hill

Caveland Lodge. *Moderate.* In Carter Caves State Resort Park on Rte. 182. Lodge & family efficiency cottages. Restaurant. Pool (in season); 9-hole golf year round. Park facilities: fishing year round, beach, boating, pedal boats, miniature golf, riding (seasonal). Some pets allowed. State operated. Open year round.

Owensboro

Holiday Inn. *Moderate.* US 60W. Appealing rooms. Free airport transportation. Restaurant, bar, entertainment. Pool (heated), play area. Kennels.

Imperial Inn. *Inexpensive.* 2609 New Hartford Rd. Some studios. Play area, pool (heated). Coffee shop; restaurant near.

Paducah

Holiday Inn. *Expensive.* 727 Joe Clifton Dr. Amusement park near. Some studios. Courtesy airport transportation. Pool (heated). Restaurant, entertainment. Kennel.

Best Western Paducah Inn. *Moderate to Expensive.* 1379 S. Irving Cobb Dr. Pool, restaurant, bar, entertainment. Some pets permitted.

Diplomat Inn Embers. *Moderate.* 2701 H. C. Mathis Dr. Appealing rooms. Restaurant, entertainment. Pool. Pets allowed.

Paducah TraveLodge. *Moderate.* 1234 Broadway. Some rooms with balconies. Pets admitted. Pool (heated). Restaurant near.

Red Lion Inn (formerly Ramada Inn). *Moderate.* Usual good quality. Restaurant, entertainment. Pool (heated). Pets accepted.

Days Inn. *Inexpensive.* I-24 and US 60W. Cafe, pool. Pets allowed.

Pikeville

Holiday Inn. *Expensive.* 146 S. Mayo Trail. Handsome rooms. Rooftop restaurant. Pool.

Pinson. *Inexpensive.* Pike Ave. at 2nd St. Restaurant (closed Sun.). Some pets permitted.

Pineville

Evans Lodge. *Moderate to Expensive.* In Pine Mountain State Resort Park on US 25E. Lodge & family efficiency cottages. Pool, 9-hole & miniature golf (seasonal).

Game room. Park facilities: fishing (year round), riding, beach, water-skiing (seasonal). Some pets accepted. State operated. Seasonal rates.

Prestonburg

May Lodge. *Moderate.* In Jenny Wiley State Resort Park on Rte. 80. Charming native stone & timber lodge. Restaurant. Pools (seasonal); 9-hole golf, game room. Park facilities: fishing, boating (year round), riding, beach, water-skiing (seasonal). Some pets accepted. State operated. Seasonal rates.

Richmond

Holiday Inn. *Moderate.* I-75 and Lancaster Eastern Bypass. Pleasant rooms & studios. Restaurant. Pool. Kennel.

Knights Inn. *Moderate.* US 25 and 421 at I-75. Color TV, pool.

Somerset

Somerset Lodge. *Inexpensive to Moderate.* 1½ mi. S. on US 27. Courtesy airport transportation. Good selection of rooms. Pool (heated), games. Restaurant. Pets accepted. Seasonal rates.

Holiday Inn. *Moderate.* 1 mi. S. on US 27. Courtesy airport transportation. Pool (heated), play area. Restaurant. Some suites. Kennel.

Williamsburg

Holiday Inn. *Moderate.* KY 92 at US 25W. Dependable standards. Some suites. Restaurant. Pool (heated). Kennel.

Williamsburg. *Inexpensive to Moderate.* KY 92 at I-75. Nicely furnished. Restaurant. Pets allowed. Pool (heated), play area.

Convenient Motor Lodge. *Inexpensive.* 1½ mi. W. jct. KY 92 and I-75. Pool (heated). Restaurant nr. Pets permitted. Seasonal rates.

Winchester

Holiday Inn. *Expensive.* I-64, exit 96. Customary quality. Pool (heated). Restaurant. Kennel.

Best Western Country Squire. *Moderate to Expensive.* 1307 W. Lexington Rd. Some efficiencies. Restaurant. Pets accepted. Pool (heated).

Skylit Motel. *Inexpensive.* 1018 W. Lexington Ave. Color cable TV. Restaurant near. Pets allowed.

 DINING OUT. Kentucky is proud of its "country cooking," with items like Kentucky Country Ham (cured for 1½ days per pound), fried corn, Sally Lynn muffins, chess pie, corn dodgers, and jam cake. You may also enjoy hush puppies, Mississippi and Ohio River catfish and barbecued pork chops. Kentucky eating is hearty and healthy. Many worthwhile restaurants may also be found at the preceding hotels we have listed.

Restaurants are listed by price category as follows: A complete dinner may cost over $15 in our *Deluxe* category; up to $15 in *Expensive;* up to $10 in *Moderate;* up to $7.50 in *Inexpensive.* A la carte meals will bring the tab up. For a more complete explanation of restaurant categories see *Facts at Your Fingertips* at the front of this volume.

Aurora
Brass Lantern Restaurant. *Expensive.* US 68 and KY 80. 107 W. Stephen Foster Ave. Steak, teriyaki shish kebab, grasshopper pie. 5 dining rooms. Reservations except Sat. Closed Jan.-Mar.

Bardstown
Old Talbott Tavern. *Moderate to expensive.* Regional specialties, (including chess pie and country ham), home baking. Pleasant environment in historic bldg. Children's portions. Lunch and dinner.

Jones' Kentucky Home. *Moderate.* In Best Western General Nelson Motel. Wide selection includes country ham and fried chicken. Bar.

Hurst Restaurant. *Moderate.* Homecooked meals.

The Old Stable. *Moderate.* Restaurant, lounge and outdoor cafe. Features steaks, lobster, country ham, prime ribs and seafood. Open for lunch and dinner with live entertainment nightly except Sunday.

Berea
Boone Tavern. *Moderate to expensive.* Student-managed project of Berea College. Delightful colonial atmosphere. Try the spoon bread and chicken flakes "in birds' nests." Children's portions. No tipping.

Bowling Green
Golden Branding Iron. *Moderate to expensive.* 31W Bypass. Charbroiled steaks; make your own salad. Don't miss the fudge nut pie. Children's portions.

Brandenburg
Doe Run Inn. *Moderate to expensive.* Ky. 448 S. Jct. Ky. 1638. Picturesque country inn & restaurant. Features Smorgasborg and regional dishes. Dinner only.

Covington
El Greco. *Inexpensive to expensive.* 2440 Alexandria Pike. Continental-American cuisine, specializing in steak and seafood. Attractive.

Gatehouse Tavern. *Inexpensive to expensive.* Buttermilk Pike, at Drawbridge Motor Inn. Excellent steak, crab legs. Salad bar. Old English decor with wine waiters dressed as monks.

Town & Country. *Inexpensive to expensive.* 1622 Dixie Hwy. Good meals. Kentucky hamsteak vies with skillet-fried chicken as menu favorites. Intimate atmosphere. Dancing, entertainment. Children's portions. Lunch, dinner and midnight snack.

Mick Noll's Covington Haus. *Moderate.* 100 West 6th Street. An 1865 building which served as a firehouse until 1975, when it was refurbished into a fine restaurant serving German and American food and drink. German music.

Danville
ABC Grill. *Moderate.* Homecooked food, pies a specialty.

Elmwood Inn. *Moderate.* Old fashioned meals served in 1880s building.

Harrodsburg
Beaumont Inn. *Moderate to expensive.* KY 68, 127 Country ham and corn pudding are tops. Own baking. Gracious service.

Trustees House. *Moderate.* Shakertown at Pleasant Hill. A part of reconstructed Pleasant Hill Family Houses. Excellent traditional Shaker and Kentucky food served by waitresses in Shaker dress. Open for all meals at set hours. Children's portions. No tipping.

Lexington

Stanley Demos Coach House Restaurant. *Expensive.* 855 S. Broadway. Continental cuisine with gazpacho, Dover sole, red snapper and steak Diane. Open for lunch and dinner. Music. Jackets required at dinner.

Levas. *Moderate to expensive.* 141 W. Vine St. Greek cuisine. Own baking. Children's portions. Family-owned for more than 50 years.

Little Inn. *Moderate to expensive.* 1144 Winchester Rd. Charbroiled specialties and country ham. Buffet lunch Mon. Fri. Children's portions. Open from lunch through dinner.

Red Lion. *Inexpensive to expensive.* In Campbell House Hotel, 1375 Harrodsburg Rd. Steak, lobster, seafood. Children's portions.

Louisville

Old House. *Expensive to deluxe.* 432 S. 5 St. Good selection of French specialties, from onion soup to crêpes Suzette. Early 19th-century house. Open from lunch through dinner. Closed Sun.

Captain's Quarters. *Expensive.* Upper River Rd. at Harrod's Creek. Charming luncheon and supper club. Prime ribs specialty. Entertainment, dancing.

Casa Grisanti. *Expensive.* 1000 E. Liberty St. N. Italian, American dishes. Fettucine and canelloni lead the list of pastas. Family-owned. Impeccable service, dramatic decor.

Embassy Supper Club. *Expensive.* 4625 Shelbyville Rd. Continental cuisine. *Duck à l'orange* a favorite. Open for lunch and dinner. Special after-theater menu from 10:30 p.m.

Bauer's Since 1870. *Moderate to expensive.* 3612 Brownsboro Rd. Popular. German dishes well prepared. Bar, pianist on weekends. Childrens portions.

Bill Boland's Dining Room. *Moderate to expensive.* 3708 Bardstown Rd. Unpretentious 150-year-old farmhouse offers hearty American food in intimate dining rooms. Specialties include steaks, chicken Eugenie, country ham. Children's portions. Friendly, personalized service.

Flagship Restaurant. *Moderate to expensive.* Atop Galt House Hotel. Savor excellent beef and seafood specialties, along with dramatic views of Louisville and the Ohio River.

Hasenour's. *Moderate to expensive.* 1028 Barrett Ave. Fine German (sauerbraten) and regional (country ham) dishes. Music. Open from lunch through dinner daily; Sun. dinner only. Children's portions. Family-owned.

Kunz's The Dutchman. *Moderate to expensive.* 526 S. 4 St. Attractive. Tasty American and German food. Bars. Open lunch through late supper. Closed Sun.

Stouffer's Top of the Tower. *Moderate to expensive.* 101 S. Fifth St., atop 38-story First National Bank and Trust Company. View most of Jefferson County and a stretch of the "Beautiful Ohio" as you feast on such popular Stouffer specialties as pepper steak, beef tenderloin en brochette, roast duckling à l'orange.

Normandy Inn. *Moderate.* 644 W. Washington St. French and American dishes. Roast suckling pig a favorite. Chef-owned. Weekend entertainment. Open for lunch and dinner. Closed Sun.

Owensboro
Skyline Room. *Moderate to expensive.* OBC Tower Hotel, 1926 Triplett St. Unusual 12th-floor dining room offers fine view and food. Steak and prime ribs are staples. Open from breakfast through lunch; for dinner and late snacks. Closed Sun. Children's portions.

Gabe's. *Moderate.* 18th and Triplett Sts. Pleasant atmosphere and nice selection of good food. Lobster tank. Open from lunch through dinner. Buffet lunch. Children's portions. Entertainment, dancing.

Paducah
Stacey's. *Inexpensive to expensive.* 1300 Broadway. Prime ribs specialty. Buffet lunch. Children's portions. Open from early breakfast through late supper. Closed Sun.

Perryville
Elmwood Inn. *Moderate.* 205 Fourth St. Southern fried chicken, country ham, fresh vegetables, fluffy biscuits in elegant classic-columned antebellum plantation home. A favorite of the late Colonel Sanders, who liked the chicken with cream gravy here about as well as his own Kentucky Fried.

Winchester
Old South Inn. *Moderate.* 218 S. Maple St. Country ham, home-baked goods served in Southern mansion. Open from lunch through dinner. Closed Wed.

LOUISIANA

Romantic Outpost of the Old World

BY
KATHERINE SPIELMANN

Katherine Spielmann regularly writes and edits travel books and features.

New Orleans is the home of a unique attraction: the French Quarter, or *Vieux Carré* ("Old Square"), which comprises the original town laid out by the French. There is nothing quite like the atmosphere of these narrow streets with their lovingly restored old buildings, flower-filled patios, antique shops and coffee bars. And for a change of pace after browsing among the Quarter's architectural charms, there are world-famous restaurants, the honky-tonk strip along Bourbon Street, and a few remaining places where authentic New Orleans jazz is still played.

The old buildings of the Quarter are built flush with the *banquette* (sidewalk), with flower- and shrub-crowded patios and courtyards to the rear. Many of these may be visited. In spring, wisteria twines its heavy, grape-like clusters of flowers over wrought-iron balconies, while the courtyards blaze with hedgerows of red and pink azaleas.

A good place to refresh oneself is in the coffee bars of the French Market (toward the end of the walking tour given below). The specialties here include Creole or French (dark-roasted, chicory-flavored) coffee drunk with milk *(café au lait)* and the unperforated square French doughnuts *(beignets)*.

Walking Tour of French Quarter

Walking in the oldest part of New Orleans is much more fun than driving. It's also more practical. You can go at your own pace, pausing to browse and enjoy. Allow about three hours for the tour or longer, if you wish to stop at those sites that are open to the public.

In case you wish to take an abbreviated tour, Items 14–16 and 18–25 are recommended as especially representative of the French Quarter.

A good place to start is at the Visitor Information Center of the Greater New Orleans Tourist and Convention Commission (1) at 334 Royal Street. Here you can have a cup of coffee, pick up brochures and enjoy looking at the building that was the Old Bank of Louisiana. Completed in 1826, this building and the others at this intersection comprised the financial hub of New Orleans.

What distinguishes the Quarter from the rest of the city is that within its area of about a square mile, strict legal ordinances have preserved its original character. Not only are the facades the original ones of French and Spanish design, they are painted in the original colors. This experiment in maintaining historic charm has insured that after over two hundred years the harmony of fanciful iron grillwork, intimate courtyards, and classic French lines remains undisturbed.

Neatly bounded by Decatur Street and the Mississippi River on one side, and by Canal, North Rampart, and Esplanade on the other three, the Quarter is just the right size for a walking tour. In this way, the original creation of architects Latrobe, the Galliers, the De Pouillys, and the Dakins can be examined in the course of one leisurely walk.

Picking up the walking tour, cross Royal to 339 Royal Street (2). The Old Bank of the United States was built in 1800. Its balcony railings are exceptionally good examples of hand-forged (wrought) ironwork.

Cross Conti Street to 401 Royal Street (3) to the Old Louisiana State Bank. Note the bank's monogram ("LB") in the delicate wrought iron of the balcony railing. The Louisiana State Bank, which opened for business in 1821, was designed by Benjamin H. Latrobe, one of the architects of the U.S. Capitol at Washington.

The large white building across the street is the New Orleans Court Building, 400 Royal (4). Erected in 1908-09, this marble edifice occupies a square of ground formerly covered by buildings from the Spanish era. It houses the Louisiana Wildlife and Fisheries Museum.

Across the street at 417 Royal Street (5), Casa Faurie is today a famous restaurant (Brennan's). This mansion was built soon after 1801 for the maternal grandfather of the French Impressionist painter Edgar Degas. In 1805 the newly organized Banque de la Louisiana bought the property, and the bank's monogram ("BL") was added to the balcony railing. In 1819 the bank passed out of existence, and the building became a social center of the city. When General Andrew Jackson visited New Orleans in 1828 he was entertained at several lavish banquets at this house. Later it was sold to Judge Alonzo Morphy, whose son Paul was the chess champion of the world by the time he was 21.

The cross street ahead of you is St. Louis. Turn left and go a block and a half to 820 St. Louis Street (6). This is the Hermann House (The Grima House), built by Samuel Hermann, a well-to-do commission merchant, about 1823. He sold it to Felix Grima, a prominent attorney and notary in 1844. Today it is owned by the Christian Women's Exchange.

Retrace your steps to Royal and turn left. In the middle of the block is 520 Royal Street, Maison Seignouret (7). Originally built in 1816, it was occupied by François Seignouret, a noted furniture maker. It was later owned by the Brulator family, hence the name "Brulator Court." It now houses the radio and TV station WDSU. The patio is open to the public.

Across Royal is 533 Royal Street, Merieult House (8). This building, constructed in 1792, was one of the few that escaped the fire of 1794. It now houses the Kemper and Leila Williams Foundation's Historic New Orleans Collection of maps, prints, drawings, documents and artifacts.

Cross the street to 536 Royal (9). Casa de Comercio is an excellent example of forthright Spanish architecture in New Orleans. This building was built shortly after the December 1794 fire.

Recross Royal to 537 Royal and 710 Toulouse Streets. (10), Court of Two Lions. Much of the novel *Anthony Adverse* was based on the life of Vincent Nolte, who bought this property in 1819 from Jean François Merieult. On the Toulouse Street side is a wide wooden gate in a high wall, with the pillars surmounted by a pair of stone lions.

Return to Royal. Walk one block to St. Peter. Turn left and go to 714 St. Peter Street (11), LeMonnier House. Built in 1829 for Dr. Yves LeMonnier, this house was acquired in 1860 by Antoine Alciatoire, its most notable occupant. Antoine operated a boarding house, and his fame for preparing succulent dishes eventually led to his opening the restaurant that today is known as Antoine's.

Only a few steps away is 718 St. Peter Street (12), Maison de Flechier. It is thought to have been built by the planter Etienne Marie de Flechier just after the disastrous fire of 1794. A bar now occupies both the building and the magnificent courtyard.

Return to Royal. At the opposite corner is 640 Royal Street (13), Maison LeMonnier, known as the "first skyscraper." The three-story structure was built in 1811.

Now turn off Royal into St. Peter. A little more than half a block along is the Spanish Arsenal at 615 St. Peter Street (14). During the years of Spanish dominance this was the site of the prison, or *calabozo*. After 1803 the State of Louisiana constructed an arsenal on this spot. Now the building is part of the Louisiana State Museum complex.

To see the rear of the Spanish Arsenal you should turn left from St. Peter into the short Cabildo Alley, then right into a longer passageway. This is Pirate's Alley (15). Legend has it that Jackson conferred here with freebooters Jean and Pierre Lafitte about the forthcoming defense of New Orleans, but the Alley simply did not exist at that time. It was cut sixteen years later in 1831.

Now walk toward Royal Street. On your right is Royal at Orleans Street, behind the St. Louis Cathedral (16) or Cathedral Garden. The marble monument in the center of this small iron-fenced garden was erected by the Minister of the Navy under Napoleon III to honor thirty French Marines who gave their lives serving as volunteer nurses during a Louisiana yellow fever epidemic. It is also called St. Athony's Square in memory of the most beloved individual in the colony's history, a priest, Antonio de Sedella, who came to the Louisiana colony in 1779.

Cross Royal to Orleans and walk half a block. On your right is a hotel (717 Orleans Street). In the section above the main entrance is a substantial portion of the Orleans Ballroom, or Salle d'Orleans (17). Erected in 1817, this fine ballroom was the setting for the naughty-nice quadroon balls, where mothers would offer their virginal golden-skinned daughters to the aristocratic white men of the city. Each mother hoped that a wealthy man would choose her daughter to be his concubine, setting her up, often for life, in a little house in a special section of the city a few blocks from the ballroom.

Go back to Royal and turn left. On the far side of the Cathedral Garden from Pirate's Alley is Père Antoine's Alley (18), Royal to Chartres Street, between the Cathedral and the Presbytère. Cut in 1831, this passageway memorializes the beloved Capuchin priest Antonio de Sedella.

Follow this passage to its far end (Chartres Street). As you emerge, turn left. The large gray building with iron fence in its arches is The Presbytère (19). The first edifice on this site, a small Capuchin monastery, was destroyed by fire in 1788. In 1793 rich Don Andres Almonester Roxas began construction of what he called a Casa Curial, which in French is a Presbytère, or residence for the clergy serving the parish church. In 1794 fire swept through the structure again. The U.S. took over the Territory in 1803 and completed the building in 1813. But never did it serve as either Casa Curial or Presbytère. In 1853 the city purchased it from the wardens of the Cathedral, and it is now part of the Louisiana State Museum.

As you face the front of the Presbytère, to your left is St. Louis Cathedral (20). This is the oldest active Cathedral in the United States and the third church on this site. The present building dates from 1789-94. In 1964 Pope Paul VI designated it a minor basilica.

Next door, again to the left, is the Cabildo (21). During Spanish rule this structure housed the governing council, or Cabildo, of the colony. The first structure on this site was erected in 1770 but burned in 1788. What you see was built during the period from 1795 to 1799. The balcony railing has been called the finest work from the Spanish period in New Orleans. From this building France, then Spain, then France again, then the United States, the Confederate States and finally the United States again, have governed. On the second floor in 1803 France ceded the territory of the Louisiana Purchase to the U.S. Today a part of the Louisiana State Museum, the Cabildo displays such important items as the "founding stone" of the colony (1699) and the death mask of Napoleon Bonaparte.

Presbytère, Cathedral and Cabildo face the green oasis called Jackson Square (22). Established in 1721 as a drill field, it was known for more than a century as the Place d'Armes (under the French flag) or the Plaza de Armas (under Spain). The plaza acquired its current name in 1848. The statue of General Jackson on his rearing horse was the work of sculptor Clark Mills and was put in place in 1856. It is the world's first equestrian statue with more than one hoof unsupported.

Bordering Jackson Square on two sides you will see the Pontalba Buildings (23). Micaela Almonester de Pontalba, daughter of the colony's richest man in the Spanish period, built the great twin buildings which bear her name. Her plan was to offer luxury apartments and fine ground floor offices and shops. Work was begun in 1849 and both buildings were completed in 1851. The City of New Orleans now owns the St. Peter Street building and the Louisiana State Museum the St. Ann Street one.

At about the middle of the Pontalba Building on St. Ann Street is 525 St. Ann, the 1850 House (24). Here a three-story section of one of the two Pontalba Buildings has been beautifully restored to present a typical New Orleans dwelling of 1850.

As you leave the 1850 House go to your left on St. Ann. At the first corner (Decatur Street) that long, low structure across the street is part of the French Market (25), across from Jackson Square. The French Market dominates a bend of the Mississippi River that forms the waterfront perimeter of the historic French Quarter. Its buildings are distinguished by graceful arcades and stately colonnades that have been a vibrant part of the New Orleans scene for more than 160 years. The French Market is anchored at its downriver end by the popular farmers' market area of open sheds filled with fresh fruits and vegetables. In the Market are longtime shopkeepers as well as many new shops, bistros, coffee stands and craft stalls.

A block down Chartres is the Old Ursulines Convent, 1114 Chartres Street (26). This is one of the oldest structures in the Mississippi Valley. The Sisters of St. Ursula moved into the building in 1749. Theirs was the first nunnery in Louisiana, and they conducted the first Catholic school, the first Indian school, the first Negro school and the first orphanage. The sisters taught the colony's daughters at this site until 1824, then moved to another location outside the city. The Archdiocese of New Orleans is presently restoring the building. The Convent housed the Louisiana State Legislature from 1831 to 1834.

Across Chartres at 1113 Chartres Street is LeCarpentier House, or Beauregard House (27). A New Orleans auctioneer named Joseph Le-Carpentier built this handsome residence in 1827 on land he bought from the Ursuline nuns. With him lived his daughter and her husband, attorney Alonzo Morphy. Here, during the bleak winter of 1866-67 following the end of the Civil War, Confederate General P.G.T. Beauregard, "the Great Creole," rented a room. In recent years the house and garden were the property and residence of the prolific novelist Frances Parkinson Keyes, who adopted New Orleans as her home and wrote many books about the region.

In the same block is Soniat House at 1133 Chartres Street (28.) About 1829 wealthy, aristocratic planter Joseph Soniat duFossat built this place as a townhouse. In the 1860s the wrought iron with which Monsieur deFossat had embellished his home was torn away and replaced by the admirable castiron lacework it now wears.

Proceed to Governor Nicholls Street and turn left to the Clay House at number 618-20 (29). This is a residence built about 1828 by John Clay for his wife. Clay's brother was the famous statesman Henry Clay.

Another building was added after 1871, which in the 1890s was used by Frances Xavier Cabrini—now St. Frances Cabrini—as a schoolhouse.

At the next corner (Royal Street), on your left is a tall building of considerable interest: LaLaurie House at 1140 Royal (30). This is the city's most famous private residence, constructed before 1831 by Louis Barthelemy de MacCarthy. One of his five children, Delphine LaLaurie, acquired the house from her father in August 1831, and it became the scene of brilliant social events. But there was talk about the house: why did the servants seem so broken in spirit and physically emaciated? In 1833 a neighbor accused the glamorous Delphine LaLaurie of mercilessly lashing a small slave girl. Madame LaLaurie was merely fined. Then, on the night of April 10, 1834, a fire broke out. Neighbors attempting to save the contents of the house crashed through a locked door and found seven wretched, starving creatures chained leg and neck in the most painful positions, unable to move. A newspaper the next day suggested that Madame LaLaurie herself had set the fire. Citizens began to mass outside the unhappy house. Suddenly a carriage burst out of the gate and raced away, with the LaLauries in the back. The crowd proceeded to tear down the house in anger. The wrecked building was later restored, but the LaLauries never returned. Not alive, that is. After she died in Europe some years later, Delphine's body was brought back and buried secretly. Ever since, some say, the house has been haunted by groans, screams and the savage hissing of whips.

Cross Royal and enter Governor Nicholls Street again. On your right is Thierry House, number 721. (31). This house, erected in 1814 for Jean Baptiste Thierry, embodies as much of the spirit of ancient Greece as its nineteen-year-old architect, Henry Latrobe, was able to give it, concentrating chiefly on the portico. This modest place started the Greek Revival that so influenced Louisiana architecture.

Go back to Royal. Turn right. On your left will be the Gallier House, 1132 Royal Street (32). James Gallier, Jr., was one of the most illustrious in a long line of notable architects in the city. In 1857 he bought a lot here, then designed and built this residence (1857 or 1858). It has been lovingly restored, presenting an excellent opportunity to see how the wealthy people of New Orleans lived just after the middle of the last century.

As you come out of the Gallier House, turn left, then right at Ursulines Street. Walk one block to Bourbon. Turn left for another block, reaching St. Philip. On the far corner of Bourbon and St. Philip is LaFitte's Blacksmith Shop (33) at 941 Bourbon Street. Just when this place was built or by whom is unknown. The oldest record of ownership dates back to 1772. Legend has it that this was a smithy operated by the dashing brothers Lafitte, the "hero" pirates of New Orleans.

Now return to Royal and turn right. In the middle of the block at 915 Royal stands the Cornstalk Fence (34). The old edifice that once stood here burned, but its most interesting feature remains—a cast-iron fence representing stalks and ears of corn intertwined with morning glory vines and blossoms. There is only one other like it in the city (at 1448 Fourth Street). The fence was cast in Philadelphia by the Wood & Perot foundry and shipped by sea to Dr. Joseph Secondo Biamenti, who bought the house in 1834 and placed the fence around it.

Across the street and a few steps to your right are the Miltenberger Houses, 900-906-910 Royal Street (35). The Widow Miltenberger built the houses in 1838 for her three sons. Her great-granddaughter, Alice Heine, was born in 1910. Alice might be described as the city's greatest social success; she married first the Duc de Richelieu, becoming a duchess, and then Prince Louis of Monaco, becoming a princess.

Continue on Royal to Dumaine. Turn left. About a third of a block from Royal, on the opposite side of Dumaine, is a raised house with a recessed gallery, reminiscent of what is known as West Indian architecture. This place is "Madame John's Legacy," The House of Jean Pascal, at 632 Dumaine Street (36). Many researchers insist it is the oldest building in the Mississippi Valley. The great fire of Good Friday, 1788, which almost totally destroyed New Orleans, also burned this house, but it was soon rebuilt. Records, though scanty, indicate that it was originally erected after the arrival of a ship's captain, Jean Pascal, who reached New Orleans on January 15, 1726. There have been many owners. The current one is the Louisiana State Museum, which renovated the place and fitted it with furniture of the period. The name "Madame John's Legacy" was given to it in a fictional story, *Tite Poulette,* by George Washington Cable.

This ends your walking tour. Now you're on your own.

Beyond the French Quarter

The Garden District offers an interesting contrast to the French Quarter. Instead of buildings fronting the sidewalk with courtyards or patios hidden from the public in the rear, this area has old mansions, most in Greek Revival style, built on spacious grounds abounding with shade trees, shrubbery, and flowers.

A fifteen-minute drive away from the Quarter are the exquisitely beautiful estate gardens of Longue Vue, with a series of cloistered gardens around the spacious greensward and topiary art of the Spanish Court. Each smaller garden has a motif (dolphin fountain, Japanese wall, etc.) whose mood is carried out in the choice of blooms and colors.

The Louisiana Superdome, opened on August 3, 1975, is the world's largest enclosed stadium-arena, covering 52 acres and reaching 27 stories high. It seats more than 80,000 and houses major sports events, including the Sugar Bowl football games; leading entertainers, circuses, trade shows. The Superdome is home of the New Orleans Saints of the NFL. Tours of the Superdome are conducted daily except during certain events; for information write: Tour Director, Louisiana Superdome, 1500 Poydras St., New Orleans, LA 70113.

The New Orleans Museum of Art at City Park has permanent collections of 19th- and 20th-century French paintings and sculpture, and a distinguished pre-Columbian art collection.

The old cemeteries of New Orleans are intriguing; most burial is in tombs aboveground, because of the once-high water table in the swamp-surrounded city. On All Saints Day, November 1, the graves are laden with flowers. It is recommended that visitors go in groups.

For exploring without a car, try the St. Charles Ave. streetcar. It runs under live oaks and past old houses with leaded glass doors, through the garden district, past Tulane and Loyola Universities, to the place where

Points of Interest

1) Absinthe House
2) Broulatour House
3) Cabildo
4) City Hall
5) Civic Center
6) Concert Hall
7) Confederate Memorial Hall
8) Culture Center
9) Eads Plaza
10) French Market
11) Grima House
12) International House
13) International Trade Mart
14) Jazz Museum
15) Lafitte's Blacksmith Shop
16) Louisiana Maritime Museum
17) Louisiana Superdome
18) Lee Monument
19) Little Theater
20) Mme John's Legacy
21) Municipal Auditorium
22) Musee Conti
23) Napoleon House
24) Cid Sazarac Coffee House
25) Orpheum Theater
26) Saint Louis Cathedral
27) Sieur George's House
28) Tulane University Medical Center
29) Ursuline Convent

NEW ORLEANS
DOWNTOWN

PRIEUR

S. ROMAN

N. PRIEUR

CANAL ST.

IBERVILLE

N. ROMAN

ST. LOUIS

ORLEANS AVE.

ST. ANN

DERBIGNY

N. DERBIGNY

N. DERBIGNY

10

CLEVELAND

N. ROBERTSON

ST. PETER

N. ROBERTSON

N. VILLERE

N. VILLERE

ST. PHILIP

MARAIS

GOV. NICHOLLS

ESPLANADE AVE.

LA SALLE

28

6

CULTURE CENTER

21

Beauregard Square

8

Elk Place

BASIN ST.

N. RAMPART ST.

25

V I E U X

C A R R E

COMMON

CANAL ST.

IBERVILLE

BIENVILLE

BURGUNDY

22

TOULOUSE

ST. PETER

ORLEANS

ST. ANN

BURGUNDY

DAUPHINE

URSULINES

GOV. NICHOLLS

BARRACKS

ESPLANADE AVE.

11

HARLES AVE.

1

14

ROYAL

EXCHANGE

CHARTRES

24

CONTI

BOURBON ST.

19

2

26

27

3

DUMAINE

20

16

12

23

Jackson Square

29

AP

DECATUR

DECATUR

COMMON

10

ard of
ade

ETERS

13

9

MISSISSIPPI   RIVER

ALGIERS

the avenue meets the Mississippi River levee. A free ferry across the river leaves every twenty four minutes from the foot of Canal St. and offers a good view of the Cathedral and Jackson Square. Check bookshops for *Trolley Tours,* a sightseeing guide to the streetcar route.

PRACTICAL INFORMATION FOR NEW ORLEANS

HOW TO GET THERE. *By air:* New Orleans is served by Braniff, Continental, Delta, Eastern, American, Republic, Northwest Orient, Lacsa, Texas International, Aviateca, Northwest, Sahsa, Taca, Southwest, Pan-American, Ozark, British Airways. There are direct flights to New Orleans from many cities within the U.S. and from many other countries such as Mexico, Honduras, Guatemala, Puerto Rico and Venezuela to mention some. The airport at New Orleans has many of its facilities adapted to the handicapped and elderly, including available medical service. It is easy to get into, and then get around in once inside, and restroom facilities for the handicapped (wheelchairs included) are available.

By car: I-10 connects with Baton Rouge, Lafayette, Houston, Tex., and points west with New Orleans; I-10 also comes in from Mississippi to the east; I-55 connects New Orleans with Jackson, Miss., Memphis, Tenn., and points to the north; I-59 also comes into New Orleans from Mississippi.

By train: Amtrak and Southern Railways will get you to New Orleans.

By bus: New Orleans is served primarily by Trailways, Colonial Trailways, Greyhound and Venice bus lines. These lines make connections with many other bus lines. Charter buses from all over the country come into New Orleans regularly.

By ship: Passenger and cargo liners from all parts of the world make calls.

HOW TO GET AROUND. There is limousine and bus service from the airport.

By car: American International, Avis, Budget, Dollar, Econocar, Hertz, National, Thirfty all have offices at or near the airport.

By bus: The "Streetcar Named Desire" has been replaced by a bus.

By streetcar: Streetcars still run on St. Charles and Carrollton, starting from Canal St.

By horsecab: Several horse-drawn surreys are available for riding through the French Quarter.

SEASONAL EVENTS. *Carnival* climaxes on *Mardi Gras* (Shrove Tuesday), which varies annually as the 41st day before Easter Sunday, not counting Sundays. Two-week *Spring Fiesta* is held beginning first Friday after Easter, during which tours of the French Quarter, Garden District and plantation homes are arranged. Parade, street dancing and outdoor art show add to fun. Spring Fiesta headquarters are at 529 St. Ann St., New Orleans 70116. *Jazz and Heritage Festival* celebrates crafts, food and music in mid-Apr. There are jazz, ragtime, gospel, blues and country music concerts, parade, river cruise. Write Festival, P.O. Box 2530, New Orleans 70176.

MUSEUMS AND GALLERIES. The *Historic New Orleans Collection,* 533 Royal St., housed in 1792 Merieult House, in the Vieux Carré. Open Tues. through Sat. *Louisiana State Museum,* 751 Chartres St., housed in 1795 Cabildo located on site of the final transfer ceremonies for the Louisiana Purchase. Also includes the 1850 Pontalba House. Open Tues. through Sun.

Art: New Orleans Museum of Art, Lelong Ave., City Park. Free. Closed Mon. and holidays. *Gallier House,* 1118-32 Royal St. Decorative art museum, housed in 1857 Gallier House located on the site of the New Orleans Vieux Carre. Closed Mon. and holidays.

Special Interest: Louisiana's Maritime Museum, located in the International Trade Mart, open daily except Sunday, dedicated to the preservation of Louisiana's maritime heritage. *Pharmaceutical Museum,* 519 Chartres St. Built in 1847 for druggist Louis Dufillo, the museum reflects early history of New Orleans medicine. Open year round. *Confederate Museum,* 929 Camp St. Relics pertaining to military history; Civil War memorabilia. Closed Sundays. *Louisiana Wildlife Museum,* 400 Royal St. Natural history museum. Closed Sat. and Sun.

Others: Musee Conti Museum of Wax, 917 Conti St. Period settings of local history. Open daily except Mardi Gras and Christmas.

 HISTORIC SITES. In New Orleans the *Vieux Carre* (Old Quarter) represents a concentration of historic sites, with the apex at Jackson Square, where the old *St. Louis Basilica* has housed the Catholic See of New Orleans continuously since 1794. It was around this square that Bienville had engineers lay out the city in 1718. For over two and a half centuries the city's history has centered here. Uptown, the *Garden District's* great homes are still maintained as showplaces of the antebellum period. *U.S. Custom House,* 423 Canal St. 4-story 1849 building of granite. The site was once occupied by Fort St. Louis. Used as an office by General Benjamin F. Butler during the Union Army's occupation of New Orleans. Closed wknds. and holidays. Free. *Chalmette National Historical Park,* St. Bernard Highway, State 39. Site of the Battle of New Orleans in the War of 1812. Open daily but closed Mardi Gras.

Historic Houses: Casa Hove, One of the oldest buildings in the Mississippi Valley. Spanish architecture. Closed Sun.

 TOURS. *Bus.* Gray Line offers six tours covering various sections of the city as well as nightlife tours. A wide range of fees, with some special tours including a meal. Tours include French Quarter, Jackson Square, French Market, plantation homes and River Road, Garden District, parks, Mississippi River, bayous, Lake Pontchartrain, old cemeteries, Superdome, Bourbon Street and nightclubs. Hotel pickup and return. Other tour companies such as Southern and Dixieland also run regular tours. Destinations Unlimited offers tours with foreign-language-speaking guides in Limousines. Medicab of New Orleans offers sightseeing trips for the disabled including those in wheelchairs.

Boat. MV Voyageur leaves from foot of Canal St. for cruise into Intercoastal waterway, Bayou Barataria, and return through Harvey Canal. 5 hrs. Harbor cruise to Chalmette Battlefield, 2 hrs. *Mark Twain,* diesel-powered replica of sternwheeler steamboat, leaves Canal St. Dock for bayou trip, 5 hrs.; also a nightly dinner-dance cruise of 3 hrs. *S.S. President,* large sidewheel steamboat, offers a daily 2½ hr harbor cruise, leaving Canal St. dock. Sat. night cruise with jazz band, drinks, dancing. The 1600-passenger sternwheeler *Natchez* leaves from Toulouse St. Wharf at Jackson Square 3 times daily for 2 and 2½ hr. cruises on the Mississippi from Chalmette Battlefield to Huey P. Long Bridge. Moonlight dance cruise Sat. only. Dining rooms, cocktail lounges, snack bar. The *Commodore* leaves three times daily for a 2-hr. cruise to Chalmette National Historical Park. The smaller *Cotton Blossom* makes 1 daily 5½ hr. trip into bayou country.

On foot. The friends of the Cabildo in conjunction with the Louisiana State Museum offers walking tours Tue., Thurs. and Sat. mornings from the Presbytere on Jackson Square. Not available holidays and during Mardi Gras. Destinations Unlimited also offers walking tours with a minimum of five people. If you want to go without a guide check with Tours-on-Tape. They offer taped walking tours as well as taped driving tours.

 GARDENS. During the blooming time of camellias (late Nov. to Mar.) and azaleas (late Feb. to Apr.) New Orleans becomes a huge garden, with concentrated displays in almost all parks. Along the country roads of St. Tammany Parish, across the causeway from New Orleans, the tung trees and azaleas bloom profusely in late March. *Longue Vue Gardens,* 7 Bamboo Rd., off Metairie Rd., includes five gardens on its 8-acre site. Fountains, tropical fruit trees, roses, camellias, azaleas and a wild garden with native iris. Closed Mondays. *City Park* has a Floral Clock 25 ft. across, which operates electrically and a rose garden with azaleas, camellias and gardenias.

 STAGE AND REVUES. The burlesque queens and strippers of *Bourbon Street* are world famous, and they bring back memories and images of New Orleans' notorious Basin Street red-light district. *Saenger Performing Theater* offers regular performances. *Le Petit Theatre du Vieux Carré,* 616 St. Peter St., is one of the oldest community theater groups in the country. The Beverly Dinner Playhouse, at 217 Labarre Rd., presents performances nightly except Monday preceded by a buffet dinner. *Tulane* and *Loyola* also present meritorious productions during the school year.

 NIGHTCLUBS. On Mardi Gras day the whole downtown area and French Quarter are turned into a mammoth "day-club," with drinks (only in paper cups) on the streets and plenty of entertainment from the maskers. Throughout the year, along Bourbon St., at least every third door is a nightclub, with entertainment varying from the predominant bumps and grinds of energetic stripteasers to the music of *Al Hirt* (501 Bourbon) and *Pete Fountain* (New Orleans Hilton, Poydras St. and the Mississippi).

Fat City was never planned—it just happened. The area's high density of apartment dwellers fostered the first lounges more than 10 years ago. In 1972 several nightclub owners were driving around the area trying to create a name for the location. They saw a snowcone stand on the corner of Severn and 17th Sts. where the Lakeside Plaza sign now stands. The two boys had painted the name "Fat City" on it, to mean "you have arrived." The slang term "fat city" depicts affluence and for that reason was to become the name of the area. Just minutes from downtown New Orleans, the area is headquarters for dining and nightlife. It's bounded by Veterans Blvd., North Causeway, West Esplanade and Division Sts. Fat City consists of more than 70 shops, boutiques, restaurants and night spots. Morning Call, one of the French Quarter traditional stops for *café au lait* and *beignets,* has moved to Fat City and is open 24 hours daily.

 SHOPPING. Royal Street in the French Quarter is as filled with antique shops as Bourbon Street is with bars and nightclubs. The best American antiques may be found in the Magazine Street section. Souvenir shops are all over the French Quarter. And don't forget the delectable Creole pecan pralines.

 WHAT TO DO WITH THE CHILDREN. During the ten days or so of *Carnival* parades and especially on *Mardi Gras* (Tues. before Ash Wednesday) children are as delighted as their parents to watch and participate in masking and costuming. *Lake Pontchartrain Amusement Park* has rides. Beside the general sightseeing and walking tour of the French Quarter, several museums appeal to children: *Museé Conti,* 1917 Conti, features life-sized wax figures depicting regional legends and history. Closed Mardi Gras, Christmas. *Doll Museum,* 1218 Burgundy, closed Sun. *Puppetorium,* 514 St. Peter, story of New Orleans performed by automated marionettes; open daily. Special children's tours are available through Bonomolo Limousines and Plantation Tours, and Gray Line Tours. Tours-on-Tape offers special taped walking tours for children of the area around Jackson Square and the French Market. Located at St. Ann and Chartres Sts. Continuous shows from 10 A.M. every day.

 HOTELS AND MOTELS. Minimum night stays are required at Carnival (and during the Sugar Bowl football and sports events at the New Year) than at any other time of the year. Almost all the better hotels and motels in New Orleans have French- and Spanish-speaking staff members. Most people in South Louisiana are bilingual, speaking English and French.

Listings are in order of price category. Based on double occupancy without-meals price categories and their ranges are as follows: *Superdeluxe,* $65 and up; *Deluxe,* $50–$65; *Expensive,* $40–$50; *Moderate,* $30–$40; *Inexpensive,* under $30. For a more complete explanation of hotel and motel categories see *Facts at Your Fingertips* at the front of this volume.

New Orleans Hilton. *Superdeluxe.* Located by New Orleans cruise terminal on the Mississippi. You can get oysters on the half-shell in the lobby. Very plush and new. Everything from atrium cafes to rooftop disco.

Fairmont. *Superdeluxe.* University Pl. Restaurant, coffee shop, bar, top entertainment, color TV, sitter list, 24-hr. rm. service.

Hyatt Regency. *Superdeluxe.* Poydras St. Plaza. Opened 1976. Adjacent to Superdome. 1200 rooms & suites, 5 restaurants & lounges including revolving rooftop lounge, pool, garden patio. Spectacular indoor garden lobby 21 stories high.

International Hotel. *Superdeluxe.* 300 Canal St. Lounge, bar, restaurant, terrace dining room. Pool, sauna.

Maison de Ville. *Superdeluxe.* 727 Rue Toulouse. 18th century building, furnished with antiques. Complimentary breakfast, coffee, tea, soft drinks. Suites with kitchens available. Pool. Small pets permitted.Pool.

Marie Antoinette Hotel. *Superdeluxe.* 827 Toulouse St., in the French Quarter. Attractive rooms. Suites, dining room, dancing in the lounge. Pool.

Pontchartrain Hotel. *Superdeluxe.* 2031 St. Charles Ave. This elegant hotel has a particularly good restaurant.

Royal Orleans Hotel. *Superdeluxe.* Royal & St. Louis Sts. Located on the site and using some of the masonry of the historic old St. Louis hotel (once the state capitol), this plush hotel has a fine restaurant, cocktail lounge with jazz, and coffee shop. Second lounge and pool on rooftop.

Royal Sonesta. *Superdeluxe.* 300 Bourbon St., in the French Quarter. Well-appointed rooms. Dining rooms, pool with service at poolside. Barber shop.

Saint Ann (Formerly French Quarter Inn). *Superdeluxe.* 717 Conti St. Luxury accommodations in the French Quarter. Suites. Pool. Restaurant.

St. Louis Hotel. *Superdeluxe.* 730 Bienville St., in the French Quarter. Suites; some refrigerators. Restaurant. Continental breakfast.

Holiday Inn-Chateau Le Moyne. *Deluxe.* 301 Rue Dauphine. In the heart of the French Quarter. Restaurant, lounge with entertainment. Pool, sauna, health spa.

Bienville House. *Deluxe.* 320 Decatur St. In French Quarter. European atmosphere with iron balconies and courtyard. Restaurant, pool.

De La Poste Motor Hotel. *Expensive.* 316 Rue Chartres. Pool, babysitters.

Inn on Bourbon Street. *Deluxe.* 541 Bourbon. Free parking, pool, cocktail lounge with entertainment, 24-hour food service. Center of Quarter.

Holiday Inn-French Quarter. *Deluxe.* 124 Royal St. Member of the chain. Complimentary coffee. Kennel. Pool. Restaurant, lounge with entertainment.

Holiday Inn-Superdome. *Deluxe.* 1111 Gravier St. In Business district. Restaurant, lounge with live entertainment and 24-foot TV screen.

Maison DuPuy. *Deluxe.* 1001 Rue Toulouse. In French Quarter, near Superdome. Furnished in French Provincial style. Restaurant, cabaret with live entertainment. Food and drinks served in garden courtyard. Pool.

Marriott Hotel. *Superdeluxe.* 555 Canal St. Large hotel with lovely rooms. Dining rooms, coffee shop, lounges with entertainment. Beauty parlor, barber shop. Pool with service at poolside. List of sitters.

Monteleone Hotel. *Deluxe.* 214 Royal St. Largest hotel in French Quarter. Lobby-entrance garage. Rooftop terrace with pool.

Le Pavillon. *Deluxe.* 833 Poydras. Pool, saunas, dining room, bar. Spacious and luxurious. Near the Superdome.

Bourbon Orleans Ramada. *Deluxe.* 717 Orleans St. In the French Quarter. Very nicely furnished rooms. Refrigerators in some. Restaurant. Pool.

Chateau Motor Hotel. *Expensive.* 1001 Rue Chartres. In French Quarter. Patio and poolside cafe. Pets allowed.

Dauphine Orleans Motor Hotel. *Deluxe.* 415 Dauphine St. Continental breakfast. Bagnio Lounge. Pool, pets.

Downtown Howard Johnson's. *Deluxe.* 330 Loyola Ave. Restaurant, pool, indoor car park.

Fountain Bay Club Hotel. *Moderate.* 4040 Tulane. Three pools, coffee shop, dining room, cocktail lounge, entertainment.

Le Richelieu Motor Hotel. *Expensive.* 1234 Chartres St. Refrigerators. Pool.

New Orleans Airport Hilton Inn. *Deluxe.* Airline Hwy., opp. Airport. Putting green, shuffleboard. Free airport transportation.

Place d'Armes Motor Hotel. *Expensive.* 625 St. Ann. Pool, restaurant, patio.

Prince Conti. *Deluxe.* 830 Conti. Heart of French Quarter. Continental breakfast, bar, elegantly furnished suites.

Provincial Motel. *Expensive.* 1024 Chartres St., in French Quarter. Very pleasant rooms with antiques as part of the decor. Restaurant, pool, list of sitters.

Sheraton-Gretna Motor Inn. *Expensive.* 100 West Bank Exprwy., Gretna. Very nice rooms. Pool (heated), restaurant.

Sheraton Inn International Airport. *Expensive.* 2150 Veteran's Memorial Blvd. Restaurant, lounge with entertainment. Large pool, tennis, sauna and health spa. Airport transportation.

Vieux Carré Motor Lodge. *Expensive.* 920 N. Rampart. Sidewalk café; restaurant, bar, pool.

Warwick. *Deluxe.* 1315 Gravier St. Restaurant specializing in New Orleans seafood. Babysitters.

Olivier House. *Expensive.* 828 Toulouse. Small and loaded with atmosphere of old New Orleans.

Quality Inn. *Inexpensive to moderate.* There are three branches in New Orleans area: **Bel-Air:** 4104 Chef Menteur Hwy.; **Capri:** 2424 Tulane Ave.; **East:** 13552 Chef Menteur Hwy.; **Midtown:** 3900 Tulane Ave. All have restaurant, cocktail lounge. Pool and color TV at most.

Ramada Inn. *Moderate to expensive.* At three locations: 1021 Airline Hwy.; **Slidell:** at intersection of I-10, I-12, I-59; **Hammond:** US 51 S. Restaurant, lounge, pool.

Holiday Inn. *Moderate.* There are six branches in the New Orleans area: **East-Highrise:** US 90 & I-10; **Fat City:** Causeway Exit South at I-10; **Airport:** 2929 Williams Blvd.; **Gretna:** 100 West Bank Expwy.; **Slidell:** I-10 & US 190; **Hammond:** US 51 at Jct. I-55 & I-12. All have restaurant, lounge, pool.

Howard Johnson's Motor Lodge. *Moderate.* At two locations: **East:** 4200 Old Gentilly Rd. & I-10 at Louisa St. exit; **Airport-West:** 6401 Veterans Memorial Blvd., Metarie. Restaurant, cocktail lounge, pool.

Patio Motel (Best Western). *Moderate.* 2820 Tulane. Babysitters, family plan. Putting green, 2 pools, free parking. Washerteria.

Rodeway Inn. *Inexpensive to moderate.* At four locations: 851 Airline Hwy. (airport); 930 West Bank Expwy. in Gretna; 6322 Chef Menteur Hwy. Downtown, 1725 Tulane. Restaurant, cocktail lounge, pools.

St. Charles Hotel. *Expensive.* 2203 St. Charles St. Restaurants and lounge. Barber, beauty and other shops. Babysitters.

TraveLodge West. *Moderate.* Five locations in the area: **Downtown:** 1630 Canal; **East:** 5035 Chef Menteur; **Airport:** 2240 Veterans Blvd.; **Lake Forest:** 101000 I-10 service road; **West:** 2200 Westbank Expwy. All are moderate except Downtown, which is expensive.

La Quinta Motor Inn. *Inexpensive.* 3100 I-10 Service Rd., Metairie; and Crowder Rd. off I-10. Pool, 24-hour adjoining restaurant. Children under 12 free.

La Salle. *Inexpensive.* 1113 Canal St. In downtown shopping district. Continental breakfast. Caters especially to foreign visitors.

Scottish Inn. *Inexpensive.* 6613 W. Bank Expwy. (at Garden Rd.); and I-10 and US 190 in Slidell. Attractive place with pool, café, bar.

 DINING OUT. Fine creole cooking is a treat in New Orleans, but other cuisines can also be found here. Classic French fare is also a specialty. See the previous hotel listings for some other good restaurants. Price categories and ranges (for a complete dinner) are as follows: *Deluxe,* $15-19; *Expensive,* $10-14; *Moderate,* $5-9; *Inexpensive,* under $5. Listings are in order of price category. For a more complete explanation of restaurant categories see *Facts at Your Fingertips* at the front of this volume.

EDITOR'S CHOICES

Rating restaurants is, at best, a subjective business, and obviously a matter of personal taste. It is, therefore, difficult to call a restaurant "the best" and hope to get unanimous agreement. The restaurants listed below are our choices of the best eating places in New Orleans, and the places we would choose if we were visiting the city.

LE RUTH'S French Cuisine
Chef Warren Le Ruth owns and operates this remarkable establishment, and the limited French menu perfectly complements the intimate environment. The restaurant is three miles south of the center of the city, across the Mississippi River. Specialties include stuffed soft-shell crab, frog's legs meuniere, and a noisette of lamb for two. Excellent appetizers include Crabmeat St. Francis, and the bread is baked on the premises daily. Franklin St. (Gretna). *Deluxe.*

GALATOIRE'S French/Creole
This old-fashioned, traditional dining room accepts no reservations, but patrons don't seem to mind standing in line watching the passing scene on Bourbon St. Excellent seafood includes Trout Marguery, Trout Meuniere Amandine, and broiled pompano. Excellent appetizers are topped by Shrimp Remoulade, and the Creole gumbo is in a class by itself. 209 Bourbon St. *Deluxe.*

CARIBBEAN ROOM Continental/Creole
Located in the Pontchartrain Hotel, this pleasant establishment provides leisurely dining in its inviting dining rooms and patio. The menu is eclectic, and specialties include Shrimp Saki, Trout Veronique, Steak Diane, and a crepe souffle that must be ordered in advance. Mile-high ice cream pie provides a perfect dessert. 2031 St. Charles Ave. (Garden District). *Deluxe.*

ANTOINE'S French/Creole
This is dining in the opulent, old tradition, and regular customers even have their own personal waiters. The large wine cellar is open to the public and worth a visit. This restaurant can accurately be described as a local landmark, and specialties include Oysters Rockefeller, Pompano en Papillote, and the Tournedos. Crepes Suzette are a favorite sweet, and the menu is full of dishes that are specifically associated with this exceptional establishment. 713 St. Louis St. *Deluxe.*

COMMANDER'S PALACE. French/Creole
Choose between indoor or patio dining at this Garden District landmark, which blossoms with the grandeur of the 1880s. If you order crayfish Etouffe

or crabmeat Imperial, you may give up your landlubbering ways forever. The town turns out in force for the Sunday jazz brunch. Musicians stroll and stomp, and no two corners of the restaurant are on the ground at the same time. Eggs Basin Street make the perfect jazz accompaniment. 1403 Washington Avenue. *Expensive.*

BROUSSARD'S   French/Creole
A grand New Orleans tradition has been reopened. Most attractive interiors and the famous Bonaparte Patio. Cuisine is near perfect and prices most reasonable in the Vieux Carre. Specialties are Duck Nouvelle Orleans, Chicken Ratatouille, Oysters Gresham, Trout Conti and caramel custard. 819 Conti. *Expensive.*

MASSON'S   French Cuisine
Owned and operated by the talented chef, and a fine place for a leisurely and elegant suburban dinner. The quiche is exceptional, and every seafood item is delicious—especially the "marvels of the seas," and sauteed crab "fingers." 7200 Pontchartrain Blvd. (West End). *Expensive.*

MOSCA'S   Creole/Italian
Little atmosphere but the food is something else. Loyal crowd patronizes this restaurant. On Highway 90, in Waggaman. *Expensive.*

Other recommended restaurants:

Andrew Jackson. *Expensive.* 221 Royal St. Elegant service and atmosphere. Tour the kitchen to see the chef prepare trout Meuniere, lump crabmeat or Creole gumbo. Family-owned and operated.

Arnaud's Restaurant. *Expensive.* 811 Bienville St., at Bourbon St. World renowned French restaurant in the French Quarter. Wide selection of delectable dishes on their menu. Specialties: oysters Bienville, shrimp Arnaud and filet mignon Clemenceau. *The Richelieu Room* requires black tie. Children's portions.

Brennan's. *Expensive.* 417 Royal Street. Breakfast has gained renown, but lunch and dinner merit equal attention. Buster crabs Bernaise or poached pompano could make a seafood fancier out of anyone.

Christian's. *Expensive.* 1519 Veterans Hwy. Seafood. Bouillabaisse is a continuing favorite.

Corinne Dunbar's. *Expensive.* 1617 St. Charles Ave. Creole dishes served in a lovely antebellum home with period furnishings. The set menu changes daily.- Reservations required. Closed Sun. and Mon.

Court of Two Sisters. *Expensive.* 613 Royal St. French and Creole menu. In the French Quarter, in a beautiful garden setting.

Etienne's. *Expensive.* 3100 19th St., Metairie. French and Creole menu features trout meuniere and roast chicken.

La Louisiane. *Expensive.* 725 Iberville St. Steak, Italian dishes. Established 1835.

Manale's. *Expensive.* 1838 Napoleon Ave. A popular restaurant, established in 1913 features an Italian menu. Specialty: barbecued shrimp.

T. Pittari's. *Expensive.* 4200 S. Claiborne. Creole cuisine, lobster, beef.

Rib Room of the Royal Orleans Hotel. *Expensive.* Royal & St. Louis Sts. Specialties: rib roast and extensive English and American cuisine. Good wine cellar. Unusually attractive decor.

Sclafani's. *Expensive.* 1315 N. Causeway Blvd. Variety of Italian, American and Creole dishes, served in a Louisiana plantation-style dining room.

Turci's. *Expensive.* 3218 Magazine St. Italian, American menu. Their homemade ravioli is delicious. Children's portions. Reservations advised.

Castillo's Mexican Restaurant. *Moderate.* 620 Conti St. Mexican cuisine. Mouthwatering specialties: nopalitos, puerco en chile Colorado and chilmole Yucateco. Children's portions. Closed holidays.

Charlie Steak House and Bar. *Moderate.* 4501 Dryades St. Chicken, trout and steak are featured at this pleasant dining spot. Closed Sun., holidays.

The Embers. *Moderate.* 700 Bourbon St. Charbroiled steaks are their specialty. Intimate candlelit atmosphere.

Felix's. *Moderate.* 739 Iberville St., between Bourbon and Royal Sts. Seafood is their specialty. The oyster bar is a stopover for everyone. Closed Sun., Christmas, Mardi Gras.

Kolb's. *Moderate.* 125 St. Charles. Authentic Bavarian decor. Schnitzel à la Kolb, imported draft beer. Est. 1899.

Tujagues. *Moderate.* 823 Decatur St. Est. 1856. Well-prepared Creole and French dishes served family style. There is no menu choice. Children's portions. Sun., holidays dinner served from 11 A.M. Closed during Mardi Gras.

A & G Restaurants & Cafeterias. *Inexpensive.* Several locations: 1112 Canal St., 3 Westside Shopping Center, 3800 Dublin St., 2661 Canal St., and 4486 Veterans Blvd. Open for lunch and dinner. Closed Christmas.

Morrison Cafeterias. *Inexpensive.* At 3 locations: 4403 Chef Menteur Hwy., 5516 Veterans Blvd. and 5700 Read Blvd. American cuisine. Wide variety of well-prepared food to choose from. Open for lunch and dinner.

COFFEE HOUSES. Across the square from St. Louis Basilica and down the street are the outdoor coffee houses of the French Market. Although the famed *Morning Call* coffee house has moved to Fat City, the *Cafe Du Monde,* next to the entrance to the Moon Walk (here you can watch the ships and barges make their way along the Mississippi), and the *Cafe Maison,* located a few shops over, offer the weary tourist some of that special New Orleans coffee *(café au lait)* and mouth-watering *beignets* (square, puffy doughnuts always freshly made). Open 24 hours a day the year-round. The French Market has recently undergone a renovation, and in addition to the Moon Walk park area and a parking lot for cars, there are a half dozen shops and boutiques. In one shop you can watch pralines being made daily and can purchase cookery equipment and spices. There's a candle shop, a toy store and several snack spots, as well as a seafood house and the Farmer's Market, where shopping for fresh fruits and vegetables has been a tradition since New Orleans' earliest days. On weekends, the area next to the Farmer's Market is the Flea Market and attracts thousands of tourists and localites. Scattered through the French Quarter are countless other small coffee houses and pastry shops, while the *Gumbo Shop*, at 630 St. Peter, is the place where New Orleans natives go for gumbo and coffee.

Exploring Louisiana

Travel in Louisiana was once determined by its waterways; the vast, serpentine Mississippi and the state's innumerable lakes, rivers, and bayous. (A bayou, by the way, is a marshy inlet or tributary; the word comes from the Choctaw *Bayuk*—"small stream.") The first roads were the navigable streams. Early French explorers followed the great river south as it tumbled the silt of the east down-country toward the Gulf of Mexico. French, German, Acadian, Spanish, and American pioneers followed in time to establish settlements. Frontier river outposts became great cities and picturesque towns, and vast industrial complexes now cover ground where Indians once hunted.

Today, this watery network has been supplanted by a fine highway system, and there is a wide choice of routes for the traveler to explore. For example, if you should be driving southward through the state to New Orleans, it is possible to stop at as many as forty magnificent mansions, gardens, and plantations.

The route described in this guide begins at New Orleans and ends at Shreveport; but if you wish to return to New Orleans, it is possible to do so without retracing your path. This is because the route, in order to give the most complete coverage, outlines the shape of an hourglass, with its corners near the state's four corners and its waist at the state's central city of Alexandria.

The first leg of the journey crosses the state from New Orleans in the east to Lake Charles in the west, taking in Baton Rouge and Lafayette and lingering along the way among the charming and unique attractions of southern Louisiana. Next the route swings up on a long diagonal to Monroe in the northeast, and finally west across to Shreveport, the state's northern industrial center. As will be clear by tracing this itinerary on a map, the "hourglass" may be completed, if you wish to return to New Orleans, by striking southeast on the corresponding long diagonal from Shreveport to New Orleans.

From New Orleans

There are three ways to reach Baton Rouge by car. One way is by Airline Highway (US 61). A faster and more scenic route is along I-10. One elevated portion goes above a corner of Lake Ponchartrain and over the Bonnet Carre Spillway flood control area. The spillway does just what its name suggests; its 350 weirs provide an outlet through which, at high flood stages, the rampaging Mississippi waters may be diverted to Lake Pontchartrain. Since its construction in 1927, the spillway has saved New Orleans from floods several times.

By following the winding River Road (State 48) the visitor will travel along the Mississippi and see a procession of stately antebellum plantation homes, remnants of the class of wealthy planters before the War Between the States.

The first of these are Ormonde (not open to the public) and Destrehan (open daily), both late-18th-century plantation homes.

The River Road changes to State 44 at LaPlace, where crawfish bisque at Roussel's is a good idea if you're hungry.

See San Francisco (open daily), an authentic restoration of mid-19th-century architecture, a Gothic gem, covered with scrolls, fluted pillars and carved grillwork.

Further toward Baton Rouge, there is a free ferry at Lutcher, where you might want to take a detour across the Mighty Mississippi to see Oak Alley (open daily), with its overhead canopy of interlaced branches of huge oaks, one of the state's most famous plantation homes.

North of Oak Alley, on the River Road 2 miles north of White Castle, is Nottoway Plantation (open daily beginning July, 1980), the largest (64 rooms) and most impressive of the antebellum homes.

Come back across the river at Lutcher and continue on State Highway 44 to pass Manressa, a superb columned group of buildings, now a Jesuit retreat for laymen.

All along the River Road there are many south Louisiana-style, small, charming homes and stores amidst the many chemical plants that add to the industrial economy of Baton Rouge and New Orleans.

At Burnside, the River Road changes to LA 75. Continue to Houmas House (open daily), a magnificent restoration of home and gardens. Further on you'll pass Bocage (private), L'Hermitage (private) and Ashland Belle Helene (open and interesting, but not in good condition).

At Geismar, turn off for LA 30 and continue into Baton Rouge.

Baton Rouge

The Indians called it *Istrouma*—a tall cypress, its bark stripped to expose the ruddy wood beneath, adorned with freshly killed game. Set on the bluffs overlooking the river, it marked the boundary between the Houma and Bayougoula tribal hunting grounds. In 1699, someone in the Iberville-Bienville party pushing up the Mississippi marked the spot on his map: *le baton rouge* ("the red staff"). The name stuck.

A good place to take a first look at Baton Rouge is from the observation platform atop the thirty-four-story capitol building (open daily) dating from 1932 and the gubernatorial term of Huey Long. Three years later the colorful and unscrupulous Long, then a U.S. Senator, was assassinated in the same building. His grave and monument now face the capitol.

Amid the twenty-seven acres of formal gardens on the capitol grounds is a curious structure called the Old Arsenal Museum (closed Tuesday). The building is thought to have been used for different purposes in various eras, most recently as a Civil War prison. That it was originally a Spanish arms storehouse is suggested by details such as four-foot thick walls and winding air vents to keep out stray bullets. It is now filled with exhibits on the theme "Louisiana Under Ten Flags."

The Old Capitol, downtown at St. Philip and North Boulevard, has been fondly preserved with its hand-wrought iron fence, spiral staircase, and stained glass skylight. An unusual blend of Norman, Gothic, and Moorish styles, the building was the object of both praise and criticism upon its completion in 1847. Mark Twain called it "the Monstrosity of the Mississippi" and recommended dynamite!

Points of Interest

1) Arsenal Museum
2) Arts and Science Center
3) Cohn Memorial Arboretum
4) Geoscience Museum
5) Governor's Mansion
6) Louisiana State University
7) Magnolia Mound
8) Memorial Stadium

9) Memorial Tower and Museum
10) Museum of Natural Science
11) Old State Capitol
12) Olympia Stadium
13) LSU Rural Life Museum
14) Southern University
15) State Capitol
16) West Baton Rouge Museum

The Old State Capitol, now on the National Register of Historic Places, is open daily and has information hostesses to help you.

Across the street from the Old Capitol is the Louisiana Arts and Science Center Riverside, located in a remodeled railroad station (open daily except Mondays). Here you can find exhibits of art, natural history, anthropology, a gift shop, tea room and such, plus a marvelous viewing area of the port of Baton Rouge.

The Louisiana Arts and Science Center, at 502 North Blvd., was originally the official Governor's Residence. It has been restored and houses Louisiana Governor artifacts and excellent historical exhibits (open daily except Mondays). There is a planetarium next door.

One and one-half miles south of downtown Baton Rouge, on LA 30, is Magnolia Mound Plantation House, a French settler's cottage of 1791. It is open daily (except Mondays) and is an authentic restoration with superb furnishings and interesting out buildings and grounds.

Just south of Magnolia Mound, also on LA 30 is the LSU campus. The school's campus covers more than 200 acres; here and there are Indian mounds estimated to be over 750 years old. There are pleasant lake areas to relax in and a number of museums. The library has a collection of the "elephant folio" prints by Audubon.

The Anglo-American Museum in the Memorial Tower is a gem of a small museum, well worth seeing. LSU Rural Life Museum (Essen Lane at I-10) is a collection of 19th century buildings, including typical plantation buildings.

Two miles south of LSU on La. 42 is Mount Hope Plantation, a magnificent restoration of an early Louisiana home (1817) with West Indian influence (open daily).

Southern University, the nation's largest predominately black university, is located on the bluffs overlooking the river (5 mi. north via US 61).

There is a zoo some distance from the center of town that covers a 140-acre expanse, with walkways through forest settings for more than 400 animals. Cohn Memorial Arboretum (Foster Rd. off Comite Drive) has over 16 acres of rolling terrain covered by more than 120 varieties of trees and shrubs.

Baton Rouge Side Trips

The city may be used as a base for exploring the historic old towns of the surrounding country and the Atchafalaya Basin. Roughly 45 minutes to the west of Baton Rouge, following Interstate 10, lies Henderson, La. where one can arrange boat tours of the Atchafalaya Basin. Contact Mrs. Barbara Hanks at the McGee's Landing. To the north lie the handsome parishes of East and West Feliciana, which must be explored to get the flavor of antebellum Louisiana.

Clinton, thirty-five miles north of Baton Rouge via St. 67, has a stately white-columned courthouse dating from 1838. Facing it is Lawyer's Row, a block of five Greek Revival buildings dating from 1825-30. Scenes from *The Long Hot Summer* and *The Sound and the Fury* were filmed here. Clinton and its outskirts are an antiquarian's dream of pre-Civil War dwellings.

Jackson (State 10 from Clinton) has many old churches and attractive buildings. Further along on State 10 is St. Francisville and a cluster of fine plantation homes. Rosedown, Oakley and Catalpa are the most significant. Propinquity, Asphodel and the Cottage offer overnight accommodations.

Oakley is the place where artist-naturalist Audubon, while serving as tutor to the plantation children, observed, collected, and sketched many of the birds pictured in his monumental *Birds of America*. His method was to shoot the bird, then position it on wires in a lifelike posture for sketching. The excellently furnished and restored home is now a part of the Audubon Memorial State Park. Open daily.

Rosedown (open daily) is another superb restoration of house and grounds with complete furnishings, paintings and accessories. It's a distinguished showplace featuring a 30-acre garden inspired by Versailles, containing rare Oriental plants and statuary. There is a house and garden tour (children are welcome but must be accompanied by their parents to be admitted to the house).

North a few miles from St. Francisville, on US 61, are many more plantation homes. The Cottage Plantation has tours of grounds and out buildings, and provides overnight guest accommodations. Catalpa Plantation, open daily except during December and January, is a manor-type home with original antique furnishings. There is a free ferry at St. Francisville for river crossings, and it is worth taking to get to New Roads. This pleasant town lies on False River, actually not a river but a boomerang-shaped lake that eons ago was part of the Mississippi. (Lakes of this shape are called oxbow lakes.) About three miles northwest of town on the River Road is Labatur, an architectual gem dating from about 1800. A mile further west is another old home, Stonewall.

State 1 follows False River, on whose banks survive such handsome plantation homes as Parlange (open daily) and Austerlitz (not open; can be viewed from road). The road connects with US 190, which can be taken west to Opelousas, one of the state's oldest settlements and a very attractive town. Frontiersman Jim Bowie lived here in his youth. The food here is good, particularly the gumbo at Dedee's Restaurant. In the fall Opelousas holds a yam festival.

Magnolia Ridge, built by a Confederate officer and later commandeered as a Union headquarters, is six miles north of Opelousas on State 10.

Four miles north of town on State 182 is the quaint little town of Washington. In the same neighborhood is Arlington Plantation. Perched over its entrance is an unusual dormer wing, once a classroom for the owner's children.

From Opelousas, US 167 swings southward toward Lafayette, the "hub of Acadiana." Grand Couteau, near Sunset, has two fine old structures dating from the 1830's. St. Charles College now serves as a Jesuit novitiate, while the Sacred Heart Academy is still a girls' school. Both are beautifully landscaped with gigantic oaks and flowering shrubs.

Acadian Lafayette

Lafayette itself, a city of almost 100,000 which bills itself as the industrial and cultural center of the bayouland, is a good base from which to explore the surrounding attractions of Acadiana.

This city, which now boasts a multimillion-dollar Oil Center, was once part of the territory of the Attakapas Indians. Tourist information can

Cajun Country

be obtained from the city's tourist bureau at 16th St. and the Evangeline Thruway.

At University Ave. and Johnston St., the handsome campus of the University of Southwestern Louisiana covers more than eight hundred acres. There are horticultural laboratories, and a Maison Acadienne dedicated to the perpetuation of French and Acadian traditions.

On Mardi Gras, Lafayette's carnival celebration is second only to New Orleans' gala pre-Lenten festival, drawing upwards of 100,000 people. The popular Festivals Acadiens takes place during the third weekend in September, and features Acadian food, music, arts, crafts, and dramatic and literary presentations.

If it is the right weekend in spring for the biennial Crawfish Festival (held in even-numbered years), those who enjoy eating this shrimplike food might want to visit Breaux Bridge, nine miles northeast of Lafayette, for the celebration. Several area restaurants offering country French cuisine serve special dinners of crawfish prepared every possible way, from bisque to boiled to étouffée.

Located just south of Lafayette is The Acadian Village, an authentic Acadian community of the 1800s, and 'Round the World Tropical Gardens.

Southeast of Lafayette is St. Martinville, one of the oldest and most charming small places in Louisiana. In the early days of French and Spanish rule it was known, after the name of the regional tribe, as Poste des Attakapas. Settled in the 18th century by Acadian and French royalist refugees, the town became an early center of culture and elegant living where richly dressed nobles attended luxurious balls and operas; often it was spoken of as "Le Petit Paris."

Later, when the United States took over the Teche country, tensions between the two cultures were expressed in laws which forbade, among other things, biting off ears. The French replied by suspending municipal government until the U.S. came to terms.

The old church on Main Street, dating from 1832, may contain parts of an earlier structure dating from 1765. Exhibited inside are a baptismal font said to have been bestowed on his royalist friends by Louis XVI before his career was ended by the French Revolution, an oil painting of St. Martin, and a replica of the Lourdes grotto. Completing these unusual mementos is a statue of Evangeline, the Acadian heroine made legend in Longfellow's narrative poem, in a little cemetery outside the church. The life-size seated bronze statue was the gift of actress Dolores del Rio, who lived in St. Martinville during the filming of the movie about Evangeline.

The Evangeline Oak, on the banks of Bayou Teche at the foot of Port Street, is the most popular tourist attraction in town. Across the street is the Convent of Mercy, a very old building, once a trading post, now a school run by the Sisters of Mercy.

At the edge of St. Martinville is the attractive Longfellow-Evangeline State Commemorative Area. In this pastoral setting a museum building (the Acadian House Museum), dating from about 1765, contains rustic frontier furnishings of the 18th and 19th centuries. Cajun crafts of weaving, palmetto work, and basketry are displayed and sold in a shop housed in a reproduction of a typical small Acadian farmhouse. Picnic shelters with tables and grills are available in the park; however, camping is no longer allowed on the grounds.

About two miles out of St. Martinville on the Catahoula Road stands Oak and Pine Alley, once the site of the Durand plantation. The story is that Durand, seeking to celebrate his daughter's wedding with something unheard-of, imported giant Chinese spiders to festoon the trees with webs. The great webs were sprinkled with silver and gold dust, it is said, to form a gauzy, glittering archway for the wedding guests.

Further to the northeast is Lake Catahoula, sacred pool of the Attakapas, where there is crabbing, fishing, and a seasonal crawfish harvest.

Fourteen miles south of St. Martinville on State 182 is New Iberia, first settled by Spaniards from the Canary Islands who named it Nuevo Iberia ("New Spain"). The town, billed as "Queen City of the Teche," has a variety of attractions.

Shadows-on-the-Teche, a stately mansion in the heart of town, now the property of the National Trust for Historical Preservation, was built in 1830. Stately moss-draped trees and a formal garden of roses, camellias, azaleas, and other flowering shrubs adjoin a handsome lawn sloping to the banks of the Bayou Teche.

There is an Acadian Regional Tourist Information Center for the town, quartered in a plantation cabin built of native cypress about 1880 (US 90 at State 14). At 541 E. Main is the Gebert Oak, a magnificent specimen shading almost an entire lawn with its limbs overgrown with fern and Spanish moss. It was planted in 1831 by Mrs. Jonas Marsh over the grave of her son.

At Weeks and St. Peter streets is a seven-foot, white marble statue of the emperor Hadrian, created in Rome about 130 A.D.

Three miles east of New Iberia on the Loreauville Road (State 86) is the Justine Plantation and Bottle Museum. The house, built by slave labor in 1822, was moved by barge some fifty miles up the Bayou Teche to its present location. It is built of native cypress and has a Gothic stairway and honeycolored woodwork. The bottle museum is a quaint country store displaying a collection of rare and unusual bottles, from flasks to inkpots to Mason jars.

Six miles further east on State 86 is the Loreauville Heritage Museum. Open limited hours or by appointment. This is a complex of buildings and artifacts spanning three centuries of territorial history. They range from burial-mound objects to the Attakapas Indian Trading post to a turn-of-the-century village complete with log-cabin school, saloon, and country store. (If it's not open when you stop by, knock on the front door of the house in front of the museum, and chances are they'll open it up just for you.)

Seasonal festivals include the fall Sugar Cane Festival in New Iberia, featuring pageants, sports, and dances, and the annual Delcambre shrimp festival and fair. Delcambre, fifteen miles west of New Iberia on State 14 on the old Bayou Carline, is the home port of a colorful 150-vessel fleet of shrimpboats and seafood docks. Deep sea fishing trips are available with prior notification.

Just above Delcambre is Jefferson Island (which, like Avery and Weeks, is not really an island at all). Besides its underground caverns of salt (the eight hundred-foot shaft is no longer open to visitors) Jefferson

Island has a horticultural paradise called Live Oak Gardens. It was once a hideout of Lafitte, and legends of buried booty were substantiated when in 1923 a treasure of gold and silver coins in three pots was uncovered near the Lafitte Oaks.

Later the island was bought by Joseph Jefferson, famous 19th-century actor who portrayed Rip Van Winkle in the dramatic adaptation of Irving's story. The big house built by Jefferson in 1870 from native cypress shows a mixture of Hispano-Moorish, Gothic, and Southern architecture. (Not open to visitors.) Two-thirds of the garden were ruined when a lake and its shoreline fell into a drilled salt dome. It should be open again in Oct., 1982, almost totally restored. The opulent gardens cover twenty acres of woodland, footpaths, fountains, and formal and informal plantings.

Using New Iberia as a base for further forays, a drive nine miles south will take you to Avery Island, a stately showplace developed as a private preserve by two wealthy families. The "island" is a salt dome pushed up from sea-level marshland, producing rock salt from its mine, oil from its wells, and the world-famous Tabasco sauce from its pepper fields. For a fee, the tourist may drive through the two hundred-acre Jungle Gardens, landscaped with native and exotic plants, trees, and flowering shrubs. A giant statue of Buddha stands in a Chinese garden along the route. Bird City refuge attracts nesting egrets and herons in spring.

Weeks Island, another salt mine, is nine miles farther south; and another nine miles south is Cypremort Point, where there is swimming, fishing, and boating on West Cote Blanche Bay, an arm of the Gulf of Mexico.

Before leaving New Iberia to resume the westward journey, you might want to spend some time enjoying the town's own forty-five-acre park on the north bank of the bayou. It has tennis courts, picnic shelters, a pool, and boat-launching ramp beneath centuries-old oak trees.

From New Iberia it is best to return to Lafayette before proceeding. From there, Interstate 10 runs straight west to Lake Charles. (If you wish to curtail touring at this point, there is a choice of retracing your route to Opelousas and from there heading north to Alexandria, or striking north on State 13, further along I-10, after Rayne.)

Frog Festival at Rayne

Rayne, near I-10 and the first stopping place after Lafayette, is known as the Frog Capital of the World. There is a frog festival in the fall, celebrating the town's export of this delicacy to gourmet establishments around the country.

Crowley, eight miles further on, is the center of the country's rice production and home of the October Rice Festival. Irrigation systems transform the vast fields on either side of the highway into lakes each spring, later turning to endless acres of grain. The Chamber of Commerce can arrange visits to rice mills and to a rice experimental station.

Five miles southwest of Crowley off State 13 is the Blue Rose Museum. Built of cypress more than one hundred years ago, the building has the original pegged construction, cypress paneling, handmade bricks, and mud and moss walls. Collections of fine china, cut glass, silver, and antiques are on display. Rice cookbooks and souvenirs are sold.

Lake Charles, Louisiana's third seaport, is the center of an important petro-chemical empire. The port offers a busy scene of American and foreign ships loading and unloading. Visitors are often allowed on board. Lake Charles is the home of McNeese State University (Country Club Road, leading into University Drive). Once a neutral buffer zone between Spanish Texas and American Louisiana, this area sheltered pirates and smugglers. The early May Contraband Days, a festival featuring a water sports carnival, commemorates this tradition.

The Imperial Calcasieu Museum, Sallier and Ethel Streets, has historical exhibits with manniquins in furnished settings and a collection of original Audubon prints. The Sallier Oak is on the grounds; it was planted long ago by Charles Sallier, after whom the city is named.

About seven miles north of Lake Charles off US 171, is Sam Houston State Park. Located on the Calcasieu River amid pine-clad hills, the park's facilities include camp and picnic grounds, stone cabins, and boat facilities with launching sites. Children will enjoy the wild deer compound.

Alexandria-Pineville

Striking north from I-10 some miles east of Lake Charles, US 165 leads toward Alexandria. The drive is about seventy-five miles.

Alexandria and its twin city Pineville on the opposite bank of the Red River mark the geographical center of the state, where the earth shades from red clay to moist black. The first settlements in the area were established in the mid-1700s when a French outpost was placed on the Pineville side of Red River, which separates the two towns. They called the area "Les Rapides" because of the rapids located just above the outpost. Just above the city is the site of Bailey's Dam, an outstanding engineering achievement of the Civil War. When the fall of the Red River trapped the Union fleet above the rapids, its destruction appeared certain until Lieutenant Colonel Joseph Bailey constructed a dam which raised the water sufficiently for the Union warships to navigate the shoals.

The old national cemetery in Pineville is the resting place of war dead from the Indian, Mexican, Civil, Spanish-American, and later wars. Also in Pineville is Mt. Olivet Church, built in 1853. It escaped burning during the Civil War because it housed Union troops.

Each of the twin cities has an institution of higher learning, Louisiana College at Pineville and a branch of LSU at Alexandria.

The Alexandria Museum, open daily, is housed on the Rapides Bank Building, constructed in 1898, at the corner of Main and Murray Streets.

There is a choice of side trips to be made from Alexandria before proceeding northeast to Monroe. Some thirty miles southeast on State 1 is the Marksville Prehistoric Indian Park, containing a number of Indian mounds and a museum of Indian life and art. There are also barbecue pits. A short distance north are the ruins of Fort DeRussy, a Confederate mud fort which fell to Union forces during the 1864 Red River campaign.

All of Alexandria and many plantations and homes in the outlying area were burned during the War Between the States. However, still standing and open to the public is the Kent House, completed in 1800. It was built by the father of one of the members of the board of directors of the Louisiana Seminary of Learning, which opened in 1860 with William Tecumseh Sherman as director. Union troops also spared Rosalie Plantation and Tyrone Plantation, both owned by men serving on the Seminary board of directors.

The seminary burned in 1868 and was moved to Baton Rouge, later becoming Louisiana State University. The site, marked by signs and a few stones, is on Hwy. 71 north.

Some 14 miles northwest of Alexandria, on Bayou Rapides Road, is Hot Wells Health Resort, where mineral waters flow from the ground at a temperature of 113 degrees. Open year-round, there's a bath house, motel and restaurant, and camping grounds.

From Alexandria the most direct route to Monroe is US 165 north. However, if time permits, a westward swing to Natchitoches on State 1 allows more sightseeing. Beyond Natchitoches one can proceed east and north on State 6, US 84, and (at Winnfield) State 34.

If using this longer route, you will find places to visit near Cloutierville. Little Eva plantation is here. Robert McAlpin, a New Englander, was rumored to be the model for Simon Legree in Harriet Beecher Stowe's *Uncle Tom's Cabin*. During the Chicago World's Fair of 1893 one of the plantation's cabins was exhibited as the original home of Uncle Tom. A replica of the cabin along with the "graves" of Uncle Tom and Legree are nearby.

The Bayou Folk Museum in the same area has period furniture and displays depicting the history of the Cane River country. Those who are familiar with the work of Kate Chopin, distinguished author of *The Awakening*, will want to stop here, for the museum was once her home.

North of Cloutierville are Cane River plantations Beau Fort, Oakland, and Melrose, with its famous African House.

Natchitoches

Natchitoches, a charming river town and farm center, is the oldest town in the Louisiana Purchase territory. It was established in 1714—four years before New Orleans—by Louis Juchereau de St. Denis, who built Fort St. Jean Baptiste here as a French outpost and trading center. A replica of Fort St. Jean Baptiste is under construction and will be open to the public.

Front street on Cane River provides the most charming prospect of any town in Louisiana. Many old buildings and antebellum homes remain along the river and side streets. The attractive campus of Northwestern State University dates from the 1880's. A marker on the campus, near Caldwell Hall, identifies the site of St. Denis' home. Four miles north of Natchitoches on the Red River is a one hundred-foot bluff, Grand Ecore, where remains of Civil War entrenchments can be seen. This is also the site where the outdoor dramas and musicals are presented in a huge amphitheater during the summer months.

Once the largest trading post in the South, the quaint town holds an historical tour every fall, when many of the private homes are opened to the public. For sightseers, Natchitoches is a miniature New Orleans. It was here that the El Camino Real (King's Highway) originated, winding westward and southward all the way to Mexico City.

The Cane River Country is the home of Clementine Hunter, sometimes called "the black Grandma Moses," whose bright and gay paintings in the style of the primitive school have attracted national notice. (These are sold, by the way, at the Downtown Gallery in New Orleans, 532 Chartres.)

Visitors who reach Natchitoches during the Christmas season will find themselves winding among a fairyland of lights, for streets, buildings, riverbanks, and bridges blaze with over 140,000 lights.

Between Natchitoches and Winnfield are a complex of lakes and bayous which abound with black bass, bream white and yellow bass, crappie, catfish, and pickerel. Fishermen will have Black Lake, Black Lake Bayou, Clear Lake, Prairie Lake, Saline Bayou, Saline Lake, and Chee Chee Bay to choose from.

Continuing to Winnfield, US 84 leads through a division of Kisatchie National Forest, a huge preserve for wildlife with uncommon species of birds and plants.

Winnfield itself is the center of timber production and the scene, each fall, of the State Forest Festival. For this event the town becomes one huge lumber camp, with the townsfolk dressed in lumberjack gear. Huey Long was born on Maple Street in Winnfield, and practiced law here for several years before entering politics.

From Winnfield, State 34 north leads to Monroe. Monroe on the Ouachita ("Washitaw") River is one of Louisiana's oldest settlements, established in 1785 as Ouachita Post. Later, when the post was stockaded against Indians, it was called Fuerto Miro after the Spanish governor of Louisiana. Its present name came about after the time in 1819 when the steamboat *James Monroe* tied up here. Evidently the visit was so convivial that the townsfolk decided to commemorate it by renaming the town.

In the 19th century, Monroe was a center of cotton production and export. After the discovery that the entire parish of Ouachita rested upon a vast pool of natural gas, Monroe and West Monroe (across the river) became a thriving industrial region.

Attractions in Monroe include Layton Castle, Stubbs House, and Filhiol House. The Masur Museum is an attractive art gallery with educational and cultural exhibits, and there is a Little Theatre housed in the Strauss Playhouse. The Louisiana Purchase Gardens and Zoo has a one hundred-acre park with formal gardens, moss-laden oaks, and winding waterways. The zoo uses natural settings. *Louisiana Legend,* an outdoor drama, is presented summer evenings.

Northeast Louisiana University's campus has an art gallery, and in Hanna Hall there are geological exhibits and displays of Indian, Latin American, and African artifacts.

If there is time for an excursion to the east before heading west for Shreveport, take US 80 east, stopping first at Rayville. A dozen miles south of Rayville on State 135 is Alto, where in 1916 a gas well caught fire. It burned for fifteen years. The crater, three hundred feet across and sixty feet deep, was filled with water to create a swimming pool.

Sixteen miles east from Rayville on US 80 is Delhi, legendary hideout of Frank and Jesse James. The Carpenter House, a stagecoach inn during the 1850's, still stands here.

Poverty Point

About twenty miles from Delhi is the significant prehistoric Indian site of Poverty Point. The route is by State 17 north to Epps about sixteen miles and then right on State 134 for about five miles. A state park with a museum is located at Poverty Point.

The Poverty Point Indians, numbering perhaps as many as six thousand, built their community on terraces more than 2,700 years ago. Although for years Indians relics had been found in the neighborhood, it was not until relatively recently that excavations showed the area's importance. Dr. James A. Ford of the American Museum of Natural History said of it: "Poverty Point is in every way one of the most remarkable sites in the Americas. . . . It is undoubtedly the earliest site yet discovered in the Lower Mississippi Valley and is the most complex and interesting I have seen in this country."

Twenty miles east of Delhi on US 80 is Tallulah, not far from the Mississippi border. It has an interesting courthouse and several plantation homes.

Returning to Monroe, you can now complete the last lap of the "hourglass" tour by heading east toward Shreveport on I-20.

The route passes Ruston, a charming town and the seat of Lincoln Parish, named for Abraham Lincoln in 1873. This area was settled by emigrants from Georgia and the Carolinas who flocked here after the Louisiana Purchase in 1803. Grambling College and Louisiana Tech, an engineering school, are located here. A tourist information center is located in a restored 1890s home on North Vienna Street.

If it is spring, travelers who value scenic routes might want to take a northerly detour at Minden in order to enjoy the eighteen-mile Dogwood Trail Drive. A few miles north of Minden you can stop to see a restored Germantown community. One of the communal villages which were started in hundreds of places throughout the country during the 19th century by various religious and progressive groups, this one dates from 1836. A few of the original buildings still remain, along with the cemetery. The experiment lasted from 1836 to 1871.

Also near Minden is a pine seedling farm that sends out millions of seedlings annually.

To reach the Dogwood Trail Drive, head north on State 7 about four miles west of Minden. At Springhill, the Drive winds west on State 157 to Plain Dealing. It is a drive through the state's highest hills, among flowering dogwood, redbud, and wild flowers.

Shreveport

Shreveport, now a bustling industrial city, has an early history marked by slow and tentative beginnings. The earliest settlers were the Caddo Indians, who built dome-shaped straw houses in circular communities on the bluffs overlooking Red River and its tributaries.

In 1832, modern Shreveport was founded by a group including Captain Henry Shreve, an American trader and steamboat builder. Development of the area was hindered by the presence of a logjam in the Red River, where driftwood, snags, and treetrunks had accumulated for a century and a half. Captain Shreve, who had already aided Louisiana once by bringing supplies to General Jackson in 1814, now invented a battering-ram type vessel to clear away the "Great Raft," as the log jam was called, cutting a navigable channel through it. In 1835, the town was purchased from the Caddos for $80,000.

Today, Shreveport, situated in the center of the Ark-La-Tex (the combined corners of Arkansas, Louisiana and Texas), is one of the country's leading oil- and gas-providing areas as well as a financial, cultural and recreational center for the region.

There are three major annual events at Shreveport. In fall, the State Fair attracts half a million visitors during its ten-day run with music (the city considers itself a Country-Western capital), auto races, rodeo exhibitions, arts and crafts displays, carnival rides, band concerts, and fireworks. Adjacent to the fairgrounds is the Louisiana State Exhibit Museum with its doughnut-shaped exhibit building containing dioramas, an art gallery, historical murals, archeological relics and planetarium.

Another big event is the ten-day Holiday in Dixie each April. It is a round of flower shows, sports competitions, an air show, carnival, treasure hunt, pet show, two fancy-dress balls, and a grand finale parade. The city's brochure promises ten days "packed with a sort of leisurely frenzy!"

Then there's the Red River Revel, held in fall, which is "a celebration of the arts" on the riverfront.

Civil War students will be interested in the site of Fort Humbug, whose weapons were hollowed logs blackened to simulate cannon. This "defense" was set up during the Red River Campaign of 1864 to dissuade Union General Banks from attacking. However, since Banks never reached Shreveport, having been routed in the battles of Mansfield and Pleasant Hill, Fort Humbug was never called upon to fire its unfireable cannon.

There is a branch of LSU and Southern University at Shreveport, and Centenary College, oldest liberal arts college west of the Mississippi, is here, too. A Methodist institution, Centenary was founded in 1825. The Marjorie Lyons playhouse presents dramas throughout the year. Community Theatre has always been active in Shreveport. Besides the Shreveport Little Theatre, there's also the Gaslight Players and a Gilbert and Sullivan Society. With its own symphony orchestra, concerts and opera performances are common occurrences. Famed pianist Van Cliburn makes his home in Shreveport.

The R. W. Norton Art Gallery, on Creswell Ave. in a forty-acre wooded and landscaped park, with azalea gardens, has thirteen exhibition galleries containing European and American painting, tapestries, sculpture, and silverwork. It has a double-elephant folio edition of Audubon's *Birds of America.*

A fascinating display of France's Jean Despujols paintings and drawings of Indochina, which he did between 1936 and 1938, are housed in the Meadows Museum of Art on the Centenary College campus.

The Barnwell Cultural Center, near the city's business district, is an imposing modern structure dedicated to art and horticulture. Plantings are sheltered in a 7,850-square-foot domed conservatory.

Cross Lake, at the city's western edge, offers fishing, hunting, boating, and water sports.

KRMD broadcasts weekly performances of the Louisiana Hayride. The broadcast originates at Hayride USA near Bossier City. One of the Hayride's most famous performers of the past—and it's had nearly all the good ones even remotely connected with the Country and Western field—was Elvis Presley. Hayride USA also has a restaurant and lounge, and dances are held regularly.

The American Rose Center, with its Windsound Carillon Towers, is also located west of Shreveport. Rustic paths wander through 118 acres of water, trees and breathtaking roses in various garden settings.

If you've never seen frisbee golf played, drive along the Clyde Fant Memorial Parkway by Veterans Park. There's even a course laid out for the frisbee throwers.

Across the river in Bossier City is the mammoth Barksdale Air Force Base. For entertainment while in Shreveport, you might try Shreve Square, a cluster of nightclubs, restaurants and shops. There's also what's referred to as the "Bossier City Strip."

Bossier City is home of Louisiana Downs thoroughbred racetrack, with its completely glass-enclosed, air-conditioned club house, grandstand and several restaurants. Track season runs late spring into fall.

The "hourglass" tour is now complete, although, as mentioned before, it is possible to return to New Orleans by a different southerly route, taking in such sights as Mansfield, Many, and Hodges Gardens, 4,700 acres of natural scenic woodlands and formal gardens complete with waterfalls, streams and a beautiful, serene lake. Adjacent to the Gardens is a motel with golf course and tennis courts. Many is just a few miles to the east from Toledo Bend Lake, a bass fisherman's delight that extends north and south along the Louisiana-Texas border. Mansfield is the site of one of the most famous battles ever fought on Louisiana soil. Both sides claimed victory in this bitter battle during the War Between the States, a battle that involved 30,000 men and left thousands dead or wounded. But whether or not you continue, you will have savored during your trip an extraordinary range of flavorsome contrasts: such is the many-layered richness of Louisiana's cultures, histories, and ambiences.

PRACTICAL INFORMATION FOR LOUISIANA

 FACTS & FIGURES. Louisiana was named for Louis XIV of France. Its nicknames are *Bayou State, Sportsman's Paradise, Pelican State.* The magnolia is the state flower; bald cypress, the state tree. The brown pelican is the state bird. "Union, Justice, and Confidence" is the state motto. *Give Me Louisiana* and Jimmy Davis' *You Are My Sunshine* are the state songs.

Baton Rouge is the state capital. The state population is about 3,800,000.

With the exception of some low hill country in the northern part of the state, Louisiana is flat, low Mississippi Delta country. The extreme southern area is a watery region of swamps, marshes, and bayous, the home of trappers, fishermen, and oil (Louisiana is second only to Texas in petroleum output). It is also the second largest mineral producer in the country and first in the annual fur catch. Fishing, both salt and fresh water, is important both to the state's economy and to its sportsmen. Timber is another important source of revenue, and tropical and subtropical crops flourish. Cotton, rice and sugar-cane fields line the fertile banks of the broad Mississippi, which courses down the state to the great port of New Orleans and the Gulf of Mexico. The climate is one of mild winters, hot summers and high humidity. Louisiana is a frequent victim of tornadoes, and the coastal areas lie in the tropical hurricane belt.

HOW TO GET THERE. *By air:* New Orleans may be reached from cities within the U.S.A. on direct flights of: Braniff, Continental, Delta, Eastern, Ozark, Texas International, Southwest and United airlines. Baton Rouge and Monroe on direct flights of: Delta, Southern and Texas International airlines; Shreveport on direct flights of: Delta and Frontier; Alexandria on Delta and Texas International airlines; Lake Charles and Lafayette on Texas International and Commuter airlines; Fort Polk on Commuter airlines, which also serve other cities.

To New Orleans: Delta has direct flights out of Caracas, Venezuela; Aviateca and Taca have direct flights out of Merida, Mexico; Sahsa flys to Honduras and El Salvador; Braniff has a direct flight to Panama City; Aviateca has a direct flight to Guatemala City.

By car: From Picayune, Miss., you can get to New Orleans via I-59. I-55 will take you from McComb, Miss., south to Kentwood and Hammond. I-20 comes in from Vicksburg, Miss., and cuts through the state west to the Texas state line. I-10 enters the state at Vidor, Texas, and goes through the state to Slidell. In the northern part of the state I-20 comes into Shreveport from Texas and continues east. US 71 comes in from Texarkana, Ark., goes south to Shreveport and then southeast to Alexandria and New Orleans. US 61 enters the state at Woodville, Miss., goes south to Baton Rouge and then east to New Orleans. Note: H'way I is best way to go from Shreveport to Alexandria.

By train: Amtrak and Southern Railways trains enter the Union Passenger Terminal in New Orleans.

By bus: Greyhound and Trailways provide the most frequent service, tying in with other major lines. Several other smaller bus lines operate around the state.

HOW TO GET AROUND. *By air:* Delta, Texas International and Commuter airlines service cities within the state. Aircraft charter and rental services, including helicopter, are available.

By car: I-55 will take you from Kentwood to Hammond. I-20, in the north, runs west from Monroe, Ruston, Minden to Shreveport. On I-10 you can go from Slidell east through New Orleans, Baton Rouge, Lafayette, Jennings to Lake Charles. I-12 leads from Baton Rouge east to Hammond and Covington. US 61 goes from New Orleans west to Baton Rouge, then US 190 west to Opelousas. There is no interstate running from north to south through the state. To go from Shreveport to New Orleans, take US 71 to I-10. However, I-10 and I-12 are connected with I-20 by I-55 out of New Orleans through Mississippi, connecting at Jackson, Miss.

Car Rental: You can rent an *Avis, Hertz, Budget* or *National* car in Baton Rouge, Lafayette, Lake Charles, Monroe, New Orleans and Shreveport. Hertz and National also have rental offices in Alexandria, Morgan City, New Iberia and Opelousas.

By bus: Greyhound and Trailways, as well as Arrow Coach, Central Texas Bus Lines, Inc., Great Southern Coaches, Inc., Orange Belt Stages and Salter Bus Lines serve some cities within the state.

By ferry: The Mississippi River may be crossed by ferry at New Orleans, Plaquemine, White Castle, Reserve, Luling, Belle Chase, St. Francisville or at Lutcher.

TOURIST INFORMATION SERVICES. The Greater New Orleans Tourist and Convention Commission at 334 Royal St. will help you plan. The Chamber of Commerce at 334 Camp St., 527-6900, is also helpful. For the rest of the state, inquiries to specific chambers of commerce of cities and towns and to the Louisiana Tourist Development Commission, Box 44291, Baton Rouge

70804, with its 12 information centers around the state, will bring desired information.

Louisiana Wildlife & Fisheries Commission, 400 Royal St., New Orleans 70130, will supply fishing & hunting regulations.

Forest Service, Southern Region, 50 Seventh St., N.E., Atlanta, Ga. 30323, offers information on national forests.

 SEASONAL EVENTS. The annual *Cajun Pirogue* (Indian log canoe) *Race* is held S of New Orleans on Rte. 45 nr. *Lafitte* each year at varying times that the La. Tourist Commission, 334 Royal St., can identify.

Spring: Mardi Gras is the most famous seasonal event in the state, with all-out, 2-wk. celebration in *New Orleans; Shrove Tuesday* celebrations in *Houma* and *Lafayette.* In March, *Lafayette* annually observes the *Azalea Trail; Lake Charles* has a *House & Garden Tour;* Shreveport a 10-day, *Holiday in Dixie* festival celebrating the Louisiana Purchase. Balls, parades, water shows, art exhibits are part of festivities. Lake Charles celebrates *Contraband Day* late May to early June with a water sports carnival.

Summer: The Morehouse rodeo takes place in *Bastrop* in June; the *KC fishing rodeo* in *Houma,* $3, is also in June, while *Ruston* celebrates its *Peach Festival* late in the month. *Many* has its *Arts & Crafts Festival* and Lafayette has its *Food Fest* in June. *Houma's Tarpon Rodeo* takes place in July, $5. *Winnsboro* has a *Deep South Rodeo,* 3 nights in mid-Aug.

Fall: This is the time of harvest festivals: *La. Sugar Cane Fair & Festival, New Iberia,* Sept.; *Festival Acadiens, Lafayette,* Sept.; *International Rice Festival & Frog Derby, Crowley; Sauce Piquante Festival* and *Pirogue Races* in *Raceland; Yambilee Festival* in *Opelousas* all take place in Oct. *Natchitoches* offers its *Historic Plantation Tour* the 2nd weekend in Oct. *Louisiana State Fair,* Shreveport, Oct. Zwolle's *Hot Tamale Festival* is also in Oct.

Winter: Sugar Bowl Festival begins right after Christmas, culminating in Sugar Bowl Football Classic on New Year's Day. *Battle of New Orleans* is celebrated in February at *Calmette National Historical Park.*

 NATIONAL PARKS AND FORESTS. Campsites and trailer space, as well as picnicking facilities are available throughout the nearly 600,000 acres of the *Kisatchie National Forest* in central and northwest Louisiana. Eleven recreation centers, open year round. Most are located on lakes or streams; and all have grills and sanitary facilities. A nominal charge is made for fishing, for duck hunting, and for boats. Reservations should be made through the Forest Service, U.S.D.A., Box 471, Alexandria 71360.

Chalmette National Historical Park, E of New Orleans on State 46, commemorates the last battle of the War of 1812. The American victory here assured westward expansion, and Gen. Andrew Jackson became nationally known. Beauregard House, an antebellum mansion, serves as information center, with exhibits and audio visual program concerning the battle of New Orleans. The 1-mi. battlefield tour road begins at Chalmette National Cemetery. Closed Shrove Tuesday, Christmas.

 STATE PARKS. There are 25 state parks and commemorative areas in Louisiana, all but three permit picnicking, 10 permit camping and four have cabins.

Audubon Memorial State Park, nr. *St. Francisville* on State 965, is the site of Oakley Plantation House, a museum of Audubon memorabilia, with period furnishings. Formal garden, picnicking, hiking trails. *Bogue Falaya Wayside Park, Covington,* has a natural beach, picnicking on its 13 acres. *Fort Jesup State Monument,* 6 mi. E of *Many* on State 6, is the site of the antebellum garrison. Replicas of 2-story brick and frame building and an original army field kitchen. Museum, picnicking. *Fort Pike State Monument,* US 90, 30 mi. E of New Orleans. Picnicking. *Lake D'Arbonne State Park,* off Rte. 33 W of Rte. 15 nr. *Farmerville,* 90-acre wooded lakeside area with picnicking, boating, water skiing. *Longfellow-Evangeline State Park,* 3 mi. NE of *St. Martinville* on Rte. 31, on banks of Bayou Teche, has restored Acadian house, kitchen garden, craft shop, replica of Acadian cottage. Museum, picnicking, swimming, boating, fishing. *E.D. White State Park* on Rt. 1 North of Thibodaux features a museum in the 1790 boyhood home of U.S. Chief Justice White.

CAMPING OUT. Ten of the state parks provide campsites.

Chemin à Haut State Park, 522 acres E of Rte. 139, 10 mi. N of *Bastrop,* is portion of road used by Indians. Picnicking, swimming, boating, fishing, camping. *Chicot State Park,* 6,500 acres in Evangeline Parish, 6 mi. N of *Ville Platte* on State 3042, features an artificial lake, picnicking, fishing, camping, swimming, water sports. *Fairview Riverside Park,* 2 mi. E of *Madisonville* on State 22, is 98-acre woodland on banks of Tchefuncte River. Picnicking, camping, fishing, swimming. *Fontainebleau State Park* in *Mandeville* on US 190, has nature trails, ruins of a plantation brickyard and sugar mill, camping, picnicking, water sports.

Grand Isle State Park, on State 1, in *Jefferson Parish,* is an 140-acre site with access to Gulf of Mexico. Beach, fishing, jetties, camping facilities, picnicking. 50c fee for day use for all wheeled vehicles. *Lake Bistineau State Park,* E of State 163 nr. *Doyline.* 750-acre pine forest. Picnicking, swimming, camping. *Lake Bruin State Park,* E of US 65 nr. *St. Joseph.* 50 acres, with picnicking, swimming, camping, boating, fishing. *Lake Claiborne State Park,* 7 mi. SE of Homer, on State 146. 97-acre woodland area, with picnicking, swimming, camping, fishing.

Sam Houston State Park, 12 mi. N of *Lake Charles* on State 378. Densely wooded, 1,068-acre tract with lagoons, nature trails. Picnicking, boating, fishing, water skiing, camping.

TRAILER TIPS. The Federal forest area, *Kisatchie,* provides trailer space at six of its recreational areas, but no connections.

Of the state parks listed above, all but Grand Isle have water and electricity hookups with dump stations. Because Louisiana is an outdoors state, commercial campsites complete with all hookups can be found around the state, not only on the main highways and interstates, but in interesting places off the beaten path. Permits for trailers over legal size may be obtained from the Division of State Police, Permit Section, P.O. Box 1791, Baton Rouge. Oversize are those with length over 60 feet; width of 8 feet; and height of 13 feet, 6 inches. Others require no permits.

HOT SPRINGS. The state-owned and operated *Hot Wells Health Resort,* with adjoining comfortable motel and restaurant, is on State 121 nr. *Boyce,* about 20 mi. from Alexandria. Hydrotherapy equipment and state-approved masseurs provided. The resort has a foot pool with the mineral water and an open-air swimming pool.

MUSEUMS AND GALLERIES. *Lafayette Museum,* 1122 Lafayette St., *Lafayette,* was home of Gov. Alexandre Mouton. Furniture, historical documents, portraits, Indian artifacts. Tours. Closed Mon. & holidays.

Imperial Calcasieu Museum, 204 W. Sallier St., *Lake Charles,* contains Victorian period furnishings, Gay Nineties barber shop, glass, crystal. Tour. Closed New Year's, Easter, Christmas wk. Free. *Bayou Folk Museum,* off State 1 in *Cloutierville,* nr. Natchitoches, displays an extensive collection of period pieces, artifacts and memorabilia of the area. Sat. & Sun. only.

Louisiana State Exhibit Museum, 3015 Greenwood Rd., *Shreveport,* tells history of state through murals, dioramas. Glass, china, paper money, Indian artifact collections. Free.

In *Baton Rouge,* the *Old Arsenal Museum* houses historical exhibits in bldg. used by Federal troops during Civil War. The *Rural Life Museum,* Burden Research Center on LSU campus, is comprised of blacksmith shop, general store, overseer's cottage typical of 18th- & 19th-century plantation life.

Hanna Hall at *Monroe's* Northeast Louisiana U. campus, houses American Indian, Latin American and African artifacts.

Loreauville Heritage Museum, 9 mi. NE of New Iberia in *Loreauville,* is a 40-unit village and farm, telling history of territory. Dawn to dusk.

Art Exhibits. *Art Center for Southwestern Louisiana,* Girard Park Dr., *Lafayette.* Permanent and changing exhibits. Closed New Year's, Mardi Gras, Thanksgiving, Christmas.

McNeese State U. Auditorium Gallery, Lake Charles, has monthly exhibits by students, faculty, guest artists. Closed school vacations.

R. W. Norton Art Gallery, Creswell Ave., *Shreveport,* features a large collection of Remington and Russell works, also has fine permanent collection of American, European paintings and sculpture. Closed Mon., holidays. Free.

Meadows Museum of Art on Centenary College campus, has a collection of paintings and drawings of Indochina by Jean Despujols.

Altus Museum at Alto is primarily a "doctor's" museum.

In *Monroe, Masur Museum of Art* has regular exhibits, and *Bryan Hall Art Gallery,* Northeast Louisiana U. campus, sponsors shows by American and foreign artists, students and faculty during the school year. Free.

Special Interest Museums. In *Baton Rouge,* LSU's *Geoscience Museum, Museum of Natural Science,* Foster Hall. *Louisiana Arts & Science Center & Planetarium,* 502 North Blvd., houses paintings, sculpture, cultural, historical, scientific exhibits. Closed Mardi Gras, holidays. Planetarium shows: late May to Labor Day. Museum free. *Museum of Natural History,* LSU campus.

Natural History Museum & Planetarium, 637 Girard Park Dr., *Lafayette,* maintains an environmental trail, changing exhibits. Closed Mardi Gras, holidays. Museum free.

HISTORIC SITES. Throughout Louisiana are numerous antebellum homes, many open to the public. *Kent House State Commemorative Area,* in *Alexandria,* is the oldest house in central Louisiana. On 4-acre site, *Oakley,* on State 965, approx. 25 mi. N of Baton Rouge in Audubon Memorial State Park, has Audubon memorabilia. Mon. to Sat., 9 to 4:45, Sun. from 1. Closed major holidays. *Rosedown,* on State 10, E of *St. Francisville,* has antique furnishings, 17th-century gardens. *Cottage Plantation* was started in 1795. On grounds are smokehouse, school, slave cabins. 6 mi. N of *St. Francisville. Locust Grove Cemetery,* NE of *St. Francisville* on US 61, contains graves of Sarah Knox Taylor, wife of Jefferson Davis, and Gen. Eleazar W. Ripley, War of 1812 hero. *Fort Jesup State Monument,* 6 mi. E of *Many* on State 6, is site of antebellum garrison. Replicas of 2-story brick and frame bldg. and an original army field kitchen. *Mansfield Battle Park,* 4 mi. S of *Mansfield* on State 175 is site of last battle of

Civil War in La. Monuments, museum, military artifacts. Picnicking. *Marksville Prehistoric Indian State Monument,* nr. *Marksville* on State 5, is site of Indian settlement of 2,000 yrs ago, and of Civil War ammunition supply point. Museum, picnicking. State 44. 18th-century furnishings, landscaped grounds.

St. Martinville, E of New Orleans on US 90, is center of legends surrounding Longfellow's *Evangeline.* In the churchyard of *St. Martin of Tours Catholic church,* 133 S. Main St., is the grave of the poem's heroine, Emmeline Labiche. The *Evangeline Oak* still stands at the end of Port St. *Evangeline Museum,* 429 E. Bridge St., and Longfellow Evangeline State Park's *Acadian House Museum* reconstruct Acadian life.

Edward Douglass White Memorial, 5 mi. N of *Thibodaux,* on State 1, includes restored homestead of Chief Justice of Supreme Court.

Oak Alley, in *Vacherie,* is a Greek Revival mansion, built in 1830's. Live oaks line a corridor from the house to the river.

Parlange Plantation in *Mix,* State 1, is noted for rare "bousillage" architecture.

Houmas House, State 44 in *Burnside,* is a large plantation house, restored to its original state, with typical furnishings.

Near *Franklin* are two outstanding houses. *Oaklawn Manor,* 5 mi. off US 90, has a large grove of live oaks and lovely gardens. *Albania Mansion,* nr. Jeanerette, 14 mi. from Franklin on US 90, features a 3-story spiral staircase.

In Natchitoches, *Roque House,* Riverbank Dr. nr. Keyser Ave. Bridge, is a restored French Colonial home.

Shadows on the Teche, 117 E. Main St., *New Iberia,* is a gracious 2-story, 16-rm. townhouse set among live oaks. *Justine,* originally built in Franklin in 1822, was added to twice and moved to New Iberia by barge. Victorian furnishings.

In *Reserve, San Francisco Plantation* house is 2 mi. upriver on State 44. 18th-century furnishings, landscaped grounds.

Winter Quarters, Antebellum home in Newellton.

 FAMOUS LIBRARIES. Several million manuscript items of Louisiana are in the *Archives of the Louisiana State U.* at Baton Rouge, open daily 8 A.M. to 10 P.M. Also on display here are four Audubon folios, as well as about 150 framed sheets from other folios. Notable manuscripts of Lafcadio Hearn and others are available for short periods daily at *Tulane University Library* in New Orleans.

 TOURS. *Louisiana Lagniappe Tours* offers tours of Baton Rouge and nearby plantations. *Delcambre,* 15 mi. W of New Iberia on Rte. 14, offers tours aboard paddlewheeler *Cajun Belle. Passe Partout Touring Co.,* 329 Beverly Dr., Lafayette, offers special interest & offbeat tours in Acadian country. *Old Natchitoches Tours* offers city and Cane River Plantation Tour and cruises on the *Cane River Belle.*

 SPECIAL INTEREST TOURS. Alexandria's *Southern Forest Experiment Station,* 2500 Shreveport Hwy., opens its research facilities to the public Mon. to Fri.

The *U.S. Agricultural Experimental Station,* 1½ mi. S of Tallulah on US 65, conducts research into insects that attack cotton.

Carville Hospital, approx. 20 mi. S of Baton Rouge, is the only hospital in the continental U.S. which cares for victims of Hansen's disease. Tours daily.

Tours of Atchafalaya Basin are available from Henderson.

GARDENS. Avery Island's *Jungle Gardens,* off State 329 via a toll road, is a 300-acre paradise, with camellias blooming Nov. to April, iris Mar. to July, azaleas late Feb. to late Apr. Also featured are tropical plants, sunken gardens, a Chinese garden with a centuries-old Buddha, and a bird sanctuary where egrets nest.

Hodges Gardens, 15 mi. S of *Many* on US 171, is a 4,700-acre garden in a forest. There are experimental areas, wildlife refuge, wild and cultivated gardens in bloom yr. round. In Dec. there's a Christmas Light Tour. Picnicking, boating, swimming and fishing also avail.

Live Oak Gardens, (closed until Oct. 1982) on *Jefferson Island,* is a very traditional English garden, featuring azaleas, camellias, wisteria, oleanders, as well as a fountain walk and Alhambra Garden. Self-guiding trails, picnicking. There are greenhouses displaying orchids and other tropical plants, some of which can be purchased seasonally.

Rosedown Plantation and Gardens, St. Francisville, is a magnificently restored antebellum home with 17th-century style French formal gardens.

In *Monroe, Louisiana Purchase Gardens* is a 140-acre garden and zoo with over 8,000 plants and 800 animals.

In *Shreveport,* the *Barnwell Center Botanical Gardens* are open Mon. to Fri., 9 to 4:30; Sat. and Sun. from 2 to 5. The American Rose Center features roses from April through December, but other flowers and plants bloom year-round.

Walter Jacobs Nature Trail is open to the public.

Bossier's Cypress-Black Bayou Recreation Area has a 1½ mile hard surface nature trail for the handicapped and elderly.

Around the World Tropical Gardens, adjacent to the Acadian Village at Lafayette, features a horticultural walking tour of the world's warm weather areas.

Afton Villa Gardens, N. of Baton Rouge, has a Gothic gate house, beautiful gardens and a great oak alley.

Longue Vue Gardens, series of varied gardens complemented by statues, pebbled walkways, patios and graceful fountains.

 MUSIC. In *Shreveport* music enthusiasts can attend a number of concerts and musical offerings ranging from classical to country. The *Community Concert Association* brings major symphony orchestras, Metropolitan Opera stars and instrumentalists. The *Shreveport Symphony* brings guest artists, presents two performances a month during its season. The *Civic Opera Society* also brings in guest stars for its productions. Country & western fans will want to check out the *Louisiana Hayride,* broadcast over KRMD every Sat. night, followed by a big dance. *Centenary College Choir* is internationally known, regularly appears at the Convention Center, Hodges Gardens and on local TV stations. Pop band concerts are held at Centenary College's Hargrove Amphitheatre during the summer.

 STAGE AND REVUES. In *Shreveport,* one of the best known community theater groups of the country has a yr.-round *Little Theater.* Summer stock is represented by the *Gas Light Players;* Centenary College's *Jongleurs* regularly presents plays at Marjorie Lyons Playhouse.

The *Monroe Civic Center* brings Broadway plays, leading entertainers, ice shows and the circus regularly.

DRINKING LAWS. Liquor sold by package and drink at stores or establishments with a license. Sunday sales optional in some locations. None may be imported from another state. The minimum age is 18.

SPORTS. *Fishing,* both fresh- and salt-water is a year-round sport. Spanish and king mackerel, jewfish, marlin, bluefish, cobia, channel bass, pompano, red snapper and common jack are found in the coastal areas and Gulf of Mexico. Tarpon fishing below Houma and Grand Isle is becoming increasingly popular. Crawfish are found inland and are a popular food in Louisiana. Many consider Louisiana a bass fisherman's dream because of all the lakes to be found around the state. Many are manmade, which means there are lots of brush and tree stumps left, making for good bass fishing. Crappie fishing is also popular. Boats, tackle and bait are available everywhere. Nonresident fishing license costs $6; a 7-day license, $3. No license is required for salt-water fishing.

Hunting, concentrated generally during the winter, requires a non-resident license for 3 days, $10; for a season, the fee is $25, excluding bear, deer and turkey. These require an additional $20 fee. Louisiana's coastal marshes provide a winter home for ducks, turkey, wildfowl using the Mississippi flyway. Turkey, squirrel and deer inhabit the pine hills and swampland.

Licenses and information available from Wild Life and Fish Commission, 400 Royal St., New Orleans 70130.

Swimming is available at the following recreation areas: Bogue Falaya Wayside, Covington; Chemin-A-Haut, nr. Bastrop; D'Arbonne Lake, Farmerville; Fontainebleau, Mandeville; Grand Isle, off Rte. 1; Lake Bistineau, S of Doyline; Lake Bruin, NE of St. Joseph; and at Cotile Reservoir, 20 mi. W of Alexandria.

Golf is popular throughout the state. *Alexandria: Bringhurst Park,* off Masonic Dr., 9 holes. *Lafayette: City Park Golf Course,* Mudd Ave. & 8th St. *Shreveport: Andrew Querbes Park,* Gregg & Fern Sts. *Lakeside,* Milam St., *Huntington,* Pines Rd.; *New Orleans: Lakewood Country Club* sponsors Greater New Orleans Open every spring.

SPECTATOR SPORTS: New Orlean's *professional football team, Saints,* plays at Superdome. LSU's athletic teams play major competitors at Baton Rouge.

Racing: Thoroughbreds at *Evangeline Downs,* Lafayette, from early Apr.-early Sept. *Fair Grounds Race Track,* New Orleans, was established in 1872. Late Nov. to late Mar. *Jefferson Downs Race Track,* 44th St. & Williams Blvd., Kenner, has night races April to Nov. (with a short interruption during the season). Quarter-horses and thoroughbreds race at Delta Downs in Vinton for much of the year. Thoroughbreds run at Louisiana Downs, Bossier City, from late spring into the fall.

WHAT TO DO WITH THE CHILDREN. *Louisiana Purchase Gardens and Zoo,* off I-20, *Monroe,* exhibits rare animals in modern buildings, some glass-fronted, some moated. Nocturnal animals are shown under red lights. The entertainment section has a Lewis & Clark Railroad, boat rides, and other amusement rides. Baton Rouge and Alexandria also have zoos, with children's rides at Alexandria.

In *Shreveport, Ford Park* at Cross Lake on S. Lakeshore Dr., open May to Oct., daily. *Hamel's Park* is a small but good amusement park with nine outside rides, including a train and a roller coaster, and another half-dozen or so rides inside for rainy days. There's a Frisbee golf course on Clyde Fant Parkway.

INDIANS. Only one Indian reservation still exists in Louisiana. It is located nr. Charenton, about 4 mi. from Baldwin, 25 mi. W of Morgan City on US 90. Only a few Chitimacha Indians live there. A small settlement of Houmas is located nr. Kraemer (Rte. 20 and 307 N from Thibodaux), where they have their own chapel and school. The Koasati maintain their own trading post

3 mi. N of Elton. Their charmingly designed baskets, decorated with alligators, armadillos, frogs and turkeys, make fine souvenirs of the piney woods. The Tunica-Biloxi Indians maintain a trading post nr. Marksville, selling beadwork, basketry, wood carvings and metal work.

There are many ceremonial mounds in Louisiana. Among the more notable are: Poverty Point, West Carroll Parish. One of the largest in the state, believed to have been built by one of the oldest cultures in the Northern Hemisphere: Tensas Parish's Lide Mounds, off Rte. 605; Balmoral Mounds, off US 64, Newellton; Marksville's Prehistoric Indian Museum and Park; Brannin Mound in Franklin Parish, 240 ft. long, 130 ft. wide, 22 ft. high; Little River Mounds, LaSalle Parish, evident along river.

 HOTELS AND MOTELS. Most of the state's establishments are less expensive outside New Orleans. There are many "chain" motels along I-10 and I-12. One practical note: many of the motels in Baton Rouge are along US 61 from New Orleans north and US 190, which runs east-west. Both of these routes pass along the edge of the city on US Bypass 190. A few hotels and motels are within the downtown or capitol area. An Airline Highway address in Baton Rouge is located along the US 61 and 190 bypass.

Based on double occupancy without meals, price categories and ranges are as follows: *Deluxe,* $60 and up; *Expensive,* $45–$60; *Moderate,* $30–$45; *Inexpensive,* less than $30. Listings are in order of price category. For a more complete explanation of hotel and motel categories see *Facts at Your Fingertips* at the front of this volume.

Alexandria

Howard Johnson's Motor Lodge. *Expensive.* Free library. Olympic pool, nightly entertainment, free local calls.

Ramada Inn. *Expensive.* Pool, free saunas. Restaurant and cocktail lounge.

Rodeway Inn of America. *Expensive.* Pool. Restaurant and cocktail lounge adj. Free parking.

Sheraton Inn. *Expensive.* 2716 MacArthur Dr. Cafe, bar, entertainment, pool.

Alexandria TraveLodge. *Moderate.* Lounge and restaurant. Pitt Grill and shopping area nr.

Holiday Inn. *Moderate.* Member of chain. Restaurant and bar.

Baton Rouge

Baton Rouge Hilton. *Deluxe.* I-10 at College Drive. In Corporate Square, 31-store enclosed mall. 3 restaurants, 2 cocktail lounges, nightclub with live entertainment. Tennis courts, pool, health spa. Fully stocked bars in rooms.

Sheraton Baton Rouge Hotel. *Deluxe.* I-10 at College Dr. Large motor inn. Suites. Restaurant, lounge with entertainment, coffee shop. Pool (heated). Golf nr.

Capitol House. *Expensive.* Convention & Lafayette Sts. (downtown). Roof deck pool over Mississippi River. Elegant cocktail lounge and restaurant. Free lobby-entrance garage. 24-hr. cafe.

Prince Murat. *Expensive.* 1480 Nicholson Dr. Nicely decorated rooms. Pool, dining room, coffee shop, bar.

Ramada Inn. *Expensive.* 10330 Airline Hwy. Pool and kiddie pool, restaurant, bar.

Baton Rouge TraveLodge. *Moderate.* 427 Lafayette St. (downtown). Some rooms have river view. Pool, café, coin laundry.

Bellemont Motor Hotel. *Moderate.* 7370 Airline Hwy. Restaurant, coffee shop, bar, and pool.

Best Western Inn. *Moderate.* 5955 Airline Hwy. 5 miles to downtown, 7 miles to LSU.

Holiday Inn. *Moderate.* At three locations: 10455 Reiger Rd. **South:** 9940 Airline Hwy. **West:** I-10 & State 415. Coffee shop, pool, bar, free airport transportation. Kennel.

Howard Johnson's Motor Lodge. *Moderate.* 2365 College Dr. Babysitter list, restaurant, pool, shuffleboard.

Oak Manor Motor Hotel. *Moderate.* 8181 Airline Hwy. Luxurious rooms and suites on 14 acres of landscaped grounds. Old English Manor restaurant. Bar, pool, free parking.

Rodeway Inn. *Moderate.* I-10 and S. Arcadian Thruway. Pool, restaurant, cocktail lounge, live entertainment.

Days Inn. *Inexpensive.* I-10 & State 415. Pool, restaurant, play area.

Lafayette

Best Western-Evangeline Inn. *Expensive.* Restaurant, pool, lounge with entertainment.

Holiday Inn. *Expensive.* At two locations: **South:** US 90E. Airport 1 mi. Free transportation. **North:** on US 167 at jct. I-10, lounge, entertainment. Restaurant, bar, pool.

Howard Johnson's Motor Lodge. *Expensive.* Attractive rooms, color TV. Pool with service at poolside, play area. Restaurant, lounge.

Lafayette TraveLodge. *Expensive.* At two locations: **Center:** 1101 Pinhook Rd. **North:** 251 Frontage Rd. (US 167) at Willow St. Restaurant, pool, lounge with entertainment.

Rodeway Inn. *Expensive.* 24-hour restaurant, lounge with entertainment. Pool. Transportation to airport.

Sheraton Town House Motor Hotel. *Expensive.* Nice rooms, 3 dining rooms, cocktail lounge with dancing and live entertainment nightly. Pool.

Ramada Inn. *Moderate.* Restaurant, lounge with entertainment. Pool.

Imperial '400' Motel. *Inexpensive.* Pool. Business center.

Lake Charles

Downtowner Motor Inn. *Expensive.* On beautiful Lake Charles. Pool, restaurant, bar.

Howard Johnson's Motor Lodge. *Expensive.* Restaurant, bar, pools, play area. Children under 12 free.

Sheraton-Chateau Charles Motor Inn. *Expensive.* Children free. Pool. Restaurant with first-class French cuisine.

Holiday Inn. *Moderate.* Pool, restaurant, cocktail lounge.

Many

Toro Hills Hotel. *Expensive.* At entrance to the 300-acre Hodges Gardens. Spacious rooms overlooking pool and patio. Fine restaurant. Tennis courts and pro golf courses; private club.

Monroe

Holiday Inn. *Expensive.* Restaurant, pool.

Howard Johnson's Motor Lodge. *Moderate.* Across from Civic Center. Pool, play area, restaurant nr.

Ramada Inn. *Moderate.* Restaurant, grill, bar, pool, free saunas.

Rodeway Inn. *Moderate.* Glenwood Dr. in West Monroe.

Natchitoches

Holiday Inn. *Expensive.* Very pleasant rooms with color TV. Suites. Restaurant, lounge with live entertainment. Kennels. Free airport transportation.

Revere Inn Motel. *Inexpensive.* Restaurant. Kitchenettes available.

New Iberia

Holiday Inn. *Expensive.* Decor follows railroad theme in Park Station Restaurant and Railhead Lounge.

Acadiana Motor Lodge. *Moderate.* Restaurant, bar, pool. Entertainment.

Opelousas

Downtowner Motor Inn. *Inexpensive.* Pool, restaurant, and bar.

Ruston

Holiday Inn. *Moderate.* Pool and restaurant. Kennel.

Shreveport

Chateau. *Deluxe.* 201 Lake St. Cafe, bar, entertainment, pool. Free in-room movies. Free airport transportation.

Hilton Inn, Bossier. *Deluxe.* I-20 at Airline Exit. Restaurant, lounge, disco.

Regency. *Deluxe.* Spring and Lake. Free airport transportation. Restaurant, lounge.

Sheraton-Bossier Inn. *Deluxe.* 2015 Old Minden Rd., Bossier City. Attractive rooms, some with king-size beds. Suites. Restaurant, lounge with dancing and entertainment. Pool with service at poolside. Free airport transportation.

Ramada Inn. *Expensive.* 5116 Monkhouse Dr. Pool, restaurant, and cocktail lounge with dancing.

Sheraton Inn-Shreveporter. *Expensive.* 3880 Greenwood Rd. Children free; play area and pool. Luxurious rooms.

Holiday Inn. *Expensive.* Three locations. **West:** 4900 Greenwood Rd. N off I-20. **North:** 1906 N. Market St. US 71 & State 1. List of babysitters, kennel. **Bossier City:** 150 Hamilton Rd. (off I-20). All with restaurant, bar, pool, color TV and free airport transportation.

Howard Johnson's Motor Lodge. *Expensive.* 5101 Monkhouse Dr. Pool, kids playground; restaurant and lounge. Local calls are free and there is a free library and morning paper. Rates increase during State Fair.

Palace Inn. *Expensive.* 1968 Airline Dr., Bossier City. Pleasant rooms. Complimentary coffee. Babysitter list. Restaurant. Pool.

Days Inn. *Moderate.* Also in Bossier. Pools, restaurant.

Western Hills Inn. *Moderate.* 3515 E. Texas St., Bossier City. Restaurant, lounge, and pool.

 DINING OUT in Louisiana often means the same fine creole cooking you can experience in New Orleans, as well as seafood specialties and the ever-present steak houses, fried chicken emporia, and occasional oriental establishments. Because of Louisiana's proximity to our southernmost neighbor, there are also many places featuring Mexican-style cuisine. For other worthwhile restaurants, check our hotel listings.

Restaurants are listed in order of price category. Price categories and ranges, for a complete dinner, are as follows: *Expensive:* $8-$12.75; *Moderate:* $5-$8; *Inexpensive:* $3-$5. For a more complete explanation of restaurant categories see *Facts at Your Fingertips* at the front of this volume.

Alexandria

Don's Seafood. *Expensive.* Excellent French cuisine.

Rapides Cotton Gin. *Expensive.* 3807 Prescott Rd. Located in an old cotton gin. Steaks, seafood. Dinner served daily from 5:30 P.M.

Herbie K's. *Moderate.* Specialties: oysters on half shell, other seafood, Cajun dishes, and steaks. Children's portions. Closed Sun.

Plantation Manor. *Moderate.* Seafood, steak. Crab-stuffed eggplant is great. Chef owned.

Piccadilly Cafeteria. *Inexpensive.* At two locations: 1400 MacArthur Dr., in MacArthur Village Shopping Center; and 3451 Masonic Dr., in Alexandria Mall Shopping Center. Try their spaghetti and meatballs. Children's portions. Closed on Christmas.

Baton Rouge

The Chalet Brandt. *Expensive.* 7655 Old Hammond Hwy. French cuisine is featured. Swiss Chalet decor. Choose wine to complete your dinner from their excellent wine list. Chef-owned. Medaillons de veau are a favorite. Pastries made on the premises. Closed Sun.

Mike and Tony's. *Expensive.* 10270 Airline Hwy. Tempting steaks and seafood à la Louisiane highlight the menu. Children's portions. Closed Sun.

Ralph and Kacoo's. *Expensive.* 7110 Airline Hwy. Open daily. Specializes in seafood—crawfish, crab, shrimp, trout meuniere, catfish. Also in New Orleans.

The Village. *Moderate.* 8464 Airline Hwy. Excellent Italian cuisine. Pasta and pastnes are homemade. Dining room has pleasing decor. Children's portions. Closed Mon.

Piccadilly Cafeterias. *Inexpensive.* Five locations: 332 S. Sherwood Forest Blvd.; Cortana Mall, 8953 Florida Blvd.; Delmont Village, 5179 Plank Rd.; Westmoreland Village, 3164 Government St., Mid City. Excellent food for the price. Wide variety of food on the menu. A la carte.

Lafayette

Chez Pastor. *Expensive.* 1211 Pinhook Rd. Cuisine with a flavoring of Cajun and a touch of Creole.

Jacob's Fine Foods. *Expensive.* 1600 Cameron St. Very popular in the area. Relaxed and friendly atmosphere. Acadian and French cuisine. Seafood is their specialty. (shrimp de la Teche is very special). Children's portions. Closed Christmas and New Year's Day.

Lake Charles

Chateau Charles Restaurant. *Expensive.* On US 90 at the Sheraton Chateau Charles Motor Inn. Locally popular. Serves a variety of well-prepared American and Louisiana French dishes. Children's portions.

Chez Oca. *Expensive.* 815 Bayou Pines Dr. Owned by a former New Orleans chef. Coat and tie for evening requested. Wine cellar.

Plantation House. *Expensive.* Seafood (crayfish in season and crabmeat Imperial lead the list), own baking. Chef owned.

Terre Haute House. *Expensive.* 311 Hudson Lane. Features seven-course dinners.

Monroe

Bamboo Restaurant. *Moderate.* Hwy 80 East. Specializes in Chinese and American dishes.

Piccadilly Cafeteria. *Inexpensive.* In the Twin City Shopping Center. Extensive and varied menu. Closed Christmas.

Natchitoches

Lasayone's. *Inexpensive.* 622 Second St. Nationally known for its Natchitoches meat pies.

New Iberia
The French House. *Moderate.* Cajun dishes are featured at this pleasant dining spot. Try the crawfish, gumbo or other seafood as well as their steaks. Closed first 2 weeks in July; Christmas, New Year's Day; Labor Day.

Opelousas
Palace Cafe. *Moderate.* 167 W. Landry St. Gumbo, crawfish, seafood and steaks are specialties at this restaurant. Creole and Cajun menu. Family-operated since 1927.

Shreveport
Don's Seafood and Steak House. *Expensive.* 3100 Highland Av. Cajun dishes, seafood and steaks. Other Don's in Baton Rouge, New Orleans and Lafayette.

Ernest's Supper Club. *Expensive.* 612 Commerce St. Downtown. Known for its seafoods. Live entertainment.

Firenze. *Expensive.* 1846 Fairfield. A very fine, plush restaurant featuring Northern Italian and French cuisine in the Florentine manner. Adjacent lounge with live entertainment.

Sansone's. *Expensive.* 701 E. Kings Hwy. Steak, Italian and seafood dishes highlight the American, Continental menu here. There is a combo and vocalist for your listening and dancing pleasure nightly, except Sun. Children's portions. Bar is closed on Sun.

Smith's Crosslake Inn. *Expensive.* 5301 Lakeshore Dr. Seafood, steak and Crosslake catfish attract locals as well as visitors.

Cypress Inn. *Moderate.* A catfish restaurant featuring Atchafalaya catfish and char-broiled steaks. Located in nearby Benton. Closed Sunday and Monday.

Nanking Restaurant. *Moderate.* 614 Milam. In downtown Shreveport. Specializes in Chinese and American dishes. Open until 4 A.M. Closed Sundays. Local nightime gathering place of entertainers and night people.

MARYLAND

The Genteel Border State

BY
VICTOR BLOCK

Victor Block, a lifelong resident of the Maryland area, has contributed articles about the state to leading newspapers and magazines for over a decade. He has written and edited several books, and currently writes for the Joyer Travel Report, *a monthly newsletter that stresses tips on stretching the budget and travel to out-of-the-way destinations.*

You may go from Washington to Baltimore on the Baltimore-Washington Parkway, or by way of I–95 or the more crowded US 1. Once you get there, you'll enjoy the attractions of one of the most vibrant cities in the United States.

Numerous magazine and newspaper articles have recounted this dramatic turnabout. "Look What's Happened to Baltimore" is the way LIFE magazine titled a 1980 story that called Baltimore "the most downright livable major city in the U.S." It is fitting that during 1979, in the midst of this flurry of redevelopment and new construction, Baltimore celebrated its 250th anniversary.

The city's renaissance actually got underway in the early 1960s with a downtown renewal effort. Today, visitors see towering office complexes designed by such leading architects as Mies van der Rohe, I. M. Pei and Edward Durell Stone. The Inner Harbor area has been cleared of warehouses and old piers, and redeveloped into a 95-acre recreational park and plaza, site of a continuing series of ethnic festivals, concerts, art shows and other activities during much of the year. Harbor Place, opened in 1980, contains some 140 shops, boutiques and restaurants.

Neighborhood renewal and urban "homesteading" programs are continuing to transform worn, blighted sections of the city into a showcase of what imaginative restoration can accomplish. The modern $47 million convention center, which opened in 1979, is attracting major events. The subway system, when completed, will provide ready access to sightseeing attractions.

There are twin centerpieces to Baltimore, both with much to offer visitors. One is the redeveloped Inner Harbor, which serves as a reminder that the city has been a seaport since Colonial days. The picturesque setting includes the U.S. Frigate *Constellation*, the oldest navy ship still afloat, and a World War II submarine; a public marina; tour boats; rental sail and paddleboats; and the largest aquarium in the U.S.

The second attraction results from restoration of entire neighborhoods. Baltimore's redevelopment program has been cited by the International Association of Planners as the best example of urban renewal in America. Rather than following an over-all master plan for the entire city, Baltimore is focusing upon rehabilitation of its old ethnic sections. In this way, the cultural heritage of the city is preserved along with its architectural gems. As a result, visitors experience life as it has been led for generations in such distinctive communities as Fells Point, a working seaport that retains much of its early flavor; "Little Lithuania" surrounding Mencken's Union Square, and "Little Italy," east of the Inner Harbor along Lombard St.

Along with these banners of Baltimore's resurgence are numerous historical, artistic and other attractions. Be sure to see the following:

Fort McHenry, a National Monument and Historic Shrine, visited by over half a million people a year, site where the original Star-Spangled Banner flew.

The Star-Spangled Banner Flag House, home of Mary Pickersgill, who made the Star-Spangled Banner (all 1,260 square feet of it) is also open to the public. Mt. Vernon Place, where stands the first completed architectural monument to George Washington, was begun in 1815 and completed in 1829. The Place is known as one of the most beautiful city squares in America.

The Walters Art Gallery houses works of art spanning 6,000 years, and the Peale Museum, opened in 1814 and devoted to Baltimore life, also is extremely interesting. The Baltimore Museum of Art, which has a huge collection of classic and modern work, and the Baltimore & Ohio Railroad Museum both are intriguing. The latter is the greatest collection of railroad memorabilia in the world.

The Maryland Science Center would be interesting for no other reason than its irregular shape, designed by architect Edward Durrell Stone. Inside are a planetarium, observatory, museum, and other attractions. Also interesting is Shot Tower, where—from 1828 until 1892—shot was made by dropping molten lead from the top into a vat of cold water. Recently restored, the tower is open and has an excellent slide presentation.

The U.S. Frigate *Constellation*, launched in 1797 and the oldest ship in the United States Navy still afloat, is here. It is a Registered National

Historic Landmark. At the Maryland Historical Society Headquarters building, you will find a vast collection of exhibits relating to state history. Among these is the original manuscript of "The Star-Spangled Banner."

The World Trade Center, on Pratt St. between South and Gay Sts., has an observation level on the 27th floor that provides a panoramic view of the city and its port. The area overlooking the harbor resembles a ship's bridge. Attractions include a display of products handled in the port, film and slide show, and international gift shop.

Saint Elizabeth Seton House is where Elizabeth Ann Seton, founder of the American Order of the Sisters of Charity, and the first American-born Roman Catholic saint, made her home in 1806. Also open is the Edgar Allan Poe House, where Poe lived from 1832 to 1835. The Lloyd Street Synagogue, dating from 1845, is distinguished for its architectural beauty, as is the Basilica of the Assumption of the Virgin Mary, the first Catholic cathedral in the United States, designed in 1806.

You will also be able to see horseracing at a famous track, if you are in Baltimore at the right time, for Pimlico Race Course lies within the city limits. Here each spring is run the Preakness, second jewel of racing's "Triple Crown." The track includes the Jockey Hall of Fame, open to visitors during racing seasons.

Hampton House makes an interesting side trip out of the city. Reach it by turning off the Baltimore Beltway (I–695) at the sign near Towson. Hampton House, a National Historic Site, is an 18th-century mansion once owned by the Ridgely family of Maryland. Now, with all its original furnishings and works of art unchanged, it is a museum. There also are formal gardens and a tea room where luncheon is served.

National Social Security Headquarters, located on Security Blvd. (Baltimore Beltway, I–695, Exit No. 17), offers an interesting educational tour featuring its vast complex of sophisticated electronic data-processing equipment.

PRACTICAL INFORMATION FOR THE BALTIMORE AREA

HOW TO GET THERE. *By car:* Baltimore is on I–95 40 mi. north of Washington and 90 mi. south of Philadelphia. From Hagerstown in the west I–70N runs to the city, as does I–83 from Harrisburg, Pennsylvania, to the north.

By air: Baltimore-Washington International Airport, 10 mi. south of the city, is served by numerous airlines, including *American, Delta, Eastern, TWA, United and USAir.* The airport has facilities for physically handicapped persons, including reserved parking spaces, ramps, accessible rest rooms, and auto rental agencies (Avis, Hertz, and National) that, with advance notice, can provide hand-controlled cars. A five-year, $70 million expansion and renovation was completed in 1979. There's direct Amtrak train service between the airport and downtown Baltimore.

By train: Baltimore is on the *Amtrak* line. The station is at 1500 North Charles St., and the number is (800) 523–5700.

By bus: The *Trailways* terminal is located at 210 W. Fayette St. Their number is 752–1393. *Greyhound* is at Howard and Centre Sts. 727–5780.

BALTIMORE
DOWNTOWN

Points of Interest

1) Basilica of the Assumption
2) Carroll Mansion
3) City Hall
4) Civic Center
5) First Presbyterian Church
6) First Unitarian Church
7) Fish Market
8) Johns Hopkins Medical Center
9) Lexington Market
10) Maryland Historical Society
11) Maryland Science Center
12) Mechanical Theater
13) Medical College (Univ. of Maryland)
14) Otterbein Church
15) Peabody Institute
16) Peale Museum
17) Edgar Allan Poe's Grave
18) Saint Paul's Rectory
19) Shot Tower
20) Star-Spangled Banner Flag House
21) Walters Art Gallery
22) Washington Monument
23) U.S. Frigate Constellation
24) World Trade Center
25) HarborPlace
26) National Aquarium
27) U.S.S. Torsk
28) Baltimore Office of Promotion and Tourism

HOW TO GET AROUND. *By car:* The Baltimore Beltway, also known as I–695, circles the city limits. I–95, coming from the east, is called the John Kennedy Memorial Thruway outside the city, and the Harbor Tunnel Thruway in the city. Similarly, I–83 from the north is known as the Jones Falls Expressway. US Routes 1 and 40 are major east-west streets. US 1 is Belair Rd. at its eastern end, and North Ave., downtown. From the east, US 40 is Orleans St., Franklin St., Edmonson Ave., and Baltimore National Pike. From the north, State 45 is York Rd. and Greenmount Ave.

By Bus: The bus fare is 50¢, and exact change is required. Maps of the bus routes are available from the Mass Transit Administration, tel. 539–5000.

By taxi: Within the city the taxi rate is $1 when you get in and 10¢ for each 1/6 mile. If you go out of the city there is an additional charge of 15¢ per mile. *Diamond Cab Co.'s* number is 947–3333.

From the airport: A limousine will take you to the Hilton Hotel at 101 W. Fayette St. for $4.50. The limousines leave the Baltimore-Washington International Airport every 30 minutes. A taxi will cost about $10 to the downtown area.

TOURIST INFORMATION. The Baltimore Office of Promotion and Tourism, 110 W. Baltimore St., Baltimore 21201, will be glad to answer any questions. Their number is (301) 752–8632. During non-office hours, call (301) 685–8687 for a recorded announcement of activities for visitors. An information kiosk at the Inner Harbor is open in spring and summer.

NIGHTCLUBS AND BARS. For old-timers and visiting seamen, Baltimore's best known club is the *2 O'Clock*. The club is located in the 400 block of E. Baltimore St., a neon-bright strip that features the usual strip joints, burlesque, musical bars, penny arcades, shooting galleries, and, for anyone so inclined, tattoo parlors. The Block is justly famous and enjoys the greatest amount of police protection of any part of the city, especially since part of it was torn down in 1972 to make way for the city's new police headquarters.

Newer places of entertainment, including sophisticated discotheques and first-class restaurants, have opened recently in other neighborhoods—the Inner Harbor area, Charles Center, Hopkins Plaza, and near the Washington Monument. Particularly attractive is *P. J. Crickett's*, a "trendy" British-style pub near the Convention Center.

The "in" place for young adults of the T-shirt and blue jeans set is the seafaring Fells Point area at the south end of Broadway. There, British-like pubs go by such names as *The Horse You Came In On* and *Turkey Joe's*, and other spots offer variety from "Greek disco" to bluegrass.

DRINKING LAWS. The age for purchasing wine and beer is 18; other alcoholic beverages, 21. Bars, hotels and restaurants can serve alcoholic beverages from 6 A.M. to 2 A.M. Package stores closed on Sundays.

MUSIC. *The Baltimore Symphony Orchestra* season runs from mid-September to May with guest solo artists. All concerts at the Lyric, 120 W. Mt. Royal Ave., the city's oldest musical hall. Very popular also are the 10 *Saturday Night Pop Concerts*, featuring music of Gershwin, Tchaikovsky, Gilbert and Sullivan, etc.

In the summer, the *Baltimore Symphony* and a variety of jazz, bluegrass, gospel, and folk groups perform at the 2,000-seat concert pavilion adjacent to the National Aquarium at Pier 6 on E. Pratt St. The Baltimore Opera and Ballet both offer fine presentations, which are listed in local newspapers. *The Baltimore City*

Park Band performs most nights throughout the summer in various locations around the city.

STAGE AND REVUES. In the recently refurbished downtown section, the *Morris A. Mechanic Theater*, the nation's first new legitimate theater in 50 years, has replaced historic old *Ford's*, where the Booths, Joe Jefferson, Julia Marlowe and the Lunts played. Open year round, it presents musicals, comedies and drama that have been successful on Broadway or are bound there. Underground parking. Check daily newspapers for shows and prices.

Baltimore also offers the *Arena Players*, 406 Orchard St., in predominately black-produced and cast plays; *Center Stage*, 700 N. Calvert St., a professional repertory company, in such classics as Shaw's *Caesar and Cleopatra;* the *Spotlighter's*, 817 St. Paul St., a small theater-in-the-round with well-known plays, and *The Vagabonds*, on S. Broadway in Fells Point, the nation's oldest little theater company.

Baltimore Civic Center, 201 W. Baltimore St., presents everything from rock shows to ice shows and the *Ringling Bros. and Barnum & Bailey Circus*. On other nights, there's basketball, wrestling, ice hockey, and increasingly popular indoor soccer. *Lyric*, Baltimore's oldest music hall and home of the *Baltimore Symphony Orchestra*, also is host to the *Baltimore Civic Opera Co.*, the *Ballet Russe de Monte Carlo*, and touring concert performers. At 120 W. Mt. Royal Ave.

TOURS. There is much of interest to see in the National Anthem City. Details about guided bus tours are available by calling the Baltimore Office of Promotion and Tourism at 752-8632. Baltimore Patriot Harbor Cruises, Constellation Dock, Pratt St., runs daily narrated cruises aboard the *Baltimore Defender* and *Baltimore Patriot* to Fort McHenry, where they dock, and back.

Monumental Motors Tours, Inc., 3319 Pulaski Hwy., Baltimore 21224, conducts five or six tours to Georgetown, Hagerstown, and other places in Maryland during year. Prices vary according to distance. Tour Tapes of Baltimore rents portable tape players along with maps, brochures, and driving instructions so you may sightsee in your own car. There are two tours of historic and scenic attractions costing $6 each, or $10 for both. Tapes and players may be picked up from the AAA office at 1401 W. Mt. Royal Ave. and several other spots. For information, call 486–8989.

Baltimore Rent-A-Tour, 3418 Philips Dr., Baltimore 21208, conducts a variety of guided group tours to major attractions. Most popular during the spring-fall months are all-night "Insomniac Tours," offering a view of the city seen by few residents much less visitors. Reserve well ahead.

Chesapeake Bay all-day cruises are conducted on the *Port Welcome*, which leaves Constellation Dock, Pratt St., at the foot of Light St., Tues.–Sat. from June to Labor Day. Rates are $9.50 for adults, $4.75 for children. Special cruises are offered occasionally to St. Michaels and the C.&D. Canal. Tel. 383–5705.

GARDENS. Elsewhere, the first robin or the crack of a baseball bat may be the harbinger of spring, but in Baltimore the season has not officially arrived until the *Sherwood Gardens* are in bloom, usually in mid-May. Started by the late John W. Sherwood for his own pleasure, the gardens attract up to 40,000 visitors a day to see 100,000 tulips (50 varieties), 5,000 azaleas, and 10,000 clumps of pansies. Follow the crowd to 204 E. Highfield Rd., just east of 4100 block N. Charles St.

Druid Hill Park Rose Garden and Conservatory, just inside the Gwynns Fall Parkway entrance of Baltimore's largest park, has 3,900 rose bushes. The conservatory features indoor tropical plants. In March and April, 11,400 spring bulbs are in bloom. In fall mums are featured; at Christmas, poinsettias.

Cylburn Park, 4915 Greenspring Ave., presents a garden of wild flowers and trees in a natural setting. Free.

Recipient of the highest award of the Garden Club of America, the *Ladew Topiary Gardens* are considered the finest of their kind in the United States. Located near Monkton, 14 miles north of Towson and Beltway Exit 27 on Jarrettsville Pike.

HISTORIC SITES. *Basilica of the Assumption of the Blessed Virgin Mary,* Cathedral and Mulberry Sts. First Roman Catholic cathedral in the United States, its cornerstone was laid in 1806 by Bishop John Carroll at a time when more than half of the Catholics in the United States lived in Maryland. It was not completed until 1821, partly because of the War of 1812.

Babe Ruth's Birthplace, 216 Emory St. Baseball's greatest player, George Herman Ruth, was born in this tiny house on Feb. 6, 1895. The museum program includes rare photographs, exhibits, and a slide presentation.

Carroll Mansion, 800 Lombard St. Charles Carroll of Carrollton, Maryland's oldest signer of the Declaration of Independence, died here in this handsome town mansion of his son-in-law, now restored and furnished in the style of the period.

Edgar Allan Poe House, 203 Amity St. In this tiny, two-story brick house, from 1832 to 1835, the melancholy poet lived and courted his cousin, Virginia Clemm, who later became his wife. Nearby, in Westminster Churchyard, W. Fayette at Greene St., is Poe's grave. The house, a bit difficult to find, is of interest to real Poe buffs.

First Presbyterian Church, Park Ave. and Madison St. Architects still come to marvel at the 273-foot steeple of this Gothic edifice completed in 1859.

First Unitarian Church, North Charles St. at Franklin St. Built in 1819, it is considered birthplace of Unitarian Church. A small museum is behind church.

Fort McHenry, foot of Fort Ave. Overlooking Baltimore harbor, this star-shaped fort with brick walls 20 feet thick withstood the might of British fleet on Sept. 13–14, 1814. Francis Scott Key, witnessing the bombardment and the flag at dawn, was inspired to write what became the National Anthem.

H. L. Mencken Home, 1524 Hollins St. Not regularly open. The editor of *American Mercury Magazine* and Baltimore *Sunpapers* lived here all but five years of his life.

Johns Hopkins Hospital, Broadway and Monument Sts., began to acquire its world-wide reputation in 1889. Worth seeing is the figure of Christ in Carrara marble in the lobby.

Lexington Market, Lexington and Eutaw Sts. One of the oldest markets in the nation (1803), it has now been modernized but still has stallkeepers whose fathers and grandfathers had stalls there before them. This is but one (the largest) of seven city-owned markets.

Lloyd Street Synagogue, Lloyd St. off 1100 E. Baltimore St. Free. Third oldest synagogue in the United States is now a museum.

Saint Elizabeth Seton House, 600 Paca St. Free. The first home and school conducted by Elizabeth Ann Seton, a convert who founded the Sisters of Charity, and became the first American-born saint.

Mount Clare, in Carroll Park, Washington Blvd. and Monroe St. Built in 1754, the oldest house in Baltimore was home of Charles Carroll, a cousin of Charles Carroll, a Maryland signer of the Declaration of Independence. Contains period pieces.

Mount Clare Station, Pratt and Poppleton Sts. The first passenger and freight station in the United States, it was here that Samuel F. B. Morse's first telegraph message, *"What hath God wrought,"* was received. Now entrance to the B&O

Railroad Museum, which contains fine examples of early steam engines and wooden coaches. (See *What to Do with the Children.*)

Otterbein Church, 124 W. Conway St. This is the mother church of the former United Brethren congregation, now part of the United Methodist denomination. Built in 1785, its bells announced end of Revolutionary War.

St. Paul's Episcopal Church, Charles and Saratoga Sts. Known as the "The Mother Church of Baltimore." The Parish was founded in 1732; the first church on this site was built in 1739. The present one dates from 1856.

Tyson Street, 900 block north. A slum for a century, this is one of Baltimore's most colorful blocks, with its circa 1830 houses renovated by arty folks right after World War II. Open on one June Saturday each year for charity.

U.S.F. Constellation, Pratt and Light Sts. Launched in Baltimore, the oldest ship afloat and the first ship of the U.S. Navy, it earned nickname "Yankee Race Horse" when it carried U.S. Marines to Tripoli.

Washington Monument, Charles and Monument Sts. at Mount Vernon Place. Some 25,000 Baltimoreans walked or rode to a rise of ground north of the city on July 4, 1815, to see the cornerstone laying of the first architectural monument to George Washington, a 204-foot shaft which earned Baltimore the title *Monumental City.* An island of graciousness, almost in the center of town, the monument is surrounded by the city's loveliest park, an equestrian statue of General Lafayette dedicated by President Calvin Coolidge, the Walters Art Gallery, Peabody Library and Institute of Music, and Mount Vernon Place United Methodist Church, which is on site of home where Francis Scott Key died in 1843.

 MUSEUMS AND GALLERIES. With the *Maryland Institute of Art,* including its *Rinehart School of Sculpture,* in Baltimore, the city has its fair share of small art galleries, such as the *Studio North, Purnell's,* and century-old *Bendann's.* Major galleries and other museums worth a visit include:

Baltimore Museum of Art. This institution has achieved national stature for its collection of Picasso, Matisse, Manet, and Cezanne. Its $1 million Grecian building was voted by the people of Baltimore and is on land donated by Johns Hopkins University, Charles and 31st Sts. Concerts are held in its Rose Garden, where old movies are shown. Be sure to see the *Wurtzburger Sculpture Garden.* Free.

Walters Art Gallery. The 25,000-object collection acquired by William T. Walters and his son, Henry, over a period of 90 years is ranked among the five most comprehensive among American art museums that illustrate the art and archaeology of the important civilizations. It includes one of the finest Egyptology collections in the U.S. Charles and Centre Sts.

Maryland Historical Society. Besides the state's records pertaining to World War II, its library contains 40,000 books and papers about Maryland. Its 16 rooms at 201 W. Monument St. also include 250 portraits and paintings of famous Marylanders, a typical Baltimore double parlor of the 19th century and a room containing personal belongings of Betsy Patterson, wife of Napoleon's brother, Jerome. Also on view is the original manuscript of the "Star-Spangled Banner," purchased for the Society in 1933 for $26,400. Admission fee.

Star-Spangled Banner Flag House, 844 E. Pratt St. In this tiny brick house, close by the waterfront, Mrs. Mary Young Pickersgill made the huge 30-by-42-foot Star-Spangled Banner which Francis Scott Key saw "by the dawn's early light" over Fort McHenry in 1814 and which inspired him to write what became our national anthem. The flag is now preserved in a temperature-controlled glass case in the foyer of the Smithsonian Institution in Washington, D.C.

Peale Museum. Built in 1814 by Rembrandt Peale, artist son of the artist Charles Willson Peale, the oldest museum building in America made history in 1816 when it was the first building lighted with gas, later served as city hall. It features Baltimore memorabilia and Peale portraits. At 225 N. Holiday St.

The *National Aquarium* in Baltimore, so designated by Congress, opened in 1981. The largest, most technically advanced aquarium in the U.S., it rises seven stories over the Inner Harbor. The $21-million structure houses some 8,000 specimens in more than 75 exhibit tanks. Included are a tropical rain forest, a donut-shaped shark tank, a Chesapeake Bay water specimen, and a Caribbean coral reef.

Lacrosse Hall of Fame. On Johns Hopkins University campus, N. Charles St. off University Pkwy. The history of the old Indian game—as seen through trophies, old uniforms and other memorabilia—in which Johns Hopkins and other Maryland colleges and prep schools have played a leading role.

Fort George G. Meade, South of Baltimore-Washington Pkwy. Museum of Griffin Rd., off State 108. Free. The history of the First Army from the Revolutionary War to the present, including World War I's famous "Lost Battalion."

Fire Museum, 1301 York Rd., Lutherville. One man's hobby collection of antique fire engines, telegraphs and other memorabilia.

Street Car Museum. 1901 Falls Rd. A nostalgic collection of horse cars, open-air summer cars and other trolleys which once operated in Baltimore. Some provide rides on Sundays and Thursday evenings in summer over 1½ miles of track.

 SUMMER SPORTS. A favorite way to spend a Saturday afternoon or a weekday evening out is to eat peanuts and hot dogs while watching the *Orioles* play nine innings or a twilight double-header at Memorial Stadium. Game time varies. Tickets are rarely difficult to get.

The old Indian game of *lacrosse* is the national sport of Canada by legislative act, but Baltimore is the game's unofficial capital. Johns Hopkins University has held the United States intercollegiate title for more years than any other team and has twice played in the Olympics. A rough sport, games are played at most high schools and colleges from mid-March to second week of June. Mt. Washington, a club team of former college stars, organized in 1904, plays most Saturday nights at Norris Field, Falls Rd. at Kelly Ave.

Landscaped with dogwoods and pines, *Pine Ridge* is generally rated as the best of five *golf courses* owned by Baltimore City. It's on Dulaney Valley Rd. near Loch Raven. Other city-owned courses are *Mt. Pleasant, Clifton Park, Forest Park,* and nine-hole *Carroll Park.*

Good, semi-private golf courses: *All View,* State 29, South of Ellicott City; *Dulaney Springs,* in Dulaney Valley, north of Towson; *Sherwood Forest,* off State 178 between Dorrs Corner and Parole; and *Crofton,* especially good for tourists, at the Bowie turn-off on US 301. The *Anne Arundel County Municipal Dwight D. Eisenhower Memorial Golf Course,* on Generals Hwy. just west of Annapolis, near Crownsville. *University of Maryland,* for students, has driving range, College Park.

There also are 18 and some 9-hole courses in Salisbury, Ocean City, Hagerstown, Frostburg and Oakland.

With well over 50 yacht clubs around the Chesapeake Bay area, there is hardly a weekend that does not feature some class of *sailboat race.* They continue right up through the "frostbite season." Check local sports pages for places and times. Summer and winter, a good vantage point on Saturday and Sunday afternoons is along the sea wall inside the U.S. Naval Academy grounds in Annapolis.

Some 600-plus *softball* teams play every evening and on weekends under the supervision of the Baltimore City Bureau of Recreation in public parks throughout the city.

WINTER SPORTS. No sports fans are more enthusiastic or vocal than those in Baltimore. As a result, Memorial Stadium still lives up to its nickname as "the world's largest outdoor insane asylum" whenever the 1971 Super Bowl-winning *Baltimore Colts* play. Close to 40,000 season ducats are sold for the 60,000 seat bowl, so some are available. But as the season nears they grow increasingly scarce.

Boxing and wrestling have become hit-and-miss spectator sports. There are occasional matches at the Baltimore Civic Center. Former Olympic boxing champ Sugar Ray Leonard, a Maryland resident and now professional, is a local favorite.

With spring meets starting in January and fall meets ending in December, there is almost continuous *horse racing* at the following one-mile tracks: *Bowie* (Rte. 197 from the Baltimore-Washington Expressway); *Laurel* (US 1 or Baltimore-Washington Expressway); *Pimlico,* in Baltimore, and nearby *Delaware Park.* Minor tracks: *Timonium* (north of Towson via Harrisburg Expressway), and fairly near *Charles Town* across the Maryland line in Charlestown, W. Va. Transportation to all of these tracks provided daily by Baltimore Motor Coach buses from in front of Baltimore Civic Center, 201 W. Baltimore St. No reservations needed.

Night harness racing: Laurel Raceway (opposite *Laurel Race Course*); *Rosecroft* at Oxon Hill (Washington Beltway south from Baltimore-Washington Expressway); and *Ocean Downs* (Ocean City).

WHAT TO DO WITH THE CHILDREN. *Baltimore and Ohio Railroad Museum,* Poppleton and Pratt Sts., Baltimore. A collection of replicas and original iron horses from America's first railroad, assembled for the 1893 Chicago World's Fair and now displayed in an old roundhouse. Especially fun is climbing into cabooses and coaches that once were the last word in luxurious travel.

Children's Zoo in Druid Hill Park, Baltimore. Besides the usual zoological attractions, there are rabbits, chickens, goats, and cows, a train ride, a tree house, a bouncing bridge, Noah's Ark, swings, and other playground apparatus, and a carillon with 100 miniature bells. A public milking in the dairy barn takes place every day at 4 P.M.

Enchanted Forest, US 40, 14 mi. west of downtown Baltimore. A miniature-size Disneyland with rides, Mother Goose characters, Alice in Wonderland, and a 65-foot toboggan slide down Mt. Vesuvius. Open about May 15 to Oct.

Christmas Gardens. Elaborate model villages with trains and other electrically operated gadgets are especially popular in Baltimore, where they were started by immigrant German craftsmen. Besides private homes, there are traditional Christmas displays at Fire Engine Co. No. 45, located at Cross County Blvd. and Glen Ave.

Baltimore Society of Model Engineers, 225 W. Saratoga St. This permanent layout by railroad buffs is open to public New Year's Day and each Sunday in Jan.

Baltimore Symphony Orchestra presents children's concerts during the winter season.

Submarine U.S.S. *Torsk,* tied up at Pier 4, Pratt St. Known by her crew as the "Galloping Ghost of the Japanese Coast," this sub sank the last two enemy warships in World War II.

Rides on vintage trolley cars once used in Baltimore at *Baltimore Streetcar Museum,* 1901 Falls Rd. Open Sundays, and Thursday evenings in summer only.

Relive American history aboard U.S. Frigate *Constellation,* oldest ship in the U.S. Navy still afloat, launched in 1797, at Constellation Dock, Pratt St.

Fire Museum, 1301 York Rd., Lutherville. Antique fire apparatus, fire alarm telegraphs and other memorabilia of fire fighting in days of horse-drawn engines.

Some 27 city branches of *Enoch Pratt Free Library* in Baltimore City and others in Baltimore County present *movies* and *story-telling programs* for children throughout the summer and on Sat. in winter.

Designed especially for those between 8 and 15, the *Darnell Young People's Museum* at the Maryland Historical Society, Park Ave., and Monument St., Baltimore, presents Maryland history from pre-settlement days through the present time with scale-model dioramas, full-scale log cabin and colonial kitchen. Permission for children to touch.

Maryland Science Center, 601 Light St., has a variety of permanent and visiting exhibits from around the world. The star show in *Davis Planetarium* fascinates children and adults alike.

The Cloisters Children's Museum, 10440 Falls Rd., combines various types of workshops with demonstrations and entertainment—all geared to interests of the young set.

Ice-skating, mid-November to mid-March, at *Baltimore Memorial Stadium,* Charles Center, and Patterson rinks. For further information, contact the Department of Recreation and Parks, 396–7900.

HOTELS AND MOTELS. in Baltimore are characterized, with a few exceptions, by an ultra-modern atmosphere. Almost all of the old-line establishments, with traditional plush accomodations, have closed in recent years and been torn down to make way for parking lots or other commercial uses. It is wise, therefore, to check these listings carefully and to always make advance reservations.

Price categories for Baltimore may be translated into the following ranges: *Deluxe* $35 and higher, *Expensive* $22–$34, *Moderate* $13–$21 and *Inexpensive* $12 and lower. For a more complete explanation of price categories, refer to the *Facts at Your Fingertips* at the beginning of this book.

Baltimore Hilton. *Deluxe.* 101 W. Fayette St. Located in the $130 million Charles Center complex in the heart of the city's revitalized downtown area. Its 500 rooms are across the street from the Morris Mechanic Theater and only a few minutes' walk to the Baltimore Civic Center and new Convention Center. The hotel features the nationally-known Miller Bros. Restaurant, major airline offices, barber shop, coffee shop, cocktail lounge, and meeting and banquet facilities for up to 1,400 people.

The Belvedere. *Deluxe.* Charles and Chase Sts. This stately old structure, newly refurbished, has a limited number of transient rooms among the apartments. The atmosphere is quiet and subdued.

Cross Keys Inn. *Deluxe.* 5100 Falls Rd., Village of Cross Keys. Excellent rooms with a number of extra touches. Fine dining rooms, lounge with entertainment, coffee shop.

International Hotel. *Deluxe.* Baltimore-Washington International Airport, off Baltimore-Washington Expressway. Soundproof rooms are a necessary luxury here, for planes come and go day and night. Includes free parking, a swimming pool and for whiling away some hours between planes, the Bards' Tavern and Moll Flanders Pub.

Hilton Inn (Pikesville). *Deluxe.* Reisertown Rd. (US 140) at Baltimore Beltway exit 20. This Tudor-style hostelry on the outskirts of Baltimore City has 178 rooms, a shopping mall, heated swimming pool, tennis club, restaurant, large ballroom, a paneled lobby with working fireplaces and other appointments designed to make it a plush social center for Northwest Baltimore.

Holiday Inn-Airport. *Deluxe.* 6500 Elkridge Landing Rd. at Airport Rd. One mile to Baltimore-Washington International Airport, free transportation provided there.

Hyatt Regency. *Deluxe.* On the Inner Harbor at South Charles St. This 14-story, 500-room hotel, opened in 1981, is one of Baltimore's finest. It's adjacent to the Convention Center and Harbor Place. Among unusual attractions are a 6-story atrium, coffee shop with a waterfall, and rooftop restaurant and lounge. Recreational facilities include a swimming pool, 3 tennis courts, and a jogging track.

Marriott's Hunt Valley Inn. *Deluxe.* Shawan Rd. off I-83, north of Baltimore Beltway Exit 24. A resort-type inn with meeting rooms, an outstanding restaurant, indoor swimming pool, and golf course two miles away.

Sheraton-Johns Hopkins. *Deluxe.* 400 N. Broadway. Across the street from world-famous Johns Hopkins Hospital, this motor inn is modern and warmly inviting. Restaurant, cocktail lounge.

Holiday Inn-Cromwell. *Expensive.* 1100 Cromwell Bridge Rd., exit 29 from Baltimore Beltway (I-695). The typical high-rise motel of this chain, with pool, lounge, restaurant, color TV. On the northern edge of Baltimore, near Towson, Goucher College, and Timonium Fairgrounds.

Holiday Inn-Downtown. *Expensive.* 301 W. Lombard St. at Howard. This 13-story motor hotel, conveniently located just across from the Civic Center, has restaurants, a cocktail lounge and swimming pool. Circle One is a rooftop restaurant that makes one complete circle every hour, offering a good view of the city.

Holiday Inn-Glen Burnie No. 2. *Expensive.* 6301 Ritchie Hwy. State 2, off Beltway exit 3. Restaurant, cocktail lounge, outdoor pool.

Howard House. *Expensive.* 8 N. Howard St. A family-owned hotel with a restaurant and tavern.

Lord Baltimore. *Expensive.* Baltimore St. at Hanover. The city's oldest hotel, constantly being renovated, the Lord Baltimore is only one block from the Civic Center and just across the street from the Morris A. Mechanic Theater. A favorite for banquets and conventions, it has a restaurant and bar.

Quality Inn-Northwest. *Expensive.* 10 Wooded Way, Baltimore Beltway at Reisterstown Rd. (US 140), exit 20. Color TV, playground, free continental breakfast.

Quality Inn-Towson. *Expensive.* 1015 York Rd., exit 26 from the Beltway (I-695). Every convenience: modern lobby with fireplace; large swimming pool, restaurant, recreation room, baby sitters. Towson, home of Goucher College, is 8 mi. north of Baltimore.

Quality Inn-West. *Expensive.* Baltimore Beltway exit 15. Seven miles from the children's Enchanted Forest. Color TV, kitchenettes, restaurant, and lounge.

Ramada Inn. *Expensive.* Baltimore Beltway (I–695) at exit 17. The usual amenities, including restaurant and lounge. Near the Social Security Administration complex.

Abbey. *Moderate.* 723 St. Paul St. Clean, basic accommodations. Rates include continental breakfast.

Hilltop Motor Inn. *Moderate.* 1660 Whitehead Court, off Beltway exit 17. The standard motel accommodations include pool and free airport bus. The restaurant is a favorite with local people.

Howard Johnson Motor Lodge. *Moderate.* 5701 Baltimore National Pike (US 40 W), off Beltway exit 15. A high rise, with Howard Johnson restaurant next door, this older motel has a cocktail lounge, free parking and outdoor pool. Across US 40 from two large shopping centers, 6 mi. from downtown.

Harbor City Inn. *Moderate.* 1701 Russell St., exit 7 from Baltimore-Washington Parkway. A handsome modern overnight stop with elevators. Restaurant, cocktail lounge, meeting rooms, and swimming pool.

 DINING OUT in Baltimore can involve some serious exploring. Though one hears a lot about Maryland's traditional dishes—spoon bread, beaten biscuits, terrapin soup, oyster stew—the truth is that it is not so easy to find them on menus. However, those whose business it is to know say that the equal of Baltimore's Maryland roast turkey, fried chicken, crab cakes or fried Chincoteague oysters is nowhere to be found. To quote *New York Times* food editor Craig Claiborne: "Baltimore is a city worth visiting for the food alone. . . . Here one can enjoy some of the best continental and American cuisine in the country, and definitely the best seafood."

Restaurant price categories are as follows: *Deluxe* $12 and higher, *Expensive* $8–$11, *Moderate* $5–$7, *Inexpensive* below $5.00. These prices are for hors d'oeuvres or soup, entree and dessert. Not included are drinks, tax and tips. For a more complete explanation of restaurant categories refer to *Facts at Your Fingertips.*

Editors' Choices

Rating restaurants is, at best, a subjective business, and obviously a matter of personal taste. It is, therefore, difficult to call a restaurant "the best," and hope to get unanimous agreement. The restaurants listed below are our choices of the best eating places in Baltimore, and the places we would choose if we were visiting the city.

TIO PEPE   Spanish
Baltimore's salute to Spanish cuisine is a place for the gourmet, where the best of ingredients are carefully prepared and attractively presented. Service is attentive without becoming overbearing. Meals are fairly priced for the quality of the food. The building was once a townhouse, and its cellar now yields delicious Spanish wines. Average price for dinner (per person): $12. 10 E. Franklin St.

THE CHESAPEAKE   Seafood
This is the fine seafood restaurant you'd expect in this bastion of fresh finny fare. Locally caught fish and shellfish are the specialties, and they are delightfully prepared and served. The dining room is handsomely done in dark wood paneling, and the comfortable bar boasts a piano. Average price for dinner (per person) $13. 1701 North Charles Street.

HAUSSNER'S   Continental Cuisine
The dining room is a veritable art gallery, with the walls covered with paintings that range from modest to great value. Less intellectual art (nudes, to be precise) adorn the walls of the bar. The variety of the menu is impressive, from a wide selection of seafood to pig's knuckle, quail and rabbit. Average price for dinner (per person): $10. 3244 Eastern Avenue.

DANNY'S   Continental Cuisine
Gourmet American and Continental dishes are carefully prepared, many at table-side, and portions are huge. The selection of wines is as expensive as it is extensive. Dieters beware: there's a separate dessert and cordial menu. Meals are à la carte, and the bill can escalate rapidly. Average price for dinner (per person): $20. Charles and Biddle Streets.

PIMLICO HOTEL   American-Continental
Don't go to this restaurant—among the city's most popular—unless you're raven-ous. Portions—from the selection of more than two dozen appetizers to five-layer cake desserts—are huge. So is the menu. With more than a dozen beef entrees, a wide range of other American and continental specialties, and a complete Chinese section, it's difficult to decide what to order. Once you do, the food is well prepared and efficiently served. Music in the Cavalier Lounge. Valet parking. Reservations suggested. Average price for dinner (per person): $14. 5301 Park Heights Ave.

Other recommended restaurants:

American-International

Cafe des Artistes. *Deluxe.* Hopkins Plaza in the Morris A. Mechanic Theater building. Continental cuisine in an elegant setting. Opened in 1976, it became an instant success with the theater crowd. Reservations recommended.

The Crease. *Deluxe.* 27 Hopkins Plaza (in the Morris Mechanic Building). Prime rib, sirloin, shrimp scampi are some of the delectable dinners served in a New York pub atmosphere.

Maison Marconi. *Deluxe.* 106 W. Saratoga St. Mostly French food, plus some Italian specialties, served in a simple but elegant dining room. Popular with knowledgeable natives of the area.

Marriott's Hunt Valley Inn. *Deluxe.* Shawan Rd., off I–83, north of Baltimore Beltway Exit 24. The Inn is an "in" place for Baltimoreans to hold their banquets and receptions. Located out in the country, its restaurant is called *The Cinnamon Tree,* probably because the Inn is owned by McCormick & Co., the firm. A big, big menu features continental, Chesapeake and steak-house offerings. Lunch and dinner seven days a week.

Miller Brothers. *Deluxe.* 101 W. Fayette St. In the Hilton Hotel, this restaurant is on almost the same site where the original Miller Bros. stood long enough to become a famous landmark, especially for visiting show people. A varied menu, with emphasis on seafood.

Prime Rib. *Deluxe.* 1101 N. Calvert St. This sophisticated restaurant combines outstanding food with swank surroundings and excellent service. Not surprisingly, the limited menu features roast beef.

Burke's. *Expensive.* 36 Light St. This pub-style restaurant has become a magnet for the city's young executives and secretaries, not the least due to its modest cost. Excellent soups and beef stew join a menu that also features crab cakes, chili, and particularly tasty roast beef sandwiches. The onion rings are legendary, and the decorative pewter around the room is for sale.

Gino's Steak Houses. *Inexpensive.* A chain of eat-in or carry-outs, best known, in fact a password among children, for finger-lickin'-good chicken. The steak houses are fewer and more scattered. For less than $2.50 you can get a steak, baked potato, salad, beverage and dessert. Gino is Gino Marchetti, formerly of the Baltimore Colts. Look in the phone book for locations.

Hampton House Tea Room. *Inexpensive.* Hampton Lane, off Dulaney Valley Rd. The very good food here is just a part of the experience. Meals are served in the former kitchen of a Georgian mansion that is now a National Historic Landmark. You'll see a beautiful fireplace and real colonial furnishings. Lunch only.

Horn & Horn Cafeterias. *Inexpensive.* In the First Maryland Bank Building downtown and at four other city locations (see telephone book listings). Offering quality meals at reasonable prices, daily from 11 A.M. to 8 P.M.

Peabody Book Shop, Beer Stube and Bar. *Inexpensive.* 913 N. Charles St. Unique and unusual. The eatery is hidden behind the book shop. An old-time institution in downtown Baltimore, it's worth a visit for the interesting—if now somewhat seedy—atmosphere. You might prefer to skip the food and enjoy a beer.

Chinese

Golden Star. *Expensive.* 3326 Greenmount Ave. Good, reasonably priced Chinese-Cantonese food. Huge portions—one order probably will satisfy two average appetites.

New China Inn. *Expensive.* 2426 N. Charles St., near 25th St. Most Baltimoreans refer to this favorite eating place as Jimmy Wu's, for the proprietor who serves Chinese-American dishes in a tastefully modern Oriental setting. Free parking in rear.

Pagoda Inn. *Expensive.* 1010 Reisterstown Rd., Pikesville, 2 mi. south of Beltway Exit 20. Has a menu that spans the Orient. The food is Chinese, Korean, Japanese and Hawaiian. Take your pick or combine dishes from all four areas.

China Doll. *Inexpensive.* 406 Park Ave. In the heart of downtown Baltimore's Chinatown, has a Chinese-American cuisine that includes shrimp with lobster sauce. Free parking.

French

Martick's. *Deluxe.* 214 W. Mulberry St. You'll imagine you're in Paris, thanks to Morris Martick, who was. For lunch, try the Crevette au Facon de Maurice.

Italian

Velleggia's. *Deluxe.* 204–206 S. High St. A fine Italian restaurant in the heart of Little Italy, this one has been around for more than 50 years, which speaks well enough for its authentic dishes and selection of Italian wines.

Chiapparelli's. *Expensive.* 237 S. High St. In the heart of Baltimore's Little Italy since 1938, a stone's throw from the waterfront. The décor is unpretentious, but the usual array of Italian dishes is well prepared.

Russo. (formerly Maria's 300). *Expensive.* 300 Albermarle St. Near the waterfront. Besides 24 specialties, it has perhaps the widest assortment of Italian appetizers, soups, spaghetti and macaroni dishes in the city. Wines are used to flavor the black bean soup, beef *braciola* and the squid. Luncheon, cocktails and dinner.

Sabatino's. *Expensive.* 901 Fawn St. You'll think you're in Napoli when you enter. Veal dishes are the specialties, but don't overlook the shrimp marsala.

Danti's. *Moderate.* 6000 Liberty Rd. Enjoy family-style Italian cooking, such as chicken *Ma-De-Cosmo* and *Veal Viola,* named for members of the Italian owner's family, and served with old Italian wines.

DeNitti's. *Moderate.* 906 Trinity St., at High St. Pleasant and unassuming, with the usual good Italian fare—and spectacular pizza—to be expected in this section of town.

Japanese

Nichi-Bei-Kai. *Deluxe.* Two locations: In the Belvedere Hotel, and 1524 York Rd. (State 45), Lutherville. Both feature all sorts of steak, shrimp and chicken dishes, with exotic vegetables, cooked before your eyes. Make reservations.

Mexican

Tijuana Tacos. *Inexpensive.* 5847 York Rd. (State 45). A salute to Mexican cooking courtesy non-Mexicans from California. The tortillas, the paella, chile con queso and other Mexican dishes are about as authentic as you can expect this far from the border.

Seafood

Bo Brooks Crab House. *Deluxe.* 4807 Belair Rd. Hot steamed crabs bring in the crowds. For those who want the treat without the work and mess, the crabmeat is served up in soup, cakes, fluff, and imperial-style.

Chart House. *Deluxe.* Pier 4, East Pratt St., Inner Harbor. Fine food served in a colorful nautical setting.

Karson's Inn. *Deluxe.* 5100 Holabird Avenue. May be tough driving for the out-of-towner but Baltimoreans think it's worth the trek to Dundalk on the eastern outskirts of the city to order stuffed whole lobster a la Karson (lump crabmeat, mushrooms, shrimp), a house specialty.

Meushaw's. *Deluxe.* Security Blvd. and the Baltimore Beltway, exit 17. Near the National Social Security office, this restaurant, which looks out on the Baltimore Beltway from a hilltop, is a favorite with local folk on the west and northwest sides of Baltimore and its suburbs. There is a fine selection of seafood, like Maryland rock fish stuffed with crabmeat; also sour beef. Operated in conjunction with Hilltop Motor Inn.

Orchard Inn. *Deluxe.* 1528 E. Joppa Rd., W of Loch Raven Blvd. Old-fashioned sauerbraten and dumplings en casserole is a specialty served in the *Starboard, Dockside* or *Coach and Four* rooms, though half of the items on the menu are seafood. A seafood platter has a feast of backfin crab, gulf shrimp, scallops, sea perch, and a broiled half lobster. Named for an old apple orchard, most of which has been cut down to make room for more free parking. Reservations are advisable.

Original Olde Obrycki's. *Deluxe.* 1729 E. Pratt St. The setting is pleasantly Early American, but the attraction is seafood. Many people come for the crabs—especially some of the best steamed hardshells in town. Closed in winter.

Thompson's Sea Girt House. *Expensive.* 5919 York Rd., at Belvedere Ave. Only a few restaurants serve homemade crab cakes made with backfin meat. This is one of them, and it has become nationally known since it was established in 1885. Imperial crab is another delicacy.

Bertha's. *Inexpensive.* 734 S. Broadway. Mussels are the house specialty. Also features homemade desserts. If you see bumper stickers advising "Eat Bertha's Mussels," this is the spot to which they refer.

Millrace Tavern. *Inexpensive.* 5201 W. Franklintown Rd. Many Baltimoreans say that this place, which looks just like its name implies, has the best steamed crabs anywhere. Dancing on weekend evenings. Very, very casual. Shorts, slacks okay. But weekends it is hard to get a table.

Snacks

Owl Bar. *Expensive.* In Falstaff Room of The Belvedere. A delightful new restaurant and bar featuring soups, sandwiches, and quiche.

Harbor Place. *Inexpensive to Expensive.* At the Inner Harbor. A nosher's delight, with more than three dozen eateries—from carryouts featuring Caribbean, Japanese, and Greek specialties to French and seafood restaurants. There's something for most tastes, and every budget.

Friendly Ice Cream Shops. *Inexpensive.* Bright, clean eateries for a good lunch or ice cream treat. Prices are reasonable. Check a phone book for the nearest location.

Lexington Market. *Inexpensive.* Lexington and Eutaw Sts. From early morning until early evening, you may munch your way from stall to stall for as long as your appetite lasts. There's virtually endless variety—from egg rolls to seafood, corned beef to bratwurst, frozen yogurt to cheesecake.

EXPLORING MARYLAND

In the 17th century, when it began to be settled, the Eastern Shore of Maryland was no harder to get to than any other place. You reached it by horse overland and by sailing vessel over water. After 250 years these rules had changed so that you used trains and steamboats, but for some reason trains and steamboats alike were few and were run primarily for freight, not passengers. Good motor roads, airports, bridges (and bridge-tunnels) are recent in the shore's development, and the landscape consequently shows a face shaped in the past. Be prepared for antiquity as you explore this part of Maryland, for antiquity (relative, of course) is everywhere.

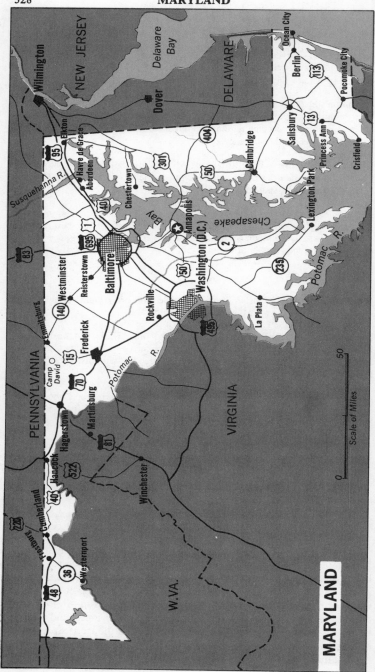

MARYLAND

The Rural Eastern Shore

The shore was settled for farming—to a large extent by Colonial land grants. Today, after 300 years, there are no large cities and the area is mainly rural. The farms are now modernized; they produce most of the broiler chickens sold in the United States, and breed race horses and beef cattle. But they are still there—they, and forests, marshes and long sandy shores that have scarcely changed at all.

Suppose you enter the Eastern Shore area by US 40 from the east. You will do so by crossing the Mason-Dixon Line. Remember this, for you are going to *see* the line later on. It is visible, though not at this point.

Keep on to Elkton. It was named Head of Elk in Revolutionary times, and armies, going south and coming north on Chesapeake Bay, embarked and disembarked at its docks. British, French, American—they came hard on one another's heels at times, as is indicated on Elkton's main street, where stands Hollingsworth Tavern. George Washington put up there one night—and the very next night Lord Howe, the British general, occupied the same room. The tavern is an office building today.

Turn off 40 onto US 213. You will soon come to the Chesapeake and Delaware Canal, dating from 1829, one of the few works of that canal-building period that is still in use. It connects Delaware and Chesapeake bays, shortening the distance between the ports of Philadelphia and Baltimore by hundreds of miles.

At the southern end of the Canal Bridge, turn off at the Old Lock Pump House sign and go to the pump house, a short distance. Here you will see the largest water wheel in the world, an engineering marvel and a National Historic Landmark. It was used from 1851 to 1927, in which period the canal was operated by locks, to raise the water level. It would move 1,200,000 gallons in an hour.

A Genuine Colonial Village

Keep on 213 to Wye Mills. In this tiny village, you will find a water mill dating from the late 17th century (which ground flour for Washington's troops at Valley Forge), a Colonial schoolhouse with original furnishings, the 1721 Wye Church with its high box pews and suspended pulpit, and Maryland's official State Tree, the Wye Oak, more than 400 years old and sometimes called a "one-tree forest." This is a genuine Colonial village, not one made to order.

Turn onto State 404 and go to the intersection of US 50. Proceed to Easton. This town, though Colonial in origin, differs from other villages in that it has been more fully discovered. Its county, Talbot, has drawn numbers of out-of-state people of wealth and today consists largely of finely-restored old estates. The effect can be felt in the town. There is a smartness to the place: antique shops of art gallery quality, the Academy of Arts, a handsome hotel (the Tidewater Inn). All are worth a visit. On the other hand, Easton's antiquity is attested to by a peculiarly eloquent structure, the Third Haven Quaker Meeting House, dating from 1682. It has its original furnishings.

How to See the Mason-Dixon Line

Take State 333 to Oxford. The town was Maryland's first and most important port of entry and is still devoted to boats; in fact, it is a

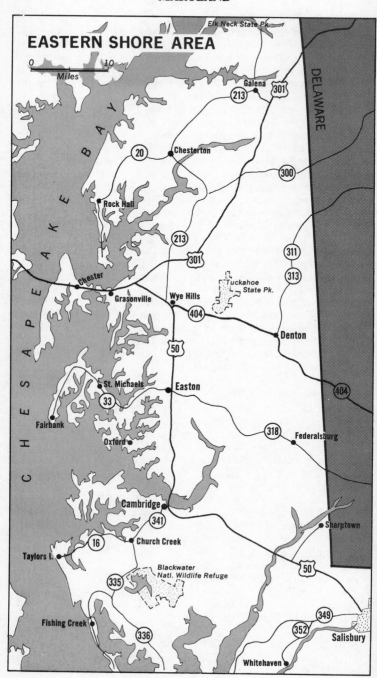

well-known center for sailing enthusiasts. In it you may visit shipyards and a sail loft. And you will certainly want to stop at the Robert Morris Inn, a well-run hotel occupying the early 18th-century home of the father of the famous Financier of the Revolution. Its dining room is excellent, its decor charming.

The oldest ferry in the United States, the Oxford Bellevue will next carry you (and up to 8 cars) across the Tred Avon River. Take State 33 to St. Michaels. For 250 years it was a shipbuilding community. Today, it has the Chesapeake Bay Maritime Museum, where relics of that work may be seen, while tied up at the museum wharf are some of the old vessels themselves. Also, there is an original 19th-century Bay lighthouse on display. See St. Mary's Square, where they still ring the bell that used to call the carpenters to work. Take a look at the Log House, an example of pioneer building with its skin peeled back, as it were, to display the workmanship. See the Cannonball House, a reminder of a joke the townspeople played on the British in the War of 1812. At that time St. Michaels was scheduled for a night's bombardment. The people, knowing what was coming, hung lanterns well up in the trees and the English gunners, taking these for the town lights, aimed high. Only one shot hit a house. That house still bears the name of the missile intended to destroy it.

Return to US 50 and go to Cambridge. Turn right on State 16 there and drive to Church Creek, where you will see the oldest Church of any denomination continuously in use in the United States: Old Trinity, built in 1675, and restored with exquisite care to its original form and materials.

Then take State 335 to Blackwater National Wildlife Refuge, administered by the Department of the Interior. One of the greatest concentrations of waterfowl in the United States is found here during the winter months; also a phenomenally large number of species of song birds. A visitors' center provides a map of trails and roads.

It was promised earlier that you would see the Mason-Dixon Line. Actually the whole line is visible and has been for 200 years. Its original stones, one a mile (with a crownstone every five miles), are still in place. But turn off 50 on State 467 and you will come upon the first stone of them all. A shelter has been erected over it and a plaque gives the history. Look well. Along this same line the United States almost broke in two.

Salisbury is the Eastern Shore's one big town. It is modern and has an up-to-the-second community center, a state college, a big country club and an industrial park. It is the heart of Maryland's vast broiler industry.

Leave Salisbury by State 349. Within a few miles you will come to two cable ferries, rarities now anywhere. Both cross the Wicomico River. The first is the Upper Ferry, the second is at Whitehaven.

Cross at Whitehaven on the old cable ferry and follow State 362 to Princess Anne, founded in 1733. A walking tour guide available at the Court House and most stores will show you prim boxwood gardens, the stately Teackle Mansion (1801) and the Washington Hotel and Inn (1744), where travelers still find comfortable lodging and good food.

Turn off US 13 onto State 667 and go west to Rehobeth. Here is the oldest Presbyterian Church in the United States, built in 1706 and open ever since.

Follow State 667 to Marion and turn south on State 413 to Crisfield. Tour boats leave here daily May-November for Smith Island, Md., twelve miles out in Chesapeake Bay, and Tangier Island, Va., 15 miles away. These islands, charted in 1608 by Captain John Smith, are unique pockets of "a faraway time," inhabited today by hardy descendants of the early settlers. Several guest houses accommodate visitors overnight, and an afternoon's visit can include a memorable family-style meal fresh from the Bay.

The *Captain Tyler* offers an afternoon boat-and-bus tour of Smith Island, plus dinner. The ferry *Jason* makes twice-daily round trips to Smith Island year-round, and the captain can arrange for dinner and lodgings at Frances Kitching's on the island. The *Island Belle II* mail-boat takes passengers to Pitchcroft Restaurant on Smith, which also has overnight accommodations. The *Spirit of '76* serves Tangier Island; both a day tour and overnight lodging are available.

From Crisfield return to Marion, take State 667 to US 13, go on 13 to US 113, and follow that to Snow Hill. There, visit the Julia Purnell Museum. It contains a vast and fantastically varied collection of antique articles. Also go out to the nearby Nassawango Furnace, the impressive ruins of a mid-19th-century iron works.

Proceed over US 113 to its intersection with US 50, and go on to Ocean City, Maryland's bustling Atlantic shore resort. There are all kinds of accommodations, from trailer camps to luxury motels, but the surf is the same for everyone—superb. The major attraction here is the fine white sand beach, but there's a bit of history as well. At the south end of the development area are several fine old hotels—including the Atlantic, which opened for business in 1875—from the early days of this resort. The shop-lined boardwalk, which covered two blocks when laid down in 1902 by several hotel owners, now spans three miles. Take time to see the new Convention Hall, which hosts a variety of shows, big band dances and other events.

Next, take State 611 to Assateague Island National Seashore. Assateague Island is 37 miles long, the northern 22 miles in Maryland and the southern portion in Virginia. A 700-acre state park at the northern end offers camping and swimming. A herd of wild ponies wanders freely here, and the park offers refuge to many species of wildfowl.

Leave Ocean City by US 50, keep on until the intersection with State 313, follow this to Federalsburg and take State 318 to the water-turned Linchester Grist Mill, marked with an Historical Society sign.

Go on from the mill to Preston, there take State 16, follow that until it runs into State 404, and follow that until it runs into US 50. Keep on until the Bay Bridge, where you end your tour of Maryland's Eastern Shore.

Before leaving this area of the state, one more stop is worthwhile. This is the Chesapeake Bay Hydraulic Model Complex, two miles south of US 50 on State 8. The worlds largest hydraulic model, covering nine acres, is used to study Bay tides and currents, salinity, preferred location of power plants and port facilities, and other factors. Tours at specified times on weekdays.

Crossing the Bay

Crossing the Bay Bridge, give a thought to the bay itself. It is America's leading inland sea, salty and containing islands with indigenous cultures. The Indians called it "Mother of Waters." Its shoreline, with tributaries, measures 25,000 miles. Captain John Smith undertook to explore it in 1608, making its circuit in an open boat, carrying a crew of sixteen. He was the first white man to take the tour. The Bay has been the route of vast commercial shipping for 250 years and is the waterway to the nation's capital. Baltimore, at its head, is one of the nation's largest ports; the United States Naval Academy fronts on its waters.

Bay craft suited for Bay conditions—skipjack, bugeye, pungy, log canoe—were designed by Bay men and worked the Bay for over a century. The clipper, designed in Baltimore, carried commercial traffic all over the seven seas. Bay goods—oysters, crabs, clams, terrapin, finfish—have produced an extensive industry of fishermen, preservers and shippers. Today, sport fishing and boating flourish; the Bay is ringed with yacht clubs, power boat clubs and marinas, while from March to mid-November, regattas are held frequently. The Bay influences the lives of all who stay about it. It is a place-personality; give it a thought as you glide overhead on its tall steel twin spans.

Pride of the Western Shore

Your first stop on the Western Shore will be Annapolis, founded in 1649, the capital since 1695. Its Colonial downtown (a National Historic Landmark) contains the State House (1772–79), the Old Treasury (1735), Maryland Inn (1782) and Middleton's Tavern (1750)—both still in use—the Hammond-Harwood House (1774), the Chase-Lloyd House (1771), William Paca House and Garden (1765), St. Anne's Church (rebuilt 1858), St. Johns College (begun 1696), and an attractive waterfront with a bustling marketplace. Guides for walking tours may be employed through Historic Annapolis Tours at the Old Treasury, State Circle, or Three Centuries Tours. The Naval Academy grounds are open daily. There are full-dress parades Wednesday afternoons in spring and fall. A harbor tour boat operates out of the city dock in the spring and summer.

Then go south on US 301. If your trip is made between April and mid-June, you will be able to see the world's greatest loose-leaf tobacco sales along your way, auctions that take place during those weeks in four southern Maryland villages, weekday mornings. Two of the towns—Upper Marlboro and La Plata—lie along 301. Visitors are welcome at the warehouses and there is no charge.

Three miles west of US 301 on State 6 is Port Tobacco, one of the oldest inhabited sites in the country. Today half a mile from the river, this restoration town was once the port of entry through which southern Maryland's vast tobacco crop was shipped abroad. It had a customs house, extensive wharves, warehouses, a courthouse, churches, and taverns. Then, due to the change of shoreline, it eventually lost its waterfront, and died. You will see three or four buildings now, including the reconstructed Courthouse, which serves as an information center and county museum, and a public square that is almost, but not quite, empty.

ANNAPOLIS AREA

For in its center flows a well that is "nobody-knows-how-old." Captain John Smith's log mentions that he filled his ship casks there in 1608.

Follow the Chapel Point Road and you will come to St. Ignatius Church (1784) and the adjoining Jesuit Chapter House, St. Thomas Manor. The church is open and the view over the valley and river is magnificent.

Now return over 301 to La Plata, turn right on State 488, and keep on to the intersection with State 5. You will presently be in St. Mary's County, the oldest part of Colonial Maryland. There has been a minimum of change here since the 17th century. The fields are still velvety with tobacco, the many tall old forests still stand, and houses and settlements remain spaciously set.

St. Mary's County Highlights

Go first to St. Mary's City, on State 5. There, go to the Old State House. You will see for yourself that there is no commercialization. The place on the riverbank where the first settlers came ashore is still covered with wild growths and is marked only by a small stone bench. You can sit there, if you wish, and think a little of the idea that entered America at this place. It was called "tolerance."

Go on to Point Lookout, still on 5. Here the ten-mile-wide Potomac rolls into the twenty-mile-wide Bay, the nearby state park offering excellent camping facilities. In the Civil War, there was a Confederate prison camp there. Two monuments have been erected to the prisoners who died, one by the Federal Government, one by Maryland. Nearby are the remnants of Fort Lincoln, where Union soldiers kept guard.

Head back north on State 235, turning right on State 245 three miles to Sotterley. This magnificent working plantation, built on land that was part of a grant from Lord Baltimore, takes its name from the Satterlee family, the last of four to live there. The oldest part of the main house was built in 1711–27. The notable woodwork includes a Chinese Chippendale staircase and shell alcoves in the drawing room, and the oldest rooms are completely wood paneled. No visit to this section of Maryland is complete without a stop at this outstanding example of a plantation house.

Continuing north along State 235, visit the Farmer's Market at Charlotte Hall. Open year-round on Wednesdays and Saturdays, it has Amish stalls, antiques, and produce stands.

Keep on State 5 to State 231. When you reach the Patuxent River, you will pass through the village of Benedict. It was at this place that the British Army which burned Washington during the War of 1812 came ashore, their transports having sailed up the Patuxent from Chesapeake Bay.

Cross the bridge; follow 231 to State 2 and 4 at Prince Frederick. Then go on 2 and 4 to the intersection with 497 (Cove Point Rd.). This will take you to Cove Point, where there is an old lighthouse.

Return to 2 and 4 and follow the road to its end at Solomons, if you are interested in fish and fishing. Not only do the fish bite well here, they also bite in unusual varieties. Strange species are not infrequently caught off Solomons. The Calvert Marine Museum is here, with exhibits related to local marine history. These include clam and oyster dredge boats, log canoes, and an 1883 lighthouse.

Head back over 2 and 4 where they divide, and take 4. It will carry you to Interstate 495 (I–95), which is the Capital Beltway. State 4 there becomes Pennsylvania Avenue and will take you to the heart of Washington, D.C. Do what sightseeing you wish in Washington, but remember that you are also in Maryland, as this state surrounds the nation's capital.

Sometime while you are in Washington, you might wish to visit two attractions in nearby Montgomery County, Md. The Mormon Temple, dedicated in 1974, is one of 16 such sacred Mormon structures throughout the world where baptisms, marriages, and other ceremonies are performed. Located at 9900 Stoneybrook Dr. in Kensington, it rises dramatically above the trees and can be seen while driving the Capital Beltway. The visitors' center is open daily, and there are tours of the temple and grounds.

A short drive away, in Gaithersburg off Interstate 270, is the National Bureau of Standards. The lobby of the administration building contains historic documents and an exhibit on the metric system. Open weekdays.

Fort Washington, off Exit 3 from the Capital Beltway, near Oxen Hill, is an immense, semi-ruined structure, with drawbridge, portcullis, battlements, and dungeons, that once guarded Washington from attack by water. A beautiful park with picnic facilities surrounds it.

Also off the Capital Beltway (Exit 30), along US 29, is Columbia, one of the earliest—and most successful—of the self-contained "new towns." Columbia welcomed its first residents in 1967, and is scheduled eventually to be home for 110,000 people. There's an audio-visual presentation at the visitors' center, and tours are available.

There also are walking and bus tours of nearby Ellicott City, off US 29 a few miles north of Columbia. Founded in 1772 along the shores of the Patapsco River, Ellicott City became one of the leading milling and manufacturing towns in the East. Among numerous remaining mid-19th century buildings are the county courthouse, Gothic-Revival Angelo Cottage and "Mount Ida," the last home to be built (in 1828) by members of the original Ellicott family.

North of Baltimore

Leave Baltimore by US 40 East and go to the Aberdeen Proving Ground, where, in the Army Ordnance Museum, you will see the greatest collection of weapons of war in the world. All American history is there, in the arms not only of our own forces but in those of our enemies as well. Examples of the latter include "Anzio Annie," still mounted on a flatcar, and the Congreve rocket that made the "red glare" above Baltimore Harbor in the War of 1812.

Then take State 136 to Norrisville. Go out Amos Lane and visit the Amos Mill. The water wheel alongside the three-story building used to be turned by overhead flow. Leave Norrisville on State 23, go to the intersection with 138, and follow 138 to Interstate 83. Cross over 83 to State 317; take that highway and go to Hampstead. There, get on State 482 and proceed to Westminster.

In this town, at Historical Society of Carroll County on Main Street, there is a rare collection of fashion model dolls, the dolls that in pre-fashion-magazine years were used by smart dressmakers to display new styles. The Historical Society has other collections, including one of unduplicated flags.

If you are touring in summer, go over State 97 to Union Mills. There you will see the Homestead, built in 1797, variously a stagecoach station, an inn, a post office, a store and a magistrate's court—while all the time serving as a home. The same family has always lived in it.

Visit the Carroll County Farm Museum, an 1850s farmhouse and barn furnished to depict 19th-century farm life. Outbuildings include a smokehouse, blacksmith shop, and craft sheds, and demonstrations of blacksmithing, broom making, weaving, and other crafts are given at designated times throughout the year.

Return to Westminster and take State 31 to New Windsor, where the Church World Service has its largest headquarters at the Brethren Service Center. Clothes, hospital equipment and medical supplies are prepared here with the assistance of voluntary labor for shipping to needy people throughout the world. In the Service's International Gift Shop, articles made by craftsmen and artists of 30 nations are offered for sale. The list includes carvings, metal work, ceramics, paintings, fabrics, furniture, garments, and toys—from Latin America, the Pacific Islands, Africa, Asia, and Europe. Prices are astonishingly low.

Leave New Windsor on State 84. Keep on to the point where 84 joins State 140. Follow State 140 and 97 to the St. Joseph's Provincial House in Emmitsburg, where the first American chapter of the Sisters of Charity was founded in 1806. Saint Elizabeth Ann Seton, the founder, cannonized in 1975, lies buried there. Visitors may have tours of the grounds and Shrine, still operated by the Sisters of Charity. The National Grotto of Lourdes, the pilgrimage site of St. Seton, is on the grounds of nearby Mt. Saint Mary's College.

Go south from Emmitsburg on US 15. On the left side of the road are the restored remains of the Catoctin Iron Furnace, built in 1774. Cannon balls for the Yorktown campaign and the plates for the iron-clad *Monitor* were cast here. Nearby are some small stone cottages that were the homes of furnace workers. This area also offers outdoor recreation at Catoctin Mountain National Park and Cunningham Falls State Park, as well as most of Maryland's covered bridges. They can be found on Old Frederick Road, off US 15, near Utica, and on MD 77 near Thurmont, at Loy's Station and Roddy Road.

Maryland's Not-so-Wild West

In Frederick, the National Historic District includes the beautiful Court House Square; the restored home of Barbara Fritchie, heroine of the Whittier ballad; the tomb of Francis Scott Key in Mt. Olivet Cemetery, where the American flag flies 24 hours a day by decree to honor the author of "The Star-Spangled Banner," plus numerous other historic attractions. To enjoy the National Historic District to the fullest, take the guided walking tour by contacting the Visitors Information Center at 19 E. Church St. in downtown Frederick.

A few miles east of Frederick on MD 144, off I–70, is New Market, the "Antiques Capital of Maryland." It is a tiny village that is almost entirely supported by the sale of antiques. More than four dozen shops, all of high quality, line its brief street. Any antiques fancier really ought to see this place.

South of Frederick is Stronghold, a private estate, the grounds of which are open to the public and well worth seeing. They include Sugarloaf Mountain, 1,281 feet high, from whose top one can look into three states. On its slopes are overlooks and picnic grounds along a well-planned drive. The view is magnificent. One reaches Stronghold by going south from Frederick on I–270 to MD 109 west via Comus.

Go by US 40 Alternate to Hagerstown. In the City Park there see the Hager House, built by the founder of the city in 1739. This building combines the aspects of a mansion and a fort, reminding the modern traveler that in 1739, this area was the American "West."

On the field of Antietam on September 17, 1862, the Union Army repulsed the first Confederate attempt to invade the North. It was the most fiercely fought single-day battle of the war. The field, a National Battlefield Site, can be reached by State 65 out of Hagerstown. The Visitors Center and Museum is a good place to begin your tour. The Burnside Bridge over Antietam Creek is an impressive stone structure and famous landmark of the battle.

Leave Hagerstown and proceed west via Interstate 70. A highway sign will direct you to Fort Frederick State Park. Here is a huge stone fort of the French and Indian War period (1756). The authentically reconstructed barracks reminds you vividly of the dangers of frontier existence.

Continue west on Interstate 70 to US 40 into Cumberland. Historic Washington St. is lined by 19th-century period houses. Visit Emmanuel Episcopal Church (1851), with its beautiful stained-glass windows; Washington's Headquarters (1755), the only remaining building of the original Fort Cumberland, used by Colonel George Washington at the beginning of his military career, and the Western Maryland Railroad Station (1913).

Through the Narrows

Keep on to Cumberland Narrows, just beyond Cumberland. Through this tall slim break in the mountain wall has passed the connecting link, whatever it was, between Mid-East and Mid-West. Now it is US 40, also called the Old National Road because it was the first Federal Highway, built in 1806 and running between Cumberland and Wheeling, West Virginia. Other east-west links through the Narrows have been the bison and Indian trails, the first military road (1755), and the first railroad (1828).

At Penn Alps, on US 40 just before you come to Grantsville, Pennsylvania Dutch food of high quality is served. Here also is a gift shop in which the arts and crafts of the mountain people are offered for sale and where crafts such as weaving, pottery, and clock making are demonstrated year-round. (Closed Sundays.) Adjoining the Penn Alps grounds is the Casselman River Bridge, now a Registered Historic National Landmark. It was part of the National Road and, when it was finished in 1814, was the longest single-arch stone bridge in the country.

Leave US 40 at Keysers Ridge, turning onto US 219. This will take you to Deep Creek Lake. Driving toward the area, one passes a road sign proclaiming Deep Creek Lake to be "Maryland's Best-Kept Secret." In many ways, it is.

This area of Maryland is called the state's "mountain playground," and Deep Creek Lake its "four seasons" mountain resort. The contrast is striking to the rest of the state: the bustling port city of Baltimore, the antiquity of Colonial Annapolis, and the sand beaches and glittering activity at Ocean City. Here, the mountains are the major physical presence. Cool mountain streams, deep forests and magnificent rolling scenery are as unchangeable as a way of life that remains much as it has been for generations.

Deep Creek Lake itself, created in 1925 by an electric company to provide water-generated power, serves as the center of a wide variety of activities on and around its 65 miles of shoreline. In summer, there is swimming, boating, water-skiing, fishing and sailing. During the winter, there's downhill skiing at the nearby Wisp Ski Area, as well as cross-country skiing, skating and snowmobiling. Other diversions—such as hiking and picnicking—are best during spring and fall.

Accommodations of various types—from luxurious condominiums, motels and inns to rustic cottages, trailer camps and campgrounds—surround the lake. Scenic attractions, as well as the ubiquitous mountains, include Swallow Falls and Muddy Creek Falls, primeval forests in a number of state parks, the Big Savage River Dam drive (where the road follows a canyon for miles), the Cranesville subarctic swamp, where there are growths to be found nowhere else on the continent except in the Arctic Circle, the beautiful farms of the Amish, and Backbone Mountain (3,360 feet high), commanding a 30-mile view.

The above is the outline of one possible tour. It is not the full list of what there is to see in the Old Line State, but it will give you an idea of how much is waiting for you should you come here.

PRACTICAL INFORMATION FOR MARYLAND

MARYLAND FACTS AND FIGURES. Maryland was named for Queen Henrietta Maria of England. Its nicknames are *Free State* and *Old Line State*. The state flower is the black-eyed susan; the state tree, the Wye Oak, a 400-plus-year-old white oak at Wye Mills; the state sport, jousting (the only state with an official sport); the state bird, the Baltimore oriole; the state dog, Chesapeake Bay Retriever; the state insect, the Baltimore Checker Spot Butterfly. *Fatti maschii parole femine* ("Manly deeds, womanly words") is the state motto. "Maryland, My Maryland" is the state song.

Annapolis, home of the U.S. Naval Academy, is the state capital. The state population is about 4,100,000, 18th in the U.S.; its area of 10,577 square miles is 42nd in size among the 50 states.

Chesapeake Bay, the long arm of the Atlantic that runs through the state from north to south, dominates the topography, economic and social character of Maryland. In 1608 Captain John Smith described it thus: "Here are mountains, hills, plaines, valleyes, rivers and brookes all running most pleasantly into a Faire Bay compassed but for the mouth with fruitful and delightsome land." The flat land of the Eastern Shore is primarily agricultural and seafood country (Maryland is famous for its oysters, crabs, fish, and clams), and the region is a paradise for sportsmen—sailing, fishing, hunting—including fox hunting. The Eastern Shore is the historical part of the state, a land of old antebellum mansions, rich in reminders of the South's colonial past. To the west of Chesapeake Bay, the land rises to rolling hills in the center of the state, a pleasant landscape dotted with historic old towns like Frederick. Western Maryland is a skinny mountainous panhandle squeezed between Pennsylvania and the Potomac River, which come to within less than two miles of each other near Hancock. The state's highest point, Backbone Mountain (3,360 feet) is here; and on Marsh Mountain there is skiing well into March. Despite its rural aspects, industry plays a dominant role in the state's economy, with most industrial activity centered around the port of Baltimore.

The climate is moderate, with cold winters and warm summers.

HOW TO GET THERE. *By car:* I–95 enters the state near Wilmington, Delaware, passing through Aberdeen and Baltimore and leaving the state south of Washington, D.C. I–70 connects central Pennsylvania and Baltimore, entering Maryland at Hancock. The primary north-south routes on the Eastern Shore are US 301, which enters the state from Middletown, Del., and US 13 from Laurel, Del. US 13 goes through Salisbury into Virginia, where it leads to the Chesapeake Bay Bridge-Tunnel connecting Cape Charles and Cape Henry, Va.

By air: There is scheduled air service to Baltimore, Hagerstown and Washington, D.C. Numerous airlines fly to Baltimore and Washington, D.C. *Allegheny Commuter* flies to Hagerstown and Salisbury.

By bus: Greyhound and Continental Trailways are the major carriers to Maryland and Baltimore is the major terminal.

By train: Amtrak has service to Wilmington, Delaware, Baltimore and Washington, D.C.

HOW TO GET AROUND. *By car:* A network of good roads, which makes it possible to speed through Maryland en route to Florida or New England, also makes it convenient to get to all parts of the state. Maryland boasts the first Federally-financed road in the original 13 United States, the National Road (US 40), which still provides a scenic route to western Pennsylvania, Ohio and the West. The new I–70 west from Baltimore also traverses the same route. I–95 does the same north and south.

By boat: The Inland Waterway traverses the Chesapeake Bay from the Chesapeake and Delaware Canal to Virginia Capes. There are approximately 60 yachting centers and 350 marinas and marine facilities along the way. Boats can be rented in Annapolis, Chestertown, Edgewater, and many other towns around the Chesapeake Bay, and in Ocean City.

TOURIST INFORMATION. Maps, brochures and information of all kinds is available from The Office of Tourist Development, Maryland Department of Economic & Community Development, 1748 Forest Dr., Annapolis 21401. Tel. (301) 269–3517.

SEASONAL EVENTS. *January.* Open house at the Governor's mansion in Annapolis is a tradition on New Year's Day. *The Vacation, Travel and Auto Show,* at the new Baltimore Convention Center. *Ratification Day* commemorates the end of the Revolutionary War in the State House at Annapolis. Late January to early February, the new Baltimore Convention Center hosts the Chesapeake Bay Boat Show. Winter horse racing gets underway at Bowie, lasting until March.

February. In Baltimore, the Convention Center becomes a temporary marina for the *Chesapeake Bay Boat Show.*

March. Maryland Day, anniversary of the landing of the first settlers in 1634, is celebrated at St. Mary's City and before the State Court House at Baltimore on the 25th. Also in Baltimore, the annual *Mason-Dixon Open Badminton Tournament,* an antique gun show and the annual *Maryland Kite Festival.* It's still cold in western Maryland, perfect for the *Annual Winterfest* at the Wisp Ski Area near Deep Creek Lake; and there are maple sugar demonstrations at Catoctin National Park and Cunningham Falls State Park near Thurmont.

April. The Chesapeake Bay Fishing Fair gets under way the first day to run until Nov. 30. *The Maryland House and Garden Pilgrimage* gets under way the last few days of April and continues into May. Also popular around Baltimore are the annual *My Lady's Manor* and the *Grand National and Maryland Hunt Cup*— timber races across big estates for gentlemen jockeys. In southern Maryland, at La Plata, Hughesville, Upper Marlboro and Wayson's Corner, tobacco auctioneers sing-song their distinctive chant over Maryland leaf from mid-April to mid-June, weekday mornings.

May. Blooming of Sherwood Gardens in Baltimore, usually in mid-May, marks the arrival of spring. The third Saturday of the month the $200,000 *Preakness* is run at Pimlico. The preceding week is *Preakness Cultural Festival* in Baltimore, with daily special events, including a parade and hot air balloon race the weekend before the race. Highly colorful, with bands, mounted drill teams, a race for lady jockeys, and picnics of crab cakes and fried chicken, it is a tradition started in 1873. "Commissioning Week" at the Naval Academy in Annapolis is one of the most colorful and photographed graduation ceremonies on any campus, and a time when nostalgic admirals return to see the traditional color-girl ceremony and parade. Almost weekly "ethnic festivals" begin in Baltimore, culminating with the gigantic City Fair in September.

June. In Annapolis, the *Arts Festival* draws crowds. Along both sides of the Bay regattas are held, while those who stay ashore begin their annual round of horse and pony shows. Fair Hill also is site of sheepdog trials and the *Delaware Highland Gathering* with traditional Scottish games, dances and bagpipes. Maryland farms are open for visiting. The Frederick Fairgrounds is the site of the *National Craft Fair.* Also in Frederick is the *Annual Carriage Driving Show* at Rose Hill Manor. The second weekend is Heritage Days in Cumberland, with tours of historic homes, exhibits and free entertainment. *Flag Day* is occasion for festivities in Baltimore, while on the Eastern Shore homage is paid to the chicken industry with three days of cookin' and eatin'. There's lots of "old-fashioned family fun" during *Grantsville Days,* including a parade, fiddlin' contest, and traditional picnic in Grantsville Park.

July. County fairs and jousting by this time are going strong. The state sport requires skilled horsemen or horsewomen, who ride nearly every Saturday for the benefit of country churches, to spear a small ring at full gallop. Jousting has its fair queens, whose colors the riders carry on their lances, but the real queens of beauty are those who compete for the title *Miss Maryland* and the right to represent the Free State at the Miss America contest in Atlantic City. Other events include *Family Picnic Day* at Carroll County Farm Museum, motorcycle races at Frederick Fairgrounds and the annual *Mid-Atlantic White Marlin Handicap Fishing Tournament* at Ocean City.

August. Dutch Picnic, said to be the largest picnic held in the state, has been an annual fixture for more than 100 years at Trinity Lutheran Church, in Smallwood, near Westminster. Not far away, at Union Mills Homestead, there's an old-fashioned corn roast. The original jousting or tilting tournament on the Eastern Shore is still held at St. Joseph's Catholic Church, Cordova, the first Wednesday. Another is at Port Republic in southern Maryland. Both tournaments are more than 100 years old. Cumberland Fairgrounds is the site of an agricultural fair the first week of August, while White Marlin and Small Boat tournaments take place at Ocean City. Tennis attracts the best of Maryland's players to tournaments in Baltimore and Mountain Lake Park, and the *Potomac River Festival* is held in Brunswick. Soft-shell clams, corn-on-the-cob and big-name entertainers have turned the *Maryland Clam Festival* at Sandy Point State Park into a popular annual event.

September. The Maryland State Fair at Timonium, six miles north of Towson on York Rd., runs the week before Labor Day, while in Crisfield, the seafood capital of the world, the *National Hard Crab Derby* is run. Labor Day sees races at Deal Island among the remaining "skipjacks"—sloops dating from as far back as the early 1900s, which are the only sail-powered fleet of workboats in the U.S.—and white water races on the Savage River near Bloomington. For those who grow nostalgic at the sight of old farm threshers, *Steam Show Days* is held at Carroll County Farm Museum. Cumberland is inland, yet each September throws a two-day seafood festival and "motorama." Down at St. Clement Island, where Maryland's first settlers landed in 1634, they hold a blessing of the fleet. But the oldest annual commemoration is *Old Defender's Day* on Sept. 12, which marks the successful defense of Baltimore against the British, and on the Sunday nearest that date a *mock bombardment at Fort McHenry* recalls the historic day. The Baltimore City Fair, the largest of its kind, takes place at the inner harbor in mid-September. Fall horse racing at Bowie.

October. Autumn Glory Time, always in the first two weeks, celebrates the fall scene in the Appalachian Mountains. Grantsville takes the opportunity to display its handicraft at the *Folk Arts Festival,* while in Oakland, Western Maryland's largest and most colorful "do," *Autumn Glory,* features parades, banjo strumming and fiddle contests. Other festivals include the *Oktoberfest* in Baltimore, one of the largest such celebrations outside Germany itself, the *Fell's Point Fun Festival,* the *Camp David Country Colorfest, Catoctin Mountain Color-fest* near Thurmont, the *Old Princess Anne Days, Fall Harvest Days* at the Carroll County Farm Museum, and the *Apple Butter Festival.* During *Heritage Weekend* in Annapolis, homes not usually open on other tours welcome visitors inside to see where history was made more than two centuries ago. The Oyster Festival at Leonardtown—with a shucking contest, entertainment and plenty of oysters and other Southern Maryland specialties to eat—has become a major seafood event. But the biggest events this month are for the nautical-minded: the *Chesapeake Appreciation Day* skipjack races off Sandy Point State Park, the in-water *U.S. Sailboat Show* and the *U.S. Yacht Show,* and the largest displays of boats afloat— at Annapolis City Dock.

November. A trumpeter from the Baltimore Symphony sounds the call for thoroughbreds that belong to such distinguished owners as Queen Elizabeth, Alfred G. Vanderbilt, and C. V. Whitney to come to the *Laurel* starting gate for the *Washington, D.C., International,* now regarded as the classic that produces the *Horse of the World.* The annual 50-mile *John F. Kennedy Hike* is held along the C&O Canal, beginning in Boonsboro. The *Annual Needlework Show* at Rose Hill Manor in Frederick.

December. The Christmas Greens Show at the Baltimore Museum of Art is a prelude to the many communities that award prizes for best-decorated doorways and houses at Christmas. Other viewings of special holiday decorations include the *Holly Tour* of downtown Baltimore homes, the candlelit *Hammond-Harwood House,* and the Paca House in Annapolis—part of that city's elaborate Christmas festivities—the 18th-century *Mount Clare* and *Charles Carroll mansions* in Baltimore and the old farm home at *Carroll County Farm Museum.* The custom of Christmas gardens in firehouses has been consolidated in recent years at Engine Co. No. 45. Another is at Towson Fire Headquarters. (See *What to Do with the Children.)* The ski season opens the 15th in Garrett and Baltimore counties.

NATIONAL PARKS AND HISTORICAL ATTRACTIONS. The bloodiest single day's fighting of the Civil War occurred along *Antietam Creek* near the town of Sharpsburg. While *Antietam National Battlefield Site* has its share of modern encroachments, much of it is still farm land as it was on September 17, 1862, when Gen. Robert E. Lee made his first unsuccessful invasion of the North. Self-conducted tours start at the Visitors' Center, which can be reached by State 34 from Alt. US 40 at Boonsboro, by State 65 from Alt. US 40 at Hagerstown.

Sometimes the black ducks, blue-winged teals, mallards and Canada geese at *Blackwater National Wildlife Refuge* on the Atlantic flyway are so numerous, it is difficult to drive along the roads of this 11,200-acre refuge near Church Creek, 11 mi. south of Cambridge, which can be reached via US 50. Over 225 species of birds and 27 species of waterfowl have been observed in a single week, as well as muskrats, raccoons, foxes and other wildlife. Hunting or fishing not allowed. Visitor center, wildlife drive and observation tower. Best times to visit are late autumn and winter.

Catoctin Mountain Park, just 3 miles west of Thurmont on MD 77, includes the site of Camp David, the Presidential retreat, which is strictly off limits. But for the public there is still a 7-mile scenic drive, 12 miles of well-marked hiking trails, two picnic areas and a modern camp for 5-day family camping from mid-April through October. Girl and Boy Scouts and other groups have primitive areas. The National Park Service conducts several interesting programs during the summer season. The park is about equidistant, 65 miles, between Washington and Baltimore, and about midway between Frederick and Gettysburg, Pa., on US 15.

Chesapeake and Ohio Canal National Historical Park. Stretching from Georgetown in the District of Columbia to Cumberland, along the Maryland bank of the twisting Potomac River, this park and its canal extend nearly 185 miles. An idea of George Washington's, the canal was started by President John Quincy Adams on July 4, 1828—the same day the Baltimore and Ohio Railroad was begun. It was not completed until 1850, by which time the railroad had made the canal obsolete. However, the waterway struggled along until 1924 despite financial disasters, the Civil War, and spring floods. Some 22 miles from Georgetown to Seneca have been restored. The canal is visible at Georgetown, Great Falls, Antietam, Harpers Ferry, Williamsport, Paw Paw, Hancock and Oldtown, where another area is open for canoeing and fishing. For more information write Superintendent, C&O Canal National Historical Park, P.O. Box 4, Sharpsburg, Md. 21782.

The story of how Francis Scott Key, a Maryland attorney and poet, was detained by the British while their fleet bombarded *Fort McHenry* at the entrance to Baltimore harbor is a familiar one. First, "in the rocket's red glare" and then "by dawn's early light," he saw the flag was still flying, wrote what became the National Anthem. Fort McHenry, with its visitor center and film story, is an inspiring place to visit. The fort, three miles from the center of the city, is readily accessible over E. Fort Ave. near the Inner Harbor. Free admission to visitor center to see film. During the summer, there are musket firing and other demonstrations.

Within sight of *Mount Vernon,* Va., on the opposite shore of the Potomac River, *Fort Washington* is an outstanding example of an early 19th-century coastal defense. George Washington selected the site, but the fort to protect the new Federal City was not begun until Dec. 1, 1809. Destroyed by the British in 1814, it was rebuilt under the direction of Maj. Pierre L'Enfant, who designed Washington, D.C. It can be reached by Indian Head Highway (State 210). Turn right 5½ mi. below District of Columbia line and follow signs. Picnic tables.

When *Hampton House* was built in 1783–90, the workmen were allowed to quit early each day to reach home before dark. The reason: wolves in the neighborhood. Now the stately Georgian mansion, with its terraced gardens, is on the outskirts of Baltimore, easily reached by driving out the Dulaney Valley Rd. from Towson. Lafayette was a guest there on his second visit to America in 1824, and the coach he used is still there. The high-ceilinged rooms contain most of their original furnishings.

Assateague Island National Seashore. After a long controversy between conservationists and private developers, President Johnson, in September 1965, signed the bill that preserves one of the largest undeveloped seashore areas on the East Coast from the blight of boarding houses, neon signs and hamburger stands. Home of the famous Chincoteague wild ponies, whose origins remain a mystery, this wild barrier beach has little on it except a camping and swimming area on the northern end, in Maryland. It can be reached by driving south on State 611, from US 50 near Ocean City, to a bridge that crosses Sinepuxent Bay.

Western Maryland: *Catoctin Furnace,* US 15, 7 mi. south of Thurmont. There are several iron furnaces in the state but this one, in the town of Catoctin, where several old log and stone houses are sole remnants of a once thriving community, is the best preserved. Cannon balls for the Yorktown campaign and plates for the ironclad *Monitor* were made here.

Paw Paw Tunnel. Built for the Chesapeake and Ohio Canal in 1839 to cut off five miles of bends in the Potomac River, this is a lasting tribute to the engineering skill of early 19th-century builders. Reached by a dirt road from the Maryland end of the Potomac River above into Paw Paw, W. Va. (State 51). *Roger Brooke Taney House,* 123 S. Bentz St., Frederick. Memorabilia of Francis Scott Key and his brother-in-law, Chief Justice Taney, who administered the oath of office to seven Presidents, including Abraham Lincoln. Slave quarters in the rear are furnished as they were about 1812. Open June through October. "Schifferstadt" at 1110 Rosemont Ave. in Frederick, a German-style farmhouse built in 1756.

Williamsport. Here the Civil War nearly ended 10 months before Appomattox. Following the Battle of Gettysburg, Lee's Army of Northern Virginia was unable to recross a rain-swollen Potomac River. But Union Gen. George Gordon Meade delayed his attack, and Lee escaped under cover of night.

Deep Creek Lake, south of US 48 along US 219. The state's largest lake is in the center of the state's largest, most western and most remote county, Garrett. Now a summer vacation and winter ski resort, it is lovely any time of the year, but especially during the "Autumn Glory Festival." Muddy Creeks Falls, the state's highest, is in *Swallow Falls State Park,* 10 miles northwest of Oakland in Swallow Falls State Forest.

 STATE PARKS AND FORESTS. Maryland has 35 parks and recreation areas, some of them small historic sites that are free. Others levy a small charge for day shelters, fireplaces, picnic tables and charcoal. Many parks have separate areas for campers. Trailers, when permitted, are limited to 29 feet in length. Dogs, except seeing-eyes, are not allowed in developed areas of parks. Hunting is allowed in some state parks.

The parks provide a variety of topography, scenery and recreational experiences. There are parks on tidewater flatlands, parks in the mountains and parks on beautiful lakes. Others are on the Chesapeake Bay and its tributaries, the Atlantic Ocean and one on an island. They include within their boundaries old forts, lighthouses, mansions, Civil War battlefields, a monument to George Washington and several famous trout streams. In *Cunningham Falls State Park,* Big Hunting Creek, with a 40-foot waterfall, has lured five presidents of the United States. Across the road is the late President Franklin Roosevelt's *Shangri-La,* later renamed *Camp David* for his grandson by President Dwight D. Eisenhower. Patapsco State Park, which runs along the Patapsco River from Baltimore Harbor to Reisterstown, has a well laid out Braille trail.

Gathland Correspondents' Memorial Arch, near Burkittsville. Reached via Rte. 17 from Middletown on Alt. US 40. On a hilltop, novelist George Alfred Townsend raised this curious monument to correspondents who, like himself, covered the Civil War. Names of World War I and II war reporters have been added by State of Maryland. Now in a state park.

George Washington's Headquarters. Riverside Park, Cumberland. This log cabin is the only remaining structure left of Fort Cumberland. It was here that young George Washington learned military strategy and later, as President, where he reviewed his troops for the last time. Open for tours at designated times during the year. *Fort Frederick,* on State 56 off I–70. Now a state park on the Potomac River, the stone fort was built in 1756 as a defense against the French and Indians, later used as prison during Revolutionary and Civil Wars. Revolutionary period military drills are presented several weekends in summer.

Maryland also has nine state forests that provide primitive camping and permit licensed hunting and fishing in season. For a complete list of parks, forests and details, write Maryland Park Service, Tawes State Office Building, Annapolis, Md. 21401.

  MUSEUMS AND GALLERIES. *Army Ordnance Museum,* Aberdeen Proving Ground, off US 40 at Aberdeen. Free. Some 15,000 weapons of our allies and enemies from the Revolutionary War to the present, including tanks from World War I to "Anzio Annie," a German V-2 rocket and the car Gen. John J. Pershing used in Mexico in 1916.

Carroll County Farm Museum, off US 140 on Center St. Extended in Westminster. A century-old farm where blacksmithing, weaving, quilting and candlemaking can be seen.

National Capital Trolley Museum, on Bonifant Rd. north of Wheaton. A collection of American and foreign streetcars of particular interest to railroad buffs and youngsters. Rides are available in some clanking, rocking old cars. Call 384-9797 for information about hours and special programs.

National Bureau of Standards, Clopper and Quince Orchard Rds., off I–270, Gaithersburg. An exhibit of the evolution of the metric system, and historic documents. Tours on Tuesdays and Fridays.

National Colonial Farm Museum, at Accokeek, Exit 37 off I–95 to State 210. A fully operating example of an 18th-century freeholder's farm. On the Potomac River directly opposite Mt. Vernon.

Calvert Marine Museum, Solomons. A museum dedicated to preservation of local marine history, featuring a lighthouse, boat models, Chesapeake Bay boats, paintings, and other exhibits.

Naval Academy Museum, just inside Gate 3, U.S. Naval Academy, Annapolis. Free. An outstanding collection of incredibly detailed model ships, plus many mementos of naval battles and heroes, such as Admiral "Bull" Halsey's saddle.

Washington County Museum of Fine Arts, in City Park, Hagerstown. Free. The only real art museum in the state outside Baltimore, this one overlooking a lake was a gift of a Hagerstown girl who married William H. Singer, Jr., a landscape artist and son of a business associate of Andrew Carnegie in the steel business. Features a new exhibit every month and Sunday afternoon concerts in fall and winter. Also in City Park is the *Hager House,* Jonathan Hager's 1739 fieldstone house, with loop holes for fighting Indians, which was in one family for 199 years.

Wildfowl Art Museum, Salisbury State College, Salisbury. This unique collection traces the history of hunting decoys, from primitive Indian rush creations of 1,000 years ago to today's elaborate "decoratives." Hundreds of fine decoys and carvings by numerous artists are displayed, including the work of two great carvers from nearby Crisfield, Lem and Steve Ward.

Chesapeake Bay Maritime Museum, on State 33 off US 50, in St. Michael's. Established in 1965 to keep alive the memories, adventures, romance and artifacts of America's great inland sea, the museum has an impressive collection of boat models, name boards, bells and figureheads, as well as a retired lightship, lighthouse and several sailing craft which can be boarded.

Julia A. Purnell Museum, on US 113 in Snow Hill. An interesting collection of local rural ca. 1800 memorabilia and artifacts, such as dentist's pliers, flatirons, hair curlers, gingerbread molds, high-wheel bicycles and Tom Thumb's bathtub.

 HISTORIC SITES. Central Maryland (all within less than an hour's drive from Baltimore): *Clara Barton House,* MacArthur Blvd. in Glen Echo, 3 mi. north of District of Columbia line. Home of the Civil War nurse who founded the American Red Cross, built for her by the grateful survivors of the 1889 Johnstown flood using lumber from emergency barracks erected while she was director. Used as Red Cross headquarters from 1897 to 1904.

White's Ferry. The only crossing of the Potomac River between Washington and Point of Rocks, this ferry has been in operation since at least 1830. Used by Gen. Jubal Early to escape after an unsuccessful raid on Washington in the last days of the Civil War. Can be reached from US 15 north of Leesburg, Va., or via State 107 from Poolesville, Md.

Southern Maryland: *Annapolis.* The capital of the Old Line State offers much for the visitor to see and most of it within easy walking distance, including *Hammond-Harwood House* (1774), called by many "the most beautiful Georgian mansion in America." St. John's, third oldest college in the United States after Harvard and William and Mary. *Chase-Lloyd House,* 22 Maryland Ave. at King George St., was built by Samuel Chase, one of the signers of the Declaration of Independence. Francis Scott Key was married in the front parlor. First floor open.

Government House, between State and Church Circles, built in 1866, is home of Maryland's governors.

The *Paca House* on Prince George St., built in 1763–65 by William Paca, a signer of the Declaration of Independence and three times Governor of Maryland, has been authentically restored. The extensive gardens have been carefully reconstructed.

Reynolds Tavern, Church Circle and Franklin St., built in 1737, is now under restoration. *State House,* on State Circle, is the nation's oldest functioning State Capitol; it was here George Washington resigned as commander-in-chief of the Revolutionary forces.

U.S. Naval Academy and Chapel, with crypt of John Paul Jones. Entrances through Maryland Ave. gate. Bancroft Hall is the largest dormitory in the world. The *Big E* ship's bell from the aircraft carrier *Enterprise* is rung after a Navy victory over Army. *Tecumseh,* a bronze replica of the figurehead from the USS *Delaware,* is the god of "C," the passing grade for midshipmen. Dress parades, Wednesday afternoons in spring. Noon meal formation in front of Bancroft Hall.

Fort Washington, 16 mi. southwest of District of Columbia line via Indian Head Highway (State 210). An excellent prototype of 19th-century coastal defenses, it was erected after British burned an earlier fort on the site in 1814.

Old State House, St. Mary's City, Rte. 5. A replica of the original, built in 1676, was erected in 1934 as part of tercentenary celebration. *Sotterley,* 3 mi. east of Hollywood, State 235. Many Marylanders say this is their favorite home. Overlooking the Patuxent River, the long, low structure, the oldest part of which was built between 1711 and 1727, has a notable Chinese Chippendale stairway and other fine hand-carved woodwork. Since it never deteriorated, it never had to be restored, and is still surrounded by a plantation-size farm.

London Town on the South River, once considered for the capital of Maryland, is being restored to its 1744–50 appearance, with a *Publik House,* log tobacco barn, and gardens. Continuous exhibits at visitors' center. Reached from Annapolis via State 2 and 253 to south shore of South River.

Smallwood's Retreat, on State 225 west off US 301. Open June to Sept. An unusually small brick colonial house, it was home of Gen. William Smallwood, a Revolutionary War hero and later governor of Maryland.

St. Clement's Island, viewed from State 242 off State 5, has an impressive 40-foot cross where the first English settlers landed in Maryland from the *Ark* and the *Dove* in 1634. "Maryland Day" every March 25 commemorates the event.

Point Lookout, the southern tip of southern Maryland, on State 5. Monument marks site of Civil War prison, whose prisoners Gen. Jubal Early hoped to free during raid on Washington. A state park is now located here, with good camping, excellent fishing and crabbing, and a 4-mile-long white-sand beach.

Eastern Shore: *Fredericktown-Georgetown* (US 213) are picturesque waterside villages on opposite sides of the Sassafras River, said to be the prettiest river in Maryland. Both were raided by the British fleet during the War of 1812. Today they are yachting centers.

Centreville, on US 213. An 18th-century town with an old courthouse and lawyers' row still in daily use. On Main St. is *Wright's Chance,* an excellent example of a colonial Eastern Shore plantation home, now a museum. In 1977, a larger-than-life statue of Queen Anne—for whom the county was named—was placed in front of the courthouse.

Wye Mills, on State 404 off US 50. Here is the location of the *Wye Oak,* Maryland's official tree, said to be well over 400 years old. Nearby is a restored 18th-century grist mill which ground flour for George Washington's army, a one-room schoolhouse and restored *Wye Church* (1721).

Old Trinity Church, Church Creek, State 16, 7 miles south of Cambridge. The oldest active church in use, built about 1675, it was restored in 1960 by daughter of Walter P. Chrysler, the auto magnate. Its 15 picturesque slip and roundabout pews seat only 100. Burial place of Anna Ella Carroll, close friend of Abraham Lincoln's who conceived the successful Tennessee campaign during the Civil War.

TOURS. *Historic Annapolis, Inc.,* Old Treasury, State Circle, Annapolis, 21401, a non-profit organization, which provides *guided walking tours* of varying lengths. Tel. 267–8149.

Three Centuries Tours, P.O. Box 29, Annapolis, 21404 meets requests for transportation and guides. General and special-interest tours, including a pub crawl and historic churches and graveyards jaunt. Tel. 263–5357.

The *Annapolitan* leaves from Pier One, Annapolis City Dock, for a cruise to *St. Michaels Maritime Museum.*

The *Harbor Queen* makes 40-minute tours of *Annapolis harbor.* Sights include Naval Academy and Bay Bridge.

The *Mustang,* a Chesapeake Bay log canoe, is available for daytime charter for groups up to six people. Passengers must supply own food.

The *Wm. B. Tennison,* a "bugeye" built in 1899, offers afternoon and evening cruises, departing from the Calvert Marine Museum dock, from spring to fall.

Cruises to *Smith Island* are available from Crisfield on tourboats during the summer.

STAGE AND REVUES. *Olney Theater,* Olney, Routes 108 and 97. Professional repertory company, with guest star in the lead. Summer months. *Toby's Dinner Theater* in Columbia. *Limestone Valley Dinner Theater,* also in Cockeysville. *Colony 7 Dinner Theater,* in Quality Inn Colony 7 Motel on Baltimore-Washington Parkway at State 32. *Harford Opera Theater,* on campus of Harford Community College, Belair. Dundalk, Catsonville, Harford Community Colleges and others also present plays on weekends on a nonregular schedule. *Garrett County Playhouse,* Beckman's Peninsula, Deep Creek Lake. A resident company presents well-known plays in an old barn during July and August. *Henry's Dinner Theater,* Hagerstown, is open weekends. The *Morris A. Mechanic Theater* features Broadway shows and pre-Broadway openings. Located in Charles Center off Baltimore St., in Baltimore.

GARDENS. *Lilypons,* a 300-acre tract of exotic water plants and 700 ponds, 8 miles south of Frederick, off State 85, is the world's largest breeding center for ornamental fish, including the prized fringetail calico and water lilies named after such famous personalities as Col. Lindbergh and Dorothy Lamour. It was named in 1932 for singer Lily Pons, a friend of the garden's developer, G. L. Thomas.

Maryland House and Gardens. This 10-day spring pilgrimage opens more than 100 outstanding homes and gardens, most of them private, in Baltimore, the horse and hunt country north of Baltimore, southern and western Maryland, and on the Eastern Shore, where many restored colonial-period homes are situated on necks or peninsulas. Boxwood is outstanding at many. One county is host each day. Please, no spike heels. Write Maryland House and Garden Pilgrimage, 600 W. Chesapeake Ave., Towson, Md. 21204, for schedule.

DRINKING LAWS. It is best to inquire locally about legal drinking restrictions, for they vary from county to county and even differ in towns in the same county. But generally, places serving alcoholic beverages are open from 6 A.M. to 2 A.M. except on Sundays and election days, when those in about half the counties are closed. Nothing can be consumed on the premises between 2 A.M. and 6 A.M. except on New Year's Day, when there are few restrictions. Persons under 21 are prohibited from purchasing distilled spirits for themselves or others. The minimum age for buying light wine and beer is 18.

HOTELS AND MOTELS. in Maryland range from first class to inexpensive, and include resorts over a century old and the latest in up-to-the-minute motels. As elsewhere in this book, hotels and motels are arranged alphabetically by community. Price categories for double-occupancy rooms in Maryland are divided into the following ranges: *Deluxe* $30 and higher, *Expensive* $20–$29, *Moderate* $11–$19 and *Inexpensive* $10 and lower. For a more complete explanation of price categories, refer to *Facts at Your Fingertips* at the beginning of this volume.

Aberdeen

Holiday Inn. *Expensive.* John F. Kennedy Hwy. (I–95) at State 22. Dining room, double beds, laundry and valet service, pool. Conveniently located near US Army's Aberdeen Proving Ground, which boasts a fine new museum of old Army tanks and weapons, Allied and enemy.

Quality Inn. *Expensive.* Aberdeen exit off I–95. A typical motel in this far-flung chain, it has color TV, a restaurant and lounge.

Red Coach Motor Inn. *Expensive.* 783 W. Belaire Ave. Located a mile from the center of town, five miles from Aberdeen Proving Ground.

Annapolis

Annapolis Hilton Inn. *Deluxe.* Compromise St. at St. Mary's St. With docking space for yachts, this is a come-by-water or come-by-land inn. The Penthouse Restaurant has dramatic views on three sides of the Severn River and the Chesapeake Bay Bridge. The varied menu places emphasis, naturally, on Maryland seafood delicacies. There's also a Skippers Pub with nautical and Colonial decor combined. Other features include outdoor swimming pool, 200-foot boardwalk, airy rooms that overlook the Annapolis Harbor, two double beds, etc.—all within a short walking distance of historic Annapolis Town and the Naval Academy.

Annapolis Terrace Motel. *Expensive.* Four mi. N. on US 50 and US 301. Convenient to Baltimore, Washington, Annapolis, and the Chesapeake Bay Bridge. All double beds. Restaurant and cocktail lounge. Swimming pool. Pets.

Holiday Inn. *Expensive.* US 50–301 at State 450. Typical of this growing chain. Reservations can be made by other Holiday Inns. Restaurant and lounge attached. All color TV. Rates are slightly higher during "Commissioning" week at the Naval Academy, the end of May.

Howard Johnson's Motor Lodge. *Expensive.* On US 50 and US 301, 4 mi. west of Chesapeake Bay Bridge. Between Annapolis and the Chesapeake Bay Bridge, only 25 mi. to Baltimore and 35 mi. to Washington. The same quality to be found in other H.J. lodges is found here. Its restaurant adjoins. Cocktails. Swimming pool. Rates are higher during Naval Academy "Commissioning" Week. Like all Annapolis-vicinity lodging places, make reservations well in advance.

Maryland Inn. *Expensive.* Church Circle. Originally built in 1778, this lodging still retains the old flavor with its hand-hewn beams and large fireplaces. There is a bar with entertainment and you can play golf nearby.

Academy Motel. *Moderate.* US 50, 301, just E of State 2. Large and modern, this facility has a swimming pool, rec. rooms for grown-ups and children. Restaurant, lounge and coffee shop.

Bel Air

Hickory Inn Motel. *Moderate.* US 1 at State 543. Small and rustic but comfortable. Air-conditioned. TV in every rm. Has the Fireside Restaurant.

Bethesda
(See also Washington, D.C. Chapter)

Bethesda Marriott. *Deluxe.* Intersection of I–495, I–270 and Wisconsin Ave. Opened 1979. Fine facilities, including indoor and outdoor pools, lighted tennis courts and meeting rooms. Excellent restaurants, lounge, and a discotheque.

Ramada Inn. *Deluxe.* 8400 Wisconsin Ave., US 240. This 5-floor motor hotel is close to US Naval Hospital. Conventional services include a coffee shop, dining room, valet service, beauty salon, swimming pool, bellmen.

Bowie

Holiday Inn. *Expensive.* Intersection of US 301 and US 50, 8 mi. E. of I–95. Located 12 mi. from Annapolis, 5 mi. from Bowie race track. Outdoor pool, restaurant and lounge.

Cambridge

Quality Inn. *Expensive.* US 50 at State 16. There is a cafe and a lounge, which has entertainment. You can enjoy the swimming pool.

Chestertown

Great Oak Lodge. *Deluxe.* This 2-story, 32-room motel is part of a 400-acre complex with pool, marina, 9-hole golf course and excellent restaurant.

White Swan Tavern. *Deluxe.* 231 High St. Charming mid-18th century tavern with five guest rooms. Continental breakfast provided.

College Park

Holiday Inn-Capital Beltway. *Deluxe.* US 1 and Capital Beltway (I–95). Outdoor pool, color TV, restaurant.

Holiday Inn-College Park. *Deluxe.* US 1, ¾ mi. S. of I–95. Suites for groups available. Restaurant and pool.

Quality Inn. *Deluxe.* US 1, 3 miles south of Capital Beltway (I–95). Near the University of Maryland. Restaurant.

Royal Pine. *Expensive.* 9113 Baltimore Blvd. A long stone's-throw from the University of Maryland's sprawling campus. Swimming pool.

Columbia

Cross Keys Inn. *Deluxe.* Wincopin Circle. This luxury inn, with its outstanding restaurant, is located on a lakefront in Maryland's well-known "new town." Available to guests are golf, tennis, handball, ice and roller skating, boating and year-round swimming.

Cumberland

Holiday Inn. *Deluxe.* South George St., State 40 exit to downtown. All color TV; lounge with live entertainment. Some noise from the nearby train yard, but still the best place to stay in town.

Algonquin Motor Inn. *Expensive.* Baltimore and Greene Sts. One of the leading hotels in city, in heart of town. Free parking, private access to rooms, color TV.

Braddock Motor Inn (Best Western). *Expensive.* US 40 W. Has a restaurant, lounge, and pool.

Colonial Manor Motor Lodge. *Expensive.* US 40, I–70, 1 mi. E of town. The "wine cellar" in the basement of this mid-19th century structure was one of the original inns along the "Old National Road."

Continental. *Expensive.* 5 mi. W on US 40. A first-rate stopping place, with restaurant, lounge, swimming pool.

Holiday Motel. *Moderate.* Bedford Rd. and US 220 N of US 40. Just a few minutes' drive from Cumberland. Comfortable. Three restaurants nearby.

Maryland. *Moderate.* Bedford Rd. (US 220), 3 mi N of town. Swimming pool, picnic area and gardens. There's a restaurant a short walk away.

Slumberland Motel. *Moderate.* US 40, 6 mi. W of town. Air-conditioned. Color TV. Near a Howard Johnson restaurant.

Easton

Mariner Motel. *Deluxe.* US 50, 1 mi. S of town. In the heart of the Maryland Tidewater Country, where colonial homes have been restored into large waterfront private estates. The usual Holiday Inn features including pool, restaurant, lounge with entertainment.

Tidewater. *Deluxe.* Harrison St. at Dover. This gracious inn is famous in these parts. It's well located to tour the charming town of Easton and historic Talbot County. Attractive swimming pool, and guests have golf and tennis privileges at nearby facilities. The Crystal and River rooms serve regional specialties.

Edgewood

Best Western Invitation Inn. *Deluxe.* 1709 Emmorton Rd., exit 4 from J.F. Kennedy Hwy. (I–95). Swimming pool and playground, plus the usual TV, air-conditioning and motel standards.

Frederick

Holiday Inn. *Deluxe.* ½ mi. W on US 40, at jct. of US 15 and I–70. Convenient to an historic and scenic area of western Maryland, as well as being 50 miles either way to Washington or Baltimore, this inn for a holiday trip has a pool, rent-a-car, kennels, a good restaurant.

Red Horse Motor Inn. *Deluxe.* US 40 and US 15, at the edge of town. The 70 rooms are clean and comfortable, and the steakhouse serves excellent beef and seafood.

Sheraton Inn. *Deluxe.* I–270 and State 85. Typical of this chain, with a restaurant, lounge, swimming pool and sauna.

Spring Bank Inn. *Deluxe.* State 355 at intersection of US 15. Restored late-19th century Victorian mansion. Most rooms share a bath. Rates include continental breakfast.

Dandee Motel and Country Inn. *Moderate.* US 40 West, four mi. W of Frederick. TV and air-conditioned. No pool. Excellent restaurant that serves family style and is popular locally.

Frostburg

Clarysville Inn. *Expensive.* 2 mi. E on US 40. One of the best in a motel-scarce area, this inn, built in 1807, offers pleasant rooms, restaurant, cocktail lounge, and swimming pool. Colonial dining room.

Gaithersburg

Washingtonian Motel and Country Club. *Deluxe.* Shady Grove Rd., 2 mi. S on I–270. A large luxurious-type motor hotel with the best in service and facilities, including a 95-foot swimming pool, lawn games, two 18-hole golf courses and tennis courts.

Glen Burnie

Holiday Inn-South No. 1. *Deluxe.* 6600 Ritchie Hwy. (State 2) off Baltimore Beltway (I–695) exit 3. The restaurant of this chain motel serves good but less expensive meals than its sister motels in the Baltimore area, otherwise its rms. and service are pretty much the same. You get TV, swimming pool, etc.

Holiday Inn-South No. 2. *Deluxe.* 6301 Ritchie Hwy., State 2, exit 3 on Baltimore Beltway. Accommodations identical. Rates slightly higher than No. 1.

Grantsville

Holiday Inn. *Deluxe.* Exit 22 off US 48 W. Dining room, lounge and disco. Heated indoor pool.

Cassleman Hotel and Inn. *Moderate.* Main St. Historic hotel has 7 bedrooms, the newer inn 40 units. Restaurant features home-style Pennsylvania Dutch cooking.

Little Meadows. *Inexpensive.* Jct. of US 40 and US 219. Small. Very little available in this area of the Appalachian Mountain region until traveler gets to Deep Creek Lake or Oakland, which is usually filled in summer season. TV. Restaurant close.

Hagerstown

Holiday Inn. *Deluxe.* 1 mi. E on US 40. Swimming pool, cocktail lounge, room service, restaurant, and all the other Holiday services, as well as convenience to Hagerstown, Antietam National Battlefield, Harpers Ferry National Park, and other historic points of interest.

Ramada Inn. *Deluxe.* 1 mile east on US 40. The adjacent Tortuga Restaurant attracts area residents as well as motel guests.

Sheraton Motor Inn. *Expensive.* 1910 Dual Hwy. All the comforts and conveniences of this well-known chain service.

Venice. *Expensive.* ½ mi. E on US 40. Good restaurant, cocktail lounge, and beautiful swimming pool with golf course just across the road from this 2-story, air-conditioned motel. Several other good eating places in the area. Rates lower from November to March.

Jessup

Holiday Inn. *Deluxe.* I–95 and State 175, Jessup exit. Guests receive free transportation to Baltimore-Washington International Airport, 8 miles away.

La Plata

Howard Johnson's Motor Lodge. *Expensive.* N on US 301. Pool and other services of this chain in an area devoted to tobacco. Restaurant adjoining.

Laurel

Colony 7 Motor Inn. *Expensive.* Baltimore-Washington Expressway, Md. 32 exit. Near the Laurel Race Course and trotting track, about midway between Baltimore and the National Capital, this is a large, luxurious motel with a fine Schrafft's Restaurant adjoining. Cocktail lounge, swimming pool and children's area. Pets.

Howard Johnson's. *Deluxe.* US 1 at Second St. If you stay here in the summer, it's good to know that poolside rooms and suites are available.

New Carrollton

Sheraton Inn. *Deluxe.* Exit 20 off I–95. Located 3 miles from the Baltimore-Washington Parkway on the Capital Beltway. There's a coffee shop, restaurant, lounge with entertainment and swimming pool.

New Market

Strawberry Inn. *Expensive.* 17 Main St. It's fitting that this town of antique shops should have a tiny country inn with pleasant accommodations and continental breakfast.

Oakland

Alpine Village. *Deluxe.* North on US 219. Motel and cottages. Facilities include a swimming beach, and boat docks. Deluxe restaurant.

Oak Mar. *Deluxe.* US 219. In-town location. Color TV.

Starlite. *Deluxe.* US 219 in Oakland. Tennis courts and restaurant. 5 minutes from golf course.

Village Inn. *Deluxe.* Marsh Hill Rd. off US 219. A year-round resort motel, near the Wisp ski area, with heated indoor pool, indoor racquetball and handball courts, and lake-front beach club. Also, the Jolly Roger dining room and lounge.

Will O' the Wisp. *Deluxe.* US 219. Accommodations in motel, cottage or condominium rooms and suites. Recreational facilities include an indoor heated pool, sauna, exercise room and sand beach.

Oak-Land Motel. *Expensive.* US 219. Located in a residential area, 10 minutes from the lake.

Point View Inn and Motel. *Expensive.* N. on US 219. This very attractive vacation motel, with restaurant and gift shop, overlooks Deep Creek Lake. Fishing, boating, swimming, and skiing.

Town Motel. *Expensive.* US 219 in Oakland. Country club nearby.

Ocean City

Beach Plaza Hotel and Bo-Con Apartments. *Deluxe.* 13th St. and Boardwalk. This little gem of a hotel isn't the newest place to stay on the beach, but it has an air of genteel elegance. The lobby is gracious, the air conditioned rooms spotlessly clean. Has an excellent restaurant, the best coffee shop in Ocean City, piano bar, and several shops.

Carousel Hotel. *Deluxe.* 118th St. and Coastal Hwy. Well-known in these parts. Restaurant, night club, disco, indoor ice rink and pool, lighted tennis courts. Rooms have kitchenettes. Open year-round.

Castle in the Sand. *Deluxe.* 37th St. on the oceanfront. An older but well-maintained motel directly on the beach. Pool. Rooms have handy kitchens, and there's a restaurant, lounge, and a coffee shop that serves delicious sandwiches.

Flagship. *Deluxe.* Boardwalk at 26th St. All ocean-view rooms with private balconies and bedrooms with two double beds. This is a luxury inn a comfortable distance up the boardwalk from the honky-tonk shops and amusement rides. Has its own dining room and a swimming pool within a pebble's throw of the famous white Ocean City beach. Open all year.

French Quarter. *Deluxe.* Baltimore Ave. at 22nd St. Open all year with an enclosed heated pool. Motel and family rooms, also 1-2-3 bedroom apartments and efficiencies. Free morning coffee. TV and phone in every room. But one block from the ocean.

Gateways. *Deluxe.* 48th St. The oceanfront Gateway Motel and recently refurbished Gateway Inn on Sinepuxent Bay have a total of 160 rooms and apartments. Heated indoor pool and Olympic-size outdoor pool. Gateway Inn houses L'Auberge, one of Ocean City's best restaurants.

Park de Ville. *Deluxe.* Oceanfront at 54th St. An apartment motel with fully equipped kitchen. Each glass-front unit of the three-story building faces the Atlantic Ocean. Besides swimming pool and ocean bathing, there is maid service and private balconies. Rooms are large, with two double beds and a hide-a-bed. Air-conditioned, naturally.

Quality Inn Boardwalk. *Deluxe.* Boardwalk at 17th St. One of the first of the open-all-year stops at Ocean City, it has an indoor heated swimming pool with sauna bath and sun deck. All rooms contain double beds and a folding door separates sleeping and living areas. Coffee shop, gift shop, soda fountain and ocean-front restaurant.

Santa Maria. *Deluxe.* On the ocean at 15th St. With more and more people coming in the winter, the Santa Maria is open year round now, with package plans for both seasons. Olympic pool. Elevator service. Its restaurant, the Captain's Table, is well-known for its steaks and seafood.

Satellite. *Deluxe.* Boardwalk and 24th St. Motel rooms with equipped kitchenettes, daily maid service except dishes. TV. Pool. Coffee shop. All rooms with private terraces.

Sheraton Fontainebleau. *Deluxe.* 10100 Coastal Hwy. It has 254 rooms, with banquet and meeting facilities, indoor pool, tennis, saunas and gourmet dining. Ocean City's Convention Hall, with monthly entertainment events year round, is nearby.

Stardust. *Deluxe.* Oceanfront at 33rd St. With attractive rooms and balconies overlooking the ocean, this is vacationing in comfort. Kitchen apartments fully equipped. Pool as well as seaside bathing. All rooms have double beds and a hide-a-bed. Daily maid service, except for dishes. Folding doors between sleeping and living-room area. Now open all year.

Surf and Sands. *Deluxe.* Boardwalk and 23rd St. A three-story motel with elevator, this modern weekend or vacation spot has light, airy rooms, wading and swimming pools, coffee shop, and is only the width of the boardwalk away from one of the best sandy shores on the Atlantic Coast.

Misty Harbor. *Expensive.* Philadelphia Ave. at 25th St. This old but well-kept motel, a short 2 blocks from the beach, has sizeable rooms at reasonable rates. Congenial hostess Susan Cropper knows Ocean City as well as anyone, and is happy to offer helpful tips on restaurants, sightseeing, etc.

Stowaway. *Expensive.* Boardwalk at 22nd St. All vacation amenities. Air-conditioning, cocktail lounge, restaurant, coffee shop, free TV, free parking, Olympic pool, kiddie pool and sun deck, plus a full block of white sandy beach in front.

Oxford

Robert Morris Inn. *Deluxe.* Morris St. Built as a home prior to 1710, with wooden-pegged paneling and hand-hewn beams. Charming accommodations, outstanding dining room. Being an old inn, don't look for phones or TV in the rooms.

Perryville

El Capitan Motel. *Moderate.* US 40, ½ mi. E. of Susquehanna River Bridge. Singles and doubles. Air-conditioned. Free TV. Restaurants are nearby.

Pocomoke City

Holiday Inn. *Deluxe.* US 13 one mile south. The Eastern Shore Room restaurant and Windjammer Lounge are popular with area residents. Rates increase slightly during the annual late-summer penning of the Chincoteague Island ponies.

Pocomoke Twin Towers. *Expensive.* US 13, 2 miles south. First-class accommodations, along with an Olympic size pool, very nice restaurant and lounge.

Royal Oak

Pasadena Inn. *Deluxe.* Eight mi. W. of Easton on State 33. This big, rambling, old resort inn is open spring, summer and fall, making available a plain but comfortable place to stay in the Chesapeake Bay country, close by such seafood centers as Tilghman's Island or the yacht races at St. Michaels. This is the kind of place to take it easy, go crabbing, fishing, visiting old estates, or playing shuffleboard. Dancing Saturday nights. Board includes three huge meals a day.

Salisbury

Holiday Inn. *Deluxe.* Delmar Rd., 3 mi. N. of Salisbury on US 13. No charge for children under 12. Double beds in all rooms. Pool. Restaurant.

Sheraton Inn. *Deluxe.* On US 13 at US 50. At the intersection of two major highways, yet conveniently located in downtown Salisbury. Has a new heated indoor swimming pool.

Howard Johnson's. *Expensive.* US 13, just N. of city limits. Midway between Wilmington and Cape Charles on the Del-Mar-Va peninsula, 30 mi. from Ocean City and Rehoboth Beach, it offers the usual H.J. restaurant, a swimming pool, and comfortable overnight accommodations.

Lord Salisbury Motel. *Moderate.* Delmar Rd., 3 mi. N. of Salisbury on US 13. Family rates. Swimming pool. Color TV. Major credit cards honored.

Temple Hill Motel. *Moderate.* S. Salisbury Blvd. and US 13. Swimming pool, in-room-coffee, color TV.

Silver Spring

Georgian. *Deluxe.* 7990 Georgia Ave. A multi-story inn with elevators and large, handsome, air-conditioned rooms.

Holiday Inn. *Deluxe.* 8777 Georgia Ave., two blocks N. of US 29 and near Exit 31 of the Capital Beltway (I–495). This 16-story motel has a rooftop swimming pool with dining terrace, 2 restaurants and a lounge.

Quality Inn. *Deluxe.* 8040–13th St., at the District of Columbia line. All the comforts for pleasant in-town visiting: color TV, pool, restaurant, and lounge. Greyhound tour bus stops at the door.

Sheraton Inn-Northwest. *Deluxe.* On US 29, in town. There are two restaurants: the Derby, and the outstanding Mamma Ragina's, serving Italian food. There is a roof-top pool.

Twin Towers. *Expensive.* Intersection of Colesville Rd. (US 29) and Georgia Ave. Right in the heart of Silver Spring. Facilities and services include roof-top pool, indoor parking, sauna and laundry rooms. Some rooms with kitchenette.

Thurmont

Cozy Motel. *Expensive.* 103 Frederick Rd., just off US 15. This modern motel has color TV, some fireplaces and—for those who want them—waterbeds. Also, a popular restaurant.

Waldorf

Holiday Inn. *Deluxe.* US 301 and St. Patrick Dr. Pool, golf, free in-room movies.

Cadillac. *Expensive.* Four mi. N. on US 301. This is one of many places on a 20-mile strip north of the Potomac River Bridge. Once known as the Las Vegas of Maryland, before slot machines were outlawed. Some motels and restaurants closed but the better ones remain.

Stardust. *Moderate.* One mi. N. on US 301. Colonial decoration in these charming rooms. The swimming pool is a good feature in summer, as it can be very hot and humid. The motel has a snack bar, and there are many steak houses along this neon strip.

Westminster

Lee's Motel. *Inexpensive.* Baltimore Blvd. Pleasant accommodations in 80 rooms. Also, a swimming pool.

Wheaton

Howard Johnson's. *Deluxe.* University Blvd. at Viers Mill Rd. A suburban Washington, D.C. location in a busy, commercial area. Amenities include color TV, sauna, and a lounge. There are many restaurants nearby.

White Marsh

Williamsburg Inn. *Moderate.* Twelve mi. E. of Baltimore on US 40. This stretch of highway between Baltimore and the Delaware line offers the traveler hundreds of accommodations. Almost all have TV, many have pools. This is among the most attractive and has a restaurant, bar, and pool.

 YOUTH HOSTELS. *Cambridge.* Cambridge Home Hostel. 1311 Race St., Cambridge 21613. Home-like atmosphere, with 10 beds available. $4.50 per person.
Grantsville. National Hotel. Grantsville 21536. Historic hotel with weekend entertainment. Double rooms about $16.

Oakland. Camp Minnitoska, Oakland 21550. 7 mi. W on Hutton Rd., right at Sanders Lane. 100 beds available in summer for $1.50 a night each. During winter, camping only.

Sandy Hook. Kiwanis Youth Hostel. 16 mi. W of Frederick; From US 340 turn left on State 180, right on Sandy Hook Rd. Route 2, Box 304, Knoxville, Md. 21758. Open April 1–Nov. 1. 30 bunks. Flush toilets, hot and cold water, showers, washing machine and dryer, electric stove, refrigerator, freezer. Overnight rate, $3–$4.

Williamsport. Falling Waters Hostel. 5 miles outside town on State 63, right on Falling Waters Rd. Route 1, Box 238-B, Williamsport, Md. 21795. Cooking facilities in this farm hostel that overlooks the Potomac River. Near the C&O Canal and bicycle path. Accommodates up to 20 people. Overnight rate $3.

 DINING OUT in Maryland can involve not only fine local dishes, but also the pleasure of a country drive culminating in the discovery of a charming restaurant or inn. There are plenty of fine spots along the highways as well, but if you have the time you should definitely try to sample some of the more out-of-the-way places.

Restaurant price categories are as follows: *Deluxe* $12 and higher, *Expensive* $8–$11, *Moderate* $5–$7, *Inexpensive* below $5.00. These prices are for hors d'ouevres or soup, entree and dessert. Not included are drinks, tax and tips. For a more complete explanation of restaurant categories refer to *Facts at Your Fingertips.*

Aberdeen

The Colonel's Choice. *Deluxe.* S. US 40. Well-prepared American food, with prime rib and crab imperial the specialties.

Annapolis

The Galleon. *Deluxe.* Md. 2 at S. River Bridge. From an interior that looks like a Spanish galleon, the view is superb of the beautiful South River, S of Annapolis. Features prime rib, one full rib, and imperial crab. Come by boat or car—docking or parking free.

Harbour House. *Deluxe.* On City Dock in old Annapolis. Touristy, but still nice. The specialty is seafood—fresh oysters and soft-shell crabs in season, and soft-shell clams, lobster and imperial crab—as well as char-broiled steaks year-round. From the second floor deck, you look over the busy harbor, which has the same configuration as it did in Colonial days.

Maryland Inn. *Deluxe.* On Church Circle, Annapolis. An inn serving the public for 200 years on historic Church Circle in the Maryland capital, the menu features 18th-century St. Mary's crab imperial, lobster, corn sticks, fish from the Chesapeake Bay and pecan pie. The wine list is attractive, and fairly priced. Entertainment Fri., Sat. and Sun. nights (when reservations are a must) in the King of France Tavern.

Middleton Tavern. *Deluxe.* 2 Market Place, Annapolis. A registered historic landmark, this eating place has a cozy atmosphere with large fireplaces. Dinners are listed on blackboards, and the spot attracts the casual boating crowd.

Wagon Wheels. *Deluxe.* On Gov. Ritchie Hwy. (Rte. 2), 6 mi. N of Annapolis. In a rustic setting that looks like country-cured ham, the specialties are seafood and steaks. A favorite dining-out spot for area families.

Dockside. *Moderate.* 22 Market Space, Annapolis. Dine in a picturesque port of Annapolis, opposite the renewed Old City Market House on City Dock. Besides aged beef and seafood dishes, a raw bar serves oysters, clams and fried hard crabs. No reservations.

Little Campus. *Moderate.* 63 Maryland Ave., Annapolis. A small but pleasant eating place that serves baked stuffed oysters, shrimp marinate, flaming shish-kabob, veal entrees and hot sandwiches, plus omeletes for a late evening meal or snack.

Bethesda

Bello Mondo. *Deluxe.* In the Bethesda Marriott Hotel, Pooks Hill Rd. Outstanding Northern Italian cuisine, elegant setting.

La Miche. *Deluxe.* 7905 Norfolk Ave. A pleasant setting and well-prepared French food. Try the fresh-fish bouillabaisse, breast of duckling.

Michel's. *Expensive.* 7904 Woodmont Ave. A little gem of a neighborhood favorite. The intimate atmosphere is country French; the entrées—including veal, roast duckling and sweetbreads—are well prepared for the price. No reservations and it's popular, so there can be a wait for lunch or dinner.

Boonsboro

Old South Mountain Inn. *Deluxe.* Alternate US 40 on top of South Mountain. A picturesque setting for an inn that dates back to the French and Indian Wars. American and Continental fare, with al fresco dining in summer.

Chestertown

Flyway Restaurant. *Deluxe.* An outstanding eating place, at Great Oak Lodge, serving 3 meals a day. Continental selections and unusual seafood delights are well prepared. Lounge. Closed in winter.

Columbia

Clyde's. *Deluxe.* Wincopin Circle. Omelet and pasta room, plus cafe with Victorian decor.

King's Contrivance. *Deluxe.* 2 mi. S. of Maryland's new town just off US 29 on Rte. 32. French cuisine in a 100-year-old Federalist mansion. Smoked shrimp and frogs' legs Provencale are among the entrees, which range from $7–$9. Reservations suggested on weekends.

The Wincopin. *Deluxe.* Cross Keys Inn, Wincopin Circle. Veal Oscar, crab imperial, and other continental and American specialties. Dinner and dance music, no cover charge.

Cresaptown

Fred Warner's German Restaurant. *Deluxe.* US 220. The Warner family has been serving authentic German food since 1928. Huge portions (doggie bags available). Sinfully rich homemade desserts.

Cumberland

Bistro. *Deluxe.* 37 N. Centre St. A surprisingly elegant setting for a small town. International cuisine prepared with a touch and beautifully presented. Each of the dining rooms is furnished with precious antiques. Worth a side trip.

Barton's Coffee House. *Moderate.* US 220 S. Overlooks the valley. Outstanding salad buffet.

Ed Mason's. *Moderate.* 1 mi. E. on US 40. Food served in both the restaurant and downstairs saloon. Entertainment.

Gehauf's. *Moderate.* US 40 adjacent to US 48 intersection. Features homemade soups and rolls.

L'Osteria. *Moderate.* US 40 E. Italian food served in 19th century inn.

Easton

Tidewater Inn. *Deluxe.* Dover and Harrison Sts. Chesapeake Bay seafood is the specialty, but steaks and chops also are excellent. Given a day's notice, the chef will prepare gourmet meals for 2, including Maryland terrapin, roast pheasant, and beef Wellington. This large dining room, with snowy white tablecloths and gracious but slightly haughty waiters, offers dining as one seldom finds it any more in this Southern-like state.

Easton Manor Restaurant. *Moderate.* US 50. Good Eastern Shore cuisine in a pleasant little dining rm. Operates in conjunction with a Quality motel.

Eastport

Spiro's. *Moderate.* 400 6th St. On the other side of the creek, so to speak. Cross the bridge at the Annapolis Yacht Club into Eastport. Greek specialties.

Ellicott City

Chez Fernand. *Deluxe.* 8141 Main St. French cuisine in the heart of this picturesque mill town.

Fallston

Blue Bell Seafood House. *Moderate.* 2607 Bel Air Rd. (US 1). Unpretentious from the outside, this enjoys a good reputation locally for its fine seafood menu.

Finksburg

Branding Iron. *Expensive.* Rte. 140. Featuring an open hearth, serves good steaks and seafood. Popular locally.

Frederick

Chez Maggy. *Deluxe.* 26 N. Market St. Marguerite (Maggy) is French, and it shows. The décor is pleasant and spotlessly clean. Menu selections are typical, but well prepared, nicely served—and some have a different twist.

Red Horse Steak House. *Expensive.* 996 W. Patrick St. You can watch your steak charcoal-broiled in a colonial decor, or enjoy cocktails at the Anvil Bar while you wait. In the Red Horse Motor Inn.

Barbara Fritchie Candystick Restaurant. *Moderate.* US 40. Counter or booths, food is good and plentiful. Try countrystyle crab soup and cheese cake. Good way stop when traveling.

Dan-Dee Country Inn. *Moderate.* US 40, five mi. W. Bountiful dinners served country style. Usually only three selections, so service is fast. Families travel 50 mi. from Baltimore to eat here, so there is sometimes a wait.

Peter Pan Inn. *Moderate.* 7 mi. S on Rte. 80, Urbana exit off I-270. Using century-old family recipes, noted for country-cured ham and fried chicken, served family style with corn fritters, this unusual restaurant has become a Maryland tradition and institution. Popular with church and other groups, which drive more than a hundred miles to eat here; there is often a wait of an hour or more to get in by the number. There are only five choices and the menu hasn't changed in 47 years. Children's portions half price.

Fredericktown

Granary. *Deluxe.* Rte. 213. A delightful view of the Sassafras River from the Cecil County side goes with the steaks, seafood, crab imperial, and soft-shell crabs. Drinks served. Since this is next to large marina, weekend reservations are advisable.

Frostburg

Au Petit Paris. *Deluxe.* Main St., US 40. In this small college town and one-time coal-mining center, such a restaurant looks out of place. But the veal cordon bleu, coq au vin, escargots and frogs legs are deliciously prepared. This Paris-like bistro, with wine cellar, is entered through a little French courtyard.

Georgetown

Kitty Knight House. *Moderate.* Rte. 213. Good menu and pleasant atmosphere in large dining room that presents a good view of yachts moored in the Sassafras River. It is said Kitty Knight saved this house from burning by the British.

Grantsville

Penn Alps. *Moderate.* US 40, one-half mi. east. Three meals a day feature Pennsylvania Dutch cooking. Try the buckwheat pancakes and applesauce bread. During the summer months, there are demonstrations of Early American crafts.

Hagerstown

Airport Restaurant. *Expensive.* Middleburg Pike, 5 miles north on US 11. A pleasant atmosphere, a favorite with Hagerstown businessmen. Next to the local airport, it serves steaks, prime ribs and seafood, takes pride in its Greek salad.

Dutch Kitchen. *Expensive.* 12 E. Washington St. (US 40). Charming place and nice menu that includes imperial crab and steak. Liquors served.

Tortuga. *Expensive.* US 40. An old establishment that serves prime ribs of beef and live Maine lobsters.

Lexington Park

Belvedere. *Deluxe.* 60 Main St. In conjunction with motor inn of same name, this is located in an area mostly of tobacco farms, long distances from eating places of any kind. Very good. Stuffed ham, fresh lobster tails, prime steaks and Chesapeake Bay seafoods, all served family style. Restaurant, like the inn, is near the Patuxent Naval Air Station and historic St. Mary's City, first capital of the colony of Mary Land.

Mount Airy

Quail Ridge Inn. *Expensive.* State 27. Good food in a rustic setting.

Oakland

Four Seasons. *Deluxe.* US 219. Small, pleasant dining room in the Will O' the Wisp resort, overlooking Deep Creek Lake. Steak, seafood and nightly Continental specials.

Red Run Inn. *Deluxe.* Mayhew Inn Rd. off US 219. Intimate dining room with salad bar, and lounge, at the shore of Deep Creek Lake. Also, cocktail and seafood lounge open in summer.

Silver Tree Inn. *Deluxe.* US 219 adjacent to the Alpine Village Inn. Surprisingly sophisticated atmosphere and good food for a mountain resort. Specializes in Italian dishes, but the steaks and seafood also are very good. The main dining room has 1890s décor, the less sumptuous annex overlooks the lake.

Cornish Manor. *Expensive.* Memorial Dr. Pleasant 18th century decor plus good food and cocktails.

Oak Mar. *Expensive.* In the Oak Mar Motel, US 219 in town. Early American atmosphere and home-style cooking.

Starlite Restaurant. *Expensive.* In the Starlite Motel, US 219. Special salad bar and breakfast of buckwheat cakes and sausage.

Chimney Corner. *Moderate.* Jct. US 50 & 219, about one mi. S of Deep Creek Lake. After sampling sugar-cured and hickory-smoked hams, bacon, and sausage, you can buy buckwheat flour, homemade preserves, and old-fashioned candy in this rustic, country-store-like dining room.

Ocean City

Bonfire. *Deluxe.* 70th St. and Coastal Hwy. Same ownership—and good food—as the Embers, listed below. Entertainment and dancing in the lounge. Specializes in steaks and lobsters but has good selection of other choices.

Captain's Table. *Deluxe.* 15th St. and the ocean. Specializes in seafood and steaks. Open all year in Santa Maria Hotel.

Center Stage. *Deluxe.* Located in the Carousel, 118th St. and the beach. Overlooks the ocean. Specialties are prime ribs, almond shrimp.

Embers. *Deluxe.* 24th St. and Philadelphia Ave. Noted as one of Ocean City's four most expensive, but still hard to get in during the height of the summer season. Specializes in charcoal-broiled steaks and live Maine lobsters. Has a nice wine list at fair prices. Dancing.

Fagar's Island. *Deluxe.* 69th St. on the Bay. A favorite both for dinner—when steaks, lobster, and seafood are featured—and at lunchtime, when over-stuffed sandwiches satisfy any appetite.

Golden Plough. *Deluxe.* 45th St. Village Shopping Center. This large, often busy restaurant offers a standard selection of good beef and seafood entrees.

L'Auberge. *Deluxe.* In the Gateway Inn, 48th St. One of Ocean City's outstanding restaurants, serving well-prepared American and continental dishes, plus fresh seafood. Tasteful decor, entertainment. Prices are high, but the food is worth the cost.

Moonraker. *Deluxe.* In the Sheraton-Fontainebleau Inn, 10100 Ocean Hwy. Beef and seafood specialties. Music and dancing.

Phillips by the Sea. *Deluxe.* In the Beach Plaza Hotel, 13th St. and Boardwalk. This comfortably elegant restaurant, affiliated with Phillips Crab House, makes a specialty of serving excellent crab dishes. But steaks and other seafood also are outstanding. The quiet setting can be a welcome escape from the hustle and bustle of most Ocean City eating places.

Phillips Crab House. *Deluxe.* 21st St. and Philadelphia Ave. Specializing in crab delicacies and seafood, this is Ocean City's most famous restaurant, where you dine under hundreds of Tiffany lamps. Almost always a waiting line but service is fast.

Phillips Seafood House. *Deluxe.* 141st St. and Coastal Hwy. Newest of the Phillips chain of fine restaurants. There's an attractive bar. The wide selection of fresh seafood is fairly priced, and portions are ample.

Wharf. *Deluxe.* 128th St. and Coastal Hwy. A nautical atmosphere, perfect for the raw bar and seafood dishes. The beef is good, too.

Oxford

Robert Morris Inn. *Expensive.* On St. 333. Seafood is the specialty in this restored inn, where bread is baked on the premises. Try the soft shell crabs, oysters (in season) prepared several ways, and homemade strawberry pie, famous in these parts. Breakfast, lunch and dinner are served, and there's a rustic tavern.

Pier Street Marina and Restaurant. *Moderate.* Pier St. Steamed crabs and beer in historic old town on the Tred Avon River, where old homes and old boatyards draw almost as many visitors as the small ferry that still operates across the river.

St. Michaels

Longfellow's. *Deluxe.* 125 Mulberry St. at the harbor. Fresh seafood the specialty. A casual but pleasant atmosphere, courteous service. Try to reserve a window table for the view.

Crab Claw. *Moderate.* Navy Point, off Main St. Next to Chesapeake Bay Maritime Museum. It is amazing how well known this second-floor room overlooking St. Michael's harbor has become. You can put on an apron and pick steamed hard crabs to your heart's content. Other crab dishes and crab cakes, too. Expect a wait of at least a half-hour, on summer weekends, for lunch or dinner.

Silver Spring

Luau Hut. *Deluxe.* 8407 Ramsey Ave. In a dark secluded spot, with bamboo decor, Polynesian, Japanese, and Korean food, with tropical drinks.

Mrs. K's Toll House. *Deluxe.* 9201 Colesville Rd. (US 29). Beautifully decorated and highlighted with early American pressed glass and other antiques. The restaurant is an attractive setting where highway tolls actually once were collected. The best entrées are fried chicken, ham, turkey and other typical American fare. Hot buttered rolls, mix-it-yourself salad with the popular house dressing and a selection of desserts top off the meal. Some long-time fans say Mrs. K's has slipped of late, but it's still popular. Reservations necessary.

Taneytown

Havilah Inn. *Expensive.* Rte. 140. This local favorite features a friendly atmosphere in a rural setting.

Thurmont

Cozy Restaurant. *Expensive.* US 15 in the Cozy Motel. Pennsylvania Dutch cooking is the specialty, and there's a soup and salad bar. Among world-famous figures who have enjoyed the food here, while on their way to the nearby Presidential retreat at Camp David, have been Presidents Franklin Roosevelt and Dwight Eisenhower, and Winston Churchill.

Urbana

Peter Pan Inn. *Moderate.* Rts. 355 and 80. Strictly for families. A limited number of entrees—fried chicken, ham, and steak—served up with all-you-can-eat platters of vegetables. The setting is "busy"—fountains, statuary, and decorative chandeliers—and so is this country-style restaurant. There are no reservations, so be prepared to wait up to an hour.

Westminster

Cockey's Tavern. *Expensive.* E. Main St. Good food served in a warm atmosphere.

Maggie's. *Expensive.* Old Washington Rd. and E. Green St. Continental and American cuisine in a 1920's atmosphere.

Seafarer's. *Moderate.* W. Main St. Tasty meals, well prepared and presented in an 18th-century tavern.

Wheaton

Sans Rival. *Deluxe.* In the Kemp Mill Shopping Center, Arcola Ave. Don't let the location in this suburb of Washington, D.C. fool you. This is a first-rate French restaurant. The veal dishes, seafood and other specialties are well-prepared and served in pleasant surroundings. Call early for reservations weekends.

MISSISSIPPI

White Pillars and Magnolias

BY
BERN KEATING

Exploring Mississippi is easy via north-south or northeast-southwest routes. From these you can reach every point of interest in the state. The three tours usually follow United States routes, in some cases portions of interstate highways.

Mississippi has four interstate highways: I-55, entering the state from Tennessee on the north and running south through Sardis, Grenada, Jackson and McComb into Louisiana; I-20, crossing the state from Meridian to Vicksburg; I-59, entering the state from Alabama near Meridian and running diagonally southwest through Laurel, Hattiesburg and Picayune into Louisiana; and I-10, paralleling the Gulf Coast from Alabama to Louisiana.

South from Tennessee

You begin the easternmost of the north-south tours by entering the state from Tennessee via US 45. Your first stop is at Corinth, first named Cross City when two railroads selected it as a junction point and later given the Grecian name. This was a vital crossroads during the Civil War. It was to Corinth the Confederates withdrew in April, 1862, after the bloody Battle of Shiloh, twenty-one miles to the north in Tennessee. The Confederates evacuated the town in May, 1862, and in October failed in an attempt to recapture the rail junction under General Van Dorn.

MISSISSIPPI

TENNESSEE
Memphis
Corinth
78
ARKANSAS
6
Clarksdale
Tupelo
Tombigbee R.
Greenwood
82
Columbus
Greenville
55
NATCHEZ TRACE PKY.
45
3
Ross Barnett Res.
Vicksburg
Meridian
Natl. Military Pk.
20
Jackson
49
59
Laurel
Brookhaven
84
Natchez
61
Pearl R.
Hattiesburg
98
Pascagoula R.
LOUISIANA
MISSISSIPPI RIVER
ALABAMA
10
Biloxi
90
Gulfport
GULF ISLANDS
NATIONAL SEASHORE
GULF OF MEXICO

0   50
Miles

One mile east on Cemetery Street, you will find the Corinth National Cemetery, established in 1866 to provide a burial place for Union soldiers who died in the vicinity. There are 5,763 graves, of which 3,993 bear no names. The soldiers represented 273 regiments from fifteen states.

Taking US 72 east from Corinth to Iuka, you can visit the J. P. Coleman State Park, 12 miles northeast of Iuka and three miles east of State 25. The 1,468-acre park, situated on a bend in the Tennessee River, affords some of the most beautiful national scenery found in the state. You can watch passing tugboats and their tows for twelve miles on the river. Modern facilities include eight air-conditioned, duplex cabins, picnic areas, tent and trailer camping sites, and a boat launching ramp. Hiking, fishing, and swimming are popular on Pickwick Lake, formed by the dam of the same name across the state line in Tennessee.

Returning to Iuka, which was the site of a Civil War engagement in 1862, you continue south thirteen miles on State 25 to explore Tishomingo State Park. Named in honor of a great Chickasaw chief, it's located three miles east of the little town of the same name. The 1,400-acre park is divided by Bear Creek, which flows into the Tennessee River. Haynes Lake and Bear Creek are noted for excellent fishing, but be prepared to man the oars—no motors are allowed.

Tupelo and Its Battlefields

Continuing south on State 25 to Fulton, and there turning west on US 78, you can reach Tupelo, a town built on what were Chickasaw lands, ceded by the Indians in the Treaty of Pontotoc in 1832. In addition to its historical importance, Tupelo also is noted as the birthplace of Elvis Presley, and for the less momentous annual birth of some three million gamefish at the Federal Fish Hatchery. The hatchery, located at 101 Elizabeth Street, is one of the oldest in the Federal system, dating back to 1902. Covering seventeen acres with fifteen ponds, it produces largemouth black bass, bluegill, redear, sunfish and channel catfish. Annually 3,000,000-odd fish are distributed for use in management of ponds and reservoirs in twenty-four counties in northern Mississippi.

Within a radius of less than twenty-five miles of Tupelo are three national battlefield sites. Oldest is Ackia Battleground National Monument, a forty-nine-acre tract, between US 78 and State 6 on the old Natchez Trace. In 1736 the Battle of Ackia was fought on this site, once the location of an Indian village. In the eighteenth century, the French had widely separated centers of influence in North America, scattered from Canada through Illinois to the lower Mississippi Valley (New Orleans and Mobile). The Chickasaws, allies of the English, occupied a strategic area separating the French positions. Bienville, governor of Louisiana, in 1736 led an expedition from New Orleans against the Chickasaws, hoping to remove them as a menace to French lines of communication. His force failed to meet with another French expedition from Illinois, and in separate attacks, both failed to defeat the Chickasaws. Bienville's forces were so badly defeated at Ackia that he was forced to withdraw to Mobile, and France's position was badly weakened during her struggle with the English in the French and Indian Wars.

Approximately 20 miles northwest of Tupelo and six miles west of Baldwin is the Brice's Cross Roads National Battlefield site, honoring both the Blue and Grey who fought here on June 10, 1864. As was the case with Rommel during his desert campaign, Sherman overextended his supply line when he invaded Georgia during 1864. Having been informed of General Forrest's plan to attack him, Sherman attempted to gain the element of surprise and had a detachment from Memphis move to engage Forrest. The Union force of some 8,000 men encountered Forrest's 4,800 at Brice's Cross Roads. After a daylong battle, the Federals were defeated, Forrest capturing all of the Federal supplies. Brice's Crossroads Museum, housed in a log-cabin pioneer home, features relics of Americana, Indian artifacts and interesting articles from the Civil War.

Nearest Tupelo is the third of the battle sites, the Tupelo National Battleground, one mile west of the downtown section of the city. The engagement here was the climax of the series of operations designed to protect Sherman's flank as he attacked Atlanta. Not content with having attacked Atlanta, the Union Army chased after General Forrest into Mississippi, ordering the expedition to "follow him to death, if it costs 10,000 men and breaks the Treasury."

The Union force of 14,000 men, which made a column fifteen miles long on the march, after fighting off Confederate raids for nine days, reached Harrisburg (today, within the Tupelo town limits) on July 13. Forrest attacked the following morning. Three assaults failed, and, low on ammunition, the Federals withdrew four miles. Forrest attacked this encampment but was driven off. The Union forces again withdrew, the Confederates following, but there were no more major attacks. Although an indecisive engagement, it served the purpose of keeping Forrest from attacking Sherman's supply line to Atlanta. After the Georgia capital fell, Sherman no longer depended upon his supply line, as he began his famous March to the Sea through Georgia, living off the land and leaving a path of destruction in his wake.

Near Tupelo also is the site of de Soto's winter camp in 1540-41. But seven miles east-southeast on State 6 is a more exciting spot. Tombigbee State Park, covering 822 acres, is famous as a fisherman's haven with its 100-acre lake. Facilities include tent and trailer camping sites, swimming area and a nature trail. Each summer, a fishing rodeo for children is held, and often the youngsters surpass their elders.

Columbus, Old Possum Town

Heading south again on State 45W, you reach Okolona, headquarters of the 65,232-acre Tombigbee National Forest, reached by either State 41 or 32. Davis and Choctaw Lakes are the two favorite recreational areas in the forest. The facilities offered are seasonal hunting and fishing, water sports and picnicking.

Continuing south on State 45W, you come to the junction with US 82. By turning east, you can visit Columbus, noted for its tree-shaded streets and beautiful, antebellum mansions. The first week in April a pilgrimage is held through nineteen of the houses. The program includes a Friendship Cemetery Observance and Parade, Candlelight Dinner, Junior Auxiliary Pageant and Ball, and tours of the city, the Air Force Base, and the campus of Mississippi University for Women. The latter, founded in 1847 as the Columbus Female Institute, was the first state-supported school in the nation to offer education exclusively for women. The home of the famous Confederate General Stephen D. Lee is now a museum containing his papers and personal belongings.

Columbus' past stretches back to the time of de Soto. The Spanish conquistador is believed to have entered what is now Mississippi in the vicinity of Columbus, in 1540. Columbus was an early stopover on the Military Road ordered built by Andrew Jackson between New Orleans and Nashville, at first being called "Possum Town," a name apparently the product of local Indian wit. In 1821 educators established the first public school in the state, while the following year Tombigbee River was the site of a historic event, the arrival of the first steamboat at Columbus.

Columbus' Friendship Cemetery was the site of the first Memorial Day observance on April 16, 1866, when the women of Columbus gathered to decorate both Confederate and Union graves. (This date is still Confederate Memorial Day in Mississippi, Alabama, Florida and Georgia.)

Heading west from Columbus on US 82, it's a short drive to Starkville, once an antebellum center of plantation life, now noted for its proximity to Mississippi State University. Established in 1878 and formerly known as Mississippi Agricultural and Mechanical College, MSU is located 1½ miles south of Starkville in the little town of State College. The 750-acre campus includes an agricultural experimental station, which utilizes much of the 4,000-acre tract assigned to the university.

Heading south on State 25, you pass through a portion of the southern section of the Tombigbee National Forest, and into Louisville. Here, change to State 15 and continue to Philadelphia, center of Mississippi's Indian country. This is the headquarters of the Choctaw Indian Agency, and the majority of the few Indians—less than 2,000—in the state live in this region. At Nanih Waiya Historic Site, 15 miles northeast off State 21, you can see the Indian facet of Mississippi history. The state park includes the Nanih Waiya Mound, the Nanih Waiya Cave, and the site of the Dancing Rabbit Treaty, which opened the state to white settlement. Currently it's a day-use area, undergoing expansion. East of Philadelphia via State 16 and 39 is Shuqualak, on US 45, one of the several Mississippi sites for bird dog National Field Trials. Southwest of Philadelphia eighteen miles on State 21 is another state park—Golden, affording swimming, fishing, picnicking, camping and canoeing.

Memorials in Meridian

Taking State 19 southeast from Philadelphia, you can reach Meridian, one of the leading industrial cities of the state, located in a region of abundant raw materials for wood and pulp industries and for textile manufacturing. The town is the site of the Jimmie Rodgers Memorial honoring one of America's most famous folk singers, grandfather of today's country music. Annually top stars in the music world gather to honor this outstanding entertainer.

Merrehope, in Meridian, is one of less than half a dozen residences left standing after the burning of the city during General William T. Sherman's fiery campaign of 1864. Included on the National Register of Historic Places, Merrehope has been restored and opened by the Meridian Restorations Foundation. During the Christmas season, Merrehope displays Christmas trees decorated in the styles of different nations.

The most direct route from Meridian to Laurel is via US 11. However, by taking a slightly longer route, US 45 to Quitman and State 512 to its junction with US 11, you can visit Clarkco State Park, a short distance north of Quitman. The 792-acre park is named for Clarke County, in which it is located. This is gently rolling land, featuring woodlands of loblolly pine, mixed with red and white oak, redbud and dogwood. Facilities include rental cabins, swimming, boating, fishing, picnicking, playfields, nature trails and tent and trailer camping.

Two sawmill men built Laurel in the piney woods of southeastern Mississippi after the Reconstruction, naming the town for the abundant flowering shrub in the area. But despite its pretty name, Laurel was a rough lumber camp for years. It began to bloom after an eastern company took over the mill and encouraged workers to buy houses. The state's first garden club was organized here in the 1890's. In contrast to its rough beginning, Laurel today has an unusual library—the Lauren Rodgers Library and Museum of Art, featuring permanent collections of American and European paintings, including works by Homer, Whistler, Corot, De Hoog and Daumier, Japanese prints, sculpture, pottery, glass and Indian relics.

Heading south from Laurel to Hattiesburg, you can sample Mississippi's I-59 interstate freeway—excellent for fast driving, but like others in the nation, not designed for sightseeing. However, you miss nothing of great import even at freeway speeds. You zip through Jones County, where, at Ellisville, nonslave-owning farmers elected a delegate to vote against secession. He didn't, and they burned him in effigy. Then they conducted guerrilla operations against the Confederates throughout the war.

Hattiesburg is another of the lumber towns in the longleaf pine belt of southern Mississippi. Only a few miles from both sections of the 500,240-acre de Soto National Forest, it still produces lumber and naval stores, but unlike many smaller neighbors which disappeared with the end of the lumber boom in the 1920's, Hattiesburg long ago diversified its industries. It is the site of the University of Southern Mississippi, specializing in teacher training. The university occupies an 840-acre campus. The town also is the site of William Carey College (founded in 1906).

Eight miles south on US 49 is the 805-acre Paul B. Johnson State Park. Tent and trailer camping sites are provided. There is a 225-acre lake, where fishing is excellent, in addition to three small ponds. Facilities for swimming, boating, picnicking and water-skiing are also available.

Twenty-two miles west of Hattiesburg via US 98 is Columbia, a small town noted for being the three-month capital of the state. The scenic Pearl River Valley is the location of the picturesque little town of Sandy Hook, situated on State 358, where the 19th-century John Ford homestead and its excellent collection of antiques and memorabilia can be seen. Throughout the years it has been used as an inn and post office. History reports that Andrew Jackson stayed here overnight on his way to the Battle of New Orleans.

From Hattiesburg, you can take four-lane highway US 49 directly into Gulfport, heart of Mississippi's sixty-five-mile seaside playground on the Gulf of Mexico.

Midstate North to South

You can begin your midstate north-to-south trip in Mississippi from several points on the Tennessee line on I-55. Probably a more interesting means of beginning your exploration can be experienced by entering the state either via US 78 from Memphis, Tenn., or via State 7. Both routes converge on Holly Springs, one of the state's antebellum jewels and once known as the Athens of the South.

Owners of many large plantations in the Carolinas and Virginia, well aware of the rich soil conducive to growing cotton in the Holly Springs vicinity, migrated to the area and settled the town in 1835. While there is much doubt as to the first settler, William Randolph from Virginia is generally considered to be the town's founder.

During this period the inevitable conflicts between cotton dynasties resulted, and legal practitioners found this the ideal place to open business. Because of this rapid growth, the town blossomed overnight into a resplendent community, with columned porches and wide lawns accenting the wealth of the plantations. Even today the restored mansions reflect the gracious living which characterized this time, and visitors from many states come to view many of the homes during the Holly Springs Pilgrimage in April.

The touch of the Civil War did not escape Holly Springs, despite her opulence, for it was here that over sixty-one minor skirmishes were fought, and in 1862, Confederate General Van Dorn dealt a crushing blow to the Union by destroying a supply base with a value estimated by General Grant at almost one million dollars. This one act stalled the attack on Vicksburg and lengthened the war by six months. The North was forced to regroup and reorganize supply lines before pressing on.

The Kate Freeman Clark Art Gallery in Holly Springs has been maintained as a memorial to one of the noted painters of the day, and visitors can see hundreds of her paintings on display here. Living a semisecluded life from 1923 until her death in 1963, Miss Clark kept many of her paintings in her home, and in later years provided funds for their display at the gallery.

A short distance south of Holly Springs on State 7 is 855-acre Wall Doxey State Park featuring lake swimming, fishing, boating, both developed and primitive camping.

Ole Miss and Oxford

Twenty-seven miles south of Holly Springs is Oxford, site of the University of Mississippi (Ole Miss). Borrowing its name from the Old World, as did many other towns, it rallied to the bugle when the Civil War broke out, sending many men to battle for the South, with the university contributing the famous regiment the Grays.

Oxford, too, was the home of one of the nation's great writers, the late William Faulkner, who lived near the university at 900 Garfield Street. Oxford is the "Jefferson" featured in so many of Faulkner's novels. In St. Peter's Cemetery is the grave of Lucius Quintus Cincinnatus Lamar, who drafted the Ordinance of Secession which was adopted by the Mississippi Convention on January 9, 1861. By a quirk of historical fate, he later became a U.S. Supreme Court Justice (1888-1893) and was noted for his work in reconciling the North and South before his death in 1893.

On Ole Miss campus in the Mary Buie Museum, founded by descendants of General Nathanael Greene of American Revolutionary War fame, are interesting displays of historic relics as well as medals and prizes awarded to Faulkner, 1949 Nobel Prize winner for literature.

Both Holly Springs and Oxford lie east of your main north-south route, but you can rejoin it (and I-55) either by taking State 4 from Holly Springs to Senatobia, or State 6 from Oxford to Batesville. If you take the first route to Senatobia, you can visit the Arkabutla Reservoir. North on I-55 is Hernando, one of several sites in Mississippi where U.S. and National Bird Dog Field Trials are held annually. Another site is at Shuqualak.

Between Senatobia and Batesville along I-55 is Sardis, near Sardis Lake and Dam. The dam is several miles east on State 315. Its water has created a thirty-mile-long lake, part of the Yazoo Basin flood control project, from the Little Tallahatchie River. John W. Kyle State Park covers 740 acres, for primitive and developed camping, with laundry facilities.

Proceeding south on either I-55 or US 51, you reach Grenada, on the eastern edge of the famous Mississippi-Yazoo Delta. Cotton always has been an economic mainstay, and now is joined by livestock raising, lumbering and nylon manufacturing. Chartered in 1836, the city developed from an important early trading post. Line Street marks the division between the old towns of Pittsburg and Tulahoma, founded by rival companies. Tired of competing and feuding, the two towns merged in 1836, celebrating the marriage of a Pittsburg man and Tulahoma maiden. Grenada was the headquarters of General Pemberton during Grant's second campaign against Vicksburg. The Grenada Historical Museum is on Poplar St.

Near Grenada are two state parks, both on the 64,000-acre Grenada Reservoir, three miles northeast of the town. Hugh White Park, located on State 8, covers 1,500 acres and features boating, swimming, fishing and camping, both primitive and developed. White also has a trailer area and a restaurant.

South of Grenada, US 51 begins to curve gradually southwestward as it heads for Jackson, the capital named in honor of Old Hickory. Near Durant, you can visit the 463-acre Holmes County State Park. It features fishing, swimming, boating, nature trails, rental cabins and camping.

Jackson, the capital, is your next stop, and well worth careful investigation. Jackson was laid out as the capital before it was even settled. In 1821, the legislature, which previously had met in Natchez and Washington, appointed a commission to select a site within twenty miles of the geographic center of the state, in the territory sold to the U.S. by the Choctaw Treaty of Doak's Stand in 1820. The commission chose Le Fleur's Bluffs, where French Canadian Louis Le Fleur had set up a trading post in 1792. The new capital was named for Andrew Jackson, and designed on a checkerboard plan with alternate squares reserved as commons. Surviving attempts to move the capital to Clinton and Port

Gibson, Jackson slowly grew and was firmly established by 1850. By the time of the Civil War, it was not only the center of state government, but also an important rail junction.

After the legislature passed the Ordinance of Secession in 1861, Miss Amanda Hilzheim produced a blue silk flag with a single star for the occasion. An Irish actor, Harry McCarthy, who was playing in town, wrote and sang three verses of the "Bonnie Blue Flag" as Mississippi withdrew from the Union. The capital played an important role in the Confederacy until 1863, when the Federal Army, commanded by General W. T. Sherman, besieged and captured it. Sherman's forces burned and looted it, but the legislature and state officials were safe, having fled previously to Columbus. Scars of the war remain. A Battlefield Park features a chain of Civil War entrenchments.

During rebuilding Jackson had to contend with hordes of Carpetbaggers, indicative of the problems of the entire South. It was here, in 1884, that Jefferson Davis last spoke to the vanquished South, and six years later the State Convention drafted the present charter.

Buildings connected with the past and present state government are important attractions for visitors to Jackson. The governor and other state officers can be located in the new state capitol, built over sixty years ago. It also houses the state Hall of Fame. The Governor's Mansion, set on grounds covering an entire block, has an exterior resembling the White House and dates from 1842. The Governor's Mansion has been restored, filled with American antiques that date from 1785 to 1840, and opened to the public. It is a National Historical Landmark. In 1908 the mansion was almost razed to make way for a commercial development. But the question was raised: "Will Mississippi destroy that which Sherman would not burn?" And the legislature voted no.

You can spend hours in the State Historical Museum, located in the Old Capitol. This aging structure, begun in 1833 and occupied by the Mississippi Legislature from 1839 until 1903, is an excellent example of Greek Revival architecture. Used later as an office building, the Old Capitol was completely restored (1959-61) at a cost of $1,600,000, excluding the cost of the furniture. The building originally cost $400,000.

During the restoration, rooms that had been modified in converting the Old Capitol to an office building were returned to their original state. Mississippi's history is capsuled by four dioramas in the building, depicting the discovery of the Mississippi River by de Soto in May, 1541; the Treaty of Doak's Stand in October, 1820, by which some 5,500,000 acres of land were opened to white civilization; the landing of the first steamboat at Natchez, December, 1811; and the running of the Confederate batteries at Vicksburg by Yankee gunboats in April, 1863, prelude to the capture of the city.

You can also inspect the restored governor's office with its ornate, authentic period furnishings, and the historic Hall of Representatives, where such important events occurred as the passage of the first law in America giving property rights to married women (1839); Andrew Jackson's address (1840); the passage of the Ordinance of Secession (1861); the Constitutional Convention of 1865, first in the South after the fall of the Confederacy; the overthrow of carpetbag government by the legislature of 1876; and Jefferson Davis' last address to the legislature (1884).

Also on the grounds is the Archives and History Building, which houses the State Department of Archives and History collections and valuable books and manuscripts.

Lovers of the outdoors will be interested in the Museum of Natural Science maintained by the State Game and Fish Commission. One feature of the museum is the excellent collection of state animals on display. There are approximately 25,000 specimens. The zoological park in Jackson is gaining one of the finest reputations in the country. A decade ago it was a sad collection of wild animals in a run-down setting. The present inventory, however, lists 748 specimens, ranking Jackson's zoo in the top 50 of the nation.

The Jackson City Hall, one block south of the Capitol on President Street, managed to survive the burning of the town by General Sherman's troops.

East of Jackson on US 80, at the edge of the Bienville National Forest, is Roosevelt State Park, covering 562 acres. It's three miles south of Morton. Facilities are similar to those in other Mississippi State Parks.

Continue south via I-55 and US 51, and in less than a hundred miles, you're approaching Louisiana. At McComb, a small railroad and manufacturing city, you can make a side trip to Percy Quin State Park, five miles southwest on State 24. Second largest in the state system, it comprises 1,680 acres, including a 675-acre lake. It provides group camping facilities, as well as rental cabins, boating, swimming, fishing, nature and bridle trails.

The Historic Mississippi River Country

No portion of the state is richer than the Mississippi River country, extending through the Delta section. Here the state's history began when de Soto first saw the mighty Father of Waters, and here French explorers cruised. Here, too, the Spanish were briefly in control, and here were fought some of the most important battles of the Civil War.

US 61, entering Mississippi from Memphis, Tennessee, provides a natural route to explore this most historic section of the state. Clarksdale is your first stop. Named for an Englishman, John Clark, it was founded after the Civil War (1868). However, it has a Civil War connection, for ten miles north is Yazoo Pass, through which General Grant attempted unsuccessfully to attack Vicksburg via inland waterways. De Soto first glimpsed the Mississippi River, in 1541, somewhere between Clarksdale and Memphis.

You have two routes south from Clarksdale. If you want to see Mississippi's big cotton market, then take US 49 and later the US 49E fork to Greenwood, which is particularly interesting during the cotton harvesting season, August to December. By taking US 61 south from Clarksdale and US 82 east from Leland, you can head for Greenville. (You also can reach Greenville by going west on US 82 from Greenwood.)

Mississippi's largest river port is not even on the river. Greenville, from its rebirth after being burned to the ground during the Civil War, steadily lost its riverfront streets to the river's currents that gnawed off great chucks of paved streets and two-story buildings. During the great flood of 1927, most of the city was under water for 70 days. Armed with a promise from the Corps of Engineers that dredges would keep open a year-round channel 9-feet deep, city fathers permitted the corps to close off the upstream opening of the branch of the river that flowed by the city, forcing all the stream into the other branch on the far side of an island facing the city. The corps left open the lower end of that chute, so that Greenville stands on a slack-water arm of the river, connected with the main channel but free of destructive currents. To take advantage of that slack water, many towboat companies and shipbuilding firms have made Greenville a kind of Liberia of the river trade.

Greenville has produced an uncommon number of writers for so small a city, among them William Alexander Percy, whose autobiography has remained in print as a standard explanation of the Old South through more than a score of printings and many decades; Hodding Carter, who won a Pulitzer Prize for his editorials defending civil rights for blacks; Shelby Foote, a prominent novelist and historian; Dave Cohn, a brilliant humorous, essayist and social historian; Ellen Douglas, a novelist who has won national awards; Bern Keating, author of 25 nonfiction books; Walker Percy, novelist and winner of the National Book Award; and Charles Bell, poet and novelist. Here you can also visit the Winterville Indian Mounds Museum and State Park. The museum has collections of archeology and Indian artifacts. At least 23 mounds are indicated in the area, 13 within the park itself. Arranged in an oval, they form two plazas, an unusual feature distinguishing Winterville from lesser sites. Development of the mounds, archaeologists say, began soon after the year 100. Winterville is a primary temple mound that ranks in size and importance with just a half dozen others in the country.

If you want to drive along the levees as close to the Mississippi River as possible, you can follow State 1 south from Greenville. An alternate route south is to follow US 82 east to Leland and then turn south on US 61. Both routes give you good views of the Delta country.

Between State 1 and US 61 west of Hollandale is the largest of the Mississippi parks, 2,441-acre Leroy Percy, with facilities similar to other major parks, plus the most spectacular natural display of live alligators in North America. Visitors view the giant beasts from a boardwalk over a swamp and wallowing hole. Because the hole is fed by hot springs, the gators are active year-round. Continue south on State 1 and take an 8-mile dogleg east on State 14 to Rolling Fork. Turn south on US 61 toward Vicksburg. However, if you want to sample further the Delta National Forest area, you can make a side trip via State 3 from Redwood to Yazoo City. You travel through low, flat, moist hardwood country bordering the 59,288-acre forest. This area is noted for fishing and squirrel, turkey, and waterfowl hunting. Near Yazoo City the first oil field in the state was discovered, the beginning of oil production in 1939 spurring a rapid industrial development. Now the city's economic base rests upon chemicals, oil refineries and cottonseed oil, as well as agriculture. It's the market center for a large farming area producing some $3 million worth of beef cattle, hogs and soybeans, corn and oats, annually.

Vicksburg and the Civil War

It's only eleven miles from Redwood to Vicksburg, the site of one of the greatest battles of the Civil War, the siege of Vicksburg. It's easy to get information about the city. There are two Tourist Information Centers, one on Washington Avenue and one across from the entrance to the military park.

Vicksburg's history stretches back to the early eighteenth century, when the French arrived (1719) and built a fort as protection against the Yazoo and Tunica Indians. The Spanish were in control in 1791 when they established Fort Nogales, but were replaced by the Americans in 1798. However, Vicksburg didn't really get started until the early nineteenth century, when, in 1812, Methodist preacher Newitt Vick and his followers arrived and established what became Vicksburg. The town was incorporated in 1825, and despite the usual river town problems resulting from an unwanted number of gamblers, highwaymen, rough flatboatmen and other unsavory characters, developed rapidly. The Mississippi became an ever more popular artery of travel in the first half of the nineteenth century.

Vicksburg's rough character can be realized easily when it's noted that the first five editors of the *Tri-weekly Sentinel,* established in 1837, died violently. Gamblers didn't like adverse comments. But the early violence was only a prelude to the Civil War, which, today, is Vicksburg's chief tourist asset.

You're impressed immediately with the fact that few cities live more intimately with the past than does Vicksburg. Today, the National Military Park surrounds it, just as the battle lines did more than a century ago, and as you tour the park in your car, you can almost visualize the battle scenes.

The Vicksburg National Military Park is not new, for it was established by Congress in 1899, when the 1,330 acres were set aside as a permanent memorial to the heroes of the Blue and the Gray. It covers the battle area of the actual siege and defense of Vicksburg (May 18 through July 3, 1863). The city surrendered on July 4, on the same day the Confederacy reached its high tide at Gettysburg. The National Cemetery here is even older than the Military Park, having been established in 1866.

The park, shaped like a great crescent, slips peacefully along the rolling hills and timbered thickets of the Mississippi River. From its visitor's center, a self-guided automobile tour winds back along the ditches and trenches where men once fought, and died, to possess control of that mighty river. Cannons, originals from the War Between the States, stare emptily out across the terrain, lining the ridges that once blocked the road to Vicksburg.

The tour passes the Louisiana Monument and Great Redoubt, the largest fort on the Confederate line; the oak tree where Grant and the Southern General, Pemberton, met to negotiate surrender, the Shirley House—the lone surviving wartime building in the park, the Third Louisiana Redan, where Federal engineers constructed a mine and exploded 2,200 pounds of powder in an attempt to blast through the Confederate stronghold, an equestrian statue of General Grant that marks his headquarters, and the National Cemetery, the final resting place for almost 17,000 Union soldiers. Thirteen thousand of them are unknown.

By June 1863, with the exception of the earthworks at Port Hudson, Vicksburg then was the only Confederate stronghold left on the Mississippi. As long as the South held this citadel, free passage of the river by the Union forces was impossible, and supplies, arms and men could be brought from Louisiana, Arkansas and Texas and sent to the Confederate armies in the East. This, then, was the stage for the Federal campaign to capture Vicksburg.

Located on the high bluffs overlooking a hairpin turn in the Mississippi, Vicksburg presented a formidable target. It was not until General Grant moved his army through the Louisiana swamps and marshes west of the river to a point thirty miles south of Vicksburg, and then crossed to the eastern side of the river that conquest was possible. His earlier attempts to approach the city from the north on the Mississippi shore had failed.

He was aided by daring maneuvers of the Federal fleet which ran under the Confederate guns on the bluffs, and, getting south of the city, was able to provide transportation for Grant's troops across the river. Porter's running past the Vicksburg guns was one of the outstanding naval operations of the war.

Operating without a base of supplies, Grant kept two Confederate armies apart, and eventually laid siege to Vicksburg. For forty-seven days and nights, the Federals and Confederates bombarded each other. Then, with no prospects of reinforcement, with few supplies and little ammunition, the Confederate garrison surrendered on July 4, 1863, and the fate of the Confederacy was sealed, although it was two years before Lee and Grant met at Appomattox Courthouse.

As you look down upon the Mississippi from the bluffs, you marvel that any gunboat could run the batteries successfully. Regarding the steep, trench-topped hills, you understand why the direct Union assaults failed. Hunger and lack of supplies, however, didn't fail, and the city fell.

If you take time to examine the numerous statues, monuments, memorials and signs, you will have a comprehensive knowledge of what took place. The detail with which the campaign is outlined is amazing. There are 898 historical tablets, 274 markers, and 230 monuments commemorating the various military organizations engaged here. As you stand reading each marker, you face in the same direction as the troops who long ago manned the position. There are also nine beautiful memorials, three equestrian statues and 150-odd busts and relief portraits. If you're interested in the ordnance of the period, examine the 128 cannons of various types mounted in the park.

The battlefield is a green, carefully manicured area now, a marked contrast to the shell-pocked terrain of the last century. But as you stand at these vantage points, it doesn't seem nearly as long ago as when you read about it in history books. It's an integral part of America, even today.

The Old Courthouse and Other Landmarks

Probably Vicksburg's most historic Civil War site is the Old Courthouse, once a favorite target of Union guns. It is now a museum containing Confederate memorabilia dealing with life in the South. There are eight display rooms featuring not only weapons of the Civil War, but also silver, glass and early handwritten documents such as receipts for slaves.

Anyone interested in flood control can learn much by visiting the U.S. Army Engineers Waterway Experiment Station on Hall's Ferry Road.

Miniature reproductions of different methods of controlling water are simulated here, and in this way scientists gain an insight into water management, whether it be for power or recreation. The working models vary in size and there are more than fifty of them to examine.

Among the antebellum houses in Vicksburg, three are of particular interest—Planters Hall, McRaven and Cedar Grove. McRaven, located at the eastern end of Harrison Street, developed from a frontier cottage built before 1797, with additions in 1836 and in 1849, the year during which it developed into its present Neo-Greek style with living wing stairway, exquisite plaster wall moldings, ceiling medalions and graceful marble fireplaces. Caught in a crossfire during the siege of Vicksburg, the house still bears shell marks visible both inside and out. John Bobb owned McRaven when General U.S. Grant came marching into Vicksburg. And on a morning in 1864, he glanced out the window and saw Federal troops in his yard. He ordered them to leave. They refused. So Bobb picked up a brick and threw it at them. When the troops returned they were carrying muskets and as Bobb walked alone in his garden, he was shot to death. It marked the first recorded incident of violence against the civilian populace during the Union occupation of Vicksburg. Grant, outraged, had the soldiers courtmartialed and hanged.

Cedar Grove, another antebellum home being restored as a civic project, is located at 2200 Oak Street. It was constructed between 1840 and 1858 by John A. Klein, prominent plantation owner and banker. Cedar Grove, too, bears Civil War scars. Mute testimony of the siege of Vicksburg can be seen in the walls, where Federal warships attempted to level the house with cannonballs but failed.

Planters Hall, at Main and Monroe streets, the third antebellum showplace in Vicksburg, has had a varied career. It was erected in 1832 as a bank, and contained a special second-story apartment for the bank president. The bank prospered until President Andrew Jackson ordered gold or silver payments for government land instead of bank notes. Banking became difficult, and operations ceased in 1848. The building was bought by the McRae family, and converted into a residence. They in turn sold it to the Vicksburg Council of Garden Clubs, who have maintained it as a museum dedicated to the true South.

Vicksburg is at the southern tip of the Delta country, from which you can cross the Mississippi into Louisiana via a large bridge. However, to complete your Mississippi state tour, you'll want to continue southward. US 61 takes you into Port Gibson, a town with a Civil War past closely linked to Vicksburg's. Port Gibson, remembered as the town Grant called "too beautiful to burn," is thirty miles south of Vicksburg and dates from 1788. US 61 enters the city along a wide thoroughfare lined by seven churches, the most famous and most photographed being the First Presbyterian, with its gold-lead, metal hand pointing skyward.

The tombstones in Port Gibson's cemeteries tell interesting tales of American history. In the Protestant Cemetery are the graves of Sam Gibson, founder of Port Gibson, and of Harmon Blennerhasset, associate of Aaron Burr in the Burr Conspiracy. Blennerhasset came to Port Gibson after his acquittal and established a plantation here. In the Catholic Cemetery is the grave of Resin P. Bowie, inventor of the famous bowie knife, first used by his brother, Jim, of Alamo fame in Texas history.

You'll want to make two side trips from Port Gibson. On Old Rodney Road, ten miles from town, are the ruins of Windsor. Built in 1861, and consisting of five stories and an observatory, it was one of the most extravagant antebellum mansions of Greek Revival style in the state. Mark Twain, while a river pilot, once used the observatory as a landmark. The mansion burned in 1890. Nearby is the ghost town of Rodney —a town the river moved away from.

No town in the state felt the blows of the Civil War more than Grand Gulf. The Confederates fortified it to harass the Federals controlling the river. Beginning in May, 1862, the Union Navy bombarded Grand Gulf in reprisal for the Confederate attacks. In June, a landing party torched much of the town. The Confederates returned, and the Federals finally sent a strong column inland after landing at Bayou Pierre. During the march, the Federals were fired upon by a field gun mounted on a railroad flatcar and protected by bales of cotton, a forerunner of the armored trains of later wars. The Federals again occupied Grand Gulf and destroyed what was left.

War returned to the area in 1863 when General Pemberton had the Confederates throw up defenses against General Grant's forces, which he feared, correctly, would bypass Vicksburg. Rebuffed in his efforts to get at Vicksburg from the north, Grant marched his army southward on the Louisiana shore in late March, intending to cross the Mississippi and capture Grand Gulf. By April 29, the Union forces were ready to attempt the crossing. Admiral Porter's ironclad squadron began a sustained attack for five hours. By then, one Union vessel had been disabled, and one of the two Confederate forts silenced, but the big guns at Fort Wade, the second fort, still boomed. The Federals called off the attack, and the next day crossed the Mississippi at Bruinsburg with little opposition. After crossing, Grant moved north to begin his siege of Vicksburg.

A four-room cottage from the early days of Grand Gulf has been reconstructed to serve as a museum. Two rooms house Civil War displays, including large naval shells hurled into the forts by gunboats, drawings of the battle by actual participants, and colorful dioramas. Scattered through the 104-acre park are the remains of Forts Cobun and Wade, including some of the best preserved, original Civil War trenches and gun emplacements existing anywhere. What's left of the town of Grand Gulf is just outside the park boundaries.

Antebellum Natchez

Natchez, only a short distance farther south on US 61, is your introduction to an antebellum town where time seems to have stood still. Don't, however, despite the flood of promotional literature, assume you're going to see nothing but antebellum mansions, ladies in hoopskirts and men in frock coats. They're for publicity picture purposes only. The town treasures its antebellum past with greater intensity than most communities, however, and profitably so, for the antebellum is its prime tourist appeal. It's also a manufacturing town, and modern buildings mingle with the dominating eighteenth and nineteenth-century structures.

There's a lesser-known side to Natchez, however. Its history of bear-grease trapping, the role of the Indians for whom it was named, and the days of Natchez-under-the-Hill which was known far and wide as a den of iniquity, remained hidden subjects of conversation, while Natchez-on-the-Hill was developing as a wealthy, dignified city.

Its history is interwoven with that of the entire Mississippi valley. La Salle visited here in 1682, as did the enterprising Bienville, who established a fort in 1716. In 1729, the Natchez massacred everyone in the settlement. Later, the French, with the aid of the Choctaws, drove the Natchez Indians from the area. Spain held control briefly, the Americans taking over in 1798. Here, in 1797, the American flag was raised for the first time in the lower Mississippi Valley, a year before the Spanish left.

After the Civil War, steamboating continued to bring some prosperity to Natchez, but the loss of the slaves from the huge plantations was a blow stunting development. Natchez was the home of Captain Tom Leathers, who built several steamboats, all named *Natchez,* including the one which ran the famous race with the *Robert E. Lee* in 1870. The prize was $20,000. And Cap'n Leathers lost because he waited in a fog bank for six hours rather than endanger the lives of his passengers. So he returned to his home, Myrtle-Terrace, broke but proud.

Undoubtedly more people visit Natchez during the annual Spring Pilgrimage (March and April) than at any other time. The Pilgrimage was established during the Great Depression of the 1930's by the more farsighted ladies of the town. Since then, it has achieved national stature, and the old has become almost a way of life. In all, thirty antebellum homes are open to the public in Natchez. Many of the houses are open daily, some only during the Pilgrimage. The complete list can be obtained from the Natchez-Adams County Chamber of Commerce, which will tell you which ones are open during your visit, and tours can be arranged.

Many of the homes have their own stories to tell. Memories of Union looters still haunt Lansdowne. But even so, many of the original furnishings remain. Green Leaves houses such treasures as letters from Jefferson Davis and a saber from the Battle of Waterloo. The Briars, an old plantation home, was the girlhood home of Varina Howell who married Jefferson Davis. The Burn served as headquarters and hospital for northern forces during the occupation of Natchez. And Melrose has the only landscape ever painted by John James Audubon.

Natchez-Under-the-Hill is nothing more today than a ghost town in the heart of a city. Once it had the reputation of being the Devil's own personal workshop, a hard-drinking, always-fighting sort of place. During those lusty times, it was said that the only thing cheaper in Natchez than a woman's body was a man's life. Developers are beginning to restore the site. Already there are a tavern and a restaurant specializing in catfish dinners. The jazz orchestra from the steamboat *Mississippi Queen* often gives an impromptu concert at the tavern when the boat ties up at the wharf only 100 yards away.

On Ellicott's Hill can be seen Connelly's Tavern, which is one of the most interesting historic buildings open to the public. Its rules were simple. Fourpence a night for bed, sixpence with supper. No more than five to sleep in one bed. No boots to be worn in bed. Organ grinders to

sleep in the washhouse. No dogs allowed upstairs. No beer allowed in
the kitchen. No razor grinders or tinkers taken in. And it was inside these
walls that former Vice-president Aaron Burr planned his defense against
the charge of treason.

Another antebellum mansion, probably the most lavish remaining in
Natchez, is Stanton Hall, built in 1851, and now owned by the Pilgrimage Garden Club. Located at Pearl and Monroe Streets, it's an imposing
white structure set beneath towering oaks. Among its outstanding features are carrara marble mantles, bronze chandeliers, enormous mirrors
from France, and a 72-foot ballroom.

Another interesting mansion is Longwood; its architecture has been
described as Moorish, Egyptian, Byzantine, and bizarre. But it was the
home and the dream of Dr. Haller Nutt, a Union sympathizer. He even
raised the American flag above Longwood during the war. So Confederate soldiers burned his cottonfields. He fed and clothed Union troops,
then watched in dismay as they marched away and put the torch to his
cotton gin, three plantations and sawmill. Suddenly, Dr. Haller had
nothing left in this world. He died of a broken heart and Longwood was
never finished.

A side trip from Natchez via US 84-98 takes you to the Homochitto
National Forest (189,072 acres), in one of the finest natural timber
growing areas in the United States. Camping, picnicking, swimming and
fishing are available.

You're less than fifty miles from the Louisiana line when you head
south from Natchez. You can cross into Louisiana at Vidalia via the
bridge at Natchez, but more than likely you'll prefer to continue southward. The Woodville area boasts two little-known sites connected to
Mississippi and American history.

The Natchez Trace

For the motorists who abhor traffic, there's the Natchez Trace, leading
southwest across the state from Tupelo to Natchez, and making accessible many historical points and accommodations.

Three state parks, with lodges, cabins and campsites available, are near
the parkway entrance at Tupelo, on US 45 just north of town. Heading
south you will find historic sites indicated by markers, with picnic spots
nearby. There's the Old Chickasaw Indian Village, a French-Indian
battleground and a nature trail just four miles from the parkway entrance. Twelve miles further you'll see where de Soto crossed the Trace
enroute to the Mississippi River and camped in the winter of 1540-41.
Past the Chickasaw Agency, relax at Davis Lake recreation area, located
twelve miles off the Trace. Farther south is another similar spot, Choctaw Lake recreation area, eighteen miles off the Trace.

At Jackson, you'll find excellent accommodations. Outstanding attractions have been described in earlier pages of this chapter. Back to the
Trace via State 18, you'll find Port Gibson, Windsor, and Rodney (also
described on previous pages), not far from the Trace.

The Natchez Trace, following the trails of Indians and wild animals,
became the link for communication between the Mississippi Territory
and Washington, D.C. But it wasn't an important frontier highway until

Thomas Jefferson, in 1801, ordered the U.S. Army to clear the road and, seven years later, appropriated $6 million for improvements.

The Natchez Trace Parkway doesn't pretend to follow the exact route of the original trail, yet all along the way you can find, and hike back along, depressions that once were the wilderness road. Markers have been erected every few miles to point out historic sites. Some are still visible: Emerald Mound, the crumbling ghost town of Rocky Springs, restored Mount Locust, an early pioneer hostelry and Tupelo Bald Cypress Swamp.

Along the Gulf Coast

Mississippi's sixty-five-mile stretch of coast bordering the Gulf of Mexico runs from the Alabama line to Louisiana and affords the state its own playground in the sun. I-10 and US 90, a four-lane highway from Pascagoula to Bay St. Louis, follows the Old Spanish Trail that ran from St. Augustine, Fla., to the missions in California. Today, there's scant evidence of the Spanish era, but the conquistadors are as much a part of the area's history as the French, English and Americans who also ruled here.

Along the blue waters of the gulf and its bayous grow colorful flowers, the dense green foliage hinting of the tropics. Moss-bearded giant oaks grow everywhere in profusion. A mixture of antebellum with twentieth-century recreation, the coast offers sun-kissed beaches and plenty of water sports—swimming, water-skiing, fishing and boating

Entering Mississippi from Alabama via US 90, your first stop is Pascagoula, a shipbuilding center that boomed during World War II. Dating from 1718, Pascagoula has had a long and colorful history, one of the main centers of attraction being the Old Spanish Fort. Designed by the Frenchman, Joseph Simon de la Pointe, the structure is a monument to the creativity of its builders. The fort was constructed from fallen trees, mud, and even sea shells. Cited as the oldest building in the area, it is now used as a museum and is filled with artifacts of historical significance. The thick mud walls even today could withstand the onslaught of cannon balls.

No one can visit Pascagoula without hearing the legend of the singing river. The Indians have lent a touch of color to the area as well, for here is the Singing Pascagoula River which emits a low humming sound. While scientists have two or three possible answers which attempt to explain the oddity, none of them are as colorful as the Indian legend. Apparently, a young warrior of the Pascagoula tribe fell in love with a princess from the powerful Biloxi tribe. He managed to spirit her away much to the anger of the Biloxis, who attacked the Pascagoulas. Upon realizing that they were outnumbered and could not win, the Pascagoulas walked into the river and drowned themselves, their death song to this day clinging to the water. Thus, the legend persists, adding color to local literature.

In this region of former French-Spanish domination, it's not surprising that Mardi Gras is a big event. Here it takes the form of an eight-week carnival ending on Shrove Tuesday. As in New Orleans and Mobile, there are parades and other festivities, the schedule growing a bit longer each year.

With numerous antebellum homes, Pascagoula has joined the growing number of cities having spring pilgrimages sponsored by garden clubs. Exact last-minute details and dates can be obtained by writing the Chamber of Commerce.

Proceeding westward on US 90, you come to Ocean Springs, original site of Biloxi when d'Iberville made his settlement in 1699. There was some question as to whether this was the site of the original settlement, but the discovery of weapons from warships in the shallow bay dispelled the doubt. For a period of over 150 years, the town did little more than exist, then the influx of tourists about the turn of the century transformed it into a resort area, and it has grown to nationwide popularity over the past years.

Neighboring Biloxi, a short distance west, is one of the key points on the Mississippi sun-and-sand strip. Founded when the original settlement of Ocean Springs was shifted here, it has been a resort since the middle of the nineteenth century when the cotton planters first indulged in seaside recreation. Biloxi is not only a beach resort, the area is also noted for the quantity of seafood it has produced since the 1870's. Since 1883, shrimp has been one of the major products, and today, the seafood industry is an important part of the city's economic life.

Twelve miles across Mississippi Sound is Ship Island, part of the Gulf Islands National Seashore and site of ruined Fort Massachusetts. Because the sound is shallow, seagoing vessels from the early days of the French colonists landed first on Ship Island. The most popular cargo was eighty maidens sent from France in the early eighteenth century to be wives of the bachelor pioneers.

Fort Massachusetts was built by orders of Jefferson Davis while he was Secretary of War. Ironically, its only military use was as a prison for Confederate captives. The British fleet and army that assaulted New Orleans during the War of 1812 was based on Ship Island. The body of their leader, Sir Edward Pakenham, felled by one of Andy Jackson's sharpshooting riflemen, was packed into a barrel of rum for shipment home. Scheduled boat service connects Ship Island with both Gulfport and Biloxi. Also lying offshore are Deer Island, only half a mile from East Beach Boulevard in Biloxi, and Horn and Cat islands. The latter, actually closer to Gulfport than Biloxi, was named Cat Island because the French explorers, unfamiliar with raccoons, mistook them for large cats.

The area around Biloxi is filled with natural beauty and the streets of the town are accented with brilliant blooms and the majesty of tall trees shading the sidewalks, while strands of Spanish moss reach down from the limbs. With its long past, it's only natural that Biloxi has numerous historical points of interest. The dyed-in-the-wool Southerners undoubtedly are most proud of Beauvoir, the Jefferson Davis Shrine and Memorial Gardens, five miles west on US 90 (W. Beach Boulevard). This was the home of the Confederate president for the last twenty-two years of his life, after his release from a Federal prison in Virginia. After Davis died in 1889, the building was converted into a home for Confederate soldiers. Later, it was converted into a Confederate shrine, including a museum housing various Davis and Confederate relics. You can see the little white cottage Davis used as his library. Here, he wrote the *Rise and Fall of the Confederate Government.* There's also a Confederate cemetery.

In the same vicinity, along US 90, is the Biloxi Lighthouse, now operated by the United States Coast Guard. Upon the death of Lincoln it was painted black, but now is white. Before automation the light was tended for sixty-two years by a mother and daughter team.

Driving along US 90, you begin to realize the tremendous extent of the beach. The highway separates the sand strip from the hotels, motels, restaurants and other appurtenances of a beach resort, affording a twenty-six-mile stretch of sand and surf. North of Biloxi on State 15 (also north of Gulfport on US 49) is the de Soto National Forest, a cool place in summer.

Between Biloxi and Gulfport occurred a famous bit of heavyweight boxing history. Here was held the bare knuckles, heavyweight championship fight in which John L. Sullivan beat Paddy Ryan, on February 7, 1882. (The last bare knuckles, heavyweight championship bout was also held in Mississippi. John L. Sullivan defeated Jack Kilrain in seventy-five rounds on July 8, 1889, at Richburg, defying the governor, who had called out the state militia to prevent the match.)

Gulfport, a short distance west, was chosen as a port site in 1887, but it was 1902 before the plans matured. When the railroad was completed through the sparsely settled sections in the southern part of the state, Gulfport became a major lumber shipping port. The town turned to the resort business in the 1920's, as a result of the Gulf and Ship Lines being purchased by the Illinois Central Railroad in 1925. The boom soon collapsed, however. After World War II, the town developed rapidly as a resort city, and today, recreation is a vital part of the economy. The deep-sea harbor extends gulfwards from a junction of US 49 and 90. On its edge is the world's most modern banana terminal, where ships can unload 9,600 stems hourly. The port, quite naturally, is used mainly by Latin American carriers.

West of Gulfport and halfway to Pass Christian is Long Beach, another of the resort communities, featuring a municipal pier. Pass Christian was a seaside resort long before the Civil War and proudly claims the South's first yacht club, founded here in 1849. Settled in 1704, Pass Christian has been a favorite vacation area for six presidents—Grant, Jackson, Theodore Roosevelt, Taylor, Truman and Wilson. It, too, has a Mardi Gras, with carnival parade and ball. Several historic homes and gardens are open to the public during the annual Garden Club Pilgrimage.

At Bay St. Louis, US 90 swings inland to cross the Louisiana border eighteen miles to the west. Bienville is credited with exploration of the area, and also with naming it after Louis IX. During the War of 1812, it was the scene of a naval engagement involving five American gunboats, which attacked a British fleet of sixty vessels in an effort to protect New Orleans. Bay St. Louis was a favorite vacation spot with wealthy planters long before the War of 1812.

Nearby, at the western end of Waveland, is Buccaneer State Park. Covering 400 acres of land, with a mile-long beach area, it was designed to be Mississippi's finest, with camping, swimming pools, tennis and shuffleboard courts, and a basketball court, as well as picnic pavilions.

Ten miles north on Jordan River, you can visit Holly Bluff Gardens, a natural woodland of giant Spanish moss-draped oaks interspersed with cypress, pine, maple and gum trees.

North and south, east and west, Mississippi offers a fascinating blend of history, mixed with modern twentieth-century hospitality, creating a vacation area of great interest. Moreover, it's Southern to the core.

PRACTICAL INFORMATION FOR MISSISSIPPI

FACTS AND FIGURES. Mississippi is a tortured spelling of a simple Algonquian Indian word misi sipi, that means "big water." The state's nickname is the Magnolia State, and, naturally, the magnolia is both the state flower and state tree. The state bird is the mocking bird. *Virtute et Armis* ("By valor and arms") is the state motto. "Go, Mississippi" is the state song.

Jackson is the state capital. The state's population of about 2.5 million people is roughly divided equally between urban and rural. Only slightly more than half that population is white; the rest is mostly black, with a scattering of Chinese in the Delta region and a band of Choctaw Indians near Philadelphia.

The tail end of the Appalachian foothills gives the northeast and some of the central areas rolling contours. In the so-called Prairie along the Alabama border and in the Mississippi-Yazoo Delta from Memphis to Vicksburg along the big river are two billiard-table-flat, tremendously fertile farmlands.

Cotton has been the major crop for most of the state's history, but recently soybeans have surpassed the old king both in acreage and dollar return. Mississippi summers are long, hot and humid. Winters are mild, but an occasional ice and snow storm is not unheard-of.

HOW TO GET THERE: *By air:* Delta and Republic have direct service into many cities in the state. American is planning service to Jackson. Take Rio from Greenville to Memphis; Royale from Jackson and Natchez to New Orleans.

By car: I-55, US 45 and US 61 go from north to south; US 82, I-20, US 84, I-10 and US 90 run from east to west.

Car rental: Avis, Hertz, Budget and National in major cities.

By train: Amtrak from Chicago to New Orleans runs over Illinois Central Gulf rails from north to south.

By bus: Greyhound and Trailways.

By ferry: From St. Joseph, La., to Port Gibson.

HOW TO GET AROUND: *By air:* Republic for local service; Rio from Memphis to Greenville; Royale from Jackson and Natchez to New Orleans.

By car: I-55, US 45 and US 61, north to south; US 82, I-20, US 84, I-10 and US 90 east to west.

By train: Amtrak over the Illinois Central Gulf system north to south.

By bus: Greyhound; Trailways; for northern local service, Arrow; and for southern service Gulf Transport.

TOURIST INFORMATION. Contact the Mississippi Department of Tourism Development, PO Box 22825, Jackson, 39205; the Mississippi Park Commission, 717 Robert E. Lee Bldg., Jackson, 39201; individual city chambers of commerce; Natchez-Adams County Chamber of Commerce, 300 N. Commerce St., 39120, for antebellum houses open to public.

MUSEUMS AND GALLERIES: Brice's Cross Roads Museum, Baldwyn. Winterville Indian Mounds Museum & State Park, Greenville. Grenada Historical Museum, Grenada, State Historical Museum, in the Old Capitol, Jackson; Old Spanish Fort, Pascagoula. Natchez Trace Parkway, Visitor Center, Tupelo. Park Museum Vicksburg National Military Park.

Art: Kate Freeman Clark Art Gallery, Holly Springs; Municipal Art Gallery, Jackson. Mary Buie Museum, Oxford, Museum of Art, Meridian. The Lauren Rogers Memorial Library and Museum of Art at Laurel deserves special mention for it houses many canvasses of the Great Masters, including Homer, Whistler, Corot, de Hoog and Daumier.

Special Interest: Mississippi Museum of Natural Science, Jackson. Military Museum, Port Gibson. Dunn-Seiler Museum (geology), Mississippi State University, Starkville. Art Center Planetarium, Jackson.

Others: Old Country Store, Lorman, River Museum and Hall of Fame, Vicksburg. Florewood River Plantation State Park, Greenwood. Grand Village of the Natchez Indians, Natchez.

 SEASONAL EVENTS. In every section of Mississippi *Annual Spring Pilgrimages* are held in early spring (Mar.-Apr.). Hoopskirted attendants greet visitors to the pre-Civil War mansions—filled with rare antiques and treasures of the antebellum past. These Pilgrimages can be enjoyed in the following cities: Bay St. Louis, Biloxi, Carrollton, Columbus, Gulfport, Hattiesburg (homes featured here were built during the first years of the 20th century); Holly Springs, Jackson (through June), Natchez, Oxford, Pascagoula, Pass Christian, Port Gibson, Raymond, Sardis, Vicksburg, Woodville. The *Gulf Coast Pilgrimage,* held during mid-March, covers eleven cities. Tours are marked and are free. The Pilgrimage is sponsored by the Mississippi Gulf Coast Council of Garden Clubs.

February: Dixie National Livestock Show and Rodeo, Jackson. 2nd week.

March: During this month there are brilliant celebrations of *Mardi Gras* at Biloxi, Pascagoula and Pass Christian. From early March to Sept. the *Dixie Showboat Players* present melodrama in Vicksburg.

April: Greenwood Arts Festival with literary lions, all-day jazz, exhibits.

May: Armed Forces Day, Keesler Air Force Base, Biloxi. *Mississippi Arts Festival,* Mississippi State Fairgrounds & Coliseum, Jackson. *Miss USA Finals,* Gulf Coast Coliseum, Biloxi.

June: Biloxi Shrimp Festival, the *Blessing of the Fleet,* and the *Shrimp King & Queen Pageant.* (1st week). A *Deep-Sea Fishing Rodeo* is also held in Biloxi.

July: Blue Angels Air Show, Naval Air Station. Meridian. *Yachting Regatta,* Biloxi. *Yachting Regatta,* Pass Christian (July 4th). *Mississippi Deep-Sea Fishing Rodeo,* Gulfport. 1st wk. of July. *Miss Mississippi Pageant,* Vicksburg Municipal Auditorium, Vicksburg.

August: Outdoor Fishermen's Club Fishing Rodeo, Pass Christian (all month).

October: Invitational Golf Tournament, Pass Christian. *Mississippi State Fair,* State Fairgrounds, Jackson (2nd wk.); *Mississippi State Horse Show,* Jackson (late Oct.).

November: Annual Jaycee Bowl, Long Beach. *Bird Dog Field Trials,* Holly Springs (late Nov.). *Frost-Bite Regatta,* Pass Christian (early Nov.).

December: Shrimp Bowl Football game: Delta Band Festival & Winter Carnival. Biloxi (early Dec.).

NATIONAL PARKS AND FORESTS. Bienville National Forest, US 80, east of Raworth, is a place where you will find all necessary camping and picnicking facilities, while fishing and hunting in season are two reasons for the influx of many campers. DeSoto National Forest is in southern Mississippi, in the Biloxi area. Again, hunting and fishing draw sportsmen from all over the state. You can also visit one of the largest tree farms in the country here. Holly Springs, Delta, and Homochitto National Forests all have good camp sites and picnic areas for the visitor. Fishing and hunting are permitted in all three. Vicksburg National Military Park, in Vicksburg, is something truly different for the traveler. As you enter the park, the Visitor Center offers you a pictorial display of the Battle of Vicksburg, fought on the site of the present park. As you walk over the surrounding countryside, dotted with memorial markers, you can see evidences of the lines of battle. Half-covered trenches mark the Union and Confederate emplacements, rusted guns and sabers, ruined forts and cannons are mute testament to the battle that won the war. The Natchez Trace Parkway is the longest, skinniest park in the federal system, a two-lane blacktop highway that retraces the ancient frontiersman's route from Nashville to Natchez. Landscaping conceals signs of industrialization in nearby towns; roadside billboards are forbidden.

 STATE PARKS. Over 16,000 acres in Mississippi have been set aside for camping and recreation. The cost of staying at one of the state areas runs according to the activities in which you want to take part. If you want to camp overnight, you will be pleased to find that there are toilet and running-water facilities in all fourteen camps. In some cases, rental cabins are available, but these are generally filled early.

Some of the better parks are: *Clarbco State Park,* US 45, south of Meridian, is an excellent place for those interested in nature study. The large freshwater lake offers facilities for all types of water sports. *Leroy Percy State Park* is on Rte. 12, west of Hollandale. If you are interested in camping but want something more modern than a bed of pine needles, you will enjoy the cabins and the lodge, both of which have good accommodations.

Percy Quin State Park, off Rte. 24 west of McComb, features water sports, with the major area of interest centering around the large lake in the Tangipahoa River. *Roosevelt State Park,* south of Morton on State 13, has all the facilities for enjoyable camping. Swimming and boating are just two of the many recreational activities you may enjoy here. *Wall Doxey State Park,* State 7, south of Holly Springs, is where you may test your piscatorial skills. Some of the best fishing waters in the state are located on this 800-acre tract.

 CAMPING OUT. The state parks, though high in acreage, have relatively few campsites (5-30 per park). Open all year, the length of visit is unrestricted. Small charge. Trailer space is available everywhere but in *Carver Point* and *Roosevelt Park.*

Hunters are drawn to the rugged timberland of Mississippi's six national forests and although quail and small game abound, campsites do not. Of the 109 available, *Davis Lake* (Tombigbee) and *Clear Springs* (Homochitto) each have 26 sites. The *Big Biloxi National Forest* campground area is very popular.

Clustered in the northwestern corner of the state, the four Corps of Engineer Lakeside parks have created the greatest number of camp sites. *Lakes Arkabutla* (500), *Sardis* (300), *Enid* (435) and *Grenada* (455) are open year round, charge no fee and have trailer space. Visit need not be limited to two weeks if permission from reservoir manager is obtained.

Magnolia State Park at Ocean Springs has all facilities, plus a boat launching ramp and a channel into the Gulf.

HISTORIC SITES. The history of Mississippi seems to center around the War Between the States, whereby much that was the Old South was reduced to a memory, with large plantations made into crumbled ruins and elegant lace into faded rags. However, in many areas of the state you will find that there are places which have been restored or preserved. In these spots you may capture some small idea of the graciousness and charm of the South before the Civil War.

Baldwyn: Brice's Cross Roads National Battlefield Site, off Rte. 370. Daily. *Biloxi: Beauvoir,* on US 90, last home of Confederate president Jefferson Davis, now a shrine and museum. *Biloxi Lighthouse,* West Beach Blvd. *Columbus: Friendship Cemetery,* origin of the first National Memorial Day observation. *Corinth: Corinth National Cemetery,* the Blue and the Gray, who died in the battle of Corinth lie side by side in this first official U.S. Cemetery. *Ship Island: Fort Massachusetts* can be reached by excursion boats twice daily from Biloxi and Gulfport. *Tupelo: Tupelo National Battlefield.* Open year round.

Vicksburg: The town teems with memorabilia of the war, including the *Vicksburg National Military Park & Cemetery.* Daily. Free. *Cedar Grove,* 2200 Oak St. 1842 mansion located at the site of the siege of Vicksburg. Open year-round. *McRaven,* 1503 Harrison. Pre-Civil war home. Opening hours vary. *Rosemont Plantation,* the boyhood home of Jefferson Davis near Woodville. Guided tours are available. Closed Jan.–Feb.

TOURS. *By boat: Sailfish Tour Boat,* 1½-hr. shrimping and oystering expedition. Leaves Biloxi, Small Craft Harbor, April–Labor Day. Island Trader. Harbor tour from Biloxi. April–Labor Day. Excursion boats make two round trips daily, leaving Biloxi and Gulfport to historic Fort Massachusetts on Ship Island. April–September. *Jefferson Davis Cruises,* leave from Vicksburg, April–Labor Day. Sat., Sun. only Sept. to Oct.

By train: Shrimp Tour Train. 50-min. tour covering 10 mi. of interesting sights, leaves from the Biloxi lighthouse March-Labor Day. Six tours daily.

SPECIAL INTEREST TOURS. *Keesler Air Force Base,* largest technical station of the U.S. Air Force, Biloxi. *John S. Ford House.* On State 35 in *Sandy Hook,* nr. Columbia. Sat., Sun.

National Space Technology Laboratory in Hancock County near Waveland. Monday through Friday at 1:15 P.M.

Mississippi Petrified Forest, in *Flora.* Only petrified forest in the eastern U.S. Open year round 8 to dark.

Old Country Store, on US 61, *Lorman.* Operating since 1875. Daily.

Jimmie Rodgers Memorial, Highland Park, *Meridian.* Year round.

Grand Gulf Military Park, Port Gibson: Open daily to sunset. *The Ruins of Windsor,* Old Rodney Rd. Remains of 4-story mansion destroyed by fire in 1890. The town of Rodney, once a bustling river port, now a ghost town.

Elvis Presley Birthplace, Tupelo. Year-round except major holidays; spring-fall 9–5; winter 12–5.

In *Vicksburg: U.S. Army Engineer Waterways Experiment Station,* Halls Ferry Rd. Mon. to Fri. 1½-hr. guided tours. Closed holidays. *National Military Park,* handsomely landscaped battlefield and museum. Year-round except Christmas.

GARDENS. *"Beauvoir,"* Jefferson Davis Shrine and Memorial Gardens, Biloxi. 50 acres of landscaped grounds.

Mynelle Gardens, 4738 Clinton Blvd., Jackson. One of the South's finest gardens. Year round, dawn to sundown. Adults $1; under 12 free. Also on the grounds is the colonial home (Old Greenbrook) of Mrs. Mynelle Hayward, with exhibits of fine antique silks and art treasures. *Wister Gardens,* Belzoni. 14 acres, 8,000 azaleas, 1,000 roses, 5,000 tulips. Swans, flamingos. Year-round, free.

Palestinian Gardens. 12 mi. NW of Lucedale. 6 mi. N of US 98.

MUSIC. Jackson is the home of Opera/South, the only professional black opera company in the U.S. Also based there is the Mississippi Opera Association that presents grand opera with a mixed cast of gifted local amateurs and big name professionals. The Delta Blues Festival is held in Greenville in September, and Meridian has the Jimmie Rodgers Memorial Festival in May. Meridian also has a Lively Arts Festival in April. Jackson has a symphony orchestra and full-time professional ballet troupe, and in May hosts the Mississippi Arts Festival. Greenville has a symphony orchestra that presents four concerts a season.

STAGE AND REVUES. Southern Exposure is presented Tuesdays, Thursday, Saturdays and Sundays during the Natchez Pilgrimage; the Confederate Pageant is presented on Mondays, Wednesdays, Fridays, and Saturdays.

DRINKING LAWS. Privately owned package stores and bars in hotels and restaurants are legal on a local option basis. Store hours 10 to 10, bars 10 A.M. to midnight. Certain designated resort area bars stay open past midnight. No Sunday sales of liquor. The drinking age is 21 for liquor, 18 for beer.

 SPORTS. *Swimming:* The world's longest man-made beach is from Biloxi to Henderson. There are also beaches at Pascagoula, Ocean Springs, Bay St. Louis, Waveland and others on the offshore islands, reached only by boat.

Boating: Most towns have launching ramps. There is powerboating in the Mississippi Sound, Escatawpa River, Pascagoula River, Bluff Creek, on Biloxi Back Bay, Ft. Bayou, Tchoutacabouffa, Biloxi, Wolf and Jordan Rivers and many bayous. Small sailboats available for rent along the beachfront at Biloxi; races on weekends.

Fishing: There is year-round freshwater, saltwater and deep-sea fishing coastwide, as well as hard and soft-shell crabbing. No license or limit on saltwater fishing. Fishing for freshwater fish requires a non-resident license. There are fishing camps on all waters in the 3 coastal counties. Deep-sea fishing rodeos are held in Biloxi, Gulfport and Pass Christian.

Deep-sea charter fishing boats are available on the Gulf at an average of $300 for parties up to six, $25 per extra head.

Aqua-planing, waterskiing, skindiving all along the coast.

Horseback riding at the Gulf Hills Riding Stables, Ocean Springs.

Hunting: Fox, coons, possums, rabbits, squirrels, deer, quail, ducks, geese and turkeys are to be found. U.S. and National bird dog Field Trials are held at Shuqualak and Hernando.

Golf: With the warm climate, golf has long been a major sport in the state. There are lush, well-planned courses to try the golfer's skill: *Gulf Hills C.C.,* a resort course, with gently rolling fairways; *Edgewater Gulf C.C.,* Biloxi, a resort course; *Broadwater Beach G.C.,* Biloxi, a tough sun resort course; *Pass Christian C.C.,* a private course, open to guests of members only; *Hickory Hill C.C.,* Pascagoula, a semi-private Earl Stone course, with seven holes dominated by water; *Sunkist C.C.,* N. Biloxi, a semi-private course with level fairways and smallish greens; *St. Andrews,* a resort course in Ocean Springs; *Banyon Views C.C.,* a municipal course with three water holes and a driving range; *Diamondhead G.C.,* Bay St. Louis, a resort course with long tees, roller-coaster greens.

Tennis: Courts in Biloxi, Gulfport, Ocean Springs and Pascagoula, on the Gulf; and since the tennis boom, courts have mushroomed in dozens of inland cities.

SPECTATOR SPORTS. *Football:* The Shrimp Bowl Football game is held at Biloxi in early Dec., but college football is king throughout the state all fall.

Golf: In Oct., the International Golf Tournament is held at Pass Christian. A professional satellite golf tournament is held each year at Hattiesburg. The oldest tournament in the state is at Greenwood.

WHAT TO DO WITH THE CHILDREN. Here in Mississippi is the opportunity for youngsters to see first hand one of the most famous sites of the War Between the States. *Vicksburg National Military Park* and the Park Museum are teeming with mementos of the battle. You will find models, maps, and displays showing the course of the battle and the influence of the terrain. After seeing the museum, take the children around the park so they may actually see the trenches and barricades restored to their natural condition.

Those curious about Southern life before the war get an accurate picture from the exhibits and pictures on display in the *Old Courthouse Museum* in Vicksburg.

Eight Flags, Biloxi. Old West atmosphere. Visitors may feed and pet tame deer. Open June-Sept.

Marine Life Aquadome, Gulfport. 6 shows daily. Interesting exhibits. Apr. to Labor Day.

National Fish Hatchery, on US 11, Meridian. Free.

National Fish Hatchery, Tupelo. Summer fishing rodeo for children. Tombigbee National Forest. Free.

Harbor Tour Train, Gulfport. A 25-minute narrated tour along the ocean front.

RECOMMENDED READING. *Historic Architecture in Mississippi,* by Mary Wallace Crocker, published by University & College Press (1973), Jackson, Miss. 39205; *Mississippi, A Guide to the Magnolia State,* by the Federal Writers (Project), published by Somerset, New York; *History of Mississippi* (2 volumes), editor R. A. McLemore, published by the University of College Press (1973), Jackson, Miss. 39205; *Boy in Rural Mississippi,* by S. G. Thigpen, Box 819, Picayune, Miss. 39466; *The Mighty Mississippi,* by Bern Keating, published by the National Geographic Society, Washington, D.C. (1971); *Antebellum Natchez,* by James D. Clayton, published by the Louisiana State University Press (1968), Baton Rouge, La. 70806.

HOTELS AND MOTELS. The Gulf Coast of Mississippi boasts several fine resort establishments and a wide selection of excellent motels on or near the gulf. Inland, the state has a more narrow range of accommodations, there being no super deluxe hostelries in the grand tradition. But these are more than compensated for by the abundance of comfortable, more modest accommodations. We have listed hotels and motels alphabetically in categories determined by double-occupancy, in-season rates. Family rates are available at almost all listings. Rates will by $3-$4 higher during Pilgrimages. *Expensive:* $40 and up; *Moderate:* $25–$40; *Inexpensive:* $20–$25. For a more complete explanation of hotel and motel categories see *Facts at Your Fingertips* at the front of this volume.

Biloxi

Broadwater Beach. *Expensive.* West Beach Blvd. (US 90). This large resort has all the facilities, including deep-sea fishing, heated pool, golf, tennis, but if none of them appeal, you can spend a quiet afternoon walking over the thirty-odd acres of terraced grounds. Free airport transportation. In-room coffee. Restaurant. Cocktail lounge with entertainment in evenings, dancing. Supervised play area.

Hilton Resort Hotel. *Expensive.* 300 Deluxe rooms, gourmet dining room, show lounge, lighted tennis courts, 18 hole championship golf course.

Royal D'Iberville. *Expensive.* 3634 W. Beach Blvd. (US 90) Pools (heated). Restaurant, cocktail lounge, entertainment, dancing.

Quality Inn Emerald Beach. *Moderate to Expensive.* 3717 W. Beach Blvd. Restaurant, bar. Limousine, tour service.

Ramada Inn. *Moderate to Expensive.* 3719 W. Beach Blvd. (US 90W). Restaurant, coffee shop, bar, dancing. Pool (heated).

Holiday Inn. *Moderate.* 92 W. Beach (US 90). Free airport transportation. Restaurant, bar, dancing. In-room coffee. Play area. Pets welcome.

Oak Manor Motel. Member of Best Western. *Moderate.* 626 Central Beach Blvd. Pool, restaurant nr.

Sea Gull. *Moderate.* W. Beach Blvd. (US 90). Here is an excellent medium-sized place for the whole family. Outdoor barbecue facilities. Some family kitchen units and cottages. Restaurant nr. Heated pool, play area.

Sun-N-Sand. *Moderate.* W. Beach Blvd. (US 90). For those who are interested in salt-water swimming, fishing and boating, this is the place. A large resort with pools. Play area. Restaurant, bar, dancing. Free airport transportation. Beautician.

Sun Tan Motel. *Moderate.* 200 Central Beach Blvd. A well-run medium-sized motel which offers many opportunities for both relaxing and sightseeing. Pool. In-room coffee. Restaurant nr.

Biloxi Rowntowner. *Inexpensive.* 115 W. Beach (US 90). Pools, play area. Restaurant, cocktail lounge, entertainment, dancing. Pets allowed.

Clarksdale

Clarksdale Uptown Motor Inn. Member of Best Western. *Inexpensive.* Central location. Restaurant, bar.

Holiday Inn. *Inexpensive.* Restaurant, bar. Free airport transportation. Pool.

Columbus

Holiday Inn. *Moderate.* Two locations on US 45. Restaurant, bar. Pets welcome.

Ramada Inn. *Moderate.* US 45N. Pool. Pets allowed. Restaurant, cocktail lounge, entertainment.

Chief Econo Inn. *Inexpensive.*

Columbus. *Inexpensive.* This well-maintained medium-sized motel seems to cater to the family vistors. Restaurant nr. Pool.

Corinth

Ramada Inn. *Moderate.* US 45 bypass. Entertainment. Beauty shop.

Holiday Inn. *Inexpensive.* Free airport transportation. Pools. Pets welcome. Restaurant, bar.

Southern. *Inexpensive.* This is a favorite meeting place for many of the local service clubs. Restaurant, bar. Play area. Pets allowed.

Windsor Inn. *Inexpensive.* Pool. Pets allowed. Restaurant.

Greenville

Coachman's Inn. *Moderate.* Pool, play area. Pets allowed. Restaurant nr.

Ramada Inn. *Moderate.* Pool, play area. Bar, entertainment.

Gilhara. *Inexpensive.* Large well-furnished rooms will add much to your comfort while you stay at this spacious motel. Pool. Pets allowed.

Holiday Inn. *Inexpensive.* Restaurant, bar. Pool. Play area.

Riverview Inn. *Inexpensive.* Restaurant, bar. Pool. Central location.

Greenwood

Downtowner Inn. *Moderate.* Restaurant, pool.

Holiday Inn. *Moderate.* Entertainment, dancing. Heated pool. Pets allowed.

Ramada Inn. *Moderate.* Dancing, entertainment.

Grenada

Day' Inn. *Inexpensive.* No frills but complete comfort.

Holiday Inn. *Inexpensive.* Restaurant, bar. Pool (heated). Pets allowed.

Hilltop Motel. *Inexpensive.* Restaurant, pool.

Ramada Inn. *Inexpensive.* Swimming pool. Restaurant.

Gulfport

Best Western. *Moderate.* Overlooks Gulf. Restaurant, bar, entertainment, dancing. Pool (heated). Pets allowed.

Holiday Inn. *Moderate.* Pools. Pets allowed. Free airport transportation. Bar, entertainment, dancing.

Moody's Fountainhead. *Moderate.* Fishing trips arranged. Restaurant, bar. Pool. Play area. Family units offered by this large motel-cottage combination. Seasonal rates.

Ramada Inn. *Moderate.* Entertainment, dancing. Heated pool. Pets allowed.

Sheraton Gulfport. *Moderate.* Heated pool, shuffle board. Entertainment, dancing.

Alamo Plaza Hotel Courts. *Inexpensive.* Large well-maintained operation, with rooms on Gulf. Family units with kitchens, outdoor barbecue facilities. Pool. Restaurant nr.

Deep South. *Inexpensive.* Pool. Restaurant nr.

Worth. *Inexpensive.* Heated pool, tennis, putting green, shuffleboard.

Hattiesburg

Carriage Inn. *Moderate.* Restaurant nr. In-room coffee.

Holiday Inn. *Moderate.* Two locations. Both have restaurant, lounge, entertainment, pool, coffee makers in room. Kennels.

Ramada Inn. *Moderate.* Pool (heated). Restaurant, bar, entertainment.

La Grace Motor Hotel. *Inexpensive.* Restaurant, pool.

Red Carpet Inn. *Inexpensive.* Restaurant, bar. In-room coffee.

Jackson

Coliseum Ramada Inn. *Moderate to Expensive.* 400 Greymont St. Pool (heated), play area. Bar, entertainment. Pets welcome.

TraveLodge-Airport. *Moderate to Expensive.* Jackson Municipal Airport above terminal blvd. Restaurant.

Admiral Benbow Inn. *Moderate.* 905 N. State. St. Restaurant, bar, entertainment. Pets allowed.

Downtowner Motor Inn. *Moderate.* 225 E. Capitol. Central location, rooftop pool (heated). Restaurant, bar, entertainment.

Holiday Inn. *Moderate.* Four locations. All have restaurant, entertainment, pool. **North:** 155 N. Frontage Rd. **Southwest:** 2649 US 80W. **Downtown:** 200 E. Amite. **Medical Center:** 2375 N. State.

Howard Johnson's Motor Lodge. *Moderate.* I-55 at McDowell Rd. Restaurant, bar. Pool. Pets allowed.

Jackson Downtown Travelodge. *Moderate.* 550 W. Capitol St. Central location of this medium-sized motel helps account for its popularity. Excellent staff. Restaurant. Pool.

Jacksonian Master Hosts Inn. *Moderate.* US 51N, 5 mi. Ideal location for the sportsman, with bowling, golf, other sports to test his skill. Restaurant, bar. Wide choice of accommodations and rates. Pools. Play area.

Ramada Inn. *Moderate.* 2275 US 80W. Pool. Restaurant, bar.

Rodeway Inn. *Moderate.* 3720 I-55N. Restaurant, bar, entertainment. Pool. Pets allowed.

Sheraton Motor Inn. *Moderate.* US 51N, I-55. The large dressing rooms will add much to your pleasure while staying here. A good-sized motor hotel with an excellent restaurant, bar, entertainment. Pool. In-room coffee.

Quality Inn Drake. *Inexpensive.* On US 80W, 2 mi. W of downtown. Restaurant.

Sun-N-Sand Motor Hotel. *Inexpensive.* 401 N. Lamar St. Restaurant, cocktail lounge, entertainment. Pool (heated). Pets allowed.

Stonewall Jackson Motor Lodge. *Inexpensive.* 1955 US 80W. Gracious staff. Medium-sized establishment. Restaurant, bar. Pool.

Laurel
Holiday Inn. *Moderate.* Free airport transportation. Bar, entertainment. Pets welcome.

Ramada Inn. *Moderate.* Typical chain operation. Sawmill Rd.

Town House. *Moderate.* This medium-sized motel is a favorite among the local gentry. The accommodations are better than average, so is the service. In-room coffee. Restaurant nr. Pool.

Long Beach
Ramada Inn. *Moderate.* Free in-room movies.

Gulf View. *Inexpensive.* Some kitchen units. Family-type.

McComb
Holiday Inn. *Moderate.* Free airport transportation. Restaurant, bar. Pool. Pets welcome.

Continental Motor Hotel. *Inexpensive.* Restaurant. Pets allowed.

Meridian
Ramada Inn. *Moderate.* Restaurant, bar. Pool, play area. Pets allowed.

Days Inn. *Inexpensive.* Swimming pool. Restaurant.

Downtowner Motor Inn. *Inexpensive.* Convenient location. Restaurant, pool.

Holiday Inn. *Inexpensive.* Two locations. Both have restaurant, bar, free airport transportation and pool.

Howard Johnson's Motor Lodge. *Moderate.* Restaurant, bar. Pool (heated). Play area. Free airport transportation. Pets welcome.

Natchez
Holiday Inn. *Moderate.* Restaurant, bar. Pool, play area.

Prentiss Motel. *Moderate.* Restaurant, cocktail lounge, entertainment. Pool (heated).

Ramada Hilltop. *Moderate.* Swimming pool. Restaurant. Superb view.

Scottish Motel. *Inexpensive.* All necessary comforts.

Ocean Springs
Gulf Hills Inn and Golf Club. *Expensive.* This is Mississippi's only first class resort, with tennis, golf, swimming pool, and horseback riding. Children are offered a summer recreation program.

Oxford

Holiday Inn. *Inexpensive.* Free airport transportation. Restaurant, bar.

Oxford Inn. *Moderate.* Typical Best Western.

Ramada Inn. *Moderate.* Swimming pool. Restaurant.

Pascagoula

La Font Inn. *Moderate* Large motel with excellent view of pool from spacious rooms. Family rates. Restaurant, bar. Pools. Play area. Pets welcome. Free airport transportation.

Holiday Inn. *Inexpensive.* Restaurant, cocktail lounge, entertainment. Pool and play area.

Longfellow House. *Inexpensive.* Housed in a magnificent beachfront mansion and surrounded by spacious grounds, this hotel offers first-rate accommodations. Restaurant, bar. In-room coffee. Play area. Pools. Medium-sized complex of hotel and motel units plus cottages. Best buy in area.

Shamrock Motel. *Inexpensive.* Restaurant, bar (beer only). Pools. Play area.

TraveLodge Motel. *Inexpensive.* Restaurant, cocktail lounge, entertainment. Free in-room coffee. Pool (heated).

Sardis

Gulf Trail Motor Lodge. *Inexpensive.* Restaurant, bar. Pool, play area. Pets allowed.

Holiday Inn. *Inexpensive.* Restaurant. Pool (heated). Play area. Pets welcome.

Starkville

Ramada Inn. *Moderate.* Entertainment, dancing.

Holiday Inn. *Inexpensive.* 1 mi. from Miss. State U. Restaurant, pool.

Plantation Bell Motor Lodge. *Inexpensive.* Well-run medium-sized motel caters to families. Restaurant. Play area. Pets welcome.

Tupelo

Holiday Inn. *Moderate.* Restaurant. Pool. Play area. Free airport transportation.

Tupelo TraveLodge. *Moderate.* Situated among many historical sites, this medium-sized motel offers an excellent jumping-off place for day trips. Pool. Restaurant nr.

Natchez Trace Inn. *Inexpensive.* Restaurant, bar, entertainment. Pool, play area. Pets welcome.

Ramada Inn. *Inexpensive.* Free airport transportation. Pools. Restaurant, bar, entertainment.

Rex Plaza. *Inexpensive.* This medium-sized motel offers all the facilities normally associated with larger operations. Restaurant, bar, entertainment. Pool.

Town House. *Inexpensive.* One of the better-run motels in the area, this well-equipped medium-sized establishment features a pleasing decor in both the lobby and rooms. Pool. Restaurant nr.

Vicksburg

Holiday Inn. *Moderate.* Restaurant, bar. Pool. Play area.

Best Western Magnolia Inn. *Inexpensive to Moderate.* Large dressing areas, tastefully decorated. Family units. Restaurant, bar, coffee shop. Play area.

Ramada Inn. *Inexpensive to Moderate.* Swimming pool. Restaurant.

Downtowner Motor Inn. *Inexpensive.* Convenient location. Restaurant, bar. Pool. Pets allowed. Southern Tea Room.

West Point

Marshall. *Inexpensive.* Pleasing decor. In-room coffee. Restaurant, pool.

 DINING OUT. Mississippi offers many traditional Southern specialties, as well as all the standard American favorites. Along the Gulf coast, be sure to try the shrimp prepared in the Creole manner, and hot gumbos or other seafood specialties. Among the Southern items to be found on many Mississippi menus: hush puppies, grits, country-style ham, and of course, Mississippi River catfish.

For other worthwhile restaurants, be sure to re-check hotel listings. Restaurants are listed in order of price category. Price ranges and categories for a complete meal are as follows: *Moderate:* $6.50–$10; *Inexpensive:* $2.50–$6.50. For a more complete explanation of restaurant categories see *Facts at Your Fingertips* at the front of this volume.

Biloxi

Baricev's. *Moderate.* 633 Central Beach Blvd. The small dock in the rear affords the owner some of the freshest seafood you can imagine. If you are a fish or shellfish fancier, be sure to stop here. Try the oysters and stuffed flounder. Overlooks the Gulf. Bar.

The Log House. *Inexpensive.* Dubuys Rd. Superior seafood.

Sea 'n' Sirloin. *Moderate.* West Beach Blvd. The stuffed sirloin is recommended, but you will find a wide selection of alternatives. Children's portions.

White Pillars. *Expensive.* 100 Rodenburg. New Orleans-style seafood. Jambalaya, gumbo, trout Clemanceau and crabmeat Lorenzo are served in an enclosed patio setting. Family-owned. Elegantly restored mansion.

The Factory. *Moderate.* A converted seafood factory that specializes in seafood. E. Beach Blvd.

Mary Mahoney's. Old French House. *Moderate.* Magnolia Mall. This converted house and slave quarters features a lounge with live entertainment, a 24-hour La Cafe, and outdoor patio dining. Specializes in po-boy sandwiches for lunch and seafood for dinner. Family-owned.

Clarksdale

Ponderosa. *Moderate.* Steaks.

Columbus

Tays. *Moderate.* Specialty: Barbecue and steak.

Sands. *Inexpensive.* Rte 49 Bypass.

Chism Trail. *Moderate* Closed Sun.

Corinth

Lloyds. *Inexpensive.* Steaks.

Greenville

Does. *Expensive.* Superb food in dubious decor.

C & G Depot. *Moderate.* Converted train station in impeccable taste. Buffet at luncheon.

How Joy. *Moderate.* Chinese food a specialty.

Morrison's. *Inexpensive.* Cafeteria.

Greenwood

Jubilees. *Moderate.* Charming bar-restaurant. Barbecued oysters, trout florentine, prime ribs. Currently best dining in area.

Grenada

Monte Cristo. *Inexpensive.* Try the homebaked goods which add a delightful touch to the baked lobster and sirloins.

Darras. Greek salad, occasionally other Greek dishes.

Gulfport

Angelo's. *Moderate.* European cuisine served in a semi-Old-World atmosphere, made even more pleasant by the large fireplace and view of the Gulf.

The Landing. *Moderate.* Lively hangout for a sporting crowd. Try weird but delicious French-fried vegetables.

Hattiesburg

Wagon Wheel Restaurant. *Inexpensive.* Good food and cheerful surroundings. Popular locally.

Speed's. *Moderate.* In-house baking. Steaks and seafood.

Holly Springs

Hitching Post. *Inexpensive.* Steak and seafood.

Holly Inn. *Inexpensive.* Steak and porkchops.

Jackson

Fishermans Wharf. *Moderate-Expensive.* Salty atmosphere.

Pavillon. *Expensive.* New, attractive decor. Superb French cuisine.

China Inn. *Moderate.* In Highland Village, Mandarin cuisine.

The Country Kitchen. *Moderate.* Weekends are the time to dine here, when you can dance to the music of a small combo. Trout is one of the best menu items. Children's portions.

Cerami's. *Moderate.* On the reservoir. First-rate Italian.

Cork 'N' Cleaver. *Moderate.* Steaks and king crab specialties. Good wine list.

King's Inn. *Moderate.* Try the charcoaled steak. Low lighting adds a touch of intimacy to the meal. Creole seafood is also featured. Open for all meals.

LeFleur's. *Moderate.* A profusion of flowers and Creole cooking. What could be more appropriate to this area? You will enjoy the beef and shrimp dishes.

Oliver's. *Moderate.* Steaks and seafood.

Laurel

Captain John's. *Moderate.* Steak and seafood.

Meridian

Weidmann's. *Moderate.* Special lobster and steak items, plus black bottom pie, make this a popular local dining spot. Children's portions.

Natchez

Carriage House. *Moderate.* Southern cooking.

Post House. *Moderate.* Oldest building in town. Charming addition to the historical scene, first-rate cuisine.

Side Track. *Moderate.* Converted railroad depot.

Cock of the Walk. *Inexpensive.* Catfish dinners only. Strawberry juleps.

Ocean Springs

Trilby's. *Moderate.* Look over the display of Gulf Coast art and clocks while waiting for a delicious dinner. Creole menu and seafood as their specialty. Open for lunch and dinner. Closed Mon.

Frenchie's. *Moderate.* Cajun-styled delicacies such as lemon fish and crawfish.

King William's Cellar. *Moderate.* Continental cooking in a historic house, the site of the springs which gave Ocean Springs its name.

Lagniappe. *Moderate.* Lagniappe is a Cajun word meaning "something extra." It describes this restaurant's Cajun and Lebanese cooking.

Oxford

Warehouse Restaurant. *Moderate.* Specialty: steaks. Closed Sun.

The Gumbo Factory. *Inexpensive.* As good as in Louisiana.

Pascagoula

Longfellow House. *Moderate.* Relaxing atmosphere. Enjoy their tempting prime ribs, seafood and steak. Open for all meals.

Tiki. *Moderate.* Strange decor but excellent seafood.

La Font Inn. *Inexpensive.* Try their seafood, soup and steak. Pastries made on the premises. Open for breakfast, lunch and dinner.

Pass Christian

Annie's. *Moderate.* A coastal favorite for Creole-American menu.

Quitman

Davidson. *Inexpensive.* Specialty: seafood.

Starkville

The Golden West. *Inexpensive.* Steak.

Tupelo

Gaslight Inn. *Moderate.* Dinner only. Jacket and tie, despite Western theme.

Hunter's. *Inexpensive.* Quiet, pleasant. Excellent shrimp.

Terrace. *Inexpensive-Moderate.* Despite inland location, serves good seafood.

Vicksburg

Tuminello's. *Moderate.* Locally popular, well-run restaurant offers European cuisine with dinner music and weekend entertainment. Children's portions.

Old Southern Tea Room. First-rate Southern cooking.

NORTH CAROLINA

Tobacco and Textbooks

BY
JOHN PHILLIPS

John Phillips is a native North Carolinian living in Raleigh. He is on the staff of State Magazine *and is a member of the North Carolina Travel Council.*

North Carolina divides itself into three major geographical regions: the Coastal Plains, the Piedmont Plateau and western North Carolina. A visitor traversing the state from east to west moves first through the broad and deep Coastal Plain, swings onto the Piedmont Plateau and then climbs into western North Carolina with its chain of mountains.

A tour of North Carolina's Coastal Plain—about 25,000 square miles, including ocean beaches—can appropriately begin where the first English expedition to the New World landed: Roanoke Island.

Lying between the mainland and long barrier islands called the Outer Banks, Roanoke is a gateway to both. The approach from the north is via US 158 and the Dare County beach resorts of Kitty Hawk, Kill Devil Hills and Nags Head. From the west and south, main routes to Roanoke Island are US 64 and 264, converging before crossing Croatan Sound on William B. Umstead Bridge.

If you visit Roanoke Island between late June and early September, a pleasant way to study the earliest history of English-speaking people in America is to see "The Lost Colony" drama at Waterside Theatre (nightly except Sundays) in Fort Raleigh National Historical Site, near

NORTH CAROLINA

Manteo. The drama does not attempt to solve the mystery of what became of the little band of English settlers who disappeared, but it relates the story of their first few months on Roanoke and describes the dream of freedom which inspired them to leave England.

The birthplace of aviation is across Roanoke Sound from Fort Raleigh, giving Dare County another unique historical attraction. In 1900, the Wright Brothers chose the sand dunes near Kitty Hawk for glider experiments which led to their success, in 1903, with the world's first powered aircraft flight. Wright Brothers National Memorial marks the spot at Kill Devil Hills, site of the first flight. Year round visitors can study its interpretive exhibits, walk up to the Monument atop the tall dune and trace the marked patterns of the earliest flights. There is an airport for light planes at Wright Memorial.

Cape Hatteras

The Cape Hatteras National Seashore embraces seventy miles of ocean front between Nags Head (on Bodie Island) and the village of Ocracoke on the southern tip of Ocracoke Island. Focal point of the National Seashore is Cape Hatteras itself where the tallest lighthouse in the U.S.A. —208 feet—protects shipping from the treacherous Diamond Shoals. This lighthouse is open daily, and visitors can climb to the observation balcony. Of the six North Carolina lighthouses operated by the Coast Guard, this is the only one regularly open to the public.

Almost all of Ocracoke Island is in the National Seashore. There are comfortable accommodations for visitors near Silver Lake, port for the toll ferry from the mainland. Between Ocracoke and the central coast are the virtually uninhabited Outer Banks of Portsmouth, Core and Shackleford, destined for preservation in the natural state as the Cape Lookout National Seashore.

The development of seaside resorts and the National Seashore has ended more than two centuries of isolation for the Outer Banks between Kitty Hawk and Ocracoke. Roads, bridges and regular ferry service make the area easily accessible. Most impressive is the Herbert C. Bonner Bridge spanning Oregon Inlet to Hatteras Island. At the northern end of the Bridge is Oregon Inlet Fishing Center, where charter boats fish the Gulf Stream and other offshore waters. Hatteras Village is another important sport-fishing center. Sport-fishing craft are also based at Wanchese on Roanoke Island and at Ocracoke. The name "Gamefish Junction" is used to describe the waters off Cape Hatteras, where the Gulf Stream and cold northern currents meet and where northern and southern species of fish abound. During World Wars I and II, Cape Hatteras became known as "Torpedo Junction" because German submarines took a heavy toll of shipping in the area. Diamond Shoals has been feared by seamen as an area that claimed so many vessels it was called "The Graveyard of the Atlantic." Salvage operations were important to the early economy of the Banks. Nags Head, it is said, earned its name because the original residents used to tie lanterns on the necks of their horses; then they rode up and down the dunes luring ships into the shoals, where they were considered fair prey for salvage operations.

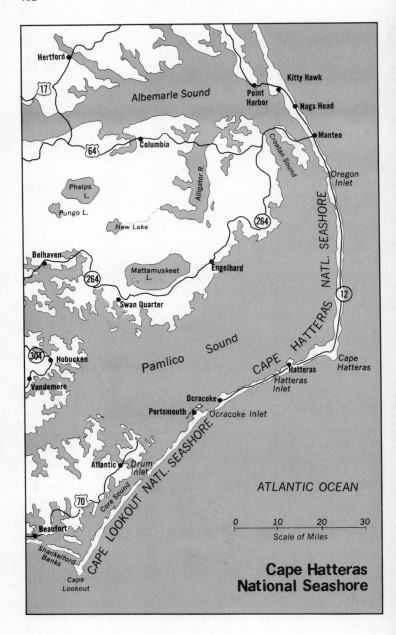

Cape Hatteras National Seashore

Animals of the National Seashore

Shore birds and migratory waterfowl annually flock by the thousands to feed along the marshlands and beaches. Within the National Seashore is Pea Island National Wildlife Refuge on Hatteras Island. Here, in company with Canada geese, swans and wild ducks, over one-half the world's population of Greater Snow geese can be seen between early November and late January. The big white birds make Pea Island the southernmost point of their winter migration from Canada and the Arctic Circle. They arrive about mid-November, and begin their return flight shortly after New Year's. The Hatteras Island Highway, State 12, passes through Pea Island. From it there are good views of the geese feeding or circling overhead in symmetrical flight patterns. There are also observation platforms and a walkway atop a dike.

While it is possible for a visitor uninterested in history to enjoy the Outer Banks in any season, few people come here without feeling the impact of the past. It is evident in the accent of the older islanders' speech, and in the skeletons of wrecked ships, the exhibits and museums. Only a few minutes away from modern resorts, it is easy to sense the loneliness of being in a vast unknown territory, which must have been part of everyday life for the first settlers and seafarers who succeeded in establishing themselves on the Banks.

In early June, the International Blue Marlin Tournament brings affluent sportsmen to the Hatteras Marlin Club. The waters off Cape Hatteras regularly produce an abundance of very large billfish. In autumn, which shares honors with spring as a prime time for channel bass fishing, there are surf-casting tournaments at Nags Head and Hatteras.

The coast of Dare County abounds in pirate lore. A placid bay near Ocracoke Village is known as "Teach's Hole" because it was the hiding place of the pirate "Blackbeard" (Edward Teach), slain there in 1718.

The Central Coast

The Outer Banks swing southwest from Cape Hatteras, which is nearly thirty miles from the mainland, to outline the central coast of the state. Beaufort Inlet divides them from Bogue Island bordering Carteret County for some twenty-five miles.

This section of North Carolina includes a large peninsula formed by the Neuse and Oak Rivers and Pamlico, Core and Bogue Sounds. From Ocracoke it is reached by toll ferry docking at Cedar Island a few miles from the eastern terminus of transcontinental US 70. Carteret County is called the "Maritime Province" because of its maze of waterfronts.

The largest Carteret community is Morehead City, one of North Carolina's two ocean ports and the base for the state's largest fleet of charter boats that take sportsmen saltwater fishing. There are also "head boats" that carry large groups (at a fixed price per person) for trolling and bottom fishing offshore. The Blue Marlin Tournament, with accompanying festivities in early June, is Morehead City's largest annual event. Morehead is the gateway to resorts on Bogue Island via a drawbridge across Bogue Sound and the channel of the Intracoastal Waterway.

Beaufort is the county seat of Carteret. It appears today much as it did long ago when it was a principal port where seafaring men built neat, white residences in the Bahamas style. Settled in 1709, Beaufort is North Carolina's third oldest town.

Between Beaufort and the fishing village of Atlantic, US 70 heads through "down east" Carteret, where farming, fishing and boat building are the main occupations. Harkers Island is accessible from US 70 by highway and bridge. Except for the spectacular Cape Lookout Lighthouse with its black and white diamond patterned painting, a marina and some fishing camps, there is no development on Core Bank or Shackleford. There are motels on Harkers. You are likely to see large cabin cruisers or commercial fishing boats under construction on the premises of the islanders' homes.

Atlantic Beach was a resort as early as the 1870's, but in those days vacationers usually stayed in Morehead City and went by boat to the shore. In 1928 the first bridge to Bogue Island was built, and since then cottage and hotel-motel development has steadily increased. South of Atlantic Beach are the resorts and residential colonies of Emerald Isle, Pine Knoll Shores, Bogue Inlet and Salter Path.

North Carolina's seaside resorts are on narrow islands that have access to both ocean and sound. This makes for a kind of "have your cake and eat it too" situation; it is easy to enjoy sheltered boating waters and ocean surf as well.

A state park surrounds old Fort Macon on the northern tip of Bogue Island. There are swimming and picnic areas among the dunes and excellent surfcasting on the Park's shoreline. The Fort is a classic example of early nineteenth-century military architecture. It was seized by Confederate forces in 1861 and captured by the Union forces the following year. Transferred to the state as a park area in 1924, the Fort was called back into active service for a few years during World War II. It is a historic shrine today and houses a small museum.

The Southeastern Coast

Between White Oak River and New River, a large area of Onslow County is in the Camp Lejeune Marine Base reservation. You can drive through the reservation on State 172, linking up with State 24 from Morehead City and Jacksonville, the largest city near the base. Historic fishing communities of this area are Swansboro on the White Oak and Snead's Ferry near New River Inlet. State 172 intersects with US 17 a little farther south, and from it you can take a side trip to Topsail Island via State 50 & 210. Topsail, which is about thirty miles long and close to the mainland of Onslow and Pender Counties, has quiet seaside resorts at Surf City and New Topsail. There are uncrowded beaches for surf bathing or fishing, ocean-fishing piers and charter boats for sound and offshore fishing. Here, as at many other points along the Carolina coast, the Intracoastal Waterway channel is in a narrow sound separating island from mainland. For some three hundred miles in eastern North Carolina, this water route for pleasure craft and freight barges threads its way though a maze of rivers and sounds.

Two large resorts of southeastern North Carolina are Wrightsville and Carolina Beaches. Wrightsville spreads across an entire island and is

reached from US 17 near Wilmington by US 74 & 76. It is one of North
Carolina's oldest resorts. There are docks for charter and pleasure craft,
plus ocean-fishing piers. Wrightsville and Masonboro Sounds, like Bogue
Sound, are highly regarded for sailing. The surf along the southeastern
beaches is usually gentle and considerably warmer than that along the
Outer Banks.

Wilmington is a historic port, year-round recreational and historic
center, and gateway to beaches and plantations. It is at the upper end
of a peninsula formed by the Cape Fear River. Giovanni de Verrazano,
navigating the mouth of the Cape Fear River, described the area as
" . . . pleasant and delectable to behold, as is possible to imagine." The
city is at the junction of US 17, 117, 74, 76, and 421. On the eastern banks
of the Cape Fear opposite downtown Wilmington, the battleship *U.S.S.
North Carolina* is enshrined in permanent moorings as a war memorial.
Visitors may board the superdreadnaught daily and Sundays year round.
From June until Labor Day a light and sound spectacular called "The
Immortal Showboat," in honor of the ship's wartime nickname, is presented nightly. Spectators watch the hour-long show from a grandstand
near the bow of the ship. The *U.S.S. North Carolina* earned twelve battle stars in the Pacific during World War II and was brought home for
honored retirement in 1963.

Wilmington greets blossom time with the North Carolina Azalea
Festival in early April. This is an extravaganza of pageants, parades,
garden tours, art exhibits and concerts. Nowhere in North Carolina do
azaleas bloom in such profusion as here and on nearby plantations. April
is the month of peak color, dramatized by backgrounds of dogwood,
pines, cypress and live oaks. Camellias bloom lavishly, too, from around
Christmas until late March. Municipal Greenfield Park has a five-mile
drive through azalea gardens bordering Lake Greenfield, and it is open
all year. Zoning and planning have preserved old homes and buildings.
The Cotton Exchange on the waterfront has been recently restored and
is delightful with its shops and restaurants. The one-time headquarters
of Cornwallis, the Burgin-Wright House, predates the Revolution. Historic Wilmington is a defined district in the city, and there are tours
available.

On the highway to Wrightsville Beach are Airlie Gardens, situated on
the grounds of an old plantation. Some fifteen miles south on State 133
to Southport is Orton Plantation. The Orton gardens feature formal and
informal plantings of camellias, azaleas and other flowers. Orton Plantation, dating from 1725, personifies the popular concept of the antebellum
South. The mansion with graceful white columns overlooks the Cape
Fear River, and the approach is a sandy road winding through enormous
trees and circling through the edge of the gardens. These gardens and
Airlie gardens are open to visitors all year.

Fort Fisher and South

US 421 skirts Greenfield Park and continues down the Cape Fear
peninsula to Carolina Beach and Fort Fisher. En route, it soars over a
wide canal that connects the lower Cape Fear and Wrightsville Sound.
Paradoxically, therefore, Carolina Beach has an insular location although it is actually North Carolina's only mainland beach. It more

nearly resembles a city than any other North Carolina seashore resort, and it has an amusement area and boardwalk in addition to cottages, motels, small hotels, shops, office buildings and restaurant. It is also an important deep-sea sport fishing center, possessing numerous facilities for all types of fishing and pleasure craft.

South of Carolina Beach are the smaller resorts of Wilmington Beach, Kure Beach and Fort Fisher State Historic Site. At Fort Fisher, a museum displays ammunition, weapons and other artifacts brought up from the submerged wrecks of Confederate blockade runners close to shore. Several embankments and gun emplacements of the Fort have been marked. The largest land-sea battle in history, up to that time, took place at Fort Fisher in January, 1865. Below Fort Fisher, US 421 dead-ends at the Rocks, a breakwater built in 1875-81 to close the New Inlet and save Wilmington's harbor by insuring a sufficient depth over the main bar at the mouth of Cape Fear. There is automobile ferry service between Fort Fisher and Southport.

The Blockade Runner Museum, on US 421 at Carolina Beach, offers exciting surprises for those who think they don't like museums. It should be a "Do Not Miss" stop on a tour of the area. It was presented a national award in 1967 as an outstanding contribution to national, state and local history. The museum presents the story of how over 2,000 ships attempted the Carolina ports through the Northern blockade, how the massive fort sought to protect them as they approached the coast and what the city was like that received the vital supplies which meant so much to the Confederacy. The presentation is done with dioramas, each with its own tape explaining the action, displaying expertly crafted models of ships that were twenty years ahead of their time. The highlight of a visit to the museum is the forty-foot diorama of Fort Fisher. The history of the fort and the blockade is presented in a fifteen-minute narration accompanied by martial music, projected pictures, the sounds of battle and smoke from the guns of the fleet. It is open all year.

Brunswick County is North Carolina's southernmost county and one of its largest. It extends from the Cape Fear banks near Wilmington to the South Carolina line. Its county seat is Southport near the mouth of the Cape Fear River. This gracious town, with its casual pattern of comfortable dwellings and tree-lined streets edged by a picturesque waterfront, is the home of the famed Southport Pilots Association. The Pilots go out in small cruisers to meet ocean vessels bound for Wilmington, and they guide them up the Cape Fear.

On the east side of lower Cape Fear River in Brunswick County, the town of Brunswick was founded in 1725. It was a flourishing river port until the American Revolution, when it was partly burned by the British. After the Revolution, the town never recovered, and it became extinct about 1830. Walls of St. Philip's Church and numerous house foundations remain. Also remaining are the massive works of Fort Anderson, a Civil War fortification erected by the Confederates; they have been improved for exhibit. There are historical markers in the area and trailside exhibits, plus a visitor-center museum off N.C. Hwy 133, south of Wilmington.

Always closely identified with shipping and commercial fishing, Southport is a key point on the Intracoastal Waterway. It has a small boat harbor completed by the State Ports Authority in 1965. From Southport one may visit the nearby resorts of Caswell, Yaupon and Long Beaches.

Fort Caswell, constructed in 1825 and manned during the Civil, Spanish-American and both World Wars, is a religious assembly grounds operated by the Baptists of North Carolina. Many of its frame buildings are in use. Between Fort Caswell and Yaupon Beach is the Oak Island Golf Club. Yaupon Beach is a peaceful resort with good accommodations. Long Beach is somewhat larger. There are growing residential colonies, highly popular with retirees at Yaupon and nearby Tranquil Harbor. South of Oak Island are the smaller seaside resorts of Holden's Beach, Ocean Isle and Sunset Beach, each on its own sandy island and linked to US 17 by highways and bridges. All have fishing piers, motels and cottages. Near the bridge to Sunset Beach is Calabash, a tiny community so famed for excellent seafood that it has twenty thriving restaurants.

The inland communities of Brunswick County are small, primarily trading centers for the surrounding farms. Shallotte has inlet and river fishing. A residential and recreation complex about seven miles inland from Southport is Boiling Spring Lakes, situated in gently rolling countryside much like the famous Sandhills of North Carolina's southern Piedmont.

Large military reservations include Camp Lejeune (as noted in the Southeastern Coast Section), the U.S. Marine Corps Air Station at Cherry Point between New Bern and Morehead City, Seymour Johnson Air Force Base at Goldsboro and Fort Bragg and Pope Air Force Base near Fayetteville. Fort Bragg is the "Home of the Airborne" as well as the famous Special Forces "Green Berets."

Fayetteville is the county seat of Cumberland, and it is on the Cape Fear River, which is navigable from here to the Atlantic Ocean. Fayetteville dates from 1739 when Highland Scots settled it as Campbelltown. The city was named for General Lafayette. The old Market House in downtown Fayetteville was built in 1838 as a produce center on the site of Convention Hall, which had been destroyed by fire in 1831. George Herman Ruth ("The Babe") hit his first home run in professional baseball while training with the Baltimore Orioles here in 1914.

The largest town in the northeastern part of the state is Elizabeth City on US 17 and the Pasquotank River, the southeastern edge of the Great Dismal Swamp. The International Cup Regatta and the Craftsman's Fair are principal fall events. The Pasquotank and Great Dismal Swamp Canal form an alternate route of the Intracoastal Waterway, and Elizabeth City is popular with yachtsmen as well as motorists.

There are fine old courthouses of Georgian architecture at Hertford and Edenton (built in 1767). The Chowan County Courthouse, Cupola House, James Iredell House, St. Paul's Church and Penelope Barker House are open year-around. It was in Edenton on October 25, 1774, that a Tea Party protesting British taxes was organized by Mrs. Penelope Barker. The Tea Party Marker at Edenton Green is on the site. St. Paul's Episcopal Church is the state's second oldest church (1730's).

Washington is called "Little Washington" to distinguish it from the nation's capital. The earliest recorded mention of the name "Washington" for the town is dated October 1, 1776, making it the first town in the country to take this name. Washington contains many historic buildings. Located on the waters of the Pamlico at the junction of US 17 and 264, the town was the home of the De Mille family and the place where Edna Ferber was inspired to write *Showboat*. William C. De Mille was a celebrated nineteenth-century playwright. His son Cecil B. De Mille, the motion picture producer, was born in Washington. Edna Ferber visited the James Adams Floating Theatre at Washington to gather material for her book. Although the locale of *Showboat* was the Mississippi River, she used Beaufort County names and copied verbatim an inscription in St. Thomas Church at Bath.

Washington's tobacco warehouses are among the many eastern North Carolina sales centers where visitors are welcomed at auctions from August until November. Others are in Rocky Mount, Wilson, Tarboro, Greenville, Williamston, Kinston, Goldsboro, Fayetteville, Lumberton, Whiteville and Smithfield. Check locally for information on sales hours. Wilson is the largest tobacco sales center in the state, leading the world in the production of flue-cured tobacco.

New Bern, a Colonial Capital

At New Bern, the first permanent colonial capital, the first state capitol building has been restored to its original elegance, and it is open (except Mondays) to visitors all year. Now known as the Tryon Palace Restoration, its gardens are on the site where Governor William Tryon supervised construction of a "seat of government and residence of the royal governor." Also at New Bern are the Fireman's Museum with horse-drawn fire equipment, the John Wright Stanly House of the 1770's and numerous other structures of classic Georgian architecture executed in brick and wood.

Among the most traveled routes through the Coastal Plain are US 17, 301, 421, 64, I-85 & I-95. Motorists in North Carolina can get off the beaten path to explore areas of unusual geographical or historical interest by using well-marked state roads connecting with the arterial highways. There is amazing variety to enjoy on the shunpikes of the Coastal Plains. In Tyrrell and Hyde Counties, State 94 runs north and south between US 264 and 64. It crosses Lake Mattamuskeet National Wildlife Refuge on a long causeway. Bird watchers enjoy seeing Canada geese and other waterfowl at their winter feeding grounds here, and there is excellent waterfowl hunting nearby. Accommodations and hunting guides are at Belhaven, Fairfield, New Holland and Swan Quarter. Another shunpike combines a free auto ferry from Currituck to Knotts Island with State 615 to Virginia Beach, Virginia. Accessible by State 55 and 111, southeast of Goldsboro, are Cliffs of the Neuse State Park and picturesque Seven Springs, which was once a famed watering place. There are motor roads into Croatan National Forest from US 70 southeast of New Bern; one of them terminates at a camping and picnic area on the Neuse River.

Turn off US 74-76 between Whiteville and Wilmington to visit Lake Waccamaw, where dark waters edged by cypress swamp offer boating, swimming and fishing. White Lake, so named because its crystal clear waters are on white sand, is just off US 701 in Bladen Lakes State Forest. Accommodations are plentiful. Pettigrew State Park, on Lake Phelps, is on a secondary road connecting with US 64 at Creswell. The Park is on portions of two early plantations, Bonarva and Somerset Place. The manor at Somerset Place is of Greek Revival Style, well-preserved. State-owned Lake Phelps has excellent fishing and is North Carolina's second largest natural lake.

Powerboat and sailing regattas are held in several communities on lakes or rivers; horse shows are annual events at Wilson, Enfield, Wilmington and Fayetteville. Benson, a trading center for rural Johnston County, celebrates harvest time each September with the annual Mule Day festival. The fourth Sunday in June signals the State Singing Convention, which brings hundreds of religious and folk singers and musicians to Benson's Singing Grove. The North Carolina Strawberry Festival is in May at Chadbourn. East Carolina University at Greenville has a summer theater on the campus, and Washington has a Summer Festival in early June.

Piedmont North Carolina

The Piedmont Plateau of central North Carolina begins at the fall line a few miles east of Raleigh and US 1 and rolls westward to the base of the Blue Ridge Divide. Within the 21,000-square-mile Piedmont are such distinctive geographical features as the Sandhills in the southeast, the Uwharrie and Sauratown mountains of the central area and large rivers. Principal lakes of the region—impounded along the Yadkin, Roanoke, Catawba and Pee Dee Rivers—offer excellent boating and fishing. The Piedmont has famous winter golf and riding centers, state parks and numerous all-year historical attractions. There are free tours of cigarette factories in several cities, and a wide choice of all-year accommodations.

Raleigh, the capital, is a good introduction to the entire state, and a convenient beginning for a tour of the Piedmont. It is on US 1 and two main east-west highways, US 70 and 64. One of the state's busiest airports serves Raleigh, Durham and Chapel Hill. Raleigh is the southeastern apex of the Research Triangle Park formed by North Carolina State University in the capital, the University of North Carolina at Chapel Hill and Duke University in Durham. The Sandhills resorts of Pinehurst and Southern Pines are seventy miles south of Raleigh.

In Raleigh, visitors can tour the historic Capitol (1840) and unusual Legislative Building, the North Carolina Museum of History in the Archives Building, the Museum of Natural History and the North Carolina Art Museum, which houses a multimillion-dollar collection of masterworks. This art museum is the first ever established with state funds in the U.S.A. All of these buildings are open free to the public and are within walking distance of one another.

The granite Capitol of Greek Revival architecture is on a six-acre square. Among the monuments on the square is an equestrian statue honoring the three Presidents born in North Carolina: Andrew Johnson, James K. Polk and Andrew Jackson. The Legislative Building, first structure ever built by any state for the exclusive use of its Senate and House of Representatives, was designed by Edward Durrell Stone and executed in marble and granite. The Capitol and Legislative buildings are open weekdays and also Saturday and Sunday afternoons. In the Capitol are the old Legislative Chambers, the permanent office of the Secretary of State and the office of the Governor. The North Carolina General Assembly convenes in the Legislative Building during January of each odd year. Visitors may observe the sessions from a gallery on the third floor.

About one mile from Capitol Square is the Andrew Johnson House, a tiny gambrel-roofed building where the 17th President was born. This historic shrine is located in Mordecai Park on Person St. and is open to the public. On N. Blount St., two blocks from the Capitol is the official residence of North Carolina's governors. This "gingerbread" mansion (1880's) has been restored recently and is adjacent to Historic Oakwood, a section where many homes of the same era have been restored. Raleigh has a marked "Capital City Trail" keyed to a leaflet describing points of interest.

Two miles W. of the Capitol is N. C. State University which is the agricultural and technical branch of the Consolidated University of N. C. with campuses at Chapel Hill, Greensboro, Charlotte, Asheville and Wilmington. The influence of N. C. State's noted School of Design is reflected in the newer buildings on campus and in the striking J. S. Dorton Arena on the State Fairgrounds a few miles south on Hillsborough St. This parabolic pavilion is used for livestock judging, rodeos and exhibits during Fair Week in October and for entertainment programs during the rest of the year.

America's Winter Golf Capital

In North Carolina's southern Piedmont the white sand and longleaf pine signify an area known as the Sandhills. Pinehurst and Southern Pines make the Sandhills the winter golf capital of America.

There are 26 courses within a 15-mile radius of the Pinehurst-Southern Pines area, including Mid-Pines, Pine Needles, Knollwood, Whispering Pines, Seven Lakes and the Southern Pines Country Club.

"Top season" in the Sandhills resorts is from October through April, but year-round vacationing in the area is now on the upswing.

Horsemen as well as golfers discovered the Sandhills in the early 1900's. The oldest organized hunt in North Carolina, the Moore County Hounds, was established at Southern Pines in 1914. Today, the Moore County Hounds turn out in traditional splendor for fox and drag hunts between November and late March. Thoroughbreds and standardbreds are trained on Sandhills tracks, and riding is a major sport in the area. In April the Stoneybrook Steeplechase at Southern Pines is a big event.

April golf tournaments in the Sandhills are among the oldest in the nation—the North and South Invitation Amateur Championship for Men and the North and South Invitation Championship for Women. Some golf courses at each of the two resorts remain open through summer; all are open from October through April.

The Sandhills resorts are popular for year-round living as well as zestful vacationing. The subtropical gardens and renowned saltwater fishing of North Carolina's southeastern coast are within a few hours drive of Pinehurst and Southern Pines. So are the mountain summer and ski resorts. In the immediate area are Gaddy's Wild Goose Refuge at Ansonville, Clarendon Gardens, crafts centers and the 57,000-acre Sandhills Wildlife Management Area with excellent field trial courses, deer hunting and fishing lakes. Dove, deer and quail hunting are within a short distance of the resort colonies. Pinehurst and the Sandhills Wildlife Management Area are settings for major field trials.

In May, Sedgefield, a suburb of Greensboro, hosts one of the South's oldest horse shows. The Sedgefield Hunt season is from Oct. until spring; visitors can arrange to ride here, as well as with other organized hunts in North Carolina.

Tryon, in the unique "Thermal Belt," is noted for its mild climate year round and enjoys year-round patronage—Northerners come here in autumn, winter and spring because of the equable climate at these seasons; Southern visitors find Tryon cooler than the lowlands in summer. Like Southern Pines and Pinehurst, Tryon has a growing colony of retirees. Horseback riding is a major sport, with the Tryon Hounds offering fox hunting between October and spring, and the Block House Steeplechase and Tryon Horse and Hound Show prominent in March and April.

Charlotte is a bustling center of trade, manufacturing, transportation and communication. Its handsome Coliseum, Ovens Auditorium and Merchandise Mart form a complex where sports, cultural events, trade fairs and expositions are held. Named for Queen Charlotte of Mecklenburg, wife of George III, the "Queen City" is North Carolina's largest convention host and is readily accessible. The Mint Museum of Art has an excellent collection of paintings and other art works. Major events at Charlotte include the Festival in the Park, featuring arts and crafts, the Carolinas Carrousel with a parade on Thanksgiving Day, flower shows and tours of homes. Charlotte's residential areas are noted for fine homes and gardens. The newest entertainment addition to this area is Carowinds Theme Park, situated on the South Carolina border, a few miles south of Charlotte. Carowinds is the largest theme park in North Carolina.

On the Catawba River a few miles north of Charlotte is Cowan's Ford Dam, which forms Lake Norman. This lake covers more than 30,000 acres, and is the largest lake in the state. Duke Power State Park and many marinas and boat launching areas give access to the lake.

Morrow Mountain State Park near Albemarle, about forty-two miles northeast of Charlotte, has swimming, boating, fishing, hiking, camping and nature study. Here you can drive a scenic road to the top of Morrow Mountain, a distinctive feature of the Uwharrie Range. The Uwharries stretch across portions of four counties and include Uwharrie National Forest. Morrow Mountain State Park is on Lake Tillery, southernmost in the series of lakes along the Yadkin and Pee Dee Rivers.

Only a short drive from Morrow Mountain is Town Creek Indian Mound State Historic Site, on an area that was the ceremonial center and burial ground for a prehistoric tribe of Indians who lived on the lower Pee Dee. A stockade, a temple mound and other features have been restored here.

In the north central Piedmont, High Point, Thomasville and Lexington are focal points of North Carolina's large furniture industry. The Southeastern Furniture Exposition Building at High Point is the center of annual furniture markets, attended by buyers from all over America and foreign countries as well.

Greensboro, founded in 1808 as county seat of Guilford County, is named for General Nathanael Green who commanded Colonial troops in the Battle of Guilford Courthouse, which was fought just beyond the present city limits. William Sidney Porter, writer of short stories under the pen name "O. Henry," was born in Greensboro. The drugstore where he worked as a youth has been reconstructed in the Greensboro Historical Museum. Textiles have always played an important part in the life of Greensboro, and the first steam-powered cotton mill in North Carolina was built here in 1828. The city has tremendous textile operations today.

Guilford Courthouse National Military Park, on US 220 northwest of Greensboro, covers 150 acres with monuments, markers and a museum. Here in March, 1781, Cornwallis won a victory over General Greene's American forces, but he was so weakened that the British surrender at Yorktown followed. The park is open year round. In spring, Greensboro, the park and surrounding countryside bloom with dogwood and redbud. During the entire year, the Greensboro War Memorial Auditorium-Coliseum is a center for athletic events, entertainment and cultural programs. Greensboro's Forest Oaks Country Club on US 421 S is the home of the famed Greater Greensboro Open Golf Tournament in April. This is one of the oldest stops on the PGA tour.

Winston-Salem, North Carolina's fourth ranking population center, is some thirty miles northwest of Greensboro and High Point. Winston-Salem is a major travel objective in its own right and a gateway to North Carolina's Blue Ridge Mountain vacationlands. It was two towns until 1913, when Winston (founded in 1849) was united with Salem (founded in 1766 by the Moravians).

Old Salem

Old Salem, in the heart of the city, is a treasury of time-mellowed buildings, reflecting—in architecture and arrangement—the middle-European heritage of its founders. The Old World charm which Salem has retained for two centuries has been enhanced with the restoration of more than thirty structures, some open as exhibition buildings and some in use as dwellings, shops or offices. Other buildings in Salem—among them Home Moravian Church (1800) and several units on the campus of Salem College—have been in continuous use since the late 1700's and early 1800's. The Brothers House, built on Salem Square in 1769 and owned and used by the Moravian Church until its restoration, is the setting for Moravian Candle Teas in early December. Visitors to the teas watch preparation of beeswax candles for the Christmas Eve Lovefeast services at the Home Church, and they are served traditional sugar cake and coffee.

Tours of Old Salem are held throughout the year. Exhibit buildings in addition to those previously mentioned are: Salem Tavern (1784); the Tavern Barn and Farm Museum; the Hiksch Tobacco Shop (1773), the oldest tobacco shop still standing in America; the John Vogler House built in 1819, the home of the village silversmith and clockmaker. Wachovia Museum, housed in the Boys' School (1794), has one of the largest collection of local antiquities in America. Old Salem is about six city blocks long by three blocks wide. As headquarters for the Moravian

Church South, Salem is the setting for religious observances that have continued since the community's earliest days. In December, the many-pointed Moravian Christmas stars light Salem doorways. The Moravian Easter Sunrise Service, which opens on Salem Square in front of the Home Church and concludes in nearby "God's Acre," the Moravian Graveyard, has been held for nearly two hundred years. During the Moravian Easter Litany, the Church Band plays antiphonally. Just before Easter, the flat white gravestones of God's Acre are scrubbed clean, and fresh flowers decorate each grave. Visitors to Salem at Easter should plan to stroll through God's Acre on Good Friday or Saturday to watch the preparations, for Easter in God's Acre is like a vast outdoor flower garden.

Eight miles west of Winston-Salem, at Clemmons, is Tanglewood Park, a former country estate willed to the people of Forsyth County by Mr. and Mrs. William Reynolds. Tanglewood has golf, camping, swimming and tennis. Center of the Park is the gracious manor house where visitors may dine.

At the western edge of Winston-Salem is Wake Forest University, opened in 1834 at Wake Forest, North Carolina, near Raleigh, and relocated on its present three-hundred-acre campus in the early 1950's.

Winston-Salem is the largest auction center for marketing flue-cured tobacco in the Old Belt. Auctions begin in September and continue until after Thanksgiving.

Two of North Carolina's state parks are located within 30 miles of Winston-Salem: Hanging Rock State Park and Pilot Mountain State Park. Near Wilkesboro, west of Winston-Salem on US 421, is the W. Kerr Scott Reservoir in the Blue Ridge foothills. The U.S. Corps of Engineers maintains campgrounds and boat launching facilities here. There are also powerboat races in summer.

Kerr Scott Reservoir is not to be confused with Kerr Lake, which is some 170 miles east near Henderson, and has an eight-hundred-mile shoreline extending into Virginia. Kerr Lake is impounded by the John H. Kerr Dam on the Roanoke River in Virginia. On the North Carolina shores of the lake are areas for picnicking, camping and boating. North Carolina's Kerr Reservoir Development Commission administers these recreational facilities. The Carolina Sailing Club sponsors regattas on Kerr Lake, the largest being the Governor's Cup in June. There is excellent fishing for bass, panfish and landlocked striped bass or "rockfish." The lake is used extensively by residents of the Triangle or Capital area.

Durham and Chapel Hill

Durham, only twenty-three miles from the capital, is a ranking industrial center, leading tobacco market of the Middle Belt and home of Duke University, one of the largest institutions of higher learning in the Southeast. The history of Durham is a fascinating chapter of the "American success story." Durham was only a small village when, in 1865, General W. T. Sherman received the surrender of General Joseph E. Johnston a few miles west at Bennett Place, a historic site open all year. Among the Durham County residents mustered out of the Confederate Army when the Civil War ended was Washington Duke, who walked

Points of Interest

1) Bennett Place
2) Duke Homestead
3) Duke University Campus
4) Museum of Life and Science
5) North Carolina Central University
6) Planetarium, University of N.C.
7) Research Triangle

Durham, Chapel Hill

137 miles home to his farm to begin civilian life again. The Dukes, like most of their neighbors, grew tobacco. Washington Duke began grinding tobacco which he packaged and sold. By 1874, Duke and his three sons were established in Durham as manufacturers of smoking tobacco. Within a few years, they were producing cigarettes for domestic sale and export; the growth of the huge American Tobacco empire and other manufacturing enterprises began in their city. It has been said that James B. Duke did with tobacco what Rockefeller did with oil and Carnegie with steel. He endowed the University (formerly Trinity College), which bears his family name and is principal beneficiary of the Duke Endowment.

Duke University has a Gothic West Campus and Georgian East Campus on 7,500 acres of rolling land a few miles west of Durham. Duke Chapel, a Gothic structure, has a spire rising 210 feet above the West Campus and houses an 18th century Flentrop organ, the second largest Flentrop in the world, the largest one being in Rotterdam, Holland. Nearby are the Sarah P. Duke Memorial Gardens with extensive formal and informal landscaping. The gardens offer a succession of blooms from early spring through late autumn.

The Duke family homestead, three miles north of Durham via US 501, is a small, white frame dwelling built in 1851 by Washington Duke. Restored and containing its original furnishings, it is open on Sunday afternoons, April through September.

Thomas Wolfe, who began his literary career as a student at the University of North Carolina, once described Chapel Hill as a place that "beats every other town all hollow." Situated on a hilltop at the eastern edge of the Piedmont Plateau, the town was named for New Hope Chapel of the Church of England. The site of New Hope Chapel is now occupied by the gracious Carolina Inn. The University of North Carolina was the first state university to open its doors to students. Chapel Hill has a growing colony of year-round residents who have chosen this community for its "stimulating serenity." Among them are playwrights, novelists, distinguished educators, scientists and artists.

Morehead Planetarium, first planetarium ever built on a college campus, was the gift of University benefactor John Motley Morehead. There are daily shows held here for the public. The Planetarium Rose Garden is built around a mammoth sun dial showing international time around the world. The U.S. astronauts come to the Planetarium for study in preparation for their space flights. The Old Well, symbol of the University, is a famous landmark on the campus. In the Monogram Club is Carl Boettcher's huge woodcarving of an "around the world" circus parade. The William Hayes Ackland Memorial Art Museum on the campus has a fine permanent collection and features special exhibits, while Coker Arboretum is a five-acre botanical garden nearby.

About fifteen miles north of Chapel Hill is historic Hillsborough, established in 1754 and once capital of the Colony of North Carolina, containing many public buildings and residences with historical associations. In Hillsborough is the site of the hanging of six of the Regulators whose uprising against the British culminated in defeat at the Battle of Alamance on May 16, 1771. Alamance Battleground, five miles south of Burlington, is a historic site open all year. Many historians regard the

Battle of Alamance as the first major conflict of the American Revolution. It stimulated the westward movement of freedom-loving colonists, seeking new homes on the Southern Appalachian frontier. Their story is told in the outdoor drama *Horn in the West* at Boone in the Blue Ridge Mountains. Daniel Boone's trail to Kentucky began in Hillsborough where prominent citizens were partners in the company sponsoring his expeditions.

The old Orange County Courthouse with its Museum, the Masonic Hall, several churches and numerous other buildings of historical interest are open all year in Hillsborough. This is a place to visit at leisure for an insight into America's past. Only a short drive from contemporary hotels and motor lodges in the Triangle area, Hillsborough's accommodations are appropriate to the town's atmosphere of history—the Colonial Inn was built in 1781, and meals are available.

From the Piedmont Triangle area of High Point, Greensboro and Winston-Salem, I-85 and I-40 are the arterial routes toward the Southern Appalachians.

Western North Carolina, "Land of the Sky"

In 1794, French botanist Andre Michaux climbed Grandfather Mountain and sang the "Marseillaise," triumphantly believing he had discovered the highest point in North America. He hadn't, but there's such a "top of the world" feeling in surveying one's surroundings from promontories in western North Carolina that Michaux's enthusiasm is understandable. These Southern Appalachian Mountains—the Blue Ridge, Great Smokies, Blacks, Nantahalas and others—range in height from 5,000 feet to more than 6,000 feet. Their soft, rich tapestry of foliage is laced with tumbling streams and accented with massive rock outcroppings. Colors and visibility change constantly with atmospheric conditions and the seasons.

Mount Mitchell (6,684 feet) is the highest mountain east of the Mississippi River and one of the forty-nine peaks in North Carolina reaching 6,000 feet or more. Grandfather Mountain (5,964 feet) is the tallest peak in the Blue Ridge.

The Cherokee Indians were the first to explore and live in North Carolina. The haze that hangs over the high country was called "Sahkanaga" by the Cherokees, meaning the "Great Blue Hills of God." We know the area as the Great Smoky Mountains. Some 5,000 Cherokees live here today on their reservation adjoining the Great Smoky Mountains National Park and the Blue Ridge Parkway. Elsewhere in western North Carolina live descendents of the pioneers who began building homes in the mountains shortly before the Revolutionary War, and of settlers who came later from Virginia, Pennsylvania and other states.

Contrast is dramatic in most sections of the highlands. Hewn-log dwellings are reminders of the past. The present is here in twentieth-century architecture and culture. The future's pattern is indicated by the construction of superhighways, suburban residential areas, shopping centers and malls. You can visit a satellite tracking facility at the edge of forests looking much as they did centuries ago. There are cluttered country stores, sleek specialty shops, department stores and craft centers ranging from quaint to contemporary. The southern prong of the "Wilderness Road" crosses the Blue Ridge Parkway near the town of Boone. Each summer the outdoor drama *Horn in the West* tells the story of Daniel Boone and his fellow frontiersmen. At Asheville's Mountain Dance and Folk Festival in August and Mountain Youth Jamboree in March, you'll see natives of the area presenting traditional music and dances of the Southern Appalachians. At Fontana Village and other resorts you'll learn the intricate paces of Western-style square dances as well as those of local origin. It's a rare festival, fair or celebration in the mountains that doesn't feature at least one of the teams of clog dancers for which the region is noted. Traditional hymns are heard at the "Singing on the Mountain" at Grandfather Mountain on the fourth Sunday in June.

A Forest Kingdom

Western North Carolina's region is a huge "sample case" of vegetation, minerals and fauna as well as a fascinating complex of scenery. Botanists have classified over 145 varieties of trees and more than one thousand other plants in these mountains, and evergreen forests on higher peaks and slopes more closely resemble those of Canada than the Carolinas. In October the region is a riot of color when the hardwoods turn to crimson and gold accented by evergreens and the distant tones of blue which give the Blue Ridge and Great Smokies their names. There are two rules of thumb to remember in planning to see the autumn foliage parade. One is that color begins in the high elevations and moves down the slopes—the earlier your trip, the higher the places you should plan to visit. The other is that most generally distributed coloration usually occurs between October 10 and 25. In most areas below three thousand feet, it continues until November.

Spring comes later and lingers into June at elevations above five thousand feet. Its patterns of flowers and foliage, like those of autumn, vary according to altitudes, but they move upward. In April, small ground flowers decorate forest floors, while hardwoods assume tones of soft pink and pale green as their leaves unfurl. The snowy white of dogwood and silverbell appears in April and May. The "big three" of the mountain flower parade—laurel, flame azalea and purple rhododendron—begin blooming in late May and make their biggest displays in June. Tall white rhododendron blooms in late June; numerous wildflowers bloom all summer.

To natural advantages, the region has added varied accommodations, golf courses, swimming pools, riding stables, hiking trails, theme parks, festivals and sports events. There are summer theaters and two outdoor historical dramas, arts and crafts colonies, summer camps for boys and girls, religious assembly grounds and historical attractions. In a region of few natural lakes, huge power projects provide boating, fishing and water-skiing.

Snow-skiing is the growing winter sport. North Carolina is the southern-most state where skiing is possible extensively, and there are several ski resorts currently developed—Appalachian Ski Mountain at Blowing Rock; Beech Mountain and Sugar Mountain at Banner Elk; Seven Devils and Mill Ridge near Boone; Cataloochee near Waynesville; High Meadows at Roaring Gap; Sapphire Valley at Sapphire and Wolf Laurel at

Mars Hill. North Carolina enjoys a mild year-around climate, but frequently natural snow is available. However, when Mother Nature won't cooperate, all the Tar Heel slopes are equipped with artificial snow-making equipment so that skiing may continue as long as the temperature permits. Skiing is enjoyed from December until early March.

Western North Carolina's resorts and towns are small to medium-sized, and its largest city, Asheville, is traditionally a resort as well as a county seat, trading center and gateway to the entire state. A chateau constructed by George W. Vanderbilt and a modest residence that was once a boarding house for "summer people" are two noted Asheville attractions. The chateau is Biltmore House, completed in 1895 in French Renaissance style. Biltmore House is furnished with antiques and art works from all over the world. Its Norman banquet hall is 72 X 40 feet, with a vaulted ceiling 75 feet high. The house is on a 12,000-acre estate and includes the Biltmore Dairy Farm. Residence, gardens and dairy are open to visitors year around. The original Vanderbilt holdings consisted of some 125,000 acres, including Mount Pisgah. Much of this acreage was deeded to North Carolina by Mr. Vanderbilt's widow, and it became the nucleus of the Pisgah National Forest.

Asheville's Famous Sons

The boarding house at 48 Spruce Street is the Thomas Wolfe Memorial, "Dixieland" in Wolfe's first novel, *Look Homeward, Angel.* Preserved as a literary shrine, it contains furnishings and personal possessions in use when Wolfe's mother opened the family home to paying guests. Pack Memorial Library nearby has the many different editions of Wolfe's books in various languages, together with correspondence, clippings and most books and articles written about Asheville's famous native son.

Thomas Wolfe and O. Henry are buried in Riverside Cemetery at Asheville. The marble angel which inspired the title of Wolfe's first novel is in Oakdale Cemetery at Hendersonville, twenty-five miles south of Asheville.

Asheville is headquarters for the Southern Highland Handicraft Guild and scene of the annual Crafts Fair in August. The Guild has a crafts center at 930 Tunnel Road (US 70) and also a downtown shop. The Guild operates a crafts center from May through October in the old manor house in Moses Memorial Park on the Blue Ridge Parkway. Artisans from many Southern states are Guild members, as are North Carolina's two noted crafts schools—Penland near Spruce Pine and the John C. Campbell Folk School at Brasstown. Guild centers, the two schools, the Fair and numerous crafts shops throughout western North Carolina are excellent introductions to the crafts of the region, and they have information about visiting individual craftsmen in their workshops or homes.

The Blue Ridge Parkway

A high-altitude route for pleasure travel between Shenandoah National Park in Virginia and the Great Smoky Mountains National Park entrance near Cherokee is the Blue Ridge Parkway. This is a scenic drive and offers varied recreational opportunities. It also illustrates the history, geology and culture of the mountains through such features as the Museum of North Carolina Minerals, pioneer dwellings, crafts centers, nature trails and exhibits. There are campgrounds, picnic areas and scenic overlooks. It should be emphasized that the Parkway is for optional travel, principally in spring, summer and autumn. Highest sections (in the Mount Mitchell area) and the entire seventy-five miles of Parkway west of Asheville may be closed from early November until mid-April due to bad weather. Snow and ice may also cause winter closure of some of the sections which are normally open all year. Other mountain highways are open all year, with the exception of the spur highway to Clingman's Dome in the Great Smoky Mountains National Park and a few U.S. Forest Service or privately built roads, which are not intended for through traffic.

The Cherokee Indian Reservation

Half of the Great Smoky Mountains National Park is within the state. US 441 is the transmountain highway through the Park; it enters North Carolina a few miles south of Franklin, links up with many other highways, and on the Cherokee Indian Reservation it meets US 19 and the Blue Ridge Parkway.

Cherokee is the largest town on the Reservation. Here the Indians relate their history through the outdoor drama *Unto These Hills* (late June through August). Oconaluftee Indian Village shows how the Cherokee lived two centuries ago. This is an outstanding attraction and is open from May through October. Baskets, pottery and other crafts produced in the village are sold at the Qualla Arts Cooperative and other shops of the area.

Cherokee's "Main Street" is lined with shops. Many of the mass-produced items come from manufacturing concerns operating on the Reservation and employing Cherokees. Among the numerous motels at Cherokee is the Boundary Tree, a tribal enterprise. Craftsmen and guides at Oconaluftee Village and actors in *Unto These Hills* wear traditional Cherokee costume, but the "chiefs" who greet visitors at most shops dress in Sioux-style feathers and buckskin. "Chiefing" has been a time-honored occupation for the tribesmen ever since visitors began coming to the Reservation; but the Eastern Band of the Cherokees has only one practical chief, who is elected by the tribe. Most Cherokees dress just like any other mountain people.

In the Park, one of the oldest uplands on earth, the Great Smokies Divide zigzags through from northeast to southwest for seventy-one miles along the North Carolina-Tennessee line for a few miles west of Cherokee. For thirty-six miles along its crest, the range maintains an altitude in excess of 5,000 feet. Sixteen peaks rise to more than 6,000 feet. Tallest is Clingman's Dome (6,643 feet). There's a paved road from US 441 to a parking overlook near the summit. From the overlook a hiking trail leads to the observation tower at the highest point.

At the Park entrance near Cherokee is Smokemont Ranger Station, with pioneer exhibits and farmstead showing how yesterday's settlers lived. In the Park are some seventy-five miles of paved roads, plus an equal amount of secondary roads, and over seven hundred miles of marked trails for hiking or horseback riding. There are short self-guiding trails at points of unusual interest like the evergreen "rain forest" on Clingman's Dome. Park campgrounds in North Carolina are at Deep Creek near Bryson City, Smokemont on US 441 and Balsam Mountain near Heintooga Overlook. Trout streams are open from May through August, but except for the fish that may be taken under special regulations, the Park is a sanctuary for every living thing.

For direct all-year travel between the Great Smokies and Asheville, US 19 and 19-23 can be used in combination with I-40. Waynesville, county seat of Haywood, is the largest city within twenty-five miles of the North Carolina boundary of the Great Smokies Park. The town is highly popular with travelers and seasonal residents because of its variety of accommodations, its golf course and its proximity to both the Parkway and the Great Smokies Park. Nearby is Lake Junaluska, a resort as well as a religious assembly, and Maggie Valley. Maggie Valley is 4,000 feet above sea level, with tall mountains on either side. For several miles along US 19, Maggie is intensively developed with motels, restaurants, shops and recreation facilities.

Square Dancing Areas

Canton, bypassed by a link of I-40 between Asheville and Waynesville, has one of the oldest and largest Labor Day celebrations in North Carolina.

Bryson City, on US 19 a few miles southwest of Cherokee, is a noted gateway to the Great Smokies Park and Cherokee Reservation. It is near the headwaters of Fontana Lake, which extends for some thirty miles along the southern boundary of the Park. Areas of Nantahala Forest also adjoin the lake, which is impounded by the highest dam in the TVA system. Main highways lead to the dam and Fontana Village resort from US 10 and State 28, which has views of the lake at several points, and State 129 through Robbinsville and the Lake Santeetlah area. Fontana Village—with lodge, cottages, boat docks, golf, swimming, tennis, square dancing, riding and other features—is the largest strictly resort community in the Great Smokies. The resort was developed from the community built to house the workers who rushed Fontana Dam to completion during World War II.

At the dam there are observation areas and a visitor center. Below Fontana, waters of the Little Tennessee River also form Lake Cheoah.

Lake Santeetlah, another nearby power lake, is surrounded by Nantahala Forest. Accessible by a loop road, which turns off 129 near Robbinsville and circles the lake, is Joyce Kilmer Forest, a 3,800-acre tract of virgin timber preserved as a memorial to the poet who wrote "Trees." There is a forest service campground near the entrance to the Forest; within the Forest are hiking trails. Snowbird Mountain Lodge is nearby.

The first transmountain wagon train in this century was initiated by North Carolina and Tennessee in 1957 to call attention to the need for a road across the mountains in the Joyce Kilmer Forest area. With the road assured, the wagon train continues as an annual event in other areas of southwestern North Carolina. Both Andrews and Murphy have been its destinations in the past, as well as Franklin. Sponsors of the wagon train say it will continue as a feature of the Fourth of July holiday season. In the Blue Ridge Mountain country north of Asheville, the citizens of

Watauga and Wilkes counties staged a "Daniel Boone Wagon Train" in 1963. This wagon train has become an annual trip from North Wilkesboro to Boone, with overnight encampments enroute.

Near Spruce Pine, Burnsville and Bakersville is Roan Mountain, respectfully referred to as "The Roan." It rises to 6,285 feet on the North Carolina-Tennessee line and for nearly six miles never dips below 5,800 feet. The Roan has what has been called the world's largest natural garden of Catawba rhododendrons, and North Carolina's Rhododendron Queen is crowned here during the Rhododendron Festival in late June. On the Roan, reached by Highway 261 and a U.S. Forest Service road, is a recreation area of Pisgah National Forest. The rhododendron here is usually most colorful between June 15-25.

The origin of the name "Roan" is lost in legend, but Mt. Mitchell is named for the man who first measured its height and later lost his life while attempting to verify his findings. He was Dr. Elisha Mitchell, a professor at the University of North Carolina. His tomb is at the foot of the observation tower atop the mountain. The tower is in Mt. Mitchell State Park, and the Park was the first established of the state's parks. The Park is reached by a paved highway (State 128) which connects with the Blue Ridge Parkway.

Among the Blue Ridge Parkway recreational areas north of Asheville is Linville Falls, where the Linville River plunges into Linville Gorge. The gorge itself is a wilderness area in Pisgah National Forest. From several overlooks along the Parkway in this area, and from Wiseman's View on the rim of the gorge, are seen the mysterious Brown Mountain Lights which rise over a wooded peak in Burke County. They have never been explained by scientific theory or investigation. The dark of the moon in August is regarded as best for seeing this phenomenon.

Boone-Blowing Rock-Banner Elk

The visitor to the Boone-Blowing Rock-Banner Elk area finds himself in a section of North Carolina that offers many entertainment features, as well as beauty. Between Boone and Blowing Rock is one of the area's most popular attractions—"Tweetsie," a narrow-gauge train, so named because of its plaintive whistle. Tweetsie is located in a setting which includes a frontier-type village and amusement park.

Blowing Rock, adjacent to the Parkway and the eastern slope of the Blue Ridge Divide, is almost entirely a resort. The town is named for The Blowing Rock, a formation which takes its name from air currents which swirl upward around it. Golf and tennis are available at Blowing Rock and at nearby Boone, Linville and Newland. In 1962-63, the Boone-Blowing Rock-Banner Elk area became a winter sports center with the establishment of the following ski areas—Appalachian Ski Mountain, Beech Mountain, Mill Ridge, Seven Devils and Sugar Mountain. In this area, as in the Waynesville-Maggie Valley area to the southwest, skiing has given a lively new look to winter, with accommodations remaining open. In mid-June the "Land of Oz" atop Beech Mountain opens, offering one of the most unusual attractions in the area. It is open daily through Labor Day and from Labor Day through October on weekends only.

The Museum of North Carolina Minerals, on the Parkway at its junction with US 226, displays a sampler of the more than three hundred different kinds of gems and minerals found in North Carolina. Spruce Pine, six miles west of the Parkway, has a Gems and Minerals Festival in early August. "Rock shops" here and elsewhere in the mountains have information and equipment for collectors or "rockhounds." Franklin, a substantial community in southwestern North Carolina, is famous as a center of ruby making. The Cowee Valley and other localities nearby were once a source of commercially mined gems. Since the early 1950's, the ruby fields have been opened, and visitors can pay a small fee to "dig, find and keep." Findings often include sapphires as well as rubies.

Carl Sandburg's Home

Near Hendersonville on US 25 is Flat Rock, the home of the late Carl Sandburg. Mr. Sandburg's home has been appointed a National Historic Site. At the Flat Rock Playhouse, the Vagabond Players—North Carolina's oldest professional stock company—present plays from later June until Labor Day.

The area around Hendersonville and Brevard has over fifty percent of the summer camps for boys and girls. This is a multimillion-dollar industry for western North Carolina. Also in this area are several religious assembly grounds maintained by various denominations for summer conferences, study, retreats and recreation. Largest are Lake Junaluska (Methodist) and Montreat (Presbyterian) on US 70 west of Asheville. Evangelist Billy Graham lives at Montreat.

Near Brevard, US 276 enters the oldest section of Pisgah National Forest and crosses the Blue Ridge Parkway to link up with 23-19A and 19 at Waynesville to the west. The Cradle of Forestry in America, the site of the first forestry school in America, has a visitor center just off US 276. Beside the highway are Sliding Rock and Looking Glass Falls on the Davidson River. There are also Forest Service picnic areas and campgrounds along this route.

Pisgah National Forest covers 479,232 acres of western North Carolina, with its tracts of land widely scattered. Nantahala National Forest is comprised of 449,869 acres in southwestern North Carolina. Both have campgrounds, picnic areas, game management lands that offer hunting and trout fishing.

About eighteen miles west of Brevard and near the small community of Rosman on US 64 is the National Aeronautics and Space Administration Data Acquisition Facility, which tracks satellites. It is open to visitors daily and Sundays.

In the Sapphire country a little farther west, distinctive resorts along US 64 are Lake Toxaway, Sapphire, Cashiers and Highlands. Golf is one of the featured attractions. There are ski slopes at Sapphire Valley. The highest cliffs in eastern America are on Whiteside Mountain near Highlands. Highlands, four thousand feet above sea level, has been a summer resort for almost a century, and "summer people" greatly outnumber its year-round population.

Between Highlands and Franklin, US 64 negotiates the walls of Cullasaja Gorge and passes Bridal Veil Falls, Dry Falls and several Nantahala Forest recreation areas. You can drive an automobile under Bridal Veil and walk behind the waters of Dry Falls without getting wet.

The Nantahala Mountains rise sharply around Franklin. There is a Forest Service road to the top of Wayah Bald, where native pink and flame azaleas bloom in early June.

Southwest of Franklin, US 64 continues to the extreme southwestern corner of North Carolina, where the largest town is Murphy. Lake Hiwassee and Lake Chatuge offer fishing and boating and have resort developments on their shores.

North Carolinians say "from Manteo to Murphy" to describe the east-west extent of their state—it is over five hundred miles from one of these points to another. The entire trip can be made on US 64, although newer and wider highways cut down the driving time.

Two scenic approaches to Asheville and western North Carolina from the Piedmont are US 74 and I-40. After crossing the state from the coast via Charlotte in the southern Piedmont, US 74 approaches Asheville through Hickory Nut Gorge, where Chimney Rock and Lake Lure are noted features. Chimney Rock is accessible by a paved motor road and an elevator in the Rock itself. There are sports car hill climbs in spring and fall, and the Rock is open all year. As it nears the mountains, I-40 commands expansive views of the blue wall of the mountain ranges north of Asheville and then climbs the Eastern Continental Divide between Old Fort and Black Mountain.

PRACTICAL INFORMATION FOR NORTH CAROLINA

FACTS AND FIGURES. The state was named for Charles I of England. Its nicknames are the "Old North State" and the "Tar Heel State." The state flower is the dogwood; the cardinal is the state bird. *Esse Quam Videri* ("To be, rather than to seem") is the state motto. Raleigh is the state capital, and the population of North Carolina is 5,082,059.

HOW TO GET THERE. *By air:* Interstate airlines serving major North Carolina cities are: Piedmont, Delta, Eastern, United, US Air and Altair. Intrastate lines are: Wheeler, Sunbird, Mid-South and Atlantis. Limousine service available at all major airports.

By train: Amtrak trains go into Rocky Mount, Raleigh, Fayetteville, Hamlet and Southern Pines/Pinehurst. Southern Railway also has passenger service.

By car: A tourist is given a taste of "Tar Heel" hospitality at the state's lovely Welcome Centers located on I-95 and I-85 on the Virginia and South Carolina state lines and on I-40 on the Tennessee line. I-26 and I-77 come in from South Carolina.

By bus: Good service by Greyhound and Trailways.

HOW TO GET AROUND. *By air:* See "How To Get There" section.

By car: North Carolina's state-administered highway system has more than 75,000 mi. of roads and bridges, all toll-free. I-26, I-40, I-77, I-85 and I-95, as well as US 17, US 19, US 64-264, US 70, US 220, US 221, US 258 and US 421 all have delightful rest areas with picnic tables and barbecues.

By ferry: The state operates toll-free ferries daily across Currituck Sound from Currituck to Knotts Island, Hatteras Inlet, Pamlico River, at Bayview, and Neuse River, at Minnesott Beach. Toll ferry service is available from Cedar Island to Ocracoke Island and Southport to Ft. Fisher. All state ferries carry automobiles. For ferry schedules write: Dept. of Transportation, Public Affairs Office, P.O. Box 25201, Raleigh, N.C. 27611.

By bus: In addition to Greyhound and Trailways, Seashore Transportation Co. operates within the state.

TOURIST INFORMATION. For information regarding points of interest in the state and also information about camping, hunting and fishing write to the: N. C. Travel Division, Dept. of Commerce, Raleigh, N.C. 27611. Contact the Superintendent, Park Headquarters, Cape Hatteras National Seashore, Box 457, Manteo, N.C. 27954, for information about the Cape Hatteras National Seashore. The Public Affairs Office, North Carolina Dept. of Transportation, Raleigh, N.C. 27611, can supply ferry information and highway conditions bulletins. A pamphlet listing vacation events in North Carolina can be obtained by writing: "N.C. Calendar of Events," N. C. Travel Division, Dept. of Commerce, Raleigh, N.C. 27611.

Welcome Centers are located on I-95 and I-85 on the Virginia and So. Carolina state lines and on I-40 on the Tennessee line.

SEASONAL EVENTS. Festivals, fairs and other special events usher in spring and other seasons. A sampling follows of some of the better known annual events, listed in chronological order beginning with the spring months.

Late March: Annual *Old Time Fiddlers and Blue Grass Convention,* Mooresville, N.C. The state's oldest continuous fiddlers convention.

April: *North Carolina Azalea Festival,* Wilmington, features parade, garden tours, coronation of festival royalty, dances and concerts. The festival celebrates the blooming of millions of azaleas in and around this historic port city. *Greater Greensboro Open Golf Tournament,* Greensboro; and the *Stonybrook Steeplechase* in Southern Pines.

May: *Strawberry Festival,* Chadbourn; Sports Car Hill Climb, Chimney Rock; Men's and Women's North-South Golf Championships, Pinehurst; Hang Gliding Championship Competition, Grandfather Mtn., Linville; Hang Gliding Spectacular at Jockey's Ridge, Nags Head; "World 600" Grand National Stock Car Race, Charlotte; Marlin Tournament in Wrightsville Beach.

June: *Blue Marlin Tournament,* Morehead City; *International Blue Marlin Tournament,* Hatteras; *North Carolina Rhododendron Festival,* Bakersville and Roan Mountain. *"Singing on the Mountain,"* Grandfather Mountain, Linville, held on the fourth Sunday in June—begun as a family reunion in 1925, this is an all-day program of music and picnicking that draws thousands. Also in Spivey's Corner is the unusual *National Hollerin' Contest*—an event that has grown each year and has received national television attention.

July: Wagon trains—trans-mountain treks of horse-drawn vehicles and horseback riders end with Fourth of July parades at Franklin in southwestern North Carolina and Boone in the Blue Ridge Mountains. *Highland games* and the *Gathering of the Scottish Clans,* Grandfather Mountain, Linville—caber tossing, the Highland Fling, kilts, pipe bands. *Craftsman's Fair,* Asheville, a week-long event sponsored by the Southern Highland and Handicraft Guild, whose members display their finest products and demonstrate their skills.

August: *Gems and Minerals Festival,* Spruce Pine—displays of gems and minerals from North Carolina and other states, field trips for collectors. *Blowing Rock Horse Show,* Blowing Rock—Annual Mountain Dance & Folk Festival, Asheville.

September: *North Carolina Apple Festival,* Hendersonville; *State Championship Horse Show,* Raleigh, held in the J. S. Dorton Arena on the State Fairgrounds.

October: *North Carolina State Fair,* Raleigh—one of America's oldest and largest agricultural fairs, extensive exhibits and entertainment including the State Fair Folk Festival; *"National 500" Stock Car Race,* Charlotte; and *"American 500" Stock Car Race,* Rockingham. *Senior Men's and Senior Women's North-South Golf Tournaments,* Pinehurst; Pumpkin Festival, in Spring Hope.

The spring-through-autumn schedule of flower shows in North Carolina begins in February in Wilmington and Whiteville with *camellia shows.* The *Southeastern Flower and Garden Show,* at the Charlotte Merchandise Mart in February, features extensive horticultural exhibits and also room settings with living gardens created for this annual event. Raleigh and Kinston have *rose shows* in May; Hendersonville features the *Carolina Mountain Flower and Garden Show* in the summer.

 NATIONAL PARKS. *Blue Ridge Parkway*—the motor road and its right of way are actually an elongated park for leisurely enjoyment of mountain country between Shenandoah National Park in Virginia and the North Carolina entrance to Great Smoky Mountains National Park. More than 250 miles of the Parkway have been completed in western North Carolina, where the road reaches its highest elevation (6,053 feet). There are over 100 scenic overlooks, and special recreational areas are open May through October. Except for stretches at the higher elevations, the toll-free road is normally open all year. Camper-trailers are permitted, but no commercial traffic. Maximum speed limit is 45 m.p.h., lower where posted. Pets are allowed—but only on leash or otherwise under physical, restrictive control.

Cape Hatteras National Seashore—America's first National Seashore, 45 sq. mi. on Outer Banks Islands of Bodie, Hatteras and Ocracoke, with 70 mi. of ocean beach for public use. Campgrounds, day-use centers of picnicking, surf bathing, nature trails, visitor centers and museums. Oregon Inlet Fishing Center (concession) has charter craft for deep-sea, sound or inlet fishing available spring through fall. *Pea Island National Wildlife Refuge* offers opportunities to observe shore birds and migratory waterfowl. There are up to 12,000 Greater Snow geese here between early Nov. and late Jan. There are 3 active lighthouses in the National Seashore. Cape Hatteras Lighthouse is open daily, and visitors can climb to the top. The state maintains highways through the park and operates free automobile ferries between Hatteras and Ocracoke Islands. There is also a bridge across Oregon Inlet to Hatteras Island. The northern entrance to the National Seashore is near Nags Head and is reached by US 158 and US 64-264 crossing to Outer Banks on bridges. The southern approach is from US 70 via a toll ferry between Cedar Island and Ocracoke.

Cape Lookout National Seashore embraces 58 mi. of shoreline between Ocracoke and Shackelford Banks.

Great Smoky Mountains National Park—800 sq. mi. shared equally by North Carolina and Tennessee. The main North Carolina entrance is on US 441 near Cherokee and the southern terminus of Blue Ridge Parkway. Oconaluftee Ranger Station, with Pioneer Exhibits and Farmstead, at the Park entrance, is open daily. Tent and trailer camping allowed at developed campgrounds; rough camping by permit from rangers. Pets must be kept leashed or restricted at all times. Marked hiking trails include 70 mi. of Appalachian Trailway along the crest of Great Smokies Divide. Livery stable concessionaires rent horses from June through Aug. Trout fishing mid-May to Sept. US 441 is the transmountain highway through the Park. At Newfound Gap on the North Carolina-Tennessee line, it intersects with a paved Park road to Clingman's Dome, highest peak in the Great Smokies.

Pisgah and Nantahala in the Southern Appalachians, *Uwharrie* in the Piedmont, and *Croatan* on the coastal plain are National Forests with a total area of over 1,124,000 acres, administered by the U.S. Forest Service. The forests are accessible by main highways, including sections of the Blue Ridge Parkway, and U.S. Forest Service roads. Developed recreational areas for picnicking, swimming, camping, stream and lake fishing, hiking trails, hunting in areas cooperatively managed by North Carolina Wildlife Resources Commission and the Forest Service. Pisgah and Nantahala contain the largest number of scenic and recreational features. In Nantahala National Forest is the *Joyce Kilmer Memorial Forest.* Headquarters for the National Forests in North Carolina are at 50 S. French Broad Ave., Asheville (P.O. Box 2750).

 STATE PARKS AND FORESTS. North Carolina's twenty-seven State Parks and two nature preserves range from mountaintop to seacoast. All except *Mt. Mitchell* and *Mt. Jefferson* are open year round, daily and Sun. Swimming areas and refreshment stands are open in about half of the parks from Memorial Day to Labor Day. Mt. Mitchell restaurant is open from May 1 to October 31. Vacation cabins (reservations advised mid-Apr. to Oct. 31) are found in two parks—*Morrow Mountain* and *Hanging Rock*—with tent-trailer camping in 12 of them. Campsites may be reserved for one or two weeks. Organized (group) camping facilities in two parks—*William B. Umstead,* with three sites in the Crabtree Creek Section and one in the Reedy Creek Section, and *Singletary Lake.* Youth camping (Boy Scout groups, etc.) facilities are available in several parks. For more specific information write to any individual park, Dept. of Natural and Economic Resources, Division of State Parks, P.O. Box 27687, Raleigh, N.C. 27611 or call 919/733-4181. All State Parks are wildlife sanctuaries, and firearms are prohibited.

Boone's Cave—110 acres on Yadkin River, in Davidson County, reputed to be site where Daniel Boone spent a considerable amount of time. Undeveloped. Hiking, picnicking, fishing, nature study.

Carolina Beach—Formerly known as Masonboro State Park—15 mi. S. of Wilmington, at junction of Intracoastal Waterway and the Cape Fear River. A naturalist's delight. The Venus Fly Trap is endemic to this area. Year-round tent-trailer camping, fishing, boating, nature study, hiking & picnicking.

Cliffs of the Neuse—In Wayne Co., 14 mi. SE of Goldsboro of N.C. 111. Scenic, recreation, picnicking, swimming, tent, trailer & organized camping, boat rentals, fishing, hiking, nature study & museum.

Crowder's Mountain—16 mi. W of Gastonia in Gaston Co. Has facilities for picnicking, fishing, and hiking.

Duke Power—1,328 acres on Lake Norman, 10 mi. S of Statesville off US 21. Swimming, boating, picnicking, fishing, snack bar, 33 tent-trailer campsites, hiking, nature study.

Eno River—The park lies in Durham and Orange Counties. Undeveloped. Hiking available.

Fort Macon—on Bogue Island, opposite Morehead City and Beaufort, 4 mi. from Atlantic Beach, via US 70 and state road. Historic Fort with museum, bathing, beach, surf fishing, picnicking, snack bar.

Goose Creek—In Beaufort Co., 10 mi. E. of Washington; there is a boat launch, recreation, picnicking, fishing, hiking, nature study. Rough camping.

Hammocks Beach—on Bear Island, said to be one of the most beautiful and unspoiled beaches on the Atlantic Coast, 5 mi. SE of Swansboro via Rte. 24 and 2½ mi. free ferry (no vehicles). Memorial Day to Labor Day. Bathing, beach, fishing, picnicking, snack bar, hiking, nature study.

Hanging Rock—4,040 acres in Sauratown Mountains, about 32 mi. N of Winston-Salem via Rte. 89 & 66. Picnicking, lake swimming, fishing, rental rowboats, 6 cabins (Apr. to Oct.) 74 tent/trailer campsites, hiking, nature study, snack bar, observation tower.

Jockey's Ridge—At Nags Head in Dare Co. Site of the highest sand dune on the eastern coast. The park is undeveloped but offers hiking and nature study.

Jones Lake—in Bladen Lakes State Forest via Rte. 242, 4 mi. N of Elizabethtown. Picnicking, lake swimming, boating, fishing, snack bar, tent-trailer camping, nature study.

Kerr Lake—in Vance and Warren Counties, N of Henderson. There are boat launches, recreation, picnicking, refreshment stand, swimming, tent, trailer and organized camping as well as fishing and hiking.

Medoc Mountain—15 mi. SW of Roanoke Rapids in Halifax Co. Park is scenic and has tent and organized camping, picnicking, fishing, hiking and nature study.

Merchants Millpond—nature study, fishing, hiking, picnicking, boat launch are available at this facility 5 mi. NE of Gatesville in Gates Co.

Morrow Mountain—in Uwharrie Mountains on Pee Dee River, 7 mi. E of Albermarle. Picnicking, snack bar, swimming, 6 vacation cabins (mid-Apr. to Oct.), year-round 106 tent/trailer campsites, boating, fishing, hiking, museum, historic Kron House, nature study.

Mt. Jefferson—539 acres, including Mt. Jefferson, about 1 mi. W of Jefferson in Ashe County near US 221 and Blue Ridge Parkway in northwestern North Carolina. Picnicking, hiking, nature study.

Mt. Mitchell—1,469 acres, especially noted for its beautiful natural colors in autumn. The 6,684-ft. summit of Mt. Mitchell (highest peak in U.S. east of Mississippi River), with its 39-ft. observation tower, affords a magnificent view for many miles. 35 mi. NE of Asheville via Blue Ridge Parkway and then 5 mi. to the peak. Tent camping, snack bar, restaurant, picnicking, museum, hiking, nature study. NOTE: Blue Ridge Parkway closes when icing develops on road during winter.

N.C. Zoological—5 mi. S of Asheboro, wild animals viewed in natural setting, picnicking, hiking, refreshment stand.

Pettigrew—17,360 acres, including 16,600-acre Lake Phelps, 9 mi. S of Creswell via US 64 and state road. Noted for freshwater fishing, boating, water-skiing, hiking, historic mansion and other buildings of Somerset Place Plantation. 13 tent/trailer campsites, picnicking and nature study.

Pilot Mountain—3,547 acres, including unique 5¼-mi. 300-ft. wide corridor to the Yadkin River Section, about 24 mi. N of Winston-Salem off US 52. Contains large quartzite monadnock rising 1,500 ft. above surrounding countryside, which the Indians called *Jomeokee* (the Great Guide). First phase of development now underway. Hiking, picnicking, nature study.

Raven Rock—In Harnett County, 6 mi. W of Lillington on US 421, then 3 mi. N by Rte. 1250. Outstanding 125-ft. rock formation on south bank, at "fall line" of Cape Fear River. Mountain-type trees and shrubs. Undeveloped. Picnicking, hiking, nature study, fishing in Cape Fear River.

(Theodore) Roosevelt Natural Area—a gift from family of our 26th President, to remain undeveloped in perpetuity, for nature and ecological studies. Six miles west of Atlantic Beach, 2 mi. E of Salter Path, on sound side of Bogue Island.

Singletary Lake—within Bladen Lakes State Forest, primarily for group camping. Boating, fishing.

South Mountains—Undeveloped park 13 mi. S of Morganton in Burke Co. Picnicking, organized camping, fishing and hiking are available.

Stone Mountain—5 mi. W of Roaring Gap, off US 21, about 8 mi. from Blue Ridge Parkway. Undeveloped. Picnicking, hiking, nature study. Oval-shaped granite dome over 600 ft. high, approximately 3 mi. in circumference at base.

Weymouth Woods—Sandhills Nature Preserve—"Natural Area" featuring longleaf pine and other sandhills flora and fauna. Hiking, nature study, museum.

William B. Umstead (Crabtree Creek Section)—12 mi. NW of Raleigh on US 70. Tent-trailer camping, organized group camping, picnicking, boating, fishing, hiking, nature study.

William B. Umstead (Reedy Creek Section) 10 mi. NW of Raleigh near Cary, off US 70-A & Rte. 54, also I-40. Picnicking, organized group camping, fishing, hiking, nature study.

 CAMPING OUT. There are many campgrounds in North Carolina, and visitors to the Tar Heel State can write to the N. C. Travel Division, Dept. of Commerce, Raleigh, N.C. 27611 for brochures listing these campgrounds.

 FARM VACATIONS AND GUEST RANCHES. There are two "dude ranches," located in the western part of the state, which have limited accommodations. For information write the Pisgah View Ranch, Route 1, Candler, N.C. 28715, and Cataloochee Ranch, Rte. 5, Waynesville, N.C. 28786.

  MUSEUMS AND GALLERIES. Historical: *Museum of the Cherokee Indian,* open year round and the *Oconaluftee Indian Village,* open May through Oct., Cherokee. Admission charge. *Greensboro Historical Museum,* 130 Summit Ave., Greensboro. Guided tours, lectures. Daily except Sun. and holidays. Free. *North Carolina Hall of History* in the Archives Bldg., 109 E. Jones St., Raleigh. Closed national holidays. Free. *Rowan Museum,* Salisbury. Historic houses, Indian relics. Open Tues. to Sun. Admission to the Town House and museum is free. Old Stone House: Admission charge. *Anson County Historical Society,* 210 E. Wade St., Wadesboro. A general museum and historic homes. Open Wed., Sun. Admission charge. Shaw House: open daily Feb. to May. Free; House in the Horseshoe. Admission charge. *National Society of the Colonial Dames of America in the State of North Carolina,* 224 Market St., Wilmington. A historical museum in the Burgwin-Wright House and Garden (1771). Admission charge. *Wilmington-New Hanover Museum,* 814 Market St., Wilmington. Regional history museum. Closed Mon. and national holidays. Free.

Art: *Asheville Art Museum,* 152 Pearson Dr., Ashville. Closed Mon. and holidays. *William Hayes Ackland Art Center,* Columbia and Franklin Sts., Univ. of N.C., Chapel Hill. Closed holidays and third week of Aug. Free. *Mint Museum of Art,* 501 Hempstead Place, Charlotte. Sculptures and paintings from Italian Renaissance through 20th century. Closed national and city holidays. Free. *Duke University Museum of Art,* Durham. Closed Mon., national holidays. Free. *Weatherspoon Art Gallery,* University of N.C. at Greensboro. Closed Sun. during summer term; Sat.; major academic holidays; Easter vacation; Christmas vacation and between summer session and fall term. Free. *Greenville Art Center,* 802 Evans St., Greenville. Closed national holidays, July and Aug. Free. *The Hickory Museum of Art,* 3rd St. & First Ave., N.W., Hickory. Closed Aug. and holidays. Free. *North Carolina Museum of Art,* 107 E. Morgan St., Raleigh. Collections from classical periods to modern. Closed Mon. and holidays. Free.

St. John's Art Gallery, 114 Orange St., Wilmington. Collections of paintings, sculpture and special exhibitions. Closed holidays and Sat. and Sun. in summer. Free. *Southeastern Center for Contemporary Art,* 750 Marguerite Dr., Winston-

Salem. Free. *Piedmont Craftsmen,* 936 W. Fourth St., Winston-Salem. An arts and crafts museum. Closed Sun. Free. *N.C. League of Creative Arts & Crafts* near Old Salem, Winston-Salem. Admission charge.

Special Interest Museums: *Colburn Memorial Mineral Museum,* 170 Coxe Ave., Ashville. Closed mid-Dec. to Jan. 2. Free. *Country Doctor Museum,* Vance St., Bailey. 18th- & 19th-century medical collections. Free. *Alphonso Whaling Museum,* Front St., Beaufort. Admission charge. *Hampton Mariner's Museum,* 120 Turner St., Beaufort. Free. *Blockade Runner Museum,* on US 421, Carolina Beach. Year around. Admission charge. *Morehead Planetarium,* E. Franklin St., Chapel Hill. Admission charge. *Charlotte Nature Museum,* 1658 Sterling Rd., Charlotte. Free. Closed holidays. *Museum of the Cherokee Indian,* US 441, Cherokee. Open year around. Admission charge. *N.C. Museum of Life & Science,* 433 Murray Ave., Durham. Museum, life-sized natural history and space exhibits. Closed Mon. *Museum of the Albermarle,* Rte. 3, Elizabeth City. Old farming implements, Indian artifacts. Closed Mon. and holidays. Admission charge. *82nd Airborne Division War Memorial Museum,* Ardennes St., Fort Bragg, a military museum. Closed Mon. Free. *Schiele Museum of Natural History and Planetarium,* 1500 E. Garrison Blvd., Gastonia. Closed Mon. Free. *Natural Science Center,* 4301 Lawndale Dr., Greensboro. Closed holidays. Free. *Kings Mountain National Military Park,* Kings Mountain. Free. *Museum of the Sea,* Manteo. Free. *Bodie Island Visitor Center,* Manteo. Housed in c. 1872 Bodie Island Coast Guard Station and quarters. Free. *Ocracoke Visitor Center,* Manteo. Free.

New Bern Firemen's Museum, 421 Broad St., New Bern. Closed 1 wk. in July. Admission charge. *North Carolina State Museum, Bicentennial Plaza, Raleigh. Natural history indigenous to the state. Free. *Rocky Mount Children's Museum,* Sunset Park, Rocky Mount. Natural sciences, geology, mini-zoo. *Museum of North Carolina Minerals,* Blue Ridge Pkwy., Spruce Pine. Closed Nov. to May. Free. *Nature Science Museum,* Reynolda Village, Winston-Salem. Free. *Morehead Planetarium:* Closed Sun. and major holidays. Admission charge.

HISTORIC SITES. *Thomas Wolfe Memorial,* 40 Spruce St., Asheville. Admission charge. *Historic Bath State Historic Site,* Bath. Admission charge. *Alamance Battleground,* 6 mi. S of Burlington on Rte. 62. This 1771 Battleground is the site of typical frontier dwelling (Allen House). Visitor Center, slide program. Tues. to Sun. Free. *Fort Fisher State Historic Site,* on US 421, 6 mi. S of Carolina Beach. Coastal defense fort that provided protection for Confederate blockade runners. Visitor center museum. Daily, all year. Free. *Somerset Place State Historic Site,* Creswell. Free. *Moores Creek National Military Park.* Near Currie, site of first battle of Revolutionary War in North Carolina. Monuments, markers, museum. Free. *Bennett Place State Historic Site,* Durham, has a visitor center and is open Sept. to May wknds., during June to Aug. Tues to Sat.; Free. The Bennett House is also open to visitors. *Historic Edenton, Inc.,* S. Broad St., Edenton. Free admission to Barker House Visitor Center Museum. Historic Houses are also open to the public: Cupola house (1725); Chowan county Courthouse (1767); James Iredell house (1759); and St. Paul's Episcopal Church (1736). Admission charge. *Market House,* Market Square, Fayetteville, open on a restricted basis. A square building with cupola, it is a rare example of the English form of town hall with open, arcaded ground floor surmounted by public rooms on the 2nd floor. *Guilford Courthouse National Military Park,* New Garden Rd. & Old Battleground Rds., Greensboro. Free. *Wright Brothers National Memorial.* Kill Devil Hill on US 158. Story of aviation and the Wright Brothers in reconstructed camp buildings. Daily, all year. Free. *Caswell-Neuse State Historic Site.* Kinston. Closed Mon. Free. *Roanoke Island Historical Park,* Manteo, has an Indian Village Museum and is located on the site that was selected for the first

English colony attempt in America. Admission charge. *Carson House, Inc., Rte. 4, Marion. Open wkdays by appointment; wknds. 2 to 5. Admission charge. Town Creek Indian Mound State Historic Site,* Rte. 3, Mount Gilead. Closed Mon. Free. *Attmore-Oliver House,* 511 Broad St., New Bern. Closed on national holidays. Admission charge. *Stevenson House,* 611 Pollock St., New Bern. Admission charge. *Bentonville Battleground State Historic Site,* Newton Grove. Free. *James K. Polk Birthplace State Historic Site,* Pineville. Free. *Andrew Johnson Memorial,* Raleigh. Closed Sat. Admission charge. *The State Capitol,* Capitol Square, and the Legislative Building ("State House"), Jones St., in Raleigh, are open to the public and guides are available Free. *State Capitol,* Capitol Square, Raleigh, is open to the public. Built 1833-40, this building is one of the country's finest Greek Revival structures. *Fort Raleigh National Historic Site* on Roanoke Island (Highways 64 & 264). Exhibits illustrate the first English colonization attempts. In July and Aug. there are guided tours. Open all year. Free. *House in the Horseshoe State Historic Site,* Rte. 3, Sanford. Closed Mon. Free. *Brunswick Town State Historic Site,* 225 Pine Grove Dr., Southport. Free. *Zebulon B. Vance Birthplace State Historic Site,* Weaverville. Closed Mon. Free. *Bethabara Park,* on outskirts of Winston-Salem, first Moravian settlement in North Carolina, is open daily Easter-Thanksgiving. Free. *Old Salem,* Winston-Salem. Restored 1776 Moravian Congregational town. Seven buildings are open to the public: The John Vogler House (1819); Market-Fire House Museum (1803); Miksch Tobacco Shop and Garden; Salem Tavern; Single Brothers' House; Wachovia Museum; and Winkler Bakery. Craft demonstrations, guided tours, special holiday events. Combination or single admission tickets may be bought. *Duke Homestead* near Durham. 1852 ancestral Duke home. *Ft. Dobbs.* Near Statesville. Circa 1756. Named for Royal Gov. Arthur Dobbs. Visitor center. *Carl Sandburg Home* at Flat Rock. Home is open for visitors.

 SPECIAL INTEREST TOURS. *Biltmore House and Gardens* Asheville. Admission charge. *Fontana Dam,* on Rte. 28 (between US 19 & US 129) is the tallest dam east of the Rocky Mts. The powerhouse lobby and balcony are open to visitors daily. A free incline railway operates daily carrying passengers from the overlook to the base of the dam. A panoramic view of the dam is a feature of this ride. *Cooleemee Plantation House,* on US 64, Fork. Visitors are welcome to walk through the grounds and garden May to Labor Day. Wed., Sat. and Sun. Admission charge. *Cowee Ruby Mines,* on Rte. 28, Franklin, are open during the daylight hours from Apr. to Oct. You may dig for rubies here. Other gem mines are the Hiddenite & Emerald mine at Hiddenite, and the Big Crabtree mine, at Spruce Pine. Rates depend upon the mine selected.

Chinqua-Penn Plantation House, Rte. 3, Reidsville. Closed Mon. *U.S.S. North Carolina Battleship Memorial,* moored on the west bank of Cape Fear River, Wilmington, is open daily. *Orton Plantation,* US 17 & Rte. 133, Wilmington, is open daily year round. Admission charge.

Rea House, Winston-Salem, open Tues. to Sat., including holidays except Christmas Day. Closed Mondays and from Jan. 2 to Feb. 1. Admission charge.

Pea Island National Wildlife Refuge, Manteo, is open weekdays. Closed wknds. and holidays. Free.

Tryon Palace Restoration, 613 Pollock St., New Bern. Admission charge. Tryon Palace. Admission charge. Tryon Gardens. Admission charge. Stanly House. Admission charge. Closed Mon.

Tryon Palace Restoration, 613 Pollock St., New Bern. Admission charge. Tryon Palace. Admission charge. Tryon Gardens. Admission charge. Stanly House. Admission charge. Closed Mon.

 GARDENS. *Craggy Gardens,* 17 mi. NE of Asheville, on the Blue Ridge Pkwy., is just beautiful when the rhododendron is in bloom about mid-June. Open May to Oct. *Daniel Boone Native Gardens,* Horn in the West Dr., in Boone. Closed Nov.-Apr.; adult admission charged but children under 12 free, if accompanied by an adult. *North Carolina Botanical Garden,* Coker Hall, Univ. of N.C., Chapel Hill, is open daily. Free. *Sarah P. Duke Memorial Gardens,* on the campus of Duke University, in Durham, has a constant display of annuals, perennials and ornamental shrubs. Period of peak bloom is the month of April. Open daily. Free. *Clarendon Gardens,* Linden Rd., Pinehurst, is open mid-Sept. to Apr. Free. Closed Christmas week. *Elizabethan Garden,* Fort Raleigh National Historic Site on Roanoke Isl. Open daily. Admission charge but children under 12 free. Children under 16 must be accompanied by a parent. *Greenfield Gardens,* on US 421, are open daily. Free. The 185-acre park includes a lake, zoo, scenic boat rides, amusement park, as well as lovely gardens. The *Airlie Azalea Gardens,* on US 76, Wrightsville Beach, contain not only thousands of azaleas but also camellias and many rare plants. Open daily from the end of Mar. to end of Sept. During the blooming season (usually Apr.); children under 12 free.

 MUSIC. In North Carolina cities and towns, and on the University campuses, concerts of various types are scheduled at every session. In late winter and early spring, the North Carolina Symphony gives concerts on statewide tours; information about this is available from the Manager of the North Carolina Symphony, Memorial Auditorium, Raleigh, N.C.

Brevard Music Center is the home of the Transylvania Music Camp. It offers varied music concerts while the Camp is in session from July to mid-Aug. For further information write: Business Manager, Brevard Music Center, P.O. Box 592, Brevard 28712.

Mountain Dance and Folk Festival at Asheville, founded in 1927, is held in early Aug. It features instrumentalists, ballad singers and dancers from all parts of the Southern Appalachians. For information write: Asheville Chamber of Commerce, Asheville.

Old Time Fiddler's Convention, at Union Grove in Iredell County, is held on the Fri. and Sat. before Easter at the Union Grove School. Old-time and modern bands (string instruments only) present folk and country music. For information write: Box 38, Union Grove, N.C.

 STAGE AND REVUES. *The Lost Colony,* outdoor historical drama, Manteo, 8:30 P.M. Mon. and Sat., late June to Labor Day. *Unto These Hills,* outdoor historical drama, Cherokee, 8:45 P.M. Mon. to Sat., late June to Aug. Reserved seats. *Horn in the West,* outdoor historical drama, Boone. 8:45 P.M. Tues. to Sun., late June through Aug. *From This Day Forward,* outdoor historical drama, Valdese. Early July through late August. *Strike at the Wind,* outdoor historical drama, Pembroke. Thursday through Saturday nights, late June to mid-August. *The Immortal Showboat,* sound-and-light spectacular at the USS *North Carolina Battleship Memorial,* Wilmington, at 8 nightly, June to Labor Day.

Summer theaters which present a different play or musical each week between late June and Labor Day are the *Flat Rock Playhouse,* Flat Rock; *Charlotte Summer Theatre,* Charlotte; *East Carolina College Summer Theatre,* Greenville; *Thomas Wolfe Playhouse,* Asheville, and the *Parkway Playhouse,* Burnsville.

For dinner theatres see restaurant listings for Charlotte, Greensboro and Raleigh.

DRINKING LAWS. Local option under state control governs sale of alcoholic beverages. Distilled spirits are sold legally in package stores controlled by the N.C. Board of Alcoholic Control or "ABC." There are ABC stores in approximately half the coastal and Piedmont counties and in some cities and towns of the mountain counties. Some municipalities allow "mixed beverages" to be served in properly licensed restaurants. Under state law, no person under 21 years of age may purchase any alcoholic beverage containing over 14% alcohol.

SUMMER SPORTS. Summer is tops for aquatic sports throughout the state and for trail riding and golf in the mountains.

Water sports: The surf bathing season begins in May and continues into late autumn. Except in very high mountain localities, swimming and water-skiing are also enjoyed from May to Sept. or Oct. In the mountains, they are best in June to Aug.

Bathing: While the greatest activity in boating and sailing is in summer, these sports extend to spring and fall in most sections of the state, and are year round along the coast. Lakes, rivers and sounds provide ideal environs for the use of pleasure craft and water skis. Marinas and public boat launching areas are numerous on lakes, rivers and coastal sounds. Along the 265 miles of Intracoastal Waterway in North Carolina, there are more than 80 marinas and other facilities for yachts and smaller craft. Detailed information about the Waterway in North Carolina is in the Southern Edition of the *Inland Waterway Guide,* published at 25 W. Broward St., Fort Lauderdale, Fla.

Fishing: The angler's choice in North Carolina ranges from mountain trout to blue marlin. Trout waters in the Blue Ridge and Great Smokies are open from April through summer. There is no closed season on any other species of freshwater game fish, or on the game fish taken along North Carolina's coast and offshore. Surf-fishing for channel bass is best spring through autumn; offshore fishing is prime between May and late autumn. The *Blue Marlin Tournament* at Wrightsville Beach is in late May; also a Blue Marlin Tournament at Morehead City and the International Blue Marlin Tournament at Hatteras are held in early June. No license is required for saltwater fishing. Charter craft, fully equipped for deep-sea, inlet or sound fishing, are available at Oregon Inlet near Nags Head, Hatteras, Morehead City, Wrightsville and Carolina Beaches, Topsail Island, Southport and several other points along the coast. Some 30 ocean-fishing piers are open from Apr. to Oct. They charge a nominal fee for fishing privileges, sell bait and rent tackle. For nonresidents, seasonal freshwater licenses are available—a five-day permit and a one-day permit. Either entitles the licensee to fish for all freshwater fish except mountain trout. The nonresident trout fishing license is required in addition to the regular fishing license or permit.

Golf is a year-round sport with over 300 courses open every month. Mountain courses, however, are at their best from May through Oct.; many are closed in winter. Caddies and electric golf carts are available at most courses. The "Sandhills" of N.C. are famous for their courses and the #2 course at the Pinehurst C.C. ranks among the top ten of America's 100 greatest golf course. For a complete listing of North Carolina's golf resorts from the mountains to the coast, write for the pamphlet "N.C., Golf State U.S.A.", Travel & Promotion Division, Box 27687, Raleigh, N.C. 27611.

Horseback riding is at its best in the mountains during summer and year round throughout the state. It is most popular at the mid-south resorts of the Sandhills and in Tryon from autumn through spring. Horses for ring or trail riding are available at many mountain resorts, and there are riding concessions in the Great

Smoky Mountains Park. Cataloochee Ranch, Waynesville, is headquarters each summer for a ten-day Great Smokies Trail Ride, sponsored by the American Forestry Association through its Trail Riders of the Wilderness Program. Stables that rent and board horses and give riding instructions are located near most of the larger cities. Riding with hounds on organized hunts enlivens the sports scene at Southern Pines, Tryon, Sedgefield, Charlotte and Raleigh from Oct. to Mar. There are spring steeplechase meetings at Southern Pines and Tryon.

Hiking: There are hundreds of miles of marked trails, including 200 miles of the Appalachian Trail, following the topmost mountain ridges through the Great Smoky Mountains Park and Pisgah and Nantahala national forests. The western part of the state has the greatest number of hiking trails. Spring, summer and fall are the best times to use them.

Tennis: is one of the fastest growing year-around sports in North Carolina. There are new courts currently under construction throughout the state. Some are membership clubs, and some are open to the general public. There are both indoor and outdoor courts: *Sugar Mountain* and *Beech Mountain* at Banner Elk, *Pinehurst* resorts, the *Outer Banks Racquet Club* at Nags Head, *Tanglewood Park* in Clemmons, *Sapphire Valley,* Sapphire, and *Wolfe Laurel* near Mars Hill. Inquire locally for further information.

WINTER SPORTS. Most sports are year round in many areas of the state, especially in the mid-southern regions.

Hunting seasons begin in Sept. with dove shooting and continue through late winter. There is a varied pattern of open seasons on bear, boar, deer, small game animals, quail, ruffled grouse, marsh hens, ducks and Canada geese. Lake Mattamuskeet and Currituck Sound, near the coast, are famous for waterfowl hunting. Further information on current fishing and hunting regulations may be obtained from the North Carolina Wildlife Resources Commission, Raleigh.

Snow-skiing in the mountain areas starts, weather permitting, in Dec. and continues until early Mar. Ski areas in North Carolina include: Sugar Mtn., Beech Mtn., Seven Devils, Mill Ridge, Appalachian Ski Mtn. near Banner Elk, Blowing Rock & Boone; Wolf Laurel Ski Slope at Mars Hill; Sapphire Valley at Sapphire, Cataloochee near Waynesville and High Meadows at Roaring Gap.

SPECTATOR SPORTS. The Charlotte Motor Speedway in Charlotte features NASCAR sanctioned late-model stock car races in May (World 600) and Oct. (National 500). The North Carolina Motor Speedway on US 74, between Rockingham and Hamlet, is the site for NASCAR races for late-model stock cars in Mar. (Carolina 500) and in Oct. (American 500). Motorcycle and sports car racing are done on the infield road course.

Golf: One of the country's major golf tournaments is the Greater Greensboro Open, held in April in Greensboro.

Boating: There are sailing regattas on Kerr Lake, near Henderson, and other lakes, and on sounds in the vicinity of Kitty Hawk and Manteo. Wrightsville Beach and Morehead City. Powerboat races are featured on the Pasquotank River at Elizabeth City and on several inland lakes, including Lake Wheeler near Raleigh.

Horse races: Over 300 standardbreds are trained at Pinehurst during the winter. Harness-horse race matinees and time trials are featured here in spring. Betting is illegal in North Carolina, and there are no pari-mutuels.

College. North Carolina has six major colleges which play full schedules in nearly all intercollegiate athletics. Duke University at Durham, the University of North Carolina at Chapel Hill, North Carolina State University at Raleigh and Wake Forest University at Winston-Salem are all members of the Atlantic Coast Conference. Davidson College at Davidson & Appalachian State Univ. at Boone are members of the Southern Conference. East Carolina University in Greenville is independent. There are approximately 50 additional 4-yr. and junior colleges that participate in athletics on a smaller scale.

Hang gliding: The enthusiast of this new sport can watch the "daredevils" of today floating from the highest sand dune on the eastern coast (Jockey's Ridge at Nags Head) or from the lofty peaks of Grandfather Mountain at Linville, N.C. (The world Hang Gliding championships take place at Grandfather Mountain.)

 SHOPPING. Shopping facilities are numerous and varied in North Carolina. The larger cities and towns have good department stores and specialty shops. In various sections of the state there are shops and centers that offer fine opportunities to purchase handicrafts or textiles—two products for which the state is noted. There are many large suburban shopping centers and malls in the major cities.

Along main highways in the vicinity of Concord, Kannapolis, Charlotte, Burlington, Raleigh, Durham, Southern Pines and other towns, there are numerous shops which sell North Carolina textiles and apparel at reduced prices. The *Country Store* in Elkin is a retail outlet for woolen fabrics manufactured locally by Chatham Mills. *Fieldcrest Mills* operates an outlet store in the Eden area.

In addition to presenting the Craftsman's Fairs each year, the Guild oeprates 3 craft shops: *Allanstand,* 16 College St., and *Guild Crafts,* 930 Tunnel Rd., both in Asheville; the *Parkway Craft Center,* at the Moses Cone Memorial Park, Blowing Rock. When visiting the *Craftsman's Fair of the Southern Highlands,* which runs for five days in July at the New Civic Center, Asheville, you will be impressed by the variety of crafts offered for sale.

A *Flea Market* is held in Raleigh at the State Fairgrounds each Sat. & Sun. (except during the month of Oct.); also in Charlotte there is a Flea Market held the first weekend of each month at the Metrolina Fairgrounds. These are great places to shop, look or just pass the time of day.

A paperback for sale for folks planning a trip through the mountains, *Shopping 'Round the Mountains,* is a guide to antique and junk shops, mountain crafts, specialty shops of many kinds, factory outlets. Order through: "Shopping 'round the Mountains", P.O. Box 657, Skyland, N.C. 28776.

 WHAT TO DO WITH THE CHILDREN. Most North Carolina resorts cater to families and provide recreation for children. Among the many attractions which have a special appeal to youngsters, and are interesting to adults as well, are: The *USS North Carolina Battleship Memorial,* Wilmington. Visitors board a 35,000-ton super-dreadnaught, explore its hulk, and then see the ship's museum. The Memorial is open daily year round, and a sound-and-light spectacular tells its story nightly from mid-Apr. to Labor Day. *Tweetsie Railroad,* Blowing Rock, a 3-mi. scenic ride on a narrow-gauge railroad with steam locomotive. "Indian attacks" and a "train robbery" enliven the trip. There's a sky lift to an amusement park above the railroad station. Open daily June to Labor Day, Sat. and Sun. only from Labor Day to Oct. 31. There is a general admission charge; children under 5 free. *Gaddy's Goose Refuge.* US 52 nr. Ansonville. From 10,000 to 12,000 wild Canada geese can be fed by hand and photographed at close range between October and April. *Ghost Mountain Park,* Maggie Valley, US 19. Sky lift and incline railway to re-created Western town staffed by appropriately costumed "residents." "Gun fights" every hour. Stagecoach rides, blacksmith shop, soda shop, etc. Daily May to Oct. *Cherokee Indian Reservation,* US 19 and 441, at entrance to Great Smoky Mountains National Park. In summer there is the outdoor drama *Unto These Hills.* The Oconaluftee Indian Village, sponsored by the non-profit Cherokee Historical Association, displays how Cherokees lived 200 years ago. *Grandfather Mountain,* Linville. Open Apr. to Nov. 15. Mile-high swinging bridge offers visitors breathtaking view of Blue Ridge Mountains and valleys. Building at crest of mountain houses US Weather Bureau Station, snack bar, gift shop. Live bears ("Mildred" and her cubs) can be seen in their natural habitat in a beautiful, newly completed "environmental compound."

Land of Oz, atop Beech Mountain at Banner Elk. Ski lift, gondolas or buses to the top of the mountain where you can follow Dorothy's "Yellow Brick Road" and encounter the Cowardly Lion, Tin Man, Straw Man, the Munchkins and Witches. The road terminates at Emerald City with amphitheater for a show featuring the characters of Oz. Also, snack bar, gift shops and Oz Museum. Open daily mid-June to Labor day, Labor Day to late Oct., Sat. & Sun only. *Carowinds*—N.C.'s newest theme park. 161 acres which straddle the North and South Carolina boundary line. This is the home of "Thunder Road", an exciting double roller coaster. The park is easily reached by I-77 ten mi. S of Charlotte and offers fun for everyone with rides, shows and exhibits. *The North Carolina Zoological Park,* located at Purgatory Mountain, a few miles south of Asheboro, south off US 64 onto Cox Rd. The Zoo is in its first stages of construction. It is open to the public as a primitive recreational area for daytime use. Picnicking, hiking and walking nature trails. For further information contact North Carolina Zoological Authority, Raleigh 27603. *Santa's Land,* on US 19, Cherokee, is open daily. Admission charge. *Frontierland,* on US 19, Cherokee, is open daily May to Oct. 31. Admission charge. *Cyclorama of the Cherokee Indian,* on US 19, Cherokee, is open 9 to 9 daily June to Labor Day; 9 to 5 Labor Day to Nov. 1 and Apr. to June 1. Admission charge.; under 6 free. *Oconaluftee Indian Village,* on US 441, in Cherokee. Guided tours daily from May to mid-Oct. Closed rest of the year. Admission charge.

Daniel Boone Railroad Park, off I-85 in Hillsborough. Amusement park open wknds, noon to dark from June to Labor Day. Closed rest of the year. A 2½-mi. train ride is also featured.

Three new Marine Resource Centers located in Fort Fisher, Manteo, & Atlantic Beach offer oceanographic and marine exhibits which are of great interest to coastal visitors and vacationers.

INDIANS. North Carolina is the home of the Eastern Band of the Cherokee Indians. Their reservation—the Qualla Boundary—covers 56,000 acres adjoining the Great Smoky Mountains National Park and has some 4,500 Cherokee Indian residents. The reservation is organized and governed under a charter issued by the state of North Carolina in 1889, and it is subject to regulations established by the tribe and the U.S. Government. The Cherokees are both U.S. and North Carolina citizens and enjoy full voting privileges. The largest community on the reservation is Cherokee, which serves as administrative headquarters for the reservation, and it is a famous year-around tourist objective.

HOTELS AND MOTELS. Travelers in North Carolina will find accommodations in all price ranges. National chains, such as Quality Courts, Holiday Inns, Ramada Inns, Howard Johnsons, Hilton Inns and the "Economy" motels such as Scottish Inns and Econotels are located throughout the state. Television, telephones, heat and air conditioning are standard equipment. Except at a very few inexpensive hotels in downtown locations, free parking is standard.

Subject to change these inflation-prone days, the accommodations listed are according to price catagories. Please note these are *average prices.* Coastal and mountain resorts have seasonal rates. Categories and price ranges are: *Deluxe,* $50 up; *Expensive,* $36 to $50; *Moderate,* $26 to $35; *Inexpensive,* under $26. For a more complete explanation of hotel and motel categories see *Facts at Your Fingertips* at the front of this volume.

Asheboro

Holiday Inn. *Moderate.* Suites. Restaurant. Pool, golf privileges.

Sir Robert Motel. *Inexpensive.* Restaurant and pool. Open year round.

Asheville

Grove Park Inn. *Deluxe.* Macon Ave. To the massive native stone building of this distinctive resort completed in 1913, two wings have been added, one of them motel style and the other multistory with a ballroom. On the slopes of Beaucatcher Mountain, the Inn has terraced grounds overlooking golf course (guests may play), pool and tennis courts. Restaurants, gift shops.

Great Smokies Hilton. *Expensive.* 1 Hilton Inn Dr. Pool, golf course, indoor-outdoor tennis courts, restaurant and lounge. Seasonal rates.

Capri Motor Inn. *Moderate.* 29 Tunnel Rd. Pool, restaurant.

Downtowner Motor Inn. *Moderate.* 120 Patton Ave. A high-rise motor inn convenient to stores, restaurant, City Auditorium, hotels. Pool, dining.

Holiday Inn. *Moderate.* At three locations: 201 Tunnel Rd. (Central); US 70E, Rt. 2 (East); US 19 at I-40 (West). Pool, golf privileges.

Howard Johnson's Motor Lodge. *Moderate.* 190 Hendersonville Rd. Restaurant, pool and playground.

Quality Inn Intown. *Moderate.* 100 Tunnel Rd. Pleasant rms, many with a balcony, overlooking spacious grounds. Heated pool, play area. Restaurant nr.

Ramada Inn. *Moderate.* US 70 & 74, about 1 mi. E of center. Pool, dining rm., gift shop.

Sheraton Motor Inn. *Moderate.* Woodfin & Market Sts. Restaurant, pool, play area, golf privileges.

Atlantic Beach

Atlantis Lodge. *Expensive.* Secluded oceanfront location, 3 mi. from central resort area. Rms., kitchenettes.

Sea Hawk Motel. *Expensive.* Oceanfront. Attractive rms., many with refrigerators. Pool, beach. Golf privileges.

The Whaler Inn. *Expensive.* Ocean front. Comfortable accommodations for any month of the year. Good restaurant. Seasonal rates.

Holiday Inn. *Moderate.* On the ocean. Some rms. with kitchenettes. Restaurant. Seasonal rates.

John Yancey Motor Hotel. *Moderate.* On ocean, pool, restaurant, golf privileges. Seasonal rates.

Ramada Inn. *Moderate.* Salter Path Rd. Good accommodations, restaurant, recreation. Seasonal rates. Open year round.

Banner Elk

Holiday Inn. *Moderate.* All services, located near ski resort at Sugar Mtn.

NORTH CAROLINA

Belhaven

River Forest Manor. *Moderate.* Gracious old mansion, circa 1900; 600 E. Main St. Dining room features buffet smorgasbord. Antique furnished rooms. Sportsman's paradise. 25 rooms. Dock for boating enthusiasts.

Blowing Rock

Green Park Inn. *Deluxe.* A spacious white-frame resort hostelry adjoining the Blowing Rock Golf Course. Dining rm. Season Apr. to Nov. AP.

Hound Ears Lodge and Club. *Deluxe.* A picturesque resort with its own golf course and ski slopes. Dining rm. Rms in chalets and main club building. Year round. AP.

Appalachian Motel. *Moderate.* Attractive grounds with small lake. Year round. Restaurants nr.

Azalea Garden Motel. *Moderate.* Comfortable rms. on attractively landscaped grounds. Open mid-Mar. to end of Dec. Restaurant nr.

Hillwinds Inn. *Moderate.* Inviting, spacious rms. Barn Restaurant.

Yonahlossee Motel. *Moderate.* Restaurant, heated pool.

Boone

Cardinal Motel. *Moderate.* Restaurant. Pool. Year round.

Center for Continuing Education. *Moderate.* Enjoy spacious rooms, beautiful view and excellent food. On Appalachian State Univ. campus and run by University.

Holiday Inn. *Moderate.* Color TV. Restaurant, pool.

Plaza Motel. *Moderate.* Pool. Year round.

Ramada Inn. *Moderate.* Restaurant, pool, TV.

Brevard

Brevard Motor Lodge. *Moderate.* Pool. Year round.

Imperial Motor Lodge. *Moderate.* Pool. 26 rms. Year round.

Bryson City

Fryemont Inn. *Moderate.* Comfortable facilities, pool, restaurant. Season May through Oct.

Hemlock Inn. *Moderate.* A quiet, comfortable lodge with a secluded location off US 19. Restaurant. Season May to Nov.

Myers Court. *Moderate.* Well-maintained motel. Pool (heated), play area. Restaurant nr.

Bennett's Court. *Inexpensive.* Pool. Downtown location with restaurants nr.

Burlington

Best Western Burlington. *Moderate.* Great lounge with live entertainment. Heated pool, near factory outlet stores & Elon College.

Holiday Inn. *Moderate.* Pool, restaurant. Display room offering information and maps for famed outlet stores in area.

Ramada Inn. *Moderate.* Double-story motel. Restaurant, lounge with entertainment. Pool, play area.

Burnsville

Mtn. View Motel. *Inexpensive.* Open year round. Comfortable. Restaurant nearby.

Nu-Wray Inn. *Inexpensive.* On village square. A charming old inn with early American atmosphere. Meals served family-style are famous featuring Southern specialties (no Sun. night meal). Season Apr. through Dec.

Buxton

Cape Hatteras Court. *Moderate.* Pool. Restaurants and beach nr. Season Mar. to Dec. with lowered rates in spring and autumn. 15 cottages equipped for housekeeping.

Cape Pines Motel. *Moderate.* Year round. Restaurant nr.

Falcon Motel. *Moderate.* Hatteras Light opp. Spacious rms. Some kitchen units. Pool. Restaurant nr. Year-round.

Candler

Pisgah View Ranch. *Deluxe.* Picturesque rural setting. Family-style dining, tennis court, square dancing, horseback riding. Popular with families. American plan. Year round.

Canton

Pisgah Inn. *Moderate.* A mountaintop lodge in Pisgah National Forest. Hiking trails, spectacular views. Dining rm. Season May to Nov.

Carolina Beach

Accordion Motel. *Moderate.* On ocean near business section and amusement area. Restaurant nr. Season: Apr. to Nov. 30.

King's Motel. *Moderate.* Ocean front, kitchenettes, pool, restaurant.

Cashiers

High Hampton Inn and Country Club. *Deluxe.* A distinctive resort facility with its own golf course, lake, riding, stables, and tennis courts. Dining rm., gift shop. Special program for children in summer. Season May to Dec. FAP.

Oakmont Lodge Motel. *Moderate.* All-year golf and tennis available. Restaurant nearby.

Cedar Island

Driftwood Motel. *Moderate.* At Ocracoke Ferry landing on US 70 East. Dining room features local seafood.

Chapel Hill

Carolina Inn. *Moderate.* Lovely Inn owned and operated by University of North Carolina. Restaurant features excellent buffet.

Holiday Inn. *Moderate.* Attractive rms. with color TV, pool, restaurant.

Charlotte

Radisson Plaza Hotel. *Deluxe.* Two NCNB Plaza, in downtown Charlotte. A new hotel offering excellent facilities. Heated pool. Reflections Restaurant features gourmet foods.

Sheraton Center. *Expensive.* At new civic and convention center. McDowell St. Restaurants and shops.

Best Western. *Moderate.* At three locations: Charlotte Airport; Charlottetown Inn on Kings Dr.; Coliseum, Independence Blvd. Lounge, restaurants, pool.

Holiday Inn. *Moderate.* At four locations: 3815 N. Tryon; **Airport,** 2707 Little Rock Rd. & I-85; **Coliseum,** 2701 E. Independence Blvd.; **North,** I-85 at Sugar Creek Exit; Excellent facilities.

Howard Johnson Motor Lodge. *Moderate.* 118 Woodlawn Rd.; Restaurant, pool.

Manger Motor Inn. *Moderate.* 631 N. Tryon St. A three-story motor inn conveniently near business section. Pool, restaurant. Year round.

Ramada Inn. *Moderate.* At three locations: **Coliseum:** 3501 E. Independence Blvd. **North:** 4330 I-85N; I-77 S. at Clanton Rd. Rms. are tastefully decorated. Pool. Restaurant.

Cherokee

Boundary Tree Motor Court. *Moderate.* On US 441 between village and entrance to Great Smoky Mountains National Park. Operated by Cherokee Indians. Pool and dining rm., snack bar, play area. Some rms. with kitchenettes, in stone buildings.

Cool Waters Motel. *Moderate.* Kitchenettes, pool, tennis privileges.

Craig's Motel. *Moderate.* Comfortable. Restaurant, pool.

Ela Motor Court. *Moderate.* Inviting, well-maintained motel. Pool, play area. Fishing available. Open May to end of Oct.

Holiday Inn. *Moderate.* Suites. Color TV. Restaurant. Trout fishing. Seasonal rates. Open year-round.

Newfound Lodge. *Moderate.* Dining rm., gift shop. Season Apr. to Dec.

Dillsboro

Jarrett House. *Inexpensive.* A comfortable inn built in 1890, well known for its dining rm. featuring Southern specialties, season Apr. to Dec.

Durham

The Hilton Inn. *Moderate.* 8-story motor inn. Spacious rms. with color TV. Health Club.

Carolina-Duke Motor Inn. *Moderate.* 2517 Guess Rd. Large motor inn with comfortable rooms. New Steak & Prime rib restaurant.

Downtowner. *Moderate.* Large, five-story motel with well-appointed rms. Color TV. Restaurant. Pool.

Holiday Inn. *Moderate.* Restaurant and lounge. Near Duke Univ.

Howard Johnson's Motor Lodge. *Moderate.* Double-story motor inn. Rms. have balconies or patios. Color TV. Restaurant, pool.

Ramada Inn. *Moderate.* At two locations: I-85 & Guess Rd.; Downtown I-40 & Duke St.

Edenton
Coach House Inn. *Moderate.* US 17. Pool, restaurant.

Elizabeth City
Holiday Inn. *Moderate.* Pool, restaurant.

Fayetteville
Bordeaux Motor Inn/Convention Center. *Moderate.* Complete family recreation, bowling, skating rink, cinemas, restaurants. Shopping center.

Holiday Inn. *Moderate.* Pool, Copper Hearth Restaurant.

Quality Inn-Ambassador. *Moderate.* Pool, golf package available. Pancake House.

Quality Inn Americana. *Moderate.* Pool, playground, TV. Adj. restaurant.

Ramada Inn. *Moderate.* 4-story motor inn. Color TV. Suites. Pool heated, play area. Restaurant.

St. James Inn. *Moderate.* Large motor inn with attractive rms. Color TV. Restaurant. Oyster bar in lounge. Sauna. Ice available on each floor.

Heart of Fayetteville Motel. *Inexpensive.* Suites. Color TV, 2 pools (one indoor). Health Club (extra charge).

Flat Rock
Woodfields Inn. *Moderate.* Historic inn near Flat Rock Playhouse. 21 rooms. Period decor. Excellent dining room but only evening meal served. Season June through Oct.

Fontana Dam
Fontana Resort. *Moderate.* Lodge, cottages, riding, golf, planned recreation. Lodge open all year. Cottages: Apr. 1 to Thanksgiving wknd. Lower rates in winter season.

Franklin
Franklin Lodge. *Moderate.* Golfview Dr. Seasonal. Some units with kitchens. MAP.

Quality Inn Town. *Moderate.* On the Little Tennessee River. Nicely furnished rms. Color TV. Restaurant nr. Pool.

Goldsboro
Holiday Inn. *Moderate.* Restaurant and pool. Year round.

Perk's Motel. *Moderate.* W. Grantham St. at Hwy 70. Well-appointed rooms, excellent restaurant.

Days Inn. *Inexpensive.* Comfortable, well-maintained. Pool, restaurant.

Greensboro

Albert Pick Motor Inn. *Moderate.* I-40 at Rte. 68. Nr. airport. Restaurant, pool, golf privileges.

The Hilton Inn. *Moderate.* 830 W. Market St. 10-story motor inn. Elevators. Lovely rms. with color TV and balconies. Restaurant, lounge with entertainment, dancing.

Holiday Inn. *Moderate.* At two locations: Four Seasons: I-40 at High Point Rd.; Airport: I-40 & St. 68. Restaurant, pool.

Howard Johnson's Motor Lodge. *Moderate.* Three locations: North, I-85 at S. Elm St.; Coliseum, I-40 at High Point Rd. (heated pool, health club) & I-85 S. at Osborne Rd. TV, lounge.

Quality Inn Central. *Moderate.* At two locations: 1000 W. Market St. Double-story motel. Color TV. Some efficiencies. Restaurant. Pool; Oaks. 1118 Summit Ave. Motel situated on lovely landscaped grounds. Many rms. have refrigerators. Restaurant nr. Pool (heated), play area, putting green, shuffleboard.

Ramada Inn. *Moderate.* I-85 & S. Elm St. Nicely furnished rms. Restaurant. Pool (heated), play area.

Sheraton Motor Inn. *Moderate.* I-85 at S. Elm St. Pool, restaurant. Airport and Coliseum nr.

Smith's Ranch Motel. *Inexpensive.* 2210 Randleman Rd. Well-maintained motel. Color TV. Nr. restaurant. Pool, play area, shuffleboard.

South Gate Inn. *Inexpensive.* I-85 at US 220 S. Comfortable. Excellent restaurant.

Greenville

Holiday Inn. *Moderate.* Memorial Dr. Pool, tavern, excellent restaurant.

Ramada Inn. *Moderate.* Hwy. 264 Bypass. Near East Carolina Univ. & shopping center. Pool, live entertainment.

Harker's Island

Calico Jack's Inn. *Moderate.* Season mid-Mar. to mid-Dec. Dining rm., pool.

Cape Lookout Motel. *Inexpensive.* All year. Comfortable, and good restaurant.

Hatteras

Hatteras Marlin Motel. *Moderate.* Airconditioned, TV. Pool. Kitchenettes. Open year-round. Near charter boat docks.

Sea Gull Motel. *Moderate.* Nr. beach. Season March to Dec. Restaurant nearby.

Henderson

Holiday Inn. *Moderate.* Near Kerr Lake. Rest., color TV, lounge, entertainment. Pool (heated).

Hendersonville

Dutch Inn. *Moderate.* Pool and restaurant. Year round.

Holiday Inn. *Moderate.* I-26 & US 64 E. Suites. Restaurant.

Ramada Inn. *Moderate.* I-26 & US 64 E. Pool, lounge, entertainment.

Briarwood Motel. *Inexpensive.* 1510 Greenville Hwy. Pool, picnic ground. Restaurant nr. Kitchenettes.

Hickory

Holiday Inn. *Moderate.* Centrally located with pool, coffee shop and restaurant.

Howard Johnson's Motor Lodge. *Moderate.* Inviting rms., lounge, restaurant.

Sheraton Motor Inn. *Moderate.* Heated pool, lounge, restaurant.

Hickory Motor Lodge. *Inexpensive.* Comfortable facilities. Pool, TV.

Mull's Motel. *Inexpensive.* Excellent restaurant. Pool.

Highlands

Lee's Inn. *Deluxe.* A well-known N.C. resort. American plan. Dining rm. and pool, club lounge. Golf privileges. Inn and motel rms. Highest mountain inn in eastern America. Season May to Nov.

Skyline Lodge & Village. *Expensive.* Year-round. Restaurant, pool, golf & tennis.

High Point

Holiday Inn. *Moderate.* At two locations: W. Green Dr. Pool and dining rm. Year round; **Downtown.** 236 S. Main St. Convenient to business section. Good restaurant.

Howard Johnson's Motor Lodge. *Moderate.* Lounge, color TV.

Hillsborough

Colonial Inn. *Inexpensive.* A small, pleasant inn built in 1759. Dining room features good Southern foods; ham, chicken, home-made breads.

Daniel Boone Inn & Campground. *Inexpensive.* Cafeteria, playground, antique music museum, "village" shops, ice-skating rink.

Jacksonville

Holiday Inn. *Moderate.* 701 Marine Blvd. Pool, lounge, restaurant.

Horne's Motor Lodge. *Moderate.* Double-story motel. Restaurant. Pool, play area.

Howard Johnson's Motor Lodge. US 17 N. *Moderate.* Restaurant & pool. Year round.

Red Carpet Inn. *Moderate.* 246 Wilmington Hwy. Restaurant, pool.

Thunderbird Inn. *Moderate.* Pool, play area. restaurant.

Master Hosts Town House. *Moderate.* Hwy. 17 N. Nicely furnished rms. Good restaurant. Pool.

Kill Devil Hills
(also see **Nags Head**)

The Sea Ranch. *Expensive.* On the ocean. Spacious, attractive rms. Efficiencies. Restaurant. Beach, pool (indoor and outdoor), surf fishing, enclosed tennis courts. MAP, AP available.

Tan-a-Rama Motel. *Expensive.* Delightful efficiency apts., oceanfront.

Cavalier Motor Court. *Moderate.* On ocean, nr. Wright Brothers National Memorial. Pool, play area. Housekeeping cottages and rms. with kitchenettes. Year round.

John Yancey Motor Hotel. *Moderate.* Oceanfront resort with pool. Dining rm., club lounge.

Kinston

Holiday Inn. *Moderate.* Restaurant. Pool.

Kinstonian Motel. *Inexpensive.* Pool, restaurant; convention/meeting facilities.

Laurinburg

Holiday Inn. *Moderate.* Restaurant, pool, play area.

Scotland Inn. *Moderate.* Golf and tennis privileges. Pool and restaurant.

Lexington

Holiday Inn. *Moderate.* Pool, restaurant.

Linville

Eseeola Lodge. *Deluxe.* Rustic 1892 inn with modern facilities. Dining room, pool, golf, riding. AP. Season early May to mid-Oct.

Pixie Motel. *Inexpensive.* TV, restaurant.

Little Switzerland

The Big Lynn Lodge. *Moderate.* Cottages & motel. Season May through Oct. MAP available.

The Chalet Motor Lodge. *Moderate.* Swiss-style chalet, lovely rooms, tennis, golf, pool, restaurant, lounge.

Lumberton

Holiday Inn. *Moderate.* US 301-A, I-95 & Rte. 211. Restaurant, pool, color TV.

Howard Johnson's Motor Lodge. *Moderate.* Double-decker motor inn. Rms. have private balconies or patios. Restaurant. Pool.

Ramada Inn. *Moderate.* Lighted tennis courts, pool, restaurant, lounge.

Red Carpet Inn Best Western. *Inexpensive.* Inviting rms. Restaurant, pool.

Maggie Valley

Cataloochee Ranch. *Expensive.* Family ranch. Am. plan. Accommodations for 40 guests. Riding, tennis, fishing, swimming.

Maggie Valley Country Club & Motor Lodges. *Expensive.* Year-round. Golf, pool, lounge, restaurant. Beautiful setting.

Holiday Inn. *Moderate.* Seasonal rates. Nr. ski slopes & tourist attractions. Restaurant.

Manteo

Duke of Dare Motor Lodge. *Moderate.* Pool, year round.

Manteo Motel-Elizabethan Manor. *Moderate.* Comfortable motel. Restaurant, pool, spacious grounds.

Morehead City

Buccaneer Motor Lodge. *Moderate.* Pool and restaurant. Year round.

Morehead Motor Inn. *Moderate.* Pool. Year round.

Nags Head
(also see **Kill Devil Hills**)

Cabana East. *Expensive.* Efficiencies, suites, Ocean and pool swimming.

Sea Oatel. *Expensive.* Oceanfront, pool, restaurant.

Carolinian Motor Hotel. *Moderate.* Oceanfront, pool, restaurant, lounge. Year round. Children's program in summer.

Holiday Inn. *Moderate.* On the ocean. Some kitchenettes. Restaurant, lounge with entertainment. Seasonal rates.

New Bern

Holiday Inn. *Moderate.* Restaurant, pool, year round.

Quality Inn Palace. *Moderate.* Pool, play area, restaurant.

Ramada Inn. *Moderate.* Overlooking Neuse River. Rms. are nicely decorated. Color TV. Restaurant. Pool, play area.

Ocracoke

Harborside Motel. *Moderate.* Pleasant rms., some with kitchens, overlook the harbor. Dock & boat ramp available. Season Easter to Thanksgiving.

The Island Inn. *Moderate.* On Silver Lake harbor, in village. Dining rm. Jeeps, guides, and boats for hunters and fishermen. Year round.

Pony Island Motel. *Moderate.* Restaurant. Year round.

Pinehurst

Foxfire Golf & Country Club. *Deluxe.* Year round, villas, tennis, Pool heated. MAP.

Pine Crest Inn. *Expensive.* Restaurant, putting green, golf, bar, MAP.

Pinehurst Hotel. *Expensive.* Distinguished resort. Six championship golf courses, 24 tennis courts. Excellent dining room.

Raleigh

Mission Valley Inn. *Moderate.* Avent Ferry Rd. & Western Blvd. At shopping center. Excellent restaurant.

Hilton Inn. *Moderate.* 1701 Hillsborough St. nr. State University. Pool, restaurant, club room. Live entertainment.

Holiday Inn. *Moderate.* At two locations: **North:** On US 1, 401 **Downtown:** 320 Hillsborough St. Color TV. Restaurant. Pool.

Howard Johnson's Motor Lodge. *Moderate.* 2 locations: US 1, 401, and on Hwy. 70 W. at Crabtree Valley. Spacious grounds, restaurant, pool, play area.

Plantation Inn. *Moderate.* US 1 N. Restaurant, putting green, pool, fishing lake.

Ranch Motel. *Moderate.* US 70 W. Restaurant, color TV, pool. Near large shopping center.

Royal Villa. *Moderate.* US 70 W. Pool, dining, entertainment. Mexican decor.

Sheraton Motor Inn. *Moderate.* 2 Locations: US 70 W & Creedmore Rd. at Crabtree Valley Mall; US 1 N. Good restaurants and entertainment.

Velvet Cloak. *Moderate.* 1505 Hillsborough St. Year-round pool, restaurant, club room.

Research Triangle Park

Governors Inn. *Moderate.* Restaurant, club room, pool. Live entertainment.

Roanoke Rapids

Holiday Inn. *Moderate.* Color TV. Restaurant, pool, play area.

Quality Inn. *Moderate.* Restaurant, play area, pool.

Roaring Gap

High Meadows Inn. *Moderate.* Year round. Restaurant, pool, golf, ski slope.

Robbinsville

Snowbird Mountain Lodge. *Deluxe.* Mountaintop lodge, season late May to Nov. Excellent cuisine. No children under 12. AP.

Rocky Mount

Carleton House. *Moderate.* 215 N. Church St. Dining rm.

Holiday Inn. *Moderate.* 2 locations: I-95 N. and **Downtown:** 425 N. Church St. Pool, restaurant. Year round.

Howard Johnson's Motor Lodge. *Moderate.* Restaurant, pool, play area, putting green.

Ramada Inn. *Moderate.* Nicely decorated rms. Restaurant. Pool (heated), play area

Days Inn. *Inexpensive.* Color TV, pool, play area, gift shop. Tasty World restaurant.

Salisbury

Howard Johnson's Motor Lodge. *Moderate.* Pool, restaurant.

Holiday Inn. *Inexpensive.* Restaurant & pool.

Sanford

Holiday Inn. *Moderate.* Double-story motor inn. Suites. Restaurant, pool, golf privileges.

Palomino Motel. *Inexpensive.* Restaurant. Year round.

Sapphire

Fairfield Inn. *Expensive.* Old mountain inn, cottages also available. Good dining room.

Sea Level

Sea Level Inn. *Moderate.* Attractive setting. Dining rm., boat docks. Year round.

Smithfield

Holiday Inn. *Moderate.* Restaurant. Pool, play area.

Howard Johnson's Motor Lodge. *Moderate.* Nicely furnished rms. Restaurant. Pool, play area.

Days Inn. *Inexpensive.* Color TV, pool, play area, gift shop. Tasty World restaurant.

Southern Pines

Mid Pines Club. *Deluxe.* Resort facility with 18-hole golf course. Dining rm. Rms. in main building and Golftel. Year round. FAP.

Pine Needles Lodges and Country Club. *Deluxe.* Resort with 18-hole golf course, pool, dining rm. Year round. AP.

Holiday Inn. *Moderate.* Restaurant, pool, golf privileges. Year round.

Howard Johnson's Motor Lodge. *Moderate.* Pool, restaurant, putting green, golf privileges. Year round.

Sheraton Motor Inn. *Moderate.* Pool, restaurant, club room.

Southport
Sea Captain Motor Lodge. *Moderate.* Kitchenettes, pool, restaurant.

Riverside Motel. *Inexpensive.* Small. Restaurant nr.

Topsail Beach
Breezeway Motel. *Moderate.* Channel Blvd. On the inlet, restaurant, pool, lounge and pier.

The Jolly Roger Motel. *Moderate.* Oceanfront, rms., efficiencies. Year round.

Sea Vista Motel. *Moderate.* Ocean front, TV, efficiency apts., rooms. Nearby restaurant.

The Topsail Motel. *Moderate.* Rm., apts., cottages. Oceanfront.

Washington
Holiday Inn. *Moderate.* Color TV. Restaurant. Pool.

Washington Motel. *Moderate.* Restaurant, pool. Year round. Golf privileges.

Waynesville
Waynesville Country Club Inn. *Deluxe.* Resort with 18-hole golf course. Dining rm. Seasonal rates.

Heath Lodge. *Moderate.* 900 Dolan Rd. Season late May through late Oct. Rustic mountain inn. Excellent dining.

Queen's Farm. *Moderate.* Dude ranch. Season May to Sept.

Oak Park Motor Inn. *Inexpensive.* Spacious, nicely furnished rms. Restaurant.

Williamston
Holiday Inn. *Moderate.* Color TV in very pleasant rms. Restaurant, pool, kennels.

Best Western–Ross Motel. *Moderate.* Comfortable accommodations. Restaurant. Pool with service at poolside.

Wilmington
Best Western Carolinian. *Moderate.* Pool. Year round.

Holiday Inn. *Moderate.* Large motor inn. Restaurant. Pool heated, kennel.

Ramada Inn. *Moderate.* Double-story motor inn with nicely furnished rms. Restaurant, lounge with dancing and entertainment. Pool heated, play area.

Wilmington Hilton Inn. *Moderate.* Opp. battleship *USS Carolina.* Pool, restaurant. Convenient to Historic homes and restored waterfront area.

Americano Motel. *Inexpensive.* Pleasant accommodations. Color TV. Restaurant nr. Pool.

El Berta Motel. *Inexpensive.* Restaurant, pool. Year round.

Wilson

Heart of Wilson. *Moderate.* Attractive, double-story motel. Restaurant, pool.

Holiday Inn. *Moderate.* Restaurant, pool.

Winston-Salem

Hyatt House. *Deluxe.* 300 W. 5th St. Downtown at Convention center. Ice skating, pool, restaurant, lounge.

Downtowner. *Moderate.* Large motel. Suites. Color TV. Restaurant, pool.

Hilton Inn. *Moderate.* Restaurant, pool, bar.

Holiday Inn. *Moderate.* At three locations: **Central:** 127 S. Cherry St.; **West:** Silas Creek Pkwy. & I-40.; **North:** N. Cherry-Marshall Expwy. Dining rm., pool.

Howard Johnson's Motor Lodge. *Moderate.* Pool, restaurant, nr. shopping center.

Sheraton Motor Inn. *Moderate.* Pool, bar, cafeteria.

Tanglewood Motor Lodge. *Moderate.* Hwy. 158 W. off I-40. Manor House and motel accommodations. Golf, riding, pool. Restaurant, snack bars.

Wrightsville Beach

Blockade Runner Hotel. *Expensive.* Oceanfront. Restaurant, pool, play area, bar.

Holiday Inn. *Expensive.* On the Atlantic Ocean. Very nice rms. with balconies. Restaurant. Beach. Pool heated, shuffleboard. Boats available.

Waterway Motor Lodge. *Moderate.* Pool, restaurants nr., morning coffee.

 DINING OUT. The choice of good places to eat in North Carolina is extremely varied, including restaurants specializing in international cuisine, in several of the larger cities. Local specialties in Eastern North Carolina and a number of Piedmont localities include barbecued pork and chicken, fresh seafood, fried chicken and country ham. Hush puppies, made from corn meal batter and fried in deep fat, almost always accompany both fish and barbecue here. Grits is another Southern specialty widely served in North Carolina, usually with breakfast. There is also a wide selection of places which feature steaks and roast prime ribs of beef. The price range for restaurant meals in North Carolina is somewhat lower than in metropolitan areas of the Northeast. Restaurants are listed according to price category. Categories and ranges for a complete evening meal are as follows: *Moderate:* $6-$10; *Expensive:* $11 and up. For a more complete explanation of restaurant categories see *Facts at Your Fingertips* at the front of this volume.

Asheville

Weaverville Milling Company. *Expensive.* A few mi. N. of Asheville on Hwy. 19-23. A 1900's grist mill presents a rustic atmosphere for its patrons enjoying live entertainment and gourmet buffet dinners. Open nightly except Mon. All ABC permits. Reservations.

Three Brothers Restaurant. *Moderate.* 183 Haywood St. Good home cooked foods, steaks, seafood. Wine list. Brown bagging permitted.

Etowah Valley Golf Club. *Moderate.* On US 64 at Etowah between Hendersonville & Brevard. Dinner only. Elegance in dining.

Jareds. *Expensive.* Reservations suggested. Nationally known French restaurant. Crepes a specialty.

Mountaineer Steak House. *Moderate.* 148 Tunnel Rd. Daily 4 P.M. to midnight, specializing in steaks, rib roasts and beef kabob.

Bavarian Cellar. *Moderate.* Tunnel Rd. shopping center. German & Italian dinners. Continental sandwiches.

Beaufort

Clawson's Emporium Cookery & Saloon. *Moderate.* Good food served in 1890's atmosphere.

Belhaven

River Forest Manor. *Moderate.* Famous for its three-tiered buffet "groaning board." Great atmosphere.

Blowing Rock

The Farm House. *Moderate.* Overlooks the John's River Gorge. Features prime rib, country ham and served by college students who also "serve up" night-club entertainment. Open daily June to early autumn.

Boone

Daniel Boone Inn. *Moderate.* Family style restaurant offering country style steak, chicken, ham and biscuits.

Marvin's Garden Restaurant. *Moderate.* Excellent natural foods, unique garden atmosphere.

Burnsville

The Nu-Wray Inn. *Moderate.* This old inn on Burnsville's Town Square is one of North Carolina's best known landmarks. Food served family style. No menus. Beef, chicken and hickory smoked ham presented in this "Southern-board" style. Breakfast, lunch, dinner. Season Apr. through Dec.

Calabash

There are 20 restaurants in this tiny fishing village. All are excellent and all are moderately priced.

Chapel Hill

Slug's At The Pines. *Expensive.* Charcoal steaks and Imperial crab are specialties.

Carolina Coffee Shop. *Moderate.* E. Franklin St. 1922 Chapel Hill landmark. Enjoy informal dining and excellent food. Closed Mondays.

The Peddler Steak House. *Moderate.* Good steaks and salad bar. Wine; brown-bagging permitted.

Villa Teo. *Moderate.* International delicacies. Dinner. Brunch served Sundays. Reservations advised.

Charlotte

Epicurean. *Expensive.* 1324 East Blvd. Steaks, seafood are specialties featured in a very attractive setting. Beer & wine. Closed Sun. Chef-owned.

Slug's Tower Suite. *Expensive.* Jefferson First Union Towers. Enjoy a magnificent view from the top of the Towers and a delectable meal.

Open Kitchen. *Moderate.* 1318 W. Morehead St. International cuisine.

Slug's Rib. *Moderate.* 3911 E. Independence Blvd. Dinner only. Closed Sun. "The Residence of Prime Ribs."

Victoria Station. *Moderate.* Prime ribs and potable spirits. Enjoy good food in authentic railroad cars.

Gus's Original Forty-Niner. *Moderate.* Hwy. 49 E. nr. UNC at Charlotte. Lunch & dinner. American & Italian.

Slug's Choice. *Moderate.* Southpark Shopping Center. Excellent beef, salad bar.

Boar's Head Restaurant. *Moderate.* 3101 N. Sharon Amity Rd. Salad bar, beef a specialty. Delightful lounge.

Dillsboro

Jarrett House. *Moderate.* A comfortable old inn which has been in operation for more than 70 years. Country ham and fried chicken with fresh vegetables and hot biscuits are regional specialties found here.

Durham

Mr. Harvey's Bistro. *Expensive.* Excellent French cuisine; also other Continental dishes.

Olde House Restaurant. *Expensive.* Continental & American. Good wine list. Delightful setting.

Saddle & Fox. *Expensive.* A steak house and oyster bar with supper club atmosphere. Children's portions. Try the shore dinner for two.

Bullock's Bar-b-cue. *Moderate.* This is a specialty of the area. Worth trying.

Darryl's 1890. *Moderate.* Hwy. 15-501 halfway between Durham & Chapel Hill. Wonderful atmosphere, lunch and dinner. Excellent food.

Hartman's Steak House. *Moderate.* Dinner only. Specialty is steak, but other delicious food is available. Closed Sun.

The Ivy Room Restaurant and Delicatessen. *Moderate.* Good food for whole family.

Fayetteville

Capt. Jim's Seafood Shack. *Moderate.* 2103 Owen Dr. Worth trying.

Flat Rock

Woodfields Inn. *Moderate.* Oldest continuously operated inn in the state. Southern fare, though beef Stroganoff & home-grown vegetables a specialty. Dinner only.

Goldsboro

Griffin's Barbecue. *Moderate.* 806 S. George St. Specializes in barbecued pork and chicken.

Greensboro

Brass Gate Restaurant-Holiday Inn Four Seasons. *Moderate.* Excellent food.

Darryl's 1808. *Moderate.* 2102 N. Church St. Lunch & dinner. Good sandwiches, steaks, pizzas in period restaurant.

Le Chateau. *Moderate.* Two locations: Friendly Shopping Center, 508 Teague St. Steaks cut to your desired thickness. Good salad bar.

The Pepper Mill. *Moderate.* I-40 at Guilford-Jamestown Rd. Varied menu, good food.

Greenville

Darryl's. *Moderate.* Good Italian and American dishes served in a delightful atmosphere.

The Gathering Place. *Moderate.* Dickenson Ave. Fine dining. Reservations requested.

Hickory

Mull's Restaurant. *Moderate.* Hickory bypass. A good variety of well-prepared foods in pleasant atmosphere.

High Point

Plank Road Depot. *Expensive.* Victorian room in this renovated railroad depot serves roast beef only. Reservations suggested. More informal and less expensive dining in two other dining areas.

Top of the Mart. *Moderate.* Good food. Great view.

Highlands

Highlander Restaurant. *Moderate.* Simple, tasty, homemade foods.

Hillsborough

The Colonial Inn. *Moderate.* 1759 Inn serving excellent Southern fare.

Kenansville

Country Squire. *Moderate.* Relaxing early American atmosphere. Menu varied, but beef is a specialty.

Kinston

King's Restaurant. *Moderate.* Barbecue is the specialty but the menu is varied.

Maggie Valley

Geisha Gardens. *Expensive.* Japanese Restaurant & Tea Room. Evenings by advance reservations only.

Manteo

Duchess of Dare Restaurant. *Moderate.* Family-type restaurant. Varied menu.

Marion

Crossbow International. *Moderate.* Restaurant is known statewide. A gourmet's delight. International cuisine.

Morehead City

Captain Bill's Waterfront Restaurant. *Moderate.* Seafood and steaks and "Down East" lemon pie are the specialties. Children's portions. Overlooks fishing fleet.

Mrs. Willis' Restaurant. *Moderate.* Just what the reader imagines, home cooked food. Very good.

Sanitary Fish Market and Restaurant. *Moderate.* Seafood is the specialty but menu is varied. Closed mid-Dec. to Jan.

Mount Airy

Ray's Star-Lite Restaurant. *Moderate.* The food here is consistently good. Buffet luncheon.

Nags Head—Kill Devil Hills

A Restaurant by George. *Expensive.* Great atmosphere. Excellent food.

Seafare Restaurant. *Expensive.* American cuisine featuring She Crab Soup and lemon chess pie. Dinner. Entertainment Sat. nights.

Dareolina Cove. *Moderate.* A popular restaurant with a varied menu including good seafood and steaks. Adjoins the Sea Oatel Motor Lodge.

Evans Crab House. *Moderate.* Located in Kill Devil Hills. Its crab dishes help make it one of the area's excellent restaurants.

Owen's Restaurant. *Moderate.* In Nags Head, good food in pleasant surroundings.

Spencer's Sea Food Safari. *Moderate.* Good coastal eating. Located in Nags Head. Highlights nautical decor and strawberry pie.

New Bern

Harvey Mansion Restaurant. *Moderate.* Features fresh seafood and other favorites. Enjoy delightful atmosphere of this restored 200-yr.-old mansion.

Henderson House. *Moderate.* Old, historic inn. Ever tried peanut soup? A specialty for lunch here. Lunch served Tues. through Sat. Dinner, Fri. & Sat.

Raleigh

The Angus Barn. *Expensive.* Raleigh-Durham Hwy. (US 70). Unique atmosphere and fine food in a spacious big red barn; collection of antiques and old farm tools. Steaks and rare prime ribs of beef are specialties. Open every night, reservations recommended.

The Charter Room. *Expensive.* Located in Velvet Cloak Inn. Reservations required. Not for those in a hurry. A dinner here is meant to be an experience.

Swains Charcoal Steak House. *Expensive.* US 64 E. Good steak is the specialty. Beer and wine served.

Atlanta Station. *Moderate.* Excellent steaks and salad bar. Restaurant is located in converted railroad depot. Very attractive.

Balentine's. *Moderate.* 410 Oberlin Rd. Specializing in Southern food. Attractive cafeteria located in Cameron Village Shopping Center.

Colonnade Restaurant. *Moderate.* Located in Ramada Inn-Crabtree. Fresh trout is a gourmet's treat. Crêpes also featured.

Darryl's 1840 Restaurant. *Moderate.* Falls of Neuse Rd., **Darryl's 1849 Restaurant,** US 70 W., and **Darryl's 1906 Restaurant,** 1906 Hillsborough St. Fascinating decor and excellent food.

Don Murray's Barbecue. *Moderate.* Pork & chicken barbecue, brunswick stew & hushpuppies.

Joel Lane Restaurant. *Moderate.* Located in Mission Valley Inn. Very good food. Lovely setting.

Neptune's Galley. *Moderate.* Good seafood; steamed oysters in season.

Ragamuffins. *Moderate.* In North Hills Mall. Try the cauliflower soup, good salads & crêpes, all accompanied with muffins. Lunch and dinner menus.

Top of the Tower Restaurant. *Moderate.* In Holiday Inn-Downtown. Great view and good food.

Villa Capri. *Moderate.* 3622 Wade Ave. in Ridgewood Shopping Center. Good Italian cuisine.

Rocky Mount
Buck Overton's Barbecue. *Moderate.* Good pork barbecue.

Rosman
Red Lion Inn. *Moderate.* Reservations. Dinner only. Specialties: steaks, trout, homemade desserts. Season mid-Mar. to mid-Dec.

Shatley Springs
Shatley Springs. *Moderate.* Family-style meals. Features chicken & homemade breads. Seasonal.

Smithfield-Selma
French Country Inn. *Expensive.* Reservations only. Old colonial home is setting for excellent French cuisine. Located in small town of Selma.

Southern Pines—Pinehurst
Pine Crest Inn. *Moderate.* Dogwood Rd., Pinehurst. Features special dinner every night, also seafood, prime beef.

Spruce Pines
Beam's Restaurant. *Moderate.* Reservations. Patrons from far away come to Beam's to enjoy its Cantonese delicacies.

Tryon
Pine Crest Inn. *Moderate.* Attractive decor and atmosphere, delicious food. Open all year. Near business section of Tryon.

Mimosa Inn. *Moderate.* The dining room of this all-year resort inn is a charming setting, and the food is excellent. Unusual vegetable dishes and hot breads.

Waynesville
Heath Lodge. *Moderate.* Reservations required if not guest of Lodge. Lazy-susan tables laden with southern-style foods. Season May to Oct.

Wilmington And
Wrightsville Beach

The Bridge Tender. *Expensive.* At Intracoastal Waterway drawbridge. On the waterway. Excellent seafood and steaks.

The Gray Gables. *Expensive.* On the Waterway. Airlie Rd. Stuffed flounder a specialty.

King Neptune. *Expensive.* One of Wrightsville Beach's most well-known seafood restaurants. Good dining.

Cortley's Old Fashioned Deli. *Moderate.* 316 Nutt St. in Cotton Exchange, Wilmington. Located in newly restored area of Old Wilmington waterfront.

The Marina. *Moderate.* Seafood is the specialty and the restaurant has a picturesque location adjacent to marina on Intracoastal Waterway.

The Pepper Mill. *Moderate.* On the Plaza at Wrightsville Beach. Delicious food. Try the Crab Louis.

Stemmerman's Grocery. *Moderate.* Front & Orange Sts., Wilmington. Upstairs and Downstairs restaurants. Sandwiches to steaks.

Tuesday's. *Moderate.* Period restaurant. Brunch, lunch and dinner. Enjoyable atmosphere and food.

Winston-Salem

Canterbury Inn. *Expensive.* Corner of Country Club and Peace Haven Rds. Mon.-Sat. Minimum charge on Fri. & Sat. Excellent food, features Prime Rib and outstanding salad bar.

Berry's Restaurant. *Moderate.* Small and intimate. Specialties are crepes. Good wine list.

Darryl's 1913 Restaurant. *Moderate.* Brownsboro Rd. Food always good. Atmosphere fantastic.

Salem Tavern. *Moderate.* Old Salem. Specialty food served in an early 19th-century atmosphere.

Staley's Charcoal Steak House. *Moderate.* Steaks are the specialty. A variety of fish (flounder and trout) is also recommended. Chef-owned.

Valentino Restaurant. *Moderate.* Gourmet Italian cuisine. Very good.

Zevely House 1815. *Moderate.* Corner of 4th & Summit Sts. American & European dishes served in authentically restored oldest house in Winston-Salem. Casual atmosphere, excellent food.

SOUTH CAROLINA

Cradle of the Confederacy

BY
GEORGE DREHER

George Dreher was director of the South Carolina Travel Council for eight years, and is presently with the Carolina Motor Club AAA. Mr. Dreher is a resident of Columbia, South Carolina, and has traveled extensively throughout the South.

From the foothills of the Blue Ridge Mountains in the Up Country, to the sandhills of the Midlands, and on to the sparkling white sand beaches of the Low Country—South Carolina has a wide diversity of attractions to match the tastes of almost any visitor. Her history is preserved for all to see, but along with historic sites there are contemporary attractions, many designed for family entertainment.

Since the early 1960's South Carolina has been a leader of industrial expansion in the Southeast. The textile industry leads all others in the state and has created thousands of new jobs. Precision tool making, chemicals, and metal-working also thrive here.

But industrial expansion has not diminished the tradition most honored in South Carolina—Southern hospitality. The visitor's first evidence of this noted hospitality could well be found while stopping at Carowinds theme park, shared by North and South Carolina.

Just 13 miles north of Rock Hill and 10 miles south of Charlotte, North Carolina, on I-77, Carowinds re-creates the culture and heritage of the Carolinas. It holds seven major historical areas, a narrow-gauge

SOUTH CAROLINA

railroad which encircles the park, a modernistic monorail, and over a hundred rides. Camping is available.

At Rock Hill the Catawba Indian tribes occupied 144,000 acres from 1652-1840, and the York County Historical Commission has placed eleven markers in the area. A major recreation center in Rock Hill is Joslin Park, named for A. O. Joslin of Providence, R.I., who established the world's largest bleachery here. Glencairn Gardens is a gift from Dr. Bigger, who started Glencairn as a hobby in a thickly wooded deer park next to his home. It reaches its peak in April, when thousands of red, white, and pink azaleas bloom. The nature museum, US. 21 and Mt. Gallant Rd., contains numerous lifelike wild animals from various countries and small live animals and birds. The restored Lansford Canal is a new attraction. Also here are Fort Mill, headquarters for Springs Cotton Mills, and Confederate Park.

From Rock Hill it is only a short drive west over State 161 to sites which have been termed "turning points" in the Revolutionary War—Kings Mountain and Cowpens. Kings Mountain National Military Park comprises 6 square miles and includes the battlefield and monuments, a museum with interesting artifacts and a diorama of the battle. Adjoining Kings Mountain State Park (6,141 acres) are family campgrounds and two summer youth camps. A dramatic battle was fought here on October 7, 1780, when outnumbered, ill-trained colonists conquered British troops to take the summit. The Visitor Center exhibits battle routes of the opposing forces, plus a scenic diorama.

A breechloading Ferguson rifle is also on display at the Center—invented by, and named after, the British major who fought and lost at Kings Mountain. Summers, there are "living history" demonstrations.

Leaving Kings Mountain, join State 216, turn left to I-85, and left again to Blacksburg. This quiet little town has new life these days, brought about by ultramodern textile mills. One, a Deering Milliken enterprise, was designed by Swiss engineers with watchmaker accuracy. An older established firm, a Chicago-owned mattress maker, is Burton-Dixie Corporation, at US 29 and State 5. The townspeople have conducted a clean-up campaign since the new mills were built—a vast change from when the place was called Stark's Folly because pioneers thought the land worthless.

Vineyards are another new commercial development. Growers sell Concord and Fredonia grapes through a cooperative. Not long ago these rolling hills were cotton fields.

A few miles southeast lies Cherokee Falls, formerly a popular Carolina watering spa. Cherokee Indians lived in these parts—farmers plowing their fields often find arrowheads and, sometimes, small pieces of pottery. The area has deposits of monazite, used in gas lamps, and thorium; limestone deposits are the best in the state, and gold prospecting has been resumed by Canadian interests near Smyrna.

Now drive to Gaffney on Routes I-85, US 29, State 18, 150 and County 82. It is a good idea to carry tire chains in upper South Carolina if you are traveling December through March, as snowfalls have increased in recent years. Late afternoon rain squalls prevail August through September. During spring, the woods blossom with dogwood and the Judas tree, with yellow jessamine, Carolina's state flower, and later, cowslips, wild azalea, violets of many kinds and woodbine. Thousands of peach blossoms cover the countryside like a delicate pink cloud. South Carolina is the largest peach producer in the South, and over half the state's peaches are grown within a 50-mile radius of Gaffney stretching toward the southwest.

This is old Cherokee and Creek Indian tribal country and was named for Captain Michael Gaffney, the first Irish settler. Besides being a great peach growing area, Gaffney is a pioneer textile manufacturing center. Limestone College, located here, is one of the oldest senior colleges for women in the South. In former days it was the Limestone Hotel, a watering spa for the horse-racing set from Charleston who spent summers here.

A visit to Sunny Slope Farms peach sheds near Gaffney, is pleasant in summer. Owned by the Ciggiano family, well known for their orchards in Italy, the farm handles 10,000 bushels of peaches a day from a 1,500-acre orchard.

Cowpens National Battlefield Site, 11 miles southwest on US 29 to junction State 110, marks a victorious battle over the British in 1781. Cowpens was an iron ore district, and a foundry produced pots, pans, skillets and wash tubs. Many of these fat-bellied tubs now dot the countryside sprouting geraniums, ferns, and flowers.

On I-85, having departed either Gaffney or Cowpens National Battlefield site, drive west toward Spartanburg. (There's a rest area seven miles ahead but no facilities.) The railroad overpass is the Clinchfield, an old and profitable coal-carrying line bringing tons of fuel daily from West Virginia, Tennessee and Pennsylvania mines to the atomic energy plant at Aiken.

You can find good local eating at numerous fish camps along this route. Most are open on weekends and specialize in catfish, catfish stew, some with trout, and hush puppies. Generally you are served all you can eat for a nominal sum. Bring your own liquor is the rule, although a few camps may have beer. Local people can steer you to the best fish camps down by the rivers, often via unpaved roads, which are worth negotiating for the whopping servings and warm hospitality.

Spartanburg, on I-85 and US 29, is the world's peach capital. The thousands of flowering shrubs, fruit trees and bulbs you will see blooming during spring and summer have been planted by local garden clubs.

Converse College for women, Wofford College for men, a junior college, General Hospital School of Nursing, two business colleges and the South Carolina School for the Deaf and Blind are located here. Converse was founded in 1890 and named for Marie Converse, the daughter of a textile leader. Each year a Contemporary and a Baroque Music Festival are staged, and faculty members present a Faculty Artist Recital Series. Converse also has an art gallery, a chamber orchestra, a Chorale, and an Opera Workshop that presents frequent programs. Wofford College is the home of the Black Music-Art Center, where exhibits of local and visiting artists are open to the public. The Spartanburg Music Foundation sponsors a symphony orchestra, Spring Music Festival, and the concert series.

A Center of Art and Industry

Art is actively promoted in Spartanburg by the Art Association, the Art Club, and the Artists' Guild. Traveling exhibitions, workshops, lecturers, and indoor and sidewalk exhibits designed to encourage local and regional artists are maintained.

The County Historical Association sponsors tours to landmarks of historical interest and lectures, and has restored Walnut Grove Plantation, the home of Kate Barry, Revolutionary War heroine. Interesting exhibits are on display in the regional museum, 501 Otis Blvd.

Spartanburg has become a textile and manufacturing center in recent years. At Chesnee (17 miles north on US 221), Spartan Mills opened a $25-million plant, and when Captain John Montgomery, the founder, dedicated his first mill he celebrated by serving roast turkey with all the fixings on a platform atop the chimney.

Spartanburg is named for the Spartan Regiment, formed in 1776. It was the Spartan Rifles under General Daniel Morgan who fought and won the day at the Battle of Cowpens.

Next is Greenville, thirty-one miles west from Spartanburg on I-85 or US 29. It was named in 1821 for General Nathanael Greene, a Revolutionary War hero.

Industrial engineering here centers around J. E. Sirrine & Co., US 29 bypass and US 276, whose leaders have blueprinted most of the major plants in the southeast. The firm's founders came from Connecticut to make wagons and buggies. The major mineral resource in the county is vermiculite. Seal fur auctions at the Memorial Auditorium are held in the fall, and they attract international buyers.

Bob Jones University, an interdenominational school at US 29 North on Wade Hampton Blvd., has a museum of sacred art containing European paintings from the thirteenth through the seventeenth centuries. Among them are works by Tintoretto, Titian, Veronese, Rubens, and Van Dyck. The collection is effectively displayed in a series of magnificent rooms including two Gothic chambers. A diorama depicts Biblical household scenes, and you also will see trees and herbs mentioned in the Bible. A second collection is on display in the ultra-modern Greenville County Art Museum, 420 College St., which also boasts the nation's most complete permanent collection of Andrew Wyeth paintings, along with other impressive collections of North American art.

On US 25 North visit Furman University's Baptist Museum. Although Baptist is the largest Christian denomination represented in Greenville, there are more than 185 churches of twenty-six different faiths in the city. One of the oldest is Christ Episcopal Church, built in 1829. It was designed by Joel Poinsett, for whom the Christmas Poinsettia is named.

Interesting historical spots in Greenville include the Rock House, Buncombe Road, home of Revolutionist Billy Young "That Terror to the Tories"; Batesville Mill at Pelham, first mill in Greenville County; Poinsett Bridge honoring Joel Poinsett; the old gun works, located where the railroad crosses the road to J. P. Stevens' Dunean Mill; White Hall, 310 W. Earle Ct., summer home of Henry Middleton, son of Arthur Middleton, signer of the Declaration of Independence, built in 1810; and the Shriners' Crippled Children's Hospital, on bypass 291, the only one in the continental US.

Seven miles north of Easley on State 8 is Pickens, whose Historical Museum, Room 204, Pickens County Court House, displays pioneer and Indian mementoes. Pick up State 183 west and drive to its intersection with State 130, where the Duke Power Company's Keowee-Toxaway Visitors' Center has an audio-visual tour of the history of energy which includes a thunderstorm, a room of the planets, a working waterwheel, a reconstructed coal mine, and many other exhibits. The giant power project here has flooded archeological sites that have witnessed a visit by the Spanish explorer Hernando do Soto, settlements of the Cherokee Indians, and Fort Prince George, a wilderness outpost during pioneer days.

Clemson, southwest from Easley on US 123, is in the foothills of the Blue Ridge Mountains and the home of Clemson University, founded by Thomas Green Clemson, son-in-law of the South Carolina statesman, John C. Calhoun. The latter bequeathed most of his estate to the school, including his home, Fort Hill. Open to the public, the house contains many of its original furnishings, including a fine mahogany sideboard made of paneling from the officer's quarters of the frigate *Constitution*. In the parlor are a Duncan Phyfe sofa, once the property of General George Washington (the carved eagles on the back were said to be used as models for those on the first American silver dollar), and a marble-topped pier table, similar to one owned by James Madison in the White House. In the dining room is a sword of Colonel Ranson Calhoun, killed in a duel with Alfred Rhett of Charleston. An old spring house and Calhoun's office are in separate buildings. A Confederate one-cent postage stamp and $100 and $1,000 notes bore the statesman's likeness.

On the campus, near the agriculture building, stands Hanover House. It was built in 1716 as a plantation home; frame, with two huge chimneys of handmade brick, and named for the royal House of Hanover in England. In 1940 it was moved from the Low Country near Moncks Corner when the Santee-Cooper power dam was planned and given to Clemson for preservation.

Clemson's campus is bounded on the west by Hartwell Lake, where students and townspeople enjoy boating and waterskiing. In the Horticultural Ornamental Gardens on the campus, there's a teahouse (by the lake), a pagoda and a pioneer complex.

Oconee State Park (and area), via US 123, State 28 & 107, a restful retreat near Stump House Mountain, has a beautiful lake for picnicking or fishing. Musical names bestowed on many Oconee locations by the Indians are constant reminders of their way of life. Tamasee in Cherokee means "place of the sunlight of God." An old witch doctor buried a ruby-like gem, thought to have healing rays, in the vicinity—thus the name. The Tugaloo River in Cherokee means "two," an apt name, since the river converges with the Chattooga. One of the more comical is Coneross Creek, which means "the place where the duck fell off"—no doubt one of the many marsh ducks which can be found along the river's margins in autumn. Jocassee Valley means "place of the lost one." A daughter of a famous chief is said to have strayed in the valley and was never found. Keowee is "where the mulberry grows in bounteous stands." Near Fort Prince George, which stood on the Keowee River, several old mulberry trees are still standing. Oconee itself is derived from the Indian word Uk-oo-na, meaning "the water eyes of the hills." Waterfalls such as Whitewater Falls, Issaqueena Falls and High Falls, and countless others hidden away in dark precipices, abound in the area.

En route to Oconee you will pass by Seneca, named for the old Seneca Cherokee nation, and then through West Union and the Salem/Long Creek area. This is the center of a new apple industry, with a crop worth a half million dollars annually. Groucho Marx, the comedian, was one of the major owners. An apple festival, barbecue, square dance, golf classic and parade draws as many as 30,000 people each year. Walhalla is next on State 28, drawing its name from Norse mythology, meaning "beautiful garden of immortal heroes." There is a fish hatchery on State 107, one of the nation's largest, providing a million trout for restocking mountain streams in the Hartwell and Clark Hill Lakes area. The Chattooga River with a picnic area is nearby.

For Pendleton (and area), take US 76 and branch left on State 88. See the Old Farmer's Hall, oldest in the United States, with a post office on the first floor; the original banner carried by Wade Hampton's Red Shirts and the cannon used by the Red Shirt Company during the Civil War—it was last fired in celebration of Grover Cleveland's election as President. Near the cannon is a sun dial given the Farmer's Society by Col. Francis Huger, known as the liberator of the Marquis de Lafayette, from the dungeon of Olmütz.

Also visit the Old Stone Church and cemetery with its many historic graves. Of Presbyterian faith, it was founded in 1789. The building of rough field stone erected by John Rusk replaces the original log church two miles away. "Printer" John Miller, publisher of the famous *Junius Letters* in England, donated seventeen acres to the church and cemetery. The Calhoun Chapter of the United Daughters of the Confederacy erected an amphitheatre on the church grounds for Memorial Day meetings.

Among many historic homes in this section is Woodlawn, near the Old Stone Church—once the residence of a famous clergyman, the Reverend Jasper Adams. San Salvadore, on the Seneca River, was built by Major Samuel Taylor and named for a soldier killed by Indians on his place.

Pendleton Foundation for Historic Preservation has opened to the public Ashtabula House, three miles north on State 88. It holds antiques and relics, and the dining room and outside kitchen are restored.

Anderson, on US 76 and State 28 southwest from Clemson, is one of the state's five largest cities, named for General Robert Anderson, a Revolutionary War hero. It had one of the first hydroelectric plants in the United States and was nicknamed The Electric City. Power was derived from a plant at Portman Shoals on the Seneca River, now inundated by the Hartwell reservoir.

A textile center with fifteen large mills, Anderson produces cottons, synthetics, blends and plastics, and has also become known as the fiberglass center of the world. The city manufactures many allied products as well, from fiberglass fishing rods to garments. Good farmland—producing soybeans, cotton, pimientos, corn, wheat, oats, barley, hay, lespedesa, sorghum, peaches, pecans, apples and grapes—surrounds

Anderson which justly endorses the local radio and TV call letters—WAIM—meaning: "Where agriculture and industry meet."

Hartwell Lake Reservoir, fifteen miles west of Anderson, has 960 miles of shoreline. Hernando de Soto, it is claimed, made an inland tour of the area in the 1500's, seeking gold. He found mussels instead and an Indian princess, who presented him with a strand of pearls. In 1965 the mussels reappeared in shoreline sands, and the pearl business may one day revive as a tourist interest. The area now has marinas and 3,500 boats. At Broadway Lake, a large residential section, national water-ski competitions are held, numerous boat-launching ramps, camping and picnic facilities are available, and navigation maps of the lake can be obtained free from the *Anderson Independent.*

The Hartwell Project is a multipurpose development comprising a concrete dam flanked by earth embankments, a reservoir and a power plant. Hartwell Dam operates in conjunction with the Clark Hill Project for the reduction of flood damages, generation of hydroelectric power—and also the regulation of river flow in the interest of navigation below Augusta, Georgia.

From Anderson, State 28 leads southeast to historic Abbeville, named for Abbeville, France, home of Dr. John de la Howe, an early settler here, schoolmaster, and founder of an industrial training school.

First Cry for Secession

On November 22, 1860, some three thousand persons gathered on Magazine Hill—now Secession Hill—to hear orators of the Southern cause and to choose delegates to a state convention. When the cry for secession went up in the South, the first formal voice came from Abbeville. A monument marks the event at the entrance on Secession Ave. Abbeville did not stop with lighting the fuse of secession. Many of its men fought in the War Between the States, and its women served in hospitals.

Death gasps of the Confederacy rattled clearly when President Jefferson Davis and his cabinet moved out of Richmond, Virginia, southward. On May 2, 1865, Armstead Burt invited President Davis and his cabinet to spend the evening in Abbeville, and it was decided that further resistance was useless. Jefferson Davis, President of the Confederacy, his full cabinet and six Confederate generals held their last formal meeting here. The government was disbanded, and cabinet members split up the next day to go their own way. The Burt House, now known as Stark House, with the room where the fateful decision was made, is kept much as it was that evening. Built more than 100 years ago by Squire Lesley, a lawyer from Ireland, and later purchased by Burt, it stands at the fork of State 28 and 20.

Many old churches and homes 150 years old are located in and around Abbeville. Trinity Episcopal, just off the square, one of the most visited, was organized October 16, 1842. There are historic names on the interior walls and tombstones. Organized in 1768, Upper Long Cane Church on State 20, two miles north of Abbeville, has a graveyard with veterans of ten wars. William Randolph Hearst's great-great-grandfather lived in the area before the Hearsts moved west to Missouri and California. Patric Noble's home—he became governor in the early 1800's—still stands. His son, Edward, was a signer of the Ordinance of Secession. Murals on the wall of the State Bank and Trust Co. depict historic people and incidents in and around Abbeville.

An unusual antique store, called Noah's Ark, lies just off the square. The contents change constantly and range from history books to iron bathtubs, old locks and keys to a church pew.

The Opera House was once one of the grandest in the Southeast. This showplace on the square retains some of its original majestic grandeur amidst fallen plaster, creaking hinged doors and gilded box seats. Show troupes came from up north in the 1900's and through World War II and performers paraded in the square before the 5 P.M. opening. Every show played to standing room only, with as many as 1,500 arriving by special train from other cities.

In front of the Opera House and City Hall is a monument to a World War II hero in France, Thomas Howie, "The Major of St. Lo."

From Abbeville, State 72 leads east to Greenwood, a diversified mill town. The late James C. Self built homes, churches, a fine hospital and other community buildings here. He had a strong interest in bells, and brought a bell foundry to Greenwood after hearing its bells in the Netherlands Building at the 1939 New York World's Fair. Each bronze bell is cast and turned by hand, the formula being handed down through the family.

The George Park Seed Co. in Greenwood is one of the nation's largest and even has its own post office to handle worldwide orders. The greenhouses and exhibit halls are open for inspection weekdays, and the gardens are open Sundays. Something is blooming from seed every day. The company is two miles from town; ask directions in Greenwood, as there are three ways to get there.

Two fine old homes, both on State 10 and open by appointment, are the Frazier Pressley House and Stony Point House. The first, at the end of a long cedar avenue, has square pillars, is octagon-shaped, and has a widow's walk on the roof. The second was begun by William Smith in 1825 and completed by his son, Joel Smith. The brick house was recently restored by the Donald Hawthorne family. On State 10 is Promised Land, a Civil War Federal Government Black relocation project of several thousand acres.

At Ninety-six, nine miles east on State 34, is the Old Star Fort occupied by Loyalist troops during the American Revolution.

From Greenwood to McCormick, follow US 221 south through Bradley, named for pioneer Irishman, Patrick Bradley. Turn right on State 10. Signs direct you to the Presbyterian Church with its old graveyard. One stone reads "Patrick Calhoun—in memory of Mrs. Catherine Calhoun aged 76 years who with 22 others was here murdered by the Indians the first of Feb. 1760." Continue on 10 to the Long Cane Creek covered bridge, one of three in South Carolina. State 10 runs into State 28; turn right, drive two miles to McCormick. The town was named for Cyrus McCormick of Illinois, inventor of the reaper. He owned thousands of acres in the county and gave most of the land on which the town is built. At the railroad station are the remains of a once-prosperous gold mining operation, the Dorn mine. Gold was discovered accidentally by hounds digging the creekside while on a fox hunt. The mine became the second largest in the state and yielded about a million dollars in gold.

Orators and Camellias

From McCormick, motor down State 28 onto US 221 and turn left at State 23 to Edgefield. You will be parallel to Clarks Hill Reservoir on your right, and a power dam. Named for a blacksmith, the area has good camping sites and fishing. Then through two villages, Plumb Branch and Parksville, to Modoc. Turn left on State 23 and drive to Edgefield, through pine seedling reforestation sections. This county claims more statesmen and politicians than any other South Carolina locality: orators, ten state governors, senators, congressmen and adventurers. The people here are individualists. Families enjoy famous old homes, sit on priceless chairs, eat from antique tables and pluck camellias from ancestral gardens.

In Edgefield pick up a "City of Edgefield Historic Map" from the *Edgefield Advertiser* newspaper, established in 1844 and located on the square. Have a meal at the Plantation House, also on the square. Visit Magnolia Dale on Norris St., surrounded front and side by magnolia trees planted 100 years ago. The museum on the second floor is filled with mementoes, photos and historical manuscripts. The house was given to the Edgefield Historical Society by the Kendall Company, of Boston. The Kendall Historical Map Room is at 900 Sumter St., Columbia.

Oakley Park is the Red Shirt Shrine Museum. Maintained by the Daughters of the Confederacy, it has many portraits, furnishings and interior decorations. On the second floor are maps, histories and clothes of bygone days. The house was built in 1835 by Daniel Byrd, descendant of the Virginia Byrds.

Many tourists go to Edgefield to check ancestral dates in five church graveyards. Trinity Episcopal, Simpkins at Wigfall, is one of the largest —Edmund B. Bacon deeded the land in 1836 for one dollar. Others are at Willowbrook Cemetery, the first Baptist Church, and Presbyterian Church on Church Street, Methodist at Norris Street, and St. Mary's Catholic on Bumcomb Street.

Edgefield has many historic private homes. Cedar Grove, US 25 North, was built in 1805 by the grandsons of Michael Blocker, one of the first Prussian families in America. It has handblocked wallpaper from Paris painted in pre-Revolutionary days, fine carved mantel moldings, and a double-deck piazza overlooking a terraced rose garden. The family cemetery is in the rear. The original Blocker Plantation house, built in 1775, was burned.

Pine House, on US 25, also known as Piney Woods Plantation, originally was the site of a tavern, on a one-thousand-acre grant, later inherited by Frances Van Swearingen Ezekiel McClendon in 1791. General Washington had a meal here, spent the night and changed horses. The tavern was across the road from the present Pine House. Carroll Hill, Bumcomb and Pickens Sts., was built by Chancellor James Parsons Carroll, signer of the Ordinance of Secession and representative in both branches of the legislature.

Halcyon Grove on Bumcomb St. was the town house of Governor Andrew Pickens, Jr., the son of General Andrew Pickens. It was later bought by Governor Francis Wilkinson Pickens, Minister to the Russian Imperial Court in St. Petersburg from 1858 to 1860. Pickens' beautiful third wife, the former Lucy Holcomb, was the toast of Russia. Their daughter, born in Russia, was named Olga Liva Lucy Holcomb Dousc- hka Francesca Pickens. This young, beautiful American Joan of Arc, clad in red silk, stood beside Wade Hampton on the balcony of Oakley Plantation House as he rallied the crowd to the cause of the Confederacy with his spirited talk. The Pickens beauty mounted her horse, held the Red Shirt Banner high, and led 1,500 men in a triumphant parade. She is buried near her father in the Willowbrook cemetery. The tombstone reads only Douschka.

From Edgefield, State 19 runs southeast to Aiken, named for William Aiken, Sr., prosperous cotton merchant whose son became governor. The region is noted for sports in general and thoroughbreds in particular, with hundreds of events both for spectators and participants. Any Sun- day afternoon, January through April, for instance, you can buy a ticket to one of the weekend polo matches. But if horses are not your cup of tea, then you'll find fine tennis courts or golf greens at your disposal. Quail and dove shooting and fishing are popular. Mayfield's Museum, on State 19N, exhibits Indian, early American and Confederate relics, in- cluding an Andrew Jackson collection.

Diapers—and H-Bombs

About 12 miles south is the AEC-Savannah River or H-Bomb plant. The Atomic Energy Commission property includes a 2,800-acre pond used as a cooling basin for water from plant reactors and for an ecology laboratory. The Commission also maintains a large technical film library. The AEC has increased production of Cobalt 60 for industry, medicine and research.

In the vicinity are mountains of creamy or grayish-colored kaolin mines. These are some of the largest and purest clay deposits in the United States, used for many things from wallpaper to glue, paints, or facial mudpacks. One of the newest industries in the area is the Owens- Corning Fibreglas plant.

It's time for a side trip. Graniteville lies five miles west of Aiken on US 1, and is an old textile community in the Horse Creek Valley. The Graniteville Company chain of textile mills which William Gregg found- ed in 1845 has grown to its present-day eleven plants; owns some fifteen thousand acres of land; and maintains a fine recreation center. The cloth shop, opposite St. Paul Espiscopal Church, is worth a stop to see and perhaps buy products from the mills.

A lover of people, Gregg gave five friends fifty acres each, with the stipulation that they would build homes in Graniteville and live there at least one season in the year. The iron grillwork from his own home, which burned, may be seen at the Grace Estate.

Johnston, nicknamed "The Diaper City," on State 23, 121, 191, is so called because the Riegel plant here produces 90,000 dozen diapers a week. Deering Milliken has a large woolen mill here. This textile and farming community grew from a depot on a main line railroad, the Charlotte, Columbia and Augusta. In recent years cotton crops have been replaced by peaches, grapes, pecans and livestock. The horse show is a major annual event.

From Aiken, I-20 angles northeast to Columbia, the state capital and a university city. The site was selected in 1786 when the Low and Up Country people wanted a Midland location for their state government. John Gabriel Guignard, surveyor general, laid out the city with lovely, wide streets.

The State House, a three-story granite building of Italian Renaissance style, was designed by John R. Niernesee, begun in 1851, but not completed until 1907. Bronze stars on the south and west facades mark scars made by Sherman's shells in 1865. On the first landing, north of the building, is a life-sized bronze statue of George Washington, his staff broken by Sherman's men. Inside the lobby is a life-sized plaster statue of John C. Calhoun, South Carolina's most distinguished statesman. It was used as a model for the marble statue in the Statuary Hall at Washington. On the landings of the wrought-iron stairway are two bronze plaques, one honoring South Carolina's signers of the Declaration of Independence: Thomas Lynch, Jr., Thomas Heyward, Jr., Arthur Middleton and Edward Rutledge. The other honors the state's signers of the Constitution; Judge Rutledge, Charles Cotesworth Pinckney, Charles Pinckney, and Pierce Butler.

The South Carolina flag, adopted in 1777, features a white palmetto tree and a crescent moon. The crescent was taken from the hats of the men who defended Fort Moultrie against the British. The palmetto, the state tree, is a variety of palm that grows along the Southeast Coast, and an ironwork replica of the tree stands in the Capitol grounds to honor the famous Palmetto Regiment which helped win the Mexican War of 1847.

A number of monuments to South Carolina's history stand in the hilltop park surrounding the State House in a setting of sweeping lawns, rose beds, old magnolia and oak trees, evergreens, and Chinese fan trees.

The twenty-eighth President of the United States, Woodrow Wilson, born in Virginia, lived in Columbia at 1705 Hampton St., now a museum.

For genealogists, the South Carolina Department of Archives and History is a storehouse of information. Early South Carolina was a melting pot for people of English, French, Scottish, Welsh, Eastern European, Swiss, and German stock. The American Revolution, Plantation Era and the War Between the States caused South Carolinians to migrate to all parts of the country.

Nowadays a balance of manufacturing, government, trade, services, banking, and agriculture goes to make up Columbia's economy. In fifteen years, some twenty-two different industries have opened, three in a 400-acre industrial park. A technical education center trains students in electronics, engineering, chemistry and related studies. Fort Jackson, outside the city, is one of the nation's largest infantry training centers, with a yearly average turnover of 23,000 recruits. Northwest of the city, via US 176 and State 213, the atomic electric generating station at Parr produces some 17,000 kilowatts.

The first week of April marks the Spring Festival, when tours of homes and gardens attract thousands. The city's fine new Riverbanks Zoological Park, 500 Wildlife Parkway, is one of the nation's most modern.

Creatures roam freely in natural habitat areas—there are no cages or bars. There's also a huge, impressive aviary where birds fly about in settings which reflect their geographic origins.

Thirty-two miles northeast of Columbia on US 1 is the oldest inland town in the state, Camden. Dating from 1732, it was settled by Quakers from Ireland, who first named it Fredericksburg, then Pine Tree Hill—and finally Camden, honoring Lord Camden. Two great battles of the Revolution were fought here—and in the Civil War the town was an important railroad center and storehouse, with a hospital for the wounded.

Headquarters of Cornwallis

Historic Camden is a restoration of the Revolutionary period. You can enter two restored log houses filled with museum exhibits and miniature dioramas; here even the soldiers' buttons are perfectly detailed. There is a model of the original town of eighty buildings, adapted from General Nathanael Greene's maps, and winding trails are lined with historic markers and restored fort sites.

When the British departed from Camden in 1781, they left remains of the old town wall and six surrounding forts, the Kershaw House where General Cornwallis headquartered and a large powder magazine. They also left swords, cannon balls, muskets and other valuable pieces of history that are on display. Trails cover much of the sixty wooded areas and you can go over them in an electric cart. Helpful guides will show you everything when you arrive and treat you to something the British never got in Camden at that time—real Southern hospitality.

Camden's fame now is its industry—DuPont built their first South Carolina plant here, in the 1950's—and sports. Fox hunting in the fall, winter stabling and horse training, plus the Carolina Cup Steeplechase, in March, are important.

At Sumter, US 76, 378, the Palmetto Pigeon Plant, founded by Attorney Wendell M. Levi, is the largest of its kind in the world, marketing 100,000 squabs a year.

From Columbia, drive south on I-26 about 41 miles to State 33, then west four miles, to Orangeburg and the fifty-five-acre Edisto Memorial Gardens. Acres of azaleas bloom in profusion, peaking in April, amid tall, moss-draped cypress, crab apple and flowering dogwood. The more than 6,000 rose bushes provide masses of color all summer. Orangeburg has golf, bird hunting and freshwater game fish in the numerous lakes and the Edisto River. A Federal Fish Hatchery, on 150 landscaped acres, breeds bass, redbreast, bream and other local fish. Salley Archives Building, on Middleton St., is open on request.

From Orangeburg take US 21 to its junction with US 17. Turn right for Yemassee, a wonderful area for flowers and vegatables. S. H. Kress and his brother, of dimestore fame, grew their bulbs at a plantation here.

Continue on US 17 through Sheldon. At Gardens Corner turn south onto US 21 to Beaufort, where British merchants once made forturnes in cotton and indigo. Browse around the old homes, built high for coolness, with spacious porches and old-fashioned gardens of camellias, jessamine, oleanders, and wisteria mingled with moss-bearded oak trees. Many of the houses were made of tabby, from crushed oyster shells, and some homes are open to visitors at azalea time in the spring. One is the home of Emily, unforgettable character in the novel *Sea Island Lady;* it has wide verandas, basement tunnel-porches and double front V stairs. Another interesting home is Verdier House on Bay Street, from which General Lafayette addressed the people of Beaufort.

The old arsenal built in 1795, now Beaufort Museum, contains several ancient cannons, an old steam fire engine, Indian arrowheads, Confederate money, stuffed snakes, alligator skulls, antebellum costumes and proclamations of the Secession. The Chamber of Commerce can furnish self-guided tour folders as well as a host of other information about the area.

The landscape here varies from high bluffs, densely wooded with subtropical growth, to sloping sandy beaches. Beaufort has one of the best natural harbors on the coast, with forty public boat landings, a yacht harbor and club. The South Atlantic Sailing Regatta is held during the annual Water Festival in July. Sailing and water-skiing are very much part of the scene. Crabbing and shrimping are big business in these sea islands, and one constantly sees small boats plying the waterways. The Atomic Age has not changed the quaintness and congenial tranquility of Beaufort.

The islands of Beaufort County include: Barnwell and Little Barnwell, named for John Barnwell, a Colonial hero from Ireland and a well-known Indian fighter, later known as "Tuscarora Jack;" Buzzard's Island named for its numerous buzzards; Bermuda Island, named by early settlers for their former home; Bull Island which recalls the Bull family of Colonial days, whose land grants extended from the Savannah to the Combahee rivers; Chisolm Island where Dr. Robert Chisolm grew and shipped olives until Federal troops destroyed his trees, using them for firewood; Coosaw Island, whose Indian name means Old Creek; and Fripp Island, which got its name from a family of planters who came from St. Helena in 1725 and recently has been developed by several South Carolina businessmen into a vacation paradise.

Most of Hunting Island is a state park, and is inhabited by many deer, raccoon and other game, with flocks of local and migratory birds and waterfowl. The beach has hard, smooth sand at low tide, and a width of four of five hundred feet. This palm-tree-lined resort overlooks St. Helena Sound, on the outer banks of the chain of sixty-four Golden Islands of Beaufort County. St. Helena Island was named in 1526 by Pedro de Quexos, a Spaniard who had set sail from Florida. He suddenly came upon the island and in prayerful gratitude he thanked his Saint, Elena, for leading him to such bountiful land.

Let's go on a side trip, from Beaufort to historic Port Royal, on State 281. Named by Jean Ribaut in 1562, when he expressed admiration for the wide sound and harbor, saying: "It is one of the greatest and fairest havens of the world, where without danger, all the ships of the world might anchor." Captain Robert Sanford sailed in here, with Dr. Henry Woodward, the English surgeon, who stayed as hostage while an Indian sailed back to England with Sanford. Woodward, then captured by Spaniards, was taken to the East Indies, where he was picked up in 1670 by an English vessel. He returned and went to Charles Towne where he introduced Madagascar rice to Carolina. During the Civil War, while the

Confederates were concentrated in Charles Towne, Federal forces landed sixteen ships with 12,000 men at Port Royal. They kept possession of the Sound for the duration of the war.

Back into the car now, and off to Hilton Head Island on State 170 to the junction with US 278, then south and east. The island takes its name from British Captain William Hilton, 1663. Here at Hilton Head the golfer will find twelve beautifully sculptured courses including Harbour Town, site of the famous Heritage Golf Classic in March. And he just may see an alligator basking in the sun at one of the water hazards. For the tennis enthusiast there are unmatched courts with the latest in surfacing. Boaters may rent power craft or sailing vessels. Or you can dock your own boat at one of the island's marinas.

Swimmers and sun lovers will delight in the warm, white sand that gently meets with the Atlantic. Bicyclists will find more than twelve miles of bike paths. And fishermen can try the island's inlets and bays or the challenge of the Gulf Stream for deep-sea fishing. For children there are day-long programmed activities directed by competent, professional staffs.

The environmentalist will find Hilton Head a haven. It is a managed development which incorporates the environment with recreational enjoyment. Hotel, motor inn and motel accommodations are plentiful, or the visitor may rent a villa-condominium at a surprisingly low price.

Walk the History Trail

Leaving Beaufort backtrack on US 21 to Gardens Corner, turn right onto US 17, then north on State 3035, passing Green Pond and Ritter to Walterboro, a relaxing spot for fishing or golf, and bird hunting in season. Arrangements for guides with dogs can be made through the Chamber of Commerce, or hotel-motel management. The camellias here are a sight to see in fall and spring.

From Walterboro follow State 64 to Jacksonboro, then US 17 to Charleston.

The citizens of Charleston have achieved a happy balance between history and progress. A major seaport and diversified industry contrast with quaint streets and beautiful architecture. Historic homes and churches are visited annually by thousands from all parts of the country and the world. A walking tour, known as the History Trail, is marked with signs in the older part of the city. Guide folders are available at the Chamber of Commerce and at many hotels, motels, and restaurants.

Each spring thousands of visitors flock to enjoy the dazzling parade of color in Charleston's famous gardens and explore the scores of restored eighteenth- and nineteenth-century homes. Since 1977, they've also come for the twelve-day Spoleto Festival U.S.A., which features opera, theater, ballet, jazz and almost every other aspect of the arts.

When summer approaches, the face of Charleston seems to change. Summertime in Charleston promises the bouquet and beauty of lush oleanders, hydrangeas, hibiscus, roses, magnolia and the ever-favorite crape myrtle. Although Cypress Gardens closes on May 1, Middleton Place Gardens and Plantation Stableyards and Magnolia Gardens remain open all year for the enjoyment of children and adults alike.

Charleston

Points of Interest

1) Charleston Museum
2) City Hall
3) Confederate Museum
4) Dock Street Theater
5) Edmondston-Alston House
6) French Huguenot Church
7) Heyward-Washington House
8) Hunley Museum
9) Manigault House
10) Medical University of South Carolina
11) Old Powder Magazine
12) Russell House
13) Sunken Gardens
14) Sword Gates
15) Visitor Information Center
16) White Point Gardens

In addition to Middleton's beautiful formal grounds and landscaped gardens (the oldest in America), the recently restored Plantation Stableyards offer an afternoon's trip back through time to the plantation life of the 1700's. Magnolia Gardens has a petting zoo with rare mini-horses. Nearby is Drayton Hall, considered the nation's finest untouched example of Georgian architecture.

Many other attractions are open throughout the summer that have particular appeal to young families with an interest in history.

Fort Sumter, where the Civil War began, can be reached by sightseeing boats departing from the Charleston Municipal Marina several times a day. Both the Fort Sumter cruise and Gray Lines's 25-mile Harbor of History Tour give the visitor a delightful boat trip and spectacular offshore views of Charleston's famous battery mansions.

Fort Moultrie on Sullivan's Island, another favorite attraction, is the site of the first decisive victory of Americans over the British during the Revolutionary War.

The Hunley Museum also provides intriguing excursions for visitors, young and old alike. Located in one of the oldest bank buildings in the United States (1798), it houses a full-scale replica of the first Confederate submarine, the *H. S. Hunley,* and other artifacts of the Civil War.

Charles Towne Landing, a beautiful state park, was built on the original 1670 landing site to commemorate Charleston's 300th birthday during South Carolina's Tricentennial Celebration in 1970. One of the most unusual parks in the country, Charles Towne Landing includes a theater and twenty-minute film showing the beauty of the Low Country; an Exhibit Pavilion whose outstanding exhibits and artifacts illustrate the first century of settlement; a Reception Center with gift shop, restaurant, and rental carts or bicycles; a 1670 Experimental Garden showing various crops grown by the early settlers; the original 1670 Settlement Site; the *Adventure,* a reproduction of a seventeenth-century trading ketch; the Animal Forest with animals indigenous to South Carolina in 1670, displayed in their natural habitat; and nearly one hundred acres of beautifully landscaped English-park type gardens with paths circling placid lagoons.

Other historic points of interest include the Charleston Museum, oldest municipal museum in America; the old City Market; the Confederate Museum; Old Slave Mart Museum and Gallery; Gibbes Art Gallery; the Old Powder Magazine, oldest public building in the city dating from 1713, and the Dock Street Theater, reproduction of the oldest theater in America. Another permanent resident of this historic city is the aircraft carrier *Yorktown,* famed "Fighting Lady" of World War II, berthed at Patriots Point across the Cooper River. Planes, helicopters, ship models, weapons are displayed on board.

Also open to the public are Charleston's three famous house museums —the Joseph Manigault House (1803), the National Russell House (1809), and the Heyward-Washington House (1770).

Those who prefer to simply walk or ride through the historic sections of Charleston may do so at their leisure by following the Walking Tour route or by taking romantic horse-drawn carriage tours. Also available are tape-recorded walking tours and bus tours. For persons interested in more comprehensive touring and individualized attention, the Charleston Guide Service offers well-trained professional guides who provide transportation and guided tours for individuals, families or larger groups.

Many summer visitors are people who have visited in the spring and are returning again—this time to enjoy a totally different Charleston. They come for the beaches, the boating, the fishing, and—most of all—the temperate summer climate. Many come to participate in or observe the many sailing regattas scheduled throughout the summer months.

Charleston County boasts four excellent beaches for sun bathing, surfing, or just building castles in the sand. Folly Beach, Sullivan's Island, the Isle of Palms, and Edisto all offer beautiful sandy beaches, featuring everything from amusement parks and fishing piers to family campsites and downright remote seclusion and privacy.

Travelers who pack a fishing pole will be delighted with the many varieties of fish abundantly pulled from freshwater and saltwater around Charleston. Surfcasting, pierfishing, deepsea fishing in the Gulf Stream, or plain old-fashioned cane-pole angling from a riverbank all provide sporting excitement for novice and veteran alike.

Twenty-three miles south of Charleston, on US 17 and State 20, Kiawah Island is being developed as a walking-scale vacation resort. The island is being left in the natural state as much as possible, with accommodations, shops, and recreational facilities all within 7-minutes walking distance. For the nature lover, there is a 2,500-foot nature boardwalk through a sunken forest, and the island's forest, lagoons, creeks, and marshes are teeming with wildlife.

Seabrook Island, twenty miles south of Charleston on US 17 to State 20, then State 90, is another private resort and residential community. Its 2,042 acres have tidal creeks and marshes, massive sand dunes, moss-draped oakes, tall pines, and miles of sandy beach. The visitor may enjoy its excellent golf course and clubhouse while vacationing in oceanside villas, cottages, and lakeside treehouses.

Lake Moultrie and Lake Marion, thirty-five miles from Charleston on US 52 on the Cooper River and at the edge of the Francis Marion National Forest, are two of the most popular inland freshwater sports sections in South Carolina. They were created by a giant hydro-electric dam at Moncks Corner and Pinopolis and cover 171,000 acres of water and 450 miles of shoreline. World records in channel catfish (fifty-eight pounds) and black crappie (five pounds) are claimed. There's a striped bass hatchery nearby and many boat ramps.

Head north on US 52, thirty-two miles from Charleston, to Moncks Corner and Mepkin Plantation. This was once the Colonial home of Henry Laurens and passed through a succession of owners, including Clare Booth Luce, who gave it to the Trappist Monks.

US 17 shoots north from Charleston to McClellanville in Bull Bay, a migratory bird refuge. The place abounds in bird names—Duck Creek, Crow Island, Bird Island. The latter is a crescent-shaped strip of sand and grass and is home to many pelicans. The young pelicans consume 150 pounds of fish before they learn to fly—at the ripe age of two months.

Their diet is principally menhaden, used commercially for processing into fertilizer. The sand dunes which stretch down the center of the isle keep the nests high and dry during tides. Other islands and parts of the mainland comprise a 60,000-acre refuge, occupying a fifteen-mile segment of the coast. There are two colonies of nesting waterfowl in the summer, 2,000 brown pelicans and 20,000 royal terns, so the sky is filled with the beautiful black and white, and brown and white birds. Near McClellanville is Hampton Plantation.

City of Ghosts and Plantations

Georgetown, north on US 701, is a city of memories, ghosts and fine plantations. Many prominent figures from pre-Revolutionary days and the Civil War were born, lived or visited here. Lafayette and DeKalb landed where Winyah Bay empties into the Atlantic. The waterway from Brookgreen to Georgetown was traveled by Theodosia Burr as she came to town to board the *Patriot*. Many legends are told of this beautiful daughter of the infamous Aaron. It is even said that she was captured by pirates and made to walk the plank, but who can believe that? Francis "Swamp Fox" Marion also lived here. On the mainland side of the bay, south of town, is Belle Island where Fort White, a sixteen-battery Confederate fort is in an excellent state of preservation.

McClellanville is a fishing center. Blues, mackerel, king mackerel (king fish), cobia, barracuda and dolphin are plentiful in season. Amberjack run up to sixty pounds.

US 17 leads to Pawley's Island, a quaint old island, a summer retreat for wealthy rice planters of the 18th and 19th centuries. Their charming plantations still grace the landscape. The beach and creek are the main attractions with fishing, clamming, crabbing, swimming, water-skiing, boating and hunting in season. A fishing pier boasts large catches; boats are available for rent or charter, either ocean-going or inland motoring. For children, there are a pavilion, bowling, miniature golf courses, and trampolines. And for the whole family, there's good eating at inns and restaurants in the area which feature fresh seafood. Continue on 17 to Brookgreen Gardens, which holds more than 350 works of American sculptors of the 19th and 20th centuries, displayed in a garden setting, and Huntington Beach State Park.

Sun Fun Capital

Myrtle Beach on US 17 is the focal point of the Grand Strand, first seen by Spanish settlers in 1526 and in the 1700s a focal point for English plantation owners. Today, it is a resort area that offers year-round vacation fun for the whole family. Accommodations are plentiful—more than 38,000 rooms—and the title "Camping Capital of the World" has been bestowed on the Strand, which contains some 15,000 campsites with more being added almost daily.

Spring and sports go hand in hand on the Grand Strand. The peak golf season runs from February through April. There's also a billfish tournament, stock car racing, horseshows and golf tournaments. Canadian-American Days, plantation tours, camellia shows, a folk music festival and the Spring Fling Festival, all provide a wide variety of springtime pleasures.

The Sun Fun Festival in June kicks off the peak summer season at Myrtle Beach and the Grand Strand. With fifty miles of free public beaches and varied amusements and recreation for young and old, everything is in full swing throughout the summer.

Fall, the Indian summer season, offers the best in saltwater sports fishing along the Grand Strand. Ocean bathing is enjoyed until November, and major fall activities include the Grand Strand Fishing Rodeo, Indian Summer Days, Thanksgiving Holiday Fiesta, golf tournaments for amateurs and pros, and music festivals.

Winter is still playtime at Myrtle Beach and the Grand Strand. Christmas Holidays Festival, a January Jamboree and George Washington Days highlight the events schedule. The Myrtle Beach Convention Center offers inside entertainment, and golf is enjoyed throughout the winter.

Ten major annual festivals and other entertainment events are staged by the Greater Myrtle Beach Chamber of Commerce (P. O. Box 2115, Myrtle Beach 29577) and other groups to provide activity throughout the fall, winter and spring seasons.

Now that your tour "from the mountains to the sea" is about to end there is a unique and exciting stopover which could well be on the route you have chosen to return to your starting point. Located on Interstate 95, US 301-501, South of the Border is a colorful complex which includes motel rooms, restaurants, shops and rides for the children. It's a great place to stop, relax and remember your visit to South Carolina.

PRACTICAL INFORMATION FOR SOUTH CAROLINA

FACTS AND FIGURES. Columbia, located in the geographical center of the state, is the capital. Population of the state is 2,918,000 (1980 Census).

The official state tree, the palmetto, has earned for the state its designation as the "Palmetto State." The state bird is the Carolina wren; the state flower, the yellow jessamine; the state stone, blue granite. The state animal is the white-tail deer, and the state fish is the striped bass. *Animis Opibusque Parati* ("Prepared in spirit and resources") and *Dum Spiro Spereo* ("While I breathe, I hope") are the state mottos.

HOW TO GET THERE. *By air:* Charleston and Columbia may be reached by direct flights of Delta, Eastern, Piedmont and Republic from out of the state. In addition, Pan-American flies into Charleston. There are direct flights to Greenville/Spartanburg on Eastern, Piedmont and Republic; to Florence and Myrtle Beach on Piedmont. Republic flies into Greenwood.

By car: Main routes coming into South Carolina include I-95 a multilane divided highway from Savannah, Georgia, into Hardeeville and continuing through the state and into North Carolina; I-20 from the Augusta, Georgia, area is also a main access to South Carolina; I-85, another multilane highway brings visitors into South Carolina from the northern part of Georgia. Main routes into the state from North Carolina include I-85, I-77 from Charlotte, N. C.; I-26 from Hendersonville; and I-95 from Lumberton into Dillon. US 17, a shoreline route, follows along from North Carolina through South Carolina and into Georgia. US 301 is another well-traveled route in and out of the state.

By bus: Trailways, Greyhound, Jefferson Lines, Inc., and Southeastern Stages, Inc. all go into South Carolina.

By train: Amtrak goes into Dillon, Florence, Kingstree, Charleston, Yemassee, Clemson, Camden, Columbia, Denmark, Spartanburg and Greenville.

 HOW TO GET AROUND. *By air:* You can travel by air within the state on Delta, Piedmont and Republic.

By car: I-95, I-20, I-26 and I-85 crisscross within the state and provide car travel. US 17, which runs along the shoreline, and US 301, an inland route, are also good. US 123, 321, 52, 78, 378 and State 72 are also in this category.

Car rental: Rental service is available at the Charleston, Columbia, and Greenville-Spartanburg airports. There are several rental firms operating in Orangeburg and Sumter.

By bus: Greyhound, Trailways, Jefferson Lines, Inc., and Southern Stages, Inc., have service within the state.

 TOURIST INFORMATION. To obtain detailed information about South Carolina write: South Carolina Division of Tourism, Room 10, Box 71, Columbia, SC 29202, or South Carolina Travel Council, 1002 Calhoun St., Columbia 29201. For information on South Carolina's two national forests, write South Carolina Wildlife and Marine Services Dept., Dutch Plaza, Bldg. D, Columbia 29202. To obtain information on the Grand Strand write: Greater Myrtle Beach Chamber of Commerce, P. O. Box 2115, Myrtle Beach 29577. Santee-Cooper Counties Promotion Offices, P.O. Box 12, Santee 29142, will supply information on the Santee-Cooper Lakes. The Hilton Head Island Chamber of Commerce, P.O. Drawer 5647, Hilton Head Island 29928, will send you complete information on what the island offers. Write Seabrook Island, P.O. Box 1000, John's Island, 29455 for information on that resort island. Complete hunting and fishing information and regulations may be obtained from the South Carolina Wildlife and Marine Resources Department, Division of Game, P.O. Box 167, Columbia 29202. Charleston Convention Bureau, P.O. Box 834, Charleston, S.C. 29402, will advise you on deep-sea fishing and charter boats.

 SEASONAL EVENTS. Much of South Carolina's history and tradition is relived through the many and varied festivals and events held throughout the state. Tours of historic homes and events such as the Annual Foothills Arts and Crafts Guild Festival return the modern-day South Carolinian to the days when craftsman used pegs instead of nails and country music was the only kind to be heard. South Carolina is also a home of such modern-day attractions as the Southern 500 Stock Car Race.

Among the regularly held events in South Carolina are:

January: January Jamboree, Myrtle Beach and the Grand Strand. Golf tournaments and awards, historic and garden tours, special sales, golf films, entertainment and package activity at hotels and motels. *Annual Georgetown Camellia Show,* Georgetown. Thousands of blooms are on display from many of the surrounding plantations, as well as from the entire state, North Carolina and Georgia.

February: Polo Matches, Aiken. Hard-riding professional and amateur polo players take to the field for some fast action every Sunday at 3:30 P.M. through April. The great international game has been played in Aiken for more than eighty years. Some of America's best polo players compete. Charleston's famous gardens—*Cypress* (open mid-Feb. to May 1), *Magnolia* and *Middleton Place Gardens and Plantation Stableyards* (both open all year) are noted for their colorful profusion of camellias and azaleas and for fine old live oak and cypress trees. Magnolia and Middleton Place are on State 61; Cypress on US 52.

March: Aiken Horse Trials, Aiken. A part of the competition in Aiken's Triple Crown. Some of the nation's finest thoroughbred horses, having wintered here, make their spring debut. *Annual Canadian-American Days,* Myrtle Beach and the Grand Strand. Folk Music Festival, parade, beach games, cruises, kids' days at amusement parks, historic tours, teenage parties, square dance, daily news from Canada, antique show, golf tournaments and awards, fishing, band concerts, tours of the Air Force Base, historic garden and industrial tours and a musical stage show. *Annual Spring Art Show,* Columbia, Mar. to Apr., presented by the Artists Guild of Columbia at the Columbia Museum of Art. *Charleston Festival of Houses,* Mar. to Apr. Afternoon and candlelight walking tours are offered. Magnificent private gardens and charming historic private homes are on display in this most historic city. The event is one of the highlights of touring the state's beautiful Low Country gardens in the spring. *Annual Carolina Cup Races,* Camden. An afternoon of forty-two steeplechase and flat races in late March or early April is sanctioned by the National Steeplechase and Hunt Association. It is a gala country blend of picnicking, renewing old friendships and racing at its best. The event is one of the earliest competitions for many thoroughbreds after an arduous winter training season. The feature race is the famed Carolina Cup, a 2-mile run over Springdale Course, one of the world's outstanding steeplechase courses.

April: Annual Sidewalk Art Show, Charleston. A display and sale of paintings and artwork by local and out-of-town artists at St. Philip's Church on Church St. This is a very colorful display in the historic section of old Charleston. *Annual World's Championship Landlocked Striped Bass Fishing Derby,* Santee and Cooper Lakes, Santee, Apr. to June. One of the world's largest freshwater fishing derbies, free to all participants. Striped bass, largemouth bass, crappie and bream division. Thousands of dollars in cash, trophies, motors and merchandise are up for grabs. *The Governor's Annual Frog-Jumping Contest.* The finest jumping frogs throughout the state compete in this dramatic contest held on Main St. in the little rural town of Springfield. Festivities also include marble shooting, horseshoe and yo-yo contest, greased pig chase, country music and dancing. Frog juice sold—10 cents a cup. *International Egg-Striking Contest.* The hardest-boiled eggs that can be found are paired in striking duels. Excitement builds with every strike of these rocklike eggs in a very colorful folk custom. Also in Springfield. *Rebel 500 Race,* Darlington. Top NASCAR stock car drivers test Darlington Raceway's 1⅜-mile oval for 500 miles. This is the second oldest race in NASCAR. *Orangeburg Rose Festival,* Orangeburg. "Miss South Carolina Queen of Roses" Beauty Pageant, rose contest with entries from all over the U.S., special show and banquet, country music, square dancing, special events for ladies and men throughout three days.

May: Annual Charleston Trident Fishing Tournament, Charleston, Berkeley and Dorchester Counties. The tournament is open to participants of all ages, free of charge. Anglers may enter the tournament by completing official entry blanks and having the entry certified at one of the numerous weigh stations. Entries must have been caught in the waters of these three counties. Offshore catches must be made in boats leaving from and returning to Charleston County. Thirty-seven species of eligible fish. Special surf, military and boat awards. *Iris Festival,* Summer, is held during the last week in May. *Spoleto Festival USA,* Charleston. The American counterpart to famed Spoleto, Italy, festival, with opera, ballet, modern and folk dance, arts, crafts, and theater. For information write Spoleto Festival USA, P. O. Box 157, Charleston 29402. Spoleto lasts from late May into early June.

June: Annual Sun Fun Festival, Myrtle Beach and the Grand Strand area. South Carolina's largest festival featuring Miss Bikini Wahine Pageant, crowning of Miss Sun Fun, two parades, Old-Fashioned Day on the Beach, National Turtle Race, South Carolina Baton Twirling Championship, archery shoot, beach games, street dances, historical excursions, treasure hunt, band concerts, fishing rodeo, golf tournaments and awards, arts and crafts shows, horse show, river cruises, watermelon eatin' contest, kids' day at amusements parks and a stock car race.

July: Mountain Rest Hillbilly Day, Mountain Rest Community. This tiny community comes alive with the pageantry of city slickers gone country: square dancing, clogging, greased pig chases and hootenanny. The twang of real hillbilly music sets the background for the enjoyment of mountain victuals served atop the beautiful Blue Ridge Mountain. *Beaufort Water Festival,* Beaufort. Parade, fishing tournament, golf tournament, beauty pageant, street dances, coronation ball, motorboat races, plays, shrimp boat parade with blessing of the fleet, and children's day activities.

August: Annual Foothills Arts and Crafts Festival, on the square in Pendleton. Exhibits, booths, artists at work in various media, crafts, demonstrations, etc.

September: Southern 500 Race, Darlington. Late-model stock car trials, parade and beauty pageant. All culminate in the annual Labor Day Southern 500, the granddaddy of all stock car races. Attendance is 75,000. *Branchville Raylrode Daze Festival,* Branchville. This festival takes you back to the days when railroads were king in this rural town. Festivities center around the railroad, which is part of the oldest line in the world, and the site of the first railroad junction. The firing up of an old steam locomotive with rides available adds reality to the event.

November: The Colonial Cup Races, Camden, feature the Colonial Cup $100,-000 International Steeplechase, which brings together the best in the U.S.A., with horses from abroad. The race is run over a special course covering 2 miles, 6½ furlongs with 18 jumps, none of which is repeated. *Chitlin Strut,* Salley. People from many areas of the Southeast come to this town to get their annual fill of chitlins, country music and dancing. Barbecue pork and chicken are available for those who don't crave the featured delicacy.

December: Annual Holiday Festival Golf Tournament, Myrtle Beach-Conway. Handicap tournament sponsored by grand Strand Area Golf Association at Quail Creek Golf Club.

 NATIONAL FORESTS. Cherokee Indians once roamed across the area now encompassed by Sumter National Forest. Colonial settlements followed, then the Revolutionary War, the Civil War and the bitter Reconstruction Period. All have left their imprint.

Named in honor of General Thomas Sumter, the "Gamecock" Revolutionary War hero, the Forest has three divisions—the *Andrew Pickens Division,* located in the Blue Ridge Mountains, and the *Long Creek* and *Enoree Divisions,* located in the rolling Piedmont section.

Visitors to the park can enjoy not only the facilities available there, but they may also visit such places as *Stumphouse Mountain Tunnel* and *Isaquenna Falls.* The tunnel, which stretches back some 1600 feet into solid granite, is the result of attempts to link Charleston with Cincinnati, Ohio, by rail. (The project failed.) Nearby is *Isaquenna Falls;* legend has it that a Creek Indian maiden escaped pursuit by leaping into the foaming falls and hiding on a small ledge.

The *Francis Marion National Forest,* located on the coastal plain north of Charleston, is named for a hero of the American Revolution, a general who was also known as the "Swamp Fox." Indians and Spanish and French explorers roamed the area, following the many waterways flanked by moss-covered gums and cypress and tall loblolly pines.

The American alligator, an endangered species, is found in the forest, as are many and varied forms of other wildlife.

The Forest is located on the Atlantic flyway of migratory birds, and in winter as many as 250 different bird species have been counted.

There are several public boat ramps and seven camping sites. The forest is divided into three Ranger Districts. The *Swamp Fox Ranger Station* and *Witherbee Ranger Station* are at Moncks Corner, the *Wambaw Ranger Station* at McClellanville. Spring fishing for bream and bass is excellent.

STATE PARKS. Thirty-four state parks enhance the state with campgrounds, well-stocked lakes, nature trails and picnic tables. The parks are open all year during daylight hours. Concessions generally close Labor Day and reopen May.

Parks and locations are: *Aiken,* 16 mi. E of Aiken off US 78; *Andrew Jackson,* 8 mi. N of Lancaster on US 521; *Baker Creek,* 3 mi. SW of McCormick on US 378; *Barnwell,* 7 mi. NE of Barnwell on State 3; *Charles Towne Landing,* on SC 171 between US 17 and I–26 near Charleston; *Cheraw,* 4 mi. SW of Cheraw on US 1; *Chester,* 3 mi. SW of Chester on State 72; *Colleton Wayside,* 11 mi. N. of Walterboro on US 15; *Croft,* 3 mi. SE of Spartanburg off State 56; *Edisto Beach,* 50 mi. SE of Charleston on State 174; *Givhans Ferry,* 16 mi. W of Summerville on State 61; *Greenwood,* 17 mi. E. of Greenwood on State 702; *Hamilton Branch,* 15 mi. SE of McCormick off US 221; *Hickory Knob,* 8 mi. SW of McCormick off US 378; *Hunting Island,* 16 mi. SE of Beaufort on US 21; *Huntington Beach,* 3 mi. S of Murrells Inlet on US 17; *Keowee-Toxaway,* on US 11 at Lake Keowee; *Kings Mountain,* 12 mi. NW of York on State 161; *Lee,* 7 mi. E of Bishopville off US 15; *Little Pee Dee,* 11 mi. SE of Dillon off State 57; *Myrtle Beach,* 3 mi. S of Myrtle Beach on US 17; *N. R. Goodale,* 2 mi. N of Camden off US 1; *Oconee,* 12 mi. NW of Walhalla off Rte. 28; *Paris Mountain,* 9 mi. N of Greenville off US 25; *Pleasant Ridge,* 22 mi. NW of Greenville off US 25; *Poinsett,* 18 mi. SW of Sumter off State 261; *Rivers Bridge,* 7 mi. SW of Ehrhardt off State 64; *Sadlers Creek,* 13 mi. SW of Anderson off US 29; *Santee,* 3 mi. NW of Santee off US 301; *Sesquicentennial,* 13 mi. NE of Columbia on US 1; *Table Rock,* 16 mi. N of Pickens off State 11; *Rose Hill,* 9 mi. SW of Union off US 176; *Old Dorchester,* 6 mi. S of Summerville on State 642.

CAMPING OUT. South Carolina's commercial campgrounds and state parks are available from the mountains to the sea, offering to the camper the crisp air of the Blue Ridge Mountains or a quiet seaside beach. Camping fees at all parks are from $5-$9 (for beachfront parks April–Aug. 31) a day per family for each site. Obtain permit from Park Superintendent before setting up camp. No advance reservations. One week maximum stay. For complete listing, write for booklet, "Mountains, Beaches, Lakes, and Other Places to Camp in South Carolina," South Carolina Division of Tourism, Room 10, Box 71, Columbia, S.C. 29202.

All commercial campgrounds provide electrical and water hookups, showers and toilet facilities. Added attractions such as swimming and fishing are offered at the following campgrounds: *Lake Hartwell KOA Kampgrounds,* Rte. 3, Anderson; *Charleston's Kampgrounds of America,* US 78, Ladsdon 29456; *Wagon Wheel CG,* Dillon, 6 mi. N on US 301; *Swamp Fox,* on I-95 (Hwy 76, Exit 157), Florence; *Rocks Pond CG,* Eutawville; *Lake Murray Family CG,* State 1, Gilbert; *Lake Pines KOA Kampground,* Hardeeville, 2 mi. N. on US 17; *Apache Family CG,* Star Rte. 2, Myrtle Beach; *Lake Arrowhead CG,* Star Rte. 2, Myrtle Beach; *Lakewood Family CG,* US 17 S, Myrtle Beach; *Pirateland Family CG,* US 17 S, Myrtle Beach; *Sherwood Forest CG,* US 17 N, Myrtle Beach; *Birch Canoe Family CG,* Myrtle Beach, US 17 & 5th Aves.; *Holiday Inn Trav-L-Park,* Myrtle Beach, 9 mi. N off US 17; *Ocean Lakes Family CG,* Myrtle Beach, 5 mi. S. on US 17 at intersection of Rte. 375; *Pebble Beach Family CG,* Myrtle Beach, on Rte. 73 (S. Ocean Blvd.); *Ponderosa Family CG,* Myrtle Beach, 10 mi. N on US 17; *Springmaid Family CG,* Myrtle Beach, S. Ocean Blvd; *Riverside Family CG,* N Myrtle Beach, 2 mi. off US 17 on Little River Neck Rd.; *Sweetwater Lake CG,* 3½ mi. from I-26, just off US 21 near Orangeburg and St. Matthews (exit I-26 onto Rte. 22, proceed 2 mi. turn right onto Sweetwater Rd. and follow signs). *Harry's Fish Camp and CG,* Pineville, off Rte. 45; *Holiday Inn Trav-L-Park of Santee-Lake Marion,* Box 520, Sumter; *Shawnee CG,* P.O. Box 137, Santee; *San-*

tee-Lake KOA Kampgrounds, Rte. 3, Box 84, Summerton; *Woodland Park CG,* York, 8 mi. W on Rte. 5.

Camping areas and trailer stopovers are maintained also at the Francis Marion National Forest, rich in historical background; Cherokee Indians, colonial settlements, Revolutionary War battles and the War Between the States all left their influence on the forest areas.

 TRAILER TIPS. The following trailer parks have hookup facilities for travel trailers: *Pine Acres Mobile Home Park,* Aiken, 1 mi. N on US 1; *The Windmill,* Bamberg, 12 mi. S on US 301 at jct. of State 64; *Rainbow Trailer Court,* 5020 Rivers Ave., 11 mi. NW on US 52, Charleston; *Crosby's Texaco,* Coosawhatchie, on US 17; *Esso Trailer Park,* Coosawhatchie, on US 17; *Johnson's Trailer Park,* 106 New St., 1 mi. N on US 301 and US 76, Florence; *Lockhaven Camper's Court,* 7 mi. S on I-95 at Interchange of State 403, Florence; *Munnerlyn's Trailer Park,* Rte. 4, 3 mi. N on US 301, Florence; *Rainbow Mobile Home Estates,* 3 mi. N on US 29, Greenville; *Fairway Trailer Park,* 1 mi. S on US 301, Manning; *Pine-View Mobile Home Park,* 10 mi. N on US 501, Myrtle Beach; *Carolina Wren Motel and Trailer Park,* 2 mi. N on US 301, Orangeburg; *Bennett's Trailer Park,* 3 mi. N of US 15, Walterboro; *North Walterboro Trailer Park,* Rte. 2, 3 mi. N on US 15, Walterboro; *Moore Mobile Manor,* 160 Oakwood Dr., Intersection of I-26 and US 378, West Columbia.

 MUSEUMS AND GALLERIES. *Beaufort: Beaufort Museum.* Craven St. Donation requested.

Charleston: Charleston Museum, 360 Meeting St. at Calhoun St. The oldest municipal museum in the United States, now in splendid new quarters, houses exhibits of pre-Columbian Indian weapons and artifacts and South Carolina history and culture. There are also planetarium shows. Admission. *Old Slave Mart Museum and Galleries,* 6 Chalmers St. Numerous artifacts of Negro life and history. Small admission charge. *Hunley Museum,* 50 Broad St. Exhibits of Confederate and Naval history with the focal point a replica of the Confederate States Submarine, *Hunley,* which was the first submarine to sink a surface vessel. Free. *City Hall Council Chamber,* corner of Broad & Meeting Sts. Portraits of many important leaders, including George Washington. Free. *Old Powder Magazine,* 79 Cumberland St. Built about 1713 near the city's outer wall, the museum is made of bricks cemented with oyster shell mortar. Mon. to Fri. Closed Sept. Small admission charge. *Charles Towne Landing Exposition,* 1500 Old Town Rd. An exciting 300-acre exhibition park located on the site of the first permanent settlement in South Carolina. Features movies, exhibits and an Animal Forest with species indigenous to South Carolina in 1670 displayed in their natural habitat. Daily. Small admission charge. *The Confederate Museum,* 188 Meeting St., a military museum. Small admission charge. *Citadel Archives Museum,* The Citadel, a military museum. Free. *South Carolina Historical Society,* 100 Meeting St. Free.

Clemson: Fort Hill (Home of John C. Calhoun), Clemson University. Free. *Hanover House,* Clemson University. Closed Mon. Free.

Columbia: Columbia Museum of Art and Science, 1112 Bull Street, Italian Renaissance paintings from the famous collection of Samuel H. Kress Foundation; silver, miniatures, jewelry, pottery, and furniture from the historic heritage of Columbia and South Carolina are permanently displayed. Also exhibits of the sciences, natural history, art and history. Planetarium is also a feature here (small admission fee). Open Tues. to Sat. *Midlands Exposition Center, South Carolina State Historical Museum,* 1615 Blanding St. A general museum housed in 1820 Hampton-Preston mansion. Children free. *South Carolina Confederate Relic Room and Museum,* World War Memorial Bldg., Sumter at Pendleton. A history museum open Mon. to Fri.; by appointment only on Sat. Check for closing dates. Free.

Florence: Florence Museum, 558 Spruce St. A general museum. Closed holidays. Free. *Georgetown: The Rice Museum,* Front & Screven Sts. A history museum housed in the Old Market Bldg. (1835), located on the site of the Old Market. Small admission. *Greenville: Greenville County Art Museum,* 420 College St., has nation's largest collection of Andrew Wyeth paintings, other permanent North American collections, numerous changing exhibits, lectures, concerts. Free. *Greenwood: The Museum,* Phoenix St. A general museum. Closed Christmas, Easter, and Thanksgiving. Free.

Lancaster: Andrew Jackson State Historical Park, 8 mi. N on US 521. The park contains a museum. Free. Open Mon.-Sat. *Rock Hill: Children's Nature Museum of York County,* Rte. 4, Box 211. Free. Closed Mon. *Spartanburg: Spartanburg County Regional Museum,* 501 Otis Blvd. Closed Mon. and national holidays. Free.

Art Galleries. *Charleston: Gibbs Art Gallery,* 135 Meeting St. Closed Mon., nat'l. hol. Free. *Clemson: Rudolph Lee Gallery,* College of Architecture, Lee Hall, Clemson University. Free. *Greenville: Bob Jones University Collection of Sacred Art,* at Bob Jones University. Closed Mon. and holidays. Free. *Sumter: Sumter Art Gallery,* 219 West Liberty St. Open daily. Free.

Special Interest Museums. *Florence: Florence Air Museum,* on US 301, 2 mi. N of Florence. Open daily. Admission. *Myrtle Beach: South Carolina Hall of Fame,* Myrtle Beach Convention Center. Astronaut Col. Charles M. Duke, Jr., a member of the Apollo 16 team that went to the moon in 1973, was the first member of the Hall of Fame. Open Mon. to Fri. *St. Matthews: Calhoun County Museum,* Railroad Ave., in the Calhoun County Library. Open Mon. to Fri. also by appointment. *Santee: Wings and Wheels Exhibition,* on US 301, US 15 and I-95. World's largest private collection of antique automobiles and airplanes. Open daily. Admission charge. *Darlington: The Joe Weatherly Stock Car Museum,* at Darlington Raceway. Open daily May to Sept.; (except holidays) Mon. to Fri. the rest of the year. Closed Sat. and holidays. Free.

 HISTORIC SITES. Historic Camden, easily accessible from US 521 & 1, is a restoration of the Revolutionary period. When the British left Camden in 1781, they left behind swords, muskets, cannon balls and other valuable pieces of history. They also left remains of the old town wall and six surrounding forts, the Kershaw house which General Cornwallis used as his headquarters and a large powder magazine. Visitors can find out about the town, the people and the battles in two restored log houses filled with unique museum exhibits. Walk through the restoration site along winding trails lined with historic markers, take a bicycle tour of the 60 wooded acres, or go on an electric cart. Closed Mon. Small admission charge.

Charleston, site of the first settlement and where the "first shot" of the Civil War was fired, is rich in historical sites. Its many and varied historic sites are listed in brochures which may be obtained from the Charleston Trident Chamber of Commerce, P.O. Box 975, Charleston 29402. *Fort Sumter National Monument,* in Charleston Harbor, may be reached by tour boats from Municipal Marina throughout the year. Trips per day vary. Monument open daily. Free.

Many historic churches may be seen in Charleston: *First Baptist Church,* 61-65 Church St., the oldest Baptist congregation in South Carolina, the present church begun in 1819. *St. Michael's Episcopal Church,* S.E. corner of Broad & Meeting Sts. The first service was held Feb. 1, 1761. Its bells have crossed the Atlantic Ocean five times. George Washington and Marquis de Lafayette both worshipped here when visiting Charleston. *French Huguenot Church,* S.E. corner of Church & Queen Sts., site of three successive Huguenot Churches. The present edifice, begun in 1844, was designed by Edward Brickell White. Only Huguenot church in America adhering exactly to the liturgy of the French Protestant Church. *St. Philip's Protestant Episcopal Church,* Church St., north of Queen. The present building was begun in 1835. In its two cemeteries lie many distinguished South Carolinians including John C. Calhoun. *St. John's Lutheran Church,* 10-12 Archdale St., one block west of King.

Historic homes open to the public for a small admission fee in Charleston are: *Nathaniel Russell House,* 51 Meeting St. *Joseph Manigault House,* 350 Meeting St. May 2 to Feb. 28, Tues. to Sun. Mar. to Apr. daily. *Heyward-Washington House,* 87 Church St. Open year round. *Thomas Elfe House,* 54 Queen St. Open year round. The *Arch Building* was constructed in the early 1800's and used as a "public house" for wagon masters and their helpers coming through Charleston.

Also in Charleston, the *Dock Street Theatre,* a restoration of the oldest playhouse in America, is open Mon. to Sat., Oct. to May.

Columbia, the capital of the geographical center of the state, offers the visitor much to see and enjoy. Stop at the State House, recognized as "one of the notable buildings of the world," and enter through the north entrance at the corner of Main and Gervais Sts. Bronze stars mark spots where shells from Sherman's army struck during occupation of the city in 1865. It's open weekdays and Sat. Just across from the State House, on Sumter St., is Trinity Episcopal Church, built in 1864. In the churchyard near the famous old "Governor's Oak" are graves of five South Carolina governors and other prominent citizens. And just down a few blocks on Sumter Street, you can enter the noted "Horseshoe" of the University of South Carolina.

Other historic points of interest include: *First Baptist Church,* 1306 Hampton St., built in 1859. The first Secession Convention met here on Dec. 17, 1860, but was moved to Charleston due to a smallpox epidemic. *Robert Mills Historic House and Park,* a restoration. This showplace of national architectural significance was designed by the famous Washington Monument architect, Robert Mills. The mansion was built in 1823 for the merchant prince Ainsley Hall. Closed Mon. Small admission charge.

Historic Pendleton grew from a crossroads of the Cherokee Trading Path to the Low Country and the Catawba Trading Path into Virginia. In existence since 1790, early Pendleton was described as "a grand center of society and trade, one of the foremost pioneer towns in the South." The Pendleton District historically comprised the present-day counties of Anderson, Oconee and Pickens in the northwesternmost part of the state. Included in the Pendleton District are such places as *Farmer's Hall (1826)* oldest such hall in the nation; beautiful *St. Pauls Episcopal Church* (1822) with its hand-pumped organ and slave gallery; and Hunter's Store building (1850), where many items of past eras are on display.

Cowpens National Battlefield Site, 11 mi. NW of Gaffney and 18 mi. NE of Spartanburg is a 1½ acre area with a monument to commemorate the battle. Free. *Kings Mountain National Military Park,* south of the town of Kings Mountain, off I-85, has a museum and visitor center. Park and headquarters building, open daily. Closed Christmas. Free.

 TOURS. *By boat: Charleston: Gray Line Harbor Tour:* 2¼ hours. Daily. Tour departs from the Gray Line Pier. *Chattooga River Rafting Adventures,* Long Creek. Shoot the rapids on guided 7-hr. raft trip. All equipment and lunch furnished. Two-week advance reservations required. Wknds in May and Sept.; daily during summer months.

By bus: Gray Line Bus Tour of Historic Charleston. 2¼ -hr. tours originate from the Francis Marion Hotel. Daily.

By train: Departing each morning and afternoon, the *Georgetown Historic Tour Train* provides guided tours of the original Old Georgetown. The train leaves the Chamber of Commerce building, located at 1001 Front St. For further information, contact the Chamber of Commerce, Front St., Georgetown, S. C.

On foot: Charleston Walking Tours offers an interesting self-guided tour through old historic Charleston. Pamphlets may be obtained at the Charleston Convention Bureau.

Others: Golden Leaves Tour, Table Rock State Park, cycling tour of the beautiful South Carolina mountain country takes place annually in Oct. Cyclists camp out Fri. night at the park, ride 60 mi. Sat. and 40 mi. Sun.

 SPECIAL INTEREST TOURS. *Trails:* Retrace the flight of the President of the Confederacy, Jefferson Davis, through South Carolina after the fall of Richmond in 1865. The *Jefferson Davis Trail* winds through small towns, farmland, forests and rolling hills removed from interstate travel. Much of the countryside on this Trail has changed so little since the nineteenth century that the visitor feels like he is going back through time.

Along the route the visitor will see "CS" signs keyed to a printed guide with special points of interest marked with numbered signs. Guide and sign numbers start at the northern border of South Carolina, where Jefferson Davis entered above Fort Mill.

Another tour which is distinctively signed is the *George Washington Trail.* When President Washington visited South Carolina in 1791, he followed the old King's Highway down the East Coast. This route is marked as the Coastal Section of the George Washington Trail from the South Carolina Welcome Center near Little River on US 17 to Savannah, where the President crossed over into Georgia. The Central Section of the Trail follows the route the President followed when he returned to South Carolina at the present town of North August. The Washington Trail is clearly marked with distinctive "Washington Coach" signs.

To obtain brochures which show the routings of both the Jefferson Davis Trail and the George Washington Trail write: South Carolina Division of Tourism, Room 10, Box 71, Columbia, S.C. 29202.

Georgetown has tours of *plantations and town houses* sponsored by the Women of Prince George, Winyah Episcopal Church. These annual tours are held in the second week of April. The plantations and houses, many over a hundred years old, are privately owned and are open to the public only at this time each year. Tours take a different route daily, showing plantations along the Black, Pee Dee, Santee, and Waccamaw rivers. Plantations dating back to land grants from King George II retain names of ancestral homes of the founders from England and Scotland. At some, original slave quarters are still intact, and vestiges of the once powerful rice-planting industry are in evidence. Rice was the chief means of support for many years in thousands of coastal areas. Indigo culture, too, had a brief span of prosperity. Several plantation homes are maintained, in whole or in part, in the style of antebellum hospitality and luxurious living. Histories of the houses and maps showing the routes for the day are provided. Tours are not conducted, and visitors provide their own transportation. Only small buses can go on the tours because of many low-hanging oak limbs. *Hopsewee Plantation,* 12 mi. S on US 17. Open Mon., Wed., Thurs. and Fri. Closed holidays. Fee.

Churches, the parishes of which were established more than two hundred years ago, are also open to visitors. Visitors have an opportunity to see many beautiful pieces of silver used in church services for decades. Box lunches and tickets are on sale at the parish house, Highmarket St.

Greenwood: Annual Greenwood County Historical Homes Tour (usually in April) is sponsored by the Greenwood County Chamber of Commerce. For more information contact the Greenwood County Chamber of Commerce, 404 Main St., Greenwood, S.C. 29646.

Charleston: Boone Hall Plantation, on US 17 8 mi. N of the city. Small admission charge. *Charleston Naval Base Tour* is offered year round each Sat. and Sun. Enter the Base at South Gate off Spruill Ave. The ships on display are designated and can be boarded and inspected by visitors.

Pendleton: Tours conducted by the Pendleton District Historical and Recreational Commission during the year feature many of Oconee County's Apple Orchards. In the spring at blossom time and in the fall during the harvest, special apple tours are conducted by PDHRC. For more information on these tours, write Pendleton District Historical and Recreational Commission (PDHRC), 125 East Queen St., P. O. Box 234, Pendleton 29670.

GARDENS. *Charleston: Middleton Place,* one of the world's outstanding landscaped gardens, is America's oldest. It was begun by the Middleton family in 1741, and completed a decade later. The first camellias planted in the New World were brought to Middleton by Andre Michaux, the botanist. They line pathways, their petals dropping to form pink, white and striped carpets. In spring, azaleas blossom across the landscaped terraces, around butterfly lakes and along formal walks. At the Plantation Stableyards, a variety of domestic animals and barnyard fowl, as well as artifacts, tools and farm implements have been assembled to tell the story of the economy which supported the self-contained plantation communities of the 18th and 19th centuries. Separate admissions for stableyards and garden (one fee) and Middleton House. Special group rates. Open daily all year. Rte. 61, 15 mi. N of Charleston toward Summerville or just off I-26, Summerville exit. *Cypress Gardens* might be described as "mysterious," with its lagoons of black water, in which centuries-old cypress trees grow. Its islands and banks are studded with flowers. Floral displays begin with the camellias and daffodils, giving way in early spring to multihued azaleas. Boat or walking tours may be taken through Cypress. Restaurant for lunch and tea. Special rates for groups and military personnel. Boat tour extra. Open daily Feb. 15 to May 1. Off State 52, from I-26, 23 mi. N of Charleston. *Magnolia Gardens* is a fairyland of flowers. It has a special charm and a spirit that often has an almost hypnotic effect on visitors. No camera has ever fully captured its grandeur, nor can words adequately describe it. Growing in Magnolia Gardens are camellias so old that they are now trees, forming part of its collection of over 500 varieties. Live oaks, hung with shadowy shawls of moss, and gnarled cypress complement the thousands of azaleas, flowering bulbs and shrubs and the trailing yellow jessamine (official state flower). Admission. Special group rates. Open daily all year. Rte. 61, 10 mi. N of Charleston toward Summerville, just off I-26, Summerville exit. *Hampton Park* adjoins The Citadel (South Carolina's military college). It occupies a part of the grounds that were devoted to the Interstate and West Indian Exposition (1901-2), in which 31 states and territories participated. Hampton Park has gorgeous displays of azaleas and other flowers, a sunken garden, a pool, rose-bordered walks, pavilions, aviary, and zoo. Open all year. Free.

Summerville: The azalea gardens of Summerville, planted informally, rival Charleston's magnolia on a much smaller scale. One of the main varieties of azaleas growing along the banks of the streams is the "Pride of Summerville," a pleasing shade of pink. Tall trees drip festoons of gray moss. The *Summerville Municipal Gardens,* near junction US 17 and 78, off I-26, are open all year, but the best season is spring. Free.

Georgetown: Belle Isle Gardens, off US 17, 5 mi. S of the city, is a 5,000-acre expanse of landscaped grounds planted in azaleas and other flora. It occupies old rice fields of a plantation. Located here was Battery White during the Civil War. Open every day except Christmas, Nov. to Aug. Admission charge.

Murrells Inlet: Brookgreen Gardens, US 17, 18 mi. S of Myrtle Beach, is an outdoor museum of sculpture. The gardens contain more than 350 pieces representing the history of American sculpture from the nineteenth century. Sculpture in the gardens includes works by Anna Hyatt Huntington who, with her husband, developed Brookgreen. Across the highway is "Atalaya," former home of the Huntingtons. The castle-like home is a part of Huntington Beach State Park. Open daily except Christmas. Admission.

Orangeburg: Edisto Memorial Gardens, US 301, 21, in city limits, just off I-26, were created less than 40 years ago from a dismal, swampy area extending along the banks of the North Edisto River. Tall cypress, crabapple and flowering dogwood are surrounded by plantings of azaleas which reach their peak in April. Edisto has 6,000 rose bushes, and its 110 varieties provide a veritable mass of blooms from early spring until frost. Open all year. Free.

Sumter: Swan Lake Gardens are so called because of their beautiful black Australian and white muted English swans that live on the lake. The gardens also are noted for their six million Japanese irises, which reach full bloom in late spring and are the focal point for an annual "Iris Festival." The festival is held the last week in May. Free.

Darlington: Williamson Park, located just off Spring St. on the northeast side of Darlington-US 52; SC 34, 11 mi. from I-20, is municipally owned. It is planted with hundreds of native shrubs and flowers, including azaleas, camellias and irises. Open all year. Free.

Hartsville: in *Kalmia Gardens.* Rte. 151, 2 mi W of the city, 12 mi. from I-95, both Up Country and Low Country flora are found. Kalmia is a 24-acre arboretum with over 700 varieties of trees and shrubs. The dominant species, from which the gardens take their name, is Kalmia latifolia, the mountain laurel. The pale pastels of the blossoms range from white to rose-colored and have purple markings within; the terminal clusters of blossoms remind one of pink parasols. Open all year. Free.

Columbia: The gardens of the *State House* are pretty in every season. To be seen on the beautifully planted grounds, both alive and as a cast-iron replica, is the palmetto (sabal palm), South Carolina's official state tree. One block of Senate St. to the rear of the building, is lined with living palmettoes. The replica, created by South Carolina's famous ironsmith, Christopher Werner—who also designed the sword gates at the Sword Gate House in Charleston—is so realistic that birds build their nests in the fronds in springtime. The tree was erected as a memorial to South Carolinians who died in the Mexican War. The small garden of the *Columbia Museum of Art,* 1519 Senate St., is located in the rear of the Science Museum. It contains more than 50 species of native South Carolina flora and some fauna. The garden is divided into three sections, representing South Carolina's Low Country, Midlands, and Up Country, with flora representative of all. Open daily except Mon. 10 to 5; Sun. 2 to 6. Free. The grounds of the *University of South Carolina* contain two beautiful small gardens. At the horseshoe of the old campus on Sumter St. is the *Memorial Garden* in the rear of the South Carolina Library. Borders in the garden are defined by clipped hedges of dwarf holly. Year round bloom comes from azaleas, roses, camellias, and other flowers. The other garden, reached through a small doorway in the old brick wall on Pendleton St., between Marion and Bull, is landscaped with a fountain and formal beds of floribunda roses, bordered by sasanquas and azaleas. It is beautiful in spring. Open all year. Free.

STAGE AND REVUES. In Columbia the *Town Theatre,* 1012 Sumter St. is one of the oldest little theater organizations in the nation. It has been in continuous operation since 1919. Six plays are performed annually. In Charleston is the *Dock Street Theater,* opened in 1736. Original scripts, Broadway plays, Shakespearean and 18th century classics are performed. For list and dates of presentation write: Charleston Convention Bureau, P.O. Box 834, Charleston, S.C. 29402.

DRINKING LAWS. Mixed drinks may be purchased in licensed restaurants, hotels and motels. Liquor is served in a miniature bottle, which the purchaser may mix or have mixed according to his taste. Liquor is sold by the bottle in state-licensed package stores. Hours of operation are from sunrise to sunset. No sales on Sundays, election days, New Year's Day, July 4, Thanksgiving and Christmas. Wine and beer are available in most restaurants, or may be purchased in grocery stores.

SUMMER SPORTS. *Swimming, golf, fishing, surfboarding*—they're all there in addition to a background of white sand, warm sun and blue sky on South Carolina's beaches.

The Grand Strand, with Myrtle Beach at its center, is a sparkling 60-mile strip of sand and surf stretching from the quaint fishing village of Little River to historic Georgetown. Known as the Sun Fun Capital, the Grand Strand offers 50 mi. of free public beaches, a mild climate and unpolluted waters.

For the *golfer,* there are 35 courses that add as much fame to the Strand as the white beaches. Unlimited accommodations, superb dining facilities, attractive prices and the largest variety of courses of any resort in America have all contributed to the designation of the Strand as "The Coastal Golf Capital of the U.S.A."

Harbour Town Links, Hilton Head Island, ranks among the second ten of America's 100 greatest; Dunes G. & B.C., Myrtle Beach, among the fourth ten; and Greenville Country Club among the second fifty, according to "Golf Digest." Also recommended are two located in No. Myrtle Beach; five in Myrtle Beach; two in Ocean Drive Beach; two in Charleston; 11 on Hilton Head Island; two in Aiken; and courses on Pawley's Island; Crescent Beach; Litchfield Beach; Fripp Island; Columbia; Santee; and Florence.

For the *fishing* enthusiast, the Strand offers 13 fishing piers. Or the fisherman can join the host of visitors surf-fishing. And charter boats for deep-sea fishing are available all along the Strand.

Charter boats for deep-sea fishing from Charleston provide rods, reels and bait.

South Carolina's streams, lakes and rivers offer the avid angler the opportunity to catch rainbow and brown trout in the mountainous areas of the western counties—Oconee, Pickens and Greenville. Or he may choose the Santee—Cooper Lakes, which are most noted for their nationally famous landlocked striped bass.

Charleston boasts four excellent beaches where *surf-bathing* and *water sports* are enjoyed. Folly, Sullivans Island, Isle of Palms and Edisto attract thousands of visitors each season. Attractive cottages are available by the week, month or season. Motel accommodations are limited.

Remote, beautiful Hilton Head Island offers the ultimate in accommodations, food, golf and subtropical beaches. There are 12 golf courses on the Island, including the Harbour Town Golf Links where the annual Heritage Golf Classic is staged.

Hilton Head offers a wide variety of fishing pleasures—a variety in both species and habitat. From the wide beaches for surf-fishing to the quiet saltwater lagoons, a fisherman will find a variety of catches. Also challenging are the bays and saltwater creeks and the warm Gulf Stream waters where big game fishing takes place.

Fishing boats and guided charter boats are available and fishing tackle is included in the charter boat rate.

WINTER SPORTS. *Hunting* in South Carolina is both a tradition and a sport. Alligators and all birds of prey are protected and may not be hunted. Deer, fox, mink, muskrat, oppossum, otter rabbit, racoon, skunk and squirrel may be hunted in season and within bag limits. Domestic game birds include the wild turkey, mourning dove, bobwhite quail, ruffed grouse, Wilson snipe, woodcock, marsh hen and duck.

SPECTATOR SPORTS. *Aiken: Polo* can be enjoyed each Sun. afternoon from Jan. through part of April. Admission. *Beaufort:* the *South Atlantic Sailing Regatta* is held during the Beaufort Water Festival in mid-July.

SHOPPING. Handcrafted rope hammocks can be purchased at various shops on Pawley's Island on U.S. 17.The craft came from Africa and was practiced by ancestors of the craftsmen in the shop. Other handicrafts are also on display.

Basket weaving can be seen along US 17, north of Charleston. Numerous stands display this African craft.

In Charleston, *Historic Charleston Reproductions,* 105 Broad St., and *The Thomas Elfe Workshop,* 54 Queen St., have reproductions of Charleston furniture and accessories, porcelains, brass, china, lamps, crystal, silver, pewter. You'll also find woven seagrass and palmetto baskets at the *City Market.*

WHAT TO DO WITH THE CHILDREN. *Carowinds,* a magic-land theme park designed for family entertainment, is 85 miles north of Columbia. Follow US 21 N to Rock Hill and then I-77 to the park. On the border of the Carolinas, it's actually an "inter-state" park, shared by North and South Carolina. In 73 acres of excitement, Carowinds combines the thrills of over a hundred rides and attractions with exhibits and settings that re-create the culture and heritage of the Carolinas. Plantation Square, Queen's Colony, Indian Thicket, Country Crossroads, Pirate Island, Frontier Outpost and Contemporary Carolinas are the theme areas that take you from yesterday to tomorrow. An authentic narrow-gauge steam locomotive encircles the park and a sleek monorail offers automated transportation. All rides, shows, exhibits and attractions are included in the price of a ticket. Camping facilities are available. Rock Hill offers motels and good restaurants. For rates and information contact: Group Sales, The Carowinds Corp., P.O. Box 15514, Charlotte 28210.

Keowee-Toxaway Visitors Center, north of Clemson and accessible from State Rtes. 130 and 183, is the focal point for visitors to one of the largest nuclear generating stations. The modernistic center uses colorful, animated displays and exhibits to take visitors on a magical trip through the history of energy. It is unique in that the displays involve the visitor in what is being seen. A working waterwheel, a thunderstorm and other reality exhibits create an environment not possible with static displays. Free.

Middleton Place Gardens and Plantation Stableyards, on State 61, 16 mi. north of Charleston and US 17 toward Summerville. At the Stableyards, kids not only may see domestic animals such as sheep, cows, pigs, horses, chickens, and peacocks, but may even take a ride in a mule-drawn wagon. Open daily, year-round. Admission.

Historic Camden, on US 521 in Camden, offers Revolutionary War museum exhibits, bicycle and electric cart tours, and a petting zoo for kids. Closed Mondays unless a holiday. Admission.

Also: A "family fun mecca," *Myrtle Beach* offers Guinness Hall of World Records; Sportsworld, with disco roller skating and dancing; Ripley's Believe It or Not Museum; Wild Rapids and Water Boggan water slides; and Grand Prix, with racing on real race cars, bumper boats and go-karts. *Brookgreen Gardens* features a zoo completely stocked with local coastal animals and fowl. Open 9 to 5:30. *Charles Towne Landing,* 1500 Old Town Rd., Charleston, features an Animal Forest with animals native to South Carolina in 1670, displayed in their natural surroundings. Open daily. Admission; 5 and under free. The *National Fish Hatchery,* Lakeview Dr., Orangeburg, is open daily. Free. The *Walhalla Federal Fish Hatchery,* in the Sumter National Forest, approx. 19 mi. NW on Rte. 107, Walhalla, is open daily. Free. *Riverbanks Zoological Park,* 500 Wildlife Pkwy., Columbia, has daily penguin and sea lion feedings.

HOTELS AND MOTELS. Traditional Southern hospitality is the one ingredient common to all the hotels and motels in South Carolina. The facilities range from the modestly designed, which cater to the traveling man, to the lush and ornate, which cater to regional and national conventions.

Accommodations are listed according to their category. Based on double occupancy, price categories and ranges are as follows: *Deluxe,* $54 and up; *Expensive,* $41–$53; *Moderate,* $31–$40; and *Inexpensive,* under $31. For a more complete explanation of hotel and motel categories see *Facts at Your Fingertips* at the front of this volume.

Anderson

Howard Johnson's Motor Lodge. *Moderate.* US 76 and SC 28, jct. I-85. 10 min. from airport and downtown. Cocktail lounge and restaurant, pool, golf privileges.

Holiday Inn. *Moderate.* 3025 N. Main St. Restaurant, lounge. Color TV, pool, wading pool, playground.

Best Western University Inn. *Inexpensive.* 3430 Clemson Blvd. Under 12, free. Pool. Pets. Café and lounge. Entertainment and dancing.

Calhoun Motor Lodge. *Inexpensive.* 110 Sharp St. Free coffee in rooms. Pool.

Days Inn. *Inexpensive.* I-85 and SC 187. Pool, play area, gift shop, some efficiencies. Tasty World restaurant.

Beaufort

Ramada Inn. *Moderate to Expensive.* 3127 Boundary St. Entertainment, cocktail lounge, restaurant. Swimming pool. Rooms for handicapped.

Sea Island Motel. *Moderate.* 1015 Bay St. Dining room. Pool.

Joyland Motel. *Inexpensive.* 2½ mi. N.W. on 21, 1 block N. of SC 170. Pool. Golf privileges. Kitchenettes and cabana units available.

Lord Carteret Motel. *Inexpensive.* 301 Carteret St. Kitchenettes available. Refrigerators. Pets.

Camden

Holiday Inn. *Moderate.* 4 mi. S.W. on US 1, 601. Color cable TV. Restaurant. Kennel. Pool (heated). Golf privileges.

Hampton Park Inn. *Inexpensive.* 322 DeKalb St. Color TV, dining room. Pool.

Mona Lisa. *Inexpensive.* 1011 W. DeKalb St. Pleasant rooms. Restaurant. Pets. Pool.

Charleston

Battery Carriage House. *Deluxe.* 20 S. Battery St. Delightful small luxury guest house has 10 beautifully furnished antebellum apartments, all with kitchen facilities. Color TV, continental breakfast, bicycles for touring city.

Indigo Inn. *Deluxe.* One Maiden Lane. In heart of historic district, Inn offers 18th-century ease, 20th-century comfort. Continental breakfast, daily newspapers are provided.

Mills House Hotel. *Deluxe.* 115 Meeting St. Antique furnishings, glowing chandeliers give unusual charm and ambience to historic hostelry, reconstructed with all 20th-century amenities. Beautifully furnished lobby, guest rooms. Lounge, live entertainment, pool. Part of Holiday Inn system.

Sheraton-Charleston Hotel. *Deluxe.* 70 Lockwood Blvd., 1 blk. N of U.S. 17. City's newest luxury hotel is elegantly furnished, has own concierge. Heated outdoor pool, jogging track, lighted tennis courts, golf privileges. Dining rooms, entertainment in lounge.

Swordgate Inn. *Deluxe.* 111 Tradd St. Several rooms available in small intimate inn off courtyard of 18th-century house. No credit cards.

Holiday Inn–Riverview. *Expensive.* US 17 at Ashley River. Circular style. Golf and tennis package plans available. Dining room. Entertainment. Pool.

Howard Johnson's Motor Lodge. *Expensive.* Jct. I-26 and SC 642. Inviting rooms open onto private balconies or patios. Restaurant. Pool. Guided historic tours available.

Vendue Inn. *Deluxe.* 19 Vendue Range. Luxurious guest rooms feature canopied and poster beds, Oriental rugs, 18th-century furniture. Complimentary wine and cheese served in courtyard. Continental breakfast.

Holiday Inn. *Moderate to Expensive.* Two locations, both with dining rooms, pools and kennels. **Airport:** I-26 at Aviation Ave. Live entertainment. **Downtown:** Calhoun & Meeting Sts. Lounge, entertainment. (Also see Mills House and Holiday Inn-Riverview listing above.)

Best Western King Charles Inn. *Moderate to Expensive.* 237 Meeting St. Dining room, pool, cocktail lounge., entertainment, dancing. Color TV. Handicapped facilities.

Francis Marion Hotel. *Moderate.* 385 King St. Landmark downtown hotel has been beautifully renovated. Lounge, superb dining in Swamp Fox Room.

Golden Eagle Motor Inn. *Moderate.* 155 Meeting St. Well-maintained, two-story motor inn. Dining room. Pool. Golf privileges.

Heart of Charleston. *Moderate.* 200 Meeting St. Pool, coffee shop, cocktail lounge.

Econo-Travel. *Inexpensive.* 5169 Rivers Ave. Color TV. Pets. Restaurant adjacent.

Knight's Inn. *Inexpensive.* 1 mile from airport, 2355 Aviation Ave. Some refrigerators. Kitchenettes available.

SOUTH CAROLINA 489

Clemson

The Clemson House. *Moderate.* Hwys. 76 & 123. Operated by Clemson University.

Holiday Inn of Clemson. *Moderate.* US 123 and 76. Restaurant, lounge, pool. Color TV. On Hartwell Lake; marina, boating, fishing. Golf privileges.

Thunderbird. *Inexpensive.* 2 mi. E. on 123. Cribs free. Pool.

Columbia

Carolina Inn. *Expensive.* 937 Assembly St. Dining room. Pool. Pets. Entertainment.

Holiday Inn. *Expensive.* Two locations. All have restaurant, pool, kennels. **Northwest:** US 1 jct. I-26. Free airport transportation. Live entertainment. Playground. **City Center:** 630 Assembly St. Dining room. Live entertainment.

Quality Inns. *Expensive.* Two locations: I-20 at Broad River Rd.; 1539 Horseshoe Dr. Color cable TV, some kitchenettes. Pools, restaurants, lounges. Handicapped facilities.

Best Western Inn. *Moderate to Expensive.* Two locations: 4502 Devine St., I-26 and SC 215. Both have restaurants, lounges, pools. I-26 Inn has live entertainment, is near Riverbanks Zoo.

Ramada Inn. *Moderate to Expensive.* US 378 at I-26. Spacious, comfortable rooms. Suites. Gourmet restaurant, nightly entertainment. pool. Pets.

Downtowner. *Moderate.* 1301 Main St. Member of the chain. Nicely furnished rooms. Suites available. Dining room. Pool (heated), service at poolside. Pets accepted.

Tremont Motor Inn. *Moderate.* 111 Knox Abbott Dr. Coffee shop. Playground. Some refrigerators. Pool.

Howard Johnson's. *Inexpensive to Moderate.* Two locations. Both have rooms with balconies or patios, restaurant, pool, play area. **North:** Bush River Rd., jct. I-126 and I-26; **West:** Knox Abbott Dr. & State St. Poolside service.

Days Inn. *Inexpensive.* Two locations: Jct. I-26, S.C. 215; I-20, U.S. 1. Tasty World restaurant. Pool.

Greenville

Sheraton Motor Inn. *Expensive.* 1001 S. Church St. A six-story motor inn with very attractive rooms. Restaurant. Pool. Golf privileges. Small pets.

Sheraton-Palmetto Inn. *Expensive.* 4295 Augusta Rd., at Jct. US 25, I-85. Dining room, dancing, entertainment. Color TV, pool.

Best Western Traveleze Motor Inn. *Moderate.* 2800 Laurens Rd. Dining room, cocktail lounge. Pool. Pets.

Golden Eagle Motor Inn (Textile Hall). *Moderate.* 540 Pleasantburg Dr. A large motor inn with inviting rooms. Dining room. Pool. Entertainment. Free local calls.

Holiday Inn. *Moderate.* Two locations: 27 S. Pleasantburg Dr., and I-85 at Exit 46. Both have dining rooms, entertainment, pools, color TV, kennels.

Howard Johnson's Motor Lodge (Downtown). *Moderate.* Church St. and Augusta Rd. Lovely rooms. Restaurant. Pool. Play area. Pets.

Howard Johnson's Motor Lodge (South). *Moderate.* Jct. US 25 and 291. Dining room. Pool. Private patios and balconies.

Ramada Inn. *Moderate.* 1314 S. Pleasantburg Dr. Pool. Dining room, lounge, color TV. Pets.

Days Inn. *Inexpensive.* I-85 and US 276. Pool. Play area. Gift shop. Tasty World restaurant; service station.

Quality Inn Colonial. *Inexpensive.* Wade Hampton Blvd. Nice rooms. Restaurant. Pool with service at poolside. Play area. Small pets.

Hilton Head Island

Adventure Inn. *Deluxe.* Golf privileges. Villas, cabanas, 2-story resort homes. Pool. Kitchenettes available. Pets.

Hilton Head Inn. *Deluxe.* Oceanfront. Beautifully furnished rooms with contemporary decor, also villas and cottages. Dining rooms, lounges, entertainment. Pool. Complete resort facilities of Sea Pines Plantation: superb golf, tennis, children's programs. Numerous vacation packages.

Hyatt at Palmetto Dunes. *Deluxe.* Oceanfront. Superb resort hotel has fine dining in elegant Hugo's, lounges, live entertainment, pool. Golf, tennis, all resort facilities at neighboring Palmetto Dunes.

Marriott's Hilton Head Resort. *Deluxe.* Oceanfront, in Shipyard Plantation. Dramatically beautiful new luxury hotel has spectacular five-story atrium lobby, fine dining rooms, lounges, pool bar, bar, exercise rooms, saunas. Golf, tennis at adjacent Hilton Head Golf and Racquet Clubs.

Holiday Inn. *Expensive to Deluxe.* Large motor hotel with comfortable rooms. Ocean view. Restaurant, disco, lounge. Golf, tennis, marina privileges.

Port Royal Inn. *Moderate to expensive.* A double-story inn on the ocean plus housekeeping cottages. Spacious rooms. Game room, entertainment, pets welcome. Dining, pool, golf, tennis at Port Royal Plantation.

Sea Crest Motel. *Moderate to expensive.* Golf privileges, putting green. Oceanfront. Pool (heated). Kitchenettes available. Superb Captains Table Dining Room specializes in Continental European cuisine.

Kiawah Island

Kiawah Island Inn. *Deluxe.* US 17 South and SC 20, P.O. Box 12910. Oceanfront setting on lush, wooded island. Accommodations in inn and villas. Excellent dining rooms, lounge, entertainment. Golf, tennis, children's programs, pools, bicycling, sauna, complete resort activities. Numerous vacation packages.

Myrtle Beach

(All rates higher during May 1- Labor Day season)

Myrtle Beach Hilton Hotel. *Deluxe.* Beachside, in Arcadian Shores. Luxury resort hotel has 14-story atrium lobby. Continental dining in elegant Alfredo's, lounges, entertainment. Shopping, social program, tennis, golfing on championship course. All rooms oceanfront.

Sheraton Myrtle Beach Inn. *Deluxe.* 7100 N. Ocean Blvd. Superb dining, dancing in Pinnacle Supper Club. Lounges, entertainment, tennis club, golf privileges. All rooms oceanfront.

The Breakers Golf and Beach Lodge. *Expensive to Deluxe.* 2006 N. Ocean Blvd. Golf privileges. Oceanfront. Tennis. 2 pools. Dining room. Entertainment. Kitchenettes available.

Ocean Dunes. *Expensive to Deluxe.* 74th Ave. N. Golf privileges. Oceanfront. Tennis. Pool. Dining room. Entertainment.

The Beach House Motor Inn. *Expensive.* 6800 N. Ocean Blvd. Golf privileges. Oceanfront. Heated pool. Free continental breakfast. Kitchenettes available.

Captain's Quarters Motor Inn. *Expensive.* 901 S. Ocean Blvd. Very inviting rooms, all with refrigerator and private balcony. Rooftop coffee shop. Pool (heated). Beach. Shuffleboard. Play area. Fishing. Golf privileges. Golf and tennis Package Plans available.

Caravelle Resort Motel. *Expensive.* 6900 N. Ocean Blvd. Golf privileges. Oceanfront. Tennis. Pool. Dining room. Kitchenettes available.

The Driftwood on the Oceanfront. *Expensive.* 1600 N. Ocean Blvd. Oceanfront motel. Spacious, attractive rooms. Efficiencies. Coffee shop. Pool (heated). Beach and surf fishing. Golf package plans available.

Hawaii Kai Motor Inn. *Expensive.* 1105 S. Ocean Blvd. On the ocean. Refrigerator in each room. Restaurant. Pool (heated). Play area. Shuffleboard. Beach. Golf Package Plan available.

Holiday Inn. *Expensive.* Three locations. **Downtown:** 6th Ave. S. & Ocean Blvd. Entertainment, tennis, oceanfront. **North:** 2713 Ocean Blvd. S., North Myrtle Beach. On the ocean. Restaurant, entertainment, fishing facilities. **Surfside:** on US 17 at 48th Ave. N. Golf Package Plan available. Kennels.

Ocean Reef. *Expensive.* 601 S. Ocean Blvd. On the ocean. Spacious rooms with refrigerators. Some suites, efficiencies. Coffee shop. Pool (heated). 18-hole putting green. Shuffleboard. Play area. Golf Package Plan available.

Pan-American Motor Inn. *Expensive.* 5300 N. Ocean Blvd. Coffee shop. Oceanfront. Attractive rooms open onto private balconies. Pool. Tennis, golf privileges.

The Poindexter Motel. *Expensive.* 1702 N. Ocean Blvd. Spacious rooms with refrigerators. Pool. Golf privileges. Pets.

Quality Inn Caribbean. *Expensive.* 3000 N. Ocean Blvd. at 30 Ave. Oceanfront. Attractive rooms with private balconies. Room service. Pool (heated). Shuffleboard. Restaurant. Golf privileges.

Sea Mist Resort. *Expensive to Deluxe.* 1200 S. Ocean Blvd. Large motel on the ocean. Some efficiencies. Three pools. Putting green. Tennis. Play area. Beach, surf fishing. Restaurant. Golf Package Plan available.

Thunderbird Motor Inn. *Expensive.* 7300 N. Ocean Blvd. 2-bedroom apartments and executive suites available. Golf Package Plan available. Dining room. Heated pool. Putting green.

Dunes Village Lodge. *Moderate to Expensive.* 5200 N. Ocean Blvd. Oceanfront. Apartments available. Tennis. Golf privileges. Heated pool. Dining room.

Holiday Inn. *Moderate.* 1200 N. Ocean Blvd. Apartments available. Penthouse restaurant. Golf privileges. Not a member of the chain.

Jamaican. *Moderate to Expensive.* 3006 N. Ocean Blvd. Kitchenettes available. Refrigerators in many rooms. Balconies. Pool.

Ocean Spray Motel. *Moderate.* 1304 S. Ocean Blvd. Family oriented. Pools; restaurant adjacent.

Patricia Inn and Court. *Moderate to Deluxe.* 2702 N. Ocean Blvd. On the ocean. Kitchens available. Pool (heated). Dining room. Game room. Golf privileges. Tennis.

St. John's Inn. *Moderate to Expensive.* 6801 N. Ocean Blvd. at 69th Ave. Rooms decorated in Spanish motif with view of the garden or the ocean. Restaurant, bar with dancing and entertainment during season. Pool (heated). Beach across the road. Shuffleboard. Golf privileges.

South Wind Resort. *Moderate to Expensive.* 5310 N. Ocean Blvd. On the ocean. Apartments accommodate up to seven persons. Private screened porch overlooking pool and ocean. Restaurant. Putting green. Pool (heated). Sauna. Play area. Golf Package Plan available.

Swamp Fox Motor Inn and Restaurant. *Moderate to Expensive.* 2311 S. Ocean Blvd. Oceanfront. Spacious rooms with private balconies. Some kitchens. Three pools. Putting green. Shuffleboard. Play area. Beach, surf fishing. Golf Package plan available.

Tiki Motel. *Moderate.* 2501 S. Ocean Blvd. Family apartments available. On the beach. Pool (heated). Shuffleboard. Golf privileges. Dining room. Tennis. Some refrigerators.

Cherry Tree Inn. *Inexpensive.* 5400 N. Ocean Blvd. Oceanfront motel. Kitchens available. Pool (heated). Golf privileges. Golf Package Plan available.

Jade Tree Motor Inn. *Inexpensive to Expensive.* 5308 N. Ocean Blvd. Coffee shop. Golf privileges. Oceanfront. Heated pool. Playground.

Lakeside Motel. *Inexpensive.* 6805 N. Kings Hwy. Pool, playground, putting green, lawn games. Own lake, fishing, boating. Picnic tables. Family-oriented. Restaurant nearby.

Spartanburg

Holiday Inn of Spartanburg. *Moderate.* Jct. I-85 and I-26. Dining room. Pool. Playground. Kennels.

Howard Johnson's Motor Lodge. *Moderate.* 343 Hearon Circle. Very pleasant rooms. Pool. Play area. Pets permitted. Complimentary coffee. Restaurant.

Ramada Inn. *Moderate.* 1000 Hearon Circle. Coffee shop. Meeting rooms. Pool. Playground. Pets.

TraveLodge. *Moderate.* 416 E. Main St. Inviting rooms. Restaurant nr. Pool (heated). Pets.

Heart of Spartanburg. *Inexpensive.* 542 N. Church St. Comfortable rooms. Pool. Free coffee in rooms. Restaurant adjacent.

Sumter
Holiday Inn of Sumter. *Moderate.* 226 N. Washington St. Golf privileges. Pool. Restaurant. Kennel.

Mt. Vernon Inn. *Inexpensive.* Broad at Washington St. Nicely furnished rooms. Pool. Dining room. Golf privileges.

 DINING OUT. South Carolina's traditions include a reputation for good food, with its table fare varying over the distinctive geographical sections of the state. Menus vary from country ham and grits with red-eye gravy in the Up Country, to the renowned "she-crab soup" of Charleston. But throughout the state you'll find many restaurants serving good food at economical prices.

Restaurants are listed according to their category. The categories and price ranges for a complete dinner are as follows: *Expensive,* $12 and up; *Moderate,* $7–$11; *Inexpensive,* under $7. For a more complete explanation of restaurant categories see *Facts at Your Fingertips* at the front of this volume.

Anderson
Best Western University Inn. *Moderate.* 3430 Clemson Blvd. Tasteful room, varied menu. Entertainment in lounge adjacent.

Holiday Inn. *Moderate.* 3025 N. Main St. American cuisine. Favorite with local groups. Entertainment in lounge.

Charleston
Barbadoes Restaurant-Mills House Hotel. *Expensive.* Queen and Meeting Sts. Gourmet/Continental cuisine in elegant surroundings. She-crab soup and lobster Calhoun lead on list of superior dishes. Jacket and tie at dinner.

The East Bay Trading Company. *Expensive.* East Bay and Queen Sts. Stately brick structure, former warehouse, features seafood, Continental and native cuisine on three levels wrapped around skylight-topped atrium. Antiques, artifacts, lavish greenery lend a warm, serene atmosphere.

Perdita's. *Expensive.* 10 Exchange St. Continental cuisine served in Old World atmosphere. Children's portions. Small, elegant, low key, this is one of the South's best dining rooms. Reservations essential!

The Colony House. *Moderate to expensive.* 35 Prioleau St. Specialty: Low Country dishes, seafood. Baked pompano is a favorite.

Henry's. *Moderate.* 54 Market St. Rambling, unpretentious restaurant is a great local favorite. Ask to be seated in the bar!

The Ice House. *Moderate.* 188 Meeting St., in historic City Market. Seafoods, steaks, Carolina Low Country specialties. Clever decor features artifacts from "ice house" days.

The Market Place. *Moderate.* 32 Market Street. In old seamen's church. Seafood and beef specialties. Rather formal atmosphere.

Trawler Restaurant. *Moderate.* US 17N. Mt. Pleasant. Family dining. Specialties: fish stew and shrimp à la Newburg.

Harold's Cabin. *Inexpensive.* Meeting St. Piggly Wiggly. In-the-know Charlestonians drop by for lunch, and you should, too. Ideal place to shop for take-home treats.

Lorelei. *Inexpensive.* Shem Creek, US 17N. Family dining. Specialty is seafood.

Columbia

Chandelier Room. *Expensive.* In Carolina Townhouse, 1615 Genvais St. Elegant decor. Beef and seafood specialties. Salad bar.

Le Petit Chateau. *Expensive.* 4423 Devine St. Mostly French cuisine. Good wine list. Music.

Stadium Steak House. *Moderate.* 402 Blossom St. Beef and steaks only. Outstanding bar. Evenings only.

The Market. *Moderate.* 1205 Assembly St. Convenient to major hotels. Large dining facilities, with excellent service. Steaks, seafood (red snapper and lobster). Children's portions.

Morrison's Cafeteria. *Inexpensive.* US 176, Dutch Square Mall. Member of one of South's leading chains. Does own baking. Roast beef a specialty.

Winner's Circle Restaurant. *Inexpensive.* 1111 Green St. Home cooking featuring Southern specialties. Local favorite.

Greenville

Ye Olde Fireplace. *Expensive.* 291 Pleasantburg Dr. Children's portions. Exceptionally well-prepared steak and seafood. Entertainment.

Vince Perone's Restaurants. *Moderate to Expensive.* 1 E. Antrim Dr. Unusual combination of two quite different dining establishments. The Lighter Side features deli items. The elegant Forum offers superb Italian, Continental, seafood specialties, extensive wine list. Also, cocktails, lounge, dancing. Great local favorite. Reservations advised in The Forum.

Capri's. *Moderate.* Good Italian food at four locations.

Charcoal Steak Houses. *Moderate.* There are five of them with low lights, carpets and combo, great favorites. All about the same price and type.

Morrison's. *Inexpensive.* McAlister Square, Pleasantburg Dr. Branch of popular cafeteria chain serves lunch and dinner.

Hilton Head Island

Fulvio's. *Expensive.* 33 New Orleans Rd. Continental dining with emphasis on Italian specialties.

The Boilers. *Moderate.* U.S. 278, 1 mi. from bridge. Fine fresh seafood. Family favorite.

Hudson's. *Moderate.* Shrimp Docks, Skull Creek. Superb fresh seafood from own docks. Local favorite.

Myrtle Beach

Christy's. *Moderate to expensive.* 2 mi. S. on US 17. Crab au gratin, lobster and prime ribs are specialties. Background music, entertainment, dancing.

Slug's Rib. *Moderate to expensive.* U.S. 17 N. Superb restaurant serves only one entree—prime rib of beef.

Crab House. *Moderate.* U.S. 17 N. on Restaurant Row. All-you-can-eat seafood. Casual dress.

Rice Planter's Restaurant. *Moderate.* 6707 N. Kings Highway (US 17). Delightful large establishment, but amazingly rapid service. Specialties: crab fingers, shrimp creole, pecan pie. Children's portions.

Sea Captain's House. *Moderate.* 3002 N. Ocean Blvd. Informal restaurant at the edge of the ocean. Own pastries. Specialties: grasshopper pie and seafood. Children's portions. Lunch and dinner. Closed Dec. & Jan. Also at Murrells Inlet.

Yardarm. *Moderate.* N. Kings Highway (US 17). Wide variety seafood and steaks. Courteous, fast service. Topgrade.

Hoskins Restaurant. *Inexpensive.* On US 301. Main St. N. Myrtle Beach. Maritime decor. Seafood, steaks, and Southern fried chicken for the entire family.

Mammy's Kitchen. *Inexpensive.* 1014 N. Kings Highway (US 17). Very popular with locals as well as beach visitors. Nr. downtown and amusement center.

Ponderosa Steak Barn. *Inexpensive.* 707 S. Kings Hwy. Rapid service, with particular care in cooking to order.

Western Sizzlin' Steak House. *Inexpensive.* 2300 S. Kings Hwy. Family restaurant with over 28 varieties of beef.

Spartanburg

Four Seasons Steak House. *Expensive.* 880 S. Pine St. Features beef and fresh seafood. Children's plates. Reservations advised.

Hallmark Cafeteria. *Inexpensive.* In Pinewood Shopping Center, Byrnes Blvd. Popular locally. Usual cafeteria specialties plus home-baked breads and desserts.

TENNESSEE

Walking Horses and Moving Music

BY
JUSTIN FAHERTY

Justin Faherty is a former executive of the St. Louis Globe Democrat, *the New York* Herald Tribune, *and the Bergen (N.J.)* Record. *He has written for newspapers on all 50 of the United States.*

The twin cities of Bristol, straddling the Tennessee-Virginia line, are popular gateways to Tennessee because of their strategic location. In the north of Tennessee are the great population centers. To the south is a magnificent outdoor playground featuring beautiful mountains, picturesque, man-made lakes impounded by TVA dams, and the Great Smoky Mountains National Park, for years the nation's most heavily visited national park.

The mountains, reaching heights of more than 6,000 feet, are a part of the Appalachians. Their natural beauty is preserved along the Tennessee-North Carolina border by the Great Smoky Mountains National Park and the Cherokee National Forest, which the sprawling 505,000-acre Park splits into two sections.

Many southbound visitors will head directly for the Great Smoky Mountains National Park via Gatlinburg, the charming resort community that abuts the park entrance. Others will prefer a more leisurely course. For the latter, US 421 southeast thirty-two miles to Mountain City will provide arresting views of the lake impounded by TVA's South Holston Dam and the dam itself. US 421 crosses the Appalachian Trail.

Nashville

Points of Interest

1) Belmont College
2) David Lipscomb College
3) Fisk University
4) Fort Nashborough
5) Greek Parthenon
6) Meharry Medical College
7) Opryland U.S.A.
8) Peabody College
9) State Capitol
10) State Fairgrounds
11) Trevecca College
12) Vanderbilt University

TENNESSEE

Turning southwest at Mountain City on State 67, the scenic-minded will be rewarded with views of mountain-cradled Watauga Lake, another TVA impoundment, starting near Butler and continuing to the intersection with US 321. Proceeding on US 321, it is nine miles to Hampton. If you are here in early summer, turn south on US 19E and go thirteen miles to Roan Mountain. Atop the mountain marvel at the hundreds of acres of purple and white rhododendron, which blossom between mid-June and early July.

From Roan Mountain return to Hampton, and then go six miles on US 321 to Elizabethton. It was here in 1772 that a group of settlers organized the Watauga Association and adopted a constitution—the first written document of its kind to be drawn up by freemen born on the American continent. A monument on the courthouse lawn commemorates the action.

It's nine miles from Elizabethton to Johnson City via US 321. Johnson City is a major burley tobacco auction market, as well as a railroad center. Two TVA dams are within easy driving distance, Boone and Fort Patrick Henry. Boone Dam, ten miles north, backs up a sixteen-mile-long lake. Fort Patrick Henry Dam, up the road, forms a ten-mile lake.

Tennessee Valley Authority lakes have a total shoreline of 10,000 miles, exceeding that of the Great Lakes. Fishing, boating, swimming and camping are permitted. Information is available from public safety officers at TVA dams.

Near Johnson City is one of Tennessee's oldest houses, Rocky Mount, seven miles northeast on US 19W, 411, and 11E. Those coming directly from Bristol on this multiple-number route will pass the two-and-a-half-story house, built in 1770 by William Cobb, a signer of the Articles of the Watauga. Twenty years later, when Tennessee became part of the territory of the United States south of the River Ohio, this house became Governor William Blount's headquarters and thus the new territory's first capitol.

South of Johnson City on US 411 and 11E is Jonesboro, oldest town in Tennessee, founded in 1779. The free state of Franklin was organized here in 1784 with John Sevier as governor. A twenty-one-year-old Andrew Jackson migrated here from North Carolina in 1788 to practice law for two years. Among the old buildings to see in this town is the Methodist Church, dating from 1845, at 215 W. Main Street.

Davy Was Born Here

On US 11E, near the little town of Limestone, is Davy Crockett Birthplace Park. On five acres along the Nolichucky River, the cabin where Crockett was born in 1786 has been reconstructed, a building for tourist information built, and pleasant picnic grounds provided. The limestone marker dates from the mid-1880's. Greeneville, twenty-two miles southwest of Jonesboro, was the home of Andrew Johnson, who became President following Lincoln's assassination. The city, founded in 1783, was named for Nathanael Greene, a general in the American Revolutionary War.

In downtown Greeneville, the town's most noted citizen is honored with the Andrew Johnson National Historic Site, containing his modest tailor shop and home and his burial place. Johnson's political career saw him successively as alderman, congressman, governor, senator, vice president, president, and then senator again.

From Newport, follow State 32 south to a junction with State 73, below Cosby, and then proceed southwest to Gatlinburg. This is real mountain driving, with hairpin turns and steep grades.

Visitors quickly see why the mountains got the name Great Smokies. A smoky blue mist is suspended above them much of the time. On clear days, it is possible to glimpse such famous peaks as Mt. Guyot (6,621 feet) and Mt. LeConte (6,593 feet).

Gatlinburg—Entrance to the Smokies

Gatlinburg lives for tourists. The little village has a permanent population of approximately 3,000, yet it can accommodate 23,000 people per night in its several hotels and almost 150 motels. Crafts shops line its Main Street. As the western entrance to the Great Smoky Mountains National Park, it sees a major share of the park's more than 8,000,000 annual visitors.

Great virgin forests and wildflowers of incredible beauty cover the mountains, which have an altitude of 5,000 feet for thirty-six miles along the main crest. Sixteen peaks rise over 6,000 feet. The park is a glorious show of nature at any season, although some portions are closed in the wintertime. Summer and autumn are popular seasons.

From Gatlinburg drive southeast on US 441 to Newfound Gap for one of the most beautiful views of the park. For hikers or riders there are trails; the Appalachian Trail winds along the state line.

Among the attractions at Gatlinburg is the Smoky Sky Lift, a half-mile cable car ride up Crockett Mountain. There is skiing from mid-December through February at Gatlinburg Ski Resort, and a double chair lift carries summer sightseers. In town, the American Historical Wax Museum features 120 historical figures grouped in appropriate scenes. In a more meditative vein, on River Road, there is Christus Gardens, where well-known incidents in the life of Christ are re-created by full-size wax models in a marble cloister.

At Smoky Mountains Trout Farms (there's one two miles east of town on State 73 and another to the north on US 441), anglers can catch all the trout they want for free.

Goldrush Junction, on US 441, is a replica of a Pioneer Village. A narrow-gauge railroad offers a scenic five-mile ride. On the same road is Magic World where storybook tales are enacted and there are rides and a picnic area.

Old barns have a way of radically changing identities; one, on US 441, for years an old tobacco-curing barn, is now a pottery shop, Pigeon Forge Pottery. A second old building open to visitors is the Old Mill, which has been grinding away for at least 125 years.

If you follow State 73 west from Gatlinburg, you can take a short side trip to Cades Cove, a typical mountain settlement isolated from change until recent times. Many of the pioneer buildings remain or have been restored, and a meandering circle tour of the valley enables visitors to see the various points of interest easily. Cades Cove campground is a popular spot.

Return to State 73, proceed to the twin cities of Maryville and Alcoa. Maryville was a pioneer town. Sam Houston attended Maryville Academy (now Maryville College) here. Alcoa was founded in 1913 by the Aluminum Company of America.

En route to Knoxville, off US 129, you can visit the restored Sam Houston Schoolhouse, six miles northeast of Maryville. Houston, who taught at the school from spring until fall of 1812, later served as congressman from Tennessee and as the state's governor before moving on to Oklahoma and Texas.

Site of the gala 1982 World's Fair, Knoxville, on the Tennessee River, dates from 1786 and was named in honor of Henry Knox, Secretary of War from 1785 to 1794. Its first settlers were traders. Knoxville in its early days was distinguished for its lively and colorful goings-on instead of its drawing-room charm.

Antebellum Mansions

East Tennessee, mostly an area of small farms, was, in general, loyal to the Union. The siege of Knoxville in 1863 was a Confederate attempt to dislodge Union troops stationed there. After the war many of these Northern men returned to Knoxville to settle.

Knoxville grew rapidly and today is a city of varied industry, with textiles, marble, lumber and tobacco prominent in the economy. The University of Tennessee, TVA headquarters, and the Knox County seat are here.

Points of interest in the city range in time from territorial days to antebellum to modern. Knoxville's earliest link to the past is the Blount Mansion at 200 West Hill Avenue. It was built in 1792 for territorial governor William Blount.

Blount, a talented pioneer, was a member of the Continental Congress and the Constitutional Convention. He served under President Washington as a territorial governor and drafted Tennessee's first constitution. Upon Tennessee's admission to the Union he was elected to the United States Senate and served from Aug. 2, 1796 until his expulsion July 8, 1797. He was active in a plan to incite the Creeks and Cherokees to aid the British in conquering the Spanish territory of West Florida. During impeachment proceedings in Philadelphia, he was elected to the State Senate in Tennessee. When it convened, Dec. 3, 1797, he was chosen Speaker. He died in Knoxville, March 21, 1800, and is buried in the First Presbyterian Church Cemetery.

Attractions on the University of Tennessee campus include the Estes Kefauver Memorial Library, the Frank H. McClung Museum, and Neyland Stadium, home turf of the great Volunteer football teams. It has a seating capacity of 70,000.

The city's antebellum link is provided by Confederate Memorial Hall, 3148 Kingston Pike, a beautiful mansion maintained by the United Daughters of the Confederacy.

Six miles east of Knoxville on Thorngrove Pike is the stately Ramsey House, built in 1797 by Francis Alexander Ramsey. Reputed to be the first stone house in Knox County, it is an excellent example of the finer homes that replaced log cabins in the late eighteenth century.

Birthplace of the Bomb

Before heading south via US 11 to Chattanooga, visit Oak Ridge, once a top-secret atom bomb town. There are guided tours, demonstrations, and exhibits at the American Museum of Science and Energy on Jefferson Circle, conducted by the U.S. Atomic Energy Commission.

Nine miles south of Oak Ridge on State 95 is the Melton Hill Dam, a TVA dam finished in 1963. The dam forms a forty-four-mile-long lake and provides sufficient water for barge transportation to Clinton on the Clinch River, most upstream point on the TVA waterway system.

South on US 11, near Lenoir City, the motorist will come to Fort Loudoun Dam, another of the TVA constructions. There are docks and fishing facilities along the shore of its lake.

Continuing south, you pass through Athens and Cleveland. The latter is the gateway to three TVA dams that control the Ocoee River. If you're really adventurous, you can make arrangements in Cleveland with the game supervisor about hunting wild boar in the Cherokee National Forest.

US 11 leads on to Chattanooga, a lovely city set in the midst of steep mountain ridges. Great Indian trails joined here—the Great War Path over Lookout Mountain, the Shawnee Trail going north from Williams Island, and the Suck Creek Trail. Chattanooga became a Cherokee trading center, called Ross's Landing after the Scotch-Cherokees who were its operators. It was the starting point of the "Trail of Tears," when the Cherokees were forced in 1837 to move to lands west of the Mississippi.

In 1838, the name Ross's Landing was changed to Chattanooga, probably from a Creek word meaning "rock rising to a point."

Because of its strategic location, Chattanooga was an important prize in the Civil War; three battles were fought nearby, at Chickamauga Creek, Lookout Mountain, and Missionary Ridge. The eventual victory of Union forces in November, 1863, provided Sherman with a supply base for his Atlanta campaign.

South of the city, in Georgia, is the Chickamauga and Chattanooga National Military Park. Its nine separate parts include Point Park on Lookout Mountain, Signal Point on Signal Mountain, Missionary Ridge, Orchard Knob. Park Headquarters are just below Chattanooga in North Georgia, site of one of America's bloodiest battles—Chickamauga (34,500 casualties in 3 days). Two thousand markers and monuments commemorate the men who died in these battles.

Civil War Battlegrounds

Chattanooga has a variety of attractions to offer the visitor. The movie *The Great Locomotive Chase* documented the role the locomotive *General* played in local Civil War history. Captain James J. Andrews, with twenty-one other Federal raiders, managed to seize the train near Marietta, Georgia, and move north along the track toward Chattanooga, destroying track and bridges as they went, while another Confederate engine, the *Yonah,* was gaining on them all the while. Andrews' raiders attempted to escape in the woods near the Tennessee line but all were captured. One of the nation's largest National Cemeteries is located in the Center of Chattanooga (US 11 and US 64). Captain Andrews is buried here, as are the other heroes of the "Chase."

The city is the home of the University of Tennessee at Chattanooga on McCallie Avenue, founded in 1886 as the U.S. Grant University.

The top of Lookout Mountain, that "rock rising to a point," can be reached on what may well be the world's steepest passenger railroad, overcoming a seventy-two per cent grade as it approaches the top.

You can also drive up Lookout Mountain via Lookout Mountain Road or Ochs Highway, reaching an elevation of 2,225 feet, some 1,700 feet above the city. The view is spectacular. It was here that the Battle Above the Clouds was fought in 1863.

Point Park, atop Lookout Mountain, offers a magnificent view of the Tennessee River's Moccasin Bend and the city below. The Ochs Memorial Museum and Observatory are located here.

Opposite the park, the Lookout Mountain Museum contains Civil War items, Indian relics, and dioramas. Nearby is Cravens House, built in 1856 and reconstructed on the original foundations.

If you've driven around the countryside, you have noticed many a farmer's barn with signs urging you to see Ruby Falls and Rock City on Lookout Mountain. These may be the two most heavily advertised sights south of the Ohio River. The twin caves of Ruby Falls-Lookout Mountain, on Lookout Mountain Scenic Highway, are deep in the mountains. An elevator takes sightseers 1,120 feet down to view the 145-foot fall of water. Colorful stalactites and stalagmites, many enormous, add to the interest.

The second attraction, Rock City Gardens, offers relief from concentrated museum sightseeing. Reached via State 58, the scenery in these ten acres is beautiful. There are special attractions planned for children.

"Confederama" is an unusual diversion located at the foot of Lookout Mountain, at 3742 Tennessee Avenue. It is an attempt to show, using miniature soldiers on a scaled-down battleground, the Chattanooga Campaign.

Nine miles north of the city, on US 127, is Signal Mountain, another high point giving a majestic view. Below is the Tennessee River, running through the "Grand Canyon" of the Tennessee.

Two Tennessee Valley Authority dams in the Chattanooga area are worth visiting. East on State 153 are Chickamauga Dam and Chickamauga Lake, the latter covering 34,500 acres and having 810 miles of shoreline. Booker T. Washington State Park borders this lake, as does Harrison Bay State Park farther north. Seven miles west, off US 41, is TVA's Nickajack Dam.

Farther northwest on US 41 is Monteagle. From July 4 to August 30, the Chautauqua Assembly shifts the emphasis in this charming Cumberland Mountain town from nature to art. Since 1882, concerts, art classes and lectures have made this a special place every summer.

Continuing westward, the suggested route is US 64 and 41A via Sewanee to Winchester.

Sewanee, six miles west, centers around both the University of the South, with its handsome campus covering 10,000 acres, and the Sewanee Academy, a preparatory school.

From Winchester follow US 41A north to Tullahoma, site of the Arnold Engineering Development Center's giant wind tunnels and the University of Tennessee's handsome new Space Institute. Next town is Shelbyville. This is Tennessee walking horse country. Each year in August the Tennessee Walking Horse National Celebration is held in Shelbyville. To the west, in Columbia, you can tour the fine old home where James K. Polk, our eleventh president, lived as a boy. The house was built by Polk's father, Samuel, in 1816, and has been restored by the Polk Memorial Association.

The Natchez Trace

Taking US 43 from Columbia southwest toward Lawrenceburg, you can make a side trip at Summertown on State 20 to the Meriwether Lewis Monument on the Natchez Trace, the old road which ran from Nashville to Natchez, Mississippi. Lewis, leader of the Lewis and Clark expedition, was mysteriously killed in 1809 near this spot at Grinder's Inn. His grave alongside the historic Trace (which has been converted into a national parkway) is marked by a symbolic broken column.

Returning to US 43, and turning westward on US 64 at Lawrenceburg, you reach David Crockett State Park, a 950-acre recreational area and another state memorial to the hero of the Alamo. Here Davy Crockett lived, served as magistrate, and operated a mill.

Four miles before you reach Waynesboro, there's a natural bridge, seven miles north of US 64 on a country road. The 41-foot long limestone bridge arches over a gurgling mountain stream.

Westward on US 64 is the little town of Crump, where a five-mile side trip south on State 22 leads to Shiloh National Military Park. Here in April 1862 one of the fiercest battles of the Civil War was fought. It became known as "Bloody Shiloh"; both North and South were shocked by the carnage. Markers and other materials graphically explain the action to the visitor.

Returning to US 64, continue west to reach Memphis, largest city in the state.

Modern Memphis

Memphis, capital of the mid-South and one of the South's largest cities, is a progressive, forward-looking metropolis mindful of the past. A visitor senses the contrast when he stands amid the Civil War relics in Confederate Park and looks at the downtown skyscrapers.

Before the white man came Memphis was one of the villages of the Chickasaw Indians living along the Mississippi River. Andrew Jackson, later president, was one of the founders of the city and is credited with naming it for the ancient Egyptian city on the Nile. The name means "place of good abode."

Late in developing, Memphis had only about 500 people when it was incorporated in 1826. Today the metropolitan area population is more than 800,000. A manufacturing, wholesale, and commercial center, it is the world's largest cotton market, and the world's largest hardwood lumber center. There are numerous lumber mills and furniture plants. Cotton's status is evident in the unique row of cotton merchants on famous Front Street. An important event is the annual Cotton Carnival each May.

In PeeWee's Saloon on storied Beale Street, W.C. Handy blew those first lonesome notes and became the "Father of the Blues." And in a Memphis recording studio Elvis Presley launched the career that was to make him for a time the "King of Rock 'n' Roll." Tourist attractions include the statue of Handy in Handy Park, and Presley's showplace home, Graceland.

Although a busy center of commerce, Memphis has many attractions for visitors. For the art-minded, a visit to the Brooks Memorial Art Gallery in Overton Park is a must. It boasts outstanding collections of American and European paintings, as well as porcelain figurines.

The Museum of Natural History and Industrial Arts, at 3050 Central Avenue, is housed in a former private home dubbed "The Pink Palace" because of its unique Georgia pink marble exterior. Among its natural history exhibits, the African collection is outstanding.

The Magevney House is the oldest pioneer home in Memphis and is located on Adams Street. Built in 1831, the house was originally owned by Eugene Magevney, an Irish-born pioneer schoolteacher, typical of the thousands of immigrants who helped develop the state.

Six miles south of Memphis on US 61 and 4½ miles west on Mitchell Road is Chucalissa, a prehistoric Indian village. This was one of the string of Indian communities along the Mississippi which disappeared between de Soto's visit in 1541 and the arrival of the French in 1673. Resurrected through careful excavation, the rebuilt village consists of grass-thatched huts and a great conical temple on a flat-topped mound. There are also an excavated cemetery and a modern museum.

In Memphis again, the Overton Park Zoo, located at McLean Boulevard and North Parkway, is always a delight for children. There are more than a thousand animals and fish on display, as well as a children's circus in summer.

North of Memphis on the Mississippi River bluffs is Meeman-Shelby State Park, consisting of 12,512 acres. It's located eleven miles west of Millington off US 51.

Slated to open mid-summer on Mud Island in the Mississippi River is the $50-million Mississippi River Museum, a 50-acre complex dedicated to life on the lower Mississippi.

Casey Jones

From Memphis, drive northeast to Jackson on Interstate 40. Jackson was the home of John Luther "Casey" Jones, who rode into immortality on the "Cannon Ball Express" in the famous 1900 railroad wreck on the Illinois Central line at Vaughn, Mississippi. (The original version of the song that tells his story was written by Wallace Saunders, of Canton, Mississippi, Casey's engineer wiper.) The Casey Jones Home and Museum at Casey Jones Village, five miles northwest via US 45 bypass, displays an engine similar to the one he was piloting that fatal night, plus other nostalgic reminders of railroading in the good old days. You also can see his grave in the Jackson cemetery at Royal and Hardee streets.

Twenty-six miles northeast of Jackson via Interstate 40 is Tennessee's biggest state-owned recreational area: 43,000-acre Natchez Trace State Park, with three lakes. Not on the main tour route, but worth the trip.

By taking US 45 north from Jackson to Trenton and then State 104 west to Dyersburg, you're well on your way to the Reelfoot Lake area in northwestern Tennessee. First, however, at Trenton you can take a twelve-mile side trip to Rutherford, site of Davy Crockett's last Tennessee home. In 1822, Crockett came to West Tennessee, settling first in what is now Crockett County and then moving north to the Rutherford Fork of the Obion River. He lived there until 1835, adding to his reputation as a bear hunter and serving three terms as a member of the U.S. Congress. Defeated in his last campaign for Congress, he moved to Texas, dying less than a year later in the Battle of the Alamo. The grave of Rebecca Hawkins Crockett, his mother, has been moved to the site.

Returning to Trenton, follow State 104 to Dyersburg; there change to State 78 and proceed north to Tiptonville, gateway to the Reelfoot Lake area. Unlike so many Tennessee lakes, this one was created, not by TVA, but by the earthquakes of 1811-12. The depression left by the quakes was gradually filled by the Mississippi River, making a lake of 14,500 acres. Weird shapes of the old forest emerging above the water give it a primeval kind of beauty. Below the surface, many species of fish have natural breeding grounds. Giant cypresses along the shore add to Reelfoot's fantastic appeal. Over 250 kinds of birds and other wild creatures inhabit the lake area. Reelfoot Lake State Park is south of the lake and Reelfoot Wildlife Refuge Area to the north.

Continuing east on State 21 to its junction with State 22, follow along the lake and then swing east through Union City to Dresden. Changing to State 54, continue to Paris, a growing resort area due to its proximity to Kentucky Lake on the Tennessee River, fourteen miles to the east. Formed by the largest of the TVA dams, Kentucky Lake is 184 miles long, extending south into Tennessee.

Pick up US 79 at Paris to proceed northeast to Paris Landing State Park on Kentucky Lake. The 800-acre park is eighteen miles northeast of Paris and provides, among other things, beautiful campgrounds on the lake.

Leaving Paris Landing, US 79 skirts the southern border of Land Between the Lakes—an elongated strip of 170,000 acres flanked on the west by Kentucky Lake, formed by a Tennessee Valley Authority dam on the Tennessee River, and on the east by Lake Barkley, formed by a U.S. Engineers' dam on the Cumberland River. State 49, taking off from US 79, leads northward through Land Between the Lakes, which is being developed by Tennessee Valley Authority as a national demonstration in outdoor recreation development and conservation education. There are some developed family campgrounds, primitive camping areas, nature trails, and a variety of wildlife.

US 79 leads east to Fort Donelson National Military Park, one mile west of Dover. Here in February, 1862, General Ulysses S. Grant captured first Fort Henry and then Fort Donelson. When the Confederate commander requested a truce, Grant made his historic ultimatum: "Unconditional and immediate surrender." The victory was one of the early Union gains. The national military park contains the well-preserved fort and earthworks, as well as the Dover Tavern in which the surrender occurred.

US 79 from Dover to Clarksville skirts the southern edge of the Fort Campbell Military Reservation, the headquarters of the 101st Airborne Division. Off US 79, four miles east of Clarksville—named in 1784 for Revolutionary War General George Rogers Clark—is Dunbar Cave Park, featuring a swimming pool as well as an underground guided tour.

At Clarksville, turn south on State 48, destination Dickson. For spelunkers, Ruskin Cave is twelve miles northwest of Dickson off US 70. There's a one-hour tour.

Just east of Dickson on the way to Tennessee's capital, Nashville, is Montgomery Bell State Park.

Attractions of Nashville

There are numerous things to see in and around the capital. The Nashville Chamber of Commerce, 161 4th Avenue N, Nashville, TN 37219, has an excellent detailed map listing the city and area attractions.

The settlement of Nashville was begun in 1779 under the leadership of James Robertson. In 1780 Robertson and a group of pioneers built Fort Nashborough on the west bank of the Cumberland River. This log stockade has been reconstructed at First Avenue North and Church Street, near its original location. Although surrounded by a modern city, the authenticity of the reconstructed blockhouses and cabins makes it easy to imagine the pioneers seeking shelter here from the Indians.

By the 1830's, the log construction of Nashville's public buildings began to be replaced by limestone and marble. On Charlotte Avenue between Sixth and Seventh avenues, the State Capitol, designed by William Strickland and finished in 1855, is an impressive example of Greek Revival architecture.

In 1862 the Capitol was renamed Fort Johnson, a stockade having been built around it when Union forces occupied the city. In December, 1864, the Confederates under General John B. Hood attempted to regain the city; they were unsuccessful, and Hood's army broke up.

Another local landmark that recalls ancient Greece is the full-scale reconstruction of the Greek Parthenon.

One becomes so accustomed to Tennessee's display of its love of Greek symmetry, that the Downtown Presbyterian Church, Church Street and Fifth Avenue North, seems even more of an oddity in this gracious Southern city. Here William Strickland deserted the Greeks in favor of the Egyptians. Although the church has been rebuilt twice since first constructed in 1816, it retains its Egyptian temple aspect in general structure and architectural detail.

It is not only because of its buildings that Nashville has been called the "Athens of the South." The city has also displayed a special interest in the arts and education. Vanderbilt University, on West End Avenue, is perhaps the best known of its many educational institutions. Chartered in 1872, it now has more than 10,000 students. The George Peabody College for Teachers, Scarritt College, Belmont College, Meharry Medical College and Fisk University are only a few of the other colleges here. Some have their own collections of fine art.

Near Vanderbilt, at 1908 Grand Avenue, is The Upper Room. In its chapel on the second floor, of Georgian design, is a chancel which re-creates the room in Leonardo da Vinci's painting *The Last Supper*.

For historical exhibits, visit the Children's Museum at 724 Second Avenue South (where you will also find exhibits of natural history and science), the Tennessee State Museum in the two-block War Memorial Building honoring the dead of World War I, and the Capitol.

Grand Ole Opry

Nashville is up to date too, a center for manufacturing, insurance, banking, and agriculture. The original Grand Ole Opry at Fifth Avenue downtown is closed, but music is alive and well at the new Grand Ole Opry at 2800 Opryland Drive, about six miles out of town.

Nashville can be used as a base for further explorations into history. Southwest, off US 70S, is the estate of Belle Meade, once the site of the Dunham Station on the Natchez Trace. This mansion is quite imposing, with a portico rising two stories. A Greek Revival building, it was constructed by General William Giles Harding in 1853. Another building, erected by John Harding in 1798, a "dog-trot" house—two cabins linked by a roofed passageway—typical of early Tennessee homes, is used as a museum. The stables at Belle Meade at one time were justly famous for breeding some of the world's finest racehorses, among them Iroquois, who won the English Derby in 1881.

If you return to Nashville by US 31, six miles south of town, off the highway, you will come to Travellers Rest. Andrew Jackson, Lafayette and Sam Houston are among those who have visited this house, a clapboard of two stories built in 1820.

One of the most popular attractions in the Nashville area is The Hermitage, the hauntingly beautiful home of Andrew Jackson. It is thirteen miles east of Nashville on US 70. The interior furnishings are the exact pieces used by Jackson and his wife, Rachel. And Rachel's garden is kept according to her design. The tombs of Jackson and his wife are at one corner of the formal garden, along with the graves of others close to the family.

Leaving Nashville on US 41, driving southeast, the first town you reach is Smyrna. Turn left on State 104 and go east one mile to reach the Sam Davis Home, a historic site honoring the nineteen-year-old Confederate hero. A Confederate scout, he was captured by Union forces and hanged as a spy for refusing to betray the Union man who had given him information. This was his boyhood home. His body is buried here.

Farther south on US 41, about thirty miles out of Nashville, is the Stones River National Battlefield, covering 324 acres. This was the scene of the Battle of Stones River, which took place from December 31, 1862, to January 2, 1863, resulting in high casualties on both sides without giving either a real victory. The graves or markers of over 6,000 Union soldiers are in the twenty-acre cemetery.

A few miles farther and you reach Murfreesboro, capital of Tennessee from 1819 to 1825. On North Maney Avenue is Oaklands, one of the outstanding houses in Middle Tennessee. Built in three periods, it developed into a beautiful antebellum home. Prior to the Civil War, its guests included such personages as John Bell, presidential candidate against Lincoln in 1860, and Leonidas Polk, the bishop-general.

Eighteen miles north, on US 231, is the 8,300-acre Cedars of Lebanon State Park. Its forest of red cedar is believed to be the largest in the nation.

Driving east on US 70S the destination is McMinnville and Warren County, which has more than 125 certified growers of fruit trees, shade trees, and other plants, making it one of the nation's largest centers for the production of nursery stock. There is excellent fishing in Center Hill Lake and other waters in the area. Cumberland Caverns, seven miles east of McMinnville, is described as America's largest cave.

Twelve miles northeast of McMinnville on US 70S is Rock Island. A dam here at the confluence of two streams and near where another comes in backs up all three.

At Sparta the route is north on State 42 to Cookeville, home of Tennessee Tech, and then nineteen miles to Livingston. Here a side trip may be taken to Dale Hollow Dam near Celina off State 52, with the route passing the entrance to Standing Stone State Park, which has swimming pool, fishing lake, restaurant and furnished cabins. Returning to Livingston, turn east on State 52 through Jamestown and Rugby Road, to the Junction with US 27. This rugged area is Tennessee's "upper Cumberland country." It has produced such sons as Sergeant Alvin C. York, reared at Pall Mall north of Jamestown and Secretary of State Cordell Hull, who grew up to the west near Carthage. Near Jamestown is another state park, Pickett.

After joining US 27, proceed north for a few miles to the intersection with State 63, then drive east to Caryville, gateway to the 850-acre Cove Lake Park, located two miles north on US 25W. South of Caryville on State 71 is Norris Dam, named for the Nebraska Senator, George W. Norris, who co-sponsored the legislation establishing the TVA. The dam was the first built by the authority; it forms a seventy-two-mile-long lake.

From Caryville follow US 25W north to State 63, and take the latter northeast to Harrogate and Cumberland Gap. Through the famous Cumberland Gap, hacked clear by Daniel Boone and other frontiersmen, flooded westward-bound settlers. In 1959, the Cumberland Gap area was dedicated as a national historical park covering thirty-two square miles in Kentucky, Tennessee and Virginia. The park contains approximately two miles of the Wilderness Road, Civil War fortifications and the Tri-State Peak from which all three states are visible. The visitor center is located near Middlesboro, Kentucky.

Continue the tour route by taking US 25E southwest to its junction with US 11W, and follow the latter highway to Rogersville. En route, by taking a side trip on State 32 to Morristown, you can visit the reconstructed Crockett Tavern and Museum. It was at this six-room tavern operated by his father that Davy Crockett spent his youth. On the wall of one room is the proverbial coonskin cap and rifle similar to Crockett's Old Betsy.

From Rogersville, continue east on US 11W into Kingsport, where, six miles south on US 23, is 1,000-acre Warriors' Path State Park on Lake Patrick Henry.

It's twenty-four miles from Kingsport to Bristol. This marks the end of your grand tour of Tennessee, encompassing the mountains, the blue-grass country and the Mississippi River, pioneer points of interest and

Civil War battlefields, the TVA and Oak Ridge—the old and the new. Tennessee can be a rewarding experience for anyone.

PRACTICAL INFORMATION FOR TENNESSEE

FACTS AND FIGURES. The state derives its name from *Tenassee,* the ancient capital of the Cherokee Indians. Its nickname is the Volunteer State. The iris is the state flower; the tulip poplar, the state tree; the mockingbird, the state bird. "Agriculture and Commerce" is the state motto. "My Homeland Tennessee" is the state song.

Nashville, population 469,000, is the state capital. The state population (1980 Census) is 4,357,000.

HOW TO GET THERE. *By air:* To Memphis and Nashville there are direct flights on U.S. Air, American, Braniff, Delta, Eastern, Piedmont and Republic. In addition, Ozark has direct flights to Nashville; Frontier, Texas International and United to Memphis. Knoxville may be reached on direct flights of American, Delta, Piedmont and United; Chattanooga on Delta, Eastern and Republic; Tri-City Airport on Piedmont, Republic and United; Clarksville on Ozark; and Jackson on Republic.

From Canada Nashville may be reached on direct flights of American out of Toronto; connecting flights of U.S. Air out of Montreal and Hamilton; Memphis may be reached on connecting flights of U.S. Air out of Montreal; connecting flights of United and Delta out of Toronto.

By car: There are a number of interstate highways to bring the visitor into the state. I-65 runs from Alabama through Tennessee into Kentucky. I-55 comes from Mississippi into Memphis and out of Tennessee into Arkansas. I-40 comes in from Arkansas to Memphis, through Nashville and Knoxville and into North Carolina. I-81 comes in from Bristol, Virginia, to Bristol, Tennessee, and on to Knoxville. I-24 comes from Georgia up to Nashville. I-75 from Georgia to Chattanooga, up to Knoxville and into Kentucky.

By bus: There is good service into the state: Greyhound and Trailways; ABC Coach Lines, Arrow Coach Lines, Crown Transit Lines, Inc., Great Southern Coaches, Inc., Gulf Transport Co., Illini-Swallow Lines, Inc., Indiana Motor Bus Co., Jefferson Lines, Mid-Continent Coaches, Inc. Oklahoma Transport Co., Short Way Lines, Southeastern Stages, Inc., Southwestern Transit Co., Inc., Sunnyland Stages, T.N.M. & O. Coaches, Inc., and Wells Bus Line.

By train: Amtrak trains serve Memphis and Dyersburg from Chicago and New Orleans.

By boat: The *Delta Queen* and *Mississippi Queen* overnight river steamboats include Memphis in their cruise schedules.

HOW TO GET AROUND. *By air:* US Air, American, Braniff, Delta, Ozark, Piedmont, Republic, Eastern and United serve cities within the state.

By car: Tennessee has interstate highways criss-crossing within the state to make traveling by car a breeze. I-40 runs from Memphis through the middle of the state into North Carolina; I-65 divides the state and runs north and south; I-24, I-75 and I-81 complete the picture. US 51, 70, 79, 64, 45, 231, 431, 41, 27, 11 and 11W & 11E help visitors tour the state conveniently.

Car rental: Avis or Hertz cars may be rented in Chattanooga, Kingsport, Knoxville, Memphis and Nashville. In addition, Hertz has rental offices in Bristol, Jackson, Johnson City, Oak Ridge and Smyrna.

By bus: Greyhound and Trailways, as well as ABC Coach Lines, Brooks, Continental 5-Star, Great Southern Coaches, Gulf Transport Co., Illini-Swallow Lines, Inc., Jefferson Lines, Inc., Okalahoma Transport Co., Short Way Lines, Southeastern Stages, Inc. and Tri-State Bus Lines, Inc. serve some cities within the state.

By boat: For an unusual carefree vacation, consider renting a houseboat and cruise the beautiful Great Lakes of Tennessee at your own pace. Boats accommodate 6 to 8 persons and may be rented by the day or week. Contact: Chattanooga Area Convention Visitors Bureau, 1001 Market Street, Chattanooga 37402 for further information.

 TOURIST INFORMATION. Thirteen Welcome Centers, conveniently located on the interstate highways entering Tennessee, are in operation 24 hours a day. Information about area attractions may be obtained, rest rooms and free pamphlets are available to visitors. For information and pamphlets on the state write Department of Tourist Development, P.O. Box 23170, Nashville, TN 37202. For complete information on facilities at any of the 47 state parks, natural areas and historic sites, write the Tennessee Department of Conservation, Division of State Parks, 2611 West End Ave., Nashville 37203. To obtain detailed information on the Great Smoky Mountains National Park, write Park Superintendent, Great Smoky Mountains National Park, Gatlinburg 37738. The Forest Supervisor, Cherokee National Forest, Box 400, Cleveland 37311, will supply information pertinent to the Cherokee National Forest. Individual pamphlets with information on the following subjects: Tennessee's camping, fishing, golfing, canoeing, events, wildflowers, the State Capitol and facts on the state of Tennessee can be obtained by writing: Tennessee Department of Conservation, Division of Tourist Information, 2611 West End Ave., Nashville 37203.

Write Information Office, Tennessee Valley Authority, Knoxville 37902, for information about TVA activities. Recreation maps which show routes to all types of shoreline recreation areas, including public access areas and wildlife management areas are available for the various lakes in the Tennessee River system. Navigation charts and maps are also published by TVA for its major reservoirs. Copies may be obtained from: TVA Maps, Knoxville 37902, or Chattanooga 37401.

Public Information Office, Tennessee Department of Transportation, 106 Highway Building, Nashville 37219; Tennessee Dept. of Conservation, Division of Tourist Promotion, 2611 West End Ave., Nashville 37203; Public Relations Department, Tennessee Game & Fish Commission, Ellington Agricultural Center, Nashville 37204. Tennessee Historical Commission, Room 422, State Library and Archives Building, Nashville 37202; and U.S. Corps of Engineers, P.O. Box 1070, Nashville 37202, are helpful addresses for the visitor to obtain information on many aspects of Tennessee's activities.

Information on fishing and hunting and licenses may be obtained from the Tennessee Wildlife Resources Agency, Box 40747, Ellington Agricultural Center, Nashville 37402.

 SEASONAL EVENTS. February: *National Bird Dog Field Trials.* Grand Junction, 3rd wk.

March: A *St. Patrick's Day celebration* takes place, complete with parades, costumes and games, Erin. The "Wearing O' The Green" at its best. *The Tennessee Pilgrimate* is arranged by the Association for the Preservation of Tennessee Antiquities. Tours of historic Tennessee homes and other sites are featured in various Tennessee cities, 3rd. wk.

April: *Ramp Festival,* Cosby, paying tribute to this rare member of the onion family; public *Fish fry,* Paris, billed as the world's largest. Tours of beautiful homes and gardens, concerts, antique shows and art exhibits are seen at the

Dogwood Arts Festival, Knoxville. Naturalists gather to observe wildflowers that are native to the region at the *Wildflower Pilgrimage,* held the 3rd wk. at Gatlinburg. Spring Festival at Crossville.

May: *Memphis in May International Festival* honoring "King Cotton." *Strawberry Festival,* Humboldt, with horseshows, parades, beauty contests, street dances and band contests. All held during the 1st wk. *Strawberry Festival,* Dayton. The *Franklin Rodeo,* Franklin, a full-fledged, action-packed Wild West rodeo. 1st wk. *Old Timers Day,* Dickson, is the highlight on the last Sat. Local people wear old costumes and ride in old buggies and wagons in parades. *Iroquois Steeplechase,* Nashville, thoroughbred horseraces, 2nd Saturday.

June: *Rhododendron Festival* atop Roan Mountain near Elizabethton. *International Country Music Fanfare,* in Nashville.

July: *Old Time Fiddlers Jamboree,* Smithville.

August: The *Tennessee Walking Horse National Celebration,* Shelbyville. Some of the finest horses complete in one of the nation's best-known championships.

September: A *State Fair,* Nashville. Exhibits and competitions in all areas imaginable, from horse drawing to jelly. *Banana Festival,* in South Fulton, the 2nd week in Sept. The citizens celebrate their part as the main distribution point for all bananas shipped to the U.S. During Sept./Oct. there are other major fairs in the state: *Mid-South Fair* in Memphis.

October: *Craftsman's Fair* at Gatlinburg. *Fall Color Cruise,* Chattanooga, last 2 weekends, featuring boating and driving along Tennessee River, music, dancing, festivities.

December: *Nashville Christmas Parade,* on Dec. 1. One of the biggest parades in the state, featuring more than 20 bands and 50 floats. *Christmas Trees of Many Lands,* Cheekwood Fine Arts Center, Cheek Rd., Nashville, displays various types of Christmas decorations used by people of foreign lands. *Maid of Cotton Pageant,* Memphis.

 NATIONAL PARKS AND FORESTS. The famous *Great Smoky Mountains National Park* covers a 720-square-mile area of eastern Tennessee and western North Carolina. It is a land of mountains and vales, of waterfalls and cascades, in which over 130 species of trees stand tall in its woodlands. Unusual features of the park are the pioneer and mountaineer homes. An interesting, restored group of these is located at Cades Cove. Wildlife is abundant throughout the Park, as are flowering trees and shrubs. Hiking is one of the favorite pursuits here, and there are about 70 miles of Appalachian Trail, serviced by seven shelters spaced a day's walk from each other. There is a camping site at Chimneys, Tennessee, several modern tent and trailer camp sites within the Park, and hotels at nearby Asheville, Knoxville, and Gatlinburg. The park is open all year.

Tennessee's *Cherokee National Forest* covers 596,000 acres in a wonder-world of forests, streams, gorges and waterfalls. Its many lakes include 6,400-acre Watauga, 1,900-acre Parksville. Wildlife is abundant, including wild Russian boar, sometimes seen by campers. Other outstanding features of the Forest include the beautiful Tellico River, 5,000-foot Unaka Mountain. Trout fishing is excellent in many areas, but check regulations as fishing and hunting is only by special permit in some areas of the forest. Within this vast wilderness are 30 camping sites.

STATE PARKS. Tennessee's state parks are among the nation's finest. There are 43 in operation. Accommodations range from campsites to suites in modern, motel-type inns at up to $30 a day. Furnished housekeeping cabins are available at weekly rates in 14 parks. There are swimming, boating, fishing, and 8 parks have golf courses. Many of the parks overlook lakes and have sandy beaches. All parks are wildlife refuges. Playing fields include tennis courts, baseball diamonds, and softball and badminton places. Hiking trails, bridle paths and horses are available at some. There are excellent restaurants and dining rooms, and convenient picnic places. The parks are popular, so reservations for overnight accommodations should be made well in advance.

TRAILER TIPS. Most of Tennessee's state parks and some of the state historic areas provide camping for tents or trailers or both. Camp sites are obtained on a first-come, first-served basis. For full information write Department of Tourist Development, P.O. Box 23170, Nashville, TN 37202. In several parks cabins are available from mid-May to mid-Sept. Rentals are mostly by the week and reservations should be made at the park of your choice.

Excellent camping and trailer facilities also are available in the Cherokee National Forest and the Great Smoky Mountains National Park in East Tennessee, the Tennessee Valley Authority's Land Between the Lakes recreation area in West Tennessee, and the Cumberland Gap National Historical Park in Northeast Tennessee.

MUSEUMS AND GALLERIES. Historical. Bell Buckle: *Junior Room Museum,* Webb School, a restored 1886 classroom on campus of prestigious preparatory school.

Benton: *Old Fort Marr,* an historic building (1813). Guided tours daily.

Harrogate: *Lincoln Memorial University* has a history museum with exhibits on Abraham Lincoln and the Civil War.

Johnson City: *Carroll Reece Museum,* East Tennessee State University, a general museum.

Knoxville: *Frank H. McClung Museum,* University of Tennessee, a general museum. Closed holidays. *Students' Museum, Inc.,* 3816 Oakland Ave., a natural science museum.

Memphis: *Chucalissa Indian Village and Museum,* 1987 Indian Village Dr. *E. H. Little Gallery,* Memphis State University Campus, a general museum. Closed during the summer and national holidays. *Memphis Pink Palace Museum,* 3050 Central Ave., was the palatial former home of Clarence Saunders, inventor of the self-service grocery. Its wide assortment of exhibits ranges from African big game trophies to an absorbing children's section.

Nashville: *The Children's Museum,* 724 2nd Ave. S., a children's general museum, housed in 1853 original building of the old University of Nashville. A planetarium is also a featured attraction. *Tennessee State Museum,* 301 Capitol Blvd., a general museum. *Travellers' Rest Museum House,* off US 31 on Farrell Pkwy, is a general museum located in the 1790 home of Judge John Overton.

Vonore: Fort Loudoun, off US 441, a general museum with collections on agriculture, archeology, botany and artifacts from the Cherokee Indians.

Art Galleries. Chattanooga: *George Thomas Hunter Gallery of Art,* 10 Bluff View, housed in a 1904 home at the site of a Civil War battery guarding the Tennessee River.

Cowan: *Cowan Railroad Museum* in vintage small-town station, exhibiting grand era of passenger trains.

Johnson City: *Elizabeth Slocumb Gallery,* Department of Art, East Tennessee State University.

Kingsport: *Kingsport Fine Arts Center,* 440 E. Sullivan.

514 TENNESSEE

Knoxville: *Dulin Gallery of Art,* 3100 Kingston Pike.

Memphis: *Brooks Memorial Art Gallery.* Overton Park. Sculpture and paintings including the million-dollar Kress collection.

Nashville: *Carl Van Vechten Gallery of Fine Arts,* Fisk University, 18th Ave. and Jackson St. N., an art gallery and museum, housed on the site of a Civil War fort. *George Peabody College Museum,* 21st Ave., an art museum. *Vanderbilt University Gallery,* 1801 Station B, 23rd at West End Ave. *Watkins Institute,* Sixth and Church, an art gallery. *Tennessee Botanical Gardens and Fine Arts Center,* Cheekwood, Cheek Rd., an art center and botanical gardens.

 SPECIAL INTEREST MUSEUMS. Chattanooga: *Harris Swift, Museum of Religious and Ceremonial Arts and Library of Rare Books,* 526 Vine St. *Houston Antique Museum,* 201 High St. It houses a collection of 15,000 pitchers, china, copper and gold luster, as well as rare porcelains and furniture. *Hall of Presidents Wax Museum.* Foot of Lookout Mt. *Tennessee Valley Railroad Museum.* No. Chamberlain Ave., at the foot of historic Missionary Ridge. *Lookout Mountain Museum,* in Point Park on Lookout Mountain. Excellent Indian exhibits as well as armor and weapons from the Civil War.

Gatlinburg: *American Historical Wax Museum,* on US 441.

Jackson: *Casey Jones Home and Railroad Museum,* 211 West Chester St., a railroad museum in the former home of Casey Jones.

Knoxville: *Knoxville 1982 World's Fair,* on 70-acre downtown site. Eight International Pavilions, Hall of Industry and States, with dioramas and exhibits.

Memphis: *Overton Park Zoo and Aquarium.*

Nashville: *Baptist Museum of Dargan-Carver Library,* 127 9th Ave., N., a religious museum. *Country Music Hall of Fame and Museum,* 4 Music Square E. *John F. Kennedy Memorial Center,* 1308-16th Ave., S., a commemorative museum. *Nashville Parthenon,* Centennial Park. World's only replica of the famous Athenian temple. *Cumberland Museum & Science Center,* 800 Ridley Ave., in Ft. Negley Park.

Oak Ridge: *American Museum of Science and Energy,* Jefferson Circle, a science and technology museum.

Sewanee: *Fine Arts Gallery of the University of the South,* arts and crafts museum.

Pigeon Forge: *Smoky Mountain Car Museum,* on US 441.

 HISTORIC SITES. Because of its geographical location. Tennessee was a Civil War battleground as well as one of the more important states in the westward movement of the pioneers. The names of Crockett and Boone echo through the rich history of the state.

A small park outside of Limestone, near Greeneville, houses the birthplace of *Davy Crockett,* while to the east of Morristown you will find the *Crockett Tavern and Museum,* once run by Davy's father. You will be intrigued by the fine collection of Early American tools on display. In the Rutherford area is a copy of the *Davy Crockett Cabin* in which he lived while serving in the Congress of the United States. Many of the furnishings in the house were actually owned by Davy, including a chair that he made himself.

Chattanooga: Lookout Mountain: *Cravens House,* an 1856 Civil War home.

Columbia: *Ancestral home of James K. Polk,* 301 W. 7th St. Closed Dec. 25. The rooms have been restored, and they contain many mementos of the life of the 11th president of the United States.

Dover: *Fort Donelson National Military Park,* off US 79, has a military museum with many items from the Civil War.

Franklin: *The Carter House* is a grim reminder of the bloody battle of Franklin. Now fully restored, the house is furnished with some of the finest period furniture available.

Gallatin: *Cragfont.* The 1798-1802 home of General James Winchester of the Revolution and War of 1812.

Gatlinburg: *Cades Cove Open-Air Museum* in the Great Smoky Mountains National Park, a village museum on the site of a former pioneer community, preserved to show a way of life that has disappeared. The *Sugarlands Visitor Center,* also located in the Great Smoky Mountains National Park.

Greeneville: *Andrew Johnson National Historic Site,* Depot St., is open to the public, and contains many items from the life of this famous president.

Johnson City: *Tipton-Haynes Living Historical Farm,* Erwin Hwy. 19W. Historic buildings are open to the public: Tipton and Haynes house, Slave Quarter, Haynes Law Office.

Jonesboro: *Tennessee's oldest town,* still one of the most historic and picturesque communities in the South, has many buildings of note. On US 411, 8 mi. W of Johnson City.

Kingsport: *1803 Netherland Inn, 1820 Exchange Place,* and *1852 Allendale* are open to the public.

Knoxville: *Blount Mansion,* 200 W. Hill Ave., 1792 office and mansion of Wm. Blount, governor of the territory south of Ohio, is open to visitors. There are several historic houses to visit in Knoxville. *Confederate Memorial Hall "Bleak House",* 3148 Kingston Pike. *Craighead-Jackson House,* 1000 State St. *General James White's home* (1786) and *White's Fort* which is restored. *"Marble Springs"* Farm Home of Governor John Sevier, Neubert Springs Rd. *Ramsey House,* Thorngrove Pike.

Maryville: *Sam Houston,* hero of the Alamo, is remembered in Tennessee by the small schoolhouse north of Maryville where he once taught.

Memphis: 1870, *Fontaine House of the James Lee Memorial,* 680-690 Adams Ave.; 1832, *The Magevney House,* 198 Adams Ave.; 1852, Mallory-Neely House, 652 Adams Ave., open to public.

Murfreesboro: *Oaklands,* N. Maney Ave., is open Apr. to Oct. *Stones River National Battlefield.*

Nashville: *Fort Nashborough,* 170 1st Ave. N. The 1780 log replica of Fort Nashborough, first settlement at Nashville, is open. *Belle Meade Mansion,* the "Queen of Tennessee Plantations," on Leake Ave. off US 70 (Harding Road). Interesting to the enthusiasts for antebellum architecture, historians, and lovers of thoroughbred horses. *The Hermitage* (1819), home of President Andrew Jackson, on Rachel's Lane; 12 mi. W of Nashville.

Piney Flats; *Rocky Mount,* on US 11E, original U.S. Territorial Capitol, has a log house, smokehouse, blacksmith's shop, outdoor kitchen.

Shiloh: *Shiloh Military Park,* site of one of the crucial battles of the Civil War, contains markers and monuments to the fallen of both sides, and many of the original emplacements are still clearly marked for the visitor.

LIBRARIES. In *Nashville,* the Public Library of Nashville and Davidson County, 8th Ave. N. & Union, is a local history library and located on the site of former gardens of President James K. Polk. Collections of books pertinent to Nashville and the state of Tennessee as well as the Nashville Authors collection are available, plus many more.

TOURS. *By car:* Drive through scenic, historic 300-acres at *Reflection Riding* in Chattanooga. Historic details are noted; nature trails give the visitor relaxed enjoyment. Quiet pools reflect the majestic mountain towering above. Open daily. You can use your own car, set your own pace, and utilize a tape recorder and prerecorded commentary for a tour of the Great Smoky Mountains National Park. The history, geology, fauna and flora found in the park are presented on the tape which can be rented at the Cooper Court and Brookside

Motels in Gatlinburg. It can also be purchased as a souvenir of your trip. You can get a magnificent view of the Great Smokies from the *Space Needle*, Airport Rd., just off the Pkwy., Gatlinburg.

By bus: WSM Scenic Tours, a 3-hr. bus tour of historic and cultural Nashville. *Gray Line Tours*, Chattanooga, Great Smokies (from Gatlinburg, Knoxville), Memphis, Nashville.

By rail: The Incline Railway, America's most amazing mile straight up the side of historic Lookout Mountain, Chattanooga, offers visitors a thrilling view of the "Scenic Center of the South." *Flaming Fall Revue*. A steam train, 2-day excursion through the mountains of Tennessee. Late Oct. Contact the Cumberland County Chamber of Commerce, P.O. Box 453, Crossville, TN 38555.

By boat: The *Memphis Queen Line Riverboats*, Riverside Dr., foot of Monroe, provides visitors with a lovely 1½-hr. cruise on the Mississippi River. The *Delta Queen* and *Mississippi Queen* steamboats offer extended river cruises from Spring to late Fall, departing from Memphis. *The Border Star*, departing from the foot of Broad St., Chattanooga, takes her passengers on a 1½-hour cruise on the Tennessee River. Boat rides on the Cumberland River are available to Nashville visitors aboard the *Belle Carol, Captain Ann* and *Nashville Showboat* featuring dinner-theater cruises. Departs from 1 Ave. N., near Fort Nashborough May-Oct. Glass bottom boats explore *The Lost Sea*, a world inside a mountain, 5 mi. from Sweetwater on US 11.

By ski lifts: The double-chaired *Sky Lift* takes visitors from the main street, Gatlinburg, across the river and up the steep incline of Crockett Mt. The *Aerial Tramway* provides a 2-mi. aerial cable car ride from downtown to the Ober Gatlinburg Ski Resort, atop Mt. Harrison.

 SPECIAL INTEREST TOURS. *Bristol Caverns*, on US 421 SE, *Bristol*, is open mid-June to Labor Day.

Chattanooga: Ruby Falls, a natural waterfall 1,120 feet beneath Lookout Mountain in spectacular Lookout Mountain Caverns. Guided tours. *Canyon Land Park*, located atop Lookout Mountain, has chairlifts into the deepest gorge east of the Mississippi. Picnicking, fishing, hiking, swimming are also available to the visitor. *Rock City Gardens*, also atop Lookout Mountain, is a natural city of rocks. See seven states from Lover's Leap; cross Swing-'Along'-Bridge; *Fairyland Caverns* offer colorful scenes from fairytales in rock settings; *Mother Goose Village*, set in a cavern. *Sequoyah Caverns*, 35 mi. from Chattanooga, boasts America's prettiest caverns featuring the Looking Glass Lakes. Daily. *The Confederama*, 3742 Tennessee Ave., is an automated presentation, in miniature, visualizing in lights, guns and smoking cannon the history of the area.

Ruskin Cave, off US 70 via Yellow Creek Rd., in *Dickson*, is open daily Apr. to Oct.

Christus Gardens, housed in a structure of native marble, on River Rd., *Gatlinburg*, depicts scenes from the life of Christ. Dioramas, life-size figures and narrative are inspiring.

Memphis: From the early days in America comes the *Chucalissa Indian Village*, south of Memphis on US 61. Here you may see the restored Indian Village and learn something of a long-forgotten way of life.

Wonder Cave, in *Monteagle*, just off US 41, has onyx formations and an underground river.

Nashville: The State Capitol, between 6th and 7th Aves. N. on Charlotte Ave. Free tours. *Opryland, U.S.A.* $28-million family entertainment complex in beautiful 110-acre park setting. Live performances, exciting rides, animal exhibits and craft shows. The *Upper Room*, 1908 Grand Ave. Free. Chapel has polychrome wood carving of Leonardo da Vinci's "The Last Supper," and World Christian Fellowship Window. The Upper Room Building is where the daily devotional booklet by the same name is published.

The *Old Mill,* just off US 441 in Pigeon Forge, a water-powered mill in operation since 1830, has guided tours daily except Sun. Apr. to mid-Nov.

Forbidden Caverns, on US 411, *Sevierville,* is open daily, June to Nov.

Tuckaleechee Caverns, Rte. 73, Townsend. Guided tours, 1 hr., through the caverns. Apr. to Oct.

INDUSTRIAL TOURS. A tour is conducted by the *Tennessee Valley Authority* from its headquarters in Knoxville. The tour includes *Tennessee Valley Authority* dams, lakes, and steam-electric generating facilities in the Knoxville area. The address is Tennessee Valley Authority, Knoxville, 37902.

The George A. Dickel Distillery, near *Tullahoma,* is willing to show visitors how their product is made.

The Jos. Schlitz Brewing Co., 5151 E. Raines Rd. *Memphis,* welcomes visitors to tour the brewery and visit an authentic replica of a Mississippi River steamboat salon. Mon. to Fri. Tours on the half-hour. Free beer and pretzels.

Jack Daniel Distillery, State 55, *Lynchburg,* is the oldest registered distillery in the U.S., welcomes visitors to view the early art of making whiskey in Tennessee.

Pigeon Forge Pottery, just off US 441, *Pigeon Forge,* welcomes visitors to see craftsmen transform local clays into finished products. Workshop demonstrations Mon. to Fri. Sales displays open daily.

The American-Saint Gobain Corp., Kingsport, acquaints the visitor with the making of plate glass for all use.

The Tennessee Eastman Co., also in *Kingsport,* takes you into the world of synthetics for home and business. Also of interest in Kingsport is the *Kingsport Press Inc.,* a large publishing firm.

The Century Electric Co. in *Humboldt* and *General Electric Co., Murfreesboro,* have tours which will inform you about electric motors.

The Kingston Steam Plant, just off I-40, *Kingston,* is one of the nation's largest steam-powered electric generating plants. The visitor balcony is open daily.

GARDENS. *Memphis Botanic Garden,* 750 Cherry Rd., in Audubon Park is open daily. Flowers, trees, exotic plants and wildflowers plus elaborate gardens give the visitor a panorama of beauty and solitude in a natural setting.

MUSIC. Memphis is the home of jazz, while Nashville is the home of Grand Ole Opry and Opryland Theme Park. *Memphis:* The annual *Memphis Cotton Carnival Jazz & Blues Festival* is held the 2nd wk in May. Nashville: In June, *Country Music Fan Fair* with a large assembly of major Grand Ole Opry stars; in downtown Printer's Alley you can enjoy music ranging from country-western to pop and jazz in the *Carousel Club, Embers Showcase* and *Boots Randolph's Club.*

The well-known country music radio program *Grand Ole Opry* is presented every Fri. & Sat. night at the new Grand Ole Opry House. Sat. matinees mid-Apr. to late Oct. Contact the Grand Ole Opry Ticket Office, 2808 Opryland Dr., Nashville 37214, for schedules and advance ticket information. There are free musical concerts Sun. afternoons during July and August in the *Band Shell,* Centennial Park, Nashville.

In *Sewanee,* on weekends during June and July, concerts are held at the *Sewanee Summer Music Center.*

DRINKING LAWS. Beer is sold in all counties; hard liquor may be purchased in liquor stores in the counties of Shelby (Memphis). Davidson (Nashville), Hamilton (Chattanooga), Knox (Knoxville), Maury (Columbia), Williamson (Franklin), Lake (Tiptonville), and Dyer (Dyersburg). Stores are open 8 A.M. to 11 P.M.; closed on Sun., election days, major holidays. Liquor by-the-drink is illegal, except in Davidson County (including Nashville), Shelby County (including Memphis) and the municipalities of Clarksville, Oak Ridge, Knoxville and Chattanooga. By-the-drink sales: Mon.-Sat., 8-3 A.M.; Sun. from noon. Minimum age 18.

SUMMER SPORTS. With more than 600,000 acres of water and 10,000 mi. of shoreline, the state offers limitless opportunities for fishing, boating, water-skiing and other water sports.

Fishing: A wide variety of fish is found in the state—from bass and catfish to trout. Seventeen TVA lakes and 7 maintained by the U.S. Army Corps of Engineers offer excellent facilities. The Tenn. Game and Fish Commission operates 12 lakes, constructed and managed exclusively for the fisherman. Twenty state parks offer fishing. There is no closed fishing season in Tenn., except on trout in certain areas. On TVA and Corps of Engineers lakes, and the waters below them, the trout season is always open. There are almost 400 fishing docks and resorts on Tenn. waters. Public access ramps are plentiful and provide the fisherman an opportunity to explore most any body of water. Boats and motors can be rented at most docks and resorts; guides may also be available.

Non-resident fishing license fees are subject to change. Consult local authorities.

Canoeing: Tenn. was made to order for the canoeing enthusiast. You can shoot the rapids or float peacefully downstream on gentle rivers in the middle and western parts of the state. "Canoeing in Tenn." is available from the Tenn. Department of Tourist Development, P.O. Box 23170, Nashville, TN 37202.

Swimming, water-skiing and *boating* can be enjoyed on TVA's lakes.

Hunting: The state's naturally abundant woods, and its numerous wildlife preserves, offer a wide variety of game for the hunter. From Nov. to Apr. hunt clubs "ride to the hounds" and often entertain the *National Fox Hunters Ass'n.* In the 3rd week in Feb. the *National Field Trials Ass'n.* holds field trials for bird dogs on the Hobart Ames Plantation at Grand Junction.

Non-resident hunting license fees are subject to change. Write the Tennessee Wildlife Resources Agency, Box 40747, Ellington Agricultural Center, Nashville 37204, for up-to-date information. Permission, of course, is required to hunt on private and public lands.

Horseback riding: The most popular riding horse is the Planatation Walking Horse, bred largely in the rolling hills of Marshall and Bedford counties. This area is criss-crossed with bridle paths, and it is easy to arrange weekend or week-long trips through the countryside. There are 650 mi. of foot and horse trails in the Great Smoky Mountains Nat'l. Park.

Golfing is very big in the state. The rolling land, plus native greens and mild climate make Tenn. a great place for golfers. The season starts in late Mar. and continues through and beyond Thanksgiving. There are 165 golf courses, the majority of which are of regulation size. Public courses welcome all visitors, while some private courses will admit visitors as well. "A Golfer's Guide to Tennessee," published by the Tenn. Department of Tourist Developement, P.O. Box 23170, Nashville, TN 37202.

WINTER SPORTS. *Ober Gatlinburg Ski Resort,* Ski Mountain Rd., on Mt. Harrison, operates daily from Dec. to Mar. Three rope tows and two double chair lifts are available. Ice skating is also offered here.

SPECTATOR SPORTS. *Memphis:* In mid-Dec. two of the nation's top college football teams play in the Liberty Bowl. The *Danny Thomas Memphis Golf Classic,* at the Colonial Country Club, is held for 4 days in May.

Nashville: NASCAR stock car racing. The Grand National, Late Model Sportsman, Limited Sportsman and Mini-stock racing, take place at the Tennessee State Fairgrounds. Apr. to Oct. on Sat. On the 2nd Sat. in May, the *Iroquois Steeplechase* is held. Eight races are featured. *State Horse Show.* Ellington Agricultural Center. Late June. Every type of show horse from ponies to jumpers compete for the State's highest honors.

The *Bristol International Speedway and Drag Strip,* on US 11E, in *Bristol,* features the Southeastern 500 during mid-Mar.; the Volunteer 500 in the early part of July. The IHRA All-American Drags are held for three days in mid-Oct. Mid-June is the time for Spring National Drags, held for four days.

Major college football, basketball, track and swim meets are on view at the University of Tennessee campus, Knoxville, where Southeastern Conference and intersectional rivals come to battle the "Vols."

SHOPPING. All along the mountain roads in East Tennessee you will find craft shops, where you may buy carved wooden pieces, fine handmade furniture, handwoven cloth and rugs, patchwork quilts, pottery and other pieces of art made by the mountaineers.

Gatlinburg is a nationally recognized center for mountain crafts. You can see skilled artisans creating their handmade products in wood, leather, woven materials, metals, pottery and other art media.

Franklin is a unique village, filled with fascinating antique shops and unusual merchandise.

Overton Square, at Madison and Cooper, *Memphis,* has several unusual shops.

WHAT TO DO WITH THE CHILDREN. All of Tennessee's four major cities—Memphis, Nashville, Knoxville and Chattanooga—have parks and playgrounds. There are public swimming pools not only in the municipalities but also in many of the state parks. Exhibits in *Centennial Park* in Nashville include a locomotive, an airplane, and other items of interest to children. Swans swim placidly on a lake. And nearby is the reproduction of the Greek Parthenon.

Gatlinburg and nearby Pigeon Forge abound in commercial attractions. Among the more popular is the *Sky Lift* in Gatlinburg, which takes passengers to the top of *Crockett Mountain,* and *Goldrush Junction* in Pigeon Forge, featuring a 5-mile ride on a real steam train. If the children tire of looking at bears in *Great Smoky Mountain National Park,* take them to the *Smoky Mountain Trout Farms* in Gatlinburg or Hempton and let them fish for trout. Everything is furnished. Chilhowee Park, 3300 Magnolia Ave., Knoxville, features the *Hocus Pocus Amusement Park* and *Municipal Zoo.* A Petting Zoo is open daily except in winter. The *Fairgrounds Amusement Park* in Memphis is open daily. Games, rides and picnicking. *Opryland, U.S.A.,* 2802 Opryland Dr., a 110-acre entertainment park, is composed of 5 "towns" which highlight America's musical heritage. Rides, animal shows, craftsmen demonstrating their arts, puppet shows, complete this fun treat. *Magic World,* on US 441, and *Porpoise Island,* at the foot of the Great Smoky Mountains, Pigeon Forge, are exhibits which appeal to children.

Dale Hollow National Fish Hatchery, in Celina, just off State 53, where rainbow trout are raised, has a Visitor Center.

There are outstanding museums of special interest to children in Oak Ridge, Nashville, and Memphis. Children and adults alike marvel at the interesting and informative displays relating to atomic power and radioactive isotopes at the *Museum of Science and Energy at Oak Ridge,* birthplace of the atomic bomb. The *Children's Museum* in Nashville has fascinating displays of scientific and historical interest. It attracts youngsters from all over the country. The *Memphis Pink Palace Museum* has a specially designed section where young people may operate educational exhibits. In the same building is the planetarium, also of interest to children.

Most children enjoy seeing TVA's huge dams and steam-electric generating plants, as well as the industrial tours offered by many Tennessee manufacturers.

Fort Nashborough in Nashville is a replica of a frontier stockade. Here children can get an idea of what pioneer life was like.

Chattanooga offers a thrilling ride to the top of *Lookout Mountain* and back on the *Incline Railway,* one of the steepest in the world. Atop the mountain is *Point Park,* a museum with a collection of firearms, and other attractions, including *Rock City Gardens,* where the children may hike along mountain trails, observing natural beauty.

Tennessee, with its many mountains and variable rock formations, has a number of interesting caves and caverns. Between Sweetwater and Madisonville on State 68 is the *Lost Sea,* a large underground lake. Visitors view it from glass bottom boats. Near McMinnville is *Cumberland Caverns,* advertised as America's second largest cave. West of Gatlinburg is the *Tuckaleechee Caverns. Ruby Falls-Lookout Mountain Caves* are deep in *Lookout Mountain* near Chattanooga. Sightseers go down 1,120 feet on an elevator to view the 145-foot falls. *Wonder Cave,* 4 miles north of Monteagle, features an underground river. Other scenic caves and caverns include *Bristol Caverns* near Bristol, *Dunbar Cave* near Clarksville, which has an underground swimming pool, and *Jewel Cave,* 12 miles northwest of Dickson.

In Memphis, excursion rides on the *Mississippi River* are available aboard a paddlewheel river boat, *Memphis Queen II* or *Belle Carol,* operating from the foot of Monroe Street. The trip takes one and one-half hours.

 HOTELS AND MOTELS in Tennessee run the full range from the oldest establishments in many of the downtown urban areas to the slick-looking motels along the major highways.

Listings are in order of price category. Based on double occupancy in peak season, without meals, price categories and ranges are as follows: *Expensive:* over $40; *Moderate:* $25–$39; *Inexpensive:* under $25. For a more complete explanation of hotel and motel categories see *Facts at Your Fingertips* at the front of this volume.

Bristol

Holiday Inn. *Moderate.* Two locations: I-81 & US 11, TN 11E & 19 (536 Volunteer Pkwy.,S.) Restaurants, taprooms for beer and set-ups. Pools, some live entertainment.

Chattanooga

Choo-Choo Hilton Inn. *Expensive.* 1400 S. Market St., in Terminal Station. Luxurious rooms in the Inn and restored Victorian-era railroad parlor cars, two dining rooms, three cocktail lounges. Indoor-outdoor pools, jacuzzi, ice-skating rink, tennis. Shopping in delightful boutiques at restored 1905 Southern Railway Terminal Station.

Choo-Choo Read House *Expensive.* Broad and 9th Sts. Convenient downtown location in traditional hostelry, rooms in old and new sections. Pool, sundeck. Dining room, coffee shop, cocktail lounge, live entertainment. Free parking garage.

Sheraton Inn. *Expensive.* Two locations: 6710 Ringgold Rd., 407 Chestnut St. Restaurant, lounge with entertainment. Heated pool. Pets accepted.

Holiday Inn. *Moderate to expensive.* Four locations. All have restaurant, lounge, pool. **I-124:** 401 W. 9th St. Kennels.; **South:** 2100 S. Market St.; **Southeast:** US 41 & I-75. Free airport transportation. Kennels.; **Tiftonia:** I-24 & US 41.

Quality Inn: *Moderate to expensive.* Three locations: Cascades, 3625 Ringold Rd; South, I–75 and US 41; Downtown, 3210 S. Broad St. Dining rooms, lounges in or near Inns.

Admiral Benbow Inn. *Moderate.* 101 E 20th St., near I–24. Dining room, cocktail lounge, live entertainment, dancing. Pool.

Howard Johnson's. *Moderate.* Two locations; both with well-appointed rms., restaurant, pool, pets. **Downtown:** 100 W. 21st St.; **East Ridge:** 6616 Ringgold Rd.

King's Lodge. *Moderate.* 2400 West Side Dr. Large, attractive motor inn. Restaurant. Pool. Pets.

Days Inn and Lodge. *Inexpensive.* 1401 Mack Smith Rd., near I–74 and US 41. Family restaurant. Pool, playground, souvenir shop.

Shamrock Motel. *Inexpensive.* 5659 Brainerd Rd. Across from a regional shopping center. Family accommodations. Apartments available. Pool.

Clarksville
Holiday Inn. *Moderate.* US 41A and US 79. Dining room, cocktail lounge. Pets accepted.

Cumberland Gap
Holiday Inn. *Moderate.* US 25E. Attractive motel back from highway. Dining rm. Heated pool, play area. Kennels.

Elizabethton
Camara Inn. *Moderate.* 505 W. Elk Ave. Pleasant rms., some with refrigerators. Restaurant, pool.

Franklin
Holiday Inn. *Moderate.* I-65 and TN 96. Restaurant, pool, playground, pets.

Gatlinburg
Brookside Motel and Ranch House. *Expensive.* Roaring Fork Rd. Lovely landscaped grounds along mountain stream. Very attractive rms. Cottages also available. Restaurant opp. Heated pool.

Quality Inn Smokyland. *Expensive.* In center of town, 727 Parkway. Pools for oldsters and youngsters, in-room coffee, refrigerators in some rooms, restaurants nearby.

Ramada Inn. *Expensive.* 756 Parkway. Nearby restaurant, indoor-outdoor pools, sauna, seasonal entertainment. Fireplaces in some rooms. Private club for mixed beverages.

Sheraton Gatlinburg Hotel. *Expensive.* Cherokee Orchard and Airport Rds. Lavish facility in contemporary design on brow of mountain overlooking town. Restaurants and coffee shop, entertainment and dancing, pools and poolside services. Laundry. Varied sports offerings. Inroom movies and free parking.

Best Western. Locations include **Crossroads Motor Lodge,** *moderate to expensive,* in a downtown location on US 441, restaurant nearby, pool and some rooms with fireplaces; the **Fabulous Chalet,** *expensive,* Sunset Dr. Overlooks the Smokies, has heated pool and nearby restaurant, seasonal continental breakfasts, some fireplaces in rooms; **Twin Islands Motel,** *moderate to expensive,* in center of town on US 441, with restaurant, heated pool, fireplaces, balconies overlooking mountain stream; and **Zoder's Inn,** *moderate,* 402 Parkway, near downtown shopping, balconies overlooking stream, pool, restaurant nearby, some wood-burning fireplaces in rooms.

Bearskin Motel. *Moderate.* 955 Parkway. Accommodations in either motel or rustic cottages. Efficiencies and kitchen units available. Pool, play area.

Holiday Inn. *Moderate.* Airport Rd. Dining room, snack bar, game room, disco lounge, inroom movies, three pools with one inside.

Mountain View Hotel & Motor Lodge. *Moderate.* A vintage hostelry from early days, in center of town, 500 Parkway. Rooms in older building and new wings, dining room, pools for adults and kiddies.

Johnson City

Camara Inn. *Moderate.* 2312 Brownsmill Rd. Restaurant, pool. Some in-room refrigerators, private club.

Holiday Inn. *Moderate.* 2406 N. Roan St. Pleasant rms. Restaurant. Pool with service at poolside. Kennels.

Kingsport

Best Western Camara Inn. *Moderate.* 805 Lynn Garden Dr. Inviting rms. Refrigerators. Pool; poolside service. Restaurant.

Holiday Inn. *Moderate.* 700 Lynn Garden Dr. Double-story motel. Restaurant. Pool. Kennel.

Tennessee Motor Lodge. *Moderate.* 1017 W. Stone Dr. Comfortable rms.; most have king-size beds. Restaurant. Pool with service at poolside, sauna.

Econo-Travel Motor Hotel. *Inexpensive to moderate.* 1704 E. Stone Dr. Inviting rms. Restaurant adj. Pets welcome.

Knoxville

Holiday Inn. *Moderate to expensive.* Five locations, all with restaurants, lounges, pools. **Northeast:** 4625 Asheville Hwy. **West:** 315 Kirby Rd. **Downtown:** 2000 Chapman Hwy. **Central:** Dale Ave. at 17 St. **Alcoa-Maryville:** north of Knoxville Airport on 129.

Hyatt Regency Knoxville. *Expensive.* 500 Hill Ave. SE. A stunning contemporary modified pyramid reminiscent of Mayan-Aztec design, nine-story atrium lobby. Pool, shops, cocktail lounges with live entertainment and dancing, dining on lobby level and rooftop.

Howard Johnson's. *Moderate to expensive.* Three locations. Pools, restaurants. **North:** 118 Merchants Road. **West:** 7723 Kingston Pike. **In Town:** 3400 Chapman Hwy.

Sheraton Campus Inn. *Moderate to expensive.* 1706 W. Cumberland. On the University of Tennessee campus. Very comfortable accommodations. Suites. Restaurant. Pool; poolside service. Pets.

Sheraton West. *Moderate to expensive.* I-40 and I-75 at Cedar Bluff Rd. Spacious rms. Restaurant. Pool. Kennels.

University Travel Inn. *Moderate.* 1700 Clinch Ave. Spacious, nicely furnished rms. Dining rm. Pool.

Black Oak Motel. *Inexpensive.* 6417 Maynardville Pike. Spacious, inviting rms. Some kitchens. Pool.

Days Inn. *Inexpensive.* Lovell Rd. at I-40 and I-75. Restaurant and pool.

Tate Motel. *Inexpensive.* 6109 Clinton Hwy. Well-maintained motel. Restaurant nearby. Pool.

Lebanon
Holiday Inn. *Moderate.* US 231S and I-40. Suites. Restaurant. Pool.

Best Western Esquire Inn. *Inexpensive to moderate.* I-40 and US 231S. Pleasant rms. Pool. Restaurant.

Days Inn. *Inexpensive to moderate.* I-40 and US 231S. Pool, restaurant.

Lenoir City
King's Inn. *Moderate.* 3 mi. NW. on TN 95 Restaurant, pool, playground.

Red Carpet Inn. *Inexpensive to moderate.* Jct TN 95, I-75. Well-maintained motel. Restaurant. Pool. play area. Pets.

Memphis
Hyatt Regency Memphis. *Expensive.* 939 Ridge Lake Blvd. at I-240 Loop east of city. Contemporary high-rise, luxury rooms. Dining; lounge with entertainment and dancing; heated pool, shops, movies.

Ramada Inn. *Expensive.* Four locations. All have inviting rms., restaurant, pool. **East:** 5225 Summer Ave. **South:** 3265 Elvis Presley Blvd. Airport transportation available; **Southeast:** Lamar & Getwell; **Downtown:** 160 Union Ave.

Sheraton Convention Center Hotel. *Expensive.* 300 N. 2nd St. Located downtown near Cook Convention Center and Mississippi River, has restaurant, cocktail lounge, outdoor pool, guest laundry.

Sheraton Airport Inn. *Expensive.* 2411 Winchester Rd., on grounds of International Airport. Restaurant, lounge, shops, pool, lighted tennis courts.

Holiday Inns. *Moderate to expensive.* Memphis is the headquarters of this remarkable motel-hotel system. Flagship among the Inns in Memphis is the **River-**

mont, *expensive.* a high-rise contemporary tower overlooking the Mississippi River and the dramatic skyline of the city, with cocktail lounges, live entertainment, disco, gift shops, pools, restaurants and a gourmet roof-top dining room where music to accompany dancing and viewing are highlighted.

Other Holiday Inns in Memphis: I-40 at Macon Rd.; **Midtown,** Union Ave. at I-240; Poplar Ave. at I-240; Medical Center, 969 Madison Ave.; Union Ave. at McLean Blvd; **Holiday City,** 3728 Lamar Ave; and **International Airport** at 1441 E. Brooks Rd. All have restaurants, lounges, pools and often feature live entertainment.

Quality Inn. *Moderate to expensive.* Three locations. All have tastefully decorated rms., restaurant, pool. **Airport:** 1400 Brooks Rd. Entertainment. **East:** I-240 & Poplar. Indoor heated pool. **West:** 271 W. Alston Ave. Entertainment. Airport transportation available.

Rodeway Inn. *Moderate to expensive.* 2949 Airways Blvd. Very comfortable rms. Restaurant, lounge with entertainment. Pool.

Sheraton Skyport. *Moderate to expensive.* In the Memphis International Airport Terminal. Mini-rooms for overnight and between-flight naps. Convenient to restaurants, lounge, shops, airline and auto rental counters.

Admiral Benbow Inn. *Moderate.* Two locations, both with pleasant rooms, pool, restaurant. **Airport:** 2201 Winchester Rd.; **Midtown:** 1220 Union Ave.

Admiral Benbow Inn, Summer. *Moderate.* Inviting rms. Restaurant. Pool. Free airport transportation.

Howard Johnson's. *Moderate.* 3280 Elvis Presley Blvd. Pool, restaurant, playground, pets.

Shelby Motel. *Inexpensive.* 6803 Summer Ave. Inviting rms. Restaurant nr. Pool.

Murfreesboro

Holiday Inn. *Moderate to expensive.* Jct. TN 96 and I-24. Restaurant. Heated pool. Kennels.

Howard Johnson's. *Moderate.* Jct. US 231 and I-24. Pool, restaurant.

Ramada Inn. *Moderate.* Jct. US 231 and I-24. Well-appointed rms. Restaurant. Pool.

Quality Inn. *Moderate.* Jct. I-24 and US 231S. Opposite shopping center. Restaurant, pool.

Wayside Inn (Best Western). *Moderate.* Jct. I-24 and US 231S. Nicely decorated rms. Restaurant nr. Heated pool.

Motel Murfreesboro. *Inexpensive to moderate.* 1150 N.W. Broad St. Well-maintained motel. Restaurant. Pool.

University Inn. *Inexpensive to moderate.* 219 Broad St. Nicely furnished rms. Restaurant nr. Pool.

TENNESSEE

525

Nashville

Best Western Drake Inn. *Moderate to expensive.* 420 Murfreesboro Rd. Spacious, well-appointed rms. Some refrigerators. Restaurant. Pool.

Hyatt Regency Nashville. *Expensive.* 623 Union St. Located downtown, the luxury hotel features a stunning atrium lobby, gourmet dining room, revolving rooftop restaurant, cocktail lounges, live entertainment, dancing, shops.

Opryland Hotel. *Expensive.* 2800 Opryland Dr. at Opryland USA. Colonial design, lavish decor. Pools, dining room and restaurants, cocktail lounges with live entertainment and dancing. Boutique shopping.

Radisson Plaza Nashville. *Expensive.* 2 Commerce Pl. Striking contemporary design, downtown location. Two dining rooms, cocktails and live entertainment, heated indoor pool.

Maxwell House Hotel. *Expensive.* 2025 Metro Center Blvd. Convenient downtown location. Two dining rooms, swimming pool and saunas, lighted tennis courts, cocktail lounges with live entertainment.

Hilton Airport Inn. *Expensive.* No. 1 International Plaza. At Metropolitan Airport. 2-story motel with nicely decorated rms. Restaurant. Pool.

Holiday Inn. *Moderate to expensive.* Five locations. All have restaurant, lounge, pool, kennels. **I-24:** 350 Harding Pl. Live entertainment. **West End Ave.:** 1800 West End Ave.; **North:** 230 W. Trinity Lane. Live entertainment.; **Southeast:** 981 Murfreesboro Rd. Free airport transportation. Live entertainment.; **Vanderbilt:** 2613 West End Ave. Live entertainment.

Howard Johnson's Motor Lodge. *Expensive.* At two locations. All have restaurant, pool. Pets welcome. **North:** 2401 Brick Church Pike; **West:** 6834 Charlotte Pike.

Albert Pick Motel. *Moderate.* 320 Murfreesboro Rd. Tastefully decorated rms. Restaurant. Pool. Airport transportation available.

Quality Inn Parkway. *Moderate to expensive.* 10 Interstate Dr. A 7-story motor inn. Restaurant. Pool. Pets accepted.

Ramada Inn. *Expensive.* Four locations. All have pleasant rms. Restaurant, pool. **North:** I-65 at Trinity Lane. Pets welcome.; **Capitol Hill:** 840 James Robertson Pkwy. Pets permitted.; **South:** Harding Pl. **Airport:** I-24 and I-40, Murfreesboro Exit.

Sheraton-Nashville Hotel. *Expensive.* 920 Broadway. Spacious, nicely decorated rms. Restaurant, lounge with entertainment. Pool; poolside service.

Sheraton South Motor Inn. *Expensive.* 737 Harding Pl. Very attractive rms. Restaurant, lounge with entertainment. Heated pool. Pets accepted.

Days Inn. *Moderate.* Color TV. Restaurant. Pool, play area. Pets welcome. At four locations: **Trinity:** I-65 and Trinity Lane; **Bell Road:** I-24 and Bell Rd.; **Plus Park:** I-24 and Murfreesboro Rd.; **Old Hickory:** I-40 and Old Hickory Rd.

Congress Inn. *Moderate.* 2914 Dickerson Rd. Comfortable rms. Restaurant. Pool, play area. Color TV.

Oak Ridge

Diplomat Motel (Best Western). *Moderate.* 206 S. Illinois Ave. Double-story motel with spacious rms. Restaurant nr. Heated pool, play area.

Alexander Motor Inn. *Inexpensive.* 210 E. Madison. Nicely decorated rms. Restaurant. Pool.

 DINING OUT in Tennessee often means fresh Tennessee River catfish or such country specialties as ham with red-eye gravy (sometimes made in Tennessee with coffee instead of water). Accompanying the meal may be hush puppies or home-baked biscuits, and desserts can include such Tennessee delights as pecan pie, blueberry pie, or fruit cobbler.

Restaurants are listed according to their price category. Categories and ranges for a complete dinner are as follows: *Expensive:* over $14. *Moderate:* $8–$14. *Inexpensive:* under $8. For a more complete explanation of restaurant categories see *Facts at Your Fingertips* at the front of this volume.

Chattanooga

Chattanooga Choo-Choo. *Moderate to expensive.* Choo-Choo Hilton Inn, 1400 S. Market St., in the Terminal Station. Spacious dining room under high dome of the 1905 era railway terminal, turn-of-the century atmosphere. Steaks, chicken, seafoods. Cocktails.

Green Room. *Moderate to expensive.* Choo-Choo Read House Hotel, Broad and 9th Sts. Elegant decor. Continental dishes, background music. They serve their own baked goods and ice cream.

Fehn's. *Inexpensive.* 600 River St. An entrancing view of the river from the tables near the windows. The varied menu gives you a wide selection of steaks and seafood. Chef-owned.

S & W Cafeteria. *Inexpensive.* 824 Broad St. This modern cafeteria with a Victorian motif is one of those places where frills have been eliminated in favor of an abundance of good food at reasonable prices.

Gatlinburg

Pioneer Inn. *Expensive.* 373 Parkway, on US 441N. Novel, unusual decor. Situated to provide dining on the river. Steaks, roast beef, chicken and flaming shishkebab.

Open Hearth. *Moderate to expensive.* 1133 Parkway, on US 441. Very pleasant and friendly dining rm. with steak as their specialty. Background music.

Ogle's Buffet Restaurant. *Inexpensive.* US 441 in center of town. Wide selections of salads, vegetables, meat dishes, desserts from buffet tables. Good mountain cookery is featured. Delightful for families.

Knoxville

Volador. *Expensive.* At Hyatt Regency Hotel, 500 Hill Ave. A rooftop dining room with superb views of the city and mountains. Continental specialties feature seafoods, lamb and duckling. Each Sunday there's a lavish brunch. Al fresco dining in season.

Regas Restaurant. *Moderate.* 318 N. Gay St. Informal service and excellent food. The seafood is superb. Save rm. for fresh strawberry shortcake.

Morrison's. *Inexpensive.* West Town Mall. Cafeteria; member of excellent chain.

Memphis

Britling's. *Moderate to expensive.* 5100 Poplar Ave., Clark Tower Mall. Buffet Clambake, whole Maine Lobster or N.Y. Strip Steak. Eat as much as you want.

Four Flames. *Moderate to expensive.* 1085 Poplar Ave. Enjoy superb dining in a charming antebellum house. American, Continental cuisine. Steak, seafood (New Orleans-style) are specialties here. Lounge with entertainment. Jacket and tie a must.

Justines. *Expensive.* 919 Coward Pl. at East St. A superb restoration of an old mansion, on attractive grounds, is the setting for excellent Creole and Continental cuisine. In the summer, terrace dining. Reservations recommended.

Grisanti's. *Moderate to expensive.* 1489 Airways Blvd. Steak, veal and delicious Northern Italian preparations are specialties. On display is the world's most expensive bottle of wine, purchased by the chef-owner a few years ago.

Pancho's. *Moderate.* Two locations: **Midtown,** 1850b Union and **W. Memphis,** US 70, just over the bridge. Mexican cuisine, char-broiled steaks. Businessman's Fiesta lunch served daily.

Britling Cafeterias. *Inexpensive.* There are three of these quality cafeterias with good food. Neat, clean, and inviting. 3134 N. Thomas St.; 20 Poplar Highland Plaza; and 4550 Poplar Ave.

Nashville

Hugo's. *Expensive.* In Hyatt Regency Hotel. 623 Union St. American, French and Continental specialties feature aged beef, lamb, veal and other menu choices in a posh atmosphere.

Mario's. *Expensive.* 1915 West End Ave. Continental menu, bar, background music, elegant decor. Specialty: Italian dishes. Chef-owned.

Vizcaya. *Expensive.* 1907 West End Ave. Charming Old World atmosphere. Own baking. Specialties: seafood, paella, black beans. Spanish, Continental menu.

Brass Rail Stables. *Moderate to expensive.* 206½ Printer's Alley. Steaks, prime ribs and a variety of flambé preparations highlight the menu at this popular restaurant, situated in the downtown district and noted for lively night-time entertainment.

Morrison's. *Inexpensive.* 1720 West End Ave. Cafeteria.

VIRGINIA

A State of Mind, A Way of Life

BY
RALPH DANFORD

Ralph Danford has been a travel writer for more than twenty years. A long-time resident of Virginia, he chose that state as his home after living in various places all over the globe.

Among several approaches to Virginia, all rewarding, one of the newest follows US 13 down the rural Eastern Shore and across seventeen miles of water via the Chesapeake Bay Bridge-Tunnel. The Bridge-Tunnel, which uses four man-made islands as stepping stones across the Bay, is a convenience and a show in itself.

On back roads off US 13 along the Eastern Shore are the quiet towns of Northampton and Accomac Counties. Across ten miles of bridges and causeways lies Chincoteague Island, scene of the annual pony penning during the last week in July. Fishermen turn cowboy and herd wild ponies from Assateague Island across the channel to Chincoteague for auction on the carnival grounds.

The shaggy Chincoteague ponies, larger than a Shetland pony but smaller than a horse, are auctioned for the benefit of the island's volunteer fire department. Legend says that the ponies' ancestors swam ashore from a shipwreck in the 16th century or, alternately, that pirates put them on the island to graze.

The greater portion of Assateague is a national refuge for wildlife, including tiny Sika deer, scarcely three feet high. Native to Japan, they were released on the island in 1923 by a troop of Boy Scouts.

A visit to Assateague at any season affords spectacular displays of more than 250 kinds of birds. The winter features flocks of honking snow geese and whistling swans; spring brings sandpipers, plovers, curlews, and oyster-catchers; summer displays nesting colonies of egrets, herons, and ibises; and autumn offers migrating hawks and noisy flocks of ducks.

The Eastern Shore offers some of the best salt water fishing on the East Coast in the waters of Chesapeake Bay, and off the barrier islands along the Atlantic shore. The seafood industry is big business here with the local packers supplying the famous Chincoteague clams to the finest restaurants in North America.

On the first Wednesday in May humankind flock to Tom's Cove on Chincoteague and the Eastern Shore Annual Seafood Festival for an appetizing sea-side buffet. The Festival has become so popular since its origin in 1969 that reservations should be made before December.

Tangier Island in Chesapeake Bay has the atmosphere of a fishing village of an earlier era. A unique English is spoken here by the natives. It resembles that of their ancestors, who settled the island in 1686. Until recently the island was relatively isolated. Access is by ferry from Reedville, Va. or from Crisfield, Md. Overnight lodging is available in a guest house.

Tidewater Virginia

Leaving the Eastern Shore, the traveler crosses the Chesapeake Bay Bridge-Tunnel into a metropolitan complex encompassing Norfolk, with the world's largest naval base; Virginia Beach, with a 28 mile stretch of public beach; Chesapeake, the gateway to Dismal Swamp; and Portsmouth, site of the country's oldest ship-repair yard. An interesting introduction to the Norfolk and Portsmouth skylines are the boat tours which operate from May through October. The longer tours at sunset include the U.S. Naval Base, Norfolk, and its array of warships.

Norfolk and Tidewater Area

The first-time visitor to Norfolk may well be astonished at its variety. Long known as home port of the world's largest naval installation and as NATO's Atlantic headquarters, Norfolk plays host to an eight-day Azalea Festival in late April that honors the alliance's fourteen member-nations.

One of America's outstanding art museums, the Chrysler, is located in Norfolk. It contains the collection of Walter P. Chrysler, Jr., and includes paintings and sculpture and a comprehensive glass collection with works representative of the history of glass-making from the early Chinese period through Art Deco.

Other features of artistic merit and historical interest in Norfolk are the Hermitage Foundation Museum, with its splendid Oriental collection and lovely grounds where you can picnic; the Adam Thoroughgood House, oldest standing brick home in America: the Willoughby-Baylor House (1794); and St. Paul's Church (note the cannonball still embedded in the southeast wall) which survived a British bombardment in 1776.

VIRGINIA

Scale of Miles

0 50

NORFOLK-VIRGINIA BEACH

The house of Moses Myers, one of America's first millionaires, is a standout—hosts and hostesses in period costumes.

Norfolk's former courthouse, built in 1852, has been transformed into the General Douglas MacArthur Memorial Museum. The general is entombed in a crypt recessed in the floor of the Rotunda. Lining eight galleries are mementoes, including his crushed cap and corncob pipe. A twenty-eight-minute film traces MacArthur's career.

The major attractions of Norfolk can best be seen on a well marked drive-yourself tour, plus a walking tour in the downtown area.

Norfolk's SCOPE Convention Center houses a 12,000 seat arena, a 2,500 seat theater, meeting rooms, a great exhibit hall, and a huge underground parking facility. Everything from rock concerts and circuses through operas are held at SCOPE. The whole complex is dominated by a huge dome, which is supported by flying buttresses.

Norfolk's Ocean View Beach stretches along 15 miles of the Chesapeake Bay and offers a wide expanse of sand and a gentle surf.

Virginia Beach, one of the most popular seaside resorts on the East Coast, has combers high enough to attract the Atlantic Ocean surfing championship in July. Tucked away behind the beach and residential sections are the 2,700 acres of Seashore State Park, a melange of shady upland woods, sand dunes, and cypress swamps draped in Spanish moss.

Near the City of Chesapeake lies much of the Dismal Swamp, first surveyed by Colonel William Byrd II in 1728. George Washington and five other investors formed a company for digging ditches and draining the swamp. Fortunately for posterity, it resisted civilizing. In 1974 the U.S. Department of Interior, spurred by a lumber company's gift of fifty thousand acres, including Lake Drummond, set about making the swamp a wildlife refuge with facilities for human observers. July and August, the peak time for the pesky yellow fly, are not months for investigating Old Dismal. Inquire locally about boat tours to Lake Drummond.

From Norfolk, visitors may travel via the Hampton Roads Bridge-Tunnel to the port cities of Hampton and Newport News. Hampton is the oldest continuous English-speaking settlement in the New World. St. John's Church, built in 1728, prizes a set of communion silver made in London in 1618.

Hampton is the birthplace of one of the newest sciences. At the National Aeronautics and Space Administration's Langley Research Center America began its voyage through outer space. It was there the country's astronauts learned to walk on the moon. A space museum is open daily at the Visitor Center.

Covering sixty-three acres in Hampton, surrounded by a moat, is hexagonal Fort Monroe. During a century and a half, it held several distinguished prisoners, including Indian Chief Black Hawk and Confederate President Jefferson Davis. The brick casemate where Davis lived two years is now a museum of keepsakes from the Fort's history. From its ramparts the visitor can watch ships plying Hampton Roads and view the waters where the first ironclads, the *Monitor* and the *Merrimac*, clashed during the Civil War and changed the course of naval history.

In Newport News follow tour signs to the major points of interest, including the Mariners Museum, the War Memorial Museum of Virginia, Transportation Corps Museum at Fort Eustis, and the Newport News shipyards. From April through November a harbor cruise offers an enjoyable way of seeing the harbor area.

The Mariners Museum has an outstanding collection of miniature ships, marine paintings, figureheads, and relics from the sea. There is also an excellent marine reference library.

West on Interstate 64 from Newport News is the 23-mile Colonial Parkway connecting the information centers at Jamestown, Williamsburg, and Yorktown.

Jamestown

Jamestown, settled in 1607, was the first permanent English settlement in the New World. Start your tour at the visitor center operated by the National Park Service. Films and other displays in the museum provide background for a walking tour that includes the old church tower and the foundations of many of the original buildings. Also visit the glasshouse where craftsmen practice 17th-century glassblowing, one of the first industries of the colony, established in 1608.

A mile away from Jamestown—but not a part of it—is the Jamestown Festival Park, built by the Commonwealth of Virginia in 1957 and featuring Old and New World Pavilions. For the Old World Pavilion, tracing the settlers' origins in England, the British government provided costumed wax figures, guns, armor, coats of arms, and Captain John Smith's huge sea chest. The New World Pavilion interprets the settlers' contributions to American life, including the first representative assembly in 1619.

The Park also has a reconstructed stockade enclosing on an acre fifteen residences, a guardhouse, a storehouse, and a church. Moored at the James River dock are full-size reproductions of the tiny vessels—the *Susan Constant, Godspeed,* and *Discovery*—that brought the settlers to Jamestown in 1607, twenty years after the tragic failure to found a colony at Roanoke Island and thirteen years before the Pilgrims set foot on Plymouth Rock. What the settlers found when they landed at Jamestown is represented by a log lodge, furnished with animal skins and primitive tools, similar to the one that housed Indian Chief Powhatan and his daughter Pocahontas. A look at the raw environment underscores the Indian girl's achievement in bridging the gap between her father's Stone Age culture and the Court of St. James.

Williamsburg

In 1699 the colonists moved their seat of government from Jamestown to Middle Plantation, which originated in 1633 as a palisade between the York and James Rivers. They renamed it Williamsburg in honor of King William III, and it served as the capital of a colony whose borders reached beyond the Great Lakes to the Mississippi River and encompassed the territory of eight of our present states. In 1780, during the Revolutionary War, the capital was moved to Richmond and Williamsburg lapsed into lethargy. The town slumbered so soundly that in 1912 it forgot to hold an election.

In 1926 John D. Rockefeller, Jr. set in motion the restoration of existing buildings and the reconstruction of others, including the Governor's Palace, the elegant residence of seven royal governors and the State of Virginia's first two governors, Patrick Henry and Thomas Jefferson. Original inventories guided the furnishing of the Palace and other exhibition buildings. Careful research also went into reviving one hundred acres of greens and gardens.

Always popular are the craft shops, including the bakery, the print shop, the blacksmith's forge, and the wig-maker's shop, tended by more than 100 craftsmen and interpreters. The staff that looks after Colonial Williamsburg more than equals in number its two thousand residents during the Colonial era.

In 1693 the College of William and Mary, second oldest in the United States, was founded in Williamsburg. It has been called "Alma Mater of a Nation" becuase of notable graduates including Presidents Jefferson, Monroe, and Tyler, and Chief Justice John Marshall. The nation's oldest classroom building is the Christopher Wren building, restored by Rockefeller to its original glory.

To set the stage for a journey into the 18th century the visitor should see the thirty-seven-minute color film *The Story of a Patriot,* at the Information Center and then roam the restored area. A walk down the main thoroughfare, with the College of William and Mary at one end, the restored Colonial Capitol at the other, will confirm Franklin D. Roosevelt's observation that it is "the most historic avenue in America."

Yorktown

Within a few minutes' drive is Yorktown and, overlooking the York River, the broad meadows where the combined French and American forces led by George Washington won the climactic battle October 19, 1781, against the British troops under General Cornwallis.

In Yorktown is the home of Governor Thomas Nelson, who was serving with Washington during the siege. Sensing that American artillerymen were sparing his home, although British officers were quartered there, Nelson directed the cannon to fire upon it. Cannonballs are still imbedded in one wall.

Exhibits in the Yorktown Information Center trace the events of the three-week siege and the final assault on British redoubts. Among the displays are military tents used by Washington, dioramas of the battles, and a partially reconstructed British warship. From the Siege Line Lookout on the Information Center's roof deck, today's visitor has a view of the battlefield that Washington and Cornwallis would have envied. A self-guided tour by auto following the markers will include most of the historic sites.

Plantations and Historic Homes

Six miles east of Williamsburg on US 60 is Carter's Grove, operated by Colonial Williamsburg. The mansion was built in 1750 by the wealthy "King" Carter, and is considered one of the most beautiful in America. Many famous Americans from Washington through succeeding generations have been entertained here.

A ferry at Jamestown takes the visitor across the river to the site of Smith's Fort Plantation. Remains of the breastworks, built in 1609 by Captain John Smith, are still discernible. In 1652 Thomas Warren built a brick house, now called the Rolfe-Warren House, on property he bought from Thomas Rolfe, the son of Pocahontas and John Rolfe.

No state has more plantation houses than Virginia, and State 5 from Williamsburg to Richmond, a winding, wood-lined road, has Virginia's greatest concentration of the great houses.

West of Williamsburg is the first in the procession of mansions, Sherwood Forest, the home of President John Tyler, who chose the name because he fancied himself a political Robin Hood. The dwelling, one of the longest private houses in America, extends three hundred feet and one room deep with a central portion of three stories.

Next is Belle Air, built in 1670, one of the oldest frame dwellings in America. Then appears Evelynton, a white-columned mansion named for Evelyn Byrd and standing on land once owned by her father, Colonel William Byrd II. Belle Air by appointment only; Evelynton closed to public.

The great Byrd himself—diarist, member of the Governor's Council, founder of Richmond, explorer—built and lived in neighboring Westover. In the center of the boxwood garden is Byrd's tomb, with the stately twenty-six-line epitaph he probably composed. It speaks of his being, among other things, "a spelndid economist," a fair enough assessment of a planter who owned more than 179,000 acres.

Next in line is Berkeley, ancenstral home of a signer of the Declaration of Independence, Colonel Benjamin Harrison, and two Presidents of the United States, William Henry Harrison and Benjamin Harrison. During the Civil War in 1862 while Federal troops were tenting in Berkeley's fields, General Butterfield composed the bugle call "Taps."

Shirley Plantation, last in the line on State 5, has been in the Hill Carter family for nine generations, since 1723. It was the home of Robert E. Lee's mother, Anne Hill Carter. The original furnishings, silver, and family portraits are still in the home.

The northern neck of Virginia, lying between the Rappahannock and Potomac Rivers, is noted for producing presidents and statesmen. James Madison came from King George County and George Washington and James Monroe from Westmoreland County, as did Robert E. Lee.

Stratford Hall, home of the Lees, gave the nation a host of public servants, including twelve members of the House of Burgesses and four Governors. Thomas Lee, who began building the house about 1725, was a Burgess who became President of His Majesty's Council. Two of his sons, Richard Henry and Francis Lightfoot Lee, signed the Declaration of Independence, the only two brothers to do so. Two other sons, Arthur and William Lee, represented the United States abroad as diplomats.

Also in the parade was Light Horse Harry Lee, Washington's cavalry leader, who, as a congressman eulogized his commander, was "first in war . . . peace . . . and the heart of his country." His son was Robert E. Lee.

Stratford Hall's massive proportions fit its destiny. Designed in the shape of a capital H and constructed of brick sent to Virgnia from England, the house measures ninety by sixty feet. It has four huge chimneys at each end. Its 1,500 acres today are worked as they were when Stratford was a showplace among Colonial plantations. The house is within sight of the Potomac River and only eight miles from Wakefield, the birthplace of George Washington.

The structure at Wakefield is an approximate reproduction of the Washington birthplace. The National Park Service built it of old brick on the site of the original, which burned Christmas day in 1779—the year Washington died. Many of the Washington family furnishings are among the early 18th-century antiques. Nearby is Monrovia, where President Monroe was born. Only the site remains.

Scattered throughout Virginia are many historic homes. South of Appomattox is Red Hill Shrine, the plantation and the last home of the great patriot, Patrick Henry, whose grave is also on this site. In Norfolk, visit the oldest standing brick house in America, the Adam Thoroughgood (1636), the Georgian-Federal Willoughby-Baylor House (1794), and the elegant Moses Myers House (1792), with hosts and hostesses in period costume. Near Leesburg are Oatlands and Morven Park. Sully Plantation in Chantilly is near Dulles Airport. And another presidential birthplace, that of Woodrow Wilson, is in Staunton.

Alexandria and Mount Vernon

The nation's most celebrated home, Mount Vernon, is in northern Virginia, fifteen miles from Washington, D.C., via the George Washington Memorial Parkway.

Between 1754 and 1799, Washington developed Mount Vernon into one of the period's finest estates, enlarging the house and expanding the acreage. The most striking feature is the high-columned piazza extending the full length of the house. Here tourists relax as if it were their own.

As a seventeen-year-old surveyor's apprentice, Washington drew the first map of his home town; Alexandria. He attended Christ Church on the corner of North Washington and Cameron Streets in downtown Alexandria and socialized with other patriots at Gadsby's Tavern, recently restored, on the southwest corner of Cameron and Royal Streets. He was a member of the Friendship Fire Company, a volunteer corps.

Alexandrians insist proudly that their city offers as many buildings worth preserving as does Colonial Williamsburg. Still standing are eight hundred early buildings, many identified by bronze plaques, ranging from late Georgian and early Federal to Victorian.

Three miles west of Mount Vernon is Woodlawn Plantation, a wedding gift from George Washington to his adopted granddaughter, Eleanor Parke Custis, known as Nellie Custis, and his nephew, Major Lawrence Lewis.

Driving south, the traveler passes Pohick Church, the parish church for Mount Vernon, Woodlawn, and Gunston Hall, built in 1755 by George Mason, author of the Virginia Declaration of Rights. Gunston Hall is a story-and-a-half brick house with a steep roof accented by pairs of tall chimneys at each end.

Fredericksburg

Fredericksburg, if it wished, could contest Alexandria's claim of being Washington country. At Ferry Farm, legends say, the boy Washington cut down his father's cherry tree and threw a silver dollar across the Rappahannock River. At Charles and Lewis Streets is the cottage Washington built for his mother, Mary. At 1201 Washington Avenue is Kenmore, the home of arms manufacturer Colonel Fielding Lewis, who married Washington's sister Betty. On Caroline Street is the Apothecary

Shop of Hugh Mercer, where Washington worked while in Fredericksburg. And one of Washington's proteges, James Monroe, practiced five years in a law office at 908 Charles Street. The furnishings include the desk on which the Monroe Doctrine was prepared.

Located halfway between the two warring capitals of Richmond and Washington, Fredericksburg was a frequent target for both sides during the Civil War. Few cities saw as much strife. From Maryes Heights Lee's strongly entrenched Army of Northern Virginia threw back repeated attacks of General Burnside's Federal troops on December 13, 1862. Fierce fighting also raged in the Battle of Chancellorsville, the Wilderness, the Spotsylvania Court House.

Richmond

The traveler has easy access to Richmond via Interstate 95, I–64 or US 1.

In Richmond the two most revered structures are the Capitol, designed by Thomas Jefferson, and St. John's Church, built in 1740–41. In the white frame church at 24th and Broad Streets Patrick Henry in 1775 made his liberty-or-death speech to the Second Virginia Convention.

Down the hill from St. John's is Richmond's oldest dwelling, the Old Stone House at 1914 East Main St., built about 1737. It has been dedicated as a memorial to poet Edgar Allan Poe, who haunted the environs for twenty-six years. The blood-red Raven Room contains forty-two somber drawings from Poe's poem on that bird.

The Valentine Museum at 1015 East Clay St. is devoted to the life and history of Richmond. In the rear is a garden, a peaceful retreat from the downtown's busy streets. Richmond's first residents, the Indians, get recognition in this museum.

In the far west end, at Grove Avenue and North Boulevard, is the state-supported Virginia Museum of Fine Arts. It pioneered in launching a fleet of artmobiles, traveling galleries to put art within reach of every hamlet.

At 818 E. Marshall St. is the house Chief Justice John Marshall built about 1790 and occupied until his death in 1835.

Richmond's newest attraction is a restored commercial area dating from the mid-1700's. Known as Shockoe Slip, it is becoming an entertainment center with a variety of restaurants and small shops.

Throughout the Civil War the North's rallying cry was "On to Richmond." Now at 3215 East Broad St. there is a headquarters for the Richmond National Battlefield Park offering a road tour covering fifty-seven miles of battle lines, including Cold Harbor and Seven Pines.

Some 60 miles west of Richmond on Interstate 64 is Charlottesville, named in 1762 for Queen Charlotte, wife of George III. But it might just as well be called Jeffersonville, so thoroughly does Long Tom dominate the landscape and the intellectual atmosphere thereabouts.

Monticello

The domed mansion that is Monticello represents Jefferson's forty-one-year labor of love, of which he said: "All my wishes end where I hope my days will end—at Monticello."

To Fredericksburg
Washington, D.C.

95

Chickahominy R.

64

Amtrak Station

Charlottesville

360

Atlantic
Exposition Grounds

Creighton Rd.

Cold Harbor
Natl. Battlefield

University
of Richmond

CARY ST.

BROAD ST.

Virginia House

64

To Williamsburg

Norfolk

WILLIAMSBURG RD.

Byrd
International Airport

60

HULL ST.

COMMERCE RD.

NEW MARKET RD.

James R.

150

JEFFERSON DAVIS

Ft. Hoke

Ft. Harrison

Richmond
Natl. Battlefield

Ft. Brady

Pocahontas
State Park

95

Chester

10

Bermuda Hundred

RICHMOND AREA

The three-story building has thirty-five rooms but looks deceptively modest because twelve rooms are in the basement and a series of out-buildings, such as laundry, smoke house, dairy, stable, weaving quarters, and kitchen, is located inconspicuously beneath the long terraces terminating in two balancing chambers.

Always looking for labor-saving devices, he filled Monticello with unique features—tightly winding stairways, only twenty-four inches wide, to save space, a revolving door with shelves to serve dishes from the kitchen to the dining room in one sweeping motion, a dumbwaiter to bring wine from the cellar, a folding ladder to use in winding the cannonball clock that registers hours, days, and weeks.

Through a telescope on his mountain Jefferson watched the building of the University of Virginia, which he founded as "the last act of usefulness I can render." He designed the buildings, hired the faculty, and organized the curriculum. So well did he work that today students and faculty speak of "Mr. Jefferson" as if he were a living presence.

The Shenandoah Valley

West of Charlottesville the character of the land changes, and at times the independent temperament of the people seems to match the rugged terrain. The Blue Ridge Mountains form the great divide in Virginia. Wriggling along that range's backbone is the Skyline Drive, which runs 105 miles through Shenandoah National Park. At Afton the winding road changes its name to the Blue Ridge Parkway and continues 217 miles to the North Carolina border.

Beyond the Blue Ridge are the Allegheny Mountains and between the two ranges lies the Shenandoah Valley. At the head of the Valley, in northwest Virginia, is Winchester. Here sixteen-year-old George Washington worked as a surveyor for Lord Fairfax. His headquarters at Cork and Braddock Streets is now a museum. Winchester is the site of the annual Apple Blossom Festival, which has a nationally televised parade featuring more than 50 floats and 80 bands representing 30 states.

The Valley offers an array of natural formations, the most renowned being Natural Bridge, on Interstate 81 and US 11, and twelve miles south of Interstate 64. It rears 215 feet above Cedar Creek and is ninety feet long and from fifty to one hundred fifty feet wide. Indians called it the Bridge of God. Thomas Jefferson, who bought it from King George III for thirty shillings, termed it "the most sublime of Nature's Work." Along the edge of the Valley are numerous caves. Luray Caverns is popular for its colorful formations and the unusual stalacpipe organ.

Near the community of Mt. Solon are seven limestone columns rising high as a twelve-story building. Local residents long ago named them the Natural Chimneys because of their resemblance to huge furnaces that smeltered iron in the area prior to the Civil War.

The massive rock formations, set in a near circle against the side of a hill, also look like castle turrets and towers, an image that inspired a jousting tournament held annually on the third Saturday in August since 1821, making it America's oldest annual sporting event.

The cities of Harrisonburg and Staunton and the counties of Augusta and Rockingham have developed a regional park around the Chimneys that contains two miles of trails with scenic overlooks and recreational facilities including an Olympic-size swimming pool.

At Lexington is Washington and Lee University, named for George Washington, who endowed it, and Robert E. Lee, who was its president from the close of the Civil War to his death in 1870. On the campus is the Lee Chapel, built during his administration and housing the Valentine recumbent statue of Lee and a crypt in which are buried the General and members of his family. Visitors also may see Lee's old office and the college's museum.

Washington and Lee's neighbor is the Virginia Military Institute, "the West Point of the South," where Stonewall Jackson taught before he found fame and death as a Confederate General. VMI is the site of the research library and museum honoring another distinguished alumnus, George C. Marshall, Chief of Staff during World War II. It houses his personal papers and such relics as General Patton's helmet and General Rommel's map of El Alamein. A talking map with moving lights traces the highlights of World War II.

Just twenty miles south of Roanoke is an unusual monument—a tiny log cabin with a dirt floor—to Booker T. Washington, the black leader who was born in slavery there on a Franklin County tobacco plantation. The visitor center contains exhibits on his life and an audiovisual program interpreting his heroic quest for education for himself and his race. The reconstructed plantation is worked as it was in Booker's childhood.

Highlands of Southwest Virginia

Mountains, lakes, handicrafts, and a frontier spirit characterize this part of Virginia. One of the largest lakes is Smith Mountain Lake, forty miles long and covering 20,000 acres, with a 500-mile shoreline. Downstream seventeen miles on the Roanoke River is Leesville Lake, seventeen miles long and covering 3,400 acres with a 100-mile shoreline. Built in 1966 to generate electricity, the Smith Mountain and Leesville dams have created a vast and varied recreation area, including a 1,200-acre state park.

Fishing is a prime lure to visitors. To the usual Virginia population—largemouth and smallmouth bass, crappie, walleye pike, bream, and catfish—the Game and Inland Fisheries Commission has added landlocked striped bass, or "rock," that normally live in salt water, muskellunge native to the St. Lawrence River and Great Lakes, and rainbow and brown trout.

Moving deeper into southwest Virginia, where the Breaks Interstate Park joins Kentucky and Virginia, the visitor may see the largest canyon east of the Mississippi. More than five miles long and 1,600 feet deep, the gorge at one point nearly embraces the Towers, a pyramid of rock more than a third of a mile wide and nearly a half mile in length. The 2,670-acre park is seven miles from Elkhorn City, Kentucky, and 8 miles from Hayse, Virginia, on Ky-Va 80 off US 460.

Another impressive natural phenomenon is 100-foot-high Natural Tunnel, which curves 850 feet through rock and opens into a rockwalled chasm more than four hundred feet deep, six hundred feet in diameter, and three thousand feet around the rim. The tunnel is fourteen miles from Gate City. Natural Tunnel State Park has a visitor center open from Memorial Day to Labor Day.

Cumberland Gap

In the farthest southwest corner of Virginia is Cumberland Gap. Through that gateway in the Alleghenies passed the Wilderness Road, the main path of the immigrants who won the Northwest Territory and pushed the nation's boundary to the Mississippi River.

In 1750, leading a party of five men in locating an 800,000-acre grant for the Loyal Land Company in Virginia, Dr. Thomas Walker discovered the gap. He named the river nearby the Cumberland in honor of the Duke of Cumberland, son of King George II and Queen Caroline. Later the name was given to the gap as well.

Daniel Boone explored the pass and the rich land lying beyond it in Kentucky, and in 1775 he led thirty axemen in cutting the Wilderness Road two hundred miles from what is now Kingsport, Tennessee, to the Kentucky River.

By the end of the Revolutionary War in 1783 some 12,000 settlers had made their way into Kentucky, most of them by way of the Cumberland Gap. The pace of the westward movement quickened to a mass immigration and in 1792 Kentucky entered the Union with a population of 100,000. By 1800 the population was more than 220,000.

Cumberland Gap National Historical Park, covering thirty-two square miles, includes parts of Virginia, Tennessee, and Kentucky, and contains, along with the gap, two miles of Wilderness Road, ruins of an early iron foundry, Civil War fortifications, the Tri-State Peak, and the Pinnacle, from which visitors can see several states formed when America was starting its westward expansion.

PRACTICAL INFORMATION FOR VIRGINIA

 VIRGINIA FACTS AND FIGURES. The state is named in honor of the Virgin Queen, Elizabeth I, of England. Because of the Colony's loyalty to the Crown, Charles II called it the Old Dominion. The first Constitution, adopted June 29, 1776, termed it the Commonwealth of Virginia. Chambers of Commerce have styled it the Mother of Presidents, for having had eight native sons in the White House; the Mother of States, because under the Royal Charter of 1609 Virginia's territory included the present states of Kentucky, Ohio, Indiana, Illinois, Wisconsin, Michigan, West Virginia, and part of Minnesota; and the Mother of Statesmen for having produced such distinguished offspring as Chief Justice John Marshall, George Wythe, who taught John Marshall at the College of William and Mary, and orator Patrick Henry. The American dogwood is the state flower; the oyster, the state shellfish; the cardinal, the state bird; the foxhound, the state dog. *Sic Semper Tyrannis* ("Thus always to tyrants") is the state motto. "Carry Me Back to Old Virginia" is the state song. Lowest point: sea level, Atlantic Ocean. Highest point: 5,729 ft. Mt. Rogers, in Smyth and Grayson Counties, named for William Barton Rogers, state geographer and first president of the Massachusetts Institute of Technology. Speed limit: 55 mph, or as posted. Population is about 5,000,000, and the area of the state is 40,815 square miles. Virginia is in the Eastern Time Zone.

The Tidewater region, where much of America's history began, is a flat plain drained by four rivers, the lower Potomac, the Rappahannock, the York and the James, all of which flow into Chesapeake Bay. Richmond, the capital lies at the fall line separating this coastal plain from the Piedmont Plateau, roughly from Alexandria through Petersburg. The plateau rises into the Blue Ridge Mountains, these descend into a belt of valleys, caves and rivers bordered on the west by the Alleghenies. Richmond (pop. 249,261 is the capital).

The climate is generally mild. Spring comes early and swimming can last into October. The highly indented coastline totals 1500 miles. The western mountains are cool and pleasant in autumn, with vivid foliage displays and temperatures in the 50s and 60s.

HOW TO GET THERE. *By car:* I–95 parallels US 1 running north-south in the eastern portion of the state. I–95 passes through Washington, D.C., Richmond and Petersburg. I–81 parallels US 11 northeast-southwest in the western part of Virginia. I–64 is the major east-west route connecting Norfolk, Richmond, Charlottesville and Charleston, W. Va. The Chesapeake Bay Bridge Tunnel connects Cape Charles and Norfolk on US 13.

By Air: Cities served by regular service include Bristol, Charlottesville, Danville, Lynchburg, Newport News, Norfolk, Richmond, Roanoke, Washington, D.C. (2 airports in N. Virginia).

By train: Amtrak serves Washington, Alexandria, Fredericksburg, Richmond, Petersburg, Culpepper, Danville, Manassas, Staunton, Lynchburg, and Charlottesville. Also direct service to Williamsburg and Newport News.

By bus: Greyhound and *Trailways* throughout the state. A wide selection of motor coach tours to and through Virginia from major cities in the Northeast. Consult your travel agent.

TOURIST INFORMATION. The Virginia State Travel Service is located at 6 N. Sixth St., Richmond, VA 23219. Tel (804) 786–4484. The Travel Service also maintains offices at 11 Rockefeller Plaza, New York City (212) 245–3080; and in Washington at 906 17th St., NW (202) 293–5350. Nearly 600 travel leaflets are available at the highway information stations operated by the state.

SEASONAL EVENTS. *January:* Colonial Williamsburg starts the year with its Annual Antiques Forum in late January and early February. The Forum presents authoritative studies of Colonial furnishing, decorations and crafts. Check Colonial Williamsburg for dates and details. Also check at the appropriate locality for specifics on these Virginia events:

February: Alexandria has its annual Washington's Birthday celebration with banquets, balls and various ceremonies.

March: The Highland County Maple Sugar Festival in Monterey is the southernmost US maple sugar festival. Williamsburg, which almost always has something going, presents Candlelight Concerts in the Governor's Mansion throughout the month.

April: Early in the month is the Williamsburg Garden Symposium with lectures on horticulture and garden design and tours of the grounds. The last week of the month is Historic Garden Week all over Virginia. Norfolk has an Azalea Festival late in the month with parades and bands and tours and, of course, thousands of azaleas, all to honor the headquarters of the North Atlantic Treaty Organization. This festival is climaxed by the Coronation of the Azalea Queen, a vivid spectacle.

May: The Shenandoah Apple Blossom Festival at Winchester is one of the biggest annual events. In the first week of the month is the Seafood Festival of the Eastern Shore. At Tom's Cove on Chincoteague Island you can sample oysters, eels, crabs and fish. The Virginia Gold Cup Races at Warrenton and the Virginia Foxhound show at Oatlands, near Leesburg, bring together horse lovers from across the nation. The hunt country also has steeplechases and a variety of fall events. May also features the Virginia Beach Music Festival.

June: Wolf Trap Park, in Vienna, is the first national park devoted to the performing arts. A schedule of the world's greatest classical and popular entertainment runs from June through August. Schedules and tickets available by writing Wolf Trap, Vienna, VA 22180. Norfolk has an annual Harborfest, which varies from May to June each year. It is a salute to sailing ships of the world, culminating in a full-blown sea festival lasting all weekend. Also in June: the Hampton Jazz Festival.

July: This is a month of bluegrass music festivals at Martinsville, Narrows, Saltville, Dublin, Stuart, Middletown and Bristol. More detailed information is available through the Virginia Travel Service in Richmond. Chincoteague Volunteer Firemen's Carnival is in late July. The high point is when the little Chincoteague ponies swim the Assateague Channel. Virginia Scottish Games in Alexandria feature bagpipes, highland dances, Scottish athletic games, and Scottish foods.

August: The Virginia Highlands Arts and Crafts Festival takes place in Abingdon during the first two weeks. Along with the craft exhibits there are plays, demonstrations and classes. The East Coast Surfing Championship is held in Virginia Beach. Both professionals and amateurs compete in the two-day event. Old Fiddlers' Convention at Galax near the Blue Ridge Parkway. Jousting Tournament at Natural Chimneys is oldest continuous sporting event in America.

September. The State Fair of Virginia in Richmond is the big event this month. Over 700,000 people attend. Alexandria has boat races, maritime exhibits, concerts, and special seafoods to commemorate the days when it was an important seaport.

October: Many of the homes in the Waterford area have been preserved much as they were in the 18th and 19th centuries and open for tours during the Waterford Homes Tour and Craft Exhibit. The Highland County Fall Foliage Festival celebrates the beauty of the upland hardwood trees. For details write the Chamber of Commerce in Monterey.

November: Winter is the oyster season in the Chesapeake and the Oyster Festival in Urbanna has a full schedule of festivities and lots of oysters to eat.

December: The Christmas Walk in Historic Alexandria takes place in the first days of the month. The walk is accompanied by bagpipe players. Christmas in Williamsburg, beginning on the 19th, recaptures the spirit of Colonial Christmas.

 NATIONAL PARKS AND FORESTS. In Virginia's Appalachian mountains, including the Blue Ridge and Alleghenies, and such further subdivisions as the Massanutten and Shenandoah ranges, are more than 2 million acres of national and state forests and parks. Extending along the crest of the Blue Ridge from Front Royal south to Waynesboro is the Shenandoah National Park, featuring nearly 400 miles of foot trails, with elevations ranging from 600 to 4,000 feet. About 95 percent of the park is forested. The Skyline Drive, snaking through the park, provides 72 overlooks. From Hogback Overlook the visitor can see 11 bends in the Shenandoah River.

Virginia has two great national forests. The George Washington National Forest covers more than 1 million acres and contains the highest cascades in the Blue Ridge Mountains. The Jefferson National Forest, covering more than 600,000 acres, extends from the James River to the southwestern tip of Virginia, embracing Mount Rogers, the state's highest mountain. Camping, fishing, hunting, hiking, and an abundance of recreational opportunities exist in both of these National Forests.

On the Eastern Shore of Virginia is Assateague Island National Seashore Park, a favorite stop for migrating waterfowl as well as tourists. Just 15 miles northwest of Washington is Great Falls National Park where the Potomac cascades over a series of falls, and churns through a rocky gorge. Also near Washington, adjoining the Quantico Naval Base, is the beautifully wooded Prince William Forest Park.

STATE PARKS. Virginia's state parks are various and diverse. On or near the coast are *Seashore, Chippokes, Westmoreland.* In the Piedmont are *Pocahontas, Bear Creek Lake, Goodwin Lake-Prince Edward, Holliday Lake, Occoneechee, Staunton River,* and *Fairy Stone.* In the mountains are *Douthat, Claytor Lake, Grayson Highland* (formerly Mount Rogers), *Hungry Mother,* and *Natural Tunnel.* Five other parks are being developed at Lake Anna in Spotsylvania, *Mason Neck* in Northern Virginia, *Caledon* on the Potomac River in King George County, *Smith Mountain Lake* near Roanoke, and on the York River near Yorktown.

Low-priced vacation cabins may be rented in eight state parks for one-week periods between the Monday nearest May 1 and the Monday nearest October 8: *Clayton Lake, Douthat, Fairy Stone, Hungry Mother, Prince Edward, Seashore, Westmoreland,* and *Staunton River* are the sites which have such facilities. Information on reservations and services may be obtained from the Division of Parks, 1201 State Office Building, Capitol Square, Richmond, Va., 23219.

 CAMPING OUT. Camping is permitted at all state parks between April 1 and December 1 except designated natural areas and historic parks. To reserve a campsite or cabin, at the Virginia State Parks use the Ticketron reservation system. Reservations may be made at some Ticketron offices or by mail to Ticketron, Box 62221, Virginia Beach, Virginia 23462. Most reservations handled between March 15 and March 30. The Division of Parks, 1201 State Office Building, Richmond 23219, administers the parks and publishes a pamphlet which describes each park and the facilities offered.

There are also camping facilities at the following areas: *Blue Ridge Parkway, Shenandoah National Park, Prince William Forest Park, George Washington National Forest,* and *Jefferson National Forest.*

 TRAILER TIPS. There are more than 300 commercial and 38 publicly owned campgrounds in Virginia. The publicly owned campgrounds, usually near national and state parks and recreation areas, charge a modest daily fee. All have dumping stations and all except Longwood at Kerr Reservoir have flush toilets. Almost all have hot showers. Water and electric hookups are available at Natural Chimneys, Breaks Interstate and Gatewood Lake. *Camping in Virginia,* available from the Virginia Travel Council, 2309 E. Broad Street, Richmond, Va. 23223, has a complete list of commerical and public campgrounds and trailer parks.

  MUSEUMS AND GALLERIES. Richmond: *The Virginia Museum of Fine Arts,* the nation's first state-supported museum, continues to be a pace-setter. It has a fleet of artmobiles touring the Old Dominion, and the visitor may happen upon one of these portable galleries anywhere in the Commonwealth.

Valentine Museum reflects the history of Richmond and the life of its people. Source material for a vivid, accurate picture includes more than 20,000 photographs and the third largest costume department in the United States.

Edgar Allan Poe Museum has its home in the Old Stone House, Richmond's oldest residential building, and is filled with the melancholy poet's memorabilia and manuscripts. It succeeds in conveying a real sense of his time and mood.

White House of the Confederacy was built in 1817 and occupied by Jefferson Davis during the Civil War. The relics of both the battlefields and the home front give a graphic picture of the war.

Newport News: *The Mariners Museum* displays figureheads, boats, ropework, marinescapes, ceramics, nautical and lighthouse equipment. An absorbing show for children.

Norfolk: *Hermitage Foundation Museum* in a landscaped park is located on the Lafayette River and contains a rare collection of Eastern art.

MacArthur Memorial Museum honors General Douglas MacArthur and traces his career with memorabilia and film. Film star Gregory Peck prepared for his portrayal of the general here, and William Manchester researched his massive biography *American Caesar* here also.

Chrysler Museum contains a rich collection of European and American paintings and sculpture, as well as one of the world's great glass collections.

Big Stone Gap: *Southwest Virginia State Museum* contains exhibits tracing the region's history from frontier days to contemporary times.

Petersburg: *Quartermaster Museum,* on State 36 just inside Ft. Lee. Flags, banners, uniforms, insignia, and military mementos are featured in this unusual museum.

Williamsburg: *The Abby Aldrich Rockefeller Folk Art Center,* adjacent to the Williamsburg Inn is the largest collection of American primitive paintings and objects in the country. Given to Colonial Williamsburg by Mrs. John D. Rockefeller, Jr., it is housed in a charming 19th-century building. The Christmas display of the old-fashioned tree and toys has become a tradition in Virginia.

 HISTORIC SITES. (See also the "Exploring Virginia" section, previously.) **Richmond.** Begin with *Capital Square* and the state house designed by Thomas Jefferson. Inside is Houdon's famous statue of George Washington. From galleries in the Senate and House visitors may hear oratory from representatives who pride themselves on being members of the oldest continuous legislative body in the Western hemisphere.

Adjoining the Square, at 707 East Franklin St., is the house that was the residence of Robert E. Lee and his family during the Civil War. June through August, Tues.-Sat. 10–4, Sunday 2–5; Sept. thru May, Mon.-Fri. 10–4.

Across the street from Capital Square, at Grace and 9th Sts., is *St. Paul's Church,* where President Davis and General Lee worshipped, and where Davis received word that Richmond had to be evacuated, April 2, 1865. Open Mon. through Sat., 10 to 4, Sun. 1 to 4; services Sun. at 8 and 11.

At 818 E. Marshall St., within two blocks of Capital Square, is the house built about 1790 by Chief Justice John Marshall. It was his home for 45 years. The original furnishings and family memorabilia impart a strong sense of the Chief Justice's personality. Open Tues.–Sat. 11–4. Sundays 1–4.

St. John's Church. Patrick Henry issued his liberty-or-death ultimatum in a plain, frame church at 24th and Broad Sts. on Church Hill. Among the graves in the churchyard are those of George Wythe, Jefferson's teacher and friend, and Elizabeth Arnold Poe, mother of the poet. Open daily 10–4.

Agecroft Hall. For visitors whose taste for history antedates Jamestown, there is at 4305 Sulgrave Rd. a mansion built in the 15th century in England. In the late 1920s it was disassembled and rebuilt in Richmond on terraced lawns overlooking the James River. Open Tues. through Fri., 10 to 4, Sat. and Sun. 2 to 5.

Appomattox Court House. On April 9, 1865, retreating from Richmond and Petersburg, Lee's Army of Northern Virginia was surrounded at Appomattox Court House. After a final attempt to break the Federal lines, Lee met Union General Ulysses Grant in the home of Wilmer McLean and surrendered. Reconstructed *McLean House* is open daily 9–5:30 June 15 to Labor Day; 8:30–5 rest of year. Admission from April thru October is $1 per car, free remainder of year. Other buildings in restored village are Meeks General Store, the Woodson Law Office, Kelly House, county jail. Reconstructed courthouse contains a museum with audiovisual presentation.

Charlottesville: A tour of this area should begin with a visit to the Western Virginia Bicentennial Center located on route 20, just off I–64E. *Monticello,* the impressive estate of Thomas Jefferson, was designed and built by him between 1769 and 1809. The house contains unique architectural features, and many of Jefferson's personal effects. Open daily, March to October 8–5, rest of year 9–4:30.

Ash Lawn, the estate of James Monroe, designed by his friend, Thomas Jefferson. The house contains many of Monroe's belongings. Open daily March to Oct. 9–6, rest of year 10–6.

Michie Tavern Museum, near Monticello, is still an eating place as well as a museum of the 1700s when its guests included Jefferson, Monroe, Madison, and Lafayette.

University of Virginia, founded and planned by Jefferson. Free tours during school year.

Arlington: Arlington is a suburb of Washington, D.C., and contains the *Pentagon,* one of the world's largest office buildings, housing the Department of Defense. Free guided tours Mon.-Fri. 9–3. *Arlington National Cemetery,* the most renowned of all national cemeteries, Arlington contains the graves of such famous persons as William Jennings Bryan, Rear Adm. Robert E. Peary, John Foster Dulles, Gen. George C. Marshall, John F. Kennedy and Robert F. Kennedy. The cemetery is open daily 8 A.M. to 7 P.M., April through Sept.; 8 A.M. to 5 P.M. Oct. through Mar.

On the brow of the hill overlooking the cemetery is *Arlington House,* the mansion where young Robert E. Lee courted and married Mary Ann Randolph Custis and where they lived until the outbreak of the Civil War. Open daily 9:30 to 6, April through Labor Day; 9:30 to 4:30 the rest of the year.

Marine Corps War Memorial. At the north end of Arlington Cemetery is a 78-foot, 100-ton bronze reproduction of Joseph Rosenthal's famous photograph of Marines raising the flag on Iwo Jima.

Alexandria: Start a tour of this historic city at the Visitor Center located in Ramsay House, 221 King Street. Info on walking tours, events, maps, historic homes, antique shops, and restaurants. Also a 13 minute film on the historic sites.

Christ Church, Cameron and Washington Streets, completed in 1773. Both Washington and Robert E. Lee owned pews in this church. Open Mon.–Sat. 9–4; Sun 2–5.

Gadsby's Tavern, 134 N. Royal St. An 18th century inn frequented by Washington and other patriots. Now operated as a museum and restaurant. Museum hours Mon.–Sat. 10–5; Sun. 12–5.

George Washington National Masonic Memorial, King and Callahan St. Washington was the first master of the Alexandria Masons, and the museum includes Washington memorabilia. Open daily 9–5.

Old Presbyterian Meeting House, 321 S. Fairfax St. Built in 1774. Tomb of the Unknown Soldier of the American Revolution is in the cemetery. Open Mon.–Fri. 9–4, Sat. 9–1.

Stabler-Leadbeater Apothecary Shop, 107 S. Fairfax St. This pharmacy served George Washington and Robert E. Lee among other prominent Americans. The original furnishings, glass containers, and prescription records have remained in place from its founding in 1792. Open Mon.–Sat. 10–4:30.

Carlyle House, built in 1752, was the scene of a historic meeting in 1755 that led to the Stamp Act, the hated tax that helped provoke the American Revolution.

Mount Vernon, 9 mi south via George Washington Memorial Parkway. George Washington's home from 1754 until his death in 1799, and one of America's most beautiful colonial estates. Open daily March to Oct. 9–5; Oct to March 9–4.

Woodlawn Plantation, 3 mi W. of Mt. Vernon. A gift from George Washington to Nellie Custis (Martha Washington's granddaughter) who married Maj. Lawrence Lewis (Washington's nephew). Mansion designed by the architect of the U.S. Capitol. Open daily 9:30–4:30.

Gunston Hall, S. via George Washington Parkway and US 1. The colonial estate of George Mason, the author of the Fairfax Resolves upon which our Bill of Rights is based. Open daily 9:30–5.

Fredericksburg: Visitors should stop at the Visitor Center, 706 Caroline St., to obtain complete information on the many attractions in and around this historic city. It is difficult for any Civil War buff to fight his way out of Fredericksburg, so thick were the engagements there. *The Fredericksburg and Spotsylvania National Military Park* embraces 3,600 acres and four battlefields; Fredericksburg. Chancellorsville, the Wilderness, and Spotsylvania Courthouse. The Visitor Center at Lafayette Blvd. (US 1) and Sunken Rd. contains an electric map and Civil War relics. Open daily 9 to 5.

Near Sunken Road is a monument to the Angel of Mary's Heights, a 19-year-old Confederate, Sergeant Richard Kirkland, who, draped with canteens, made repeated trips onto the Fredericksburg battlefield to give water to wounded Federal soldiers.

Kenmore, the home of George Washington's sister, Betty Fielding Lewis, has superb plasterwork. Open Apr 1 to Oct 31, 9–5; remainder of year to 4. At the foot of Kenmore's formal garden is the home George Washington purchased in 1772 for Mary Washington, his mother. From here he left for his inauguration as President. Its hours coincide with Kenmore's.

In *James Monroe's Law Office* at 908 Charles St., the visitor may see the desk on which the Monroe Doctrine was drafted. The office, where young Monroe practiced from 1786 to 1791, has become the repository for his papers, personal belongings, and furniture used in the White House. Open daily 9 A.M. to 5 P.M.

Petersburg: *Petersburg National Battlefield Park* commemorates a series of battles where the armies of Lee and Grant fought each other for 10 months until, gradually worn down, the Confederates had to give up the defense of Richmond.

During six days in July, 1864, Federal troops planted a mine that killed 278 men and ripped a 500-yard gap in the Confederate lines. The Confederates rallied, however, and threw back the Federal assault. The deep crater that resulted from the explosion is a focal point for battlefield tours. At the park entrance is a visitor center, with a museum featuring an electronic presentation, relics, models, and maps. Open 8 to 6 daily, Memorial Day to Labor Day; 8 to 5 the rest of the year.

Williamsburg: The city of Williamsburg encompasses the largest group of restored and authentically reconstructed 18th-century buildings in the world, and is the focal point for the Virginia Historical Peninsula. For your visit, the Colonial Williamsburg free publication *This Week in Williamsburg* will prove invaluable. Check the current issue on arrival for the week's events.

Exhibition buildings and craft shops are open throughout the year. The buildings are attended by costumed, knowledgeable hosts and hostesses.

Holders of general admission tickets may purchase additional tickets to the Governor's Palace and Gardens for 20-minute carriage rides and for evening concerts and indepth tours. General admission ticket holders also may attend evening films and lectures at the Information Center and the introductory film, *The Story of a Patriot.*

The general admission ticket also covers the Tricorn Hat Tour for children during the summer, a 2½-hour expedition including the gaol (jail), bakery, palace maze, and bowling on the village green, all topped by the gift of a tricorn hat. General admission tickets also are necessary for a lanthorn (lantern) tour of selected craft shops by candlelight; concerts in the general courtroom of the capitol building on Sunday evenings, April through September; candlelight concerts by an orchestra in the Palace ballroom and supper room on Thursday evenings, April and May, September and October.

It is recommended you leave your car in the Information Center parking area and board the bus available to holders of general admission tickets. It stops at all major points of interest in the Historic Area and is within walking distance of everything else. The Information Center is adjacent to the Colonial Parkway and at the junction of US 60 and State 132. See the orientation film, *The Story of a Patriot,* shown continuously, special exhibits, bookstalls, restrooms, and the terminal for the bus. Foreign film viewers can listen, upon request, through earphones to the films' dialogue in French, German, Italian, Spanish, Japanese, Russian, and Portuguese. The *Capitol,* west end of Duke of Gloucester St. has been reconstructed, and furnished according to House of Burgesses inventories. Public goal is on Nicholson St., north of the Capitol. It is a photogenic gem for the family, who want to record on film the spectacle of being locked in stocks or cells of former prisoners and pirates. *Raleigh Tavern,* north side of Duke of Gloucester St., is a reconstructed 18th-century hotel, restaurant, meeting place and stage coach stop. All furnishings are original to the period. *Brush-Everard House,* on the Palace Green, is a charming house, garden, and outside kitchen building of 18th century merchant.

Governor's Palace, Palace Green, is the reconstructed residence and gardens of the Colonial governors. Escorted tours include the advance buildings and outbuildings. The Palace display of authentic furnishings from original inventories is worth the 30–40 minutes spent on the tour. *Wythe House,* Palace Green, was home of George Wythe, signer of the Declaration of Independence and founder of the Law School at the College of William and Mary. The *Magazine* on Market Square has an indoor display of 18th-century firearms and muskets which are fired periodically. A costumed militia and fife and drum corps carry out 18th-century drills and maneuvers complete with musket and cannon blast, twice weekly from late March through mid-October.

The Colonial craft shops. Not to be confused with the contemporary *Colonial Williamsburg Craft House* outside the Historic area. Check locations of individual shops on Colonial Williamsburg map. Craftsmen and interpreters will explain trades and demonstrate 18th-century methods and skills. In the *Tarpley* and *Prentis* stores you may buy the products. See *Spinning and Weaving,* corn meal being ground by wind power at the *Windmill,* furniture being turned at the *Cabinetmaker's Shop,* wigs being shaped at the *Wigshop,* wrought iron molded on a hand anvil at the *Blacksmith's.* Sample fresh gingerbread and cookies from the *Raleigh Bake Shop* oven, watch a book being bound at the *Printing Office* and *Book-bindery,* and mail a letter from the reconstructed first Virginia post office. The *Silversmith* displays patterns of flatware and clocks and will sell you charming jewelry made by hand in the 18th-century manner. Meanwhile, up the street the *Bootmaker* is sewing and mending and the *Milliner* will welcome you as she trims bonnets. The *Wren Building* on the campus of the College of William and Mary is open daily. The chapel, Great Hall, 3 classrooms, and convocation room may be seen. The rest is used for college activities, but the complex of campus buildings is open to the public. Stroll through the grounds.

Jamestown: Jamestown is where the first permanent English settlement in America was established, in 1607. *Jamestown Island.* Begin at the Visitor Center. Cross the footpath and bridge from the parking lot to the center. Orientation films, maps, and dioramas explain the historical significance of Jamestown. Next, follow the markers on a self-guided walk to the *Old Church Tower,* built in 1639. Its graveyard has tombstones bearing well-known family names. Built onto the Old Church Tower is the *Memorial Church,* a 1907 restoration. Nearby is the *Monument* to the General Assembly, the first legislative body in the New World. Also in the vicinity are the *Pocahontas Monument* and the *Captain John Smith Statue.*

Overlooking the river you may visualize the landing of the *Susan Constant,* the *Godspeed,* and the *Discovery* (replicas of which are at Festival Park). Continue past the *Confederate Fort* (1861), circling along the river bank beyond the Old Church to view the foundations of Virginia's first *State House, Old Townsite,* and *New Towne.* The restoration reveals to viewers the first town plan by the white men on these shores and shows clearly the ancient complex of concentrated government, rural, and residential buildings. Also visit the Jamestown Festival Park, built to commemorate the 350th anniversary of the settlement of Jamestown. The Park includes a reconstructed fort and exact duplicates of the three small ships that brought the first settlers.

Yorktown: To understand the significance of the 18th- and 19th-century events which took place in the vicinity, stop at the National Park Service Visitor Center at the east end of the Colonial Parkway. Open daily except Christmas 8–6; winter months 8:30–5. View a 12-min. orientation film and exhibits there that trace the events of the three-week siege leading to Cornwallis' surrender and the victorious conclusion of the Revolution. Terms of the British surrender were drawn up at Moore House. Markers throughout the area explain the *Battle of Yorktown.* The *Monument of Alliance and Victory,* commemorating the French assistance in America's War of Independence, is on your way to the historic houses along Main Street. The large brick mansion with the high wall and ivy is the *Nelson House. Grace Church* (Episcopal), one block off Main St., is open for Sunday services. There is parking space behind the old *York County Courthouse.* The houses on Main St. are within easy walking distance. Also visit the Yorktown Victory Center for a history of the American Revolution and a film, "The Road to Yorktown." Connecting Yorktown, Jamestown, and Williamsburg is the Colonial Parkway, with historical markers that explain major events in this region.

COURTHOUSES. The courthouses of Virginia, historically and architecturally, are important to the visitor because they embody a concept of government and plantation life from the 18th century to the present which has played a vital part in the growth of the United States. An explanation of the Virginia county system will facilitate planning interesting side trips to include these government buildings. First of all, the visitor should know that there are no towns or townships in Virginia. Forty-one cities in the state are not part of the counties, although they may be surrounded by a county on the map. County seats are identified by the words "Court House" (or "C.H.") and this should not be confused with the individual building, known as the *courthouse* (one word), housing the county government offices.

The original exterior designs of the courthouses can still be seen, but the interiors have been renovated to comply with modern needs. Visitors are welcome within the buildings during normal business hours. *Charles City Courthouse* may be viewed while visiting the great plantations on the James River. The courthouses of *Gloucester, Mathews, Lancaster, New Kent* and *Surry* counties are all located in their espective county seats. *King William Courthouse,* on Route 30 between West Point and Route 301, is particularly beautiful, inside and out. This is one of the few courthouses where a guide will assist you. *Essex Courthouse* is in Tappahannock and *King and Queen Courthouse* is 20 miles SE on Route 14. Middlesex Courthouse is in Urbanna, *Richmond County Courthouse* at Warsaw, *Northumberland* at Burgess and *Westmoreland* at Montross.

HISTORIC CHURCHES. Virginia's historic churches of the 17th and 18th century were usually located within easy riding distance of the great plantations. Many are beautiful, but all are important to American history for the role they played in the lives of the famous men who worshipped within them.

Williamsburg: *Bruton Parish Church,* Episcopal. Built between 1710 and 1715. Services regularly since the latter date. Frequent organ recitals and, during holidays, special choirs. Costumed guides. Duke of Gloucester St. Services on Sun. 8:00 A.M. and 11 A.M. *Wren Chapel* of the College of William and Mary. Non-denominational. Open daily to visitors during the school term.

Hampton: St. John's Church, built in 1622, is one of the oldest churches in continuous use. The original communion silver dates from 1619.

Smithfield: St. Luke's (formerly Old Brick Church or Benn's Church) is one of the most beautiful small churches in the state. Built in 1632, and restored in 1887.

Yorktown: *Grace Church* (Episcopal) holds services at 11 A.M. each Sunday. Erected in 1697.

Jamestown: *Old Church Tower* (1640), the only remains of the old church where John Rolfe and Pocahontas were allegedly married. Easter Sunrise service nearby.

The many beautiful old churches are occasionally hard to find, but are well worth the effort involved. The following is only a partial list of famous churches, in alphabetical order, county-by-county. Charles City County is *Westover Church,* c. 1737, attended by two Presidents (Tyler and Harrison) and continuously used by the famous Byrd family of Virginia. Near Williamsburg, on US 60, is tiny *Hickory Neck* (Episcopal). Essex County: *Vauter's Church* (erected 1720–31) is on Route 17. In Tappahannock, *Beale's Memorial* (Baptist), built in 1728, has walls two feet thick. *St. John's* (Episcopal), erected in 1849, is known for its unique wooden Gothic construction. Gloucester County: about 10 mi. N of Gloucester Point on US 17 is *Abingdon Church,* 1755, where George Washington's grandparents worshipped in the original building (1655). *Ware Church,* c. 1700, is brick and sits in a grove of trees on Route 14, east of Gloucester Court House. James City County: *Olive Branch Christian Church* (Disciples of Christ) is a 19th-century edifice also on Route 17 below Yorktown.

King and Queen County: *Colonial Church,* erected 1729, still in use as a Methodist house of worship, at Newtown. *Mattaponi Baptist Church,* built before 1824, adjoins the burial ground of the Carter Braxton family (he was a signer of the Declaration of Independence). Route 14 at Stevensville. Lancaster County: *Christ Church,* 1732, one of the very early churches of the famous Carter family, built by Robert "King" Carter, who is buried here. Between Irvington and Kilmarnock on Route 3 (presently being restored by the NPS with its original furnishings): *St. Mary's White Chapel,* original building 1669, present one 1732–34. Architecturally unique as it departs from Church of England ecclesiastical laws.

New Kent County: *St. Peter's Church,* 1701–03, where George Washington and Martha Custis allegedly were married. Prince George County (on south side of James River): *Brandon Church,* a mid-19th-century version of the original edifice, was originally part of the Brandon Plantation. Original communion silver. Westmoreland County: *Yeocomico Church,* 1706, second building, constructed of oak. Mary Ball Washington, mother of George Washington, attended services here in the 18th century. Original communion silver and font.

 MUSIC. Musical events and orchestral groups are enjoyed throughout Virginia. On a classical note, Alexandria, Arlington, Fairfax County, Norfolk, Richmond, Roanoke, and Newport News have regular symphony seasons.

The summer months are filled with country and bluegrass festivals, and a range that includes classical, jazz, and bands competing for honors.

One of the oldest festivals is at Galax, near the Blue Ridge Parkway, on the second weekend in August. It is the Old Fiddlers' Convention, with contestants of all ages playing the familiar mountain music native to the Blue Ridge area.

The Shenandoah Valley Music Festival on three weekends in July appeals to the lovers of classical music. Performances are at Orkney Springs.

The annual Virginia Beach Music Festival in May brings together high-school bands from all over the United States competing in parade and concert presentations.

In June, the Hampton Jazz Festival at the Hampton Roads Coliseum brings together the big names in jazz today.

Slightly different, the songs and music of Colonial days can be heard on Sunday evenings between April and October at the Capitol in Williamsburg.

Northern Virginia's Wolf Trap Farm at Vienna is the nation's first national park for the performing arts. An outstanding summer program that includes opera, dance, symphony, popular and classical entertainers, a National Folk Festival, special children's programs, and other related activities contribute to the wide appeal of this indoor-outdoor park. Prior to performances many people bring picnic dinners to enjoy in the park. Box office info at (703) 938–3800 during the summer season.

 STAGE AND REVUES. When Bob Porterfield was asking the General Assembly for funds for his newly created *Barter Theatre* during the Depressions, he told the legislators that Virginia wasn't getting enough after-dark entertainment. A suspicious state senator wanted to know what the showman meant by after-dark entertainment. "That, sir," retorted Porterfield, "is the kind of entertainment you can go home and talk about!"

Porterfield won his appropriation for the nation's first state-supported theater, which is still thriving at Abingdon. Barter Theatre led the way for an ever increasing number of theatres.

One of the oldest of the supper theaters is *Swift Creek Mill Playhouse* at Colonial Heights south of Richmond. It claims to be the oldest grist mill in the country and certainly boasts the finest Sally Lund bread, small loaves baked from an original recipe. Equally distinguished is Hanover's *Barksdale Theater,* north of Richmond. The nightly buffet is generous and tasty.

Other theaters offering appetizing repertoires and menus are *The Richmond Barn Dinner Theater,* the *Cavalier Playhouse* in Norfolk, *Wayside Theatre* in Middletown, the *Hayloft Dinner Theater* in Manassas, *Mill Mountain Playhouse* in Roanoke, and *The Lazy Susan Dinner Theater* at Woodbridge. During the winter the *Virginia Museum of Fine Arts* in Richmond has a season of plays and musical entertainment. In Norfolk, the Chrysler Museum Theatre offers a variety of entertainment.

Southwest Virginia bills two colorful outdoor dramas. At the *June Tolliver Playhouse* in Big Stone Gap is *The Trail of the Lonesome Pine,* based on John Fox Jr.'s novel about the fiercely independent mountaineers around him. In Radford is the production of *The Long Way Home,* the true story of a pioneer woman's escape from Indian abductors and her 43-day journey home on foot through the wilderness. A passion play is performed at Strasbourg during the summer season.

 GARDENS. *Historic Garden Week in Virginia,* occurring the last week in April, embraces the two subjects—history and gardens—that intrigue Virginians most. For a free catalog for homes and grounds on public display write Historic Garden Week in Virginia, Garden Club, 12 E. Franklin, Richmond, VA 23219.

Nature's own garden presents a changing show along the Skyline Drive and Blue Ridge Parkway with white and violet splashes of rhododendron and mountain laurel in the spring and a coat of many colors in the autumn. At those seasons few motorists object to the slow pace of the traffic. Below the Blue Ridge in Charlottesville the University of Virginia has restored its gardens, including the plants along Mr. Jefferson's famed serpentine wall. Lexington has a Memorial Garden. In Tidewater hundreds of acres of jonquils blossom in Gloucester and Mathews Counties. Norfolk's airport is set amid azaleas. Each spring Norfolk stages an *International Azalea Festival* in the Gardens-by-the-Sea honoring the North Atlantic Treaty Organization. With a helping hand from Norfolk, Richmond has planted a beautiful display of azaleas in Bryan park, off I–95. Maymont Park also has lovely lawns, giant trees, and rocky bluffs above the James River, as well as an impressive Victorian mansion. Virginia's eastern shore is a kind of Garden of Eden with fruits, vegetables, and flowers. Most of the historic homes and plantations that are open to the public feature attractive gardens and grounds. The gardens of Walter Misenheimer (on State route 10, 21 miles E. of Hopewell) have been developed privately, but are open free to the public and are especially colorful during the azalea season.

SPORTS. *Swimming* in Tidewater is superb. The major rivers and their tributaries offer choice spots. Nearly all the state parks have beaches. Along the coast Virginia is belted by fine sand: Seashore State Park on the Chesapeake Bay and False Cape State Park on the Atlantic Ocean are outstanding. Visitors have free access to the full length of Virginia Beach, as well as Ocean View in Norfolk.

Tennis courts are available at most semi-private and public country clubs, usually near the larger cities. The major cities also have numerous public courts in parks. Many local schools also open their courts to visitors.

Golf is a big sport throughout the state, and is enjoyed during all seasons. A folder, *Golf in Virginia* available through the Virginia State Travel Service describes all courses that are open to the public.

Skiing. The Old Dominion's mountains offer moderate ski slopes: the Homestead at Hot Springs, Bryce Mountain near Basye, Massanutten at Harrisonburg, Cascades at Fancy Gap, and Wintergreen.

For the *Horse-lover*, northern Virginia hunt country that surrounds Leesburg, Middleburg, and Warrenton, is the scene of many notable equestrian events that attract a national audience. In May there are the Virginia Gold Cup at Warrenton and the foxhound show at the historic Oatlands estate near Leesburg. The oldest horse show in the U.S. is at Upperville in June. Other major events are the Deep Run Hunt meet in April near Richmond, and the Middleburg Hunt Races in the fall. The Blue Ridge bridle paths in the Shenandoah Valley are also popular.

The *Commission of Game and Inland Fisheries,* P.O. Box 11104, Richmond, and local game wardens can supply you with a full set of game and fishing laws, which should be studied, as the law is enforced rigorously throughout the state. Duck hunting on the coasts and shotgun, rifle, and bow hunting in the western sections of the state are excellent. Hunting and fishing are allowed in the national forests, and the wildlife management areas with the proper credentials, in season. Hunting is prohibited in the major national parks, along the Blue Ridge Parkway, and in the Williamsburg-Jamestown-Yorktown area. The use of dogs anywhere is very limited.

Hunting in Tidewater Virginia has been made more exotic by the introduction of the Iranian black-necked pheasant and the green pheasant from Japan, which thrive in this area. Native birds which abound are quail, duck, geese and turkey. (Turkey hunting allowed in most of the state.) Hunting license required; cost: $20 for non-residents. $20 extra for bear, deer, and turkey hunting (season: mid-Nov. to early Jan.).

Fishing in Tidewater Virginia is excellent, and no license is required for salt water sport fishing. The season is year-round, and during winter, many fishermen use fresh water tackle to catch the ever-present stiped bass (rockfish). Sea bass, bonito, dolphin, flounder, marlin, shad and speckled trout are only a few of the fish found readily here. Trophies and citations available to anyone catching big fish in the Virginia Salt Water Fishing Tournament, May 1–Oct. 31 (details at all harbors). Freshwater fishing requires a license which costs $10 for non-residents of the state, an additional $7.50 license is required for fishing in stocked trout waters, and a $1 permit is needed for fishing in the National Forests. Several recommended public fishing spots include: Harrison Lake, Haynes Mill Pond, Piscataway Creek, Powell's Lake, Mattaponi River, Walker's Dam, Gardy's Pond, Cat Point Creek, Lake Anna, Smith Mtn. Lake, Lake Gaston, Chickahominy Lake and Kerr Reservoir. An excellent pamphlet on where and when to fish is available from the Commission of Game and Inland Fisheries.

DRINKING LAWS. In 1968, the state's General Assembly approved liquor-by-the-drink, the most radical change in the Alcoholic Beverage Control laws since their inception in 1934. The provisions permit "qualified establishments," meaning bona fide restaurants, not saloons, to serve mixed alcoholic beverages, subject to local option. Liberalizing of ABC laws apparently has caused no significant changes in the Commonwealth's cultural and social scene. Licensed establishments may serve mixed alcoholic beverages until 2 A.M.; most close at 1 A.M. or earlier. There are 250 ABC stores selling liquor by the package and 9,000 establishments selling beer and wine. Minimum age 21; 18 for beer.

WHAT TO DO WITH THE CHILDREN. In the belief that children are the most neglected segment of sightseers, curators at Jamestown, Williamsburg, and Yorktown have inaugurated special programs for their delight. At Jamestown children are encouraged to rummage through a chest containing clothes worn by a 9-year-old colonist with Captain John Smith. Groups are sent with maps to locate points of interest and mark their discoveries by pasting stamps in books. In Jamestown Festival Park children enjoy boarding replicas of the three sailing ships, exploring the triangular palisade, and climbing the ramparts. Festival Park has excellent facilities for picnics.

In the same sense of allowing children to participate in history, a costumed Williamsburg hostess will invite them to help straighten the Colonial furnishings in a disordered room. At Yorktown children tour the battlefield and then visit a simulated war room in the Visitors Center. There they may try on uniforms of British and American troops. The designer of the special events explains that the challenge is to bring the program directly into the child's experience.

In almost every historic shrine the alert adult may point out objects that delight a child's eye. At Monticello there is Thomas Jefferson's cannonball clock strung over the entrance. On the state's numerous battlefields are cannon and trenches good for climbing. At the White House of the Confederacy in Richmond is Robert E. Lee's sword. In Williamsburg children may sit briefly in the stocks for penitent wrongdoers. In Alexandria is a replica of the fire engine *Washington.* Langley Air Force Base has relics from man's first steps into space; the Norfolk Naval Station with its gray line of warships and the ship repair yard in Portsmouth excite the imagination. The western portion of Virginia is honeycombed with caves, underground wonderlands with colorful rock formations along Routes 11 and 340 and Interstate 81.

Two major theme parks that operate during the summer season are targets for the young set and popular with families. Near Williamsburg is the Old Country-Busch Gardens, featuring a touch of England, France, Italy and Germany. A Tudor town surrounds a version of Shakespeare's Globe Theatre. The Clydesdale horses are here, too. Sidewalk cafes and the French Follies contribute to the French atmosphere and the German village is complete with an antique carousel. North of Richmond, adjacent to I-95, is Kings Dominion, a fantasy land of rides, shows, and the wild animals of Lion Country. Roaming around the park are the cartoon characters of Hanna-Barbera. A replica of the Eiffel Tower provides an observation platform.

While in Norfolk, treat the kids to an ice cream cone at Doumar's. Abe Doumar was the inventor of the cone (1904), and the present-day Doumars still make the crisply delicious cones on the original (1905) equipment. In Norfolk's Gardens by the Sea, there's a train ride with botanical commentary.

HOTELS AND MOTELS in Virginia span a wide range. Generally, accommodations west of the Blue Ridge are less expensive than those in the Piedmont and Tidewater areas. A competitive thrust, now extending along the East Coast to Texas, originated in Virginia with Econo-Travel Motor Hotels. There are more than 40 in that economical chain spread through Virginia.

Williamsburg offers a variety of prices for lodging. The Williamsburg Chamber of Commerce, for instance, will furnish visitors with an approved list of private homes offering rooms at quite moderate prices.

The price categories in this section, for double occupancy, will average as follows: *Deluxe* $38 and up, *Expensive* $28 to $38, *Moderate* $18 to $28 and *Inexpensive* below $18. For a more complete description of these categories see the Hotels and Motels section of *Facts At Your Fingertips*.

Abingdon

Martha Washington Inn. *Expensive.* 150 W. Main St. Set back off the main street and opposite the Barter Theatre, this is an old-fashioned inn with a broad veranda. The rooms are furnished with antiques, including four-posters. The buffets in the spacious dining room are famous. Parlors are comfortable, home-like.

Alexandria

Old Town Holiday Inn. *Deluxe.* 480 King St. Colonial-style luxury hotel in heart of restored area. Indoor Pool.

Best Western Olde Colony. *Deluxe.* First & N. Washington Sts. 18 blks. N of I–95 exits I–E, I–N. Color TV. Pool. Free continental breakfasts.

Holiday Inn. *Deluxe.* 2480 Eisenhower Dr. Color TV. Pool. Pets. Free National Airport. 703–960–3400. Also at 6100 Richmond Hgwy.

The Guest Quarters. *Deluxe.* 100 S. Reynolds St. One and two bedroom suites with equipped kitchens. Hotel Service.

Presidential Gardens Hotel. *Expensive.* Mt. Vernon Ave. & Russell Rd. Apts. and suites with kitchens.

Appomattox

Traveler's Inn. *Moderate.* US 460 near State 24. Attractive, clean rooms. Call ahead as accommodations are scarce in heavy travel season. Air-conditioned.

Arlington

Arlington Hyatt at Key Bridge. *Deluxe.* 1325 Wilson Blvd. in Rosslyn. Indoor parking. 315 rooms, good dining facilities.

Sheraton National Motor Hotel. *Deluxe.* Near Pentagon at Columbia Pike and Washington Blvd. Pool, indoor parking, rooftop dining.

Stouffer's National Center Hotel. *Deluxe.* Near National Airport on US 1 at 2399 Jefferson Davis Hwy. A full facility hotel.

Best Western Arlington. *Expensive.* 2480 S. Glebe Rd., just off I–395. Pool and restaurant.

Iwo Jima Motor Hotel. *Expensive.* 1501 Arlington Blvd. on U. S. 50, close to Roosevelt Bridge. Pool, restaurant.

Bayse

Bryce Resort. *Expensive.* 3,000-acre resort with facilities for skiing, 18 hole PGA golf course, tennis courts, lake, horseback riding.

Bedford

Peaks of Otter Lodge. *Expensive.* Blue Ridge Parkway at State 43 at the foot of Flat Top and Sharp Top Mountains. Rustic but comfortable. Country-style cooking. Park Rangers explain the habits of the tame wild animals that often mosey by. Dining room overlooks lake and patient fishermen.

Blacksburg

Marriott Inn. *Expensive.* 900 Prices Fork Rd. Indoor and outdoor pools, putting green.

Sheraton Red Lion Inn. *Expensive.* 900 Plantation Rd. Spacious grounds, tennis, pool, golf. Restful and unique.

Econo-Travel Motor Hotel. *Moderate.* 3333 S. Main St. Free in room movies.

Bristol

Econo-Travel Motor Hotel. *Moderate.* 912 Commonwealth Ave. Rt. 381 exit off I–81. Convenient location.

Skyland Motel. *Inexpensive.* On US 11, 19 & 59 ¼ mi. N of exit 5, I–81, at 4748 Lee Hwy. Color TV. Pool. Playground. Restaurant adj.

Buena Vista

Barnes Motel. *Moderate.* On US 60 at 617 W. 29th St. Pool and restaurant.

Cape Charles

America House Motor Inn. *Expensive.* On US 13 at Wise Pt., N end of Chesapeake Bay Bridge-Tunnel. Resort facilities. Private beaches, Pool. Playground. Observation lookout for Bridge-Tunnel. Seafood in restaurant.

Carmel Church

Ramada Inn. *Expensive.* Off I–95 on Rt. 207. Pool, suites, restaurant.

Days Inn. *Moderate.* Off I–95 on Rt 207. Pool, restaurant. Near King's Dominion theme park.

Charlottesville

Best Western Cavalier Inn. *Expensive.* Intersection of US 29 and 250. Near the Univ. of Va. Pool. Polynesian Room.

Holiday Inn North. *Expensive.* US 29 & 250 bypass. Convenient to city, one of a complex of excellent accommodations at highway junction.

Best Western Mt. Vernon Hotel. *Expensive.* Jct. US 29 & 250 bypass. Quiet, high above the road, overlooking mountains. Fine restaurant. Protected area at rear for pets.

Chincoteague

Mariner Motel. *Expensive.* Maddox Blvd. Pool

Refuge Motor Inn. *Expensive.* Maddox Blvd. Pool, and Chincoteague ponies for petting. Overlooks wildlife refuge.

Culpeper
Econo-Travel Motor Hotel. *Moderate.* At US 15 & 29 Bypass. Free in room movies.

Sleepy Hollow Motel. *Moderate.* US 15 & 29 North on business route. Miniature golf. Restaurant nearby.

Danville
Best Western Virginia Manor Inn. *Moderate.* On US 29. Pool, room phones.

Downtowner Motel Inn. *Moderate.* 502 Main St. Heart of city.

Ford Motel. *Moderate.* On US 29. TV, room phones.

Doswell
Best Western Kings Quarters. *Deluxe.* I95 & Rt. 30. Lodging at Kings Dominion theme park. Low commercial rates off season.

Fredericksburg
Sheraton Fredericksburg Inn. *Deluxe.* State 3 at I–95. Attractive rooms, balconies or patios. Pool, wading pool, tennis, golf.

Ramada Inn. *Expensive.* I–95 and Rt. 3. Pool and restaurant.

Holiday Inn-South. *Expensive.* US 1 & I–95. Heated pool, wading pool, kennel. Golf privileges.

Thr-Rift Inn Motel. *Moderate.* US 17 at I 95. Pool, restaurant.

Thunderbird Motor Inn. *Moderate.* I–95 & Rt. 3E. (2205 Plank Rd.) Restaurant, pool.

Front Royal
Quality Inn. *Expensive.* On Rt. 522 bypass. Good dining room in addition to usual facilities.

Cool Harbor Motel. *Moderate.* N on US 340, 522. Pool, pets welcome.

Scottish Inn. *Moderate.* On US 340.

Galax
Rose Lane Motel. *Moderate.* US 58 & 221. Spacious, gracious, set back on a hill from the highway. A good place to relax.

Hampton
Chamberlain. *Expensive.* Off I–64 to Fort Monroe. Modernized, well-maintained hotel on the waterfront at Hampton Roads. Watch the world's ships glide by. Spacious rooms, terraces. Adjacent to Fort Monroe.

Sheraton Inn-Coliseum. *Expensive.* 1215 W. Mercury Blvd. Indoor pool, many facilities

Strawberry Banks Motor Inn. *Expensive.* Exit 4 from I64. Overlooks harbor, some suites with fireplaces, pool, fishing pier.

Econo-Travel Motor Hotel. *Moderate.* Two locations at 1781 N. King St., and 2708 W. Mercury Blvd.

Harrisonburg

Coachman Inn. *Moderate.* 3 mi N. on US 11. Suites, pool, restaurant.

Econo-Travel Motor Hotel. *Moderate.* Exit 64E from I–81. No pets.

Village Inn. *Moderate.* 5 mi S. on US 11. Pool, playground, restaurant.

Hillsville

Knob Hill Motor Lodge. *Moderate.* US 58 & 221. Superb views of beautiful countryside. Children and pets welcome.

Hot Springs

Homestead. *Deluxe.* Rt. 220, Warm Spring Valley. One of America's great resorts. Sports in season: skiing, skeet shooting, fishing in stocked trout stream, tennis, horseback riding, carriage drives, golfing on three 18-hole courses. Dance orchestra and movies every night.

Cascades Inn. *Deluxe.* 3 mi S of Hot Springs. The Homestead's slightly less expensive relation. Guests at Cascades may use the Homestead's resort facilities. MAP.

Irvington

Tides Inn. *Deluxe.* Off State 3. A quiet, luxurious water place for knowledgeable gentry. Open Apr.-Dec. Heated salt-water pool. Chesapeake Club for dancing. All water sports, 2 golf courses, cruises on Inn's own yacht. Poolside service. TV in lobby.

Leesburg

Quality Inn. *Expensive.* Intersection of Rt. 15 & 7 bypass. Located on 18-hole golf course with club house in hotel. Large pool, pleasant surroundings.

Lexington

Best Western Keydet-General Motel. *Expensive.* US 60 west. Quiet mountain setting, comfortable surroundings. Restaurant.

Days Inn. *Moderate.* Near exit 53 of I–64 & I–81. Pool playground.

Lexington Motel. *Moderate.* US 11A & US 11. Within easy distance of Washington and Lee University, V.M.I. and the George Marshall Research Library.

Luray

Luray Caverns Motel West. *Expensive.* On US 221 by-pass, opposite caverns. Full facilities.

Mimslyn Motor Inn. *Expensive.* W. Main St. A gracious inn used by local residents for entertaining. Pool. Small pets on leash.

Lynchburg

Holiday Inn South. *Expensive.* US 29 Expressway at Odd Fellows Rd. Pool, restaurant.

Econo-Travel Motor Hotel. *Moderate.* US 29 Expressway at stadium exit.

Thomas Motor Lodge. *Moderate.* 2 mi. N. on US 29 Restaurant nearby.

Manassas

Olde Towne Inn Motor Lodge. *Expensive.* On State 28, Center & Main Sts. Dining room, pool.

Marion

Holiday Inn. *Expensive.* Exit 17 off I–81, Jct. of US 11 east.

Quality Inn Virginia House. *Expensive.* I–81 at exit 17. pool, near state parks.

Middletown

Wayside Inn. *Expensive.* US 11 near exit 77 of I–81 at 7783 Main St. Historic restoration of colonial inn with a notable dining room.

Mt. Jackson

Best Western-Happy Day Inn. *Expensive.* Exit 69 from I–81; pool, cafeteria and restaurant.

Natural Bridge

Natural Bridge Hotel and Motor Inn. *Moderate.* On US 11 at the famed natural wonder. Gracious, modern hotel has replaced classic structure which burned. The bridge is still there.

New Market

Quality Inn-Shenandoah Valley. *Expensive.* Exit 67 off I–81; pool, sauna, dining room, cocktail lounge.

Shenvallee Lodge. *Expensive.* I–81 exit 67. Golf and other resort facilities.

Newport News

Holiday Inn. *Expensive.* US 17 at 6128 Jefferson Ave., Pool, restaurant, airport transportation.

Best Western King James Motor Hotel. *Expensive.* James River Bridge Circle and Jefferson Ave. All hotel services. Handy to Mariner's Museum, James River Country Club and Williamsburg.

Econo-Travel Motor Hotel. *Moderate.* 11845 Jefferson Ave. (Rt. 143 between I–64 & US 17). 15 mins. from Colonial Williamsburg.

Thr-rift Inn. *Moderate.* US 17 at 6129 Jefferson Ave. Complimentary coffee.

Traveler's Inn Motel. *Moderate.* US 60 at 14747 Warwick Blvd. 3 mi E. of Ft. Eustis. Pool, restaurant. Some efficiencies.

Norfolk

Omni International Hotel. *Deluxe.* 777 Waterfront Drive. Norfolk's newest showplace. First class in every respect. Cocktail lounge, with 2 restaurants and a swimming pool. Entertainment.

Holiday Inn Central. *Expensive.* 930 Va. Beach Blvd. Cocktail lounge. Restaurant and a swimming pool. Entertainment.

Holiday Inn-Scope. *Expensive.* Olney Rd. & Monticello Ave. Pool. Playground. Airport bus. Meeting rooms. Dining rooms and coffee shop. Across street from Scope Coliseum. Within easy walk of Chrysler Museum.

Sheraton Inn-Military Circle. *Expensive.* Virginia Beach Blvd. & Military Hwy. 15-story inn. Pool. Pets. Airport transportation.

Quality Inn-Lake Wright. *Moderate.* On US 13 at 6280 Northampton Blvd. ½ mi. E of Jct. I–64. Pool. Wading pool. Playground. Tennis. Extra charge, golf. Airport transportation.

Econo-Travel. *Moderate.* 3343 N Military Hwy. 1111 E. Ocean View Ave. 8 mi. NE on 60.

Petersburg

Ramada Inn. *Expensive.* I–95 Exit 3. Pool, restaurant. 1 mile from Ft. Lee.

Days Inn. *Moderate.* Exit 5 from I–95 at 2310 Indian Hills Rd. Dining room, pool.

Best Western America House Motor Inn. *Moderate.* 405 E. Washington St. The twin of the Cape Charles facility of the same name. Comfortable, colorful. Traditional decor.

Portsmouth

Imperial 400 Motel. *Moderate.* 333 Effingham. Pool, a few efficiencies.

Richmond

Holiday Inn-South. *Expensive.* West on US 60, 6346 Midlothian Tpk. Pool, restaurant.

Hotel John Marshall. *Expensive.* Franklin & 5th Sts. Located within a half block of Richmond's department stores and shops.

Quality Inn-North. *Expensive.* Parham Rd. exit from I–95 (on US 1). Putting green, pool.

Hyatt Richmond. *Expensive.* W. Broad at I–64. A fine hotel; indoor and outdoor pools.

Days Inn. *Moderate.* I–64 at Byrd Airport exit, playground, pool, restaurant.

Econo-Travel Motor Hotels. *Inexpensive.* 3 locations: 5408 Williamsburg Rd. at Byrd Airport entrance, 6523 Midlothian Turnpike, and I–95 at Willis Rd. exit.

Roanoke

Howard Johnson's Motor Lodge-Troutville. *Expensive.* Exit 44 on I–81. Full facilities.

Ramada Inn. *Expensive.* 8118 Plantation Rd. 6 mi. NW on 220 at I–81 exit 43. Heated pool. Free airport bus.

Roanoke Hotel. *Expensive.* Wells Ave. & Williamson Rd. A handsome, rambling structure in Old English decor set on high, spacious, landscaped grounds within easy walking distance of the center of downtown. Heated indoor pool.

Econo-Travel Motor Hotels. *Inexpensive.* 6221 Thirlane Ave. (I–581 & Peters Creek Rd.), and at 3816 Franklin Rd. (Intersection US 220 & Rt. 419 across from Tanglewood Mall.)

Shenandoah National Park
Big Meadows Lodge. *Moderate.* At milepost 51 on Skyline Drive (20 mi S. of Jct. US 211). Variety of accommodations and activities. Reservations advised.

Skyland Lodge. *Moderate.* At milepost 41 on Skyline Drive. Motel and cottage rooms, dining room, tap room.

Springfield
Springfield Hilton. *Expensive.* Off I–95 at Franconia exit, 6550 Loisdale Rd. Year round indoor pool, full hotel facilities.

Staunton
Hessian House Motel. *Expensive.* 10 mi S. at exit 55S on I–81. Well equipped units with patios or balconies, refrigerators, 2 pools.

Master Hosts Inn. *Expensive.* Exit 58 from I–81. Pool, restaurant, refrigerators.

Virginia Beach
Belvedere Motel. *Deluxe.* Ocean at 36th St. Glass doors opening onto private balcony. Heated pool, sun deck. Coffee shop.

Cavalier Oceanfront. *Deluxe.* 42nd St. and Atlantic Ave. Pool, rooftop supper club. Family dining room. Tennis courts. Putting green. Golf course privileges.

Diplomat Motor Inn. *Deluxe.* Ocean at 33rd St. Window wall and sliding glass doors open onto ocean veranda. Heated pool. Coffee shop. Golf.

Dunes Motor Inn. *Deluxe.* Oceanfront & 10th St. Heated pool. Guest bicycles. Shuffleboard. Game room. Dining room. Coffee shop.

Empress Motel. *Deluxe.* Oceanfront at 28th St. Pub, oceanfront balcony. Heated pool. Sundeck. Golf and beach club privileges.

Flagship. *Deluxe.* Atlantic Ave. at 6th St. Heated pool. Rooftop sun deck. Golf. Fishing. Tennis. Free bicycles.

Golden Sands. *Deluxe.* Atlantic Ave. & 14th St. Heated pool, lounge terrace. Beach and golf club privileges.

Hilton Inn. *Deluxe.* Oceanfront at 8th St. 2 pools. Patio, sun decks. Recreation room. Golf and beach club privileges. Copper Kettle Restaurant.

Holiday Inn. *Deluxe.* 25th & Oceanfront. Pool. Dining room. Coffee shop. Pets.

Howard Johnson's Motor Lodge. *Deluxe.* Oceanfront at 38th. Balconies. Pool. Restaurant. Cocktail lounge. Meeting rooms.

Kona Kai Motor Hotel. *Deluxe.* 18th at Oceanfront. Pool. Dining room. Coffee shop.

La Playa Motel. *Deluxe.* Oceanfront at 33rd St. TV. Heated pool. Coffee shop. Sun terrace. Shuffleboard. Free bicycles.

Lynn-Dee Motel. *Deluxe.* Atlantic Ave. at 11th St. Heated Pool.

Ocean House Motel. *Deluxe.* Atlantic Ave. at 31st St. Rooftop pool. Kiddie pool. Restaurant.

Princess Anne Inn. *Deluxe.* 25th St. & Oceanfront. Dining room, coffee shop. Heated pool. Golf. Tennis. Bicycles. Beach club privileges.

Ramada Inn. *Deluxe.* Oceanfront & 7th St. Oceanfront balconies. Courtesy car. Heated pool. Dining room. Lounge.

Sea Gull Motel. *Deluxe.* Oceanfront at 27th St. Heated pool. Kiddie pool. Mini-refrigerator. Morning coffee.

Seahawk Motel. *Deluxe.* 26th St. & Oceanfront. Pool. Patio. Restaurant.

Sheraton Beach Inn. *Deluxe.* Oceanfront & 36th St. Heated pool. Restaurants. Transportation to airport.

Thunderbird Motor Lodge. *Deluxe.* Oceanfront at 35th St. Dining room. Coffee shop. Pool. Club privileges.

Triton Towers. *Deluxe.* 23rd & Oceanfront. Heated pool. Sun lounge. Coffee shop. Golf club privileges.

Windjammer Motor Lodge. *Deluxe.* Oceanfront at 19th St. Heated pool. Restaurant.

Beach Carousel Motel. *Expensive.* 1300 Pacific Ave. Quiet location overlooking Holly Lake. 150 yds to beach. Pool. Sun lounge, terrace.

Carriage Inn. *Expensive.* 1500 Atlantic Ave. Quiet central courtyard, pool and terrace. TV. Coffee shop. Near fishing piers, oceanfront marina.

Econo-Travel Motor Hotels. *Inexpensive.* 2 locations: 3637 Bonney Rd. (Rosemont Rd. exit off Beach Expressway) and at 5173 Shore Dr.

Williamsburg

Best Western Patrick Henry Inn. *Deluxe.* York & Page Sts. Pool. Restaurant. Comfortable rooms. Pets. Airport bus.

Best Western Williamsburg Westpark. *Deluxe.* 1600 Richmond Rd. Yr.-round heated pool, bus to Info. Ctr. Pets.

Heritage Inn. *Deluxe.* 1324 Richmond Rd. Has restaurant and unusually large swimming pool. Accepts pets.

Holiday Inn East. *Deluxe.* 814 Capitol Landing Rd. Pool, wading pool, pets, restaurant. Similar accommodations at **Holiday Inn West,** 902 Richmond Rd.

Hospitality House. *Deluxe.* 415 Richmond Rd. Attractive Colonial decor. Pool. Shuffleboard, bicycles. Shuttle bus.

Williamsburg Inn. *Deluxe.* Francis St. Offers 102 rooms, as well as lodging in the restored area's Colonial houses. Pets, pool, golf, tennis, plantation breakfasts and late suppers.

Howard Johnson's Motor Lodge. *Deluxe.* 1800 Richmond Rd. Pool, restaurant, attractive public rooms.

Merrimac Motel. *Expensive.* Rte. 143 East. Pool. Kitchenettes available.

Motor House. *Expensive.* Info. Center Dr. Inexpensive cafeteria, pool, meeting rooms.

Princess Anne Motor Lodge. *Expensive.* 1350 Richmond Rd. Comfortable rooms, tastefully appointed. Playground. Pool.

Quality Inn-Colony. *Expensive.* Page & 2nd St. Pool. Restaurant. Snack bar. Other Quality Inns with high standards and *moderate* to *expensive* are: **Francis Nicholson.** Rt. 60, By-Pass Rd.; **Lord Paget,** 901 Capitol Landing Rd.; and **Mount Vernon,** 1700 Richmond Rd.

Ramada Inn-East. *Expensive.* 351 York St., within two blocks of historic area. Pool. Restaurant. **Ramada Inn-West** on Rte. 60 offers similar accommodations.

White Lion Motel. *Expensive.* 912 Capitol Landing Rd. Clean, attractive units, 18 with kitchens.

Williamsburg Lodge. *Expensive.* S. England St. Set in beautiful gardens adj. to restoration area. Pool, golf, tennis, excellent food at moderate costs. Outstanding convention facilities.

Econo Lodges #1 & #2. *Moderate.* 1408 & 1413 Richmond Rd.

Greenbrier Lodge. *Moderate.* 800 Capital Landing Rd. Playground, pool, fishing, English pub.

King William Inn. *Moderate.* 824 Capitol Landing Rd. Modern, quiet, central location.

Winchester

Best Western Lee-Jackson Motor Inn. *Expensive.* On US 50 & 522, exit 80 from I–81. Pool, lounge, restaurant, cable TV.

Quality Inn-Boxwood South. *Expensive.* US 11 S, exit 79 from I–81. Attractive grounds, full facilities.

Wytheville

Econo-Travel Motor Hotel. *Moderate.* Exit 23 off I–81 & I–77 to US 11 (E. Main St.).

Wythe Motor Lodge. *Inexpensive.* on US 11, exit 23 from I–81. Restaurant.

Yorktown

Yorktown Motor Lodge. *Moderate.* 3 mi. S on US 17. Offers room service, room phones, and a pool. Restaurant adj. Excellent lodgings.

 DINING OUT in Virginia can be as varied as the state's geography. US 460, from Petersburg to Suffolk, runs through peanut-and-ham country in Southside Virginia. It's as if the traveler is passing a smorgasbord all the way. On the coast, around Norfolk, Newport News, Northern Neck, and Eastern Shore, fresh seafood abounds. On the Peninsula, Colonial Williamsburg's seven dining facilities set an unflagging standard. The urban areas of Richmond and northern Virginia stimulate fine cuisine. In unpretentious places in southwest Virginia, old-style Southern cooking is at its best—and at its best, it's unbeatable. Restaurant price categories are as follows: *Deluxe* $9–$12.50. *Expensive* $6.50–

$9, *Moderate* $4–$6.50, *Inexpensive* under $4. For a more complete explanation of restaurant categories refer to *Facts at Your Fingertips.*

Alexandria
(See also Washington, D.C. chapter)

Gadsby's Tavern. *Expensive.* 130 N. Royal St. Historic restored tavern of the colonial period.

Seaport Inn. *Expensive.* 6 King St. Seafood in a long-popular waterfront dining spot.

Fish Market. *Moderate.* 105 King St. Seafood served in a retail fish market.

Taverna Cretekou. *Moderate.* 818 King St. Traditional Greek dishes served in bright Greek atmosphere.

Atlantic

Wright's Seafood Restaurant. *Inexpensive.* About 6 mi. from US 13 with a fine view of the ocean and NASA's Wallops Island. Good, home-style cooking, with fresh seafood specialties.

Berryville

Battletown Inn. *Moderate.* Intersection of US 340 & State 7. A drawing card: chicken smothered in butter.

Charlottesville

Boar's Head Inn. *Expensive.* W. on Ivy Rd. US 250. Continental cuisine, prime rib, colonial atmosphere.

The Ivy Inn. *Expensive.* 2244 Old Ivy Road of US 250 west of Charlottesville. A popular seafood specialty; steaming kettle of clams, lobster, shrimp, crab claws.

Michie Tavern. *Moderate.* Rte. 53, ½ mile below Jefferson's Monticello. Rustic structure was operated by Patrick Henry's father. One basic, tasty menu: Colonial fried chicken, black-eyed peas, stewed tomatoes, cornbread and biscuits, choice of 4 salads.

University Cafeteria. *Inexpensive.* 1517 Main St. A favorite place for University of Virginia students. Clean, wholesome meals for the entire family.

Cheriton

Paul's Restaurant. *Inexpensive.* US 13. Don't be put off by the drug store counters out front. At the rear are booths, tables, and a varied menu, including fresh-baked pies and cakes and vegetables and fish from the neighborhood.

Chincoteague

Channel Bass Inn. *Expensive.* Seafood with a European touch. Modest rooms also available.

Clarksville

Roberts Restaurant. *Moderate.* Virginia Ave. at 2nd St. on US 58. Specializing in fried chicken, country ham, steak, offering children's plates.

Fredericksburg

Allman's Pit Cooked Bar-B-Q. *Inexpensive.* A plain counter type roadside eatery known for very good barbecue.

Hanover

Hanover Tavern. *Moderate.* Rt. 301. Dining and theatre in historic stagecoach stop that catered to colonial leaders. Country dinners featured.

Great Falls

L'Auberge Chez Francois. *Expensive.* 332 Springvale Rd., Great Falls, Va. Washington's long-time favorite has moved to the country to an Alsatian-type inn. Dining here is an experience requiring reservations a week in advance. A family-owned restaurant—and superb!

Hampton

The Customs House. *Expensive.* 714 Settlers Landing Road, Old Hampton Waterfront. Excellent seafood served in a reproduction of Robert Louis Stevenson's pirate ship that sailed in *Treasure Island.*

Jamestown

Mermaid Tavern. *Inexpensive.* Jamestown Festival Park. Clean, wholesome, tasty snacks. Crab cake sandwiches.

Leesburg

Laurel Brigade Inn. *Expensive.* Rt. 7 Southern specialties. Parts of inn date from 1766. Also modest rooms at low prices.

Luray

Big Meadows Lodge. *Moderate.* On the Skyline Drive, 15 mi. north of US 33 crossing. Marvelous view from mountain ridge. Center for campers in Shenandoah National Park. Delicious food for the family. Same prices, hours, at **Skyland,** on Skyline Drive, 10 mi. south of US 211.

McLean

Evans Farm Inn. *Expensive.* Rt 123, E of I 495. Colonial atmosphere, extensive grounds, home-made desserts.

Joshua Tree. *Expensive.* On Hwy 123 at Old Dominion Drive. Beef featured in a pleasant atmosphere.

Tysons Corner Magic Pan. *Moderate.* Rt. 123 at Tysons Corner Shopping Center. Very good entree and dessert crepes.

Middleburg

Red Fox Tavern. *Expensive.* US 50, in the middle of the hunt country, a haunt for those who ride to the hounds. Restored building (c. 1728).

Norfolk

Esplanade. *Deluxe.* In the Omni International Hotel at 777 Waterfront Dr. Excellent continental cuisine in a refined dining room overlooking the harbor.

Ships Cabin. *Expensive.* 4110 East Ocean View Ave., overlooking Chesapeake Bay. Seafood shishkebab offers skewered oysters, shrimp, scallops, lobster, fish, tomatoes, onions, peppers.

Mason's Seafood Restaurant. *Inexpensive.* Choice seafood, fresh vegetables, restful atmosphere. A favorite of old Norfolkians.

Purcellville

The Inn. *Expensive.* Rt. 7. Continental/American cuisine.

Richmond

Capri. *Expensive.* 1 E. Grace St. Italian specialties, and home made pastries.

Fox Head Inn. *Expensive.* 15 mi. from Richmond at Manakin, Va. Virginia food, Southern hospitality.

La Petite France. *Expensive.* 2912 Maywill St. Take Exit Staples Mill east off I–64, turn left at third traffic light, drive 1 block and turn left. The cuisine has a genuine French accent.

Tobacco Company Restaurant. *Expensive.* 12th & Cary St. Victorian décor in restored historic area.

Morrison's Cafeteria. *Moderate.* Glenside Dr. & Broad St. off I 64. A popular chain with good variety.

Valle's Steak House. *Moderate.* 4200 Broad St. Beef and seafood. Good family dining.

Sally Bell's Kitchen. *Inexpensive.* 708 W. Grace St., 1 block off Belvedere St. A lively, always busy Richmond institution. Box lunches of spicy sandwich spreads, cheese biscuits, deviled eggs, fresh-baked tarts and cakes, all the makings of an elegant picnic.

Roanoke

Hotel Roanoke. *Expensive.* Shenandoah Ave. & Jefferson St. A rambling Stratford-on-Avon structure offering old-style hospitality in a lofty dining room.

La Maison du Gourmet. *Moderate.* 5732 Airport Rd. on Hwy 118. French Continental cuisine.

Smithfield

Smithfield Inn. *Moderate.* 112 Main St. Southern cooking featuring, of course, Smithfield ham and fried chicken. Homemade pies and cobblers. Lunch and dinner.

Surry

The Surrey House. *Inexpensive.* Superb cooking with memorable specialties—peanut-raisin pie, peanut soup, apple fritters, crab cakes.

Syria

Graves' Mountain Lodge. *Moderate.* Rte. 670 in Syria 10 mi. north of Madison on slopes of Blue Ridge. Country-style cooking and servings satisfy appetites whetted by mountain air. Open noon to 1:30 P.M., 6:30 P.M. to 7:30 P.M.; Sun. 1 P.M. to 2:30 P.M., 6 P.M. to 7:30 P.M. Lodging in cottages motel-style units.

Tappahannock

Lowery's Restaurant. *Moderate.* On State 17 in town. Seafood galore, from Rappahannock River and Chesapeake Bay. Open weekdays 6 A.M. to 9 P.M.; Sun., 7 A.M. to 9 P.M.

Virginia Beach

Three Ships Inn. *Expensive.* 3800 Shore Drive, between Chesapeake Bay Bridge-Tunnel and Lynnhaven Bridge. Early-settler decor, candlelit dinners by the fireplace or on patio. Gourmet dishes: shrimp Florentine, scallops Mornay, curries, crab imperial.

Valle's Steak House. *Moderate.* 4616 Virginia Beach Blvd. 11 A.M. to 11 P.M.; good family dining.

Wakefield

Virginia Diner. *Inexpensive.* US 460. For nearly 50 years this comfortable, unpretentious restaurant has been serving some of the region's finest food. Its ham and sausage biscuits are celebrated.

Warm Springs

Waterwheel Restaurant. *Expensive.* Gristmill Square. Fresh trout, quiches. Lunch and dinner.

The Inn at Little Washington. *Expensive.* Center on US 211, Dinner 6–9, Wed.–Sat; 4–8 Sunday. Reservations required.

White Stone

Windmill Point Marine Lodge. *Moderate.* 7 mi. east of White Stone on State 695. Fresh seafood, caught at the door.

Williamsburg

Williamsburg Inn. *Deluxe.* Francis St. Colonial Williamsburg's original dining place. A pleasing mixture of continental and regional cuisine ranging from frog legs Provencale to Virginia crab casserole. In a moderate-to-expensive range are menus at the **Cascades** on Information Center Drive and the **Williamsburg Lodge** on S. England St. An inexpensive Colonial Williamsburg dining facility is the **Motor House** at the Information Center.

Josiah Chowning's Tavern. *Expensive.* Duke of Gloucester St. in Colonial Williamsburg. Specialties here include Burnswick stew and Welsh rarebit along with spareribs, prime rib and Chesapeake Bay crabmeat. Cocktails. Children's menus. Reservations are required.

King's Arms Tavern. *Expensive.* Duke of Gloucester St. in Colonial Williamsburg. Gracious dining with waiters in period costumes. Specialties are Virginia ham, fried chicken, English lamb chops and roast beef. Try the peanut soup. Cocktails. Children's menu. Call in advance for reservations and to check end of dinner hour, which can vary.

Chickahominy House. *Moderate.* 1211 Jamestown Rd. Ham biscuits, Brunswick stew, and buttermilk pie, plus antiques. Open 8:30 A.M. to 3:30 P.M.

Christiana Campbell's Tavern. *Moderate.* Waller St. George Washington's favorite dining place in Colonial Williamsburg, specializes in seafood: Hampton crab imperial, chilled shrimp salad.

WEST VIRGINIA

The Beckoning Mountains

BY
SUSAN KRALJEVIC

Susan Kraljevic was born and brought up in White Sulphur Springs, West Virginia. She is now a publicist and freelance writer living in New York.

At one time three great Indian trails traversed the state, and today they are largely paralleled by certain state and federal highways. The Seneca Trail, which bypasses Seneca Rocks southwest of Petersburg, is closely followed by US 219 from Maryland to Virginia, with a principal fork following the South Branch of the Potomac from its mouth to Seneca Rocks and then west to the town of Elkins. The Scioto-Monongahela Trail roughly followed a path from Pennsylvania through the present cities of Morgantown and Fairmont and then to Parkersburg on the Ohio River. This route is closely followed by Interstate 79 and by US 50. The Kanawha Trail, paralleled much of the way by US 60, is in the southern part of the state, and runs generally from White Sulphur Springs to Huntington.

West Virginia roads are, for the most part, excellent hard-surface highways that provide scenic drives as they twist about the rugged terrain. Stressing the importance of its highways, twisting or otherwise, the state has launched an accelerated program of road building, giving West Virginia a first-class highway transportation system.

The Eastern Panhandle

A good place to begin a tour of the eastern portion of West Virginia is Harpers Ferry. It is the easternmost town in the state and is situated in the clawlike appendage at the north of the panhandle. The town, located on US 340, is one of old stone and brick houses, with narrow streets; it is in the process of being restored and once again resembles the way it looked in 1859 when John Brown's raiders seized the arsenal, and amply demonstrated their antipathy to slavery. The captured, including Brown, were hanged. Harpers Ferry is now a National Historical Park. It provides a Tourist Visitors Center, open from March through November. John Brown's Civil War Showcase and the John Brown Wax Museum are open year round. On a nearby hillside stands the mansion of the founder of Harpers Ferry—Robert Harper—and beyond that the ruins of St. John's Episcopal Church, with trees growing up through the nave. The area around Harpers Ferry is extraordinarily beautiful—Thomas Jefferson was one of its most ardent admirers—and from a vantage point above the town the Potomac and Shenandoah Rivers can be seen flowing together near the place where Virginia, Maryland and West Virginia meet. Contact the Appalachian Trail Conference in Harpers Ferry for hiking information. Another point of interest in the town is the Harpers Ferry Cavern, with two levels, two waterfalls and two lakes, one of which is bridged.

Two towns of interest in the immediate vicinity are Charles Town, eight miles to the southwest, and Shepherdstown, to the north. Charles Town, named after Charles Washington, George's brother, is noted for its thoroughbred horseracing and stately-mansion atmosphere. It was here that John Brown was tried for treason. Two miles west of town are the ruins of St. George's Chapel, where George Washington was accustomed to worship. Charles Town has its Mountain Heritage Arts and Crafts Festival in June and an Annual House and Garden Tour in the spring. South of Charles Town is Bunker Hill, where Morgan Morgan built the first permanent home in what is now West Virginia. To the northwest is a federal fish hatchery, in Leetown.

Shepherdstown, slightly to the north at the junction of State 48 and 45, is the oldest town in West Virginia. Once called Mecklenburg, it was settled by Germans about 1719. This quaint college town has an Annual House and Garden Tour in the spring.

If you choose, follow State 45 to Martinsburg, a city in the middle of West Virginia's apple and peach country. Belle Boyd, the Mata Hari of the South, was born and raised here, and "Boydville," the mansion of General Elisha Boyd, still stands.

From Martinsburg continue on State 9 until you reach Berkeley Springs, the oldest spa in the nation, once called Bath. The springs were then owned by Lord Fairfax and George Washington was a regular patron during the late 18th century. His yellow-ringed bathtub, fashioned from a rock-lined hollow log, is certainly worth a look. The springs are now a part of the West Virginia Park system; visitors may enjoy swimming, massage, whirlpool therapy and infrared treatments. Another historic site in the Shepherdstown area is the Rumsey Monument, also administered as a state park facility. James Rumsey, who constructed the first buildings in Berkeley Springs, operated the first successful steamboat, though he is not generally credited with its invention.

South of Berkeley Springs is Cacapon State Park, a resort that offers innumerable activities and comfortable lodging. The Sleepy Creek Public Hunting Area is also available for camping and swimming. A state fish hatchery is located at nearby Ridge.

From any one of these points, continue southwest to the town of Romney. It is located in the central portion of the eastern panhandle, at the junction of US 50 and State 28. It is the state's oldest incorporated town (dating back to 1762) and during the Civil War it changed hands fifty-six times, a trauma from which it has never quite recovered. The Confederate Monument in Indian Mound Cemetery is the first such constructed in the country (1867). Natural attractions in the area include Hanging Rocks, a strange perpendicular cliff, and two game refuges— Short Mountain and Nathaniel—where bow hunting for deer is quite the thing and where, in season, you can hunt wild turkey, deer and small game with a gun. The area is also noted for its smallmouth bass.

If you continue west on US 50 from Romney you will come to the communities of Burlington and Keyser, though Keyser is a few miles above the junction, on US 220. Both communities hold Historical Days in June. Above Keyser on State 46 stands Fort Ashby, the only extant unit in a chain of Indian forts that George Washington's troops built across the Virginia frontier in 1775. Below Keyser, at Laurel Dale, a stone marker indicates the site of the cabin where Nancy Hanks, mother of Abraham Lincoln, was born. Still farther south from Keyser, on US 50, near Mt. Storm, the new Virginia Electrical Power Company dam is located. Its 1,200-acre lake offers boating, water-skiing, fishing and swimming. Stony River Reservoir is nearby.

This is a good place to leave winding US 50 and drive across the mountainside via State 42 toward Petersburg and a broad fertile valley comparable to the Shenandoah Valley of Virginia. Now we are in one of West Virginia's most beautiful areas, near the edge of the Monongahela National Forest. Petersburg, home of the Golden Centennial Trout, is the site of the White Water weekend, held in April in conjunction with the Potomac Highland Art and Craft Show. The golden trout, actually a species of rainbow trout, was first spotted in 1954 by Harrison Shobe, who was a game warden in this part of the country. He captured this fish, which had a golden spot on its midsection, and eventually succeeded in developing a full-colored golden trout. The Petersburg Hatchery (open to the public) now stocks this unusual species in the local streams and permits may be obtained to catch them. The locale is excellent for viewing the September-October spectacle of migrating hawks, moving past the Allegheny Front.

Near Petersburg on State 28 are the Smoke Hole Caverns. They are unusual formations in the midst of mountain peaks, and were used for various purposes throughout history: the Indians smoked their meat in them; moonshiners used them for hiding their stills; and during the Civil War they were used as ammunition dumps. Just below them are the Seneca Rocks, jagged formations that loom hundreds of feet above the swift white water of the South Branch of the Potomac. It is said to be the most frequently photographed spot in West Virginia.

Thirteen miles northeast of Petersburg on US 220 is the town of Moorefield, in the South Branch Valley. It hosts the annual Hardy County Heritage weekend (a House and Garden Tour) in September. The festival features an antique auction, square-dancing, a flea market and many art and craft exhibits. The House and Garden Tour includes lovely Georgian and Victorian homes replete with 17th- and 18th-century French and Italian art and furnishings.

To the southeast of Moorefield is the Lost River State Park region. It was once owned by the Lee family of Virginia and used as a summer resort. A restored cabin from that era contains a museum. Visitors can see where Lost River disappears and then, a few miles away, resurfaces as the headwaters of the Cacapon River. There is a "family" park, open from late March to mid-December. Green Valley Farm, one of West Virginia's largest farm-vacation spots, is located here in the Lost River area.

The Lost River Park parallels the southern tip of the George Washington National Park, well worth a visit, especially if you should decide to head north on State 259 to Wardensville, which has several points of interest: an old jail built before the Civil War, the Old Stone House (1778), the Hebron Lutheran Church; and the century-old Sunnybrook Farm, built on an Indian campground. Warden Lake and two public hunting areas are in close proximity.

This tour has encompassed the points of interest within the eastern panhandle, without crossing the boundaries of the Monongahela National Forest, which runs north to south along the eastern body of the state.

The Monongahela National Forest covers 805,966 acres among the Appalachian and Allegheny Mountains. It is an area of rugged splendor, its forests and mountains encompassing 1,900 miles of stream and river, all stocked with bass and trout. A good place to begin a tour of this area would be at Davis, just within the periphery of the park, on State 93, below Mt. Storm.

Alpine Festival

Davis presents the Tucker Country Alpine Festival in February. Its Mountain State Natural and Historical Museum is open daily. At nearby Blackwater Falls State Park the Annual Wildflower Pilgrimage is held in May. The falls drop fifty-seven feet over a steep ledge into a deep, narrow canyon. There is a guest lodge on the edge of the gorge. Also deluxe cabins and a camping area, open year round. Above Davis on State 93 is the Fairfax Stone, a monument which marks the boundary of the huge land grant given to Lord Fairfax by the King of England.

For winter sports, head for Canaan Valley State Park, just below Blackwater Falls, considered one of the finest year-round facilities of its kind in the east. It contains a complete winter sports complex, an 18-hole golf course, heated swimming pool, six tennis courts, an ice-skating rink and hiking trails. There are a lodge, cabins and 34 campsites.

Below Canaan is Dolly Sods, a spot of great interest to ornithologists, who come here to study the fall migratory birds. Twelve different species of hawk have been sighted here in the fall season and the elevation exceeds four thousand feet. Camping facilities are nearby. Below Dolly

Sods, on State 32, is Harman, where the water-powered Old Mill still stone-grinds its corn meal and whole-wheat flour. Mountain Industries, a mile above Harman on State 32, is a center of native crafts; wool-carding, rugmaking, handweaving and other skills are demonstrated here and wares are sold.

From here, on the east-west US 33, the traveler has the option of traveling south on either State 28, to the east, or US 219, the Seneca Trail.

Down State 28

Almost immediately on State 28 you will encounter the Smoke Hole Recreation Area, not to be confused with the northerly Smoke Hole Caverns, previously mentioned. The Seneca Rocks are near the junction of US 33 and State 28. This forest was a burying ground for the Seneca Indians and there are many legends about the area. To the south, near Riverton, are the Seneca Caverns, a wonderland of stalactites and stalag-mites, 2,500 feet above sea level. The Indians used them as a refuge. The entire area is filled with limestone caves, some unexplored, and is also of interest to botanists, who find many incongruities in the local vegeta-tion. This is particularly true of Panther Knob, near Cherry Grove, south of Riverton on State 28, where several species of plant life indigenous to other climates can be found flourishing together. Near Cherry Grove, visit Spruce Knob, the highest point in West Virginia (4,863 feet); the observation tower there provides a splendid view of the surrounding area. This is in the Spruce Knob-Seneca Rocks National Recreation Area, and is a good place for camping.

A side trip between Riverton and Cherry Grove would be to take US 33 to Franklin, where, during September, the Treasure Mountain Festi-val is held. To the east of it is the Brandywine Recreational Area.

Continuing south on State 28, you will find three once-prosperous towns—Frank, Durbin and Bartow—with many old-time stores and buildings along their main streets.

Farther south, where State 28 joins with State 92, you will encounter Green Bank, where the National Radio Astronomy Observatory is locat-ed. It has the largest movable radio telescope in the world, with a dish antenna, measuring 300 feet in diameter, that is tuned to catch and record the sounds of the universe.

Farther south, off State 28, is one of the state's most popular tourist attractions—the Cass Scenic Railroad. In the early 1960s, when the railroad was going out of business, someone got the idea of using the old coal-burning-engine train, which had been hauling logs out of the moun-tains near Cass, for a tourist attraction. Now, open-air flatcars loaded with tourists go up and down the mountain all summer long. Thousands crowd into Cass annually for this experience and to shop at the old country store and eat in the railroad car that has become a stationary restaurant. Both two- and four-and-a-half-hour tours offer breathtaking scenery, particularly in the autumn when the foliage turns. Also in Cass are the Civil War and Wildlife Museums.

Continue south on state 28, through Minnehaha Springs, onto State 92, and you are in the Watoga State Park, largest of West Virginia's state parks (10,057 acres). Watoga is an Indian word meaning "starry waters."

Watoga has completely furnished vacation cabins (requiring advance reservation) and offers numerous activities, such as rowboating, swimming, hiking and tennis. It is an area of great scenic beauty. The park's restaurant and commissary are open between Memorial and Labor Days. Calvin W. Price Forest adjoins Watoga to the south and contains 9,482 acres of mountainous land, open for hunting and fishing.

Near Neola, farther south on State 92, lies the man-made Lake Sherwood with adjacent camping grounds. Continuing south, Avon has pure springs which froth at 92,000 gallons per minute. Nearby is Blue Bend, on Anthony Creek, a recreational area that provides extraordinary mountain views and a prospect of the Greenbrier River meandering through the valley below. At this point you are approaching the southern tip of the Monongahela National Forest, a few miles from White Sulphur Springs.

Down the Seneca Trail

If you have chosen the Seneca Trail (US 219), begin at Elkins, on the western side of the Monongahela National Forest. It is the home of the Forest's administrative headquarters, and is certainly worth a visit if the Mountain State Forest Festival is in progress (usually in early October). This four-day festival is one of the oldest and largest festivals of its kind in the eastern United States (begun in 1930). Its attractions include sawing and woodchopping contests, a jousting exhibition, and the coronation of Queen Sylvia, a yearly event held on Davis and Elkins College campus.

Near Elkins is the Bowden National Fish Hatchery. It provides forty percent of the trout for the entire state. Also near Elkins is the Stuart Recreation Area, excellent for trout fishing, swimming and picnics. Continue south on US 219 to Beverly, founded in 1790. Visit the Randolph County Historical Museum during Beverly Community Week in July. Exhibits and contests abound. Just outside Beverly, away from the commotion, there is an isolated country inn called Faraway Hills. It specializes in delicious food and gracious living.

Proceed south to Huttonsville, where the Kumbrabow State Forest is located. If you wish, take a side-trip west to the century-old community of Helvetia, founded by a handful of Swiss craftsmen. Among the town's 168 inhabitants, it is common to hear the older villagers chattering in their native tongue. Art, crafts, good food and a number of activities are featured during their annual fair, held in early September. The Helvetian children, in full regalia, perform Swiss folk dances. During the summer months, Swiss foods are served at the Hutte Restaurant, and the Art-Craft Shop sells quaint gift-items.

Backtrack to US 219 and continue south to Statyfork, home of Snowshoe, West Virginia's highest all-seasons resort. Snowshoe's huge horseshoe-shaped bowl affords a variety of ski terrain for everyone from beginner to expert. Go on to Edray, where another trout hatchery is located. Nearby Marlinton, on State 39, is the home of the Pocahontas County Museum, open from the second week in June until Labor Day. "Pioneer Days" are held in July; they recapture the spirit of the early settlers, with such activities as an old-time spelling bee, carriage rides to historical sites, turtle and frog races, antique sales and Mountain Heritage music concerts. Points of interest are the Hamlin Chapel, the old jail at Huntersville and the *Pocahontas Times* newspaper office in Marlington, where the type is still handset. Also, if you like watching hawks, Marlinton's nearby mountaintop is noted for being a hawk hangout.

Continue on US 219 through Hillsboro and out of the Monongahela National Forest. (Near Hillsboro is the birthplace of Nobel Prize-winning novelist Pearl Buck. It has been restored and is open to the public.) This route will lead through Lewisburg and, via Interstate 64, on to White Sulphur Springs, where we will begin a tour of the southern portion of West Virginia.

White Sulphur Springs to Bluefield

Southern West Virginia is noted for its sulphur springs, which have been used for health-bathing since even before the 18th-century American aristocracy discovered them. The Indians were also convinced of their restorative powers. The most famous of these resorts is White Sulphur Springs, located on US 60 at the end of State 92. The Greenbrier, a posh 6,500-acre resort hotel, is located here. It is world-famous and has attracted celebrities from all over the globe: the Duke and Duchess of Windsor, John F. Kennedy, Prime Minister Nehru and Princess Grace and Prince Rainier of Monaco are only a few. It is luxurious and expensive, presenting *haute cuisine* and opulent interiors. The architecture is Georgian, with large white columns on the facade, and the guest rooms are each uniquely decorated. It was visited frequently by Robert E. Lee prior to the Civil War. Besides presenting just about every activity you could think of, the Greenbrier's guests also benefit from diagnostic checkups at the Greenbrier Clinic. There are three 18-hole golf courses. All in all, the Greenbrier represents the notion of Southern elegance at its finest (and most expensive), in a grand setting high in the Allegheny Mountains. But in one sense it is an oasis in the midst of mountain poverty; boarded shacks and tousled-haired children dressed in dirty clothes frequently appear along the roadsides of the surrounding area. Rural poverty, it should be noted, is relatively prevalent in West Virginia, though in recent years steps have been taken to improve the lot of the Appalachian people. The problem is largely geographical; the mountainous areas are unsuitable for industry (which is a mixed blessing) and modern farming methods do not easily lend themselves to the rugged terrain.

Nearby Lewisburg, on the junction of US 219 and US 60, is the site of another spring, discovered by Andrew Lewis and his father in the 1750s. Its original name was Camp Union, later changed to Lewisburg when Lewis defeated Shawnee chieftain Cornstalk in 1774. The Old Presbyterian Church is the most notable landmark in Lewisburg. It is the oldest church in continual use west of the Alleghenies, dating from the late 1700s. Visitors may view the old slave balcony and handhewn woodwork. Old-fashioned gas lamps light the streets lined with century-old houses. There are excellent gift shops and good restaurants, particularly the restored Fort Savannah Inn, which has a rustic museum. Each May the Greenbrier Historical Society (which also operates an interesting museum) conducts a tour of historical sites. Outside of Lewisburg, at Mörlunda, is one of the state's eighteen old covered bridges. Also, in nearby Fairlea the State Fair of West Virginia takes place, in the third week in August, attracting thousands of visitors. This entire area is a spelunker's dream, for of the three hundred known caves, only two are commercially developed. Organ Cave, one of the largest in the United States, was discovered in 1704. It was visited by Jefferson in 1778 and was used by Robert E. Lee as a refuge during the Civil War.

Continue on US 219. You will pass through Second Creek, where there is a covered bridge and an old grist mill, and arrive at Union, the Monroe County Seat, settled in 1762. Their annual fair, "Farmer's Day," takes place in June. Turn east on State 3 and visit the old Rehoboth Methodist Church, consecrated by Bishop Asbury in 1785. It is the oldest church building still standing west of the Alleghenies. Farther down State 3 is Gap Mills, a once-prosperous town of water-powered grist mills and lumber and wool industry. Nearby is Mancove Lake, a 140-acre recreational complex.

Five miles south of Union is Salt Sulphur Springs, one of the state's famous spring resorts, built in 1820. It is being restored and is open to the public. At the nearby town of Zenith you can see McClung's Mill, one of the last old water mills in the state.

There are other old spring resorts of historical interest in the area—most notably Sweet Springs on State 3—but let us continue southward on US 219 toward Bluefield. Stop at Princeton if you wish to visit the Oakwood Museum, featuring a variety of antiques; it is open daily from May through September. Camp Creek Forest is located north of Princeton. Bluefield, one of the state's larger towns, has over two thousand historical exhibits at its Museum of the Hills. Also, the world's shortest interstate railroad—Ridge Runner Railroad—which travels to the top of East River Mountain.

Northwest of Bluefield on 102 is Pinnacle Rock State Park, with towering peaks of quartzite sandstone resembling the ruins of an ancient castle. Picnic facilities are provided.

North from Bluefield

Take US 19–21 north from Bluefield towards Beckley, passing by the Camp Creek State Forest. Twenty-four miles southeast of Beckley, on State 3, is the town of Hinton, surrounded by parks: the Bluestone Public Hunting and Fishing area, the 180-acre federal Bluestone Reservoir and the Bluestone Dam, 6 miles north of Hinton on the New and Bluestone Rivers (great rapids for canoe buffs). One of America's finest state parks is Pipestem on State 20 below Hinton. Named for the plant that grows here (used by Indians for the stem of their peace pipes), Pipestem offers the visitor first-class facilities, breathtaking scenery and modern luxury. The main lodge overlooks the horseshoe bend in the Bluestone Gorge more than one thousand feet below. An aerial tramway carries guests down the gorge to another vacation lodge and steak house which are inaccessible by any other means. The park has a complete recreation center with a stable and two golf courses. Visit the Studio, a unique art and crafts gallery of state handicrafts. Spring Festival is held at the park with a full roster of events. The adventurous can take white-water trips down the Bluestone River on rafts. Most park facilities are open year round.

If one chose to continue on State 20 instead of going on to Beckley, one would reach Rainelle after only thirty-three miles of driving. This is a hardwood lumber center that once grew 100,000 board-feet of timber to the acre. West Virginia's only privately operated zoo, the Ponderosa Game Preserve, displays native and imported animals and game birds and includes a craft shop, picnic area and lodging.

Now we retrace our path to US 19–21 and proceed to Beckley, "The City with a Mine of Its Own," an industrial community surrounded by fertile valleys. Beckley is in the smokeless coal region of West Virginia and coal mine tours are available here at the Beckley Exhibition Mine in New River Park, open from May through September. Beckley hosts the annual Appalachian Arts and Crafts Festival in August, a showcase for craftsfolk to display their Early American work. The art show and sale is one of the largest in the South. A new festival devoted to Black Appalachian culture, the John Henry Memorial Authentic Blues and Gospel Festival, is held on Labor Day weekend.

From Beckley swing down to the southwest through Crab Orchard, Lester, and Ravencliffe, hitting State 10 at Jesse. All of this southwestern country was the home of the legendary mountaineer of West Virginia, and it still is. You'll realize it when you continue on your journey to Logan. You'll twist through narrow-bottomed ravines wide enough to carry the highway and perhaps a small stream. You won't see many of the log shacks of movie decor, but you will see a lot of mountaineers.

Strangers in Logan used to carry guns for protection. This is the area made famous by the Hatfields and McCoys and their notorious feuding. Logan, named after the Mingo Indian chief of that name, is as peaceable and sleepy as any little mountain town can be. It is the place where former world boxing champion Jack Dempsey hardened up his muscles working in a coal mine. The Hatfield family cemetery is located a few miles nearby on a lonely slope at Sarah Ann. Devil Anse Hatfield, leader of the Hatfield clan and one of the last survivors of the feud, is buried there, his grave marked by a slab of Italian marble. In August Logan has its Logan County Art and Craft Fair. Chief Logan State Park, in the heart of the coalfields, provides daytime recreational facilities and a display of steam railroading. Below at Williamson, visit the Coal House, a structure built of sixty-five tons of bituminous coal, and used as headquarters for the city's Chamber of Commerce.

This concludes an S-shaped tour of the southern portion of West Virginia. From either Logan or Williamson the tourist can travel easily to the major West Virginia cities of Huntington and Charleston, subjects of the succeeding section.

Huntington to Charleston

Huntington, the largest city in the state, is located on the Guyandot and Ohio Rivers. Charleston, fifty miles east on Interstate 64, is the state capital. Huntington and Charleston are the cultural, economic and political centers of the state.

Huntington measures the pulse of a three-state area—West Virginia, Ohio and Kentucky. It is the metropolis to which northeastern Kentuckians and southeastern Ohio Buckeyes turn for their big-city needs. Founded in 1869 by the president of the Chesapeake and Ohio Railroad

—Collis P. Huntington—it has since early days been a major shipping point for West Virginia coal. The city contains a well-developed municipal park system of more than a thousand acres, offering swimming, picnicking and tennis. It is the home of Marshall University (named for Chief Justice John Marshall), the state's second largest educational institution. Visit the Viking Glass Company and see fine glass blown and shaped by hand. The Cabell-Wayne Historical Society is located on Eleventh Street, with many exhibits of interest. The Huntington Galleries (a combination museum and art workshop) has an outstanding collection of art, both fine and folk, and includes a priceless display of antique firearms. Other points of interest in Huntington: seasonal displays of hybrid roses at Ritter Park (open daily); Heritage Village; Cabin Creek Quilt Exhibit and Sale in October; for children, Camden Park for rides, games and concessions. At nearby Twelvepoke Creek, you can relax in the Cabwaylingo State Forest.

Driving on to Charleston on US 60, you will arrive at Milton, the home of Blenko Glass. Since 1893 Blenko has produced handblown sheet glass for churches and cathedrals, and also decorative glass. Milton hosts an annual Arts and Crafts Show in October. At Mud River see an old covered bridge. Visitors can enjoy a presentation of a Broadway show at the nearby Mountaineer Dinner Theater in Hurricane.

The Kanawha River Valley, which we are now in, is often called the chemical center of the world. The first chemical plants in West Virginia were the salt furnaces in Malden, built in 1797. Daniel Boone, scout and frontiersman, lived in the Kanawha River Valley for ten years. He was selected as one of the first members of the Virginia Legislature from Kanawha County. Follow US 60 through South Charleston, one of the largest chemical producers in the world. Gas from the Charleston area flew the famous German dirigible *Graf Zeppelin* around the world. The state's second largest Adena mound is located here in a small public park.

On to Charleston, the state capital since 1870, at the mouth of the Elk River. It began as a pioneer fort and later boomed when the salt business began in 1797. Today, besides the big business of chemicals, Charleston is a major producer of metal, synthetics and glass. Charleston's Capitol Building on the banks of the Kanawha River is recognized as one of the most beautiful buildings in the nation. Daily tours are conducted through its splendid interiors.

The $14 million Science and Cultural Center is located in the Capitol complex. It is a five-level building which houses a theater, library, archives museum, and crafts and humanities displays. All productions in the theater are free to the public.

Two beautiful mansions at Sunrise, once the home of a governor, are filled with art treasures, exhibits, a children's zoo and a modern planetarium. Charleston is the scene of the Stern Wheel Regatta in September and several art and craft shows in the spring.

The Geographical Center of West Virginia

From Charleston you may wish to drive north on US 119 to Spencer, where the Black Walnut Festival is held in October. Then follow US 33 northeast to Cedar Creek State Park, which features a newly-enlarged camping area, picnicking and fishing. At nearby Glenville attend the West Virginia State Folk Festival in June.

If you backtrack south a bit on I–79, you will arrive at Sutton, near the geographical center of West Virginia. At Sutton Lake in June the West Virginia Regatta Festival is held with boatracing, fireworks, skydiving and square-dancing. Due south is the Elk River Public Hunting Area.

Take US 19 from Sutton towards Weston. Soon you will reach the French Creek Game Farm, a 300-acre roadside park featuring animals and birds, many native to West Virginia. The farm is partly fenced to make a deer preserve. Nearby, south of Walkersville, is a covered bridge on the West Fork River. At Buckhannon (off on State 4) the West Virginia Strawberry Festival is held in the spring.

At Weston, on US 119, visit the West Virginia Specialty Glass Company, known throughout the country for its handblown stemware. Near Weston is Jackson's Mill State 4-H Camp. Jonathan "Stonewall" Jackson lived and worked here at the Old Mill until he was appointed to West Point Military Academy in 1844. The Old Mill is open to the public; inside are exhibits and machinery of the period.

Heading into Northern West Virginia

Above Jackson's Mill near West Milford is Watter's Smith Memorial State Park, a unique pioneer farm of the late 1700s, still intact, with a museum and a visitor center. There are tours in the summer, swimming and picnic sites. Follow US 19 to Clarksburg, named for General George Rogers Clark of the Revolutionary War. It began as a pioneer fort, as did so many of the cities and towns in West Virginia. Stonewall Jackson was born here. Civil War trenches can still be seen. To the west of Clarksburg, on US 50, is Salem, where the Salem College Heritage Arts Festival is held in the spring. Visit Fort New Salem, a reconstructed pioneer village complete with craftsmen, demonstrating how the early settlers lived. To the east of Clarksburg on US 50 is Grafton, where West Virginia's only National Cemetery is located. Bailey Brown, the first Union soldier to be killed in the Civil War, is buried there. Below Grafton is Tygart Lake State Park, which offers excellent family recreational facilities. The lake is thirteen miles long. Tours are given of the Tygart Dam. Adjoining the park is the 1,000-acre Pleasant Creek Public Hunting Area.

Philippi, to the south on US 119, is the site of the first land battle of the Civil War, a defeat for the Confederate forces. It also has a covered bridge, and the Audra State Park is located nearby.

But continue on from Grafton through the scenic Valley Falls State Park to Fairmont, an industrial center for glass, sheet aluminum, precision machinery and coal production. See Prickett's Fort, a Revolutionary War outpost, now restored and preserved as a park with boat-launching facilities on the Monongahela River. Fairmont hosts the Middletown Art and Craft Fair in May. West of Fairmont there are two covered bridges: Paw Paw Creek at Grant Town and Buffalo Creek at Barrackville.

North on I–79 is Morgantown, just below the Mason-Dixon Line. Here the state's first pottery manufacturing plant was operating before

1785. The pottery was shipped down the Monongahela River by keelboat to Pittsburgh, and sold at various places along the river to the early settlers. There are many glass companies in the area, including Seneca Glass Company, which makes the crystal service for the White House. West Virginia University and Medical School, the state's largest educational institution, is located here at Morgantown. The city has an experimental computer-controlled rapid-transit system, which is being developed by the university. In the spring visit the West Virginia University Arboretum with its display of over five hundred species of wildflowers, trees and plants.

At Kingwood on State 7, experience the Preston County Buckwheat Festival in September. Farther on, in Terra Alta, nestled in the Appalachian Mountains, visit the American Museum, an extraordinary exhibit of Americana, including many cherished family heirlooms from colonial days. Guides in period costume lead you through kitchens, parlors and bedrooms. Alpine Lake at Terra Alta offers skiing during the winter months.

At this point you are just minutes from the Maryland border. If you wish, before crossing, visit the Cathedral State Park near Aurora, only a few minutes away. Here are 126 acres of virgin timber, designated a Registered National Natural Landmark in 1966. They are a stunning reminder of the kind of majestic forest that once covered most of the mountainous regions of West Virginia.

The Northern Panhandle and the Ohio River Valley

The only section of the state not yet covered is the Ohio River Valley, which stretches from the tip of the northern panhandle down the western periphery of the state, meandering all the way, and largely designating the western border. Although the tourist could just as easily drive north from Huntington on State 2 or northwest from Fairmont on US 250, for our purposes it will be more suitable to begin at the northern tip.

To the Indian the word Ohio meant "river of the whitecaps." To West Virginia this river means a myriad of historic, scenic and industrial attractions. Throughout the valley are fine farms where purebred cattle are raised and where splendid orchards flourish. Start at Chester, home of Waterford Park, scene of thoroughbred horseracing in season. Chester is a large pottery manufacturing center. At nearby Newell is the largest single pottery factory in the world. To the south is Tomlinson Run State Park, with 1,398 acres for boating, hiking and swimming.

Below is Weirton, an important steel center touching three states. Visit the restored Peter Tarr Iron Furnace, the first built west of the Allegheny Mountains. Cannon balls for the War of 1812 were made here. Nearby Wellsburg, the site of the first glass plant in the state, was established in 1813 by Isaac Duval. For a side trip take State 27 east from Wellsburg and visit the Old Stone Chapel, erected in 1795. It is at Pierce Run Road, and lamplight services are held on Sunday evenings.

Due south is Wheeling, the former capital of West Virginia. An industrial river city (tobacco, steel, textiles), Wheeling has attracted German, Italian, Polish, Assyrian and Greek immigrants who have left their mark on Wheeling today. It was the site of the last battle of the Revolutionary War (which was actually over, though they didn't know it at the time), and it was here that representatives from western counties met during the Civil War to request separate statehood for West Virginia. Wheeling Downs, the state's only dog racing track, is located here. Among the things to see, other than an industrial tour which can be arranged through the Chamber of Commerce, is the Mansion House Museum, built in 1835 and furnished with Victorian pieces and containing a unique collection of glassware. It is located in Oglebay Park, one of the largest municipal parks in the country, encompassing one thousand acres. It offers year-round activities and accommodations, including a ski area and the Good Zoo. The Oglebay Institute Art and Craft Festival is held in July at the White Palace in Wheeling Park, on US 40.

Also of interest is Willow Glen, near Wheeling, a private home built of massive stone after the turn of the century for over $250,000. It is now open as a museum, where you can see the vast collection of art objects and paintings.

Twelve miles south is Moundsville, where Fostoria, the largest hand-made-glass factory in America is located. More important, though, Moundsville is the home of the Grave Creek Mound, the largest conical burial mound in America, constructed by the Adena people sometime between 800 B.C. and A.D. 500. Many of these mounds dot the Ohio River Valley.

Follow State 2 to New Martinsville, a few miles south of the Mason-Dixon Line, where the annual American Power Boat Regatta is held in September. Side trips from here could be to the Lewis Wetzel Hunting Area or to nearby Sistersville on State 2, an historic oil-boom town that hosts the annual Oil and Gas Festival in September. The Wells Inn, with guest rooms and dining, has been restored in the Victorian manner.

Twelve miles from Williamstown is Parkersburg, where the little Kanawha River joins the Ohio. At one time Parkersburg prospered from a rush for black gold in the form of oil along the Little Kanawha and Hughes rivers. But that didn't last long and Parkersburg has never been the same since. Perhaps the most fascinating thing about Parkersburg is Blennerhasset Island, open to sightseers, two miles south in the Ohio River. The 500-acre island was a wilderness paradise when Harmann Blennerhasset and Aaron Burr laid plans for establishing an empire in the Southwest. At Parkersburg's City Park visit Centennial Cabin, built in 1804. The cottage houses pioneer displays. Interesting collections can be seen at the Parkersburg Art Center, located in the former Despard home that dates from the 1870s.

Take a side trip from here to either Volcano, a former regional oil capital (on US 50), or to North Bend State Park near Cairo. At Ravenswood, farther south, is one of the world's largest aluminum plants. This town was once a part of George Washington's western holdings.

Below is Ripley, a town long noted for its Independence Day celebration. The annual Mountain State Art and Craft Fair is held at nearby Cedar Lakes. It is the oldest and largest festival in the state. Visitors are greeted by country music, the smell of good cooking and displays of thousands of handcrafted items for sale. Numerous demonstrations and exhibits: glassblowing, blacksmithing and bee handling. There are two covered bridges near Ripley, one at Left Fork Sandy Creek near Sandyville, the other at Staats Mill on Tug Fork.

To the west is Point Pleasant, where the Kanawha joins the Ohio. Tu-Endie-Wei (Indian for "where two rivers meet") Park commemorates the battle between Cornstalk and General Lewis, fought in 1774 near the park's monument. The monument itself is the first hewn-log house built in Mason County (1796), and was used by the pioneers as a tavern, church and community center. Anne Bailey, the "White Squaw of the Kanawha," a pioneer heroine and border scout, is buried nearby. Excellent duck hunting is found in the Point Pleasant area. Continuing south, Chief Cornstalk Public Hunting Area is off State 2 between Arlee and Southside.

Kenova is at the lowest point in the Ohio Valley, at the western tip of the state. The Big Sandy River joins the Ohio here, where West Virginia, Ohio and Kentucky meet. For many decades Kenova has been a rail town, a center for coal shipment into neighboring Ohio. Pass through Kenova's twin city of Ceredo, another center for handmade glass. Kenova and Ceredo are hosts for the festivities of the Virginia Point days in July.

This concludes our tour of the Ohio River Valley. From here the visitor may go on to Huntington and Charleston or cross the border into Ohio or Kentucky.

PRACTICAL INFORMATION FOR WEST VIRGINIA

 WEST VIRGINIA FACTS AND FIGURES. The state takes its name from Virginia, of which it was a part until the Civil War, when West Virginians sided with the North and broke away from the mother state. It was the 35th state to enter the Union, joining on June 20, 1863. Its nicknames are *Mountain State* and *Panhandle State.* The state flower is the *Rhododendron maximum* (big laurel); tree, sugar maple; bird, the cardinal; animal, the black bear. The state motto is *Montani Semper Liberi* ("Mountaineers are always free").

Charleston is the state capital. By the most recent figures the state population is 1,860,000 (1980 Census), the area is 24,283 square miles. The average altitude is 1,500 feet, higher than any other state east of the Mississippi. The Allegheny Mountains, part of the Appalachian chain, stretch the length of the state and are among the oldest in the world. This is the most mountainous state in the East and its landscape is deeply folded where swift rivers have cut valleys and canyons between the hills. The climate is moderate—not too cold in winter, not too hot in summer—but this is the rainiest of the Middle Atlantic states.

 HOW TO GET AROUND. *By car:* Wheeling, in the northern panhandle, is on I–70 between Washington, Pennsylvania and Martins Ferry, Ohio. I–79 runs north-south from Pittsburgh through Morgantown and Clarksburg, with traffic flowing into I–64 and I–77 at Charleston. I–64 carries traffic east-west from Huntington to White Sulphur Springs (portions are not yet completed). I–77 carries traffic from Parkersburg southeast through East Mountain tunnel at Bluefield. From Charleston to Princeton for the present it is incorporated into the West Virginia Turnpike. The southern part of the state is accessible from the West Virginia Turnpike running between Bluefield and Charleston. I–81 will take you to Martinsburg in the eastern panhandle.

By air: There are regularly scheduled flights to Charleston, Morgantown, Elkins, White Sulphur Springs, Beckley, Princeton, Huntington, and Parkersburg. Piedmont and U.S.Air are the carriers.

By bus: Trailways, Greyhound, Black and White, and *Short Way* are the major carriers in West Virginia. Charleston and Huntington are the busiest depots.

By train: Amtrak has service to Charleston, Huntington, Harpers Ferry, White Sulphur Springs, Clarksburg, Martinsburg and Cumberland, Maryland, on the border of West Virginia's eastern panhandle.

 TOURIST INFORMATION. For maps, calendars of events, or any questions you might have write Communications Div., Governor's Office of Economic & Community Development, State Capitol, Charlestown, WV 25305. The phone number is (304) 348–0400.

 SEASONAL EVENTS. *January. Rock & Mineral Show* at the Children's Museum and Planetarium in Charleston. Contact the Museum for dates.

March. The Tucker County Alpine Festival is held at Canaan Valley State Park in Davis on the first weekend of the month.

April. The first week in April has the *Petersburg White Water Weekend* for canoeists. *House and Garden Tours* at Harpers Ferry, Martinsburg, Charles Town and Shepherdstown. At the end of the month is the *Webster County Nature Tour* in Webster Springs.

May. On the second weekend of the month is the *Wildflower Pilgrimage* at Blackwater Falls State Park in Davis. Later in the month is the *West Virginia State Championship Horse Show* in Huntington.

June. The Mountain Heritage Arts & Crafts Festival is held in Harpers Ferry early in the month. Sutton Lake has a *Regatta* in the second week of June. *The State Folk Festival* at Glenville is also in the second week. *The Pearl Buck Celebration* is in Hillsboro in the third week.

July. Fayetteville, Wellsburg and South Charleston have *Fourth of July* celebrations. The *Mountain State Arts and Crafts Fair* is held around the 4th of July at Bluefield.

August. In the third week of the month is the *State Fair* at Lewisburg. The *John Henry Blues and Gospel Festival* is held on Labor Day weekend in Beckley.

September. The *Governor's Food and Agriculture Exhibition* is during the second week in Charleston. *Buckwheat Festival* is on the last weekend of the month in Kingwood.

October. The *Mountain State Forest Festival* is held in Elkins the first full weekend in October; it commemorates the more than 11 million acres of forest land in the state. The *Chrysanthemum Show* goes on all month at the greenhouses in Oglebay Park in Wheeling. There are agricultural festivals during the second week at Spencer, Thornton and Richwood.

November. Charleston has the *Annual Drawing and Graphics Exhibit* and Welch has a *Veterans Day Celebration.*

December. Harpers Ferry has an *Old Fashioned Christmas* during the first week. In the second week Parkersburg has a *Christmas Festival of the Arts* and Wheeling has a *Christmas Greens Workshop* at Olgebay Park.

For exact dates of these and other events contact the Governor's Office of Economic and Community Development, State Capitol, Charleston, 25305.

 NATIONAL FORESTS. Two national forests lie within the boundaries of West Virginia. The 805,726-acre *Monongahela National Forest* embraces the backbone of the Allegheny Mountains. The town of Elkins serves as headquarters, and one entrance to the forest is east of that town on US 33.

George Washington National Forest, covering approximately a million acres of woodland, spills over from Virginia into Hampshire and Hardy counties in northeastern West Virginia.

WEST VIRGINIA 583

Jefferson National Forest spills over from Virginia into the western part of Monroe County. The national forests offer facilities for swimming, camping (tent and trailer), picnicking, hiking, hunting and fishing. Mountain climbing is offered at some areas. Special national forest hunting and fishing licenses are required. These may be purchased at the office of any County Clerk in West Virginia.

Campfire permits are required for fires built anywhere except in grates provided at developed areas. These permits can be secured from District Rangers.

Provided at developed recreation areas are: fuel wood, tables, garbage cans and toilets. No cabins, electricity or showers. Limit of stay if area is crowded is one week, but two-week stay is usually possible. No hunting in recreation areas. Boating without motors allowed on lakes, but no rental boats are available.

 STATE PARKS. Accommodations for visitors include lodges at some parks and deluxe, standard, economy and rustic cabins. All the cabins have refrigerators and stoves but "rustic" cabins do not have running water. Deluxe cabins have heat, others have fireplaces. Reservations for all must be made in advance. For lodges, write directly to lodge offices. For cabins, write to *Division of Parks and Recreation* of the West Virginia Natural Resources Department in Charleston. You can call toll free from Indiana, Ohio, Kentucky, Pennsylvania, western New York, Maryland, Virginia, New Jersey, Delaware, North Carolina, South Carolina, and Washington, D.C.; the number is 1–800–624–8632. West Virginia residents call 1–800–642–9058.

 STATE FORESTS. West Virginia has nine state forests. All offer scenic views, hunting and fishing. Four forests have cabins: *Cabwaylingo,* near Dunlow, Rt. 152, 13 standard; *Greenbrier,* near White Sulphur Springs, 12 standard; *Kumbrabow,* near Webster Springs, 5 rustic; *Seneca,* near Dunmore, 7 rustic. Tent and trailer camping is permitted at all except *Calvin W. Price,* which adjoins *Watago State Park.* Winter sports (ice skating and skiing) are offered at *Coopers Rock,* near Morgantown. Visitors may rent horses near *Greenbrier. Camp Creek* has the best stocked trout stream in its area, near Princeton. Pre-Revolutionary ruins of iron furnaces and a powder mill may be seen at *Coopers Rock.* Featured at *Kanawha* are outstanding wildflower exhibitions in backwoods atmosphere, and many migratory birds may be seen. *Panther* is rich in legends of the panthers which roamed this forest 135 years ago, and it is said their howls still echo with the wind.

 CAMPING OUT. Note: Camping season in state parks and forests runs from late April to late fall and campsites are rented on a first-come first-serve basis. Pets on a leash are allowed.

Trailers permitted. Approved drinking water and sanitary facilities are provided in all standard and rustic campgrounds. Picnic tables and fireplaces at each campsite. Several areas have washhouses and laundry facilities. Firearms, air rifles, bow and arrows, explosives and fireworks are prohibited in state campgrounds, except in public hunting areas in season.

U.S. Corps of Engineers campsites on Ohio River near Wheeling are available but user must purchase permit.

For additional information, contact the *Office of Economic and Community Development,* State Capitol Bldg., Charleston, W. Va. A detailed directory is published annually.

584   **WEST VIRGINIA**

 FARM VACATIONS AND GUEST RANCHES. The State of West Virginia Farm Vacation Committee lists farms that take in boarders. The farms are privately operated but are inspected by the state. Among them are:

Potomac Ridge Farm in Harpers Ferry. A 130-acre farm with livestock, orchards and gardens. Canoes and boats are available.

Keister Summit, Upper Tract. 12 mi. north of Franklin. 350 acres along the Monogahela National Forest. Open year round with fishing (ice fishing in the winter), swimming, riding and hiking.

Green Valley Farms Rt. 259 at Lost City. This general farm has both rooms and cottages available. Hunters and fishermen are welcome. Riding, pond swimming and boats on Lost River nearby. Open for guests Easter through New Year's.

For a complete list write for the *West Virginia Farm Vacations* booklet at the West Virginia Department of Agriculture, Charleston 25305.

  MUSEUMS AND GALLERIES. The *Mountain State Natural and Historical Museum* in Davis has exhibits of West Virginia history, crafts and animal life. Open daily year round.

Pearl S. Buck's birthplace, in Hillsboro, has been renovated and contains many of the original furnishings from when the famous author was born. In Terra Alta, the *American Museum* has replica of 19th-century buildings and local people are the guides. Open July through October.

The Oglebay Institute Art Gallery, in Oglebay Park, Wheeling, has art exhibits all year long, also tours, lectures and film programs.

Sunrise, at 746 Myrtle Rd., Charleston, is a 16-acre estate with two mansions that provide facilities for the *Sunrise Garden Center,* the *Charleston Art Gallery* and the *Children's Museum and Planetarium.*

 GARDENS. Bluefield. *Keesling Gardens.* Thick with rhododendron, azaleas and related flowering shrubs.

Wheeling. *Oglebay Park.* Alene Kraft Memorial Garden Center. Headquarters of Wheeling Garden Club and 34 affiliated garden clubs. Full-time horticulturist.

Cranberry Glades. Arctic tundra, moss, orchids and cranberries. Rare plants and flowers.

Huntington Rose Gardens in Ritter Park, Huntington.

Municipal Parks. Wheeling. *Oglebay Park.* Over 1,000 acres. On State Route 88, two miles north of intersection of US 40. Museums, outdoor theater, garden center, pool, golf course, horseback riding, zoo, restaurant and lodge (both open year around). Cabins, 10 deluxe, 19 standard and 3 dormitory type for larger groups. Boating, dancing, fishing, hay and sleigh rides, hiking, ice skating, tennis, nature center, children's center. Noted as one of outstanding municipal parks in nation. Admission to park free. Fees vary to various activities.

 MUSIC. Marshall University in Huntington has the *Marshall Artists Series* of concerts and lectures, year round.

The *John Henry Blues and Gospel Festival* is held on Labor Day in Beckley.

The *West Virginia State Folk Festival* has authentic mountain music at Glenville in late July. Along the same lines is the *Mountain Music Festival* in Marlinton in late July.

Charleston and Parkersburg present a variety of musical events throughout the year. Contact the Chamber of Commerce in Charleston or the Travel Development Division at the State Capitol in the same city for details.

STAGE AND REVUES. Beckley. *Honey in the Rock*, and *Hatfields & McCoys*, Grandview State Park theater. Late June–last Sunday before Labor Day, nightly except Monday. Reservations: Box 1205, Beckley.

Wheeling. *Summer Entertainment Series*. Oglebay Park. June thru August; outdoor theater. *Jamboree U.S.A.* Country music every Saturday night in the Capitol Music Hall.

Hurricane. *Mountaineer Dinner Theatre*. Open year-round. Light comedy or musical preceded by a buffet meal. After the performance the cast mingles with the audience.

DRINKING LAWS. All liquor stores in West Virginia are state-owned. The minimum legal drinking age is 18. Liquor is sold by the drink in private clubs. Many hotels, motels, resorts and restaurants offer short-term club memberships enabling guests to order mixed drinks.

SUMMER SPORTS. *Boating.* Facilities available at many state parks.

Diving. Bakerton Quarries, Baker; Stoney River Dam, Grant County; Cheat Lake, 6 mi. NE of Morgantown; Quarry Run near Mt Chateau; Bull Run, Masontown; Monongahela River near Morgantown; Tygart Lake, Tygart Lake State Park; New River, Peterstown; Sutton Lake, Sutton; and Summersville Lake, Summersville.

Fishing is statewide. Trout, black bass, muskie, catfish, other species year round. Frogs mid-June–July. Ice fishing in Feb. in eastern panhandle.

Golf. Five 18-hole golf courses at the *Greenbrier* in White Sulphur Springs (complete listing available).

Horseback Riding. Babcock, Blackwater Falls, Cacapon, Lost River, Mont Chateau, Pipestem and Watoga State Parks. Oglebay Park, Wheeling.

Tournament Riding. Gear at Moorefield and Petersburg in August, at Elkins in October. Riders complete both to crown their ladies "queen" and for trophies.

Mountain Climbing. Seneca Rocks near mouth of the Seneca on US 33.

White Water Rafting. A variety of trips for novices and experienced rafters on the New and Gauley Rivers. Write to Travel–GOECD, State Capitol, Charleston, WV 25305.

WINTER SPORTS. Ice-skating at Blackwater Falls State Park, Coopers Rock State Forest, Wheeling Municipal Park, Pipestem State Park.

Skiing at Chestnut Ridge, Morgantown; Canaan Valley State Park, Davis; Oglebay Park, Wheeling; Snowshoe, Slatyfork; Alpine Lake, Terra Alta.

Official *toboggan* runs at Blackwater Falls State Park and Wheeling's Oglebay Park, where there is also *sleigh riding*.

Trapping and Hunting. Mid-Sept. through Feb. Statewide. Small game, fowl. Bow and arrow season for deer, bear and turkey. Many farms board out-of-state hunters.

SPECTATOR SPORTS. *Basketball.* All winter at West Virginia University, Morgantown; Marshall; Huntington.

Hydroplane racing at Hinton on Bluestone Lake.

Football. Fall weekends at West Virginia University, Morgantown.

Horseracing. Thoroughbreds at Charles Town Race Course 1 mi. E. of Charles Town on US 340—¾-mi. track. Nights; alternating racing dates at Shenandoah

Downs, Charles Town; Waterford Park's mile track at Chester. Wheeling Downs, Wheeling, has Greyhound dog races

Tennis. Pro/Am Tournament, Snowshoe Resort, Slatyfork. Mar.

Winter Carnival & Cross Country Ski Race, Morgantown, Feb.; *NASTAR Giant Slalom Ski Race, WV Pro Ski Race,* Snowshoe Resort, Slatyfork, Feb.

 WHAT TO DO WITH THE CHILDREN. Huntington. *Camden Park.* US 60 West. Wild animal zoo. Miniature golf, 18 amusement rides. Roller skating, penny arcade. Cafeteria. Free parking.

Charleston. *Sunrise,* 746 Myrtle Rd., a 60-year-old mansion, once a governor's residence. Contains art gallery, children's museum. Exhibits, live animals, displays, class instruction and planetarium.

Bluefield. *The Ridge Runner Railroad.* Miniature replica of an 1863 steam locomotive and three colorful coaches. Station modeled after an 1890 railroad depot. Cross Virginia state line. Three quarters of a mile run.

Cass. Ride the old steam locomotive to the top of 4,800-foot Bald Knob for a spectacular view. In the town of Cass there is a *Civil War Museum,* the *Cass Country Store* and the horse-drawn *Cass Stagecoach Line.* In nearby Green Bank is the *National Radio Observatory,* with tours of the installation.

French Creek. *French Creek Game Farm* has buffalo, peacocks, rattlesnakes and many more animals.

 HOTELS AND MOTELS in West Virginia run the full scale from elegant resorts to small, family-owned establishments. Price categories in this area, for double occupancy, will average: *DeLuxe,* $100 and up (MAP); *Expensive,* $36–$46, *Moderate,* $24–$35; *Inexpensive,* under $18.

Beckley

Ramada Inn. *Expensive.* 1940 Harper Rd. Pool, color TV. Dining room, private club. Heated pool, café, private club, entertainment.

Holiday Inn. *Moderate to Expensive.* 1924 Harper Rd. Coin laundry, pool. Pets. Dining room. Private club.

Best Western Motor Lodge. *Moderate.* 1939 Harper Rd. Restaurant nearby.

Honey-In-The-Rock. *Moderate.* 2315 S. Faxette. Pool, café.

Twin Falls Lodge. *Moderate.* 25 miles SW; Twin Falls State Park; rooms and cottages with kitchens; café; recreation facilities.

Charles House. *Inexpensive.* 233 S. Heber St. Color TV. Pets. Restaurant nearby

Berkeley Springs

Cacapon Lodge. *Moderate.* In Cacapon State Park. Fishing, golf, tennis, hiking, many outdoor activities.

Country Inn. *Inexpensive.* 207 S. Washington St. Café, private club. Color TV, weekend entertainment. Sundries, drugstore.

Park Haven Motor Lodge. *Inexpensive.* 1/4 mi. N. Cacapon State Park. Café nearby. TV, free coffee, in-room steam baths. Lawn games, picnic tables.

WEST VIRGINIA

Bluefield

Holiday Inn. *Moderate to Expensive.* 3175 E. Cumberland Rd. Heated pool, wading pool, restaurant, private club; entertainment; in-room movies.

Brier-Red Carpet Inn. *Moderate to Expensive.* 3206 E. Cumberland. Rd. Pool, café, room service, private club.

Econo-Travel Motel. *Inexpensive.* 3400 Cumberland Rd. Café nearby, pay TV.

Charleston

Holiday Inn Charleston (Charleston House). *Expensive.* 600 Kanawha Blvd. E. Pool, café, private club, entertainment.

Holiday Inn Elk River. *Expensive.* Kanawha Blvd. at Elk River. Pool, restaurant.

Holiday Inn Heart-O-Town. *Expensive.* Broad and Washington Sts.; heated pool, sauna, color TV. Dining room, lounge, live entertainment.

Ramada Inn. *Expensive.* I-64 exit 56/2nd Ave. & B Sts. Free in-room movies, heated pool. Dining room, cocktails, live entertainment.

Daniel Boone Hotel. *Moderate.* Downtown hotel. Capitol and Washington Streets. Wide choice of accommodations and rates; restaurant; coffee shop.

El Rancho Inn. *Moderate.* 2843 MacCorkle Ave. SW. Color TV, playground, free coffee. Restaurant adjacent.

Kanawha City Motor Lodge. *Moderate.* 3103 MacCorkle Ave. S.E.; free continental breakfast; free coffee.

Riviera. *Moderate.* 3313 Kanawha Blvd. E. Café adjoining.

Kanawha Terrace. *Inexpensive.* 6704 MacCorkle Ave. Pool, playground, picnic tables, grill.

Red Roof Inn. *Inexpensive.* 18 miles west on State 34, jct. I-64, in Putnam Village Shopping Center (Hurricane, WV). Café adjoining, free coffee.

Charles Town

Towne House Motor Lodge. *Moderate.* E. Washington St. Pool, café, private club. Tennis, picnic tables. In-room steam baths, color TV. Pets.

Clarksburg

Holiday Inn. *Moderate to Expensive.* 100 Lodgeville Rd., Bridgeport, WV. Pool, restaurant, entertainment.

Sheraton. *Moderate to Expensive.* 151 W. Main St. Coffee shop, restaurant, lounge. Outdoor heated pool. Pets.

Town House. *Inexpensive to Moderate.* 822 West Main St. Café across street; private club.

Elkins

Elkins Motor Lodge. *Inexpensive to Moderate.* Harrison Ave. Playground, café, private club.

Iron Horse. *Inexpensive.* Sycamore St. Café near; free coffee in rooms.

Four Seasons. *Inexpensive.* 1091 Harrison Ave. Café near; coffee in rooms.

Fairmont

Holiday Inn. *Expensive.* I-79 and Old Grafton Rd. Restaurant, pool, room service, private club. Live entertainment.

Fairmont Motor Lodge. *Inexpensive.* 1117 Fairmont Ave. at Laurel Dr. 24-hour restaurant nearby. Free coffee in lobby. Picnic tables, pool.

Franklin

Thompson's. *Inexpensive.* Jct. 33 W, 220 N. Café, playground.

Gauley Bridge

Hawks Nest Lodge. *Moderate.* Hawks Nest State Park, 1 mi. W. on US 60 tram to marina; pool, tennis, café. Color TV.

Glen Ferris Inn. *Moderate.* Overlooks Kanawha Falls. Reconstructed old inn. Café.

Grafton

Best Western Crislip Motor Lodge. *Moderate.* US 50 W, jct. 119. Café nearby; private club. Color TV, pool. Coffee in rooms.

Tygart Lake State Park Lodge. *Moderate.* 2 mi. S. off US 119, 250. Open Apr.-Oct. Cabins and tent sites. Playground, picnic spots. Lake offers fine fishing, scuba diving, swimming, boating. Café.

Hinton

Pipestem Lodge. *Moderate.* 10 mi. SW on State 20, then 3 mi. NW of entrance to Pipestem State Park. Large resort. Rooms and cottages. Open May to Oct. Two pools, sauna, playground, café, snack bar. Fishing, social program.

Coast to Coast. *Inexpensive.* 1 mi. S. on WV 3, 20. Heated pool, fishing dock, restaurant nearby. Color TV, pets.

Sandman. *Inexpensive.* 2 mi. S. on WV 3, 20. Beautiful view; fishing from back porch; cafe near; playground. Free coffee.

Huntington

Holiday Inn East. *Expensive.* 3325 US 60E. Dining room, lounge and supper club; live entertainment. Color TV, pool. Pets.

Best Western Southern Hills Motor Inn. *Moderate.* 4115 First Ave., Nitro, WV. Dining room, some pets. Sr. citizen rates.

Uptowner Inn. *Moderate.* 1415 4th Ave. Color TV, pool, wading pool. Dining room, private club, weekend dancing, entertainment.

Lewisburg

Fort Savannah Inn. *Moderate.* 204 N. Jefferson St. Café; annex in The Old Stone House, a restored inn built in the 1700s. Color TV, entertainment.

General Lewis Inn. *Moderate.* 301 E. Washington St. Picturesque inn, part of which dates back to the 1700's. Playground, fine, old-fashioned restaurant.

Old Colony Inn. *Moderate.* US 219. Color TV, free Continental breakfast.

Sunset Terrace. *Inexpensive to Moderate.* Free coffee. No café.

Marlinton

Marlinton Motor Inn. *Moderate.* 3½ mi. N. on 219. Great view of the mountains; café; private club. Color TV, free in-room coffee. Picnic tables.

Martinsburg

Holiday Inn. *Moderate to Expensive.* WV 9 at I-81. Color TV, pool, in-room steam baths. Dining room, dancing, entertainment.

Motel 81. *Moderate.* 6 mi. N. of I-81, exit 20. Some color TV, pool. Cafe.

Wheatland Motel. *Inexpensive.* 1193 Winchester Ave. Color TV, pool, playground. Restaurant near.

Morgantown

Holiday Inn. *Moderate to Expensive.* 1400 Saratoga Ave. Golf, indoor tennis, pool. Pets. Dining room, lounge, live entertainment.

Lakeview Inn and Country Club. *Moderate to Expensive.* Rt. 6, 7 mi. N. of WV 73. Two pools, poolside service, sauna, restaurant, entertainment; rates lower, Nov.-Mar. Attractive resort on 400 acres also offers golf, tennis, lawn games.

Ramada Inn. *Moderate to Expensive.* 3 mi. S. on 119 at 48 and I-79. Restaurant, private club. Color TV, pool, game room. Pets. Babysitting. Facilities for handicapped.

Parkersburg

Best Western Green Acres. *Moderate.* US 50 and I-77. Heated pool. Restaurant, lounge, coffee shop.

Holiday Inn. *Moderate.* Jct. I-77 and US 50. Restaurant, lounge, live entertainment. Pool, playground.

Uptowner Inn. *Moderate.* 415 7th St. Color TV. Pool, coffee shop, restaurant, private club.

Days Inn. *Inexpensive to Moderate.* I-77 and WV 31. Restaurant, handicapped facilities. Gasoline service.

Princeton

Holiday Inn. *Moderate to Expensive.* Jct. US 460 and WV Turnpike. Restaurant, lounge, live entertainment, dancing. Color TV, pool, wading pool.

Town 'n' Country. *Moderate.* 2 mi. E. on 219, 460, 1/4 mi. W. of I-77 exit #9. Color TV, pool, wading pool. Restaurant next door.

St. Mary's

Best Western St. Marys Motel. *Moderate.* 206 3rd. St. Color TV, pool. Restaurant and lounge nearby.

Sistersville

Wells Inn. *Moderate.* 316 Charles St. The décor is Victorian in this antique-decorated spot, an inn since 1895. Café, private club.

Sutton

Laurel Court. *Moderate.* 3 mi. N. on State 4. A beautiful setting with a combination of motel rooms and kitchen chalets. Fine family spot with playground and restaurant.

Weirton

Holiday Inn. *Moderate to Expensive.* 350 Three Springs Dr. Dining room, lounge, live entertainment. Pool. Pets.

Wheeling

Holiday Inn. *Moderate to Expensive.* I-70 at jct. 0 214, St. Clairsville, O. Pool, café, private club. Live entertainment, free HBO movies.

Holiday Inn-East. *Moderate to Expensive.* 9 mi. E. at I-70 exit 11. Pool, café, private club, entertainment, dancing. Color TV.

Wilson Lodge. *Moderate to Expensive.* Oglebay Park on State 88. Large complex of lodge, chalets, and cabanas. Wooded setting. Restaurant, playground, large pool, cocktails. Reservations required. Beautiful site in 1500-acre recreational park with many outdoor activities.

Quality Inn. *Moderate.* 2501 National Rd., 4 mi. E. at I-70 exit 5. Heated pool. Restaurants nearby.

White Sulphur Springs

Greenbrier. *Deluxe.* A luxurious resort on 6,500 acres in a magnificent setting. Hotel and cottages. Two heated pools, mineral baths, massage, golf, tennis, riding and all amenities. Social program, entertainment.

Best Western Old White. *Moderate.* 865 E. Main St. Color TV, pool. Restaurant, lounge adjacent. Open late Feb.–late Dec.

Colonial Court. *Moderate.* 1 Mi. E. on U.S. 60. Pool, picnic tables, grills. Restaurant nearby. Open mid-March to mid-Nov.

 DINING OUT in West Virginia might mean an opportunity to enjoy country-style ham (salt or sugar-cured), Southern specialties like grits or hush puppies, or such staples as steak, seafood, or fried chicken. Décor ranges from very simple in the establishments found along the highways to the elaborate dining rooms of the posh resorts.

Restaurant price categories are: *Expensive,* over $15; *Moderate,* $6–$14; *Inexpensive,* under $5. These prices are for appetizer or soup, entrée and dessert. Not included are drinks, tax and tips. In order to serve liquor in West Virginia a restaurant must have a club license. Restaurants listed here which have club licenses are so indicated.

Berkeley Springs

Country Inn. *Moderate.* 207 S. Washington St. Roast turkey, country ham, assorted seafood specialties. Garden dining in summer. Adjoins nation's oldest health spa (1748).

Charleston

Sterling Restaurant. *Expensive.* 505 Capital St. Steaks, chicken featured; open 24 hrs.; club adjacent.

The Corner Stone. *Inexpensive to Moderate.* 3103 MacCorkle Ave. SE (Kanawha City Motor Lodge). Greek-American menu. Own baking. Moussaka, grape leaf rolls are specialties.

Smiley's. 6210 MacCorkle Ave. (St. Albans, WV, Smiley's Motor Lodge.) *Moderate.* Also has private club.

Harper's Ferry

Hilltop House. *Moderate.* Retreat of Presidents. Features Southern fried chicken, baked ham, stuffed flounder.

Iron Horse Inn. *Moderate.* Potomac St. Built in 1799. Table-laden country buffets, huge sandwiches, baked Virginia ham.

Hinton

Riverside Inn. *Moderate to Expensive.* Charming colonial atmosphere. Roast goose, fruit-stuffed duckling, game are specialties. Children's plates.

Huntington

French Tavern. *Moderate.* 1925 Adams Ave. Steak, seafood, prime ribs. Beer served with dinner. Membership club.

Rebels and Redcoats Tavern. *Moderate.* 626 5th St. W. Bar. Gourmet menu. Extensive wine list.

Bailey's Cafeteria. *Inexpensive.* 410 9 St. Home cooking, luscious fresh vegetables, good selection of entrees.

Lewisburg

General Lewis Dining Room. *Inexpensive to Moderate.* General Lewis Inn, 301 E. Washington St. Fried chicken, country ham, home baking. Inn adjacent.

Parkersburg

Point of View. *Expensive.* Riverhill Rd. Membership club. Steak, seafood.

Seddon's. *Moderate.* Grand Central Mall. Adjacent to Kona Kai Club where liquor is served with Polynesian food at higher prices.

Wilmar Cafeteria. *Inexpensive.* 8th and Market Sts. Home baking.

Summerville

Country Road Inn. *Expensive.* 8 mi. on State 39. Reservation required. Italian menu—own pasta; wine, quaint house.

Wheeling

Eric's Steak House. *Moderate.* Waddle Run Rd. Continental, American menu. Wed. smorgasbord. Own baking. Children's plates.

Ernie's Esquire. *Moderate to Expensive.* On State 88S. Greek specialties and hot coquilles. Liquor served. Reservations advised.

White Sulphur Springs

The Greenbrier. *Expensive.* Superb Continental, American cuisine in elegant formal atmosphere. Impressive wine list. Strict evening dress code.

DELAWARE

A Side Trip to the Beaches and More

BY
DAVID S. HUGG

David S. Hugg is sports editor of the Delaware Coast Press *and former Tourism Promotion Director for the State of Delaware.*

Enter Delaware via the Delaware Memorial Bridge after leaving the New Jersey Turnpike. Or enter via I-95 from Philadelphia, which is just 28 miles north of Wilmington. The state's largest city, Wilmington, was settled in 1638 by Swedes, and was the first permanent white settlement in the Delaware Valley. In 1938, the Swedish people presented Delaware with a stark, bold monument to commemorate the landing. Executed by Carl Milles, this monument stands in Fort Christina State Park, at the foot of Seventh Street.

Nearby is Hendrickson House, built of logs in 1690. Another memorial of colonizing Swedes is Old Swedes Church, built in 1698. Here the early Swedish and Dutch settlers attended services. Also of interest is the old Brandywine Academy, just east of the Market Street intersection with US 202, where the typical schoolroom of yesteryear can be found. The Holy Trinity (Old Swedes) Church, now a museum, has artifacts of the 1638 Swedish colonizers. The church was consecrated in 1699 and has the oldest pulpit in the country.

Before leaving the city, visitors usually pause to see the Old Town Hall (1798) and Willingtown Square, a new historic complex, in the down-town mall area. The newly-restored Grand Opera House, also part of the

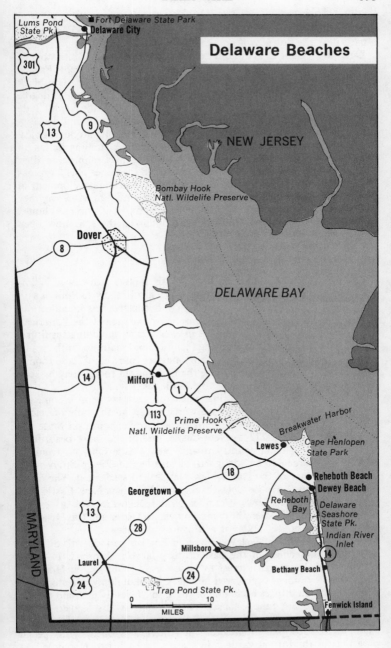

Delaware Beaches

mall, is one of the finest such buildings in the country, and the scene of many cultural activities. Wilmington is also proud of its zoo, located in a park near the downtown area and open year-round.

Delaware's giant E. I. duPont de Nemours & Co. is next. Its story of fame and wealth began in 1802 when Eleuthère Irenee du Pont, French immigrant, built a powder factory on Brandywine Creek. The black powder mill grew, and with its growth came the state's advanced degree of industrialism. The Hagley Museum, one mile north of the city off State 141, on the site of the 1802 mill, traces Delaware's industrial development through the days of water power. Its main exhibit, a topographical model of Brandywine Valley, has a miniature creek running its length to turn tiny wheels of many model mills: grist, lumber, tanning, textiles, and others. The museum also houses actual old machines plus dioramas and exhibits depicting early American history and the development of du Pont powder manufacturing. Highlight of the museum visit is a jitney ride along the Brandywine. Eleutherian Mills, du Pont's original home, furnished as it was when the last du Pont lived there, is now open year-round.

Winterthur Museum

The Winterthur Museum, on State 52, six miles northwest of Wilmington in Winterthur, the former home of Henry Francis du Pont, is said to be the largest and richest assemblage of decorative arts in collection. A gift to the state from the du Ponts, its rooms depict the American home from 1640 to 1840, complete in every detail including furniture, rugs, draperies, bric-a-brac, lighting facilities, and pictures. In the south wing, for a small admission fee visitors may see fourteen of these rooms. The balance of the museum's more than a hundred rooms may be seen by appointment. See "Museums and Galleries."

Most spectacular in the spring when the azaleas are in bloom, the sixty-acre Winterthur Gardens are worth a visit at any time of year.

Return the few miles to Wilmington and travel south on State 13, turning left on State 273 to New Castle, one of the more beautifully preserved old Colonial country towns. New Castle fans out from its central and large Green, designed by one-legged Pieter Stuyvesant, colonial governor of the Dutch New Netherland settlement. The city's Old State (Court) House dates back to 1732, when New Castle was capital of the Three Lower-Counties-on-the-Delaware. The Assembly met here until 1777, when the capital moved to Dover and this structure became a courthouse. Today it is a historical museum.

The 18th century in Delaware was an English period, with Swedish and Dutch influences of the past century largely absorbed. For this reason, there is special interest in New Castle's Old Dutch House, a 17th-century residence preserved intact. A small building of a story and a half, its design utilizes each inch of space so efficiently it is said to give a lesson to modern functionalists. This building is also said to be the state's oldest home. The George Read House, considered one of the finest examples of Georgian architecture in America, is open, with special programs in the formal gardens in season, and Christmas candlelight tours. In 1982, New Castle will celebrate the 300th anniversary of the landing of William Penn, before he went on to Philadelphia.

Driving west from New Castle on State 273, turn left at Christiana on the Old Baltimore Pike to Cooch's Bridge. The original bridge over Christina Creek was demolished long ago, yet a monument stands at today's new bridge, keeping the story of the site's events ever fresh. In 1760 Thomas Cooch built Cooch House, a building later used by the British General Cornwallis for planning battles. In 1777, Delaware's only Revolutionary War battle took place near the town. In September, 1777, after disembarkation at Head of Elk (now Elkton, Maryland), part of Lord William Howe's Philadelphia-bound British troops came through this part of the country. George Washington, not knowing which route the British would take, posted guards along all likely roads. The outpost at Cooch's Bridge attacked advance British guards, whose main body took another route. In the ensuing skirmish, the American flag first appeared in battle.

From Cooch's Bridge, travel southeast on State 72 to Delaware City, eastern terminus of the Chesapeake and Delaware Canal. This nineteen-mile waterway, constructed 1824–29, still carries oceangoing traffic between Philadelphia and Baltimore.

Boat rides are operated from the end of May to October, to nearby Fort Delaware on Pea Patch Island in the Delaware River. This old-timer river fortress was the largest Federal prison during the Civil War. Today it is a part of a state park.

Leaving Delaware City, we travel seven miles south on State 9, then cutting back to US 13 and Odessa. Visit three excellent examples of Colonial buildings: the David Wilson Mansion, the Corbit-Sharp House and the John Janvier stables. Numerous privately owned 18th- and 19th-century homes in Odessa are located on High Street or Main Street.

First European Colony

Lewes is the site of Delaware's first European colony in 1631. This town is closely associated with the piloting of boats up the Chesapeake Bay. Generations of Lewes' men have followed this occupation and their presence has given the town much of its character. In former days pilots worked as individuals, unsupervised and unorganized. When a ship stopped at the Breakwater to find a pilot, the job went to the first man who reached the vessel. Lewes' captains raced and sometimes fought each other to guide a ship up the Delaware. This colorful tradition lives no longer; today's pilots have an association with rules and laws to govern the arduous profession.

One of the city's most famous streets fronts the Lewes-Rehoboth Canal and shows the influence of these men in its name: Pilot Town Road. It is interesting to note the old homes along this road and to consider the periods of time represented by their many styles of architecture. Plan at least an hour to stroll through the Lewes Historic Complex and the Lightship Overfalls.

Lewes' showplace is the Zwaanendael Museum, a replica of Holland's Hoorn Town Hall, built in 1931 to commemorate the three hundredth anniversary of Dutch colonists landing from Hoorn. Prim, medieval, and definitely European, it contrasts delightfully with American structures all around it. At Lewes, the Lewes-Cape May Ferry can be taken for a marvelous seventy-minute ride to Cape May, N.J.

After seeing Zwaanendael, cross the bridge over the canal and drive the short distance to Cape Henlopen State Park, which includes the point where Delaware Bay meets the Atlantic Ocean. Put down a stake at the foot of a dune. Walk awhile and enjoy the area's superb views: the long cape reaching out between waters, with a colorful little village strung along the distant shore, the Breakwater, and the empty Atlantic beach stretching south. When you return, the stake will be engulfed in sand. Entire forests have been covered this way and then uncovered again as the drifting dunes follow nature's whims.

Return to Lewes to pick up State 14 south to Rehoboth Beach, annual choice of sophisticated travelers who enjoy peaceful relaxation far from city night life. They say that Rehoboth means "always room for one more sinner." In Hebrew it does mean "room" or "wide places," and casual Rehoboth offers a visitor, sinner or not, abundant sun, sand, and surf. In Henlopen Acres the pines grow to meet the shoreline and flower gardens are everywhere. Visitors usually enjoy the unpretentious old parts of town.

Lakes and Beaches

On the southern edge of the village lies Silver Lake with its enormous population of Arctic Circle geese and ducks. Wild geese are no rarity on the Delmarva Peninsula; yet at no other place can so many be seen close at hand. Silver Lake's fowl evidently have no fear, for you can walk along the shore within a few feet of them and they pay no attention. From time to time, a flock rises to fly its always-thrilling V-formation, with an infinitude of calls from bird to bird. These sights and sounds are part of Rehoboth's atmosphere.

A short drive south of Rehoboth is Dewey Beach. This resort area stands on land that dwindles to a narrow strip between the ocean and Rehoboth Bay, and its residents can easily walk to either body of water. Rehoboth Bay is salty and huge, but comparatively calm and shallow. The bay is splendid for sailing, boating, and fishing.

On the left side of the road, beyond Dewey Beach, a marker points to "Coin Beach," where visitors may enjoy personal treasure hunts. Here, for over a century, people have found English coins dating from the reign of George III. Several stories relate different versions of a ship, sunk offshore, which carried these pieces. Most of the coins are pennies, and none are of larger denomination. Why a ship carried such quantities of humble coins across the Atlantic remains a puzzle. Your chances of piling up a fortune are better after a northeaster.

At its southern extremity, Rehoboth Bay meets Indian River Bay, which connects with the ocean at Indian River Inlet, a narrow channel with a fast current. The waves along the north side of the inlet are particularly suited for surfboarding. Delaware officials have set aside two hundred yards of beach north of the inlet for exclusive use of surfboarders: Surf City. In this popular area, rubber-suited devotees ride waves and breakers in even the coldest winter weather.

Beyond the inlet is Bethany Beach, a resort area with a small year-round population. Like other Delaware shore areas, it offers sand, sun, and surf with a lack of clutter and an appreciation of nature.

PRACTICAL INFORMATION FOR DELAWARE

DELAWARE FACTS AND FIGURES. Delaware takes its name from Sir Thomas West, Lord de la Warr, Provincial Governor of Virginia. Its nicknames are "The First State" (first to ratify the U.S. Constitution), "Blue Hen State," and "Diamond State." The state flower is the peach blossom; the state tree, the American holly; the state bird, the blue hen chicken. "Liberty and Independence" is the state motto and "Our Delaware" the state song. Dover is the capital. The state's population is 595,225; and its size—96 miles long by 35 across, area 2,057 square miles—makes it 49th among the 50 states, larger only than Rhode Island. The northern part is mildly hilly; below the Chesapeake and Delaware Canal the land flattens out to sea-level in the south, and becomes scenically uninteresting. The climate is moderate, with few extremes.

HOW TO GET THERE. *By car:* I-95 runs from Philadelphia through Wilmington, then southerly to Baltimore and Washington. US 13 runs north-south down the middle of Delaware. State 14 parallels the eastern shore between Slaughter Beach and Selbyville.

By train: Amtrak has service to Wilmington, but not the rest of the state.

By bus: Greyhound has the most complete route in the state. It stops at major towns along US 13. *Trailways* also has service in Delaware.

By boat: The Cape May–Lewes Ferry connects Lewes with the southern terminus of New Jersey's Garden State Parkway. The trip is fifteen miles and takes seventy minutes.

TOURIST INFORMATION. Brochures and literature with answers to questions on Delaware are available through the Delaware State Travel Service, 630 State College Rd., Dover 19901. Travelers in Delaware can also pick up literature at the Old Court House, New Castle; Sykes House, 45 The Green, Dover; the Zwaanendael Museum at Lewes; and from the various Chambers of Commerce. Services for tour groups and bilingual guided tours can also be arranged by contacting the Delaware State Travel Service. Admission free to all state museums.

SEASONAL EVENTS. The four seasons in Delaware provide a panorama of nature's ever-changing colors and moods, providing backdrops for historical and cultural events. Spring unfolds with traditional observances: the opening of the famous Winterthur Gardens, the special tulip display at the Corbit-Sharp House in Odessa, the *Easter Sunrise Service* and *Fashion Promenade* at Rehoboth Beach and *Wilmington Garden Day.* Two important springtime festivals are *A Day in Old New Castle* and *Old Dover Days*—when Delaware's colonial capital and its present one open their homes and gardens to the public, and celebrate the advent of warm weather with colorful ceremonies. At Cape Henlopen State Park, a kite festival is held annually on Good Friday.

Summer is accentuated by beach activity—at Rehoboth Beach, Lewes, Bethany Beach, Fenwick Island and at oceanside state parks. At Lewes, restored homes are opened for public viewing and museums, through special displays, highlight the history that includes the British bombardment during the War of 1812. Up the river, to the north, summer brings launch crossings to Fort Delaware, the island bastion which long served as a principal defense of the Delaware River. The fort was also a Union prison camp during the Civil War. Inland, the Wilmington and Western Railroad's steam engine chugs between Greenbank and Hockessin, hauling visitors to picnic grounds. At Harrington, the annual *Delaware State Fair* provides a week of country fun and entertainment. Sailing, fishing, swimming and just plain sunbathing abound in resort areas. There are special exhibits by the Rehoboth Art League throughout summer months.

Autumn is especially beautiful in the hill country around the Brandywine River. Hagley Museum's Eleutherian Mills, first home of the du Pont family, open year-round, is especially attractive in the fall. The annual *Brandywine Arts Festival* is held in Josephine Gardens at Wilmington in early September. Autumn is a favorite time for antique hunting and for auctions.

As the leaves fall and winter sets in, Christmas festivities abound. Many communities open the Christmas shopping season with parades. The annual *Christmas in Odessa* finds this colonial town decorated with traditional 18th-century Christmas finery, and welcoming visitors to many private homes. A similar program in New Castle is highlighted by public caroling on the Green.

Enjoyable at any time of the year are numerous state-owned historical sites and houses, state recreation areas and parks, and ceremonies and events on public holidays.

 STATE PARKS. Most state parks are open for public use on a year-round basis with limited facilities available from November 1 through March 31. Most parks are open from 8:30 A.M. to one hour after sunset with the following exceptions: Delaware Seashore—sunrise to 11:00 P.M. and Cape Henlopen—sunrise to one hour after sunset.

Fort Delaware State Park. On Pea Patch Island, near Delaware City. A museum houses Civil War memorabilia. Used as a Union prison during the Civil War, the Fort is open Saturdays, Sundays and holidays from May 30 to Oct. 31. Boat transportation from Delaware City.

Delaware Seashore State Park. South of Rehoboth Beach, stretching from Dewey Beach to Fenwick Island. Twelve miles of ocean beach plus calm inland waters spell paradise for the swimmer, surfer, boater or fisherman. There is a bathhouse at the Indian River Inlet section. Year-round camping is available.

Cape Henlopen State Park. This sandy hook of land marks the entrance to Delaware Bay. Nature tours are available for observing the unusual flora and the many varieties of shore birds. Camping sites are also available here east of Lewes.

Trap Pond State Park. Over eight hundred acres of pine surround Trap Pond, ninety acres of deep water ideal for swimming and for small boats. Just west of Trap Pond is Trussum Pond, which contains the northernmost natural stand of cypress in the United States. East of Laurel, State 24.

Killen Pond State Park. Killen Pond is a quiet site for swimming, boating and sailing. The 70-acre pond and surrounding parklands have been left relatively undisturbed. South of Dover, east of US 13.

Brandywine Creek State Park. Rolling meadows and woodlands slope to the Brandywine River. This park offers a nature program in conjunction with Delaware Nature Education Center which is located in the park. Northwest of Wilmington, off State 100.

Lums Pond State Park. This park, with its two-hundred-acre-pond, borders on the Chesapeake and Delaware Canal. It has long been a choice family recreation area in southern New Castle County. Good swimming beach, camping facilities. Open 10 to 6.

Holts Landing State Park. A public launching ramp provides access to Indian River Bay for fishing, sailing, water-skiing and boating.

DELAWARE

MUSEUMS AND GALLERIES. *Henry Francis du Pont Winterthur Museum.* Six miles northwest of Wilmington, State 52. More than 180 period rooms covering the American domestic scene from 1640 to 1840. Gardens open spring through fall. To see main museum (100 rooms) write Reservations Office, Winterthur Museum, Winterthur, De. 19735. Fourteen rooms in south wing open without appointment.

Hagley Museum. Located on the 185-acre site of the first du Pont powder mills on Brandywine Creek, 3 miles north of Wilmington via State Rtes. 52 and 141. Indoor and outdoor exhibits depict the evolution of American industry from the colonial mills of the Brandywine Valley to the 20th-century corporate economy.

Delaware Museum of Natural History. State 52, Greenville. One hundred exhibits including 100,000 sets of birds' eggs, a million sea shells and an international collection of mammals.

Rockwood Museum. Off Washington Street Extension on Shipley Road. Home of descendants of one of city's founders and headquarters of Victorian Society of Delaware. Fine example of Rural Gothic architecture in park-like setting. Administrated by New Castle County. For appointment: (302) 571–7776.

Delaware Art Museum. At 2301 Kentmere Parkway, Wilmington. It houses Samuel and Mary R. Bancroft Collection of English Pre-Raphaelite paintings; American paintings by Howard Pyle, John Sloan and Wyeth family—including an Andrew Wyeth collection. Guided tours, lectures, films, concerts and educational workshops for children and adults.

Old Town Hall. At 512 Market Street, Wilmington. Built 1798, now the Museum of Historical Society of Delaware. Guide service.

Willingtown Square. Complex of six restored houses moved from various locations in city to site on Market Street Mall opposite Old Town Hall. Exhibits, special programs. Administered by Historical Society of Delaware.

Iron Hill Museum Old Baltimore Pike, west of Rte. 896, Newark. Collection of archaeological and geological finds; birds and mammals native to Delaware housed in former one-room school. Nature trail.

Old Court House: New Castle. Delaware's colonial capital and the county seat for many years, now a state museum.

Old Dutch House Museum. New Castle. Built in 17th century (exact date unknown). Maintained as a museum by New Castle Historical Society. Open from April 1 to November 1.

Amstel House Museum. Delaware Street, New Castle. Built about 1730, maintained as a museum by New Castle Historical Society.

Historic Odessa. On US 13, Odessa. Open are the Corbit-Sharp House (1774), Wilson-Warner house (1769), John Janvier Stable (1791), and Brick Hotel (1882) —all fine examples of Delaware Valley architecture. The two houses are fully furnished with antiques. Administered by Winterthur Museum.

Delaware State Museum. Governor's Avenue, Dover. Housed in four buildings with exhibits of many phases of Delaware life. Especially interesting is the Eldridge Reeves Johnson collection of old talking machines and records. (He was founder of Victor Talking Machine Co.)

Island Field Archaeological Museum. Off U.S. 113, near Frederica at South Bowers Beach. Prehistoric Indian cemetery and museum of Indian relics. Excavation still going on. Open March 1–Nov. 30.

Lewes Marine Museum. Front and Bank Streets, Lewes. Known also as Cannonball House (a British cannonball fired during the War of 1812 is lodged in the foundation). Marine exhibits. Open June 15 through Labor Day.

Rehoboth Art League. Henlopen Acres. Exhibits and summer classes. Open daily through summer.

HISTORIC SITES. *Lewes Historic Complex.* At 3rd and Shipcarpenter Streets, Lewes. Thompson Country Store; Rabbit's Ferry House, a small 18th-century farmhouse; Burton-Ingram House, ca. 1800, typical of the architecture in this fishing village; and the Plank House, 1700 or earlier. Also interesting, the Lightship Overfalls. Open June 15 through Labor Day.

Cooch's Bridge. Off State 896, south of Newark. In 1777 this was the scene of the only battle of the Revolutionary War fought in Delaware. Tradition states that here the Stars and Stripes were first flown in land battle.

Old Swedes Church. At 7th Street, Wilmington. Built in 1698, believed to be the oldest Protestant Church still in use in America. Guide service.

Fort Christina. Foot of Seventh Street, Wilmington. Site of first permanent settlement in Delaware, in 1638.

Barratt's Chapel. One mile north of Frederica on US 113. Erected in 1780, known as "The Cradle of Methodism in America." Here the decision to organize the Methodist Episcopal Church was reached in 1784. Interesting Dutch architecture.

Parson Thorne Mansion. Milford. Built around 1740, once the home of the Reverend Parson Thorne, Milford's founder; and, later, famous Delaware statesman John M. Clayton. Open by appointment only: call (302) 422–9593.

Zwaanendael Museum: Lewes. Erected in 1931 to commemorate first settlement in Delaware by Dutch in 1631. Interesting Dutch architecture.

Octagonal School House. On State 9, east of Dover. Built in 1836, this unique octagonal schoolhouse contains a collection of textbooks published from 1800 to 1920 and other artifacts from the early days of the public school system.

John Dickinson Mansion. Off State 113 on Kitts Hummock Road, near Dover. The childhood home of John Dickinson (1732–1808). "Penman of the Revolution." Built in 1740.

Fenwick Island Lighthouse. Near junction of State Rtes. 54 and 14, and state line at Fenwick Island. Adjacent to the base is the first marker on the Delaware-Maryland boundary, a crownstone placed by Provincial surveyors in 1751, twelve years before Mason and Dixon were sent from England to survey the north-south line.

Old Welsh Tract Baptist Church. Welsh Tract Road, west of State 896, Newark. The oldest Primitive Baptist Church Congregation in the United States was begun here in 1701. Present church, constructed in 1746, has mark where a British cannonball went through the building during the Battle of Cooch's Bridge, 1777. Services held on the second Sunday of each month at 11:00 A.M.

Old St. Anne's Episcopal Church. On State 896, Middletown. Graced by one of the state's oldest linden trees, St. Anne's was built about 1768 by the parish founded in 1705.

Legislative Hall. Legislative Avenue, Dover. Built in 1933. Houses the General Assembly, offices of the Governor and Lieutenant Governor. Portraits of military heroes and former Delaware statesmen on display.

Hall of Records. Duke of York Street, Dover. Public archives of state housed here, including original royal grant from Charles II to James, Duke of York (1682). Groups should make advance arrangements: call (302) 678–4651.

Old State House and Supreme Court. The Green, Dover. Supreme Court Wing features the Stanley Arthur mural *Delaware Troops Leaving Dover,* 1776 and Denis A. Volozan's portrait of George Washington. Fine restoration, recently completed.

Immanuel Episcopal Church-on-the-Green. New Castle. Built 1703, the first Church of England parish in Delaware. Destroyed by fire; under reconstruction.

Old Presbyterian Church. On 2nd Street, New Castle. Originally a Dutch Reformed Church congregation formed in 1656; the Presbyterians took it over in the latter part of the 17th century. Present church was built in 1707 and became the mother church for congregations in the Cumberland and Shenandoah Valleys.

St. George's Chapel. Road 285, Indian River Hundred, near Angola. Built in 1794, a Georgian church with outstanding woodwork. Services in summer, Sundays at 11:00 A.M. May be seen by arrangement with All Saints Church, Rehoboth Beach.

Prince George's Chapel. State 26, Dagsboro. Original unpainted pine interior with galleries and barrel-ceiling room are features of this church built in 1757. Annual service held the Sunday after Christmas. Open by appointment; call (302) 227–7202.

Great Cypress Swamp. Trussum Pond, near Laurel. Contains the northernmost natural stand of cypress in the United States. Follow direction signs from Trap Pond State Park (State 24, west of Laurel) for best view.

Christ Church, Broad Creek. Three miles east of Laurel on State 24. Built in 1771, it is famous for its unpainted heart-of-pine interior. Open Memorial Day through Labor Day on Sundays. Annual service on Whitsunday.

Woodland Ferry. Five miles northeast of Laurel, Road 78. A three-car cable ferry operates sunup 'til sundown, crossing the Nanticoke River. A ferry of one sort or another has operated here since 1793. Crossing is free.

Mason-Dixon Monument. West of Delmar, via State 54. Double crownstone erected in 1768 by Charles Mason and Jeremiah Dixon as the southern end of north-south portion of the Mason-Dixon line, which resolved boundary dispute between Calvert and Penn families.

The Circle. Georgetown. Laid out in 1791, this picturesque "town circle" in the heart of Sussex County has the graceful Sussex County Courthouse on its east side.

Old Christ Church. Water Street, Dover. Built in 1734. Caesar Rodney, a signer of the Declaration of Independence and Delaware's hero, is buried in the churchyard.

The Green. Dover. Laid out in accordance with William Penn's order of 1683. Sykes Building, No. 45, built in 1812 by Dr. James Sykes, has visitors' information.

Governor's House. (Woodburn). Kings Highway, Dover. Built about 1790, once a station of the "underground railroad" of pre-Civil War days. Open Saturdays, 2 to 4, usually hosted by governor's wife.

Duck Creek Village. Off Rte. 13, north of Smyrna. "The Lindens," erected 1765, typical of a miller's home in the late colonial era.

Bombay Hook National Wildlife Refuge. Off State 9, north of Leipsic. 15,110-acre haven for migrating and wintering waterfowl. Open daily from sunrise to sunset.

Allee House. Dutch Neck Road, off State 9, east of Smyrna. Built by a member of the Huguenot Allee family about 1753. It is a fine example of a country house of the Queen Anne style, with interesting architectural details and excellent workmanship both inside and out.

Hale-Byrnes House. South of Stanton at junction of State Rtes. 4 and 7. Built about 1740. General Washington and his officers met here in September, 1777, prior to the Battle of Brandywine. Open by appointment only. Call (302) 994–1777.

Buena Vista. Eight miles south of Wilmington on US 13. Built in 1847, once home of John M. Clayton, President Zachary Taylor's Secretary of State. Used by governor and other dignitaries for special parties.

DRINKING LAWS. In Delaware the minimum legal drinking age for all kinds of alcoholic beverages is 20.

SPORTS. For the outdoor-minded, there are activities galore in Delaware. The state's fine ocean beaches attract innumerable summer vacationists. The largest resort is Rehoboth Beach, where, in addition to swimming, there are facilities for surf-fishing, golf and tennis.

Increasingly popular with those seeking quiet seaside relaxation are Bethany Beach and Fenwick Island, along Delaware's southern coast. Here there are *ocean bathing* and *fishing*, plus good *crabbing* and *boating* in nearby bays. South of Rehoboth Beach, between the Atlantic Ocean and the Rehoboth and Indian River Bays, is state-owned land—the Delaware Seashore State Park—where there are both ocean bathing and shallow inland-water swimming for youngsters. This is a pleasant place for an all-day outing. There are picnic tables available, and there is a good choice of restaurants nearby. Families with small children might also like the calm waters of Delaware Bay at Lewes, as well as the small-town waterfront atmosphere of this unpretentious vacation area. At Cape Henlopen State Park, 162 campsites with shower houses, swimming, bath house, beach equipment rental, fishing pier. Write Park Office, Cape Henlopen State Park, Lewes, De. 19958.

Crabbing, clamming, and fishing are favorite activities for many Delawareans. Offshore bottom fishing is done in Delaware Bay from what are called "head boats." These depart early each morning from docks at Bowers, Mispillion Light (east of Milford), Lewes and Indian River Inlet. They generally stock everything the angler will need—including bait and tackle. There are also good surf casting and deep-water fishing. The more than 50 ponds and lakes in the state offer an abundance of fresh-water angling. All fishermen, resident and non-resident, more than 15 years of age, must purchase licenses (resident, $4.20; non-resident, $9.50). There is a special license for non-residents for seven consecutive days for $3.20.

There is excellent duck and goose shooting on the fringe of the marshes along the Delaware River and Delaware Bay. The upland hunter will find small game and whitetail deer plentiful along the Chesapeake and the Delaware Canal and in the Little Creek and Petersburg wildlife areas.

Sailing and *motorboating* are particularly popular along the eastern seaboard, and ramps for launching small boats are conveniently situated here. All motorboats in Delaware waters must be registered, but this is quickly and inexpensively accomplished by contacting the Department of Natural Resources and Environmental Control, William Penn Street, Dover, Delaware 19901.

For those who prefer land to aquatic sports, public golf and tennis facilities are available in many locations. In Dewey Beach, the new sport is *hot-tubbing*, at Naturally Hot Hot Tubs, Reed St. and Rte. 1. Reservations suggested: 227-2390.

Horse-racing enthusiasts come to Delaware for the big-time *thoroughbred racing* at Delaware Park in Stanton. All the top standard breeds in the nation vie for trotting and pacing honors at Brandywine Raceway, near Wilmington, and at the State Fair Grounds at Harrington. Both harness and thoroughbred racing and thrilling automobile races are scheduled at Dover Downs, at Dover, the state's newest, multimillion-dollar track.

HOTELS AND MOTELS in Delaware range from plain, comfortable roadside establishments in the country to the luxury (and high prices) of some Rehoboth Beach hostelries. The price categories in this section are for double occupancy: *Deluxe* $40 and up, *Expensive* $30–$40; *Moderate rate* $25–$30; and *Inexpensive* below $25. For a more complete description of these categories see the Hotels and Motels section of *Facts at Your Fingertips* at the front of this volume.

Bethany Beach

Sea Crest Lodge. *Deluxe.* Garfield Park and Atlantic Ave. Good accommodations here facing the ocean with a restaurant adjacent. Open April–Nov. TV in rooms. Baby sitter list and a restaurant adjacent.

Blue Surf. *Expensive.* Boardwalk at Garfield Ave. A resort-type motel which accepts married couples and families only. Some rooms have a view of the ocean. Baby sitter list and a restaurant across the street.

Nomad Village. *Expensive.* Ocean Highway, 2½ mi. S on State 14. A modern lodge with a pool and playground. Some individual units with kitchens. Restaurant a short distance away. Pets OK.

Summer Place. *Expensive.* 2 mi. S on State 14. Located on 5 acres with a grill and picnic tables. Pool, beauty shop and baby sitter list. Restaurant nearby.

Fenwick Island

Mason Dixon. *Deluxe.* Selbyville Road at Ocean Hwy. (State 14). A small, resort-type motel open from late June until Labor Day. Pool, playground, pets OK, adjacent restaurant, picnic tables and grills.

Sands Beach Resort Motel. *Expensive.* Ocean Hwy on State 14. Open from May 15 through Sept. Playground. Opposite a restaurant.

Seaside. *Expensive.* Ocean Hwy. on State 14. A small oceanside operation open from May to Sept. 14. Pool, baby sitter list.

Coral Sands. *Moderate.* N. Carolina and Bunting Ave. Has picnic tables and grills. Open Memorial Day through Sept. Baby sitter list. Restaurant a block away.

Lewes

Angler's. *Moderate.* Angler's Rd. and Market St. Very nice rooms here, many overlooking the canal. Opposite a marina. Minimum stay 3 days during July, Aug. and holiday weekends. Baby sitter list. Restaurant opposite. Seasonal rates.

New Castle

Ramada Inn. *Expensive.* 1 mi. S. of Del. Mem. Bridge at jct. of US 13 and I–295. Pool, restaurant.

Dutch Village. *Moderate.* Du Pont Hwy. 3 mi. S of Del. Mem. Bridge on US 13. Rooms here are clean and attractive. Pool, adjacent restaurant. Pets OK. A Quality Inn.

Gateway Motor Inn. *Moderate.* US 13 and US 40, 1½ mi. S of Del. Mem. Bridge. Pool, playground, adjacent restaurant. Some efficiencies.

Howard Johnson's Motor Lodge. *Moderate.* US 40 and I–295 at Del. Mem. Bridge plaza. Two heated pools, sauna, steam room. Pets OK. Restaurant.

Skyways Motor Lodge. *Moderate.* On US 13 and US 40 3½ mi. S of Del. Mem. Bridge. The rooms here are nicely decorated. Pool, restaurant. Pets OK.

Rehoboth Beach

Henlopen Hotel. *Deluxe.* Best Western Hotel on boardwalk. Closed Nov. 1–April 1. Horizon Room on top floor serves excellent meals. Two lounges, entertainment, ocean swimming. Condominiums.

Atlantic Sands. *Deluxe.* On boardwalk. Pool, restaurant, color TV, 4 stories, elevators. During the summer season there is a minimum stay of a week.

Breakers. *Expensive.* Handy to Convention Center and restaurants.

Hobo Beach. *Expensive.* Clayton St. and Ocean. Pool, restaurant and baby sitter list. 3-day minimum on weekends. Open Easter to early Oct.

Frances Anne. *Expensive.* ¾ mi. W of Rehoboth on State 14. Closed mid-Oct. to mid-March. One mile from restaurant.

Sea-Esta. *Expensive.* Ocean Highway, Dewey Beach (State 14). Nice motel. On weekends 2-3 day minimum. Closed Oct. through Mar. Babysitter list, ½ block from 24-hr. restaurant.

Shirl Ann. *Expensive to deluxe. (depending on season).* 2 Olive St., at Boardwalk. Rooms here are clean and comfortable. Open Easter week through Oct. Restaurants nearby.

Seaford

Sunrise. *Moderate.* 2 mi. N. on Rte. 13. Playground, pets OK. 24-hour restaurant 1 mi. away.

Wilmington

Brandywine Hilton. *Deluxe.* I–95 at Naamans Rd. Pool, restaurant, Tiffany Lounge.

Du Pont Hotel. *Deluxe.* Market St. at 11th. Grand old hotel operated in finest tradition. Two topnotch restaurants, cafeteria, lounge. Close to Market Street Mall, Grand Opera House. Limo service to Philadelphia International Airport. Free parking in garage.

Radisson—Wilmington. *Deluxe.* Customs Plaza, 700 King St. Two restaurants, indoor pool, whirlpool. Limousine service to Phila. International Airport.

El Capitan Motor Hotel. *Expensive.* 1807 Concord Pike. Nicely furnished rooms with restaurant adjacent. Color TV.

Holiday Inn. *Expensive.* I–95 at 273. Horseless Carriage Restaurant on premises. Pets O.K.; pool, weekend entertainment.

Holiday Inn North. *Expensive.* 4000 Concord Pike. Pool, playground, restaurant, kennel. Baby sitter list.

Sheraton-Brandywine Inn. *Expensive.* 4727 Concord Pike. Next to Brandywine College. Heated pool, restaurant. Limo service to Philadelphia airport. Car rentals.

Sheraton Motor Inn. *Expensive.* I–95 at 273. Pool, restaurant, exceptional salad bar.

 DINING OUT in Delaware often means chicken, since the state raises a great deal of poultry; it can also mean crabmeat, often in some exotic form—crab Imperial, crab cakes or deviled crabs. You might also want to sample stuffed crab, or baked, steamed or soft shell crabs.

Restaurant price categories are as follows: *Deluxe* $15.00 and up, *Expensive* $10 and up, *Moderate* $5.00–$10.00; and *Inexpensive* below $5.00. Not included are drinks and tips. For a more complete explanation of restaurant categories refer to *Facts at Your Fingertips.*

Arden

Candlelight Dinner Theater. *Deluxe.* Always a good show, superb buffet. Reservations needed. Open Thursday through Sunday.

Bethany Beach

Holiday House. *Expensive.* Jct. State 14 and State 26. A pleasant spot on the Boardwalk. Highlights here are seafood and smorgasbords. Open all year.

Fenwick Island

Fenwick Crab House. *Expensive.* In Fenwick Shopping Center on State 14. The atmosphere is nautical and baking is done on the premises. Specializes in seafood, chicken and steak. Children's plates.

Lewes

Angler's Restaurant. *Expensive.* Canal Bank, off State 14 and State 18. A good place to fill up on seafood. Cocktail lounge.

Lou Ianire's. *Moderate.* Seafood, Italian dishes, Sunday brunch. On waterfront.

Little Creek

Village Inn. *Expensive.* Rte. 80 E. of Dover. Fine seafood.

Milford

Leounes. *Expensive.* State 113 north of Milford. A famous name for fine food in Delaware. Seafood dishes, prime ribs, steaks. Cocktails. Dinner reservations a must.

New Castle

New Castle Inn. *Moderate to Expensive.* Decor in keeping with colonial setting, on The Green.

Rehoboth Beach

Dinner Bell. *Expensive.* Christian and 2 Sts. Chicken, crab and steak are the specialties. Cocktails. Children's plates. Baking done on the premises.

Fran O'Brien's. *Deluxe.* Popular night spot. Steaks, ribs, seafood, good wine list.

Sir Boyce's Pub. *Expensive.* On main highway near Dewey Beach. Nice atmosphere, excellent service, good beef and seafood.

Avenue. *Moderate.* 32 Rehoboth Ave., 1 block from the Boardwalk. A friendly place featuring seafood and prime ribs with homemade rolls and pastries. Cocktail lounge, children's menu.

Crab Pot. *Moderate.* 112 Rehoboth Ave. A nautical decor with seafood the specialty and a takeout menu. Cocktails. Children's plates. Try Big Red Crab.

Wilmington

Hotel du Pont. *Deluxe.* 11 and Market Sts. Pleasant dining rooms with a wide variety of selections. Children's menu. Cocktails. Considered best in area by most critics. Sunday brunch in Green Room is a delight.

Columbus Inn. *Expensive.* 2216 Penna. Ave. An elegantly furnished Early American mansion serving steak and prime ribs. Special soups and desserts. Cocktails. Children's plates. Jackets after 5 P.M.

Constantinou's House of Beef. *Expensive.* 1616 Delaware Ave. The atmosphere is Mediterranean with prime beef and flambé dishes the specialties. Baking is done on the premises and there is an open grill. Children's plates.

Crab Shack. *Expensive.* Du Pont Pkway. Wonderful seafood dishes, specializing in crab delicacies. Extensive wine list, live music. Very popular place—be prepared to wait for a table.

Leounes' Town Talk. *Expensive.* 213 W. 11th St. Good seafood their specialty.

Picciotti's *Expensive.* 1641 W. 4th St. If you're hankering for good Italian food, this may be the best in town.

Lynnhaven Inn. *Expensive.* du Pont Pkway across from Wilmington airport. Both seafood and beef are well handled here. Try the crab Imperial. Cocktails.

Town Wharf. *Expensive.* Market Street Mall. Favorite downtown spot for seafood.

Winkler's. *Expensive.* 1419 French St. A long established local favorite featuring seafood and prime ribs. Delicious pastry and rolls made on the premises. Children's menu and cocktails.

The Rathskeller. *Moderate.* Market Street Mall. Good deli-type sandwiches; dinners, sidewalk cafe.

Romel's. *Moderate.* In the Fairfax Shopping Center, Concord Pike. Good variety, salad bar, excellent desserts, generous portions.

Stage Door. *Moderate.* In Grand Opera House. Excellent drinks, late-night suppers, fun atmosphere.

H.A. Winston's. *Moderate.* Independence Mall, US 202, north Wilmington. Gourmet hamburger concoctions, fun decor. You'll find Winston's in Newark and Dover, too.

Charcoal Pit. *Inexpensive.* 2600 Concord Pike. This is a friendly place specializing in quarter-pound hamburgers, with half the menu devoted to ice cream creations. It has a 14-foot open hearth. Best steak sandwiches in town.

INDEX

(The letters H and R indicate hotel and restaurant listings.)

FACTS AT YOUR FINGERTIPS

(See also practical information sections for each chapter.)

KENTUCKY

Practical Information

Geographical

TENNESSEE

Practical Information

Geographical

VIRGINIA

Practical Information

Geographical

616 INDEX

WEST VIRGINIA

Practical Information

Geographical